mANAGING
ORGANISATIONAL
cHANGE

2nd
AUSTRALASIAN
EDITION

mANAGING
ORGANISATIONAL
cHANGE

2nd AUSTRALASIAN EDITION

Fiona **GRAETZ**
Deakin University

Malcolm **RIMMER**
LaTrobe University

Ann **LAWRENCE**
Deakin University

Aaron **SMITH**
LaTrobe University

WILEY

John Wiley & Sons Australia, Ltd

Second edition published 2006 by
John Wiley & Sons Australia, Ltd
42 McDougall Street, Milton Qld 4064

Offices also in Sydney and Melbourne

First edition published 2002

Typeset in 11/14 Horley Old Style

© Fiona Graetz, Malcolm Rimmer, Ann Lawrence and
Aaron Smith, 2002, 2006

National Library of Australia
Cataloguing-in-Publication data

Managing organisational change.

    2nd Australasian ed.
    Includes index.
    ISBN-13   9 78047080 7040.
    ISBN-10   0 470 80704 0

    1. Organisational change — Management.
    2. Industrial management. I. Graetz, Fiona, 1955– .

658.406

Cover and internal design images: © Digital Vision

Edited by Robi van Nooten

Printed in Singapore by
Markono Print Media Pte Ltd

10 9 8 7 6 5 4 3 2 1

Fiona Graetz

Fiona Graetz is a lecturer at Bowater School of Management and Marketing, Deakin University. Fiona's master's research drew on case study analysis to examine strategies for successfully executing and implementing organisational change. She has published a number of papers in the area of organisational change and strategic thinking. Fiona is the unit chair of the MBA Strategic Management Unit and the unit Managing Transitions and Change in the Graduate Diploma of HRM program run jointly by the Australian Human Resources Institute and DeakinPrime.

Malcolm Rimmer

Malcolm Rimmer is the former Head of the Bowater School of Management and Marketing, Deakin University, Burwood. He was also the director of the Centre for Change Management at Deakin University. He has recently joined La Trobe University as Head of the School of Business. Professor Rimmer is a well-known author, speaker and lecturer in HRM and industrial relations. He is considered one of Australia's experts on best practice, a vital part of any research into organisational change.

Ann Lawrence

Ann Lawrence is a senior lecturer in the Deakin Business School. Ann's Master's research examined the effect of individual and organisational value congruence on occupational groups and organisational effectiveness. She has published numerous papers on Human Resource Development, individual–organisational value congruence in organisations, and ethical values in HRM. Ann is the unit chair of Human Resource Management in the Deakin Graduate School's MBA program. She is also the unit chair of 'Managing HR for Strategic Outcomes' and 'Enhancing Organisational Learning' in the Graduate Diploma of HR program run jointly by the Australian Human Resources Institute and DeakinPrime.

Aaron Smith

Aaron Smith is an Associate Professor and Director of Research in the School of Sport, Tourism and Hospitality Management at La Trobe University. Aaron has consulted in policy, governance, marketing, leadership, change management, human resource and performance management to a diverse range of organisations including multinational corporations, professional sporting clubs, national and state sport associations, entertainment companies, local governments, and private enterprise. As a researcher, Aaron has investigated sport policy, corporate governance and organisational structure within a range of contexts and organisational agendas including change management and globalisation. He is a co-author of several books that consider sport policy, corporate change, global change, marketing and management best practice.

BRIEF CONTENTS

CONTENTS

ACKNOWLEDGEMENTS

The authors wish to thank the following reviewers: Erica French (Queensland University of Technology), Priscilla Leece (University of Western Sydney), Nuzhat Lotia (University of Melbourne), and Gavin Schwarz (University of New South Wales).

The authors and publisher would like to thank the following copyright holders, organisations and individuals for their permission to reproduce copyright material in this book.

Images

P. 113: from *Managing Change for Competitive Success* by Andrew Pettigrew & Richard Whipp, Blackwell Business, © 1993. **p. 248:** from 'Beyond the charismatic leader: leadership and organizational change' by D. Nadler & M. Tushman, © 1990 by The Regents of the University of California. Reprinted from the *California Management Review*, vol. 32, no.2. By permission of the Regents. **pp. 133, 349:** from *Reinventing Competitiveness: Achieving best practice in Australia* by Rimmer et al, 1996 © Commonwealth of Australia. **p. 96:** Reprinted by permission of *Harvard Business Review* from R. S. Kaplan & D. A. Norton, 'The balanced scorecard: measures that drive performance'. Jan–Feb 1992, p. 72 © 1991 by the Harvard Business School Publishing Corporation. All rights reserved. **p. 98:** Reprinted by permission of *Harvard Business Review* from R. S. Kaplan & D. A. Norton, 'Measuring the Strategic Readiness of Intangible Assets', Feb. 2004, p. 55 © 2004 by the Harvard Business School Publishing Corporation. All rights reserved. **p. 323:** Reprinted by permission of Harvard Business School Press from *The HR Scorecard: Linking People, Strategy and Performance* by Becker et al, © 2001 Harvard Business School Publishing Corporation. All rights reserved. **p. 314:** Malcom Rimmer, from *Benchmarking Australia* by J. MacNeil, J. Cupples, J. Testi and M. Rimmer, Longman Melbourne 1993. **p. 193:** from *Beyond the Boundaries: Leading and Creating the Successful Enterprise 2e* by D. Stace & D. Dunphy, © 2001, McGraw-Hill Australia. **p. 252:** from page 109 of *Beyond the Boundaries: Leading and Creating the Successful Enterprise* by D. Stace & D. Dunphy © 2001 McGraw-Hill Australia. **p. 91:** from 'Learning and Knowledge-Based Organisation: Theory and Practice in a Public Sector Organisation', paper presented by P. Hagel & F. Graetz at ANZAM 1996. Reprinted with permission. **p. 121:** Reproduced from Field and Ford, *Managing Organisational Learning from Rhetoric to Reality*. © Pearson Education Australia, 1995, p. 23. **p. 343:** Reproduced from Carlopio, Andrewartha & Armstrong, *Developing Management Skills 2e* © Pearson Education Australia, 2001, p. 110. **p. 59:** from *Exploring Corporate Strategy 5e* by G. Johnson & K. Scholes, © 1999 Prentice Hall Europe, reprinted by permission of Pearson Education Ltd. **pp. 364, 365:** Reproduced with permission from the William Angliss Institute of TAFE and David Weston.

Text

Pp. 376–82: Reproduced with permission from Autoliv Australia. **pp. 42–3:** Reproduced with permission from Catherine Fox. **p. 216:** This material is taken from *Human capital: external reporting framework* by CIPD, 2003, with the permission of the publisher, the Chartered Institute of Personnel and Development, London. **pp. 331–2:** Deborah Tarrant Elsevier. Extract from article 'Minding and Mining the Periphery' by John Seely Brown, reprinted from *Long Range Planning*, no. 37, 2004, pp. 143–51 with permission from Elsevier. **p. 318:** adapted from Appendix A in 'Managing and reporting knowledge-based resources and processes in research organisations: specifics, lessons learned and perspectives', pp. 47–8, by K. H. Leitner and C. Warden, *Management Accounting Research*, vol. 15 no. 1, 2001 with permission from Elsevier. **p. 289:** Republished with permission, Emerald Group Publishing Limited, www.emeraldinsight.com. **pp. 107–8:** Reproduced with permission from Emma Connors. **p. 169:** © Eric Wilson. **p. 315:** Reproduced with permission from the Global Compact Office of the United Nations. **pp. 111–12:** Reproduced with permission from Greg Combet. **p. 97:** Reprinted from *Having trouble with your strategy? Then map it*, by Robert S. Kaplan and David P. Norton, © 2000 Harvard Business School Publishing Corporation. All rights reserved. **pp. 146–7:** Reprinted from *The Ambidextrous Organization* by Charles O'Reilly and Michael Tushman, © 2004 Harvard Business School Publishing Corporation. All rights reserved. **p. 322:** Reprinted by permission of Harvard Business School Press from *The HR Scorecard: Linking People, Strategy and Performance* by B. Becker et al. Boston MA 2001 © 2001 by the Harvard Business School Publishing Corporation. All rights reserved. **p. 41:** Reproduced courtesy of Phil Ruthven, Chairman, IBISWorld Business Information. **pp. 92–3:** Extract from 'Dynamic Capabilities and Strategic Management' by David J. Teece, Gary Pisano and Amy Shuen in *Strategic Management Journal*, vol. 18, p. 313, 1997, © John Wiley & Sons Limited. Reprinted with permission. **p. 131:** Adapted from 'Fed's democratic revolution' by Nicholas Way, *BRW*, September 2004 and reproduced with permission. **pp. 185–6:** Reproduced with permission from Linda Heron. **p. 84:** Reproduced with permission from Mark Lawson. **p. 231:** Extract from p. 155 of *Beyond the Boundaries: Leading and Recreating the Successful Enterprise 2e* by D. Dunphy et al © McGraw-Hill Australia. Adapted with the permission of The Free Press, a division of Simon & Schuster Adult Publishing Group, from *A Force for Change: How Leadership Differs from Management* by John P. Kotter, Inc. All rights reserved. **p. 210:** Reproduced with permission from Paul Dougas and Andrew O'Keeffe. **p. 57:** Reproduced with the permission of Paul Robinson. **pp. 111–12:** Reproduced with permission from Peter Hendy. **p. 354:** Osterman, Paul: *Securing Prosperity*. © 1999 The Century Foundation. Published by Princeton University Press. Reprinted by permission of Princeton University Press. **pp. 153–4:** Reprinted by permission of Sage Publications Ltd from A. M. Pettigrew and R. Whittington, 'Complementaries in Action: Organizational Change and Performance in Unilever 1985–2002' in *Innovative Forms of Organizing* © Sage Publications 2003. **p. 183:** Reproduced from 'Linking HRM and performance' by David E. Guest, p. 270 *International Journal of Human Resource Management*, vol. 8 1997 © Taylor and Francis Ltd. **p. 202:** Reproduced with permission from Wayne Cascio. **pp. 362–74, 367, 373:** Reproduced with permission from the William Angliss Institute of TAFE and David Weston.

Every effort has been made to trace the ownership of copyright material. Information that will enable the publisher to rectify any error or omission in subsequent editions will be welcome. In such cases, please contact the Permissions Section of John Wiley & Sons Australia, Ltd, who will arrange for the payment of the usual fee.

1

INTRODUCTION TO CHANGE MANAGEMENT

OPENING CASE

Growth means change at Flight Centre

When in 1973 Graham Turner bought an old bus for £400 and started offering budget double-decker bus tours around Europe, few would have predicted that it would be the start of one of the world's most successful travel agencies. In fact, Turner, with his business partner Geoff Lomas, developed several successful travel-related businesses before focusing their efforts on one, Flight Centre. Now with more than 1300 stores across a handful of countries, Turner and Lomas have leveraged Flight Centre to create a suite of brands, including Great Holiday Escape, Student Flights, Overseas Working Holidays and a range of others.

Growth has been at the centre of the Flight Centre strategy. To Turner, Lomas and their managerial team, this strategy has meant managing through constant change, positive though it invariably has been. Faced with the turmoil of radical growth, Flight Centre drew up ten philosophies, or principles, that they have embraced as a compass to help navigate the turbulence of their success. This set of guidelines relates to:

- employees
- customers
- profit
- ownership
- incentives
- brightness of future
- standard systems — one best way
- a lean operational structure
- taking responsibility
- egalitarianism and unity in the workplace.

One example of these principles of navigation is the egalitarian philosophy, which serves to ensure equal privileges across the organisation throughout all levels. This approach translates to policies emphasising promotion from within the company, and discouragement of separate offices, receptionists, secretaries and other perks. A second example reflects the commitment to a lean operating structure. In Flight Centre, all employees work within small teams, generally of no more than eight people in one shop. Groups of shops interact forming a community, or what they refer to as a 'tribe'. This sense of tribalism encourages responsibility and unity. It also discourages a 'silo' mentality (where individuals are only concerned with their own job activities). The consequence is a lean and responsive working group. A corporate governance policy for the company is available on the Internet.

But even for Flight Centre, a model of success, change from growth has brought about a number of serious management challenges. For example, the company has problems with high staff turnover. Despite winning an award in 2002–03 for being an excellent employer, the company has experienced between 20 and 30 per cent annual turnover of staff. Some staff leave when the initial period of excitement and learning concludes. Others find the performance requirements too confronting. Others still become dissatisfied when their hard work does not bring kudos or other job perks that are common in the business world. The base salary is low, a uniform is mandatory for everyone, and there are no fancy offices or company cars. For some former employees, these conditions are reflective of the company's exclusive focus on growth and profit. For many current employees, the conditions of work are the reason they stay. Flight Centre has come to terms with high staff turnover as a symptom of change. Endemic change is a feature of success, and it is never easy.

For Flight Centre Corporate Governance statements see: www.flightcentrelimited.com

Introduction

We begin this book with two assumptions. The first is that change is a normal part of business life. Change is not something that has to be done when things are going badly. As the opening case exemplifies, even the best performing companies still have to manage change. In fact, it is our second assumption that an organisation's ability to manage change will have a significant effect on its performance and prosperity. Both of these assumptions are supported with evidence in every chapter. However, successful change management is immensely challenging. We make this point in the next section by considering the problems and issues that organisations and managers face in bringing about change.

A second major component of the change management challenge is the magnitude and frequency of changes occurring in the business environment. This element provides a weighty impetus for the management of organisational change in the first place. This issue is important because it places organisational change into a real world context. We discuss the drivers of business change in the second major section of this chapter.

In the third major section of the chapter, we provide an overview of the perspectives on change that have provided the seeds of change theories. In doing this we acknowledge the breadth of explanations that have been invented to explain change and we note their respective strengths and weaknesses. Towards the end of the chapter, we highlight the perspectives employed in this book, as well as the framework we use to explore change. Last, we foreshadow the other chapters and what the reader may expect from them.

The change problem

Why is managing organisational change so difficult? After all, there is no shortage of scholars and consultants searching for the right approach, and no lack of practitioners prepared to employ the latest 'thinking'. As a result, business in Australia has been exposed to a proliferation of management approaches, all of which have been associated with change transitions. Australian businesses have been quality managed, re-engineered, downsized, outsourced, empowered and 'scorecarded'. Standards like ISO 9000 and Six Sigma have been used along with concepts such as benchmarking, best practice and high-performance organisations. Knowledge has been managed and organisations have 'learned'. Some managers have looked for the key in a new interpretation of the business environment, like that suggested by the idea of an Experience Economy or through electronic commerce. Flat structures, culture, shareholder value, management by walking around, listening to customers, teams and Just-in-Time are all part of contemporary business parlance. When these are not enough to manage the intricacies of change, some business leaders have embraced complexity theory, and if that didn't go well, chaos theory was always an option, keeping in mind the Peter[1] and Dilbert[2] Principles: the former states that employees within a hierarchical organisation advance to their highest level of competence, are then promoted to a level where they are incompetent, and then stay in that position; the latter refers to the theory that companies should promote their worst employees to management in order to prevent them from directly affecting the consumer's experience of the company.

Unfortunately, while each of the many approaches to change has some utility, the very nature of change tends to make them only temporarily practical, and more often than not their introduction increases resistance, instability, mistrust, anxiety and cynicism.[3] In fact, the research on change interventions is very clear. Most fail.

But why does change so often go wrong during both the formulation and implementation stages? To begin with, since change is initiated by the conception of its need, an inaccurate perception in the first instance can preclude a change attempt from success. Skewed perceptions of the need for change can take many forms: an inability to imagine an organisation's place in the future; the refusal to accept the importance of undesirable information; a clinging to old ways of thinking despite a new business context; different assumptions held by decision-makers; and communication barriers or even silence, mitigating the delivery or reception of all information pertinent to change.

Change can also fail as a consequence of a lack of motivation held by organisational members. These can include the high costs of change, particularly when it involves the introduction of expensive new technologies, sacrifices made by one product or section of the organisation to bolster under-performing areas, the potential loss of systemic comforts and perks of the job, past unsuccessful attempts at change and personal interest in change held by different employees, managers and other gatekeepers. These motivational deficiencies lead to curtailed innovation in change solutions. Sometimes, for example, environmental turbulence is so great that fast decisions are needed, and careful analysis is an ill-afforded luxury. Alternatively, a reactionary mindset, inadequate strategic vision or a lack of commitment to change by senior management will encourage the introduction of change solutions that are inadequate or merely a replacement of a new problem for old.

Problems can also occur during the implementation of change. In a practical sense, implementation is characterised by what has to be done differently in organisational operations on the first day that the 'change' comes into effect. This can go wrong in a number of ways. For example, those charged with implementation may not consider the changes to be the most efficient or appropriate actions. Alternatively, they may be charged with implementing a vague notion, such as improving quality, without a structure for its introduction, or even an impractical goal, like increased productivity, but without additional resources, new technologies or techniques. These problems can lead to dispute, stress or inactivity, often manifesting in politics and resistance. Typically, resistance is at its most virulent when change conflicts with deep-held values of organisational members, or when the social status and hierarchical effects of change are not thought through.

To add insult to injury, change can also be complicated and ultimately obstructed by other problems associated by organisational dimensions such as leadership inaction and uncertainty, embedded ways of working that are difficult to change without replacing the bulk of employees, the difficulty of coordinating a large group of people to all behave differently at the same time, a lack of resources, knowledge or capabilities to make change — a problem exacerbated by incomplete or inadequate re-training — and plain old cynicism about the intelligence or usefulness of the intended change in the first place.

To summarise, change can go wrong for reasons associated with human psychology, engrained systems and institutionalised ideas as well as conflicting cultural standards. Making matters worse for change initiators, these dimensions interact, and even counteract each other, in ways that sometimes makes finding the real obstacle to change quite troublesome. For example, Australian employees and managers tend to be egalitarian in orientation, and lean naturally towards cooperative team environments. On the other hand, employees and managers remain conscious of status and hierarchy, and prefer to know where they fit into power relationships. Similarly, the team context facilitates shared responsibility for decisions, but also protection from the personal risk of poor decisions.[4]

Tension is a by-product of change. Most specifically, the management of change can be characterised as a tension between conformity in 'know-how' versus 'know-why'. The former is relatively benign in that it can be undertaken mechanically, but the latter is dangerous, because it reflects the acceptance of assumptions, values and ideals.[5] In other words, change management is so difficult because the act of physically changing an organisation's activities is not enough; change leaders also have to change the patterns of thinking held by managers and employees. For this reason, the management of change will never be a matter of introducing the latest fad, but this does not mean that they have no place in the change process. For the variety of paradigms, tools and techniques associated with change management to be assessed properly, a systematic and careful analysis of a number of organisational dimensions and environmental variables is warranted. Such is the goal of this book.

Change in the 'new' business environment

A staggering volume of literature proclaims that we live in times of unprecedented change, although it less often reflects on the historical evidence that suggests every generation since the industrial revolution has made the same observation.[6] We are obviously not impartial about any assumptions we might make about living in times of unprecedented and unparalleled change. Nevertheless, it is difficult to ignore the experiential evidence that the rate of change is increasing, driven at least partly by technological escalation in the Western, developed world. Perhaps the only conclusions we can draw with confidence are that change is a relatively stable feature in civilisation and that the nature of change in a period defines its dominant characteristics.

The last few decades of business in Asia–Pacific have been distinguished by changes to the business environment. Although some of these changes have introduced new opportunities, many have also been traumatic, and the cause of some significant organisational casualties. In fact, the business environment has never simultaneously offered so much promise and despair. Change is no longer something that is needed periodically; it is a business constant.

Despite the rhetoric about globalisation and the 'new economy', the nature and role of change management have shifted substantially over the past two decades. For example, only a decade ago, business commentators were beginning to think about differences between management and leadership, the former about direction within organisational boundaries and the latter about changing those boundaries altogether. It is this boundary shifting that has been, and continues to be, the source of great strain and uncertainty for business, because new boundaries are being imposed upon it constantly.

Globalisation and trade liberalisation has been one of the chief drivers of change encouraging competition and potential efficiency for producers, as well as choice and value for consumers. The dismantling of many trade barriers was a hallmark of the 1980s boom years, which led into a rapid phase of globalisation, technological development and financial market uncertainty. This practice has also heralded the arrival of a cutthroat marketplace, where businesses that cannot keep pace are sacrificed at the altar of consumerism. Despite the change imperatives that it demands, Australia has been an enthusiastic participant in the globalisation process, particularly in Asia–Pacific. East Asia accounts for over half of Australia's total exports, and the figure is steadily rising. There can be little doubt that the fate of many Australian manufacturers and service providers, from agriculture to education, rests with the trade relationships formed in Asia.

Similarly, technology in the new millennium seems likely to continue challenging the conventional boundaries of business. While the tyranny of distance is being removed in great strides, when service from business is required, it is increasingly difficult to find a human being to talk to on the other end of a phone, and when one is found they are invariably offering their advice from New Delhi. Thus, as business shifts towards more efficient service practices, so too do consumer expectations, increasingly reflected by feelings of marginalisation and cynicism. Our wallets may be open, but our hearts are yet to be won.

The structure of Australian business has also undergone transformation. Diverse, family-owned businesses are giving way to corporate conglomerates with the interests of shareholders foremost in their minds, and many of them foreign-owned. This movement towards shareholder return on investment has added pressure to corporate management and, in some cases, has led to financial malfeasance and ruthless takeover activity.

Against the scenery of consumer scepticism, rampant technological escalation and burgeoning global trade, one of the key challenges for Australia is finding the right people for the job. In one of the ironies that change management often brings, the generation charged with restoring consumer faith, introducing new technologies and storming the world stage is the same one currently predisposed to undermine the baby-boomer values of material accumulation, a strong work ethic and traditional family roles. Australian youth is comfortable with cultural interaction and technological progress, but is also characterised by a free-agency, individualist mentality. At the same time as this situation is good news for business more interested in innovation than compliance, it also means that the currency of future business is knowledge, and that this knowledge is no longer considered the rights of an employer for life, but is auctioned to the highest bidder in the marketplace.

Add to these challenges the complications of war, SARS, uncertain economic progress, environmental degradation and security risks, which all take the challenges facing Australian enterprises to new levels. It is clear that change management is more important than ever before, but more than that, the readers of this book will find that their careers will be distinguished by their capacity to bring about change and prosper in a business environment wherein change is the only certainty.

PERSPECTIVES

Change and the business environment

In the mid-1990s amongst Australia's largest and most successful companies were Qantas, Coles Myer and Telstra. Despite some ups and downs, each of these organisations remained at the pinnacle of Australian business in 2005. This might suggest that 1995–2005 was a period of stability and certainty. However, although the changes that business faced in this period can sometimes be overstated, each of these companies underwent substantial change, illustrating their response to a turbulent environment.

Qantas faced off a number of challenges including the Lindsay Fox and Solomon Lew led resurrection of the now divested Ansett, as well as an abundance of new entrants such as Compass I and II, Impulse and Freedom Air. In addition, in early 2005, another budget airline, OzJet was announced. In response to Virgin Blue, Qantas created Jetstar, with the intention of competing at the leisure end of the market, where it viewed growth as viable.

Similarly, Coles Myer was under immense pressure to perform following a flat period early in the new millennium. Coles Myer's response to marketplace change was to expand into a range of new business sectors that it believed would help to leverage its supermarket and retail shopping strengths. Along with more than 2000 stores throughout Australia and New Zealand, the company expanded into petrol, liquor and pharmacy products. Some of this new business involved moving into uncharted territory for the retail giant: for example, the Coles Myer jump into petrol sales, driven by its competitor Woolworths's successful approach. At the same time, Coles Myer decided to terminate the long-standing card which entitled Coles Myer shareholders to between a 3 and 7.5 per cent discount, but which cost the company around $170 million annually.

In November 1997, the government sold one-third of Telstra followed by a 1999 second public offering. This turned the telecommunications organisation into Australia's largest foray into privatisation. With all of its implications for quality services, competition, shareholder versus community return, government debt and political ideology, the Telstra privatisation foreshadowed a governmental reaction to change in the business environment. In a number of industries where government owns utilities, at both the federal and state level, it now plays nothing more than a regulatory role. In fact, government market reforms have required the introduction of a host of new regulatory agencies including the Australian Competition and Consumer Commission, the National Competition Council as well as dozens of state-based regulators.

Qantas, Coles Myer and Telstra each tackled the changes they perceived in the business environment by undergoing significant change, from privatisation to merger. Perhaps one commonality is that every change was designed to bolster the competitive positioning of the companies in an increasingly hostile arena. Indeed, many companies were not able to change, leading to an unprecedented string of corporate collapses including Ansett, One Tel, HIH, Impulse Airlines, Harris Scarfe and Franklins.

Perspectives on managing organisational change

Depending upon what text, article or web site one reads, organisational change can be like an organism, a machine, a military conflict, a game of chess, a mind game, a building, a jigsaw, a species, a power struggle, a personal relationship or an archaeological dig. Furthermore, within these broad perspectives on organisational change can be found more specific metaphors and analogies, where change is likened to everything from spider plants[7] to theatres[8] and even the Towel of Babel![9] As Palmer and Dunford[10] point out, although the intention of such metaphors is to cultivate insight and cut through the rhetoric of change management, frequently their effect is the reverse. In addition, from a research viewpoint the use of metaphors can also encourage fragmentation and isolated streams of thinking that do not necessarily enrich each other. As a result, before we go any further in this text, it is important that we provide an inventory of different change management perspectives, because although they are useful in the conceptualisation of change, the volume and inconsistency between different views can confuse even the most clear-thinking reader or practitioner. While we cannot pretend that the range and meanings of perspectives are not complex, it is our hope that discussing them in the first chapter of this book might help structure thinking later. It is also part of our obligation to make it clear where our approach fits in, which we also tackle later in this chapter.

Perspectives on organisational change are the foundation for theoretical inspiration. Since our minds are effectively pattern-matching machines, the ability to attribute a pattern that we already recognise and understand to a feature of organisational change is useful because it helps to smooth out some of the complexities in favour of something that is well understood. Many perspectives that have been used to explain certain aspects of change have held up in empirical testing, which indicates the staggering diversity of change in organisations, and the equally staggering volume of descriptions and explanations that have been formulated to aid its explanation. In other words, change can be seen quite legitimately through a range of lenses or perspectives. In describing these lenses, it is our hope that readers will not feel confined to one, but will recognise that the power of metaphors and perspectives is not found in a single sweeping solution, but rather in a newfound awareness that there are many perspectives in the tool-bag of the change engineer. As the previous sentence illustrates by using two construction metaphors, it is common to discuss change management while implicitly embracing certain perspectives, even if it is not deliberate. Our hope is that these unconscious assumptions about organisational change might become more overt to the reader as a consequence of the following section.

The search for one comprehensive theory to describe all forms of change is probably futile, if for no other reason than because each manager or analyst looks from a different viewpoint, and therefore inevitably sees what they are looking for. Part of the reason why so many different perspectives on organisational change have emerged is because there is not really an accepted and conventional definition for organisational change in the first place. For example, at the simplest level, organisational change can be seen as the movement away from a present state towards a future state.[11] It has also been viewed as the alterations at the broadest level among individuals, groups, and at the collective level across the entire organisation.[12] Another view again suggests that organisational change is the observation of difference over time in one or more dimensions of an entity.[13] However organisational change is defined, generic statements such as these cannot reflect the diverse assumptions inherent in different perspectives. For example, one typical assumption has to do with the pace of organisational change — whether rapid or slow. A definition of organisational change that is meaningful to managers and theorists depends upon how an assumption such as this is resolved.

There have been a few noteworthy attempts to conflate the diverse perspectives and metaphors of change to a handful of categories. Van de Ven and Poole[14] suggested that there are four main types of change management perspectives, which they labelled Life-cycle, Teleology, Dialectics and Evolution. Life-cycle is concerned with the growth and development that organisms undergo during their lives. Change is the inevitable progression through birth, growth, maturation, decline and death. Teleology (the branch of philosophy that is concerned with purpose) emphasises the goals of an organisation and its activities towards their realisation. Here, change is about the driving intentions of an organisation and its systematic attempts to realise them. Dialectics focuses on the interaction between competing political forces within an organisation. Adversarial groups compete for resources, power and control and, in so doing, encourage or obstruct change. Evolution draws on biology to illustrate that change is a process of adaptation within environmental constraints.

Similar to the four perspectives explained by Van de Ven and Poole, Kezar[15], proposes six types of perspectives on organisational change: Evolutionary, Teleological, Life-cycle, Dialectical, Social Cognition, and Cultural. Four of Kezar's categories are identical, but she adds the Social Cognition and Cultural perspectives to the list. The Social Cognition perspective assumes that change is linked to learning and mental processes such as sense making and mental models. In other words, change comes about because individuals see a need to grow, learn, and modify their behaviour. In the Cultural perspective, change occurs naturally as a response to alterations in the environment, where experiences of change are shared as a consequence of common values and norms.

From this brief explanation of two typologies, or frameworks, of change perspectives, it should already be apparent that perspectives can make some fundamentally different assumptions about the nature and implementation of change. With this in mind, we think it worthwhile to explore these assumptions in greater detail, as well as the implications they have on theory development. In the following section, we use a more comprehensive typology of ten organisational change perspectives as a framework for commentary.[16]

1 The biological perspective

More than any other, the **biological perspective** has proven the most attractive source of metaphors to appropriate for use by organisational change theorists. Part of the reason is that the natural world has, on the surface at least, much in common with business. In biology, for example, constant change in reaction to environmental circumstances is quite normal, all within the context of a ruthless struggle for survival and prosperity.

Biology has been employed in several distinctly different, but often confused, ways.[17] Hannan and Freeman[18] developed one of the first theoretical forays employing a biological perspective, in what they termed **population ecology**. Theirs was a biological view of industrial behaviour, which when further built upon by McKelvey and Aldrich[19], was concerned with incremental change within industries rather than in individual organisations. This focus on change within a whole industry is extremely important in the view of population ecologists because it helps to explain what configurations individual organisations should take to be the most successful. Taking the biological perspective to its fullest extent, population ecologists consider populations of similar organisations (industries) to be analogous to organic species. Species are governed by the machinations of Darwinian evolution, where accidental mutations or variations in genetic lines bestow advantages to a few individual organisms allowing them to become more effective reproducers, which in turn, allow them to over-contribute to the gene pool of the species. Eventually, the original mutations become consistent characteristics in the species.

Population ecologists apply similar Darwinian thinking to industries and organisations. Certain individual organisations make minor changes, which confer upon them competitive advantages that allow them to gain greater market share. In time, these new advantages are picked up by other organisations and are established as industrial standards. In this sense, industries evolve just like species — as a best fit to their environment.[20] This in itself suggests to population ecologists that populations of organisations adapt over time to environmental pressures, but do so like their biological counterparts, rather slowly.

The other way of using a biological perspective to explain organisational change is encapsulated by **life-cycle theory**. As we noted earlier, this approach considers change from the perspective of an individual organism as it is born, grows, matures and ultimately dies.[21] Similarly, an organisation goes through start up, expansion, maturity and divestment. Organisational change is merely the transition along this curve of natural progression.[22] Change from this perspective is slow but inevitable.

Although these two biological perspectives have proven enormously useful and have generated a significant body of research and commentary, they are constantly being misinterpreted and misused. This misinterpretation is a result of confusion about the unit of analysis each focuses upon. If indeed the biological metaphor is going to be used correctly in a technical sense, organisations should not be spoken of as evolutionary entities. In fact, population ecology is about the evolution of industries not organisations. In contrast, the life-cycle approach is exclusively concerned with individual organisations.

The invocation of technical, Darwinian correctness imposes two problems for organisational change theorists. First, while biological evolution is about species (or populations of organisms) where individual organisms do not have personal volition for genetic change, individual organisations do have some choice about their 'genetic' or structural composition. As a result, it is reasonable and correct to consider an individual organisation 'adaptive'. Organisations do evolve, but organisms do not. Second, the accurate transposition of the biological versions of both population ecology (evolutionary) and life-cycle approaches, insist that change is always slow and steady. However, organisational change is not strictly incremental; it can also be fast and unexpected. This possibility has been explored in the application of another biological theory, the **punctuated equilibrium** model. Based on the controversial theory developed by Gould and Eldridge[23], the model suggests that evolution is generally incremental or static, but is punctuated by radical short-term change. In application to change management, the punctuated equilibrium model suggests that industries are transformed occasionally in between periods of stability.[24]

2 The rational perspective

Where organisational change theorists have embraced the biological perspective with enthusiasm, their counterparts in practice tend to view change from the rational perspective. Also described as strategic change, the **rational perspective** is concerned with the alignment between an organisation's structure/competencies with its environment.[25] Importantly, this alignment is within the power of managers to manipulate because they are charged with the best use of resources to achieve organisational objectives.[26] Furthermore, as soon as objectives have been specified, the process of organisational change is simply the by-product of sound planning and execution. This process explains the popularity of the perspective with management practitioners and consultants. Change is held firmly in the hands of organisational leaders, its success a reflection of their capacity to translate objectives into piecemeal actions, while circumventing environmental boundaries.

In addition to strategic change, the rational perspective is sometimes more formally referred to as a teleological theory because, like the branch of philosophy it is named for, it is focused on purpose or meaning. As a result, the rational perspective assumes that the intended final destination of an organisation is the guiding power behind change attempts. This assumption presupposes that the strategy process is central to organisational change and that organisations themselves are purposeful and adaptive.[27] Rationality also assumes that change makes is causal. It comes about in a linear and straightforward way, the predictable result of the planned interventions of change managers.[28] Strategic choice theorists[29] belong to the rational perspective camp as do the voluminous number of self-declared change management experts and 'gurus', who write books explaining their own interpretation of a rational change intervention, invariably involving a sequence of key steps.[30]

The obvious strength of the rational perspective is that it is prescriptive and logical. Change comes about for a reason, and the purpose of the change manager is to make sure that they provide the right reasons in the right order. This way, bringing about change is just a matter of planning carefully for its introduction. To some extent, of course, this is axiomatic. If an organisation's leaders have any chance of changing their organisation the way they want, without relying on luck, they must take a rational perspective of some type. As a result, it is difficult for anyone commenting on change to be helpful unless they can offer some prescriptive and rational action that flows from their advice. The other side of rational change, however, is that it seldom recognises the complexities of change and the impact that external, unplanned circumstances can have on an organisation. Reality has a way of diverging rather quickly from idealised plans.

3 The institutional perspective

Like the biologically inspired population ecology perspective, the **institutional perspective** is most interested in industries rather than organisations, and views the shaping force to be the pressure within the industrial environment to conform to common standards. Unlike population ecology specifically, and biological metaphors in general, where the pressure to conform is a function of fitting the environment, the institutional perspective recognises that pressure to conform might come from other organisations as well as social, governmental, legal, cultural or other pressures.[31] In this respect, institutionalists depart significantly from biologically-inclined theorists. Although they share a view about the importance of industries to change in organisations, the pressure on all organisations towards commonality — what institutionalists call isomorphism — can come about from any number of pressures, rather than the imperative to match the environment. In other words, organisations change because external forces make them take certain forms, like finance institutions that are heavily regulated by government and industrial standards. Despite the fact that the environment might encourage these organisations to be flexible and responsive, institutional forces tend to slow them down with regulations and strict protocols. Also, unlike population ecology where the environment brings about inevitable change, institutional pressure does not necessarily have this effect of inevitability. In fact, institutional pressure often obstructs change and reinforces the status quo, a fact often observed by institutional theorists in their analysis of why change is difficult to bring about. In contrast to the rational perspective, an organisation seen through the eyes of an institutionalist does not have an almost unlimited set of choices determined by managerial strategy. Instead, strategy is confined to the actual alternatives allowed by an organisation's stakeholders, competitors, regulatory agencies, social conventions and so on. 'New' institutionalism[32] is similarly interested in pressures from the wider environment, but expands the notion in recognising that the forces encouraging organisations to accept institutionally common forms can be based on popular thinking also, such as new management 'facts'.[33]

Examining the power of the institutional environment has a number of advantages. First, changes in institutional circumstances can be anticipated thereby helping organisations to select better structures in the future.[34] In addition, organisations can better appreciate the forces that are forcing them to conform, when in reality they need to find sources of distinctiveness for competitive advantage. However, these are rational responses to an awareness of institutional forces, whereas the institutional perspective tends to assume that organisational change is prescribed by forces outside of its control.

4 The resource perspective

The **resource perspective**, also known as resource dependence or resource-based theory, takes the view that the acquisition and deployment of resources is the critical activity for survival and prosperity.[35] Change, therefore, is the process through which organisations acquire, grow and utilise resources. Of particular importance is the recognition that organisational resources — human, financial, knowledge-based and others — are pivotal assets that can be combined in unique and powerful ways in order to bring about change.[36] Since the utilisation of resources is under the control of organisational leaders, management competence is considered amongst the most important of assets.[37] In fact, the only limitations upon an organisation's capacity to change are the capabilities of its leaders to manage their resource assets in such a way as to bring it about, and the fact that organisations are unable to generate internally all the different types of resources they need in order to survive and prosper. The consequence of this situation is a reliance on the environment for critical resources. Part of the key to change is that managers must develop strategies for reducing the uncertainty of the environment, which may be more or less generous in terms of essential resources. For some this approach may involve mergers, partnerships or public listing.

The resource-based view of organisations has developed into a well-established view within strategic management.[38] An argument may therefore be made that it might be considered a derivation of the rational perspective when applied to organisational change. This argument is reasonable in that it does take a basically rational, strategic approach to change. Bharadwaj, for example, commented that 'firms compete on the basis of "unique" corporate resources that are valuable, rare, difficult to imitate, and non-substitutable by other resources'.[39] While this quotation illustrates the importance of the strategic management of resources, it also highlights the assumption that organisations are unique in composition and that their unique nature is founded upon resource assets or, perhaps even, resource liabilities. This assumption in itself implies that while change might necessitate strategy, successful strategic change is going to be different in every organisation because of its unique starting point. In an important way, this assumption undermines a platform of the rational approach to change: systematic planning will always bring about successful organisational change. This cannot be the case if the resource perspective is an accurate view of change because some organisations will be incapable of shifting their unique, difficult to imitate, non-substitutable resources towards their desired goals, particularly if the necessary resources for change are unavailable from the environment. Put simply, some organisations are so resource deficient and their environments so unkind that no amount of planning will bring about change unless they acquire the resources they need. These may be financial or knowledge-driven, including the possibility that an organisation may not have the senior management capable of envisioning change, and cannot attract those who are. Moreover, sometimes the returns on an organisation's competitive advantages may not be reflected in performance, but are appropriated by other resource-hungry stakeholders.[40] In addition, a strategic plan may not be enough to bring about change in certain organisations that are mired in deeply entrenched circumstances, or are bottled-up by institutional pressures to conform. Unlike the institutional perspective, the resource perspective best explains deviance rather than conformity, which differentiates it from a purely rational view of change where the strategy process itself represents a form of conformity, and there is no expectation that the resources essential for change may reside outside the organisation itself.

5 The contingency perspective

The **contingency perspective** explains organisational change from a behavioural viewpoint where managers should make decisions taking into account the circumstances of change.[41] The best actions to initiate change come back to two words: 'it depends'. In fact, the best course of action is one that is fundamentally situational, matched to the needs of the circumstances. For example, introducing change in the military might be autocratic whereas change in a small business might be consultative.

Organisational change within a contingency perspective is based on the management of the alignment between three main factors: technology, structure and size.[42] It is this fit that governs organisational success in change attempts, and also explains why change is so troublesome to manage smoothly. The degree of fit between different organisational components that are most relevant to the situation at hand should be the ones considered for change.[43] Furthermore, efficiency demands within competitive environments force managers to modify their organisation's composition over the long term.[44] The environment therefore plays an important role to the contingency perspective of change but, unlike institutionalists, there are not necessarily pressures towards conformity. Managers must simply respond by making decisions about the best way of responding.[45]

The great strength of the contingency perspective when applied to the management of change is that it encourages thinking about the most important facets of the organisation within the boundaries of environmental circumstances. Change can subsequently take any form and is not restricted by any further theoretical conditions or prescriptive approaches. However, the limitations of the contingency perspective are that it does not help to determine which issues or events are the most important, or indeed what to do about them after they are identified. In this regard, contingency advocates are natural adversaries of rational change supporters, who tend to see change from a linear view where the same set of best practices can be applied to any organisation in any situation. It is one thing to see change management as a situational intervention; an observation that in itself is almost obvious anyway. But it is another challenge to decide what to do about it. It is also yet to be determined whether there is one best and unique way for each individual organisation.

6 The psychological perspective

Common amidst rational metaphors of change is engineering language where change is a perfunctory process and human beings are merely another construction material to be shaped and placed in the correct location. In contrast to this mechanical interpretation of people in the change process, organisational (and industrial) psychology and social psychology[46] have developed the view that the individual experience of change is not just a part of the change management process, but is the most important component of it. As a result, those assuming a **psychological perspective** of change are principally concerned with the human side of the change experience.[47] Where evolutionary (biological) and institutional metaphors are focused on the industry, and the rational and resource perspective on the organisation, as the key units of change, the psychological perspective is fixed on the individual as the most important unit to study.

Emerging from a fundamentally psychological perspective of organisational change are the twin approaches of **organisational development** (OD) and **change transitions**. OD employs knowledge from the applied behavioural sciences in order to understand individuals' experiences of change through action research and appropriate intervention.[48] The fundamental premise of OD is that resistance to change can be understood and diminished if employees are considered as the pivotal organisational resources to be managed with care and sensitivity. Similarly, the management of change transitions implies that the impact of organisational change is psychologically and emotionally traumatic for employees.[49] Because of this inherent anxiety inspired by organisational change, a transitions approach treats change like a psychiatrist treats mental illness, constantly evaluating, diagnosing and treating, until like Kubler-Ross's[50] stages of death and dying, change can be transitioned from denial to acceptance. According to Antonacopoulou and Gabriel[51], understanding the personal feelings and emotions of employees is the most important part of making successful change transitions. In some cases, psychologically-aware change managers advocate that employees should be 'empowered', or given greater control of their own activities. It is probably also noteworthy that the psychological perspective has been employed by a movement insisting that the true secret to managing psychological adjustments to change can be found in the 'spiritual' meaning behind work.[52]

As an approach to the management of change, the psychological perspective can be manifestly useful in helping to understand resistance and general dissatisfaction. However, the individual as the unit of change analysis and intervention also means that it is weaker when it comes to dealing with the systems and strategies that organisations rely upon for the production and delivery of their products and service.

7 The political perspective

Advocates of the **political perspective** observe organisational change from the viewpoint of power and conflict. Kick-started by Marx and Hegel, this approach, which is sometimes referred to as the dialectical perspective, explains change as the fight for control of organisations in order to bring about a specific ideological or positional agenda; a process generally referred to as politics.[53] Simply put, change is driven by the desire of individuals and groups to introduce new philosophies, approaches or ideas into the organisation. Since this process means the displacement of an existing status quo, change is marked by the acquisition of sufficient power to make a challenge, and inevitably culminates in conflict stimulated by clashing beliefs.[54]

From a practical viewpoint, since the political perspective illuminates change as a conflict-driven phenomenon, common change-related activities include bargaining, lobbying, persuasion, propaganda, manipulation, influence, intimidation, posturing and the application of various types of power.[55] In this way, the political perspective is also intensely social; people and the human characteristics of seeking influence while assuming that their beliefs are correct, are at the heart of the political perspective. As a result, the strength of the political perspective can be found in its authenticity. Anyone who has ever worked in an organisation has been exposed to change encouraged by politics or has seen how politics is used to obstruct change. However, the political perspective tends to view change as an adversarial event where successful organisational change is a function of power. Clearly, this assumption is somewhat ruthless and treats organisational members as pawns to be controlled.

8 The cultural perspective

As with many metaphors of change, the **cultural perspective** draws its inspiration from another field of study, in this case anthropology, the social science that studies the origins and social relationships of human beings. In 1979, Pettigrew[56] applied anthropological thinking to an organisational context, creating the concept of organisational culture. This style of thinking has generated a change perspective that considers the study and interpretation of behavioural and social patterns of individuals within an organisation, and their responses to the environment, as an insightful window through which change can be understood. Change from the cultural perspective is seen as a quite normal reaction to changing environmental conditions.[57] Culture from this viewpoint is seen as a collection of fundamental values and attitudes that are common to members of a social group, and that subsequently set the behavioural standards or norms for all members.[58] Organisational members construct these values and attitudes collectively over time as they work their way towards the achievement of organisational goals.[59] Change management, therefore, revolves around diagnosing cultural values and setting about to change them. Some cultural researchers suggest that this process can be aided by recognising that cultural meaning is infused into every aspect of an organisation, from its visible office artefacts to the language used in memos.[60] Nevertheless, as cultural values are deeply held and shared by members of a social group, change is troublesome and time-consuming.

The cultural perspective has some similarities to the psychological perspective, which emphasises individual responses to the change experience and, as a result, is seen as an incremental process. However, the difference between the two can be seen in the chief unit of examination. The psychological perspective is concerned with the behaviour of individuals, while the cultural perspective is concerned with the common behaviours of individuals operating within groups and the organisation in general. It is the shared behaviours and experiences that are important, which are causally determined by the prevailing cultural norms. Although the cultural perspective acknowledges that individuals retain free choice about their own behaviour, it is far more interested in the reasons why they choose to behave like everyone else.[61]

The most famous cultural researcher, Schein, tends towards a combination of the psychological and cultural perspectives.[62] His psycho-dynamic view of culture suggests that it is an unconscious phenomenon, a conclusion that reinforces its problematic role in change management. Culturally-oriented change managers work towards changing the shared values held by organisational members that they consider dysfunctional or unhelpful in realising goals. They are also aware of the dangers of doing this badly, because goals that conflict with values create disaffection amongst organisational members.[63] Herein lies the double-edge of the cultural perspective sword. Culture is a powerful determinant of shared behaviour and as such its diagnosis is likely to be useful in understanding how certain changes will be received. On the other hand, like trying to change an individual's personality, cultural change is slow and difficult; its systematic introduction typically requires a more rational perspective.

9 The systems perspective

Stimulated by looking at organisations as complex machines[64], systems thinking and general systems theory, assume that an organisation is a convoluted interaction of dynamic parts. Change is not a simple causal exercise; an organisation is an open system in that it can be influenced by the environment, as well as any number of conditions affecting its parts.[65] Successful change from the **systems perspective** necessitates an awareness that even small changes to one part of an organisation will have multiple and, potentially, ongoing effects. The implication of the systems perspective is that change must be undertaken across every organisational part and using every subsystem.

A system is a set of units or entities that interrelate with each other to form a whole.[66] For example, the human body can be considered a system, with a range of additional subsystems like the muscular and respiratory systems. Just like in a body, a change in one part or subsystem will affect the others. Change, then, needs to occur across the range of subsystems. While the brain conveniently manages this process unconsciously in a human, management is responsible for systemic coordination in organisations. The systems perspective has encouraged a range of ways of undertaking this task, mainly by providing sets of guiding principles or laws about the best ways to go about doing things. Systems perspectives are therefore interested in how organisations operate and the processes that drive activity. Perhaps the best-known systems approach to change is Total Quality Management. Its architect, Deming,[67] devised 14 key guidelines that he considered applicable to any organisation. Similarly, Hammer and Champy[68] did much the same with Business Process Reengineering, while more recently, the so-called learning organisation and knowledge management are on the crest of a wave.[69] Each of these has in common a systems philosophy and a 'best practice' assumption, where each approach believes it has hit upon the most successful formula for instigating change and driving organisational prosperity.

Some systems thinkers have observed the natural world as a giant system of immeasurable complexity. Like that of biologists, their work has been borrowed by management researchers to help to model the intricacies of organisational systems, which also seem beyond understanding in terms of causal relationships. Like changes in weather patterns, organisations can exhibit changes that cannot be traced to logical causes. As a result, **complexity theory** has been used to help explain how organisations seem to totter precariously between utter chaos and rigid order.[70] Such 'chaordic' (chaos-order) change has been observed in studies and helps to show how organisations can simultaneously seem to possess incompatible characteristics. In this worldview, planned and systematic change is seen as something of a textbook prescription, rather than the actual reality of the situation. In actual fact, complexity theorists would argue that change is messy and non-linear[71], and cannot be traced to causal beginnings. The only way to understand change is therefore to see it from a holistic viewpoint, with organisations accounting for more than the sum of their parts.[72] As Peters put it, successful organisations surf at the 'edge of chaos', a point where disorder produces unexpected innovation and control ensures that it can be used.[73] The only way managers are able to understand change is to accept this contradiction.

At the other end of the complexity science continuum is **chaos theory**. Where complexity theory explains basically simple, emergent change, chaos theory explains how the combination of simple systems can lead to chaos and unpredictability.[74] Chaos theory assumes that organisations are constantly changing, tempered by occasional bouts of stability and order. It helps, conceptually at least, to appreciate why systems like organisations can appear to be random and chaotic, but actually have at their heart some simple systems.[75] It also helps to understand how organisational systems can get out of hand. The approach remains incomplete as a management tool, however, with little in the way of practical recommendations to help change.[76]

Notwithstanding the limited practical dimensions of complexity and chaos theories, which probably do not yet deserve theoretical status in change management, systems approaches have proven popular because they do culminate in prescriptive guidelines for change. The catch, however, is that few can agree on what these guidelines should be. While some have proven useful in certain circumstances, many systems-based change models are faddish and flimsy.

10 The postmodern perspective

Peter Drucker observed that sometime between 1965 and 1973 Western society passed over a cultural and economic divide, and in doing so moved from a modern to a post-modern state.[77] Unhappy with the 'modern' perspective, which is associated with the 18th century period of Enlightenment where notions of superstition and ignorance were supplanted by science, progressiveness, rationality and law, postmodernists argue that the contemporary world is too fragmented and uncertain for this philosophical approach to be relevant to the way organisations work.[78] The prevailing modern view of organisational change is that sufficient scientific analysis will ultimately reveal all that is important. A **postmodern perspective** would reject this certainty and argues for a relative position where fragmentation, the blurring of traditional boundaries (de-differentiation), the confusion of the real and unreal (hyper-reality), a mixed up interest in the past and future simultaneously (chronology), the interconnection of various different styles and fashions (pastiche) and a rejection of universal truths are prominent.[79] Knowledge, according to the postmodern perspective, is relative rather than absolute, determined by social reality rather than some universal truth.

The postmodern interpretation of change rejects attempts to explain organisations using universal, grand theories. Instead, a postmodern perspective takes the view that change is best understood through the ways organisational members construct their social reality.[80] It is an approach that is comfortable with fleeting conditions, disconti-nuity and non-causal explanations.[81] In terms of its recognition of different social realities and its non-linear foundation, postmodernism shares some ground with the cultural perspective and systems-based complexity theory. Where postmodernism departs from both is in its analysis of change where language, symbols and organ-isational artefacts are increasingly distant from real-world experience.[82]

Postmodernism as a school of management thought is itself notoriously postmodern. Fragmentation and disagreement is as common as differing views of social reality. Where for one commentator postmodern change management emphasises decentralis-ation, empowerment, flexibility, trust and reactiveness[83], a more puristic approach entirely discards any generally applied management truths.[84] The more practical version of the postmodern perspective to change encourages innovation and novel ways of doing things, irrespective of their relevance to past approaches.[85] Heavier, more soci-ologically based views of postmodernism offer managers little practical advice.

Table 1.1 on the opposite and following page summarises the ten perspectives of organisational change.[86]

TABLE 1.1	Summary of organisational change perspectives

Perspective	Nature of change	Strengths	Weaknesses	Management focus
1. Biological	Ecological; organic and evolutionary	Explains life-cycle, fitness and survival	Heavy emphasis on environment; fails to explain deliberate change	Environmental positioning; find industrial niche; progression of organisation through the life-cycle; growth
2. Rational	Directed and planned	Emphasises controllable aspects of change	Ignores or sidesteps external pressures	Strategy and planning
3. Institutional	Determined by institutional (industry) pressure	Reveals importance of industrial environment and pressures to conform	Lack of focus on need to find advantages against competitors	Industrial standards and benchmarks
4. Resource	Determined by access to resources	Shows need to acquire resources to initiate and sustain change	Assumes change cannot occur without internal resources	Acquiring and discharging resources; core competencies, particularly of management
5. Contingency	Every situation is different; fit between environment, structure and size	Illustrates dynamic nature of change and usefulness of addressing the needs of the specific situation	Easy to misread the situation and choose the wrong approach; demands an understanding of all approaches	Shifting depending upon situation
6. Psychological	Embedded in 'minds' of those affected	Highlights individual impacts and stresses of change	Can ignore systemic aspects of change in organisation (e.g. structure)	Managing employee transitions and psychological adjustments to change
7. Political	Conflict and power based	Demonstrates role of power and clashing ideology	Can ignore systemic aspects of change in organisation (e.g. structure)	Managing employee transitions and psychological adjustments to change
8. Cultural	Determined by entrenched values	Shows importance of collective beliefs and norms	Difficult to address directly	'Deep' rites, rituals and values

(continued)

Perspective	Nature of change	Strengths	Weaknesses	Management focus
9. Systems	Interconnected with all aspects of organisation	Avoids the trap of assuming that change is contained in one organisational area	Complexities of keeping track of relationships between organisational variables	Change to all constituents and components of an organisation
10. Postmodern	Rejection of universal rules	Juxtaposition of old and new explains contradictions in change	Can result in no approach to change at all and confusion about nature of change	Flexibility, empowerment and responsiveness

CHANGE MANAGEMENT IN ACTION

Cultural change and Harvey Norman

Australia's most successful retailer, Gerry Harvey, has become a household name and a superstar of entrepreneurial business. As Chairman of the retail giant Harvey Norman, Gerry Harvey sits at the helm of one of the largest and most prominent retail chains in Australia's history. While it might seem obvious that part of Harvey's success must lie in his business methods, his approach is one that has embraced constant change, and organisational culture management.

The secret to Harvey's approach has been to cultivate and develop an organisational culture — a set of values, beliefs and attitudes — amongst his employees that matched the needs of the retail environment. For example, the retail sector is highly changeable in terms of trends and fashion. Never afraid of trying something new, Harvey was the first retail leader to recognise the potential of the home computer market. This was a trend that the retail chain capitalised upon well before its competitors were able to respond. For Harvey, the best approach is to give a good idea room to grow. This notion is strongly embedded in the thinking of employees at Harvey Norman. Harvey is well known for providing resources for ideas and then letting employees get on with it. He recognises the importance of letting change occur in small fits and starts that are consistent with the needs of the retail market.

While it is common for franchises to adopt some principles and characteristics of their founders, most Harvey Norman franchisees have deliberately duplicated Harvey's approach to culture. Part of this approach has been to become part of the local community. This has advantages in allowing the franchise operators to become intimately familiar with the local business environment, the changing needs of customers and to demonstrate good corporate citizenship. For example, most franchise operators live very close to their stores, have their children in local schools, provide work to local contractors and provide financial support to local charities, schools and clubs. They also tend to work closely with local media.

Harvey's business model relies on change to succeed. This is because his very assumptions about the marketplace and opportunity pivot upon changing consumer preferences. Harvey was recorded in Richard Walsh's book, *Executive Material*, as arguing that he makes money three ways: the initial development profit; the profit from ownership of the franchise properties; and the retail profit from the franchisee. As a result, Harvey is happy for change to come about. If the retail sector is strong, he makes money in franchisee profit, and if it is slow and consumers have returned to more conservative buying, real estate prices tend to rise. The cultures of his businesses are infused with an entrepreneurial spirit.

Source: Based on R. Walsh 2002, *Executive Material*, Sydney, Allen & Unwin.

Perspectives in this book

Having mapped the range of different and sometimes competing theoretical bases of organisational change, it is important that we acknowledge our own predispositions. The most important observation to make is that we invoke different perspectives when they bolster a better understanding of a change event. In this way, we are not fixed in our assumptions about the nature of change. We think this is a healthy approach, and we would encourage readers to be flexible in their own conceptualisation of change. Change is complex and there are not always patterns and logic to be found where we may seek them. But an awareness of different perspectives provides a better set of analytical views to help.

Throughout this book we touch on all of the perspectives and acknowledge that they all have utility at various times and in various circumstances. Perhaps in this way we are contingency-friendly. The limitation with the contingency approach, however, is that there are few guidelines, and little prescriptive advice to provide in a book. Although we realise that plans often depart from reality, we also encourage a rational perspective to change management. In the end, we feel it is better to have a plan than not to, even if an uncertain environment means that planning is a never-ending process.

Our approach to change management is also fundamentally systems-based. We feel that the best way to tackle change is to do so holistically rather than compartmentally.

Two chapters, chapter 8, 'Power and resistance to change', and chapter 10, 'The problems of human adjustment and economic sustainability', consider the political and psychological perspectives respectively. Equally, as we explain in our conceptual overview, we view culture, knowledge and technology as important facilitators or affecters of change, thereby incorporating the cultural and contingency (which is interested in the fit amongst technology, size and structure) perspectives. It may also be noticeable that we invoke language inspired by various perspectives including the biological in order to help explain a concept or change activity.

In general, we have not been afraid to use a perspective when we feel it is relevant and useful. But, to be objective, this book does not try to cover all perspectives equitably. For example, it is far more rational and systems-focused than it is psychology and politically focused. Part of the reason for this imbalance is that we do try to offer some practical tools for introducing change in each chapter, and particularly in chapter 4, 'Change tools'. This advice is mostly rational and systemic, as most advice on change tends to be. We also acknowledge our own preference for these two perspectives as a guiding framework for managing change. In our view, they can better encompass the other perspectives when useful rather than the reverse.

It is common for businesses to complain about how environmental change has had a negative effect upon their financial performance. Implicit in such observations is the assumption that many changes occur beyond the power of individual organisations to control. It is in the modelling of change within these circumstances that institutional theory and the biological evolution perspective are particularly revealing. For example, the tourism industry has, since September 2001, suffered threats of terrorism, added to ongoing issues associated with the high turnover of casual labour, job insecurity, poor returns on investment and increases in the price of oil. Some of these forces can be usefully conceptualised within the biological evolution perspective. From this viewpoint, the environmental forces imposed upon the tourism industry are selection pressures acting to change the composition of organisations that survive and prosper.

Sometimes, however, changes affecting industries are stimulated as a result of decisions made by other stakeholders and players. For example, building, and occupational health and safety regulations have added significantly to the costs of many tourism businesses including hotels and restaurants. From insurance premiums to new taxes and reporting guidelines, tourism enterprises are compelled to invest more money and time into providing a business infrastructure than ever before. From a change perspectives analysis of these imperatives, institutional theory can be used to account for a range of pressures coming from government and other agencies, all acting simultaneously to compel conformity. This perspective is particularly useful when explaining the effect of new changes that all organisations in an industry have to manage in the same way. It is more limited in explaining rapid change, however.

Another derivative of the biological perspective, the punctuated equilibrium model, finds its best context in explaining rapid change. An example can be found in the radical changes that the Australian fashion industry has undergone in the past decade: the reduction of trade tariffs, shifting of production overseas to utilise cheap Asian labour, the changeover from manual methods of design to computer-aided technologies, and the global integration of ordering and distribution. All of these factors have acted to force a punctuated equilibrium of sorts, where the relative stability of the past has been cut through by severe environmental change. In the case of the fashion industry, the equilibrium might be seen to have returned with a new order in its place. In practical terms this approach has meant that the activities of different sized organisations have been further differentiated than ever before. The now fewer large organisations are preoccupied with low-end, inexpensive fashion that can be produced offshore in bulk. In contrast, the highly competitive and fragmented smaller fashion houses are geared towards the high end of the market, where differentiation, exclusivity and high prices are essential.

The lesson here is that every theoretical change perspective can be matched to certain circumstances and events in which it commands a broad and logical explanatory power. However, the addition of further complexities can reduce its utility as a single method for change description.

Managing organisational change: an analytical framework

Work on organisational change is sometimes afflicted by alarmingly contagious outbreaks of insanity. As Donaldson observed, the study of change is subservient to a proliferation of academic theories and practical solutions, many of which claim to possess the organisational change panacea and yet frequently are at odds.[87] This book does not proffer another change management model, but instead provides a critical discussion of the theoretical and practical tools and issues that face organisations and managers when they confront change. The change management 'holy grail' is an illusion. Nevertheless, we have already examined a myriad of useful perspectives and techniques that can bolster change efforts. It remains our commitment, however, to avoid the abovementioned 'contagion'.

This book is structured around an analytical framework. The purpose of the framework is to provide a foundation for conceptualising the relationships between the numerous constituents of change management. In particular, the framework seeks to give students a platform from which to explore the complexities of organisational change. The framework is typological in nature. That is, it tries to help students categorise aspects of change (which are considered in different chapters of this book), as well as reveal the issues that affect change (which are dealt with implicitly in each chapter). We divide the management of organisational change (and the chapters contained in this book) into four parts or quadrants (figure 1.1).

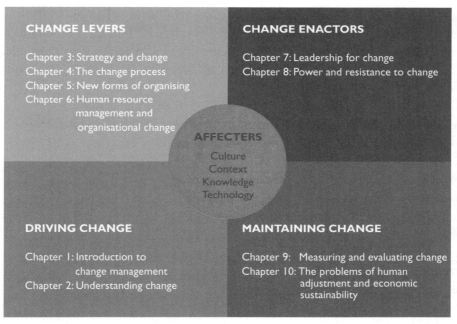

FIGURE 1.1: Managing organisational change — an analytical framework

The first section of this book, represented in the bottom-left quadrant, is about *driving change*. It considers the factors associated with recognising when change is necessary. While organisational change management is complex, requiring the simultaneous implementation of a range of activities, change cannot be managed until an organisation recognises that change forces are at work. To that end, we begin by introducing the importance of understanding the many faces of change and the many drivers that may stimulate it. Chapters 1 and 2 form this section.

The second section, represented by the upper-left quadrant, is about *change levers*. It highlights the tools, techniques and practices that are employed to facilitate planned change. Levers are the pivot points at which 'mechanical advantage' is applied to maximise change success. We demonstrate that organisational change can be effectively leveraged with the use of certain management concepts. In this section of the book, we introduce you to the use of strategy in change in chapter 3, to the change process in chapter 4, to new forms of organising in chapter 5 and to the impact of human resource management strategies in chapter 6.

The third section, reflected in the upper-right quadrant, is about *change enactors*. These factors ease or obstruct the operation of the change levers. Like change lubricants, enactors improve the efficiency of the tools that are being used to apply leverage. In this section, we examine the relationship between leadership and change (chapter 7), and the role of power and resistance to change (chapter 8).

The section represented by the lower-right quadrant is about *maintaining change*. We consider the necessary and sufficient requirements for ongoing change, exploring the process of measuring and evaluating change in chapter 9, and examining issues of sustainable change (along with the problems of human adjustment to change) in chapter 10.

While the four quadrants reflect the thematic sections of this book, a number of critical issues associated with change are considered in every chapter. In the analytical framework in figure 1.1, these factors are labelled *affecters*. This term illustrates the role of these variables in influencing all constituents of the change process. Throughout the book, we consistently return to themes or variables that affect change. We note four variables:

1. *culture* — the set of values and beliefs common to an organisation
2. *context* — the market and environment in which an organisation operates
3. *knowledge* — the set of learning processes and 'wisdom' that an organisation has accumulated
4. *technology* — the operating systems, physical machinery and equipment that an organisation employs to deliver its products or manage its internal processes.

Each of these affecters is important enough to demand a chapter in its own right. We agree that they all are important, but we also believe each is too important to limit to a single chapter that considers its impact discretely and independently. Given that affecters cross all boundaries, we have chosen to examine their impact in each chapter at points where they can best be discussed. Affecters such as culture return chapter after chapter as ongoing themes. Also, the case studies contained in this book pay special attention to the role of affecters on change.

In the writing and research on the management of change, the problem is not in finding consensus about its presence, but in finding agreement on just about everything else. Disagreement about the catalyst that stimulates change often exists — for example, does change originate from within the organisation or from 'external pressures'? The ambiguity does not end there. Was the internally stimulated change strategically driven or merely unintended 'fire fighting'? Was the externally imposed change a factor of deliberate industry transformation or simply a natural evolution?

A common method for observing and conceptualising change is to establish its underpinning force.[88] This 'impetus' or 'catalyst' typically is classified according to its source. An internally driven change, such as one introduced deliberately by management, can be contrasted with another change that an organisation involuntarily assumes as a result of an external circumstance, or what some researchers call an external 'jolt'.[89]

Similarly, the degree of premeditation can be used to contrast the nature of change.[90] Planned changes may display certain characteristics uncommon in unplanned changes. Irrespective of the stimulus for change, many writers acknowledge that change is the process of overcoming some form of organisational inertia[91], and that change management is concerned with finding the delicate balance between stability and dynamism. The objective of finding this elusive equilibrium should be a match between an organisation and its context or environment. To put it in the business vernacular: to find success, an organisation must have a 'fit' between its primary products and the needs of the marketplace.

The rapidity with which an organisation should be capable of responding to the need for change also is the subject of debate. Some researchers, such as Laughlin[92], have demonstrated that external disturbances can be so prodigious that an organisation may be permanently incapacitated or worse unless it can respond immediately. In contrast, others such as Fox-Wolfgramm, Boal and Hunt[93], insist that all change other than life and death is incremental and should be implemented with a commensurate gradient. Moss-Kanter, Stein and Jick take the middle ground, arguing that successful change comes from swift action — what they call 'bold strokes' — followed by slow, 'long marches'.[94]

Within the *driving change* section of this book, we attempt to determine exactly what organisational change entails, how it comes about, its constituents and its impact on organisations. These ambiguities are tackled in chapter 2, 'Understanding change', in which we explain the effect of the contemporary business environment and describe the challenges for Australian organisations when confronting discontinuous change. These changes demand non-traditional management and leadership skills, and necessitate breaking out of the established organisational paradigm and developing alternative configurations. Further, we take a systems view of change. In other words, these new ways of operating and strategising presuppose a holistic approach to managing organisational change, where the organisation is viewed as a dynamic, open system of interdependent parts, which embraces both the hard and soft dilemmas of change. The capability to balance these variables with strategic activities, leadership and cultural renewal is the critical success factor for managing change successfully.

Further disagreement may be found concerning the best management tools for instituting change. Some of the most common management practices associated with successful change outcomes are strategy formation and strategic planning. Hamel and Prahalad note that change programs are effective only if they are undertaken with 'strategic' intentions.[95] In other words, if the change is undertaken with the deliberate aim of improving the alignment between an organisation and its marketplace, then it has a greater chance of succeeding. Thus, to some, change is synonymous with the technique of planning and with notions of strategic positioning.[96] In addition, goal-setting, analysis of competitors' circumstances, careful review of resource allocation, risk management and performance measurement are all common elements in 'proper' strategy formulation.[97] Accordingly, correct and bold strategy formulation is a pivotal dimension governing business success.[98]

Within the *change levers* section of this book, we explore the concept of strategy, the role of strategic planning and thinking in the strategy-making process, and the relationship between strategy and change in chapter 3. We explain the critical and complementary activities of strategic thinking and strategic planning to demonstrate the importance of creative problem-solving and rational documentation. We examine the importance of identifying core competencies and capabilities as drivers of organisational direction and change, culminating in a challenge to the traditional pillars of organisational success: structures, systems and processes. Strategy and planning remain fundamental elements of the change process, but need to venture beyond the conventional bastions of influence to manoeuvre an organisation around the hazards of modern business life.

The practices of those organisations that manage to navigate change successfully by carefully balancing their strategic imperatives and internal capabilities are worth considering in greater depth. Chapter 4 deals with those activities, programs and tools that managers use to achieve organisational change. Although this presentation may seem to lead to an inventory of change management fashion, such a catalogue misses a critical dimension of the change process. The process of change in any organisation must be understood within the context of its unique 'change history', rather than as the application of change tools in isolation. Change histories are largely individual, shaped by a special combination of people, organisational characteristics and environmental challenges.

Chapter 5 attempts to draw together themes contained in the previous section by examining the most recent developments in organisational design and speculating about the future of these configurations. Given the pressures of external factors such as globalisation, deregulation, privatisation and technology integration within the 'new economy', we note the unprecedented demand for greater responsiveness and innovation within Australian organisations. In particular, organisations must balance the 'hard', rational, quantitative approach to managing organisations with a 'softer', more qualitative, intuitive, people-focused approach. This balancing requires further internal adjustments, whereby changes to structure must be accompanied by corresponding changes to systems. Our review of new forms of organising demonstrates, however, that organisations are not completely rejecting old structures, systems and processes in favour of the new; instead, they are developing more comprehensive configurations that facilitate accountability, cooperation, strategy formulation, operational decision-making, empowerment and control. We note that the impact of human resources on this process is substantial.

The final element in the *change levers* section is chapter 6, which discusses the relevance of the human resource management function in organisational change. We evaluate the application of strategic human resource management and human resource policies and practices aligned to any change goals as pivot-points for change initiatives. Underestimating the impact of these policies can be catastrophic, because behavioural change throughout an organisation is a function of employees' capacity and willingness to modify their activities and attitudes. The careful management of human resources through specialist, senior and line management is therefore critical, particularly given that the realisation of the strategic objectives depends on the cooperation of employees. This interdependence can be viewed quite clearly through an examination of human resource functions such as recruitment and selection, job design, training and development, remuneration, evaluation and even termination. Just as prudent human resource management can facilitate change, however, capricious activities that fail to acknowledge the importance of this powerful change determinant can lead to leadership challenges, power struggles and resistance.

Successful management of change, therefore, is not purely a function of the effective discharge of management activities and tasks, or of the implementation of the most recent fad. Senior leadership also may powerfully influence the management of change. While management and leadership may be distinguished from each other, both are fundamental components of the change experience — each role having dimensions that come into play depending on the context and situation. The dimensions of leadership and power, and their impact on change are scrutinised in the first of two chapters in the *change enactors* section.

In chapter 7, we consider the effect that leaders may have on the promotion and sustenance of change throughout an organisation. While leaders remain the driving character in change initiatives, charisma and perseverance are inadequate sustainers of change behaviour. If new behaviours are to be instilled throughout an organisation, then change leadership cannot be the sole prerogative of senior managers. Managers also must construct a network of change agents at all levels. Leaders are instrumental in formulating strategy, communicating the new direction, empowering organisational members to respond and, ultimately, rewarding successful achievements. Perhaps most importantly, a leader must be seen to possess a character commensurate with their significance. Honesty, integrity, charisma, confidence, energy and discipline are among the prerequisites. The changing face of organisations also calls for adaptable, operational leadership combined with highly developed interpersonal communication skills to blend the powerful triumvirate of strategic advancement, systemic improvements and delicate human resource management.

Although strong leadership can add further mechanical advantage to change levers, theories of leadership struggle to come to terms with resistance to change and the often unwritten political dimensions of change, such as power. Chapter 8 reveals the mechanisms through which power is used to prevent or facilitate change by manipulating the behaviour of others. It also reveals the forms in which change is resisted by structural, systemic or human barriers. We identify the bases of power that individuals control and the politically derived sources of power that deliver these bases, which subsequently can be employed in a range of ways, such as through conflict, the suppression of debate and the reinforcement of cultural values. We also consider the fashionable concept of empowerment. While empowerment is a potentially powerful and practical method of facilitating employee ownership of the change process, we counsel that it is sometimes met with cynicism and antagonism when used as a tool merely to dampen resistance. We note that organisational members may resist change out of fear, because it is impractical or difficult, or because it challenges the ways 'things have always been done in the past'. We observe, however, that resistance can be softened or crushed via the use of a variety of techniques, including participation, education, facilitation, negotiation, manipulation and coercion. While the success of these approaches can vary depending on a range of issues associated with the context of the change being proposed, it also can depend on the specifications of those assessing success. With this in mind, the outcome of change interventions often is overlooked or under-examined.

Chapter 9, the first chapter in the *maintaining change* section, seeks to redress this common weakness in change management. We begin by differentiating the common measurement of change in general from the more troublesome measurement of change programs in particular. A number of broad measurement techniques are highlighted, including financial, strategic and benchmarking models. Each possesses its own unique advantages and disadvantages. The relevance of suitable research also is noted, because evaluating change programs often requires more customised techniques. The high-performance work system, total quality management programs, the human resources scorecard and action research are examined as methods for undertaking the measurement and evaluation of change activities. None may be considered complete or without flaw; all, however, may be considered useful. The adequate measurement of change programs presupposes ongoing change efforts or, at least, adjustments. Without correct feedback, however, these ongoing adjustments may be abandoned before the change program has a chance to work properly. Chapter 10 considers this issue within two contexts: first, the personal adjustments that individuals face when confronted by change; and second, the axiom that change programs will survive only if they pass economic tests.

In chapter 10, we note that the direction of a change program may be slow, hesitant or circuitous over time. One explanation for this lack of reliability may be that managers and employees experience difficulty in adjusting to the new attitudes that go with the new systems. We examine, therefore, the role of transitions — that is, the process of personal psychological adjustment to change — in the success of change management programs. We discuss the nature of the changes to which people must adjust, the transition process and the relationship between change and stress in the workplace.

Chapter 10 also examines the economic cost–benefit tests that change programs must pass if they are to be sustained and developed in the long term. These economic tests revolve around the necessity of the change program to demonstrate a net financial benefit. We caution that change programs can be difficult to sustain because demonstrating these paybacks may be problematic. This difficulty can be exacerbated when the benefits have not had time to reveal themselves, because part of the change program was overlooked or because the change direction is incompatible with the organisation's core values or ideology.

Using this text with case studies

This book provides a holistic view of managing organisational change. The contents are targeted at senior undergraduates and postgraduates studying organisational change. Each chapter contains discussion questions and learning exercises. These may be useful for interactive class discussions and activities. Cases are used throughout the chapters to reinforce the contents with a practical application. Three cases are included as discrete sections at the end of the book, to provide more substantial practical guidance. We have endeavoured to provide a balance between theory, technique and example. As we have already noted, the role of affecters such as culture, context, knowledge and technology is significant in each of these cases, as are the role of time and the evolution of a change program. Two ambitions were uppermost in importance in our choice and development of case content.

First, we endeavoured to provide a rich mix of industrial experience. This is exemplified in our three end-of-book cases, which include a domestic education institution (case 1, William Angliss Institute of TAFE), a multinational automotive safety systems manufacturer (case 2, Autoliv Australia) and a pulp and paper manufacturer (case 3, Norske Skog Boyer mill, Tasmania).

Second, we sought a range of change management programs and practices with a particular emphasis on the importance of examining change over time. The William Angliss Institute of TAFE case scrutinises over a decade of change from 1993 to 2004. The case explores changes across the organisational design dimensions of structures (delayering, decentralising, project-based organising), processes (communications, IT and HR practices such as team building) and boundaries (outsourcing, strategic alliances, downscoping). There are strong links between the William Angliss Institute of TAFE case and chapters 5 and 7. The Autoliv case focuses on the human resources changes that have occurred in the organisation, and the impact of an approach that considers teamwork and empowerment pivotal. It also reviews the relationship between the human resources changes and the broader strategic objectives of the company. Chapters 3, 6 and 8 are particularly relevant to the Autoliv case study. The Norske Skog Boyer mill case study charts the implementation of best practice initiatives from 1991 to 2004. In so doing, the case provides plentiful examples where theory and practice have not met neatly, and demonstrates the importance of a sustainable change process. The theoretical underpinnings of the Norske Skog Boyer mill experiences are detailed in chapters 4, 9 and 10. In addition, it is worth noting that the generic principles contained in this chapter and the contextual overview highlighted in chapter 2 are relevant to each of the three cases.

In summary, this book contains ten chapters that constitute the principal content and three cases exploring how the theory fits into practice. We have recommendations concerning the division of this information if the book is employed as the basis for a thirteen-week teaching period. First, we believe chapters 4, 6 and 8 are particularly demanding in terms of length and content. We suggest that one or more of these chapters can be usefully split over two weeks. The case sections also can be used for one or two weeks in total and can be effectively supplemented by additional case studies not included in this book (or with the practical experiences of students). These cases are ideal for discussing the difficulties of implementing holistic change and provide an insight into the systems nature of the concept in practice.

As we noted earlier, there is sometimes little agreement on the exact relationship between the variables associated with change, their content and ultimately their best application. As exemplified by our cases, the enigma is complicated by the time frame within which the change is sought. Brooks argued that fundamental change takes three generations of management to be fully implemented.[99] The challenge of senior management, therefore, is to find ways of accelerating this process, where all activities are strategically structured around this goal. Kotter, on the other hand, advises that change can be made comparatively quickly.[100] Collins appropriately notes that change management theory is convoluted with an 'attendant baggage' of management buzzwords, which tend to be propagated by management 'gurus' who go out of their way to create unnecessarily evangelical models and frameworks.[101]

The most difficult aspect of reviewing the theories and management practices that are linked to successful change is separating them from each other. As we have indicated, there is some compelling evidence that an interdependent relationship exists among the elements we present in each of the following nine chapters. Culture (chapters 2 and 8), for example, can be the concept underpinning an organisation's strategy (chapters 3 and 7), systems (chapter 4 and 7) and structure (chapter 5). But culture is not always considered reciprocally derived from the interaction of organisational members (chapters 6 and 9) with strategies, systems and structures in the first place.

In practice, we argue consistently throughout this text that it is impossible to change one dimension of an organisation without having an impact on another. We have attempted to demonstrate this 'systems' interrelationship beyond dispute. We acknowledge, however, that the precise nature of this relationship is contested. Stace and Dunphy highlight distinct levels within which change interventions may occur, such as strategic analysis and cultural renewal.[102] While we may find such classifications useful, we reiterate that it would remain imprudent to claim that a single, integrated and empirically demonstrable theory of organisational change management exists. Change management is an inherently complex and laborious undertaking, requiring a comprehensive understanding of an organisation's practices, people, context and values.[103]

The complexity of undertaking large-scale change is well explained by Daniel-Duck, who likens a typical organisational change to a patient undergoing five surgical procedures at the same time. Even if each individual operation is a success, the possibility still exists that the patient will die of shock. We hope that this book will, in a modest way at least, decrease this possibility.[104]

Review

In this introductory chapter, we began by explaining two assumptions: that change is a normal part of business life, and that it is a key to success. In addition to these two themes, the first section of this chapter observed that change management is exceedingly difficult to manage well. Many change interventions fail or are full of challenges. However, the alternative — not attempting to change — is always a path to failure.

The second major section in this chapter considered the magnitude and frequency of changes occurring in the business environment. The contemporary business environment is by nature turbulent, providing the catalyst for organisations to need to change in the first place. Technological changes were noted as one of the most insidious and fast moving of environmental pressures, as well as the changing expectations and knowledge of consumers.

In the third major section of the chapter, we provided an overview of the perspectives on change that have led to change theories. Ten organisational change perspectives made up this 'typology'. These perspectives are the backbone of change theory, and serve as frameworks for the conceptualisation of organisational change. The ideas, metaphors and assumptions that different commentators make about change, all stem from one or more of these perspectives. In this way, it is important to recognise the variety of ways in which change can be interpreted. The ten perspectives were biological, rational, institutional, resource, contingency, psychological, political, cultural, systems and postmodern.

This chapter culminated in the presentation of the analytical framework of the text. Four parts were explained. First, driving change reflects the factors associated with recognising when change is necessary. Second, change levers highlight the tools, techniques and practices that are employed to facilitate planned change. Third, change enactors ease or obstruct the operation of the change levers. Finally, maintaining change concerns the necessary and sufficient requirements for ongoing change, exploring the process of measuring and evaluating change, and examining issues of sustainable change.

Key terms

biological perspective. A metaphor for viewing organisational change as analogous to changes that occur in the natural world, particularly focusing upon Darwinian evolution and an organism's life-cycle, (p. 9)

change transitions. An approach to organisational change where the management of change transitions implies that the impact of organisational change is psychologically and emotionally traumatic for employees, (p. 14)

chaos theory. A systems-based view of change where the combination and accumulation of simple systems can lead to chaos and unpredictability, (p. 17)

complexity theory. A systems-oriented theory that considers some change as non-linear and emergent; a result of the complex interaction of organisational elements, (p. 17)

contingency perspective. The behavioural view of organisational change where managers should make decisions taking into account technology, structure and size, focusing on those that are the most directly relevant to circumstances, (p. 13)

cultural perspective. A view that the central issue in organisational change is the values, beliefs and norms shared by organisational members, which acts as a powerful mechanism of conformity, but is difficult to modify intentionally, (p. 15)

institutional perspective. A view of change that considers the shaping force to be the pressure within the industrial environment, including social, governmental, legal, cultural or other pressures, to encourage organisations to conform to common standards, (p. 11)

life-cycle theory. An organisational change theory inspired by biological development that views change in organisations as inevitable through a series of linear stages from birth, development and maturity through to decline and death, (p. 10)

organisational development. An approach to organisational change premised upon the view that resistance to change can be understood and diminished if employees are considered as the pivotal organisational resources to be managed with care and sensitivity, (p. 14)

political perspective. A view that assumes organisational change is driven by the desire of individuals and groups to introduce new philosophies, approaches or ideas into an organisation, causing conflict and resolved by power, (p. 15)

population ecology. An organisational change theory that uses the concept of natural selection and biological evolution to model the effects of industrial change on organisations, (p. 9)

postmodern perspective. The postmodern interpretation of change rejects attempts to explain organisations using universal, grand theories, instead taking the view that change is best understood through the ways organisational members construct their social reality, which can be manifestly different and can involve the simultaneous presence of competing or even contradictory trends and experiences, (p. 18)

psychological perspective. An approach to organisational change that concentrates on individuals' personal psychology and their reaction to change interventions, (p. 14)

punctuated equilibrium. A theory of change borrowed from an alternative view of biological evolution, where radical change interrupts periods of relative stability or incremental change, (p. 10)

rational perspective. A view concerned with the alignment between an organisation's structure and competencies and its environment, (p. 10)

resource perspective. Resource dependence or resource-based theory takes the view that the acquisition and deployment of resources is the critical activity driving change in organisations, (p. 12)

systems perspective. A change approach that views organisations as a constellation of interrelated and interdependent units or entities that work together, implying that change must be holistic, dealing with the range of organisational sub-systems with an awareness that change in one will affect the others, (p. 16)

Review questions

1. Identify the reasons why change is so troublesome in organisations. What sorts of things can go wrong?
2. Identify the impact that technological change can have on the business environment.
3. What is the main weakness of the strategic perspective to change?
4. Contrast the evolutionary approach and the life-cycle approach to describing the nature of change.
5. What is the main similarity between institutional theory and the evolutionary approach?
6. What is the advantage of taking a postmodern perspective to change?
7. Explain each of the components of the change framework employed in this text, and comment on the relationship of the framework to the change perspectives.

Discussion questions

1. Why do you think that change perspectives have developed over time to explain and describe change?
2. Do you think that managers can hold different perspectives of change in their minds at the same time during a change attempt and still be clear about their intentions?
3. Identify the change perspective that appeals to you the most. Explain why you find this perspective so appealing.

Work assignment

Change perspectives

Select an example of a change intervention with which you are familiar. It might be from a work or school experience or from a new policy introduced at a sport club you belong to. Explain the purpose of the change intervention and consider the change perspective that you think might be driving the people initiating the change. Think carefully about the assumptions you think the initiators hold about change and its nature.

Suggested further reading

Styhre, A. 2002, 'Non-linear change in organizations: Organization change management informed', *Leadership & Organization Development Journal*, 23(5/6), pp. 343–51.

Van de Ven, A. & Poole, M. 1995, 'Explaining development and change in organizations', *The Academy of Management Review*, 20(3), pp. 510–40.

Grey, C. 2003, 'The fetish of change', *Tamara: Journal of Critical Postmodern Organization Science*, 2(2), pp. 1–19.

Steiner, C. 2001, 'A role for individuality and mystery in "managing change"', *Journal of Change Management*, 14(2), pp. 150–67.

Buchanan, D. 2003, 'Getting the story straight: illusions and delusions in the organizational change process', *Tamara: Journal of Critical Postmodern Organization Science*, 2(4), pp. 7–21.

Wood, T. 2002, 'Spectacular metaphors: from theatre to cinema', *Journal of Organizational Change Management*, 15(1), pp. 11–20.

End notes

1. The Peter Principle is a theory developed by Laurence Peter, which states that employees within a hierarchical organisation advance to their highest level of competence, are then promoted to a level where they are incompetent, and then stay in that position.
2. The Dilbert Principle (coined by cartoonist Scott Adams) refers to the 1990s theory that companies should promote their worst employees to management. This would prevent them from directly affecting the consumer's experience of the company.
3. For an excellent overview of the nature and utility of management 'fads', see: E. Shapiro 1995, *Fad Surfing in the Boardroom: Reclaiming the Courage to Manage in the Age of Instant Answers*, New York, Addison-Wesley.
4. C. Steiner 2001, 'A role for individuality and mystery in "managing change"', *Journal of Change Management*, 14(2), pp. 150–67.
5. ibid.
6. C. Grey 2003, 'The fetish of change', *Tamara: Journal of Critical Postmodern Organization Science*, 2(2), pp. 1–19.
7. G. Morgan 1986, *Images of organization*, Sage Publications, Newbury Park, CA.
8. T. Wood 2002, 'Spectacular metaphors: from theatre to cinema', *Journal of Organizational Change Management*, 15(1), pp. 11–20.
9. C. Green & K. Ruhleder 1995, 'Metaphors gone awry: globalization, borderless worlds, and the Tower of Babel', *Journal of Organizational Change Management*, 8(4), pp. 55–68.
10. I. Palmer & R. Dunford 1996, 'Conflicting uses of metaphors: reconceptualizing their use in the field of organizational change', *The Academy of Management Review*, 21(3), pp. 691–717.
11. J. George & G. Jones 1995, *Understanding and managing organizational behavior*, Addison-Wesley, MA.

12. B. Burnes 1996, Managing change: *A strategic approach to organizational dynamics*, Pitman Publishing, London.

13. A. Van de Ven & M. Poole 1995, 'Explaining development and change in organizations', *The Academy of Management Review*, 20(3), pp. 510–40.

14. ibid.

15. A. Kezar 2000, *Understanding and Facilitating Change in Higher Education in the 21st Century*, Jossey-Bass, Washington DC.

16. A. Smith & B. Stewart 2006, *Models and Frames for Analysing Sport Organisations*, Meyer & Meyer, Cologne, Germany.

17. U. Witt 2004, The evolutionary perspective on organizational change and the theory of the firm, Third ETE Workshop, Sophia-Antipolis, January 29–30, pp. 1–23.

18. M. Hannan & F. Freeman 1977, 'The population ecology of organizations', *American Journal of Sociology*, 82, pp. 929–64.

19. W. McKelvey & H. Aldrich 1983, 'Populations, natural selection and applied organizational science', *Administrative Science Quarterly*, 28, pp. 101–28.

20. A. Van de Ven & M. Poole 1995, 'Explaining development and change in organizations', *The Academy of Management Review*, 20(3), pp. 510–40.

21. A. Kezar 2000, *Understanding and Facilitating Change in Higher Education in the 21st Century*, Jossey-Bass, Washington DC; A. Van de Ven & M. Poole 1995, 'Explaining development and change in organizations', *The Academy of Management Review*, 20(3), pp. 510–40.

22. A. Levy & U. Merry 1986, *Organizational Transformation: Approaches, Strategies, Theories*, Praeger, New York.

23. S. Gould & N. Eldridge 1977, 'Punctuated equilibria: the tempo and model of evolution reconsidered', *Paleobiology*, 3, pp. 115–51.

24. P. Anderson & M. Tushman 1990, 'Technological discontinuities and dominant designs: a cyclical model of technological change', *Administrative Science Quarterly*, 35, pp. 604–33; J. Kimberly & R. Miles 1980, *The organizational life-cycle*, Jossey-Bass, San Francisco.

25. A. Van de Ven & M. Poole 1995, 'Explaining development and change in organizations', *The Academy of Management Review*, 20(3), pp. 510–40.

26. N. Rajagopalan & G. Spreitzer 1997, 'Toward a theory of strategic change: a multi-lens perspective and integrative framework', *The Academy of Management Review*, 22(1), pp. 48–79.

27. A. Kezar 2000, *Understanding and Facilitating Change in Higher Education in the 21st Century*, Jossey-Bass, Washington DC; A. Van de Ven & M. Poole 1995, 'Explaining development and change in organizations', The Academy of Management Review, 20(3), pp. 510–40.

28. C. Carnall 1995, *Managing Change in Organizations*, Prentice Hall, London; D. Carr, K. Hard & W. Trahant 1996, *Managing the Change Process: A Field Book for Change Agents, Consultants, Team Leaders, and Reengineering Managers*, McGraw-Hill, New York.

29. J. Child 1972, 'Organizational structure, environment and performance: the role of strategic choice', *Sociology*, 6, pp. 1–22; K. Smith & D. Berg 1987, *Paradoxes of Group Life*, Jossey-Bass, San Francisco.

30. J. Kotter 1995, 'Leading change: Why transformation efforts fail', *Harvard Business Review*, 73(2), pp. 59–67; G. Huber & W. Glick 1995 (eds), *Organizational Change and Redesign: Ideas and Insights for Improving Performance*, Oxford University Press, New York; R. Kanter, B. Stein & T. Jick 1992, *The Challenge of Organizational Change*, The Free Press, New York.

31. R. Greenwood & C. Hinings 1996, 'Understanding radical organizational change: bringing together the old and new institutionalism', *Academy of Management Review*, 21, pp. 1022–54.

32. P. DiMaggio & W. Powell 1991, 'Introduction', in *The New Institutionalism in Organizational Analysis*, eds W.W. Powell & P.J. DiMaggio, University of Chicago Press, Chicago, pp. 1-38; P. DiMaggio & W. Powell 1983, 'The iron cage revisited: institutional isomorphism and collective rationality in organizational fields', *American Sociological Review*, 48, pp. 147–60.

33. W. Scott 1995, *Institutions and Organizations*, Sage Publications, London.

34. A. Mukherji & J. Mukherji 1998, 'Structuring organizations for the future: analyzing and managing change', *Management Decision*, 36(4), pp. 265–73.

35. J. Pfeffer & G. Salancik 1978, *The External Control of Organizations: A*

Resource Dependence Perspective, Harper & Row, New York.

36. T. Connor 2002, 'The resource-based view of strategy and its value to practising managers', *Strategic Change*, 11(6), pp. 307–16.

37. R. Grant 1991, *Contemporary strategy analysis: Concepts, Techniques, Applications*, Basil Blackwell, Cambridge, MA.

38. J. Barney 1991, 'Firm resources and sustained competitive advantage', *Journal of Management*, 17, pp. 99–120.

39. A. Bharadwaj 2000, 'A resource-based perspective on information technology capability and firm performance: an empirical investigation', *MIS Quarterly*, 24(1), pp. 169–96.

40. R, Coff 1999, 'When competitive advantage doesn't lead to performance: the resource-based view and stakeholder bargaining power', *Organization Science*, 10(2), pp. 119–34.

41. L. Donaldson 2001, *The Contingency Theory of Organizations*, Sage Publications, San Francisco.

42. J. Pfeffer 1982, *Organizations and Organizations Theory*, Pitman, Boston.

43. A. Van de Ven & R. Drazin 1985, 'The concept of fit in contingency theory', in L. Cummings & B. Staw (ed.), *Research in Organizational Behavior*, 7, pp. 333–65, JAI Press, Greenwich, CT.

44. P. Alder 1992, *Technology and the Future of Work*, Oxford University Press, New York; I. McLoughlin & J. Clark 1988, *Technological Change at Work*, Open University Press, UK.

45. R. Drazin & A. H. Van de Ven 1985, 'Alternative forms of fit in contingency theory', *Administrative Science Quarterly*, 30, pp. 514-39; J. Gerdin & J. Greve 2004, 'Forms of contingency fit in management accounting research — A critical review', *Accounting, Organizations and Society*, 29(3–4), pp. 303–26; F. Hartman & F. Moers 2003, 'Testing contingency hypotheses in budgetary research using moderated regression analysis: a second look', *Accounting, Organizations and Society*, 28(7–8), pp. 803–809.

46. K. Lewin 1947, 'Frontiers in group dynamics: concept, method and reality in social sciences: Social equilibria and social change', *Human Relations*, 1, pp. 5–41.

47. J. Iacovini 1993, 'The human side of organization change', *Training and Development*, pp. 65–8; R. Stuart 1995, 'The research context and change triggers', *Personnel Review*, 24(2), pp. 3–88.

48. W. Burke 2002, *Organizational change: Theory and Practice*, Sage Publications, Thousand Oaks, CA.

49. W. Bridges 1980, *Transitions*, Addison-Wesley, Reading, MA; W. Bridges 1992, *Managing Transitions: Making the Most of Change*, Addison-Wesley, Reading, MA; T. Jick 1990, 'Note: The recipients of change', *Harvard Business School* 9-491-039, Harvard Business School Press, Boston, MA.

50. E. Kubler-Ross 1973, *On Death and Dying*, Tavistock Publications, London.

51. E. Antonacopoulou & Y. Gabriel 2001, 'Emotion, learning and organizational change: towards an integration of psychoanalytic and other perspectives', *Journal of Organizational Change Management*, 14(5), pp. 435–51.

52. G. Dehler & M. Welsh 1994, 'Spirituality and organizational transformation: implications for the new management paradigm', *Journal of Managerial Psychology*, 9(6), pp. 17–26; D. Tourish & A. Pinnington 2002, 'Transformational leadership, corporate cultism and the spirituality paradigm: an unholy trinity in the workplace?', *Human Relations*, 55(2), pp. 147-172.

53. A. Van de Ven & M. Poole 1995, 'Explaining development and change in organizations', *The Academy of Management Review*, 20(3), pp. 510–40; K. Marx 1976, *Capital*, Penguin, Harmondsworth, United Kingdom.

54. G. Morgan 1986, *Images of Organization*, Sage Publications, Newbury Park, CA.

55. L. Bolman & T. Deal 1991, *Reframing Organizations: Artistry, Choice, and Leadership*, Jossey-Bass, San Francisco.

56. A. Pettigrew 1979, 'On studying organisational cultures', *Administrative Science Quarterly*, 24, pp. 570–81.

57. G. Morgan 1986, *Images of Organization*, Sage Publications, Newbury Park, CA.

58. E. Ogbonna & L. Harris 2002, 'Organisational culture: a ten year, two-phase study of change in the UK food retailing sector', *Journal of Management Studies*, 39, pp. 673–706.

59. E. Schein 1984, *Coming to a New Awareness of Organizational Culture*, Jossey-Bass, San Francisco.

60. F. Erdem & C. Satir 2003, 'Features of organizational culture in manufacturing organizations: a metaphorical analysis', *Work Study*, 52(3), pp. 129–35.

61. L. Heracleous 2001, 'An ethnographic study of culture in the context of organizational change', *The Journal of Applied Behavioral Science*, 37(4), pp. 426–46.

62. E. Schein 1997, *Organizational Culture and Leadership* (3rd edn), Jossey-Bass, San Francisco.

63. B. Burnes & H. James 1994, 'Culture, cognitive dissonance and the management of change', *International Journal of Operations & Production Management*, 15(8), pp. 14–33.

64. A. Kuhn 1974, *The Logic of Social Systems*, Jossey-Bass, San Francisco, CA.

65. J. Gharajedaghi 1999, *Systems Thinking: Managing Chaos and Complexity: A Platform for Designing Business Architecture*, Butterworth-Heineman, Boston, MA.

66. E. Laszlo 1972, *The Systems View of the World: The Natural Philosophy of the New Developments in the Sciences*, G. Braziller, New York.

67. W. Deming 1982, *Out of the Crisis*, MIT Press, Cambridge, Mass.

68. M. Hammer & J. Champy 1993, *Re-engineering the Corporation*, Nicholas Brealey Publishing, London.

69. B. Burnes, C. Copper & P. West 2003, 'Organisational learning: the new management paradigm?' *Management Decision*, 41(5), pp. 452–64.

70. T. Sullivan 2004, 'The viability of using various system theories to describe organisational change', *Journal of Educational Administration*, 42(1), pp. 43–54.

71. A. Styhre 2002, 'Non-linear change in organizations: organization change management informed', *Leadership & Organization Development Journal*, 23(5/6), pp. 343–51; P. Shaw 1997, 'Consulting from a complexity perspective: intervening in the shadow systems of organizations', *Journal of Organizational Change Management*, 10(3), pp. 235–50.

72. R. Marion & J. Bacon 2000, 'Organizational extinction and complex systems', *Emergence*, 1(4), pp. 71–96.

73. T. Peters 1987, *Thriving on Chaos*, Harper-Collins, New York.

74. F. Dubinskas 1994, 'On the edge of chaos', *Journal of Management Inquiry*, 3(4), pp. 355–67.

75. S. Krasner 1990 (ed.), *The Ubiquity of Chaos*, American Association for the Advancement of Science, Washington DC.

76. K. Eisenhardt & S. Brown 1999, 'Patching', *Harvard Business Review*, 77(3), pp. 72–83.

77. P. Drucker 1989, *The New Realities*, Harper & Row, New York, pp. 3–4.

78. *Theory Culture and Society: Special Issue*, June, 1988, pp. 195–208; D. Lyon 1994, *Postmodernity*, Open University Press, Buckingham, pp. 6–7; D. F. Ruccio 1991, 'Postmodernism and economics', *Journal of Post Keynesian Economics*, pp.499–500.

79. B. Thomas 2003, *Controversies in Management: Issues, Debates, Answers*, Routledge, London.

80. D. Buchanan 2003, 'Getting the story straight: illusions and delusions in the organizational change process, *Tamara: Journal of Critical Postmodern Organization Science*, 2(4), pp. 7–21.

81. R. White & R. Jacques 1995, 'Operationalizing the postmodernity construct for efficient organizational change management', *Journal of Organizational Change Management*, 8(2), pp. 45–71.

82. C. Fox 1996, 'Reinventing government as postmodern symbolic politics', *Public Administration Review*, 56(3), pp. 256–62.

83. S. Clegg 1992, 'Postmodern management?' *Journal of Organizational Change Management*, 5(2), pp. 31–49.

84. R. Gephart, T. Thatchenkery & D. Boje 1996, 'Conclusion: Restructuring organizations for future survival', in *Postmodern Management and Organization Theory*, eds D.M. Boje, R.P. Gephart & T.J. Thatchenkery, Sage, Thousand Oaks, pp. 358–64.

85. C. De Cock 1998, 'It seems to fill my head with ideas: a few thoughts on postmodernism, TQM and BPR', *Journal of Management Inquiry*, 7(2), pp. 144–53.

86. Adapted from: A. Smith & B. Stewart 2006, *Models and Frames for Analysing Sport Organisations*, Meyer and Meyer, Cologne, Germany.

87. L. Donaldson 1995, *American Anti-Management Theories of Organization: A Critique of Paradigm Proliferation*, Cambridge University Press, Cambridge.

88. J. Greenberg & R. Barron 1995, *Behavior in Organizations*, 5th edn, Prentice-Hall, Englewood Cliffs, New Jersey.

89. A. Ginsberg 1988, 'Measuring and modelling changes in strategy: theoretical foundations and empirical directions', *Strategic Management Journal*, 9, pp. 559–75; R. C. Laughlin 1991, 'Environmental disturbances and organisational transitions and transformations: some alternative models', *Organizational Studies*, vol. 12, 1991, pp. 209–32.

90. S. L. Brown & K. M. Eisenhardt 1997, 'The art of continuous change: linking complexity theory and time-paced evolution in relentlessly shifting organizations', *Administrative Science Quarterly*, 42, pp. 1–34.

91. R. Greenwood & C. R. Hinings 1996, 'Understanding radical organisational change: bringing together the old and new institutionalism', *Academy of Management Review*, 21, pp. 1022–54; C. Oliver 1992, 'The antecedents of deinstitutionalisation', *Organizational Studies*, 13, pp. 563–88; M. L. Tushman & C. A. O'Reilly 1996, 'Ambidextrous organizations: managing evolutionary and revolutionary change', *California Management Review*, 38(4), pp. 8–29.

92. R. C. Laughlin 1991, 'Environmental disturbances and organisational transitions and transformations: some alternative models', *Organizational Studies*, 12, pp. 209–32.

93. S. J. Fox-Wolfgramm, K. B. Boal & J. G. Hunt 1998, 'Organizational adaptation to institutional change: a comparative study of first-order change in prospector and defender banks', *Administrative Science Quarterly*, 43, pp. 87–126.

94. R. M. Moss-Kanter, B. A. Stein & T. D. Jick 1992, *The Challenge of Organizational Change*, The Free Press, New York.

95. G. Hamel & C. K. Prahalad 1994, 'Competing for the future', *Harvard Business School Press*, Boston.

96. H. I. Ansoff 1965, *Corporate Strategy: An Analytical Approach to Business Policy for Growth and Expansion*, McGraw-Hill, New York; M. Porter 1980, *Competitive Strategy*, The Free Press, New York.

97. P. F. Drucker 1988, 'The coming of the new organisation', *Harvard Business Review*, January–February, pp. 45–53; A. Huczynsk & D. Buchanan 1991, *Organisational Behaviour*, Prentice Hall, Hemel Hempstead, United Kingdom; J. P. Kotter 1995, 'Leading change: why transformation efforts fail', *Harvard Business Review*, 73(2), pp. 59–67.

98. C. Markides 1999, 'A dynamic view of strategy', *Sloan Management Review*, Spring, pp. 55–64; H. Mintzberg & J. Lampel 1999, 'Reflecting on the strategy process', *Sloan Management Review*, Spring, pp. 21–31; P. Williamson 1999, 'Strategy as options on the future', Sloan *Management Review*, Spring, pp. 117–27.

99. A. Brooks 1990, 'The law of civilisation and decay', Unpublished paper.

100. J. Kotter 1990, *A Force for Change*, The Free Press, New York.

101. D. Collins 1998, *Organizational Change: Sociological Perspectives*, Routledge, London.

102. D. Stace & D. Dunphy 1996, *Beyond the Boundaries: Leading and Recreating the Successful Enterprise*, McGraw-Hill, Sydney.

103. R. Hinings & R. Greenwood 1988, *The Dynamics of Strategic Change*, Basil Blackwell, Oxford; L. M. Kikulis, T. Slack & B. Hinings 1995, 'Sector specific patterns of organisational design change', *Journal of Management Studies*, 32, pp. 67–100; H. Schwartz & S. M. Davis 1981, 'Matching corporate culture and business strategy', *Organizational Dynamics*, Summer, pp. 30–8.

104. J. Daniel-Duck 1993, 'Managing change: the art of balancing', *Harvard Business Review*, December, p. 109.

2

UNDERSTANDING CHANGE

OPENING CASE

Changing guard at The Palace

The Campaign Palace is a long-standing, highly regarded Australian ad agency, which launched its best campaigns and was extremely successful through the 1980s and 1990s. By the early 2000s, however, the shining star in Australian advertising was losing its lustre and big-name clients were taking their accounts elsewhere. When WWP Group, one of the largest global advertising conglomerates acquired 'The Palace' (as it is referred to in the industry), its days as a standalone entity seemed numbered. Contrary to expectations, however, WWP Group, recognising the value of The Palace reputation and brand name, decided to give it a second lease of life. Paul Fishlock, a respected copywriter, was put in charge of its rejuvenation.

So what had gone so wrong for this once highly successful, much lauded business? When Fishlock joined as Chairman in late 2003, he found himself up against a strongly entrenched 'us and them' hierarchical structure. The agency 'creatives' enjoyed iconic, untouchable status and there was a largely impenetrable divide between them and other agency staff. As a result of this 'upstairs–downstairs' attitude, there was little communication or information sharing among agency staff and little evidence of teamwork when dealing with clients. For Fishlock, it was glaringly obvious that the advertising world had moved on but not The Palace. It was still stuck in the old routines, successful in the past, but no longer applicable in a highly competitive Australian market where they were vying for business against heavyweight global conglomerates.

Fishlock's change strategy encompassed two key aims: redesign workplace systems and structures to allow greater collaboration and information-sharing; and break down the 'us and them' divide by fostering a more open, cooperative culture that valued everyone's contribution — one which recognised that good ideas were not just the preserve of 'creatives' (art directors and copywriters) — and that account executives who liaise with clients play an equally critical role. It was therefore important in terms of project outcomes and customer satisfaction that these two groups understood and respected each other's contribution and worked in partnership.

Through greater project-based teamwork and information sharing, staff are working more closely together and developing a better understanding of the business and the results. Fishlock has adopted a more participative, open management style, communicating his commitment and trust in staff by sharing core financial information with them. New workplace processes, including new remuneration structures based on cross-border teams and collaborative project work have been implemented. In addition, Fishlock believes that 'healthy debate' during the creative process is critical to a project's success; therefore staff need to be willing to share ownership of ideas and be open to constructive criticism.

Both the physical and psychological barriers that have been blocking the way forward for the business are beginning to weaken but there is still much to be done and there will be the inevitable casualties along the way. The move to team-based workgroups and a more participative, collaborative workplace culture where ideas were now open to scrutiny and challenge proved difficult for some agency staff that decided to leave. This has allowed new people to join who have no allegiance to the organisation's past but a clear stake in its future.

Source: Adapted from Catherine Fox 2004, 'Palace Revolution', *AFR BOSS*, May, pp. 46–7.

Introduction

Despite the wholesale changes that were taking place in its external environment, why did The Palace doggedly persevere with business as usual? As the opening case highlights, organisations need to guard against two key dangers spawned by success: complacency and myopia. Rather than pursuing a more innovative, risk-taking course to sustain their competitive edge, organisations tend to become locked into the tried-and-true formulae of past successes, even when these no longer meet the changing demands and expectations of consumers and a radically altered industry environment.

We all have experienced change; it is nothing new. People's tendency to resist changes to the established ways of working with which they are familiar and comfortable is well documented. In fifteenth-century Italy, Florentine nobleman and philosopher, Machiavelli, wrote with feeling about the risks associated with implementing change. From his experience, change initiatives received lukewarm support at best and made dangerous enemies of those who felt that their power and position were threatened. More recently, Jack Welch, General Electric's chief executive officer from 1981 to 2001, expressed similar sentiments. One of the things he learned when implementing large-scale organisational change throughout General Electric was that 'change has no constituency. People like the status quo. They like the way it was. When you start changing things, the good old days look better and better. You've got to be prepared for massive resistance.'[1]

As this chapter will illustrate, The Palace was so internally focused that it initially ignored the guiding management principles that organisations operating in today's business environment must consider if they are to manage **discontinuous change** and remain competitive. The chapter explores in detail the guiding management principles that are essential for leading and managing in a **global business environment** characterised by turbulence and change. We also consider a number of different examples to analyse the application of these guiding principles. The chapter also investigates the role of corporate culture in assisting or blocking change, and considers the value of Johnson and Scholes' cultural web as a tool to audit corporate culture. In the final section, we discuss further the dilemmas of change, particularly the question of whether to pursue cultural renewal or structural change, and continuous, incremental adaptation or radical transformation.

Drivers of change: the change experience

If change is such a familiar, age-old phenomenon, then why have working organisations not become more adept at managing and implementing change? Perhaps it is because change itself is undergoing metamorphosis. Until the mid-1970s, when organisations were operating in a highly protected, largely domestic industry environment against a backdrop of relative security, stability and predictability, the changes that took place were familiar, identifiable and incremental. The worldwide political, social and cultural upheavals of the 1980s (which included a recession, a stockmarket collapse, the end of the Cold War and the collapse of the Berlin Wall, the opening up of markets, industry **deregulation** and global competition), however, triggered wholesale changes to the Western business environment and, concomitantly, to the very nature and rhythm of change. Rather than undergoing evolutionary, gradual change, organisations began to experience radical, sudden and turbulent environmental shifts that defied and made obsolete the rigid, internally focused structures, systems and tactics that served so well in more benign and certain times.

The 1980s saw the dawning of the Information or Knowledge Age we live in today as advances in technology gained pace and the economic focus shifted from the manufacturing and commodities sector to the information, communications and services sector. To compete successfully in this Information Age calls for a well-educated, highly skilled, capable and self-reliant workforce. According to forecaster and strategist, Phil Ruthven, Chairman of IBISWorld, Australian business will be unable to compete on the global stage in the Knowledge Age unless it commits more resources to research and development (R&D). Ruthven defines business R&D as 'intellectual property that provides a business with the greatest opportunity for sales, innovation, growth, productivity and profitability ... a cocktail of skills, systems, patents, trademarks, brands, protocols and strategies'.[2] Ruthven points out that total business spending on R&D in 'clever countries' is up to three times more than Australian businesses spend. As table 2.1 demonstrates, Australia is eleventh on the ladder in total R&D spending as a percentage of GDP and drops even further down the rung in business R&D spending. Ruthven is encouraged, however, that growth in R&D spending in Australia since the 1980s is the seventh fastest in the Organization for Economic Co-operation and Development (OECD) group of countries.[3]

TABLE 2.1	Smartest countries: R&D spending as % of GDP*	
	Total R&D	**Business R&D**
Finland	3.4	2.4
Japan	3.0	2.3
Iceland	2.8	1.8
United States	2.7	2.1
South Korea	2.7	2.3
Germany	2.5	1.8
France	2.2	1.4
Netherlands	1.9	1.1
Canada	1.9	1.1
Britain	1.9	1.3
Australia	1.5	0.8
Czech Republic	1.3	0.8
World	2.1	1.5

* Latest figures available
Source: Department of Education, Science and Training, IBISWorld in *BRW* 18–24 March 2004, p. 69. Reproduced courtesy of Phil Ruthven, Chairman, IBISWorld Business Information.

Industry deregulation, the lowering of tariff barriers and the breathtaking pace of advances in technology and technological infrastructure have provided the impetus for global competition, global connectivity and a global economy. Technological advances, particularly the Internet, mean that geographic distance and different time zones no longer impede the transfer of information, capital or services. Technological advances in tandem with rising consumer expectations and access to global markets have contributed to shorter product life cycles and led to the need for go-to-market speed and flexibility.

The 'Change management in action' case (page 42), which looks at the engineering, technical operations and maintenance services (ETOMS) division of Qantas, illustrates how an inside-out focus, coupled with flexibility and adaptability, is an essential prerequisite for competing successfully in a highly competitive, customer-driven environment. ETOMS' internal focus (firmly anchored in the past), its paternalistic management style, its traditional, hierarchical command and control structure and its silo mentality left the organisation vulnerable and unable to respond quickly and decisively to an increasingly complex and volatile environment both locally and globally. In addition, global political conflict, terrorism, and phenomena such as severe acute respiratory syndrome (SARS) only serve to heighten the need for increased resilience and responsiveness as firms move progressively from a domestic to global strategic focus.

Changing the culture at ETOMS

Based at Sydney's Mascot Airport, ETOMS, the engineering, technical operations and maintenance services division of Qantas, plays a central role in ensuring the airline's reputation for safety and quality of service remains intact. ETOMS employs 6000 of the 34,000-strong Qantas workforce. The majority of these are male, blue-collar workers, many of whom have spent all their working lives with the airlines. It represented a stable, inwardly focused workforce operating according to values and routines established over many years of loyal service.

In a stable and benign external environment, this traditional *modus operandi* had served the organisation well. However, in the aftermath of September 11 (2001) and the SARS epidemic, the global airline industry was in damage control and not even Qantas could guarantee it would emerge unscathed. In addition, the collapse of Ansett and Virgin Blue's entrance on to the domestic stage upped the ante for Qantas on its home turf. It became abundantly clear to ETOMS management that the division's hierarchical organisational structure, autocratic and control-oriented in approach, along with the conservative steady-as-she-goes mindset that held sway, were the trappings of a bygone, more innocent and predictable era that left them dangerously ill-prepared for the challenges of the highly uncertain and volatile environment now confronting them.

Relations between management, shopfloor workers and union representatives were poor. Senior managers practised a command and control style, which was confrontational and intimidatory. Senior managers seemed remote and separate from the shopfloor, with whom they rarely communicated and where they were rarely seen. Shopfloor workers had little say in their work procedures or job design and were cynical and suspicious of management's motives. In this environment, industrial unrest was rife, with union representatives constantly at loggerheads with management.

While the ETOMS management and workers identified with the reasons for change and understood that radical change was needed, there was little understanding of what should change or how to change. Given the deeply embedded culture, those charged with articulating the what and how of change at ETOMS felt strongly that some sort of change tool, which both blue- and white-collar workers could relate to, was essential to kickstarting and driving change through the organisation; otherwise, if left to their own devices, nothing would change.

As many serious skills gaps had been identified at the management level, ETOMS decided to start with this group first. The management team was sent on intensive training courses aimed at improving their communication and interpersonal skills. The key tool used to help improve communication through ETOMS was a graphic instrument called the Strategy Map. While the executive team took some convincing that this approach would work at ETOMS, the map's use of pictures and concepts appealed to the engineers. The Strategy Map is designed like a board game and to progress through, players must review the past before planning ahead. This component was seen as very important in an organisation where 20+ years is the average length of service. The map even contains a section called 'Pity City' where players can spend time lamenting the good old days. In addition, the use of storytelling as part of the format compels people to talk through issues so that misunderstandings are less likely. 'Below-the-line' behaviour, for example, such as dominating the conversation, making snide remarks about others or not listening, is banned from meetings.

With management support, ETOMS introduced the map through the organisation with the help of some external consultants. Around 100 employees positioned at different levels of the organisation were trained as 'map guides' and charged with taking people in their area through the 12 chapters, explaining how it was meant to work and defining all key terms. The involvement of workers at all levels of the organisation in training co-workers in the use of the Strategy Map encouraged ownership and commitment to the new ways of working.

Despite initial scepticism about the value of introducing the Strategy Map to a group of burly engineers, it was received very positively. An aircraft maintenance engineer and union representative commented that while there were some doubts over the language used and the colourful diagrams, thanks to the Strategy Map, workers are now involved in making decisions about their work areas and are in direct communication with management. However, the real value, according to team members, has been its effect on behaviour. The map has helped open up areas and issues for discussion that were once taboo. As a result, there is greater honesty, respect and trust among workers and between workers and management.

As for the future of ETOMS, senior management is cautiously optimistic, recognising they still have a long way to go and that the process could falter. ETOMS General Manager, David Cox, acknowledges that it is not perfect, that there parts of the business it has not yet rolled out to, and there are still sceptics in other parts of the business. However, he views it as a never-ending journey and is encouraged by workers' observations that management is now listening to them and is out walking the talk, showing by doing. In addition, Cox points to tangible improvements in occupational health and safety, and in leadership and diversity. But, as Cox points out, if ETOMS is to have a future 'it's got to improve and the bottom line has to improve'.

Source: Adapted from Catherine Fox 2004, 'Getting in touch with their inner engines', *AFR BOSS*, March, pp. 48–53, www.afrboss.com.au. Reproduced with permission of Catherine Fox.

In many industries, technological advances also have eroded the traditional barriers to entry, such as high start-up costs and the need for economies of scale. As a result, many new smaller, nimbler companies are entering markets that traditionally have been the sanctum of industry giants. To compete against these new entrants that think global and are untrammelled by the trappings of bureaucracy and tradition, established industry giants must reinvent themselves. Consider, for example, Virgin Blue versus Qantas or Optus versus Telstra. Large organisations such as Qantas must learn to act big, but think small by flattening organisational structures and devolving authority and decision-making responsibility to smaller, semi-autonomous business units. Cooperation and communication across functional units form the ethos of the loosely coupled network organisation.[4] In this environment, autonomous business units work independently and cooperatively on projects, depending on the skills and resources needed to complete a task. This represents a fundamental shift from the traditional segmentation of skills and knowledge into discrete departments in which (often selected) information was channelled up and down the hierarchical funnel but rarely shared sideways across the organisational deck. New organisational forms are evolving, with boundaries that are fluid and permeable.[5]

The new forms of organising illustrate a radical shift in focus from the hard, more tangible elements of work organisations (strategy, structure, systems) to the soft, intangible elements (skills, staff, leadership style, shared values). In the context of a global economy that requires organisations to operate in multiple environments simultaneously, sustainable competitive advantage no longer depends on new technology, new products, market position or price. Rather, it relies on organisational capability. Ireland and Hitt, for example, refer to the remarkable 'breadth and depth' of the global economy's impact on workplace systems and structures, and the emergence in the 21st century of amoeba-like forms of organising with 'collections of workers that are subdivided into dynamic, ever-changing teams to competitively exploit the firm's unique resources, capabilities and core competences'.[6]

As the 'Opening case' (page 38) and 'Change management in action' case (page 42) each illustrate, in a customer-driven environment in which technological know-how and the ability to compete globally are universal prerequisites, a company's 'internal mode of operating drives its ability to "invent" new markets and to subsequently exploit them'.[7] Competitive advantage depends on an organisation's ability to focus on its distinctive skills and capabilities, and to develop and exploit these within a framework and culture of **continuous improvement** and innovation. Focus and innovation are considered essential ingredients for sustained high performance in a customer-driven, high-tech, global marketplace. IBISWorld data[8] reveal that organisations excelling in this environment are:

- focusing on single industries rather than diversification
- outsourcing non-core activities
- pursuing intellectual property (innovation)
- aggressively globalising their new age service industries and utilities
- leading first and managing second
- forming alliances, networks and franchises.

Flynn and Chatman define innovation as the conjunction of two processes: creating or generating new ideas; and implementing or introducing the change.[9] In other words, creativity in itself does not lead to innovation; innovation only arises if the novel product or idea is successfully implemented. If focus and innovation are precursors to sustained high performance, then what strategies must organisations pursue to develop a high-performance mindset? In the following section, we investigate the guiding management principles that organisations must heed if they are to survive and succeed in the new global business environment.

Managing discontinuous change

In contrast to the highly regulated and clearly defined boundaries of business in the 1960s and 1970s, the new global business environment of the Post-industrial Age is characterised by complexity, uncertainty and turbulence — an environment in which traditional boundaries and modes of operating are no longer sustainable or relevant. This type of random, discontinuous change — which, by definition, is fast, traumatic and revolutionary[10] — requires very different management and leadership skills if the challenges it presents are to be handled innovatively and opportunistically.

What must organisations do to turn this new era of discontinuity to their advantage and survive? Fundamental to an organisation's success in a knowledge-based world are highly trained, empowered, committed and informed employees who strive unreservedly to give their best.[11] In a competitive business environment in which product life cycles have shortened and speed to market is critical, organisations need a highly capable, multiskilled workforce that is willing and able to be 'redeployed quickly and flexibly'.[12] Shrinking product life cycles, along with the need for adaptive, quality staff and go-to-market speed and flexibility, have forced a profound re-thinking of traditional organisational systems and structures that were established to promote stability, standardisation and uniformity.

A willing and adaptive workforce is the key ingredient here. If a workforce believes management has scant regard for its welfare and sees its members as mere pawns to be moved carelessly on the shrinking work chessboard by a management interested only in increasing profits and keeping shareholders happy, then resistance, hostility and industrial unrest are inevitable outcomes. These types of fundamental workplace change need to be handled with sensitivity and maturity if they are to have worker acceptance and commitment. It is not enough to tell people that they must change; neither is it enough to give them the reasons for change. People also need to know the direction in which to change and to be given the skills, resources, recognition and rewards to help them think and act differently. (See chapter 6 for discussion on the people component of change.)

The management style, work practices, and organisational systems and structures that existed at ETOMS (see 'Change management in action' case, page 42) until very recently illustrate the *modus operandi* of the traditional workplace: decision-making and thinking were a management prerogative; management practised a command-and-control style and was seen as remote and uncaring; employee participation was limited; the workforce was mainly blue collar and male; work processes were highly formalised and routine; and occupational health and safety issues were largely ignored. Consequently, there was mutual distrust and animosity between management and workers and industrial unrest was commonplace.

In the face of massive upheaval in the global airline and tourism industries as a result of September 11 and the SARS epidemic, as well as a series of crises in the local airline industry, ETOMS recognised that it would have to change its ways if it, and ultimately Qantas, were to survive. The 'Change management in action' case and the 'Opening case' (page 38) clearly demonstrate, in the context of a complex and uncertain environment, that traditional organisational systems and structures, which combine a rigid, bureaucratic, top-down approach with historically entrenched values of stability and security, are more of a liability than an asset.[13] At The Palace, Fishlock recognised that all agency staff had to break free from the traditional organisational mindset and move to a more open, market-sensitive, participative work environment, no longer bound by the cultural and hierarchical divides of the past.

The situation at both ETOMS and The Palace also serve to illustrate that organisations require a new **holistic**, integrative approach to managing organisational change — one that recognises the organisation as a dynamic, open system of interdependent parts and embraces both hard (strategy, systems, structure) and soft issues (skills, staff, leadership style, shared values). Learning to balance and resolve the tension between hard and soft approaches to organisational change requires a single, overarching vision and focus, good management principles and processes, and a supportive and enabling corporate culture.[14] These three facets are clearly interrelated. An organisation's corporate culture — that is, its system of shared meaning and values — is shaped by the company's vision of where it wants to go and how it will get there. It will draw inspiration from and reflect the principles espoused by management. In his study of the effect of management principles on company performance, Samson[15] identified fourteen principles that guided behaviour in the world's excellent companies. Samson's fourteen principles echo many of the themes that have emerged from best-practice studies. Clear parallels can be drawn between, for example, these principles and the six common elements of best-practice firms identified by the 1986 MIT Commission on Industrial Productivity — a focus on simultaneous improvement in cost, quality and delivery; closer links to customers; closer relationships with suppliers; the effective use of technology for strategic advantage; less hierarchical and less compartmentalised organisations for greater flexibility; human resource policies that promote continual learning, teamwork, participation and flexibility. (Further reference to the MIT study appears in the discussion on best practice in chapter 4.) The fourteen principles also are reflected in the key themes and perspectives on organising for the 21st century, which we discuss in chapter 5. In examining these principles at work in organisations, it becomes clear that these are not a discrete set of unrelated items, but interact in synergy to provide a coherent and consistent framework to guide organisational values, behaviour and decision-making.

Samson's fourteen principles are:

1. alignment
2. distributed leadership
3. integration of effort
4. being out front
5. being up front
6. resourcing the medium term
7. time based
8. bias for action
9. learning focus
10. enabling disciplines
11. measurement/reporting and publication
12. customer value
13. capabilities creation
14. micro to macro.

Guiding principles for change management

In the following sections, we outline Samson's fourteen principles and consider them in relation to different organisations.

Alignment (principle 1)

Alignment occurs when employees' behaviour and mindset are compatible with the 'stated company values' and 'stated strategic direction' of the company.[16] Samson identified eight elements of alignment that 'drive the practices and behaviours of people and organisations': values, strategic direction, value chain, support functions, goals and measures, suppliers, customers and rewards.

- *Values*. This form of alignment entails creating trust and commitment, devolving authority, enabling people to work independently as well as encouraging cooperation among self-motivated, self-reliant individuals, and fostering teamwork. These elements work in synergy to raise morale and empower the workforce. A trusting, committed and empowered workforce, however, demands an organisation-wide 'commitment to values that put people first'.[17] These values must be part of the organisation dynamic and must be enacted daily in word and deed.

  Call centres are not generally regarded as the employer of choice. Yet SalesForce, a Melbourne-based call centre with 1312 full-time employees, was the 2004 winner of the annual Best Employers award, based on an Australia-wide survey of more than 35,000 employees conducted by HR consultancy firm Hewitt Associates. Survey findings indicate a strong connection between high-growth companies (best employers recorded almost double the revenue growth — 13 per cent versus 7 per cent — of other organisations) and higher levels of employee commitment. Compared with other companies surveyed, SalesForce excelled in the 'employee engagement' score, achieving a 90 per cent engagement level. For the purposes of the survey, employee engagement is defined as 'a state of emotional and intellectual involvement or commitment which goes beyond satisfaction'.[18] It was clear that SalesForce employees felt highly valued and respected and regarded themselves as key contributors to the success of the business. Hewitt Associates found that providing opportunities for employee development was integral to high commitment. The best employers inspired trust and instilled in their employees pride and a growth mindset.[19]

- *Strategic direction*. Employee needs and expectations are aligned with the company's stated strategic direction when employees understand and are committed to fulfilling the long-term goals and objectives of the organisation. A successful vision communicated by a company's top management mobilises commitment and creates energy for action within the organisation. It offers a road map of the future, generates enthusiasm, focuses attention and instils confidence. Engaging organisation members in the future direction of the business is a critical first step in enhancing change effectiveness; moreover, 'engagement is the capability that helps to form a critical mass'.[20] The involvement of senior management is also seen as fundamental to engaging and sustaining the critical mass required for effective change. It is up to them to 'set clear corporate challenges' that matter to everyone on a personal level as not only must all employees in the organisation 'find the goal emotionally compelling', they must also clearly understand how they will contribute to achieving that goal.[21]

  In 1994, Michael Paul established the first Pack & Send Store in Parramatta, Sydney. Today, he is Managing Director of a national network of 60 stores. The company's success is due in large part to Paul's unwavering vision of how he wanted to grow the business and his vigilance to market trends, both locally and globally. The company's newly revised vision is to be a 'world class retail freight operator with 110 stores Australia-wide by 2008'. Paul believes that achieving this objective depends on hiring the right people who support the company's goals and understand what needs to be done to get there. While difficult at first, Paul recognised the need to step back and yield control of the minutiae of the business and adopt a more visionary, mentoring style, allowing people to make mistakes and learn from them.[22]

- *Value chain*. Alignment of an organisation's direct value chain, such as different work processes and different functional areas (sales, marketing, product development and design, operations and so on), ensures each element of the value chain understands the contribution that all the other parts make to meet organisational goals and therefore work at optimum capacity. Value chain alignment demands a systemic, 'big picture' approach to managing people and processes in work organisations. A superior value chain ultimately means superior customer and stakeholder value. This element of alignment reflects the systems perspective discussed in chapter 1 and offers the image of organisations as part of a network of partnerships, alliances and linkages all committed to adding value to the customer. Michael Paul's wide-lens, inside-out focus at Pack & Send enabled him to monitor global freight industry trends, attend to competitor moves, and seek strategic alliances to extend the company's reach and services.[23]

- *Support functions*. It is important that 'infrastructure providers within the organisation appropriately support and are supported by those parts of the organisation that directly add value to the services and products that customers are prepared to pay for'.[24] For example, lack of communication and support between the creatives and account executives that dealt with clients at The Palace had a significant adverse impact on the organisation's ability to attract and retain its big-name clients.

- *Goals and measures*. Alignment at this level is critical to the 'efficient production of quality goods and services'.[25] Moreover, senior managers need to implement and communicate goals and measures. It is their responsibility to define the direction, set performance goals and gain the support of other key stakeholders who will help the performance goals and measures to cascade down through the organisation.

  Jackson refers to organisational processes as the dynamic drivers that 'translate purpose and values into the daily activities of the organisation'. Operational planning and performance measurement and review represent the two key work processes. As he comments, operational planning flows from a company's strategic goals and objectives. As an example, Jackson refers to the annual planning process at Cendant Membership Services, based in the United Kingdom. At the start of the planning process, a booklet detailing the company's complete business plan is distributed to each employee. The booklet also includes an introductory letter from the managing director, a purpose statement, key business objectives and goals, and departmental objectives. To ensure the entire company is aligned to the same goals, each department notes its objectives under common headings. Workshops are held for all staff to discuss company goals and objectives. In addition, each staff member receives a copy of the company's vision displayed in diagrammatic form and is asked to consider how they will contribute to that vision. Drawing on these discussions, each business area is responsible for shaping and creating what it plans to do to fulfil these overarching goals and objectives.[26]

- *Suppliers*. Alignment with suppliers is essential for ensuring the highest standards, the most suitable products, improved costs to the customer and a mutually fulfilling partnership. Stace and Dunphy point out that 65 per cent of the value adding in automotive manufacturing tends to come from work undertaken by suppliers, while 60–70 per cent of the cost of manufactured goods arises from material and purchased components. It is of much greater value, therefore, to concentrate on nurturing excellent supplier relationships rather than trying to increase profits by seeking further efficiencies in plant processes.[27]

Consider, for example, Cochlear, the bionic ear implant company. With the help of academics at the Australian Graduate School of Management (AGSM), Cochlear has set out to identify, and improve its relationship with, key suppliers. Identifying key suppliers is seen as a critical first step in adopting best-practice supply chains. Supplier importance is calculated according to risk and partnership potential.[28] Cochlear assesses all its suppliers on soft (relationship) and hard (transactional) measures. The supplier's value is quantified according to the Pareto principle (the 80/20 rule) where its most valued suppliers make up no more than 20 per cent but demand the company spend 80 per cent of its time on them.[29] According to one supplier, this approach has reduced time delays significantly and there is 'much faster throughput and faster R&D' because the supplier now does the sub-assembly rather than Cochlear. This has resulted in 'efficiency gains of 10 to 15% and a 5% cost reduction', which adds up to millions of dollars.[30]

- *Customers*. Being sensitive and responsive to customer needs and expectations ensures that the organisation is attuned to shifts in the marketplace. Stace and Dunphy refer to one organisation's practice of using a range of indicators to determine what leads to customer satisfaction. They found that customers experienced high levels of satisfaction when telephone enquiries were answered within ten seconds (measured by a meter reading on staff phones) and customer letters were answered within two days (measured by an audit). Finally, an annual customer survey measured whether overall customer satisfaction remained above 90 per cent.[31]
- *Rewards*. Alignment of rewards (such as career progression, bonuses and other incentives, peer recognition and increased status, and skills development) with consistent employee behaviour can be a potent means of reinforcing and sustaining desired new behaviours. Consider the argument that 'what gets rewarded, gets repeated'.[32] Yet, management generally underestimates the power of signals and symbols in effecting strategic change. Jackson, for example, refers to recognition and rewards as 'underused motivational tools'. He cites simple schemes that companies have implemented which have had a significant impact on job performance and motivation. One example is Pizza Hut in the United Kingdom, where managers are able to present employees with an awards cheque at any time to recognise outstanding work performance. Employees are able to accumulate these in exchange for prizes such as an overseas holiday.[33]

Distributed leadership (principle 2)

As we discuss in chapter 3, effective leaders in high-performing companies are no longer involved in the detail of organisational operations, but are more concerned with crafting strategy and confronting the challenges involved in leading change. They devolve responsibility for operational decision-making and performance improvement to experienced and trusted individuals in formal positions of authority operating at different levels of the organisation[34], working either independently or cooperatively in teams. Effective senior managers appreciate, in a complex and fluid business environment, that the days when all the answers could be found at the top are gone; they need to be able to rely on capable and trusted personnel distributed across the entire organisation. Drawing on his leadership studies, Kotter argues that the more complex and fluid the business environment, the more crucial it becomes to have leaders across the entire organisation.[35] Companies that he found were successful in this regard actively sought to develop leadership qualities in young employees. Many discovered that the process of decentralising to smaller business units devolved responsibility to less senior staff and created a more challenging work environment.

These themes are reiterated in the studies undertaken by Turner and Crawford, who spent six years investigating 243 cases of corporate change in Australia and New Zealand. They found that empowerment — along with commitment, understanding and *esprit de corps* — has a strong positive relationship with change effectiveness. They note, however, that empowerment 'not only means having the authority, power or freedom to act, it also means having the skills and resources to take action'.[36] Indeed, devolving authority to people who lack the necessary skills and resources to behave and act differently will be likely to achieve nothing other than resentment and hostility.

Integration of effort (principle 3)

Allied to the principle of *distributed leadership*, senior managers of excellent companies understand that only organisations that are flatter, less hierarchical, more interested in involving employees in their work, more open and more concerned about integration across functional departments can be responsive to a changing environment. This means breaking down the traditional barriers between functional areas, involving able employees at all levels of the organisation in the planning and decision-making processes, and encouraging the cross-fertilisation and sharing of ideas among different business areas. Professor Barry Posner, Dean of the Leavey School of Business, Santa Clara University, underlines this point when he argues that 'new attitudes require successful organisations to provide employees with a culture that encourages them to not only come up with new ideas but to take some of the first steps to implement them. Part of that is devolution, a flattening of the organisation and requires bold thinking.'[37]

Being out front (principle 4)

Being out front is about being an industry leader in all aspects — in customer requirements and customer responsiveness, environmental policy and practice, industry standards, supplier partnership development, quality, product design and features, and technology management.[38] This principle underpins the importance of feedback mechanisms that provide timely, accurate information on individual and organisational performance. 3M, for example, skilfully combines technical innovation with clarity of purpose and focus. At 3M, organisation members continually pose the question 'What can we do that will delight our customers?'.[39]

Being up front (principle 5)

Up-front companies communicate honestly and openly with everyone (staff, customers, suppliers), and act with integrity. They are imbued with a 'transparency' of action and a 'culture of openness' and information sharing.[40] This principle clearly links with the principles of *alignment*, *distributed leadership* and *integration of effort*, underlining the interplay between these principles and how they support and strengthen each other. Of concern for Australian corporations is the 2004 *Eye on Australia* study, which found that the majority of employees and consumers do not trust corporate Australia. According to the findings, 84 per cent of Australian consumers and employees believe that corporate Australia is only interested in profits; 83 per cent perceive companies as greedy and around 66 per cent consider them untrustworthy and heartless.[41] What, if any, brands are getting it right? Among those brands that Australian consumers seem to trust the most are Australia Post, Herron and Aussie Home Loans. Australia Post is perceived as putting people before profits. Australia Post Managing Director, Graeme John, believes strongly in honesty and transparency and has 'infused Australia Post with his ethics'.[42] Similarly, the face of Aussie Home Loans, friendly, down-to-earth John Symonds, is seen not only as honest and straight talking but also *caring*. Thanks to his signature cry, 'at Aussie, we'll save you' many disenchanted Australians moved their loans from the major banks which were seen as selfish and heartless, and definitely only in it for the money. In 2000, Herron won public support because of its swift and decisive action in response to an extortion attempt and the discovery of contaminated paracetamol tablets. The company immediately ordered the removal of all Herron products from retail outlets nationwide and called a press conference to report what had occurred and to outline the steps being taken to ensure public safety. As a result of its openness and honesty over the incident, when Herron products ultimately returned to the super-market shelves, the company was overwhelmed by consumer support for the brand.[43]

Resourcing the medium term (principle 6)

Excellent companies are not interested in the quick fix, but in their long-term strategic health. They are able to balance effectively their short-term operations with their medium-term development and growth issues. Paul Kerin, Professor of Business Strategy at Melbourne Business School, for example, argues that the latest faddism for 'top-line growth' tends to destroy rather than create value. In this regard, the most successful organisation leaders don't jump on the latest bandwagon, but demonstrate discipline and judgement and instil this approach into followers. For example, when Mark McInnes became CEO at David Jones, he viewed department stores as a 'mature format' to be 'managed for value, not growth'. By communicating and instilling a committed and disciplined approach to this simple but effective strategy, David Jones' shareholder value had almost doubled in one year.[44]

Time based (principle 7)

Speed of response, coupled with continual innovation, has developed as a critical organisational value. Professor Mark Dodgson, Director of the Technology and Innovation Management Centre at the University of Queensland, stresses that 'innovation drives competitiveness. It constructs value and creates efficiencies.'[45] The ability of organisations to influence or predict accurately the shifts in consumer needs or expectations, and to respond flexibly and on time, will increasingly determine their survival and competitive edge. To manage and compress cycle times, organisations must underpin excellent cost, quality and flexibility with quality improvement and process management capability.[46]

Bias for action (principle 8)

In companies with a bias for action, people at all levels are open and responsive to change. These companies recognise that planning and consultation need to be translated into decisive action. They enact decisions in both words and deeds, which foster a climate of trust, commitment and cooperation. Mark Dodgson refers to innovation as both an outcome and a process, a fusion of 'managerial decisions, organisational structures and combinations of resources and skills' through which new products and services are realised, but it is the connections and interchange between the components of the innovation process that are crucial to sustainable competitive advantage.[47] Consequently, if sustainable competitive advantage depends on continuous innovation, a *bias for action*, which presupposes a willingness to share information, knowledge, ideas and expertise, emerges as a key pre-requisite. Procter and Gamble, for example, employs a system of 'connect and develop' that facilitates connections between sources of new ideas and solutions to problems.[48]

Learning focus (principle 9)

In leading companies, learning is seen as a critical factor for all employees, not just the prerogative of senior managers. Samson notes that excellent companies 'work actively to transfer knowledge to others' and 'invest in the brains of all of their employees'.[49] In a survey of the 100 fastest growing small and medium-sized companies, *BRW Fast 100* found that only 28 per cent of these companies identified financial rewards as the key to motivating staff. According to Therese Rein, Managing Director of Ingeus, a recruiting and training company, 'work is about being part of a community, being part of a team, about developing and learning, and having the opportunity to do that.' She argues that when organisation members understand and are committed to the organisation's values and can see how their work underpins these, it motivates them to contribute 'huge amounts of discretionary effort'.[50]

Enabling disciplines (principle 10)

In adhering to this principle, an organisation 'invests in policies, procedures and standards and applies a strong systems perspective in everything it does'.[51] In boundaryless organisations that encourage cooperative individualism, enabling disciplines provide 'loose–tight couplings'[52], allowing 'creativity, innovation, and speed, while instilling coordination, focus and control'.[53] What is it, for example, about Macquarie Bank that makes it an 'employer of choice'? Based on a survey of Macquarie Bank's 5700 employees worldwide, Elizabeth O'Leary, Head of Recruitment and Careers, says the critical 'employment value proposition' is the freedom within defined boundaries offered to employees. 'There's a culture of enabling individuals to explore options within frameworks. It promotes entrepreneurialism and drive.'[54]

Measurement/reporting and publication (principle 11)

An organisation needs both tactical and strategic information to help it manage its business and assess its future.[55] This principle is clearly tied to the principle of being *up front*. It requires an openness and willingness to share information and knowledge and, most importantly, to act on that information quickly and decisively to exploit opportunities or resolve problems. In the best companies that Samson studied, employees had ready access to information centres in which graphic representations of 'performance attributes and trends' were displayed on bulletin boards. 'This builds commitment in the workplace, helps everyone understand the causal effect between actions and performance and builds an alignment between workers and their managerial control systems'.[56]

If continuous improvement and learning are the catchphrases of high-performance organisations, then regular performance measurement and review are integral to this approach. As Jackson points out, however, there is 'a relationship between the frequency of the cycles of measurement, learning, and the opportunity for improvement available to an organisation'. If, for example, an organisation conducts customer satisfaction surveys once a year, then this provides only one true opportunity to analyse performance and address problems, when significant gains are more likely to be achieved by doing this weekly or monthly. The success of this approach depends on user-friendly measurement systems, easily accessible data and skilled people who have the resources and motivation to implement improved work processes in identified problem areas.[57] At Flight Centre, an incentive-based business, where everyone is employed on a low base retainer, constant feedback is the key with performance monitoring conducted 'daily, weekly and monthly' and team leaders trained to consider at all times what employees need to be more successful.[58] (For more detailed discussion on measuring and evaluating organisational processes, see chapter 9.)

Customer value (principle 12)

Leading companies go to great lengths to 'stay close to the customer'. Their distinctive qualities are their ability to:
- create new customer demands
- predict changes in customer needs before they actually happen
- identify customer needs that the customer cannot articulate for themselves
- relentlessly pursue previously unserved customers.[59]

'Customer passion' from the Chief Executive down is regarded as essential for 'maximising customer value'. In firms enjoying superior financial performance, senior managers are 'spending more time concentrating on the organisation's assets outside the firm relative to those controlled directly from within — that is, the customer base'.[60]

Capabilities creation (principle 13)

In leading companies, 'business and organisational capabilities are defined and prioritised and drive critical development and investment decisions'.[61] The fact that a company's superior and distinctive capabilities are essential prerequisites for superior and distinctive customer value that attracts new customers and ensures existing customers return underscores the nexus between capabilities creation and driving customer value.

Consider Pack & Send, discussed earlier. The company has invested considerable time and resources into strategic planning, drawing on information from a range of sources, both local and global. This approach has resulted in a clearly framed strategic direction that is challenging, yet realistic and achievable. Within this clearly defined strategic framework, the Pack & Send franchises work relatively autonomously, with Michael Paul, Managing Director, removed from the day-to-day detail of the business, and taking on a more consultative, mentoring role.

Micro to macro (principle 14)

Leading companies understand that a systemic, 'big picture' approach is essential to understanding how each part of an organisation and each individual connects with each other and contributes to overall business success. They recognise the interdependence and interplay among the multiple facets of organisational life, and the importance of an inside-out approach.

Competing in the new economy: the role of guiding principles

Discussion of the fourteen guiding principles for change management has attempted to illustrate the point made earlier that these are not discrete, unrelated factors that an organisation must attend to independently. On the contrary, it is only by recognising and understanding how the fourteen principles overlap, strengthen and support each other that their potential to assist an organisation compete and succeed in the new business environment will be realised.

The discussion and illustration of the fourteen management principles should demonstrate that the development of powerful, distinctive organisational capabilities depends on balancing and conciliating both hard and soft issues. Innovation and focus are the key themes underpinning the principles. On the soft side, these demand highly skilled, highly motivated, committed and empowered employees who are well informed and understand how their efforts contribute to overall company success, and who are willing to seize the initiative and take responsibility for their actions. Fundamental to unleashing the skills and capabilities of employees is strong, 'personalised' leadership at the top with 'distributed' leadership, such that individuals in formal positions of authority operate at different levels of the organisation.[62] Many of the examples included in the discussion on the fourteen guiding principles attest to this. Realisation of the key themes of innovation and focus also depends on the hard, tangible issues that support, legitimise and serve to coordinate and focus the intangibles. These are addressed through the principles *resourcing the medium term, enabling disciplines*, and *measurement/reporting and publication*.

The synergies that evolve from linking and aligning the fourteen management principles makes even more compelling the argument for 'helicopter' vision — that is, vision that can not only appraise the pattern of organisational life, but also look beyond the organisation and national boundaries to trends in diverse industries around the world, to prepare for the unknowable as well as the knowable elements of the future.

The preceding discussion illustrates that the fourteen guiding principles for change management — which focus on aligning employee values and behaviour; encouraging distributed leadership and integration of effort; being out front and up front; working to enhance customer value and ensure flexibility, quality and speed of delivery; and fostering learning and investment in core capabilities — are incompatible with an organisational mindset that restricts people and processes to functional, linear modes of thinking and acting. On the contrary, these principles help shape an organisational culture whose strength derives from a holistic, interactive and integrated approach to the organisation's internal and external environments. They embody a distinctive organisational paradigm — one that is able to balance and integrate both the hard and soft dilemmas that modern working organisations must inevitably experience in an environment characterised by flux and uncertainty.

Dilemmas of change

Stace and Dunphy suggest that managers and change agents must recognise and attend to five dilemmas when managing the change process: adaptive or rational strategy development; cultural or structural change; continuous improvement or radical transformation; empowerment or leadership and command; and economic or social goals.[63] As they argue, it is easy to reject one approach for the other because they seem to represent diametrically opposite views. The culture at Macquarie Bank, for example, is described as loose–tight. Its non-hierarchical management approach and entrepreneurial spirit encourage high levels of autonomy and discretionary power within a strong risk management framework (the 'tight' component of the cultural equation). Macquarie Bank's Chief Executive Officer, Allan Moss, believes that an adaptive, dynamic corporate culture, in partnership with a coherent and coordinated approach to doing business, are essential to success in a global marketplace where customers demand quality, consistency and reliability.[64]

These dilemmas reflect the ongoing tension between continuity and change in organisations. It means managing the dynamics of human interaction and responses to external perturbations alongside institutionalised structures, systems and routines, and harnessing this dynamic to challenge existing practices where these are no longer appropriate. This explanation illustrates that the key to managing change is learning how to balance and conciliate what often appear as conflicting dilemmas — that is, skilfully merging:

- **rational strategic planning** *with* **adaptive strategic thinking**. Rational strategic planning sets the direction, considers resources and budgeting, and provides a clearly defined focus and vision of future possibilities. Adaptive strategic thinking highlights the notion of strategy as a, trial-and-error learning process, of having the ability to change and adapt in a largely unknown environment (see chapter 3 for further discussion).

- **cultural renewal** (that is, surfacing and challenging the core values, beliefs and assumptions, or 'the way we do things around here') *with* structural change (that is, improving operational efficiencies through tangible changes to existing organisational work processes, systems and reporting structures). An innovative, creative culture depends on equally dynamic, adaptive and thoughtfully designed organisational systems and structures to sustain and support it. The importance of aligning systems and structure with culture is nowhere better illustrated than at National@Docklands, where the new workplace has been carefully designed to nurture an open, cooperative, egalitarian, flexible and dynamic corporate culture (see 'Perspectives: New ways of working').

- **empowerment** *with* strong leadership at the top. The need for strong leadership that provides a clear overarching vision and focus seems particularly critical in the new-age, boundary-less organisation, which must learn to balance the need for autonomy with the need for interdependence. The focus of the leaders' role has shifted, however, from power and control to their skills as teachers, counsellors and negotiators, reflecting a mindset shift from 'leadership as personal achievement to leadership as organisational capability'.[65] Professor Roger Collins argues that excellent chief executives allow others to be leaders by 'encouraging autonomous work groups and the concept of **self-leadership**'.[66] As discussed earlier in this chapter, given the urgent need for organisations to develop their intellectual capital and pursue innovation, the concept of self-leadership, or taking charge of one's own destiny, emerges as integral to building a learning organisation.

   Leaders need to integrate the hard rational, analytical, planning, organising and controlling skills with the soft human relations skills. Although the hierarchy of responsibility may still exist, if the principle of *distributed leadership* is to be realised, then the uni-directional, top-down chain of command must be replaced by influences from a variety of sources and levels (see chapter 7 for further discussion on leadership for change).[67]

- continual, **incremental adaptation** *with* **radical transformation**, when sudden, unexpected environmental shifts occur that require decisive, unilateral action. Those who support the gradual, incrementalist approach to managing organisational change point out that an organisation cannot change the colour of its spots and adopt new behaviours overnight. Advocates of radical transformational change believe, however, that incrementalism is not possible for many companies that need to change their very identity. Many would argue, for example, that the National Australia Bank has little time for navel gazing or a softly-softly approach to change if it is to overcome the widespread alarm and concerns generated after the Bank's foreign exchange fiasco and the ensuing public brawls that erupted in the Bank's upper echelons.

- social goals *with* economic goals. 'Economic rationalism' is concerned primarily with maximising shareholder value. While the role of market forces has preoccupied decision-making in Western, capitalist societies, it is now being challenged by the view that the corporation has responsibilities to a much wider range of stakeholders. As the guiding principles suggest, and later chapters of this book also attest to, managers in high-performing organisations recognise the importance of building a strong, values-based corporate culture and establishing a wide network of 'collaborative and mutually supportive relationships' with suppliers, customers, employees and the wider community to ensure the ongoing success and viability of their business.[68]

PERSPECTIVES   New ways of working

NAB's Campus MLC in North Sydney inspired the design of National Australia Bank's new $270 million headquarters in Melbourne's Docklands. Frank Cicutto, NAB's former Managing Director, saw the project as the physical manifestation of major cultural change, gathering together the different arms of the Bank into a 'truly integrated financial services' company. His successor, John Stewart, is also strongly committed to the new development.

The 'inclusive, informal, communicative and "gender neutral"' design and layout of National@Docklands (N@D) represent a huge cultural leap from the Corinthian and Doric columns, grand hallways, marble facades, and closed offices of NAB's old headquarters located in a 'multi-storey "masculine" high-rise' on the corner of Bourke and Collins Streets. While the previous headquarters symbolised Establishment and the power and status of the Bank, the radically new design, which drew inspiration from 'the family home, cafes, public buildings and shopping plazas', represented a generational shift to more egalitarian, informal, collaborative team-based interaction in the workplace. According to James Grose of Bligh Voller Nield, the principal architect of the project, N@D 'is all about human interaction and communication' and 'represents a dramatic shift away from the hierarchy-based workplace towards an activity-based workplace.'

The building is described as resembling a giant Rubik's cube or LEGO house. Key features of N@D are:
- the focus on light and space. In the centre of the building, an atrium rises eight storeys to a steel-framed glass ceiling.
- gangways inlaid with ironbark that crisscross the atrium linking floors and encouraging people from different parts of the Bank to connect both formally and informally.
- modular, open plan work areas. There are no private office spaces, not even for senior managers who 'are on the floor' emphasising a communal, egalitarian environment; and everyone has a view.
- Modern kitchens equipped with cooking facilities and island benches aim to link work and family; internal cafes; rest areas and study areas.

While supporters of N@D say the new workplace structures have created a more accessible, open and egalitarian working environment, others are less sanguine: 'It might be a new building but the old structures are still here. It takes more than glass and steel to change that.'

Source: Adapted from Paul Robinson 2004, 'No team room? No mahogany row? It's the office, but not as we know it', *The Age*, Saturday, 24 July, News, p. 5. Reproduced with permission of Paul Robinson; Derek Parker 2004, 'Planning the workspace', *Management Today*, September, pp. 27–9; Catherine Fox 2004, 'Oh What a Building', *AFR BOSS*, March, p. 32.

These dilemmas — particularly whether to pursue cultural or structural change, and incremental adaptation or radical transformation — are discussed further in relation to the 'Change management in action' case on ETOMS (page 42). As noted above, the dilemmas of whether to pursue rational strategic planning or adaptive strategic thinking, and empowerment or leadership and command are discussed in chapters 3 and 7 respectively.

Understanding corporate culture

Before we investigate the dilemma of whether to pursue cultural renewal or structural change at ETOMS, it is important to understand what is meant by corporate culture and to consider the various dimensions of culture. Hampden-Turner describes culture as follows:

> Culture comes from within people and is put together by them to reward the capacities that they have in common. Culture gives continuity and identity to the group. It balances contrasting contributions, and operates as a self-steering system which learns from feedback. It works as a pattern of information and can greatly facilitate the exchange of understanding. The values within a culture are more or less harmonious.[69]

Schein explains culture as:

> A pattern of basic assumptions — invented, discovered or developed by a given group as it learns to cope with the problems of external adaptation and internal integration — that has worked well enough to be considered valid and, therefore, to be taught to new members as the correct way to perceive, think, and feel in relation to these problems.[70]

As these definitions suggest, the culture of each organisation is unique, shaped by the values and beliefs of those who inhabit it. As it evolves and takes shape, culture works to coordinate and control behaviour, action and decision-making within organisations. Culture reflects, therefore, not just the explicit, written rules of an organisation, but also the unwritten, subconscious, intangible assumptions and beliefs that shape organisational behaviour and are manifested in all facets of day-to-day life. These include leadership style (empowerment or command and control); language and dress (formal or casual); ways of communicating (one-way or two-way; open and upfront or closed and carefully guarded); organisational structure (tall or flat; simple or complex; rigid or fluid, flexible and adaptive); and whom the organisation regards as heroes and winners, along with the basis of competitive success (individualistic/collective or cooperative).

Schein explains culture as operating on three levels, from the highly visible, easily identifiable aspects to the invisible, preconscious aspects of culture. These three layers of corporate culture, described below, make up the organisation's shared frame of reference or mindset.[71]

1. *Artefacts*. Usually easily identified, these are the observable products of culture, such as architecture, office layout, manner of dress, behaviour patterns, language and documents (for example, mission, objectives, strategies).

2. *Values and beliefs*. These are expressed values and beliefs about how and why things are done the way they are, which Schein refers to as 'debatable, overt, espoused values'. While values and beliefs may not be directly observable in the way in which artefacts are, they represent issues that people in the organisation can bring to the surface and discuss. Organisational members will be aware of the organisation's espoused values and beliefs regarding teamwork, customer service and risk-taking, for example. These values may provide an accurate picture of what actions may be taken in given situations, but it is important to recognise that *espoused values* may differ from *values-in-action*. Senior managers may state that innovation and

risk-taking, for example, are encouraged and rewarded in their company. If subordinates have experiences that do not match this statement, they are more likely to believe that those who play it safe and by the rules are those who are rewarded.

3. *Assumptions*. These represent the real core of the organisation's culture: the hidden, invisible aspects of organisational life that people find difficult to explain and identify. They represent a 'taken-for-granted' approach to how things should happen and consequently are extremely difficult to change. Unless these deep-seated assumptions are surfaced and challenged, however, little will change in an organisation.

Johnson and Scholes depict the components of organisational culture in the form of a cultural web (figure 2.1), underlining the synthesis between these elements and how they feed off each other.[72] At the centre of the web are the core beliefs and assumptions that represent the organisational paradigm or frame of reference. These deeply held beliefs and assumptions are pivotal to guiding and framing the other elements of organisational culture depicted in the web, which represent not only the visible, identifiable aspects of culture (such as structures and control systems) but also the less tangible, harder-to-define aspects (such as symbols and stories, routines and rituals, and power networks). By attempting to understand these intricate and often complex inter-relationships, it is possible to identify elements — both tangible and intangible — that are likely to help or hinder the direction and success of organisational change.

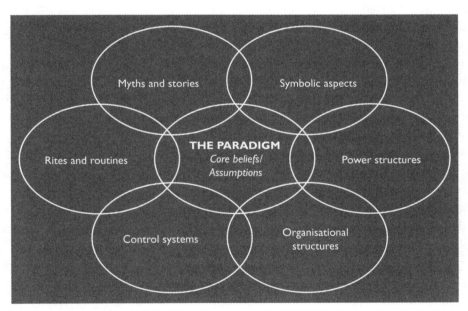

FIGURE 2.1: The cultural web

Source: From *Exploring Corporate Strategy*, 5th edition, by G. Johnson & K. Scholes, © 1999 Prentice Hall Europe. Reprinted by permission of Pearson Education Ltd.

Balogun and Hope Hailey describe the other elements of the web depicted in figure 2.1 as:[73]

• the *routine ways* in which members of the organisation behave towards each other and outsiders. They comprise the way in which things are done which at best facilitate the working of the organisation and may provide a distinctive and beneficial organisational competence, and at worst hinder progress and stymie creativity.

- the *rituals* of organisational life — such as planned special events (awards and ceremonies), training programs, promotion and assessment — that reinforce the way in which things are done and signal what is important and valued in the organisation.

- the *stories*, as told by members of the organisation to each other, outsiders, new recruits and other stakeholders, that provide the context for the present against organisational history and flag important events, personalities and mavericks who deviate from the norm. Many stories are told about the founding fathers or organisational heroes who serve as role models and become legends. At Disney, for example, Walt Disney's vision is deeply embedded in the structures, systems, language and rituals of the organisation. During induction programs, new recruits (cast members) learn that Disney is about show business; 'guests' enter a magic kingdom and as performers in a live show, the job of cast members is to entertain and make people happy.

- the more *symbolic aspects* of organisations, such as logos, offices, cars and titles, and the type of language and terminology commonly used, that become a short-hand representation of the nature of the organisation.

- the *control systems*, measurements and reward systems that emphasise what is important in the organisation, and focus attention and activity. Where people promoted are widely regarded within the organisation as being non-risk-takers, for example, this would seem to indicate that rewarding innovation is not highly valued.

- *power structures*, which are likely to be associated with the key constructs of the paradigm (figure 2.1). The most powerful managerial groupings in the organisation are likely to be the ones associated with core assumptions and beliefs about what is important. Office layout and type of furniture (status symbols), for example, may provide insights into this aspect of culture.

- the formal *organisational structure* and the more informal ways in which the organisation works. These are likely to respect power structures and, again, to delineate important relationships and emphasise what is valued in the organisation.

The cultural web provides management with a cultural audit of the organisation. It provides a means for those managing the change process to bring to the surface the hidden assumptions as well as the more readily identifiable values and beliefs. This makes it easier to identify where the change managers will encounter major roadblocks to change and where they may find supporters and allies. They can thus prioritise their change agenda and implement appropriate mechanisms to manage the change process. The web also highlights that the tangible and intangible components of culture, as with the dilemmas of change discussed earlier, are not discrete elements but work together at best to shape distinctive organisational competencies or at worst to impede the growth and development of the organisation.

Having briefly investigated the nature of culture and its composite parts, we now outline the value of the cultural web in identifying the extent of change that needs to be made to an existing organisational culture, and to those tangible and intangible aspects that underpin the existing paradigm. To do so, we draw up a cultural web using information from the 'Change management in action' case on ETOMS (page 42). The following discussion then considers ETOMS' approach to resolving the dilemmas of cultural or structural change, and incremental adaptation or radical transformation.

Applying the cultural web

In this section, we build a graphic representation of a cultural web for ETOMS prior to change based on the information given in the 'Change management in action' case. The cultural web in figure 2.2 depicts the 'taken-for-granted' aspects of the organisation and should provide an audit of the company's culture and help identify the main barriers to change. Uncovering the underlying assumptions that constitute the paradigm, however, requires a great deal of sensitivity and well-honed observation skills, because these pre-conscious assumptions often are evident only in the action and behaviour of people, not in what is expressed.

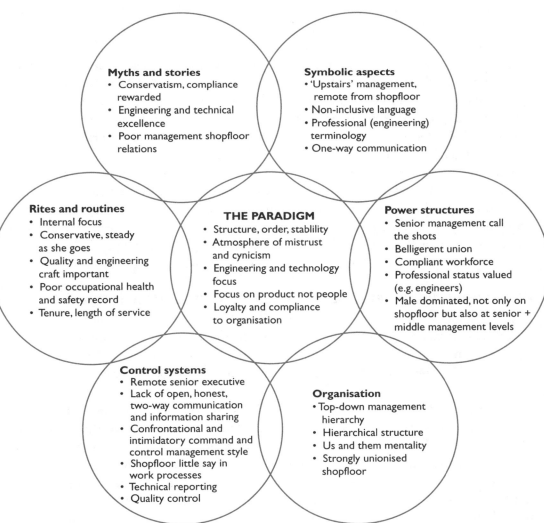

Myths and stories
- Conservatism, compliance rewarded
- Engineering and technical excellence
- Poor management shopfloor relations

Symbolic aspects
- 'Upstairs' management, remote from shopfloor
- Non-inclusive language
- Professional (engineering) terminology
- One-way communication

Rites and routines
- Internal focus
- Conservative, steady as she goes
- Quality and engineering craft important
- Poor occupational health and safety record
- Tenure, length of service

THE PARADIGM
- Structure, order, stability
- Atmosphere of mistrust and cynicism
- Engineering and technology focus
- Focus on product not people
- Loyalty and compliance to organisation

Power structures
- Senior management call the shots
- Belligerent union
- Compliant workforce
- Professional status valued (e.g. engineers)
- Male dominated, not only on shopfloor but also at senior + middle management levels

Control systems
- Remote senior executive
- Lack of open, honest, two-way communication and information sharing
- Confrontational and intimidatory command and control management style
- Shopfloor little say in work processes
- Technical reporting
- Quality control

Organisation
- Top-down management hierarchy
- Hierarchical structure
- Us and them mentality
- Strongly unionised shopfloor

FIGURE 2.2: A cultural web of ETOMS prior to change

Resolving the dilemmas of change

In this section, we examine whether ETOMS has succeeded in balancing the dilemmas of cultural renewal versus structural change; and continuous incremental adaptation versus radical transformation.

Cultural or structural change

The cultural web demonstrates the enormous difficulties that ETOMS faced in trying to break down a singularly entrenched corporate culture. Despite the growing sense of urgency, there was considerable resistance and little understanding of how to respond to the discontinuous changes taking place within a highly competitive, volatile environment. Tsoukas and Chia suggest that *how* organisations respond to external forces is shaped by internal factors and routines. Consequently, 'the pattern of response depends on an organisation's self-understanding—the historically created assumptions and interpretations of itself and its environment'.[74] While organisation members may understand the reasons for change (the *why* component of change), if self-leadership and self-directed learning have not been part of the pattern of corporate behaviour and action, they are unlikely to know either *what* needs to change or the *how-to* of change. To fulfil these elements, they must now be given the skills and resources to think and act very differently. The Strategy Map was the 'power tool' used at ETOMS to try and unlock once sacrosanct behaviours, routines, values and attitudes. The Strategy Map simultaneously targeted both the divisive hierarchical 'us and them' structure and workplace behaviours. By starting with the senior executive, the critical role this group plays in engaging others in the new ways of working through their behaviour and actions was clearly recognised. Improving senior management communication and interpersonal skills and banning 'below the line behaviour' was the first step in breaking down the hierarchical structures and encouraging more participatory, egalitarian and open management–worker relations. Consequently, structural change was integral to cultural renewal, working in tandem to break down the physical and psychological barriers that had existed for so long between workers and management.

Continuous incremental adaptation or radical transformation

As the 'Change management in action' case (page 42) illustrates, the immense shift in ETOMS' external environment — from being relatively stable, predictable and abundant, to being highly volatile, insecure and unpredictable — opened a gaping chasm between where the company was and where it needed to be to remain an industry leader.

Continuous, incremental adaptation, which focuses on increasing productivity and operational efficiency[75], represents two of the four forms of change that Stace and Dunphy observed in successful corporate transformations (discussed in further detail in chapter 7), namely *developmental* and *task-focused* transitions. However, as the ETOMS experience indicates, the process of reviewing work processes, systems and structures is not enough to change long-held values, attitudes and beliefs. In fact, it served not only to underline the gap between its existing skills and capabilities and those it urgently needed to develop to meet its changing environment, but also highlighted how current workplace structures, systems, values and behaviours were the biggest threat to its survival. As with the 'Opening case' on The Palace, ETOMS' experiences highlight the problems of the organisation that has become 'frozen by the emphatic success of the past'[76] and the difficulties involved in changing well established, carefully guarded behaviours and routines. However, if it wanted to survive in the cutthroat global airline industry, ETOMS needed to surface and challenge existing company attitudes, values and beliefs that were clearly unsustainable in such a highly competitive, volatile environment. In essence, it had to radically transform 'the way we do things around here'.

As we have seen, the ETOMS corporate transformation process focused on challenging deep-seated behaviours and providing its people with the tools and techniques to change these. In addition to the key role senior managers played in communicating the reasons for change and winning and mobilising support among other key players in the company, the involvement of 100 employees positioned at different levels of the organisation as 'map guides' served to encourage ownership and commitment among co-workers to the new ways of working. The ETOMS major change initiative, however, was the Strategy Map. Through story telling, board games, graphic mental models, and tapping into traditionally taboo areas, the Strategy Map set out to strip ETOMS of its conservative, inward-focus and remote, command and control management style and transform it into a revitalised division with an external, global focus; open and engaged management that is highly visible and engaged; an empowered workforce working in a flexible, participatory work environment in which everyone is treated with respect.

The major change initiatives implemented by ETOMS represent Stace and Dunphy's third and fourth forms of change: *charismatic transformations*, which demand radical, decisive, organisation-wide action to redefine strategic direction and develop new skills and competencies; and *turnarounds*, which represent framebreaking change (see chapter 7) in which established routines, systems and structures, values and behaviours are uncovered, questioned and recast.

In conclusion, the ETOMS experience supports the view that successfully implementing and sustaining the momentum for organisation-wide change demands a long-term, strategic approach, integrating both hard (strategy, structure, systems and technology) and soft (vision, values, behaviours and attitudes) dilemmas. The experience of ETOMS demonstrates that these dilemmas (rational or adaptive; structural or cultural; continuous improvement or radical transformation; empowerment or leadership and command; social goals or economic goals) complement and reinforce each other; to favour one over the other impedes the organisation's ability to move forwards because that approach presents a distorted, one-sided view of the organisation's situation, its strengths, weaknesses, opportunities and threats, and where it can develop distinctive, sustainable capabilities.

Stace and Dunphy's four forms of change also highlight the context-sensitive nature of change, which will indicate whether fine-tuning or framebreaking change is needed. Each organisation's change context is unique on many fronts, including the combination of environmental elements, time, place and people. In addition, organisations must be aware that solutions that worked successfully in the past may not be appropriate now and even may have disastrous consequences in a changed context.

Review

This chapter attempted to demonstrate how the direction, intensity and pace of change has increased, resulting in environmental complexity, turbulence and uncertainty. Public policy changes such as industry deregulation, the opening up of economic markets, increasing global competition, the rapid pace of technological change and the dramatic growth of service industries, effected wholesale changes to the nature of competition within and across industries, upsetting traditional boundaries and ways of doing business. In addition, global political conflict, terrorism, and phenomena such as severe acute respiratory syndrome (SARS) only serve to heighten the need for increased resilience and responsiveness as firms move progressively from a domestic to global strategic focus. Many companies were completely unprepared for these changes. Organisations quickly found that managing discontinuous change requires very different management and leadership skills and necessitates breaking out of the established organisational paradigm and developing a completely new configuration.

Discussion of the fourteen guiding management principles indicated that organisations must adopt a new, holistic approach to managing organisational change — one that views the organisation as a dynamic, open system of interdependent parts that embraces both the hard and soft dilemmas of change. You learned that to balance, and resolve the tension between, the hard and soft dilemmas, requires a single, overarching vision and focus, good management principles and processes, and a supportive and enabling culture. We drew on a number of real-life examples to consider the role of fourteen guiding management principles in framing and driving an organisation's vision, values and focus. These practical examples illustrated the synergistic nature of the guiding principles and underlined how their application can assist an organisation to compete and succeed in the new business environment.

An organisation that lives by these guiding management principles would embody a distinctive organisational paradigm, able to balance and integrate both the hard and the soft dilemmas of change, skilfully merging rational strategic planning with adaptive strategic thinking; cultural renewal with structural change; empowerment with strong, personalised leadership at the top and distributed leadership through the organisation; and incremental adaptation with radical transformation.

We further investigated the importance of balancing and integrating these dilemmas by analysing the corporate transformation process at ETOMS, as outlined in the 'Change management in action' case (page 42). At this point, we briefly considered what is meant by corporate culture, studying Schein's explanation of culture as operating at three layers of more or less visibility: artefacts, values and beliefs, and assumptions. We then considered Johnson and Scholes' depiction of organisational culture in the form of a cultural web that represents taken-for-granted aspects of organisational life. We demonstrated the power of the cultural web to provide a cultural audit and to bring to the surface any underlying assumptions by building a cultural web of the 'Change management in action' case.

In attempting to resolve the dilemmas of whether to pursue cultural or structural change, or incremental adaptation or radical transformation, we studied the evolution of the corporate transformation process at ETOMS. This case demonstrated how an organisation embarking initially on operational improvements will more than likely progress to more radical, transformational change whereby improving operations becomes an ongoing process as an organisation moves towards viewing change as a permanent item on the agenda. From these observations, we can conclude that successfully implementing and sustaining the momentum for organisation-wide change demands a long-term, strategic approach, integrating each and every one of the hard (strategy, structure, systems and technology) and the soft (vision, values, behaviours and attitudes) dilemmas.

Key terms

adaptive strategic thinking. Creative, intuitive approach to strategy-making; responding flexibly to opportunities as they emerge, (p. 55)

continuous improvement. Ongoing evaluation of work processes, systems and structures to see whether they can be improved, (p. 44)

cultural renewal. Identifying and challenging the core values, beliefs and assumptions that guide organisational thinking and action. This is about corporate cultural change. (p. 56)

deregulation. The removal of regulations governing the control of operations in, for example, the banking, telecommunications, automotive and agricultural industries. An example of deregulation is the reduction of tariff barriers on imported cars in the automotive industry. (p. 40)

discontinuous change. Rapid, turbulent, unpredictable change, forcing a radical departure from the familiar, (p. 40)

empowerment. Making employees responsible and accountable for their actions, (p. 56)

global business environment. Where competition is no longer constrained by national borders, creating a global village and economy, (p. 40)

holistic. A systemic, organisation-wide approach to change that recognises the interconnectivity of an organisation's components, (p. 45)

incremental adaptation. Predictable, familiar change that is managed as a series of small, gradual steps made within the context, or frame, of the current set of organisational strategies and components. It focuses on individual organisational components/subsystems rather than the entire organisation — for example, improving work processes, systems and structures to increase efficiency and productivity. (p. 56)

radical transformation. Revolutionary, framebreaking organisation-wide change that addresses fundamental changes in the definition of the business, shifts of power and changes in organisational culture (that is, changes in established behaviour patterns, routines and rituals, and so on), (p. 56)

rational strategic planning. A formal, systematic approach to strategy formulation, (p. 55)

self-leadership. Taking charge of one's own destiny, one's own learning and development, (p. 56)

Review questions

1. Define the concept 'drivers of change'. What have been the key external drivers of change for the industry within which your organisation operates?
2. What is meant by the term 'intellectual capital'? Give examples.
3. What is the difference between continuous and discontinuous change?
4. Describe the newly emerging organisational paradigm.
5. What does distributed leadership mean?
6. Distinguish between the principles 'being out front' and 'being up front'.
7. Describe the hard and soft components of each of the five dilemmas of change, noting which are hard and which are soft.
8. Describe Schein's three levels of culture. Provide illustrations from your organisation of each.

Discussion questions

1. Are the dilemmas of change complementary or mutually exclusive? Support your answer.
2. 'Innovation drives competitiveness.' Prepare a response to this statement. In your response, define innovation.
3. Outline and provide examples of the different elements of the cultural web.
4. Figure 2.2 (page 61) represents a cultural web of ETOMS (see 'Change management in action' case, page 42) prior to change. Review and amend this to reflect the culture at ETOMS post-change.

Work assignment

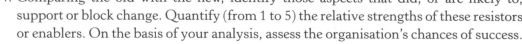

Using a cultural web to analyse corporate culture
Work individually or in groups (maximum of four).

Total time: 40–60 minutes

For this work assignment, you are required to audit the culture of your organisation, or an organisation that you are familiar with.

1. Individually, read through the section 'Understanding corporate culture' in this chapter. Analyse the web developed from the 'Change management in action' case (page 42) to make sure you understand what the elements of the web comprise.
2. Use the web to build a cultural framework that represents the organisation where you work, or with which you are familiar, *before* the change project was implemented (or, if the change project is still at proposal stage, develop a cultural web that represents the current situation within the organisation).
3. Now use the cultural web to build a framework of the organisation *after* change was implemented or as you would like to see it.
4. Comparing the old with the new, identify those aspects that did, or are likely to, support or block change. Quantify (from 1 to 5) the relative strengths of these resistors or enablers. On the basis of your analysis, assess the organisation's chances of success.

Suggested further reading

Balogun, J. & Hope Hailey, V. 2004, *Exploring Strategic Change*, 2nd edn, Pearson Education Limited, England.

Gupta, Anil K. & Govindarajan, Vijay 2002, 'Cultivating a global mindset', *Academy of Management Executive*, 16(1), pp. 116–26.

Stace, D. & Dunphy, D. 2001, *Beyond the Boundaries: Leading and Recreating the Successful Enterprise*, 2nd edn, McGraw-Hill, Sydney.

Tsoukas, H. & Chia, R. 2002, 'On Organisational Becoming: rethinking Organisational Change', *Organization Science*, 13(5), pp. 567–82.

End notes

1. R. Duane Ireland & Michael A. Hitt 1999, 'Achieving and maintaining strategic competitiveness in the 21st century: the role of strategic leadership', *Academy of Management Executive*, 13(1), pp. 43–57.

2. Fortune 1993, 'Jack Welch's lessons for success', *Fortune*, 25 January.

3. Phil Ruthven 2004, 'The cleverish country', *BRW*, 18–24 March, p. 69.

4. Ruthven 2004, op. cit.

5. D. Limerick & B. Cunnington 1993, *Managing the New Organisation*, Business and Professional Publishing, Sydney, p. 38.

6. R. M. Kanter, B. A. Stein & T. D. Jick 1992, *The Challenge of Organizational Change*, The Free Press, New York, p. 12.

7. Y. Doz & H. Thanheiser 1993, 'Regaining competitiveness: a process of organisational renewal', in *Strategic Thinking: Leadership and the Management of Change*, eds J. Hendry & G. Johnson, with J. Newton, John Wiley & Sons, Chichester, pp. 293–310; R. W. Beatty & D. O. Ulrich 1991, 'Re-energizing the mature organization', *Organizational Dynamics*, 20(1), pp. 16–30.

8. P. K. Ruthven 1999, 'Foreword', in *How Big Business Performs: Private Performance and Public Policy*, eds P. Dawkins, M. Harris & S. King, Allen & Unwin, St Leonards, New South Wales, p. viii of pp. v–ix.

9. Francis J. Flynn & Jennifer A. Chatman 2004, 'Strong Cultures and Innovation', in *Managing Strategic Innovation and Change*, 2nd edn, eds Michael L. Tushman & Philip Anderson, Oxford University Press, Oxford, p. 235 of pp. 234–251.

10. P. F. Drucker 1969, *The Age of Discontinuity*, Harper & Row, New York; D. Stace & D. Dunphy 1996, *Beyond the Boundaries*, McGraw-Hill, Sydney.

11. D. A. Nadler & M. L. Tushman 1999, 'The organization of the future: strategic imperatives and core competencies for the 21st century', *Organizational Dynamics*, 28(1), pp. 45–60; D. Stace & D. Dunphy 2001, *Beyond the Boundaries: Leading and Recreating the Successful Enterprise*, 2nd edn, McGraw-Hill, Sydney.

12. P. Cappelli, L. Bassi, H. Katz, D. Knoke, P. Osterman & M. Useem 1997, *Change at Work*, Oxford University Press, New York, p. 31.

13. See, for example, D. Ulrich & M. F. Wiersema 1989, 'Gaining strategic and organizational capability in a turbulent business environment', *The Academy of Management Executive*, 3(2), pp. 115–22; D. Limerick & B. Cunnington 1993, *Managing the New Organisation*, Business and Professional Publishing, Sydney; H. Bahrami 1992, 'The emerging flexible organization: perspectives from Silicon Valley', *California Management Review*, 34(4), pp. 33–52; R. W. Beatty & D. O. Ulrich 1991, 'Re-energizing the mature organization', *Organizational Dynamics*, 20(1), pp. 16–30.

14. P. Dawkins, M. Harris & S King 1999, 'The private performance of big business: an overview', in *How Big Business Performs: Private Performance and Public Policy*, eds P. Dawkins, M. Harris & S. King, Allen & Unwin, St Leonards, New South Wales, chapter 4, pp. 47–54; D. Samson 1999, 'Management principles and profitability', in *How Big Business*

Performs: Private Performance and Public Policy, eds P. Dawkins, M. Harris & S. King, Allen & Unwin, St Leonards, New South Wales, chapter 8, pp. 91–107.

15. Samson, op. cit., p. 94.
16. Samson, op. cit., p. 95.
17. G. Dessler 1999, 'How to earn your employees' commitment', *The Academy of Management Executive*, 13(2), pp. 58–67; J. Pfeffer & J. F. Veiga 1999, 'Putting people first for organizational success', *Academy of Management Executive*, 13(2), pp. 37–48.
18. Catherine Fox 2004, 'Choose me', *AFR BOSS*, 7(5), pp. 18–24.
19. Catherine Fox 2004, 'When it comes to the bottom line', *AFR BOSS* 7(5), p. 24.
20. D. Turner & M. Crawford 1998, *Change Power: Capabilities that Drive Corporate Renewal*, Business and Professional Publishing, Sydney, pp. 92–3.
21. G. Hamel & C. K. Prahalad 1994, *Competing for the Future*, Harvard Business School Press, Boston, p. 136.
22. Deborah Tarrant 2004, 'Strategic planning works for Pack & Send', *Management Today*, May, p. 40.
23. ibid.
24. Samson, op. cit., p. 96.
25. ibid.
26. D. Jackson 2000, *Becoming Dynamic: Creating and Sustaining the Dynamic Organisation*, Macmillan Business, London, pp. 124–7.
27. Stace & Dunphy, op. cit., p. 212.
28. David James 2004, 'Cochlear gets cosy', *Business Review Weekly*, 29 July – 4 August, pp. 62–3.
29. ibid, p. 63.
30. ibid, p. 63.
31. Stace & Dunphy, op. cit., p. 58.
32. B. Bertsch, & R. Williams 1994, 'How Multinational CEOs Make Change Programmes Stick', *Long Range Planning*, 27(5), p. 18 of pp. 12–24.
33. Jackson, op. cit., p. 134.
34. R. J. Butler, D. H. R. Price, P. D. Coates & R. H. Pike 1998, 'Organising for innovation: loose or tight control?', *Long Range Planning*, 31(5), pp. 775–82; C. Handy 1997, 'New language of organising', *Executive Excellence*, May, pp. 13–14; D. Jackson 1997, *Dynamic Organisations: The Challenge of Change*, Macmillan Business, London, p. 100; R. Whipp & A. Pettigrew 1993, 'Leading change and the management of competition', in *Strategic*

Thinking: Leadership and the Management of Change, eds J. Hendry & G. Johnson with J. Newton, John Wiley & Sons, Chichester, p. 210 of pp. 199–228.
35. J. P. Kotter 1995, 'Leading change: why transformation efforts fail', *Harvard Business Review*, pp. 59–67; J. P. Kotter 1990, 'What leaders really do', *Harvard Business Review*, May–June, pp. 103–11.
36. D. Turner & M. Crawford, 1998, *Change Power: Capabilities that Drive Corporate Renewal*, Business & Professional Publishing, Warriewood, NSW, p. 76.
37. Susan Owens 2004, 'Talent and ideas will make the difference,' *Management Today*, March, pp. 44–6.
38. Samson, op. cit., p. 98.
39. Mark Dodgson 2004, 'Innovate or die', *Business Review Weekly*, August 19–25, p. 54.
40. ibid., p. 98.
41. Simon Lloyd 2004, 'Greedy, Boring, Dishonest, Faceless', *Business Review Weekly*, 22–28 April, pp. 33–9.
42. ibid, p. 34.
43. ibid, p. 34.
44. Paul Kerin 2004, 'Create value', *Business Review Weekly*, 19–25 August, p. 55.
45. Mark Dodgson, op. cit.
46. Samson, op. cit., pp. 99–100.
47. Mark Dodgson, op. cit.
48. ibid.
49. Samson, op. cit., p. 100.
50. Jacqui Walker 2003, 'Secrets of profitability', *Business Review Weekly*, 15–21 May, pp. 68–9.
51. Samson, op. cit., p. 94.
52. T. J. Peters & R. H. Waterman Jr 1982, *In Search of Excellence*, Harper & Row, New York, p. 318; N. M. Tichy & M. A. Devanna 1990, *The Transformational Leader*, John Wiley & Sons, New York, p. 267.
53. Bahrami, op. cit., p. 37.
54. Deborah Tarrant 2004, 'The key to becoming an employer of choice', *Management Today*, September, p. 20 of pp. 19–21.
55. Jackson 1997, op. cit., p. 80.
56. Samson, op. cit., p. 101.
57. Jackson 2000, op. cit., p. 129.
58. Deborah Tarrant 2004, 'Employer of Choice', *Management Today*, September, pp. 19–21.
59. Samson, op. cit., p. 102.
60. John Roberts 2004, 'Customer passion', *Business Review Weekly*, 19–25 August,

pp. 52–3. (John Roberts holds a joint appointment as Professor of Marketing at the AGSM and the London Business School.)

61. Samson, op. cit., pp. 94, 103.
62. Butler, Price, Coates & Pike, op. cit., pp. 775–82; Handy, op. cit., p. 16; Jackson 1997, op. cit., p. 100; Whipp & Pettigrew, op. cit., p. 210.
63. Stace & D. Dunphy 2001, op. cit.
64. S. Owens 2001, 'Keepers of the corporate soul', *Australian Financial Review*, 28 April, p. 4.
65. Roger Collins 2004, 'Leadership', *Business Review Weekly*, 19–25 August, p. 55.
66. ibid.
67. C. Hampden-Turner 1994, *Corporate Culture: How to Generate Organisational Strength and Lasting Commercial Advantage*, Piatkus, London, p. 168; Kanter et al., op. cit., p. 12.
68. Dunphy & Griffiths, op. cit., p. 156; Stace & Dunphy, op. cit., p. 13.
69. Hampden-Turner, op. cit., p. 21.
70. E. H. Schein 1985, *Organizational Culture and Leadership*, Jossey-Bass, San Francisco, cited in Hampden-Turner, op. cit., p. 21.
71. E. H. Schein 1990, 'Organisational culture: what it is and how to change it', in *Human Resource Management in International Firms*, ed. P. Evans, Macmillan; E. H. Schein 1981, 'Does Japanese management style have a message for American managers?', *Sloan Management Review*, Fall, p. 64.
72. G. Johnson & K. Scholes 2002, *Exploring Corporate Strategy*, 6th edn, Prentice Hall, Harlow, United Kingdom, p. 230.
73. Julia Balogun & Veronica Hope Hailey 2004, *Exploring Strategic Change*, 2nd edn, Pearson Education Limited, England, p. 243.
74. H. Tsoukas & R. Chia 2002, 'On Organizational Becoming: rethinking Organizational Change', *Organization Science*, 13(5), p. 578 of pp. 567–82.
75. Stace & Dunphy, op. cit., pp. 106–18.
76. G. Lewis, J. Clark & B. Moss 1988, 'BHP reorganises for global competition', in *Australian Strategic Management: Concepts, Context and Cases*, eds G. Lewis, A. Morkel & G. Hubbard, Prentice Hall, Sydney, pp. 283–96.

3

STRATEGY AND CHANGE

OPENING CASE

Fit and focused at Pacific Brands

In 2001, the large manufacturing conglomerate, Pacific Dunlop (PacDun), sold off its Pacific Brands division to a private equity consortium for $730 million. Once Pacific Dunlop's cash cow, Pacific Brands was in bad shape with a debt of $570 million, having been neglected and milked dry to bolster other ailing businesses in the PacDun group. Yet, just three years later, Pacific Brands (PacBrands) is reputed to be worth more than $1 billion, with sales revenue up 4.7 per cent to $1.5 billion for the 2004 financial year ended 30 June. How did this transformation occur?

As one of the many and diverse group of businesses (including tyres, batteries, footwear and ice cream) within Pacific Dunlop, Pacific Brands had to share systems and resources with an unrelated collection of companies that were managed as an entity rather than allowed to operate as individual businesses, a framework which Paul Moore, current CEO of Pacific Brands, refers to as 'averaging'. It had little control over its own destiny and could do little more than watch as its profits were syphoned off to support others in the group.

After being accustomed to dealing with the complex bureaucratic systems and structures of a large public company for many years, Pacific Brands and Paul Moore (who had been with Pacific Dunlop for 25 years) had to learn to think and act very differently. Within a private equity structure, Moore learned quickly that a more decisive, entrepreneurial and opportunistic management style was essential.

Brave New Way, PacBrands' turnaround project, aimed 'to reduce costs by driving complexity out of the business and making operations "better, easier, faster"'. Focus and innovation, underpinned by a new mindset that valued and rewarded flexibility, speed of response, accountability and responsibility, formed the cornerstone of the organisation's new strategic direction. Unprofitable factories were closed, the workforce was slashed, non-core brands were sold off, and much of its manufacturing activities were outsourced or, as in the case of labour-intensive manufacturing, moved offshore. This has allowed Pacific Brands to focus on building and integrating its design, marketing and distribution capabilities. Its brand development strategy has played a significant part in lifting Pacific Brands' margin and market share. A central plank of this focused, revival strategy has been to concentrate on re-energising one or two key brands, familiar to every Australian household, but which had been left to languish. Its innovative marketing campaign for Bonds, for example, featuring Australian personalities Sarah O'Hare and Pat Rafter as 'ambassadors' rejuvenated the Bonds label, increased consumer awareness and saw double-digit sales growth to $180 million in 2003. With the successful revitalisation of its core brands, PacBrands is extending its brands (e.g. from Bonds underwear to outerwear) and considering 'emerging export opportunities', particularly to the United States and the United Kingdom.

Significant investment has also been made in developing the marketing and brand management skills of the company's staff. While PacBrands recognised early on that the company's core brands were its 'unsung heroes', it realised that the business potential depended ultimately on the investment made in developing the creativity and skills of its people. 'It's the innovation of people that create the products that go into market and are snapped up by consumers. If we don't invest in people, eventually we don't have a business.'

Source: Adapted from David Crowe 2004, 'The big push', *AFR BOSS*, February, accessed on 3 September 2004 at www.afrboss.com.au/printmagazine.asp?doc_id=23014; Stephen Bartholomeusz 2004, 'Pacific Brands returns from wilderness', *Sydney Morning Herald*, 28 February, accessed on 3 September 2004 at www.smh.com.au/articles/2004/02/27/1077676966944.html; Ian Porter 2004, 'Brave new world for Pac-Brands', *The Age*, 2 March, accessed on 7 September at www.theage.com.au/articles/2004/03/01/1078117364502.html?oneclick=true; Paul Moore, Chief Executive Officer 2004, *Pacific Brands Results Presentation for the period ended 30 June 2004*, 31 August, accessed on 3 September at www.pacificbrands.com.au/ir/2004FinancialResults.asp.

Introduction

In Chapter 2, 'Understanding Change', we noted that focus and innovation are emerging as key factors for success in a customer-driven, high-tech, global marketplace. We found that organisations performing well in this environment are focusing on single industries rather than diversification; are exiting or outsourcing non-core activities; are valuing and developing their intellectual capital; are leading first and managing second; and are seeking a global reach through networks, partnerships and alliances. If we now compare Pacific Brands' strategic trajectory over the past few years with these high performance characteristics, it rates very well. It has divested itself of non-core businesses; it has recognised that its people are integral to the company's ongoing success, and has committed significant time and resources into developing their skills and knowledge base; it has adopted a more flexible, responsive 'go to market' structure and is focused on developing and extending its design, marketing and distribution expertise, thereby enhancing its research and development infrastructure and innovative capacity. By focusing on building capabilities in the design, marketing and distribution of core brands, PacBrands has established an extensive range of networks, partnerships and alliances with suppliers, manufacturers and other stakeholders based locally and over-seas. It is now strategically positioned to take advantage of emerging export opportunities and step on to the global stage.

The strategic refocus and repositioning at PacBrands point to the key actions that Hamel and Prahalad, in their landmark book *Competing for the Future*, considered senior managers needed to take if their companies were to survive and succeed. They drew up a scorecard for companies to rate whether they spend too much time trying to preserve the past and not enough time creating the future. In their view, **strategic thinking** must be driven by a clear point of view about the future of the industry in which an organisation operates. Furthermore, business leaders should be concerned first and foremost with how they would like their particular industry to evolve; what skills and capabilities their business must develop to ensure it will occupy the industry high ground; and how to organise for opportunities that may not fit neatly within the boundaries of the firm's current business units and divisions.

This chapter seeks to define what we mean by **strategy** and explores the relationship between strategy-making and change. It studies the concepts of **strategic planning** and thinking, and the distinctive but complementary role that each plays in the strategy-making process. Given the increasing complexity and dynamism of organisational environments, the need to develop corresponding 'dynamic capabilities' and respond creatively and realistically to those concerns posed above becomes even more urgent. An organisation can achieve this response only by encouraging and developing the capacity among members working at different levels of the organisation to think stra-tegically. In this context, the impact of culture on strategy development and organisational learning is explored also in this chapter. The 'Change management in action' case (page 87) on the Holden HFV6 Plant looks at one organisation's attempts to develop the creativity and 'whole-brain power' of its people through training in **emotional intelligence**. The section on organisational capabilities explores the con-cepts of resources, capabilities and core competencies and examines how resources, capabilities and competencies when linked and working together synergistically can create core competencies. We also consider the use of the balanced scorecard strategy map approach to identify an organisation's tangible and intangible assets. The balanced scorecard strategy map reinforces the view that valued innovators in today's Infor-mation Age are organisations who prize their intangible assets and recognise knowledge and learning as central to effective strategy-making. Without a solid knowledge and learning base that is constantly looking at ways to innovate and grow, the seeds for sound strategy development and implementation are unlikely to take hold.

Towards a definition of strategy

Strategy is a term used in many different settings, which makes it at once familiar but at the same time quite difficult to categorically define. In the context of organisations, strategy is generally seen as a plan or direction-setting framework that addresses key questions such as: What business are we in?; What do we aspire to become?; and What course of action, as well as resources and capabilities, are needed to achieve our goals and objectives? Answering these questions requires a sound understanding of an organisation's internal strengths and weaknesses (e.g. human, financial and physical), and external opportunities and threats (e.g. exchange rates, competition, technology, market shifts, legislative and political changes).

Further highlighting the complexities of strategy and what it encompasses, Mintzberg puts forward five formal definitions of strategy as a plan, a ploy, a pattern, a position and a perspective (table 3.1).[1] It is helpful in understanding the concept of strategy to study these definitions further.

TABLE 3.1 Five Ps for strategy	
Strategy as *plan*	Consciously intended course of action
Strategy as *ploy*	Specific manoeuvre to outwit opponents
Strategy as *pattern*	Pattern in a stream of actions
Strategy as *position*	Position in relation to organisation's environment
Strategy as *perspective*	Organisation's shared mindset

As we have suggested, for most people strategy is generally perceived as a *plan* — a consciously intended course of action that is premeditated and deliberate, with strategies realised as intended. Planned strategies can be of a general or specific nature. An example of a general strategy is 'to be number one in our business'; and a more specific strategy would outline the steps that must be implemented to achieve this general strategy. Mintzberg's concept of strategy as a *ploy* represents a specific plan. It also suggests a certain artfulness or cunning, and essentially involves engaging in specific tactics to outmanoeuvre or outsmart opponents.

Strategy also can be viewed as a *pattern* in a stream of actions taken by members of an organisation. The pattern explains regular behaviour or actions that emerge over time. Whether intended or not, these routines in behaviour come to represent the strategy. If strategy as a plan refers to **deliberate strategy** that may or may not be realised, then strategy as a pattern suggests unplanned, **emergent strategy** where patterns or routines are realised despite (or in the absence of) intentions.[2]

Position concerns an organisation's strategic positioning in relation to its environment. By asking questions such as: 'How do we go about creating a market niche?' or 'How do we protect ourselves?', an organisation scans its external environment and monitors trends that may affect the organisational/environmental 'fit'. As highlighted in the 'Opening case', **strategic positioning** is about exploiting core capabilities that differentiate the organisation from its competitors, finding what will provide that competitive edge. Strategic positioning also suggests that strategy may come about in opportunistic ways to take advantage of changes in the environment, or as a firm develops or acquires new skills and competencies. An organisation's strategic positioning in relation to its environment may be constrained, however, when strategy is imposed by external forces outside the organisation's control (for example, legislative or government policy changes, the globalisation of markets, the diffusion of technological and organisational practices).

While strategy as a position seeks to place the organisation in its external environment, strategy as a *perspective* looks inside the 'mind' of the organisation, trying to understand its shared world view. Strategy as a perspective 'is to the organisation what personality is to the individual'.[3] Perspective represents the shared mindset of the organisation — its values and belief system that frame organisational action and behaviour. As the heart and soul of the organisation, perspective, unlike plans or positions, is very difficult (if not impossible) to change. The definition of strategy as perspective is clearly linked to the concept of organisational culture which you were introduced to in chapter 2 and is explored further later in this chapter.

The key concepts of deliberate, intended strategy (as a plan and position) and emergent, unplanned strategy (as a pattern in a stream of decisions) lie at each end of the continuum of strategy formation. At one extreme, strategy as a plan represents the traditional, rational approach to strategic planning that first took hold in the 1960s and 1970s. It advocated a highly systematic, structured approach to strategy formation. Strategic decision-making was seen as a precise process that could be successfully accomplished with the use of prescribed tools and techniques. As you can imagine, the seductive simplicity of following a clearly defined sequence of activities — such as those set out in figure 3.1 — made it a very popular management tool.

1. Establish the strategic objectives (which may be at the corporate, business and/or functional levels) in line with the organisation's stated goals outlined in the mission statement.
2. Conduct an analysis of the organisation's internal and external strategic position. This involves considering other players in the industry; the organisation's own strengths and weaknesses (people skills and resources, hardware, technological resources and know-how, financial position and so on); and the macro environment.
3. Re-evaluate what the organisation hopes to achieve (objectives and goals).
4. Consider the alternatives available in line with the position established in steps 1–3.
5. Evaluate and select the best option — the one that 'fits' the organisational culture and takes advantage of organisational strengths (or the weaknesses of others) in terms of the internal and external environment.
6. Implement and monitor the preferred strategy. This stage includes establishing the resources and controls to manage the plan.

FIGURE 3.1: Rational approach to strategic planning

This step-by-step 'cookbook' approach suggests that strategic decision-making is a precise process with action clearly following the planning and selection phase. Such a linear approach to strategic planning limits an organisation's ability to change course or carry out any fine-tuning as soon as the implementation phase is underway; an organisation would find it very difficult to respond to, or take advantage of, changing circumstances in either its micro or macro environment. The problem is that the rational model, while offering a clear, understandable, systematic approach to strategic planning, contains many assumptions that are unsustainable in reality.[4] The rational model implies that the strategic management process is always 'deliberate' — that is, that strategies are realised exactly as they were intended.[5] In reality, because strategy is more typically about organisations feeling their way through an uncertain and complex environment, the intended strategies often are not realised or only part of what is intended becomes reality. Consequently, while an organisation may begin with a rational plan, what evolves may be something quite different from the actual intention; and the successful or realised strategies are often emergent strategies, which have evolved as part of a pattern in a stream of actions, as opposed to a preconceived plan.[6]

The key characteristics of strategy and strategic decision-making outlined by Johnson and Scholes illustrate the complex nature of strategy.[7] These researchers explain that strategy and strategic decisions are concerned with: the direction and scope of an organisation's activities over the long-term; matching an organisation's activities with the environment; and matching an organisation's activities with its resource capability. Strategic decisions also have major resource implications, because they can have an impact not only on an organisation's ability to take advantage of present opportunities, but also on its ability to identify and develop resource capability for future initiatives. Consequently, strategic decisions impact on decisions and activities at the operational level. In addition, the substance of strategy is influenced by the beliefs, values and expectations of key **stakeholders**, who are those in positions of power within and around the company. Finally, strategic decisions influence the long-term direction of the firm.

Organisational effectiveness versus strategy

In attempting to distinguish between operational effectiveness and strategy, Porter argues that 'operational effectiveness means performing similar activities *better* than rivals perform them'.[8] In his view, operational effectiveness encompasses the concept of best practice. He states that operational effectiveness is about 'implementing the best equipment, the new IT, improving management techniques, eliminating waste'.[9] Operational effectiveness is sought through changes to workplace systems, structures and conditions, or through the introduction of new technologies. However, these measures are not usually enough to ensure competitive advantage over the long-term. In contrast, as noted earlier, strategic positioning, or competitive strategy, is about being *different*. It depends on a firm's ability to perform activities differently or to perform different activities from those of rivals to achieve competitive advantage. Hamel and Valikangas, for example, suggest that 'a company can be operationally efficient and strategically inefficient. It can maximise the efficiency of its existing programs and processes and yet fail to find and fund the unconventional ideas and initiatives that might yield an even higher return.'[10] The risk in focusing on organisational effectiveness at the expense of strategy is that competitors are quick to seek out and imitate the key characteristics of high-performing organisations operating in the same industry. As a result, a company's once superior products, features or services become indistinguishable from those of its rivals. To achieve sustainable competitive advantage requires a whole-system approach that examines, captures and builds on the unique range of skills and resources at the organisation's disposal. This approach supports the argument for value innovation, which focuses on building the dynamic capabilities of the firm, rather than simply adopting a competition-based strategy.

Take the example of Pacific Brands (refer to the 'Opening case'). Having emerged from the shadows of Pacific Dunlop, its parent company, a vast and complex conglomerate structure, Pacific Brands found itself in the unusual position of being able to craft its own destiny. Pacific Brands' successful strategic repositioning, by reinventing the way it did business, indicates that if a firm wants to be better than rivals over the long-term, it also must be different. It can achieve this balance only by assessing organisational effectiveness against a distinctive strategic vision or purpose as outlined by Hamel and Prahalad (see 'Introduction', page 72). The 'Opening case' illustrates the relationship between organisational effectiveness and strategy where organisational effectiveness reflects the plans (innovation and change through the 'Brave New Way'), systems (building its intellectual capital; developing its design, marketing, and distribution capabilities) and structures (establishing go-to-market structures that value and reward flexibility, speed of response, accountability and responsibility, and outsourcing non-core activities) that need to be in place to support the company's strategic positioning.

Strategic positioning, in turn, requires not only the ability to think creatively, but also flexibility and responsiveness to change as a company seeks out different ways of doing business. Pacific Brands, for example, focused its attention on revamping a couple of key, iconic brands that were then considered mature, mass market brands with little promise of future growth. In a few short years, Bonds was transformed from a tired, old fashioned, indifferent quality label that focused almost exclusively on men's underwear to a funky, contemporary must-have range of underwear and leisure outerwear for men and women. PacBrands' brand development strategy, that combined creative product innovation and design with an extensive yet deceptively simple marketing campaign using young Australian personalities as 'Bonds ambassadors', was so successful in raising consumer awareness that Bonds rose from industry dog to Australia's leading underwear brand in 2003.

To be able to follow the rational approach to the letter and realise strategies exactly as intended requires an entirely predictable, acquiescent environment.[11] Given the turbulent, largely uncertain environment that organisations are typically experiencing today — a result of many factors, including deregulation, the globalisation of businesses, the rapid pace of technological change and the removal of tariff barriers — the rational top–down approach, with action separated from implementation, becomes unworkable. On the other hand, strategy as an emergent, incremental pattern in a stream of actions recognises that strategy formulation and implementation cannot and should not be orderly or discrete.[12]

Quinn terms this process of strategy development **logical incrementalism**; that is, organisations 'learn by doing'. In this sort of environment, learning is a critical factor for all employees, not just the prerogative of senior managers. Samson points out that excellent companies 'work actively to transfer knowledge to others' and 'invest in the brains of all of their employees'.[13] (Chapter 2 contains a detailed discussion of Samson's guiding principles for change management.) The problem for many firms is that past successes tend to dominate current strategic thinking and they experience enormous difficulty in attempting to unlock the long-standing, programmed routines and behaviours that now prevent them from moving forwards. This illustrates a danger of strategy development as the outcome of cultural processes. As shown in chapter 2, organisational culture 'is the deeper level of basic assumptions and beliefs that are shared by members of an organisation, that operate unconsciously and define in a basic taken-for-granted fashion an organisation's view of itself and its environment'.[14] These taken-for-granted assumptions and routines are shaped by an organisation's 'collective experience'[15] and what brought success in the past. This can result in strategic inertia, however, as organisations become mesmerised by past events and adopt a conservative, risk-averse approach to strategy development. Hamel and Valikangas astutely observe that 'institutions falter when they invest too much in "what is" and too little in "what could be".' As they see it 'legacy strategies have powerful constituencies; embryonic strategies do not'.[16] The problems of challenging the assumptions of deeply entrenched routines and patterns of behaviour are highlighted in the 'Change management in action' case (page 87) on the Holden HFV6 Plant. That company recognised, in an environment characterised by flux and uncertainty, that a capacity for innovative, divergent strategic thinking, which challenged existing routines and assumptions, was essential if the company was to remain an industry leader. The problem facing senior management at the Holden plant was how to stimulate more innovative and cooperative behaviour and action among management and the shopfloor. Training in emotional intelligence was seen as the best means to open up dialogue, raise self-awareness and turn around the traditional 'hard-wired' mindset.

Quinn argues that truly effective strategy-making cannot rely on a rigid set of predetermined routines, but must be dynamic, opportunistic, flexible and adaptive:

> The validity of a strategy lies not in the pristine clarity or rigorously maintained structure, but in its capacity to capture the initiative, to deal with unknowable events, to redeploy and concentrate resources as new opportunities and thrusts emerge and thus to use resources most effectively toward selected goals.[17]

This view of strategy-making as a creative, dynamic, responsive and often intuitive process within the framework of a largely unpredictable environment fits more closely with the concept of strategic thinking. Mintzberg argues that strategic planning and thinking involve two distinct thought processes: planning concerns *analysis*, which is about establishing and formalising systems and procedures; and thinking involves *synthesis*, which is about encouraging intuitive, innovative and creative thinking at all levels of the organisation.[18] Does this approach mean that strategic planning and thinking are incompatible or irreconcilable opposites? Can planning and thinking co-exist harmoniously? These questions are discussed and the concept of strategic thinking is analysed further in the following sections.

Defining strategic thinking

From the preceding discussion, it is clear that the traditional prescriptive model of strategic planning, which served organisations well in times of relative plenty and stability, is no longer tenable in the context of the complex and uncertain environment that confronts most organisations today. This situation is particularly so in industries that are driven by technological change and that face increasing competition as a result of deregulation and privatisation.[19] Traditionally, strategy was 'about building long-term defensible positions or sustainable competitive advantage'.[20] Today, however, strategy must focus on continual adaptation and improvement, and be 'constantly shifting and evolving in ways that surprise and confound the competition'.[21] As we have stressed previously, it is about moving from a competition-based focus to a value-innovation focus that invests in building the 'dynamic capabilities' of the organisation by developing and integrating its knowledge, skills and resources.

'The heart of strategic thinking is to be strongest at the decisive point.' An organisation needs to identify what sets it apart and commit to building its skills and know-how in this area, whether it is in operational excellence; product leadership; or customer intimacy.[22] Consider the success of Virgin Blue and REX in Australia. Undeterred by lack of access to landing slots at major airports in Australia, they turned their attention to regional centres not frequented by the major carriers and made this their point of difference and 'created positions of strategic strength'.[23] As suggested earlier, an organisation needs to be able to identify what is important to the organisation and then ensure it has the capabilities to make it a reality. Virgin Blue and REX recognised that they were not in the same league as the major carriers and would only lose if they tried to play the same game. Instead, they looked for a strategic point of difference that would allow them to maximise their strengths and cancel out their weaknesses.[24]

In the face of an unpredictable, highly volatile and competitive marketplace, a capacity for divergent strategic thinking (rather than conservative, convergent strategic planning) that takes place at multiple organisational levels is 'central to creating and sustaining competitive advantage'.[25] Whereas senior management has long recognised the value of being able to think strategically, the challenge now is to build strategic thinking capabilities at middle and lower levels of management. Figure 3.2 compares the traditional strategic planning approach with the processes of strategic thinking.

As figure 3.2 illustrates, while strategic planning assumes a stable environment in which the future is clear and predictable, strategic thinking views the future as largely undefined, which we can only imagine. The belief that strategy formulation and implementation are interlinked and non-sequential components of the strategy-making process is fundamental to the concept of strategic thinking (point 2). This core tenet is linked inextricably to the two following points: the process of strategy-making not only requires a holistic, systems approach that recognises the interconnectivity and interdependence of organisation, but also is largely about the management of organisational change. Points 5 and 6 suggest that while efficiency and productivity are still important, strategic thinking depends on individuals acting autonomously and collectively, committed to a clear, shared vision and sense of purpose. Planning is not *ad hoc*, but is flexible and fluid enough to allow for opportunistic, strategic adaptation as events unfold and circumstances change.

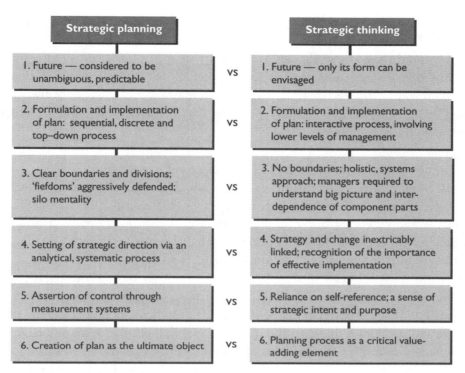

Strategic planning		Strategic thinking
1. Future — considered to be unambiguous, predictable	vs	1. Future — only its form can be envisaged
2. Formulation and implementation of plan: sequential, discrete and top–down process	vs	2. Formulation and implementation of plan: interactive process, involving lower levels of management
3. Clear boundaries and divisions; 'fiefdoms' aggressively defended; silo mentality	vs	3. No boundaries; holistic, systems approach; managers required to understand big picture and inter-dependence of component parts
4. Setting of strategic direction via an analytical, systematic process	vs	4. Strategy and change inextricably linked; recognition of the importance of effective implementation
5. Assertion of control through measurement systems	vs	5. Reliance on self-reference; a sense of strategic intent and purpose
6. Creation of plan as the ultimate object	vs	6. Planning process as a critical value-adding element

FIGURE 3.2: Traditional strategic planning approach versus strategic thinking

Traditionally, strategic planning was largely the domain of senior management. Middle management was charged with ensuring decisions were operationalised down the line. As figure 3.2 illustrates, however, the substance of strategic thinking challenges the traditional tenets on how planning should be undertaken and who should be involved in it.[26] This approach also begs the question, if middle and lower levels of managements have never been called on to 'think' strategically in the past, how can they be encouraged to do so now? The 'Change management in action' case (page 87) demonstrates how Holden used emotional intelligence training to develop the leadership and strategic thinking capabilities of organisation members at every level of its new state-of the-art manufacturing plant in Port Melbourne. The LEAD Program aimed to build a leadership culture among teams on the shopfloor as well as among the group's senior managers. Through emotional intelligence training, it aimed to develop decision-making and communication skills and equip all organisation members with the skills and tools that would help them better understand others; manage conflict; and control their emotions. By involving everyone in the program, senior management at Holden signalled its recognition that the knowledge and experience of those at the 'coalface' can add critical, valuable input to strategic decision-making.

Strategic thinking has been described variously as the ability to:

- see external opportunities and integrate these into the business (what Eisenhardt refers to as the ability to integrate decisions and tactics)[27]
- think laterally and intuitively — a person who demonstrates exceptional 'quality of understanding', 'an immense instinctive feel' and a 'superior grasp of the business'[28]

- deal with novelty and ambiguity, interpret and evaluate events and data, and determine what action needs to be taken[29]
- transfer and diffuse knowledge/information
- build multiple, simultaneous alternatives, working with a greater range of options than their more cautious, slow-response counterparts would think to be feasible.[30]

Based on her research into strategic thinking, Liedtka posits the following five major attributes of strategic thinking.

- *A systems or holistic view.* A strategic thinker understands how parts of the organisation influence each other, as well as their different environments.
- *A focus on intent.* **Strategic intent** is about creating 'stretch'. In contrast with the traditional strategic planning approach that focuses on creating a 'fit' between existing resources and emerging opportunities, strategic intent intentionally creates a substantial 'misfit' between these. Hamel and Prahalad state that the key aim of strategic intent is to impart a sense of direction, discovery and destiny.[31]
- *Thinking in time.* Strategic thinkers understand the interconnectivity of past, present and future. As discussed in the following section, scenario planning is being used increasingly to 'incorporate thinking in time'. It provides a tool for sketching possible futures and stimulates thinking about alternatives that otherwise might be ignored.
- *Hypothesis driven.* Hypothesis generating and testing is central to strategic thinking activities. By asking the creative question 'What if?' followed by the critical question 'If ..., then ...?', strategic thinking spans the analytic–intuitive dichotomy that Mintzberg refers to in his definition of thinking as synthesis and planning as analysis (mentioned earlier).
- *Intelligently opportunistic.* This attribute refers to the intellectual capacity to recognise and take advantage of newly emerging opportunities.[32]

If we compare Liedtka's five major attributes with the five preceding definitions of strategic thinking, then we see a similar pattern between them. The first two definitions — the ability to see external opportunities and integrate these back into the business; and the ability to demonstrate exceptional 'quality of understanding' and 'a superior grasp of the business' — reflect a systems or holistic view. A person with this view can see the 'big picture' and use individual and shared knowledge, intuition, insight and experience to act opportunistically.

Second, strategic intent — that is, using strategy to create stretch and leverage, and to convey a sense of direction, destiny and discovery — is reflected in all five definitions of strategic thinking. It involves the ability to integrate decisions and tactics; to think laterally and intuitively; to deal with novelty and ambiguity; and to transfer and diffuse knowledge and information. The latter is particularly critical if management is to succeed in harnessing the skills and competencies of people working at different levels of the organisation and thereby maximise its strategic capabilities.

As illustrated in the ability to deal with novelty and ambiguity, strategic intent also encompasses thinking in time, Liedtka's third attribute — particularly the ability to sketch multiple, simultaneous scenarios for the future. As a strategic intent, it deliberately seeks to disturb the organisation's equilibrium by opening, rather than closing, gaps between external demands and internal capabilities[33], daring to probe not only the identified unknown, but also what we have not identified as the unknown.[34]

This ability to think in time and sketch possible futures leads into Liedtka's attribute of being hypothesis driven, deliberately challenging the existing mindset. Posing hypothetical questions avoids the analytic–intuitive dichotomy that is typical of traditional strategic planning, because this hypothetical approach fosters both creative and critical thinking.[35] Finally, by sketching possible futures and questioning accepted wisdom, strategic thinking invokes the capacity to be intelligently opportunistic, to recognise and take advantage of newly emerging opportunities.

This discussion further underlines the need for a new strategic framework that embraces a **value-innovation focus** and encourages thinking and acting at multiple levels of the organisation. In today's knowledge era where an organisation's intellectual capital represents its most valuable resource, Kim and Mauborgne believe that value innovation is the 'essence of strategy'.[36] In the context of managing change and uncertainty, Demos, Chung and Beck also point to the importance of a value-innovation focus. They stress the need for people and process capabilities that can address simultaneously the factors for 'creating value (producing strategic innovation in products, processes and business models); aligning people to value (leading and motivating and stimulating people to become higher performance "human engines"); and delivering value (capturing the profits and other results that are promised by every strategy)'.[37] Value innovation, captured in the attributes of strategic thinking, embraces the principles of the learning organisation with its commitment to continuous improvement, trial-and-error learning and adaptation.

Thus, the ability to *think strategically* gives new meaning and insight to the process of strategic planning. This approach recognises that strategic thinking and planning are 'distinct, but interrelated and complementary thought processes'[38] that must sustain and support each other for effective strategic management. Heracleous for instance observes that 'creative, ground-breaking strategies emerging from strategic thinking still have to be operationalised through convergent and analytical thought' (strategic planning).[39] Figure 3.3 (page 82) depicts the distinct but complementary thought processes of strategic thinking and planning. As integral components of the strategic management framework, there need to be moments of convergence and moments of divergence — a synergistic tension that reconciles creativity with rationalism and pragmatism, and blends synthetic with analytic, critical thinking.[40]

Finding a balance between the two domains of strategic planning (deliberate, predetermined, rational, analytical thinking) and strategic thinking (emergent, creative, intuitive thinking) is important. By walking this fine line, strategy-making avoids the pitfalls of adopting either the over-rationalistic, prescriptive, 'steady as she goes' approach or launching into 'pie in the sky' schemes with no direction or focus, which are more than likely doomed to fail. Recognising and valuing the creative tension between strategic thinking and planning provides a driving force within the strategy-making process, as described by Mintzberg and Waters:

> . . . strategy formation walks on two feet, one deliberate, the other emergent . . . managing requires a light deft touch — to direct in order to realise intentions while at the same time responding to an unfolding pattern of action. The relative emphasis may shift from time to time but not the requirement to attend to both sides of this phenomenon.[41]

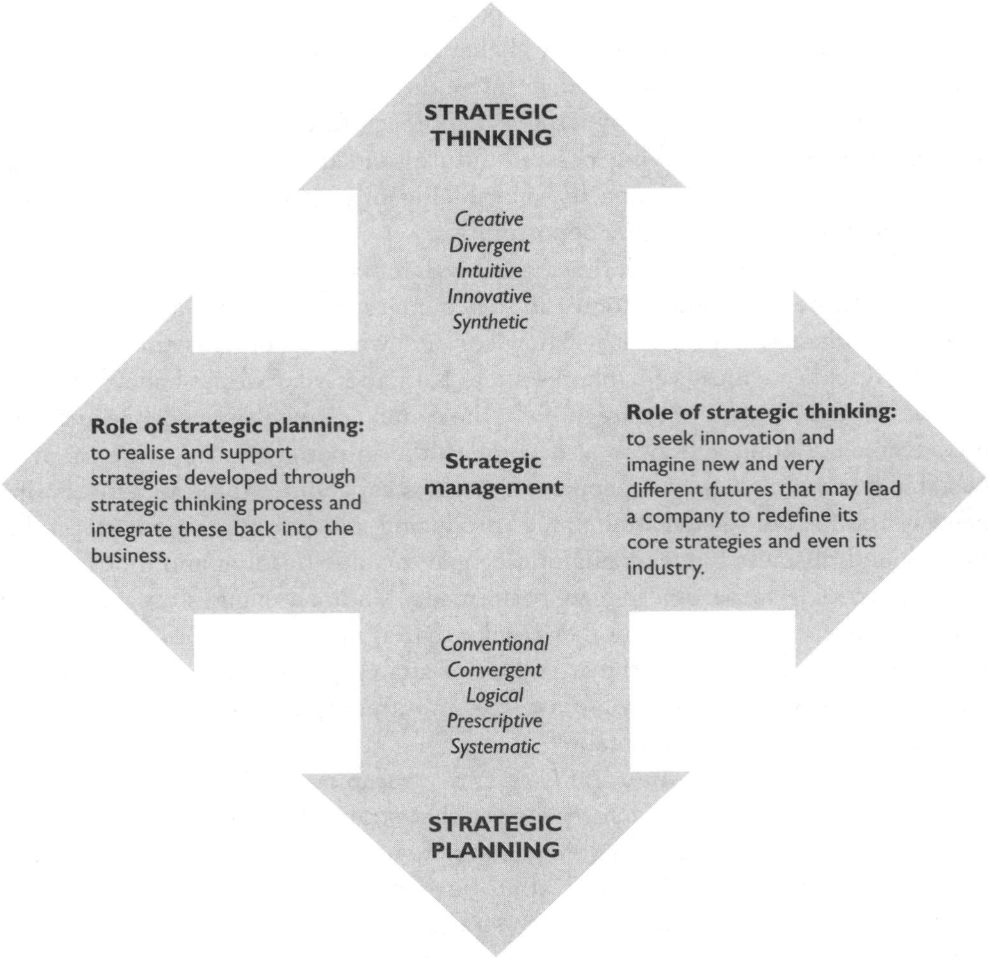

FIGURE 3.3: Strategic thinking and strategic planning

A good planning capability would encompass both domains. Business leaders wishing to compete successfully in an environment characterised by complexity, uncertainty and unpredictability need to develop strategic thinking capabilities not only at the top level, but through many levels of the organisation as well. What can leaders do to make the planning process more flexible, creative and innovative? And how do they involve others in this process in a way that will stimulate and link strategic thinking to planning at multiple levels? Scenario planning is one tool that many organisations committed to redesigning their strategic planning are using with some success. Art Kleiner, in a tribute to Pierre Wack, the 'father' of scenario planning, defines scenario planning as 'the use of alternative stories about the future, many with improbable and dramatic twists, to develop strategy'.[42] Pierre Wack introduced scenario planning to Royal Dutch/Shell in the late 1960s. As we see in the following section, scenario planning is useful in, first, bringing to the surface and challenging those taken-for-granted assumptions (which often are based on what brought success in the past) that members of an organisation share and which define an organisation's view of itself and its environment, and, second, forcing the organisation to think the unthinkable.

Scenario planning, which attempts to provide a balance between creativity and rationalism, synthesis and analysis, is discussed in the following section. Examples of scenario planning (or lack thereof) are given to help explain its function and purpose.

Scenario planning

Scenario planning has become a recognised tool for stimulating strategic thinking because it goes beyond the traditional financial and forecast-based planning approaches.[43] Scenario planning does not set out to predict the future; however, 'through superior anticipation, flexible strategies, and dynamic monitoring' that evolves from imagining a range of possible futures, Schoemaker argues that companies can extend the boundaries of what they can control over what they can't control.[44] Scenarios are written as stories that give those involved the opportunity to 'tap into their powers of intuition and imagination in a way not possible with purely rational exercises'.[45] Schoemaker describes scenario planning as a 'thinking tool and communication device that aid the managerial mind rather than replace it'.[46] As such, it is particularly valuable in times of high uncertainty and complexity because it serves to challenge the **status quo**.

By identifying trends and uncertainties in an organisation's macro environment, scenario planning:
- provides a tool for sketching possible futures
- attempts to capture a range of options
- stimulates thinking about alternatives, which otherwise might be ignored
- challenges the prevailing mindset.[47]

Scenario planning also attempts to compensate for two common errors in organisational decision-making: underprediction of change and overprediction of change. (We alluded to this problem in the previous section when discussing the need to find a balance between adopting an over-rationalistic, formulaic stance and spinning out of control.) Scenario planning avoids these problems by dividing knowledge into elements that a person knows about with some degree of certainty and elements that are considered uncertain or unknowable.[48]

Scenario planning is particularly useful where:
- environmental uncertainty is high
- there have been too many costly surprises in the past
- a company is slow to perceive or generate new opportunities
- the quality of strategic thinking is low (planning is too routinised, for example)
- the industry in which a company operates has experienced, or is about to experience, significant change (for example, the telecommunications or airlines industry)
- a common language and framework is desired, without stifling diversity
- strong differences of opinion exist, with each having merit
- competitors are using scenario planning.[49]

The basic steps for developing scenarios are to:
1. define the issues
2. identify the major stakeholders
3. gather and analyse trend data—a list of external forces that may impact on the issues identified in step 1

4. identify uncertainties — factors or events whose outcomes are uncertain and would significantly affect the chosen issues

5. sketch out a number of different scenarios, a set of 'what-if' stories that draw on the trend data to construct a narrative that is *plausible* (credible, a soundly argued story), *creative* (provides unique insights and breadth of thought), and *consistent* (combines analysis and synthesis).[50] These scenarios would generally include a best-case scenario, a middle-of-the-road scenario and a worst-case scenario.

6. assess the implications of each scenario

7. reassess your company's vision in light of the scenarios.[51] See 'Perspectives' on scenario planning for examples of scenario planning in the workplace.

PERSPECTIVES   Scenario planning

Case 1

At the time of One.Tel's collapse, the mobiles division of Optus had already, a year or so earlier, role-played senior management's meeting with the One.Tel administrator to discuss its purchase of One.Tel's subscribers. When Optus management discussed the One.Tel collapse scenario, it was just one of a series of 'what-ifs' they worked through as they scanned environmental trends and uncertainties. While they discerned signs of trouble at One.Tel, they did not at the time believe that this was the most likely scenario. As a result of their diligence, when the unimaginable happened, they were ready to step in quickly and forge a deal to transfer over 100,000 new subscribers to their network.

Case 2

Ericsson, the Swedish telecommunications equipment maker, which has been operating in Australia since the early 1900s, has used scenario planning with some success for several years now. Every two years, the company undertakes a major review of the telecommunications industry and draws up a range of scenarios based on its comprehensive study. In one such review, they identified three possible scenarios. The first, called 'grand traditionalonie', was based on the view that the major carriers would continue their domination of the marketplace. The second, called 'service mania', proceeded from the standpoint that those companies providing Internet and information services would dominate the market. The third, named 'up and away', was premised on domination by the hardware manufacturers, because consumers who buy a PC happily accept whatever services and software come with it. Within a year of this review, the 'up and away' scenario was emerging as the industry model.

Source: Adapted from Mark Lawson January 2002, 'What if?', *AFR BOSS*, accessed at www.afrboss.com.au/magarticle .asp?doc_id=18688&listed_months=32 on 14 September 2004. Reproduced with permission from Mark Lawson.

Further developing the themes incorporated in scenario planning, Day and Schoemaker, in their graphically titled article 'Driving Through the Fog: Managing at the Edge', talk about the importance of developing an organisation's peripheral vision. As they observe, it is very easy to miss or ignore early warning signs emerging on the periphery 'especially when the focal view paints such a clear and compelling picture from a very different frame of reference'.[52] Day and Schoemaker give the example of Enron Federal Credit Union where the 'unthinkable' was put forward at a scenario planning workshop held in the late 1990s.[53] The question posed was: 'What would happen if Enron ceased to exist?' As a result, the Credit Union recognised that it relied too heavily on its business with Enron and moved to extend its membership base and marketing capabilities. This proactive response to a 'what-if' scenario meant the credit union was able to continue business as usual when a few years later the unimaginable happened and Enron Corporation collapsed in spectacular fashion.

The periphery is defined as 'wherever your attention is not', bearing in mind that all things are relative and one organisation's periphery could be another's central core.[54] The difficulty for any organisation is deciding, with limited resources, where to direct its attention and the degree of intensity it needs to expend in so doing. As Day and Schoemaker put it:

> The challenge of peripheral vision is to fly reconnaissance missions over these areas *without* devoting the full attention of the organisation to them. This requires that the organisation has the capacity to identify what is important in these areas and to know when to turn the organisation's full attention to these new areas. . . . The key question to ask is whether your organisation is too narrowly or broadly focused. And a related question is whether the organisation has the requisite skill set and capacity to handle whatever information is gleaned from the periphery. . . . There are no simple formulae to answer these critical questions; they require wisdom, experience, and, above all, a strategic perspective.[55]

The issues raised in this quote point again to the importance of intangible assets, having the foresight to develop critical human (skills and knowledge), information (IT systems and client databases) and organisation (leadership and culture) capabilities and then deploy these effectively to implement strategy. In a later section, we explore the value of the balanced scorecard strategy map as a tool for plotting how to convert an organisation's assets into key strategic outcomes.

Seely Brown asks the question 'How do we become better at understanding the periphery?'[56] He argues: 'Managers need to move from managing continuity to managing discontinuity.' Discontinuities are like 'ripples in the pond' which, if we take note of them, 'can help us see and understand the periphery more clearly, but we first have to be aware of the water (i.e. the context or background) of the pond itself and be able to see the changes and differences. This requires individuals and organisations *with the capacity to sense the periphery, learn and respond from that sense making and learn to unlearn and see differently.*'[57] [our emphasis] The difficulty is getting people to unlearn and discern new patterns or inconsistencies because 'we end up interpreting new information in terms of our existing mental models and context'.[58] As a result, we often ignore or dismiss something that is different because we cannot interpret or unpack it using our existing tools of reference. IBM serves as the classic example of an organisation that failed to mind its periphery. Industry leader in mainframe computers through the 1970s, IBM dismissed the signs that the personal computer market was gathering momentum and as a consequence spent the 1980s playing catch-up to new upstarts like Compaq. Digital Equipment Corporation (DEC) was likewise caught napping with then DEC President, Ken Olson, famously quoted as saying in 1977, 'There is no reason for any individual to have a computer in their home.'[59]

Seely Brown argues that 'knowledge and learning are often created and spread through the interactions of communities of practice and other social networks. . . . Information becomes knowledge through the collaboration, narration and improvisation of these communities'.[60] He puts forward a number of tactics for building knowledge by tapping into and mining the periphery. These include building social networks; establishing listening posts; and developing communities of practice.

- *Building social networks*. This tactic refers to internal boundary-spanning units that are specifically set up to sense and respond to the periphery and act as the intermediary point bringing together, and sharing information with, disparate parts of the organisation. Smits and Groeneveld, for example, refer to the Rabobank Group, a 'broad-based financial services provider' based in the Netherlands, which has established a 'future centre' whose function is to 'create broader support and better conditions for innovation and renewal initiatives'. It allows employees from different parts of the organisation with different skills, knowledge and expertise to come together in a multi-disciplinary setting completely removed from their daily work environment and the attached structures, politics and hierarchies.[61] We also learned in earlier chapters how organisations are redesigning the workplace to create friendly spaces where organisation members are more likely to 'bump' into each other and meet and exchange information informally (see, for example, chapter 2).

- *Establishing listening posts*. This includes paying attention to employees who are at the coal-face, who act as boundary spanners and scanners interfacing with customers and clients, suppliers and distributors. In turn, the organisation's customers, suppliers and other external stakeholders, operating at the periphery, provide a valuable means of building knowledge and learning about emerging trends, changing expectations and new opportunities. The news may not always be good news, but if it is taken on board, it adds to the organisation's set of experiences, helps challenge existing patterns of thinking and identifies what the organisation must unlearn in order to create new ideas and new ways of looking at things. Seely Brown suggests that 'the key is to create a social fabric that encourages disparate points of view and that affords creative abrasion between them'.[62]

- *Developing communities of practice*. Seely Brown refers to the ability to 'link and learn from the knowledge of diverse employees who live on the customer-facing periphery' of the organisation. For example, as part of the Eureka Project at Xerox, a central database was created which linked together 23,000 technical representatives, working for Xerox in various parts of the world. The database enabled them to share knowledge and learn from each other's experiences working on different technical problems or machine faults, in different environments and contexts, and the creative solutions often applied to diagnose and fix these. It is estimated that Xerox saved more than US$100 million in the first years of the Eureka Project.[63]

The above discussion on scenario planning and the importance of 'mining the periphery' reinforce Kim and Mauborgne's assertion that value innovation is the 'essence of strategy'.[64] As with value innovation, scenario planning and the concomitant need for peripheral vision embrace the principles of the learning organisation with its commitment to continuous improvement, trial-and-error learning and adaptation.

Building emotional intelligence capacity at Holden Australia

In 2000, Holden started to put together a team that would oversee the building and preparation of its new High Feature V6 (HFV6) Plant. The $400 million state-of-the-art facility, which opened in Port Melbourne in late 2003, was forecast to turn over $450 million of exports annually. The new factory, pivotal to Holden's future in Australia, was destined to set a new industry standard.

By the end of 2001, the hand-picked team had grown to 30 people, among them planners, manufacturing engineers, systems engineers and production personnel selected for their specific skills and expertise. They were charged as a team with the task of getting the factory up and running as quickly and as smoothly as possible. A relatively simple concept in theory, but the practice proved to be anything but straightforward. Within a short space of time, the so-called team was beset with troubles that had nothing to do with plant operations, and everything to do with different personalities, and competing skills, agendas and priorities.

While a few members of the team of 30 were recruited externally, the rest were drawn from disparate parts of the organisation. The majority were long-serving organisation members who had spent 20 years or more in the same job and were used to working in a specific environment with the same group of workmates who all knew each other well. They were now expected to bond instantly with a group of strangers in an alien environment while familiarising themselves with new equipment and facilities. Amidst these unrealistic expectations, it was hardly surprising that tensions in the group were high and opposing factions began to form. In this setting, communication and cooperation was negligible and hostile at best. While a key issue was the tension between management and workers on the shopfloor, it was described as 'a whole of culture problem', not just a leadership problem.

Holden HR Director, Andrea Grant, also noted that people issues not technical skills were the crux of the problem. While the need for 'hard' skills might seem obvious in a manufacturing setting, 'soft' skills, particularly good interpersonal skills,

are just as important because 'the modular nature of the work requires high levels of productivity and coordination, which in turn hinges on good communication'. Melbourne consultants, Learning Dimensions, recruited to address these problems, custom-designed a program called LEAD — leadership through emotional intelligence, action and developing people. LEAD is 'a special intervention put in place around a team' that works well in a manufacturing environment. 'The touchy-feely' aspect of the program did cause some scepticism and resistance, but the high-profile, hands-on involvement of senior managers gave the program credibility and helped it win wider acceptance.

The LEAD program comprises six workshop modules: establishing a leadership culture; effective self-expression; understanding others; managing conflict; controlling emotions; and working effectively in teams. The original team of 30 were the first group to go through the program. With the guidance of Learning Dimensions, the team drew up a code of behaviour for the LEAD program. In the group, all team members were treated as equals and could discipline each other if any of them broke the rules of behaviour. Team members were assessed before the workshops commenced (through tests, interviews and peer review), then participated in the workshops and training modules, and assessed again at the end of the program. Their feedback was used to gauge the success of the workshops and effect further refinements to the training modules.

Key reasons for the program's success appear to be that the workers themselves recognised that they had problems and were willing to take action to resolve these; launching the plant on time was a clear goal and challenge they wanted to meet; and not least was that team members through LEAD were personally involved in developing the set of rules that underpinned new workplace values and behaviour.

Source: Adapted from Catherine Fox 2004, 'Shifting Gears', *AFR BOSS*, August, 5(8), pp. 28–32; James Thomson 2004, 'True Team Spirit', *BRW*, 18–24 March, pp. 92–3.

The issues highlighted in this 'Change management in action' case suggest that it is possible for an individual to learn, and improve his or her level of, emotional intelligence. The case also indicates a correlation between improved communication and interpersonal skills, and improved relations among team members, which in turn impacted positively on organisational commitment and workplace performance. Research suggests that it is possible and desirable for an individual to develop a more 'whole-brain' approach to his or her thinking thus improving the interaction between the left hemisphere of the brain, responsible for speech and linear, analytical and rational thought, and the right hemisphere, which is more holistic, conceptual, emotive and spatial.[65] In terms of professions, engineers, lawyers and accountants typically describe their thinking style with 'left-brain' adjectives such as logical, factual, critical and rational; while entrepreneurs, artists and playwrights, with their more visionary, risk-taking, holistic, open approach, represent 'right-brain' thinking. The left-brain adjectives sum up pretty accurately behaviours at Holden before the LEAD program began with the emphasis on 'hard' rather than 'soft' skills.

The 'Change management in action' case illustrates how individuals develop a preference for certain thinking styles, even though 'the grand design is to be whole'.[66] All parts of the brain are interconnected and we are capable of being multifunctional; however, few of us end up balancing and enabling all our mental options. Instead, preferences emerge subtly over time and are strengthened and encouraged by the environment and context in which we live, hence, in the case of Holden, the dominant left-brain engineering mentality thrived on the male-dominated shopfloor.[67] As a result, a strong correlation exists between our preferred thinking style and the skills and competencies that we acquire. Hermann notes that 'life experiences' also can help or hinder us from developing our full mental potential; for example, learning or work environments can inhibit rather than foster inquisitiveness and creativity.[68] If we consider the 'Change management in action' case, clearly the traditional command and control, individualistic work ethic in a male-dominated environment encouraged a more left-brain approach in which 'touchy feely' issues were avoided and seen as a sign of weakness. The LEAD program resulted in a more open, empathetic, 'whole-brained' approach to the way in which organisation members interacted and business was conducted that recognised and valued the skills and ideas that everyone brings to bear. In this way, organisational learning, thinking and acting become the responsibility of all members not just the senior management sanctum.

The impact of culture on strategy development and learning

In this section, we further consider the significance of culture on the development of strategy and learning. Earlier discussion on the impact of cultural processes on strategy development suggests that innovative strategy-making can thrive only within a culture of openness, information sharing, mutual trust and respect — that is, a culture that actively encourages people to ask difficult questions, to step outside the square and challenge 'the way we do things around here'. In his metaphor of the organisation as brain, Morgan suggests that three key building blocks of learning organisations are the capacity to: 'scan and anticipate change in the wider environment to detect significant variations; develop an ability to question, challenge and change operating norms and assumptions; and allow an appropriate strategic direction and pattern of organisation to emerge'.[69] These reflect the key processes that scenario planning attempts to stimulate. The importance of developing capabilities in these three areas is explored further in the following discussion.

As we saw in chapter 2, Johnson and Scholes depict the components of organisational culture in the form of a cultural web (figure 2.1, page 59).[70] The web helps expose the taken-for-granted aspects (values, beliefs and assumptions) at the core of the organisational paradigm and highlights the symbiosis between these and the surrounding political, symbolic and structural elements that underpin organisational action and behaviour. The web thus provides a framework for identifying the aspects of organisation that tend to preserve the status quo. It also can help identify the aspects of culture (for example, rituals and routines) that may be exploited to communicate and encourage new behaviours and new ways of doing things, thus improving the chances of successful strategy formation and implementation.

Crossan, Lane and Hildebrand view organisational learning as being about organisational change broadly and, more specifically, 'about the basic elements and processes by which organisations develop and grow', meaning 'growth in knowledge or understanding of the organisation, its environment and the relationship between the two'.[71] As we have seen, rational strategic planning sets the direction, considers resources and budgeting, and provides a clearly defined focus and vision of future possibilities. *Adaptive* strategic thinking, on the other hand, highlights the notion of strategy as a learning, trial-and-error process, having the ability to change and adapt in a largely unknown environment. Environmental uncertainty itself serves to challenge the traditional organisational paradigm and acts as a catalyst for innovation and change. In this environment, traditional management systems often are found wanting and organisations must search for new systems and structures that will support and encourage innovation, experimentation and learning. As noted earlier, however, trying to bring to the surface and question long-held beliefs and assumptions is a difficult task, but laying down this challenge is seen as 'a key step in creating new knowledge for the organisation'.[72]

De Long and Fahey identify four ways in which culture shapes behaviour, action (strategy-making, for example) and learning (or knowledge creation) in organisations. First, culture influences what is viewed as 'useful, important or valid knowledge in an organisation'.[73] What organisational members perceive as important is shaped by 'the way we do things around here', by the shared values and norms that govern acceptable organisational behaviour. This perception is highlighted in the well worn adage that 'what gets rewarded, gets repeated', indicating that signals and symbols consistently communicated and acted upon, will have more lasting effect than written plans or words.

Second, De Long and Fahey argue that culture 'dictates what knowledge belongs to the organisation and what knowledge remains in control of individuals or subunits'.[74] If the level of trust within an organisation is low or if the culture recognises and values individual knowledge at the expense of organisational learning, then the transfer/diffusion of knowledge between the organisation and the individuals within it is likely to be compromised. When you read the end-of-book case on William Angliss Institute of TAFE, you will note that despite the best efforts of one CEO, he regretted that silos still existed, with certain individuals protecting client information as if it were private property, and so undermining the level of knowledge available on the Institute's client database. As this case indicates, organisations only learn when the insights and skills of individuals become embodied in the routines, practices and beliefs of the organisation.[75]

Third, De Long and Fahey believe that cultural norms (the rules, expectations, rewards and punishments that shape how people interact with each other) determine how and what type of knowledge is transferred in given situations. The impact of culture on communication and information sharing within organisations can be assessed along the three dimensions of vertical interactions, horizontal interactions and special behaviours.

Vertical interaction refers to the level of knowledge and information sharing among different levels of the organisational hierarchy, particularly the degree of approachability of senior management.[76] The traditional manufacturing divide between management and the shopfloor was one key barrier to change at the Holden plant that the LEAD program effectively surfaced and challenged through the series of workshops, particularly in working through issues concerning understanding others; managing conflict; and working effectively in teams.

Horizontal interactions occur between people at the same level of the organisation and can be differentiated according to the volume of interaction, the level of cross-functional cooperation and the degree to which existing knowledge and expertise are tapped into and reused. Given an environment in which speed, abbreviated strategic life cycles and go-to-market flexibility are core strategic imperatives[77], the need for cooperation and information sharing across boundaries (between sales and marketing, for example) that allows a business to respond quickly and opportunistically to shifts in its environment is not just desirable but essential. The following quote from the chief executive officer of an Internet company illustrates this clearly:

> Increasingly sophisticated and demanding customers mean feedback and information sharing between the company's salespeople and its product developers must occur freely and regularly so that customer concerns and changing expectations are dealt with immediately. Our salespeople are attuned to what other functions in the company need, so, instead of waiting until quarterly product meetings, they are telling our product managers, 'This is what I've seen in at least ten calls during the week'.[78]

Special behaviours are promoted in cultures that 'explicitly favour knowledge sharing over knowledge acquisition'.[79] Knowledge sharing occurs where diverse and independent information is disseminated freely, where more experienced or specialist employees assume mentoring or teaching roles, and where making mistakes is recognised as an integral part of the learning process.[80]

The fourth and final point that De Long and Fahey raise concerns how an organisation's culture, with its shared values and belief systems, influences the way in which information from the external environment is selected, interpreted and disseminated through the organisation as new ideas, knowledge or routines. How individual members perceive the environment is critical to organisational learning. According to Crossan, Lane and Hildebrand, the process of individual interpretation of the environment and the creation of shared meaning from the collective experiences of an organisation result in a particular 'organisational schema'. Just as an individual schema is a 'knowledge structure that contains general rules and information for interpreting situations and guiding behaviours'[81], the organisational schema 'is the collective belief system which guides action'.[82] The processes that underpin the relationship between individual and organisational schema are depicted in figure 3.4. Figure 3.4 also illustrates the critical interplay among Morgan's three key building blocks of learning organisations (referred to on page 89).

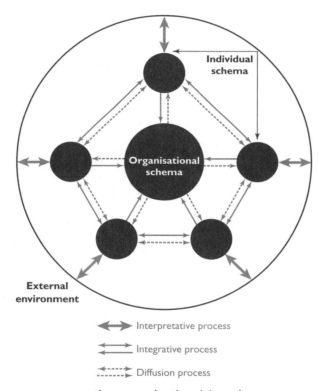

FIGURE 3.4: Key processes supporting organisational learning

Source: P. Hagel & F. Graetz 1996, 'Learning & knowledge-based organisation', Paper presented at ANZAM 1996. Reprinted with permission.

As indicated in figure 3.4, the process of interpreting occurs at the individual level. Individuals experience their environment and interpret these experiences in accordance with their personal schema. Crossan, Lane and Hildebrand argue that the potential level of interpretation of the organisation depends on the complexity of the individual schemas (that is, the ability to absorb and analyse) and the divergence among them.[83] If this process is the case, innovative strategy-making is more likely to occur within a culture that: encourages the vigorous exchange of independent and diverse views at multiple levels of the organisation; and ensures individuals interact with, and draw on stimuli from, the external environment and use this information to question assumptions, create new knowledge and pursue new business opportunities.[84]

Within the organisation, this approach depends on the ability to share, absorb and translate knowledge into action (described as interpretation, diffusion and integration in figure 3.4). Consider as an example the automobile industry. The different car manufacturers (e.g. Ford, Toyota, Holden) gather a wealth of information about their customers, yet generally have done little more with it than store it away. 'No other industry . . . has had the names, addresses and financial information on its customers for 100 years and has done less with it than the auto makers.'[85] This situation is now changing as carmakers share customer information with suppliers so that they are able to respond quickly to individual design requirements. Ford customers, for example, can watch the progress on their custom-designed car via the Internet.[86] This example at Ford highlights the importance of shifting from an industrial to information era mindset and underlines the view that knowledge, know-how and learning are core strategic issues. The concept of 'organisational learning' is being used increasingly to encapsulate what organisations must do to capture the benefits of past experience as well as change to meet future conditions. The following section considers the development of **organisational capabilities**. It also considers how culture underpins an organisation's **core capabilities**.

Developing organisational capabilities

In the preceding sections, we focused on the need for firms to develop the strategic thinking capacity of their people. We have seen that for an organisation to survive and succeed in today's 'global' world, strategic management must be about forecasting, anticipating and being creative. And senior executives are not the only ones with industry foresight. Given the opportunity to exchange ideas, information and knowledge, people from all levels of a company can help to shape its future course. To guide strategy effectively, business leaders must be able to capture and exploit the foresight that exists throughout the organisation and develop a 'dynamic capabilities' approach that is adaptive, responsive, innovative and opportunistic.[87]

In their studies of high performance, high-growth organisations, Kim and Mauborgne found that rather than trying to outperform or play copycat with their competitors, these companies pursue value innovation where the strategic focus is opportunistic and intent on 'creating fundamentally new and superior value', making their competitors irrelevant.[88] (The significance of a value-innovation focus was also discussed in the earlier section 'Defining strategic thinking'.) Kim and Mauborgne refer to competition-based strategy as a second-best, zero-sum strategy that is unsustainable because it does not create long-term wealth. On the other hand, a 'first-best' strategy through value innovation 'stimulates the demand side of the economy' by expanding existing markets and creating new ones.[89] Value innovators are knowledge-rich and prize their intangible assets (their accumulated know-how, learning and skills) over the 'traditional, finite factors of production' (the organisation's physical and financial resources). Similarly, Teece, Pisano and Shuen argue that 'if control over scarce resources is the source of economic profits, then it follows that such issues as skill acquisition, the management of knowledge and know-how, and learning become fundamental strategic issues'.[90] They point out that those excelling in the global economy are those organisations that are able to 'demonstrate timely responsiveness and rapid and flexible product innovation, coupled with the management capability to effectively coordinate and redeploy internal and external competencies'.[91] They argue that this new framework for achieving competitive advantage necessitates a 'dynamic capabilities' approach to strategy-making.

Dynamic is defined as 'the capacity to renew competences so as to achieve congruence with the changing business environment; certain innovative responses are required when time-to-market and timing are critical, the rate of technological change is rapid, and the nature of future competition and markets difficult to determine'. *Capabilities* encapsulates 'the key role of strategic management in appropriately adapting, integrating and reconfiguring internal and external organisational skills, resources and functional competences to match the requirements of a changing environment'.[92]

Business leaders have to recognise that as innovation increasingly determines a firm's competitive advantage, the firm's traditional mode of operating (its organisational capabilities) must be transformed to meet this new imperative. The key is to develop organisational capabilities that energise its people and build on other key resources. Traditionally, the focus has been on developing new products or establishing market position, rather than on internal capabilities, reflecting the difference between a competition-based and value-innovation approach to doing business as discussed earlier.[93] Schoemaker argues that there are limitations in the traditional approach of scoring the firm on a large number of attributes, such as relative strength or weakness in research and development, engineering, manufacturing, marketing, sales, product quality, product line, employee morale, compensation, reputation and so on, because not all of these attributes are of equal importance strategically. Often, these attributes are simply manifestations of fundamental characteristics that more accurately define a firm's essence.[94] So how do you track down the fundamental characteristics? Schoemaker suggests exploring core capabilities by thinking of the firm as an onion made up of layers of functions, services and production operations. Then, ask which of these truly define the firm's essence or core, and which is the periphery; for example, the outer layer for one firm may include product design, selling or even marketing, while these skills and capabilities may be the core of another firm. Schoemaker explains that 'the challenge is to think of the firm not just in terms of its visible end products but also in terms of its *invisible* assets and core capabilities'.[95] It is easy to overlook the importance of invisible or intangible assets as a resource-building capability. In some service-based businesses, for example, 'goodwill' could represent a major intangible asset of the company and may result from features such as brand name, good contacts or company image.[96] Intangible assets, therefore, are not limited to what the organisation actually owns, but also include factors outside the organisation (such as reputation and good relations with suppliers).

What, then, can help a firm distinguish between what is core and what is peripheral? Javidan suggests that first, management, as a group, needs to understand and agree on what terms like core competency, capabilities and organisational resources mean. He provides a useful conceptual framework, categorising resources, capabilities, competencies and core competencies along a continuum of increasing value and difficulty. We have depicted these different dimensions of organisational capabilities as steps on a ladder, where scaling each level creates more value, but is increasingly difficult to accomplish (see figure 3.5). At the bottom of the ladder are resources, the 'building blocks' of competencies made up of both tangible and intangible assets. These assets represent 'the inputs' into the value chain: physical resources (plant, equipment, location and assets); human resources (manpower, management training and experience) and organisational resources (culture and reputation). Capabilities are on the next rung of the ladder and are captured within functional areas (marketing, production, etc.). These assets denote the company's 'ability to exploit its resources' and represent different business processes and routines that coordinate the flow and exchange of resources. Competencies, on the next rung, flow from capabilities, providing the 'cross-functional integration and coordination of capabilities'. At the top of the ladder are *core* competencies. According to Javidan, a **core competency** 'is a collection of competencies that are widespread in the organisation'.[97] Schoemaker uses the term core capability rather than core competency. He defines a core capability as one that evolves 'slowly through collective learning and information sharing'.[98] For Hamel and Prahalad, whether the term is either capability or competency is irrelevant, the test is whether capabilities or competencies are 'core' or 'non-core'. In this book, we take a similar view. While a business leader may think of numerous capabilities that could bring success in a given industry, the greater value is in a deep understanding of those 'competencies that lie at the centre, rather than the periphery, of long-term competitive success'.[99]

As figure 3.5 illustrates, each rung draws its strength and value from the level below, resulting in increased value-added as an organisation works up the ladder, capturing and exploiting the growing network of resources, skills, knowledge and capabilities that each level offers.[100] Javidan gives the

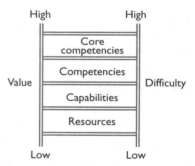

FIGURE 3.5: Organisational capabilities continuum

example of a consulting firm with offices in different locations. Over time, each office is likely to build up a unique set of skills in consulting to specific industries in their area, for example health care. Depending on how effectively the organisation as a whole is able to capitalise on this bank of specialist knowledge and expertise, it increases its value to the organisation. However, core competencies are unlikely to develop unless cooperation and willingness to share ideas and knowledge across different business units exists in the organisation. This is where organisations often become unstuck and the more people that are involved, the more complex and fraught it becomes, hence the increasing level of difficulty an organisation experiences in scaling from resources at the bottom of the ladder, through to capabilities, and competency to core competency (as illustrated in figure 3.5). These points underline the importance of earlier discussion on the impact of culture on communication and information sharing within organisations, which we learned can be assessed in terms of vertical and horizontal interactions and special behaviours. In short, unless an organisation actively encourages communication and information-sharing across vertical and horizontal intra-organisational boundaries, and promotes a culture that 'explicitly favours knowledge *sharing* over knowledge *acquisition*',[101] its ability to share, absorb and translate knowledge into action is limited. As we noted earlier, car manufacturers are beginning to recognise the untapped potential of the client database they have amassed over the years and are now taking action to value-add what they can offer customers by sharing this information with different stakeholders who can help them package and customise products to meet distinct needs.

The preceding discussion underlines the importance of adopting a holistic, 'big picture' approach to the whole process of strategy-making. Unless strategic planning is framed and underpinned by sound strategic thinking, tunnel vision develops and a short-term outcome wins over a long-term outlook. The obsession for hard facts triumphs over untried new approaches or ideas. And intangible assets are sacrificed in favour of tangible assets.

In addition, the development of core competencies or core capabilities that will be a source of sustainable competitive advantage requires an analysis of not only a firm's external environment but also its internal resource base. The resource-based view recognises that each firm is a unique amalgam of both tangible resources (for example, financial and physical assets) and intangible resources (for example, human skills, technology and reputation).[102] As we have seen, however, firms must take care that they do not overlook one set of resources in favour of another as they try to determine which assets and capabilities provide core value to the business and its strategy. The balanced scorecard approach is one method that provides a means of investigating both tangible and intangible assets, and giving them equal weight.

Balanced scorecard approach

If managers want to be competitive and add value in the long-term, they need to consider a comprehensive range of measures that offer an extensive view of the business and provide information about decisions that have already been taken. Kaplan and Norton term this holistic range of measures the 'balanced scorecard' and liken it to the dials and indicators of an aeroplane's cockpit that provide pilots with complex information at a glance.[103] The underlying strength of the **balanced scorecard approach** lies in its 'focus, simplicity, and its vision'.[104]

Kaplan and Norton support the best practice view (see chapter 4 for detailed discussion of best practice themes) that reliance on one or two measures of performance can be fatal. The balanced scorecard approach aims to force organisations away from their tendency to focus on short-term financial indicators of performance (for example, return on investment and sales growth). Kaplan and Norton suggest organisations need to review four perspectives of activities (see points 1–4 below), including both operational and financial performance. This combination allows organisations to consider 'both the drivers of performance (customer satisfaction, processes and innovation) and results' (the financials).[105] Such a four-pronged review will assist organisations to establish strategic objectives in areas that not only promote the core capabilities of the organisation, but also tap into areas that will develop future competencies (figure 3.6).

1. How do we look to customers? The *customer* perspective is the starting point on the scorecard.
2. What must we excel at? The *internal* perspective focuses on building competencies and improving operations that are critical to meeting customer needs and expectations.
3. Can we continue to improve and create value? The *innovation and learning* perspective looks at an organisation's resources and capabilities, and considers its potential to build future wealth. In particular, it focuses on individual skills and development. Traditionally, this is one area to which organisations have paid little attention.[106]
4. How do we look to shareholders? This represents the *financial* perspective that traditionally has dominated management thinking and planning.

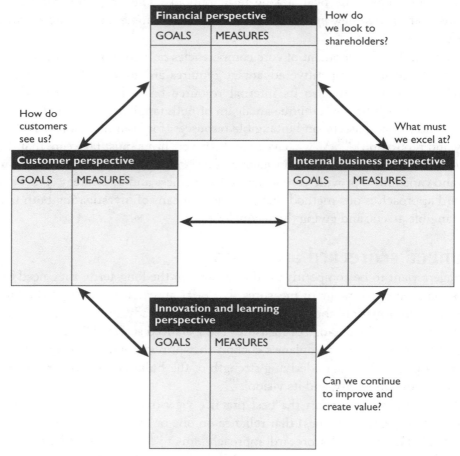

FIGURE 3.6: The balanced scorecard links performance measures

Source: Reprinted by permission of *Harvard Business Review* from R. S. Kaplan & D. A. Norton 1992, 'The balanced scorecard — measures that drive performance', January–February, p. 72 © 1991 by the Harvard Business School Publishing Corporation. All rights reserved.

The Balanced Scorecard Strategy Map

As a result of further research and work they have undertaken with many companies since introducing the Balanced Scorecard (BSC) in 1992, Kaplan and Norton have expanded the BSC into a more comprehensive framework called the Balanced Scorecard Strategy Map (see figure 3.7, page 98) that 'embeds the different items on an organisation's balanced scorecard into a cause-and-effect chain, connecting desired outcomes with the drivers of those results'.[107] The Strategy Map aims to link intangible assets to shareholder value creation through the four interrelated perspectives of the balanced scorecard referred to earlier: the *financial* perspective, which lists the tangible outcomes of strategy (ROI (return on investment), shareholder value, profitability, etc); the *customer* perspective, which defines the *value proposition* (identifying which intangibles will create value) the organisation plans to use to generate customer sales and loyalty; the *internal* perspective, which identifies the processes that create and deliver the value proposition; and the *learning and growth* perspective, which forms the basic building block of the strategy map, and identifies those intangible assets that are critical to the desired strategy.[108] Strategy maps provide organisations with the means to communicate not only their strategy, but also the processes and systems that will allow them to realise their strategic objectives. According to Kaplan and Norton, strategy maps

> ... give employees a clear line of sight into how their jobs are linked to the overall objectives of the organisation, enabling them to work in a coordinated, collaborative fashion toward the company's desired goals. The maps provide a visual representation of a company's critical objectives and the crucial relationships among them that drive organisational performance.[109]

Why use strategy maps?

During the industrial age, what mattered most were tangible assets — a firm's financial and physical resources, its land, capital and equipment. The traditional value proposition came through transforming raw materials into 'hard' products. A healthy income statement and balance sheet represented the focus of a company's business strategy. With the arrival of the Information Age, organisations learned to their cost that reliance on tangible assets alone is not enough to create long-term value, and in fact these are worthless if not underpinned and reinforced by the organisation's intangible assets (e.g. its customer relations; employee skills and knowledge; information systems; leadership). These intangibles are critical to the development of key strategic capabilities that allow the organisation to deliver value to customers, which in turn drives growth and lifts shareholder value.[110]

According to Kaplan and Norton, the best way to build a strategy map is to work from the top down, 'starting with the destination and then charting the routes that will lead there'.[111] First of all though, senior management should review the company's mission statement and core values, and from this develop its strategic vision, articulating where it is headed and how it plans to get there. Only then is it ready to start work on developing its financial strategy, where it needs to examine two key levers: revenue growth and productivity. Next, the customer value proposition is described as the 'core' of an organisation's business strategy. At this level, organisations must consider what they must do to stand apart from competitors in order to attract new customers, retain existing customers and strengthen their overall relationships with customers. This need leads them to examine their internal process capabilities, which are built around factors such as operational excellence; enhancing customer value; creating new products and services through innovation; and good corporate citizenship by promoting sound relationships with external stakeholders.[112] Underpinning the financial, customer and internal process perspectives in the strategy map is the learning and growth perspective, which 'defines the core competencies and skills, the technologies, and the corporate culture needed to support an organisation's strategy'.[113] The learning and growth perspective comprises three categories of intangible assets: human capital, information capital and organisation capital. When attempting to arrive at some definition of strategy at the beginning of this chapter, we noted that these 'bundles' of intangible assets form the foundation of every organisation's strategy and, indeed, any gaps at this level will have a major detrimental impact on the outcomes at the critical internal process level.[114]

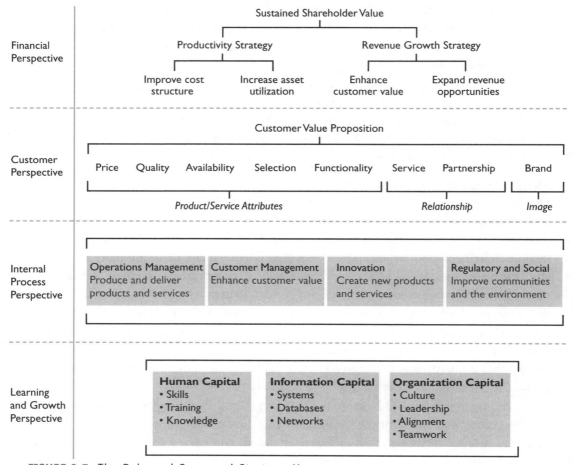

FIGURE 3.7: The Balanced Scorecard Strategy Map

Source: Reprinted by permission of *Harvard Business Review* from Robert S. Kaplan & David P. Norton 2004, 'Measuring the Strategic Readiness of Intangible Assets', February, p. 55. © 2004 by the Harvard Business School Publishing Corporation. All rights reserved.

The major advantage of strategy maps, according to Kaplan and Norton, is that they allow an organisation to identify when its scorecard is not 'truly strategic'. They point out that a common mistake organisations make is to develop *stakeholder* scorecards. Instead of building *strategy* scorecards, they develop a measurement system around their key stakeholders, namely employees, customers and shareholders. A true balanced scorecard strategy map will explain *how* it means to satisfy these key groups by mapping the action it will take within each of the four frames in the strategy map. Mapping these process elements is fundamental to the strategy. Kaplan and Norton believe strategy maps can communicate the strategy to the whole organisation. They give the example of the Mobil Speedpass used in the USA. When a customer buys petrol, the Speedpass device is passed across a photocell on the petrol pump, identifying the customer and charging the purchase against their account. A planning manager in Mobil's marketing technology group came up with the concept for a device that would automatically manage the entire purchasing transaction when he learned from the company's balanced scorecard that speed was the key to winning customer patronage and loyalty. He collaborated with a petrol pump manufacturer and a semiconductor company to develop the idea and bring it to fruition. The runaway uptake of Speedpass by consumers reinforced Mobil's value proposition of fast, friendly service and its point of differentiation from rivals.[115]

This holistic approach to performance measurement again emphasises the interdependence of, and interplay among, the multiple facets of organisational life. While it may be tempting for an organisation to deal with the quantifiable, tangible 'hard' measures first, it must not consider these in isolation or at the expense of the 'soft', qualitative measures. Both dimensions are equally critical to the identification and development of an organisation's internal resources and capabilities.

Review

This chapter explored the concept of strategy, the role of strategic planning and thinking in the strategy-making process, and the relationship between strategy and change. The discussion on strategic planning and strategic thinking led to the view that they are distinctive but complementary functions which must sustain and support each other for effective strategic management. We learned that high-level strategic thinking and emotional intelligence, which form the building blocks of an organisation's learning and knowledge capacity, are vital to a value-innovation focus and become even more critical as organisations replace the traditional 'hard-wired' approach with an entrepreneurial ethos that is more concerned with building bridges of cooperation to create high levels of synergy. The 'Opening case' (page 70) and 'Change management in action' case (page 87) both attest to this.

We then considered what tools business leaders could employ to make the planning process more flexible, creative and innovative. We studied scenario planning as a technique for stimulating strategic thinking capacity among employees. Techniques such as scenario planning are most effective when we employ both left-brain and right-brain thinking styles. The elements of left-brain thinking reflect the planning side of strategy, while right-brain thinking mirrors the creative thinking component.

We also explored the influence of culture on the development of strategy and learning. Culture comprises those taken-for-granted assumptions and routines that are shaped by an organisation's collective experience and that brought success in the past. Unchecked, the influence of culture can result in strategic inertia as organisations become frozen by the success of the past and adopt an increasingly conservative, risk-averse approach to strategy development. We learned that innovative, flexible strategy-making will flourish only in a high-trust, questioning environment in which cooperation and knowledge transfer occurs freely at multiple levels of the organisation. Within this sort of cultural framework, diverse and complementary knowledge, skills and experience interact in synergy to build a unique set of core capabilities that enhance organisational learning. This reaffirms the view that knowledge and learning, that amalgam of human, information and organisation capital are the springboard for developing an organisation's key strategic capabilities that drive its go-to-market speed and responsiveness that determine future opportunities and growth.

We then investigated factors in relation to developing organisational capabilities. We discussed the distinguishing factors that make up an organisation's resources, capabilities, competencies and core competencies and considered the characteristics that help a firm to define its core competencies and capabilities. The balanced score-card is one method of considering an organisation's tangible and intangible resources and giving them equal weight. We also examined how the balanced scorecard embedded in the strategy map provides organisations with a means of viewing strategy in a 'cohesive, integrated and systematic' manner, because it measures both intangible and tangible assets, shows the cause and effect relationships between the different scorecard perspectives (making these explicit and testable), and exposes areas of weakness.[116]

Much of the discussion in this chapter has turned around the implications of the shift in strategy-making from a competition-based approach to a value-innovation focus. Traditional strategic planning, with its focus on analysing an organisation's strength and weaknesses and aligning these with external opportunities and threats, served an organisation well in a 'hard-wired' industrial society, but is proving inadequate in today's globalised, knowledge economy where the key source of competitive advantage depends on how an organisation absorbs, analyses and shares its knowledge.[117] Our examination of strategic learning and development tools such as strategic thinking, scenario planning and the balanced scorecard strategy map add credence to the argument that skill acquisition, the management of knowledge and know-how, and learning are the building blocks of effective strategy-making in the knowledge economy.

balanced scorecard approach. A means of investigating both tangible and intangible organisational resources and giving them equal weight. It aims to force organisations away from their tendency to focus on short-term financial indicators of performance and instead view four perspectives of activities (customer, internal, innovation and learning, and financial perspectives). (p. 95)

core capabilities. Distinctive skills and technologies that provide a source of sustainable competitive advantage because they are valuable, rare/unique and not easily transferred to, or copied by, other firms, (p. 92)

core competencies. Distinctive skills and technologies that provide a source of sustainable competitive advantage because they are valuable, rare/unique and not easily transferred to, or copied by, other firms, (p. 94)

deliberate strategy. Planned, premeditated, intended strategy that may or may not be realised, (p. 73)

emergent strategy. Strategy that has evolved as part of a 'pattern in a stream of actions', as opposed to a preconceived plan, (p. 73)

emotional intelligence. Distinct from IQ and technical skills, a form of intelligence characterised by strong interpersonal skills, ability to work with others, and effectiveness in leading change, (p. 72)

logical incrementalism. The deliberate development of strategy by 'learning through doing', (p. 76)

organisational capabilities. Capabilities reflected in an organisation's shared values, assumptions and beliefs, which are manifested not only through its strategic focus, structures and systems, but also through the management style, skills and behaviour of its people. Similar to Mintzberg's definition of strategy as perspective, organisational capabilities represent the 'unconscious mind of the organisation, shaping how external change is interpreted, how strategic and tactical decisions are taken, and how internal change is managed'.[118] (p. 92)

scenario planning. A tool for stimulating strategic thinking that goes beyond the traditional financial and forecast-based planning approaches, because it can be used to capture a range of options, to stimulate thinking about alternatives that otherwise may be ignored and to challenge the prevailing organisational mindset, (p. 83)

stakeholders. Individuals or agencies with an interest or stake in the firm — for example, employees, customers, suppliers, government departments and agencies, (p. 75)

status quo. The existing state of affairs, or the 'way we do business around here', (p. 83)

strategic intent. Relentless pursuit of a certain long-term strategic objective and concentration of strategic actions on achieving that objective, even if the organisation does not have the immediate capabilities and resources. It is about creating 'stretch', or a mis-fit between resources and aspirations. (p . 80)

strategic planning. Traditional linear, rational, systematic approach to strategy formation and implementation, (p. 72)

strategic positioning. Performing different activities from those of rivals or performing similar activities in different ways, (p. 73)

strategic thinking. Creative, intuitive approach to the strategy-making process, in which strategy formation and implementation are interactive, interchangeable components, (p. 72)

strategy. The direction and scope of an organisation over the long-term — its managerial game plan for the future, which is influenced by environmental forces and resource availability, and the values and expectations of its power base (the stakeholders), (p. 72)

value-innovation focus. Organisations pursuing value innovation adopt a strategic focus that is opportunistic and intent on creating fundamentally new and superior value, making their competitors irrelevant, (p. 81)

1. Explain what Mintzberg means by strategy as plan, ploy, pattern, position and perspective.
2. Distinguish between a competition-based focus and a value-innovation focus to strategy-making.
3. Explain the difference between deliberate and emergent strategies.
4. Define and describe the five major attributes of strategic thinking outlined by Liedtka.
5. Outline the three dimensions that can be used to assess the impact of culture on communication and information sharing in organisations.
6. Explain the difference between resources, capabilities, competencies and core competencies and justify their position on the capabilities continuum.
7. Describe the purpose of the balanced scorecard strategy map and outline the functions of the four perspectives.

Discussion questions

1. Support or refute the claim that value innovation is the essence of strategy.
2. Discuss the differences between strategic planning and strategic thinking. What are the advantages and disadvantages of each?
3. What is scenario planning? Why is it considered useful in times of high uncertainty?
4. Given the turbulent and unpredictable environment facing many organisations today, consider the implications of strategy-making as a rational, planned approach versus strategy-making as an adaptive, emergent process.
5. Define tangible and intangible assets and explain their role in developing organisational capabilities. Why is it that intangible assets by themselves rarely create value?

Work assignment

Developing a balanced scorecard strategy map

Use the Balanced Scorecard Strategy Map template (see figure 3.7, page 98) to develop a strategy map of your own organisation. Remember to work from the top down:

1. *Financial perspective:* start with the financial strategy for creating shareholder value. Consider revenue growth strategy (e.g. new markets, new opportunities) and productivity strategy (e.g. improving cost structure and improved use of assets).
2. *Customer perspective:* examining how to provide greater value. This is usually assessed along three differentiators: operational excellence, customer intimacy, product leadership. Companies should aim to excel in one of these areas while 'maintaining threshold standards' in the other two.
3. *Internal process perspective:* the activities needed for creating strategic capabilities in four processes: operations management, customer management, innovation, and corporate citizenship.
4. *Learning and growth perspective:* define human, information and organisation capital needed to support the organisation's strategy.

Finally, use the strategy map you have drawn up to identify gaps or weaknesses in any of the levels of the balanced scorecard and gauge what impact these might have on achieving the strategic objectives your organisation has set.

Suggested further reading

Day, George S. & Schoemaker, Paul J. H. 2004, 'Driving Through the Fog: Managing at the Edge', *Long Range Planning*, 37, pp. 127–42.

Kaplan, Robert S. & Norton, David P. 2000, 'Having Trouble with Your Strategy? Then Map It', *Harvard Business Review*, September–October, pp. 167–76.

Kaplan, Robert S. & Norton, David P. 2004, 'Measuring the Strategic Readiness of Intangible Assets', *Harvard Business Review*, February, pp. 52–63.

Seely Brown, John 2004, 'Minding and Mining the Periphery', *Long Range Planning*, 37, pp. 143–151.

End notes

1. H. Mintzberg 1987a, 'Five Ps for strategy', in 1998, *Readings in the Strategy Process*, 3rd edn, eds H. Mintzberg & J. B. Quinn, Prentice Hall, New Jersey, pp. 10–17.
2. H. Mintzberg & J. Waters 1985a, 'Of strategies, deliberate and emergent', in 1994, *Strategy: Process, Content, Context: An International Perspective*, eds B. de Wit & R. Meyer, West Publishing, St Paul, Minneapolis, pp. 12–21.
3. Mintzberg 1987a, op. cit., p. 14.
4. G. Johnson 1987, *Strategic Management and the Management Process*, Basil Blackwell, Oxford, p. 17.
5. H. Mintzberg 1987b, 'The strategy concept I: five Ps for strategy', *California Management Review*, Fall, p. 14.
6. ibid., pp. 12–13.
7. G. Johnson & K. Scholes 2002, *Exploring Corporate Strategy*, 6th edn, Prentice Hall, London, pp. 4–11.
8. M. Porter 1996, 'What is strategy?', *Harvard Business Review*, November–December, pp. 61–78.
9. Michael Porter 2002, Extracts from Michael Porter's 'Competitive Strategy' seminar presented in Sydney, October 2002, in Helen Trinca 'Absolute Porter', *AFR BOSS*, 3(9), pp. 34-39.
10. Gary Hamel & Liisa Valikangas 2003, 'The quest for resilience', *Harvard Business Review*, September, pp. 52–63.
11. H. Mintzberg & J. A. Waters 1985b, 'Of strategies, deliberate and emergent', *Strategic Management Journal*, 6, pp. 257–72.
12. J. B. Quinn 1993, 'Managing strategies incrementally', in *Australian Strategic Management: Concepts, Context and Cases*, eds G. Lewis, A. Morkel & G. Hubbard, Prentice Hall, Sydney, p. 279 of pp. 272–82.
13. D. Samson 1999, 'Management principles and profitability', in *How Big Business Performs: Private Performance and Public Policy*, eds P. Dawkins, M. Harris & S. King, Allen & Unwin, St Leonards, New South Wales, p. 100.
14. E. Schein 1985, *Organisational Culture and Leadership*, Jossey-Bass, San Francisco, p. 6.
15. Johnson & Scholes, op. cit., p. 48.
16. Hamel & Valikangas 2003, op. cit.
17. Quinn, op. cit., p. 279.
18. H. Mintzberg 1994, 'The fall and rise of strategic planning', *Harvard Business Review*, January–February, pp. 107–14; L Heracleous 1998, 'Strategic thinking or strategic planning?', *Long Range Planning*, 31(3), pp. 481–7.
19. K. M. Eisenhardt 1990, 'Speed and strategic choice: how managers accelerate decision making', *California Management Review*, Spring, pp. 39–54.
20. K. M. Eisenhardt & S. L. Brown 1998, 'Competing on the edge: strategy as structured chaos', *Long Range Planning*, 31(5), pp. 786–9.
21. Eisenhardt & Brown, op. cit., p. 787.
22. Bruce Holland in Deborah Tarrant 2004, 'Using strategy to ambush the time bandits', *Management Today*, May, pp. 40–3.
23. ibid., p. 42.
24. ibid., p. 42.
25. J. M. Liedtka 1998, 'Linking strategic thinking with strategic planning', *Strategy and Leadership*, September–October, p. 31.
26. ibid., p. 32.
27. Eisenhardt, op. cit., p. 41.
28. ibid., p. 45; see also W. H. Agor 1988, 'The logic of intuition: how top executives make important decisions', in *Creative*

Management, ed. J. Henry, Sage Publications, London, pp. 163–76.

29. D. K. Hurst, J. C. Rush & R. E. White 1988, 'Top management teams and organisational renewal', in *Creative Management*, ed. J. Henry, Sage Publications, London, pp. 232–53.

30. Eisenhardt, op. cit., p. 46; P. J. H. Schoemaker 1995, 'Scenario planning: a tool for strategic thinking', *Sloan Management Review*, Winter, p. 26 of pp. 25–39.

31. Gary Hamel & C. K. Prahalad 1994, *Competing for the Future*, Harvard Business School Press, Boston, Massachussetts, p. 129.

32. Liedtka, op. cit., pp. 31–2.

33. Jeanne M. Liedtka & John W. Rosenblum 1996, 'Shaping conversations: making strategy, managing change', *California Management Review*, 39(1), Fall, p. 144 of pp. 141–57.

34. Schoemaker 1995, op. cit., p. 38.

35. Liedtka, op. cit., pp. 31–2.

36. W. Chan Kim & Renee Mauborgne 2004, 'Strategy, value innovation and the knowledge economy', in *Managing Strategic Innovation and Change*, 2nd edn, eds Michael L. Tushman & Philip Anderson, Oxford University Press, Oxford, p. 343 of pp. 333–46.

37. Nick Demos, Steven Chung, Michael Beck 2001, 'The new strategy and why it is new,' *Strategy+Business*, Issue 25, 4th Quarter, pp. 1–5.

38. Heracleous, op. cit., p. 482.

39. ibid., p. 485.

40. ibid.

41. Mintzberg & Waters, op. cit., p. 271.

42. Art Kleiner 2003, 'The man who saw the future', *Strategy+Business*, Culture & Change section, Issue 30, Spring, pp. 1–5.

43. P. Schoemaker 1991, 'When and how to use scenario planning: a heuristic approach with illustration', *Journal of Forecasting*, 10, pp. 549–64.

44. Paul Schoemaker 2002 *Profiting from Uncertainty: Strategies for succeeding no matter what the future brings*, Free Press. Excerpt accessed at www.simonsays.com/content/content.cfm?sid=33&pid=414774&agid=2&aid=

45. Peter Schwartz, 'Harvard Management Update', in *AFR BOSS*, November 2000. Accessed at www.afrboss.com.au/mag article.asp?doc_id=18191&rgid=2&listed _months=46

46. Schoemaker 1991, op.cit., p. 551.

47. Schoemaker 1995, op. cit.

48. ibid.

49. Schoemaker 1991, op. cit., p. 550.

50. D. G. Simpson 1992, 'Key lessons for adopting scenario planning in diversified companies', *Planning Review*, May–June, pp. 10–17 and 47–8; P. J. H. Schoemaker 1992a, 'Multiple scenario development: its conceptual and behavioral foundation', *Strategic Management Journal*, 14, 193–213; Schoemaker 1991, op. cit., p. 556.

51. Peter Schwartz, 'Harvard Management Update', in *AFR BOSS*, November 2000. Accessed at www.afrboss.com.au/mag article.asp?doc_id=18191&rgid=2&listed _months=46

52. George S. Day & Paul J. H. Schoemaker 2004, 'Driving through the fog: managing at the edge', *Long Range Planning*, 37, p. 130 of pp. 127–142.

53. ibid.

54. ibid., p. 131.

55. Day & Schoemaker 2004, op. cit., p. 132.

56. Extract from article 'Minding and Mining the Periphery' by John Seely Brown, reprinted from *Long Range Planning*, 37, 2004, pp. 143–151 with permission from Elsevier.

57. ibid.

58. ibid., p. 146.

59. Paul J. H. Schoemaker 1995, 'Scenario planning: a tool for strategic thinking', *Sloan Management Review*, Winter, p. 26 of pp.25–40; W. Chan Kim & Renee Mauborgne 1999, 'Strategy, value innovation, and the knowledge economy', *Sloan Management Review*, Spring, pp. 41–54.

60. Seely Brown 2004, op. cit., p. 147.

61. H. N. J. Smits & J. M. Groeneveld 2001, 'Reflections on strategic renewal at Rabobank: a CEO perspective', *Long Range Planning*, 34, p. 256 of pp. 249–258.

62. Seely Brown 2004, op. cit., p. 147.

63. ibid., p. 148.

64. Kim & Mauborgne 2004, op. cit., p. 343.

65. Ned Herrmann, 1996 *The Whole Brain Business Book*, McGraw-Hill, New York: p. 15; N. Herrmann 1989, *The Creative Brain*, Brain Books, Lake Lure, North Carolina.

66. Herrmann 1996, op. cit., p. 34.

67. ibid., p. 35.

68. ibid., p. 36.

69. G. Morgan 1997, *Images of Organization*, Sage, Thousand Oaks, California, p. 90.

70. Johnson & Scholes, op. cit., p. 230.

71. M. M. Crossan, H. W. Lane & T. Hilde-brand 1993, 'Organisation learning: theory to practice', in *Strategic Thinking: Leadership and the Management of Change*, eds J. Hendry & G. Johnson with J. Newton, John Wiley & Sons, Chichester, pp. 229–65.
72. D. W. De Long & L. Fahey 2000, 'Diagnosing cultural barriers to knowledge management', *The Academy of Management Executive*, 14(4), pp. 113–27.
73. ibid., p. 116.
74. ibid., p. 118.
75. Linsu Kim 2004, 'Crisis construction and organisational learning', in *Managing Strategic Innovation and Change,* 2nd edn, eds Michael L. Tushman & Philip Anderson, Oxford University Press, Oxford, pp. 375–92.
76. ibid., pp. 120–1.
77. David A. Nadler & Michael L. Tushman, 1999, 'The organisation of the future: strategic imperatives and core competencies for the 21st century', *Organisational Dynamics*, Vol. 28, No. 1, pp. 45–60.
78. De Long & Fahey, op. cit., p. 121.
79. ibid., p. 121.
80. ibid., pp. 121–2.
81. D. Norman 1988, *The Psychology of Everyday Things*, Basic Books, New York, p. 86; P. Hagel & F. Graetz 1996, 'Learning and the knowledge-based organisation: theory and practice in a public sector organisation', Paper presented at ANZAM '96 Conference, Wollongong, 4–7 December.
82. Crossan, Lane & Hildebrand, op. cit., p. 234.
83. ibid., p. 234.
84. De Long & Fahey, op. cit., pp. 123–5; J. M. Liedtka & J. W. Rosenblum 1996, 'Shaping conversations: making strategy, managing change', *California Management Review*, 39(1), pp. 141–57.
85. PricewaterhouseCoopers partner J Ferron in James Thomson 2004, 'Time to grow up', *BRW*, 25–31 March, pp. 66–7.
86. Thomson 2004, op. cit., pp. 66–7.
87. Hamel & Prahalad, op. cit.
88. Kim & Mauborgne 2004, op. cit., p. 338.
89. ibid., p. 336.
90. David J. Teece, Gary Pisano & Amy Shuen 2004, in *Managing Strategic Innovation and Change*, 2nd edn, eds Michael L. Tushman & Philip Anderson, Oxford University Press, Oxford, p. 313 of pp. 308–32.
91. ibid., p. 313.
92. ibid.
93. Y. Doz & H. Thanheiser 1993, 'A process of organisational renewal', in *Strategic Thinking: Leadership and the Management of Change*, eds J. Hendry & G. Johnson with J. Newton, John Wiley & Sons, Chichester, pp. 293–310; Liedtka & Rosenblum, op. cit., p. 143.
94. P. J. H. Schoemaker 1992b, 'How to link strategic vision to core capabilities', *Sloan Management Review*, Fall, pp. 67–81.
95. ibid., p. 75.
96. Johnson & Scholes, op. cit., p. 119.
97. Monsour Javidan 1998, 'Core competence: what does it mean in practice?' *Long Range Planning*, 31(1), pp. 60–71.
98. Schoemaker 1992b, op. cit.
99. Hamel & Prahalad, op. cit., p. 204.
100. Javidan, op. cit., p.63.
101. ibid., p. 121.
102. R. M. Grant 1993, 'Analysing resources and capabilities', in *Australian Strategic Management: Concepts, Context and Cases*, eds G. Lewis, A. Morkel & G. Hubbard, Prentice Hall, Sydney, pp. 153–79; D. J. Collis & C. A. Montgomery 1995, 'Competing on resources: strategy in the 1990s', *Harvard Business Review*, July–August, pp. 118–28.
103. R. S. Kaplan & D. A. Norton 1992, 'The balanced scorecard: measures that drive performance', *Harvard Business Review*, January–February, pp. 71–9; R. S. Kaplan & D. A. Norton 1993, 'Putting the balanced scorecard to work', *Harvard Business Review*, September–October, pp. 134–47.
104. R. S. Kaplan 1993, 'Implementing the balanced scorecard at FMC Corporation: an interview with Larry D. Brady', *Harvard Business Review*, September–October, pp. 143–7. This article recounts an interview with Brady, Executive Vice President of FMC Corporation, a large diversified US company comprising five business segments: industrial chemicals, performance chemicals, precious metals, defence systems, and machinery and equipment. Brady suggests that benefits come if the balanced scorecard is recognised and applied as 'the core of the management system, not the measurement system'. In his view, it is up to senior management whether the scorecard is used merely as a record-keeping device or as 'the lever to streamline and focus strategy that can lead to breakthrough performance'.

105. D. Jackson 1997, *Dynamic Organisations: The Challenge of Change*, Macmillan Business, London, pp. 81–6.

106. ibid., p. 81.

107. Robert S. Kaplan & David P. Norton 2000, 'Having trouble with your strategy? Then map it', *Harvard Business Review*, September–October, pp. 167–176. Reprinted from 'Having trouble with your strategy? Then map it' by Robert S. Kaplan and David P. Norton, © 2000 Harvard Business School Publishing Corporation. All rights reserved.

108. Robert S. Kaplan & David P. Norton 2004, 'Measuring the strategic readiness of intangible assets', *Harvard Business Review*, February, pp. 52–63.

109. Kaplan & Norton 2000, op. cit., p. 168.

110. ibid., p. 168–9.

111. ibid., p. 170.

112. ibid., pp. 173–4; Kaplan & Norton 2004, op. cit., p. 55.

113. Kaplan & Norton 2000, op. cit., p. 175.

114. Kaplan & Norton 2004, op. cit., p. 55.

115. Kaplan & Norton 2000, op. cit., p. 175.

116. ibid., p. 176.

117. Georg Von Krogh, Ikujiro Nonaka & Manfred Aben 2004, in eds Tushman & Anderson, op. cit., pp. 363–74.

118. T. Grundy 1992, *Implementing Strategic Change*, Kogan Page, London, p. 31.

OPENING CASE

Merging cultures: PwC meets IBM

Mergers often cause traumatic change because people suddenly lose their colleagues, status, corporate culture, and a settled way of working. But surely a top-line consulting firm would know how to handle the challenge? Or would it?

In 2002 the outgoing and incoming CEOs of IBM, Lou Gerstner and Sam Palmisano, decided to buy a consulting firm to help IBM diversify from hardware to a services business. They eventually chose the consulting arm of PricewaterhouseCoopers (PwC Consulting), which, like most of its counterparts, had fallen on hard times as technology-related consulting declined in the wake of the dot.com collapse. Like the consulting arms of other accounting firms, PwC Consulting also found its parent reacting to the post-Enron environment by distancing itself from 'possible conflicts of interest'. PwC Consulting was up for sale, and happy to go in with 'blue chip' IBM.

The merger seemed destined to cause a clash of corporate cultures. PwC had grown fat in the golden years of technology consulting. Its staff operated in a non-bureaucratised world working in small, personalised teams built around the key partners, chasing business through personal networks of customers, and savouring the 'collegiate environment' of a partnership equity structure. This *modus operandi* could not last. Free spirits find it hard in IBM, which has a hierarchical culture and a bureaucracy devoted to upholding a lot of strict rules. Those rules mean, most of all, there is a relentless focus on sales. Everyone in IBM is expected to 'make their numbers'.

In 2003 the old PwC Consulting operation failed to meet its sales targets. This brought in the IBM 'expense nazis', trimming the high-flying consultants back to cattle-class travel and grumbling about over-generous pay. If the PwC staff found this irksome, the disappointment was mutual. The IBM staff expected their new, well-connected colleagues to be opening boardroom doors for cross-selling. But this was not the style at PwC where you 'ate what you hunted'.

Pretty soon the consultants began to deliver again. At the end of 2003 IBM Australia reported a good result, and went so far as to stress that the new combined consulting business had made a major contribution. Meanwhile, cultural change was working its way through the consulting arm. One consultant who made the adjustment said 'We know the market demands answers every quarter and we know we have to provide those. I passionately believe we have done the right thing. We have created something exciting here; we are ahead of the curve.' Not all survivors were so inspired; others are reputed to have remained just for the money. As one observer put it, 'It's IBM misery versus IBM money'. And others have not survived at all, leaving because the IBM shoe squeezed too tightly. There may be a shock for those leaving trying to find their old freedom, because IBM's demands have now become the industry standard. As one ex PwC partner observed, 'Consulting is now a pretty tough business . . . quite different to what it was, say, three years ago. Cash and profitability are now paramount . . . Some have adapted well to the new environment. Others haven't.' Even consultants, it seems, can find culture change challenging.

Source: Adapted from Emma Connors 2004, 'Not drowning, dancing', *AFR BOSS*, November, pp. 22–8. Reproduced with permission from Emma Connors.

Introduction

The process of change after the merger that created PwC/IBM involved changing the PwC culture to strengthen hierarchical control, impose stricter rules, and a hunger for sales growth. While many organisations experience the change process in a similar way, the PwC/IBM **change path** remains unique because it is a product of the special conditions that applied —— the previous history, cultures and organisational characteristics of the two merging organisations. Such a customised approach to the process of change would surprise many people. They see planned change as a cue to discuss so-called 'fads' of the past two decades, like **total quality management** (TQM), **business process re-engineering**, benchmarking and other 'off-the-shelf' change tools.[1] The PwC/IBM merger case shows, however, that the change process need not involve the application of any particular **change planning tool** or change model. Change paths are the product of a particular blend of personal, organisational and environmental characteristics that make each organisation's experience of change different. Change planning tools, although often stigmatised as 'one size fits all' techniques, usually are no more than broad principles for planning change whose application demands customisation to fit an organisation.

To understand how managers implement change, it is helpful to grasp this distinction between change paths and change planning tools. Often, a complex interplay exists between the two. This interplay can be seen in the case of the Norske Skog Boyer mill (case 3) at the end of this book. Between 1991 and 1994, the firm applied a particular change planning tool — the **best practice** approach to continuous improvement by empowered teams — but its change path involved many other factors. To understand how change took place at the Boyer Mill, it is necessary to look beyond the best practice model and identify the impact of new owners, changing technologies, market pressures, the demand for better environmental protection, the influence of corporate and workplace leadership, and union–management relations, links with the local labour market and community, and much more. These factors created a unique change path or trajectory, whereby the mill implemented some of the best practice model and accomplished much of what it offered, but steered an individual course to reach that objective.

So what are change planning tools like? Two widely applied examples of a standard change planning tool can be found in the step-by-step change models of Kotter[2] and Kanter.[3] Kotter's eight-step model is perhaps the best known. It instructs managers to implement planned change in the following sequence of stages:

1. create or increase a sense of urgency
2. build the powerful guiding coalition
3. get the vision right
4. communicate for buy-in
5. empower action
6. create short-term wins
7. don't let up
8. make change stick.

Very similar to Kotter's eight-step model are the 'ten commandments' for implementing change prescribed by Kanter, Stein and Jick.[4]

Australian researchers have discovered that CEOs are attracted to such prescriptions because they provide a rational framework for implementing change. But taken literally, such models are also misleading because unexpected events are a natural partner of change.[5] Change is a journey into the unknown in which the greatest likelihood is an encounter with the unpredictable.[6] Managers should not only plan change using rational steps; they must also plan for uncertainty. The 'order' offered by a change planning tool (like those above) has to be offset against the 'disorder' that takes place in every change path as real world conditions blow the plan off course.

In this chapter, we approach the change process by looking first at the diversity of change paths in Australian organisations. A convenient starting point is to look at **Post-Fordism** (also called *flexible specialisation*), an influential model for planned organisational change throughout much of the past two decades. But as we shall see, this model is no universal template for organisations of the future, as demonstrated by the growing use of casual employees rather than highly trained and committed ones.

In the following section, we seek an explanation for diversity. This explanation is to be found in the contingency or situational approach to change. The most important Australian advocates of the **contingency model** are Dexter Dunphy and Doug Stace, whose situational model is considered at greater length in chapter 8. They argue that change strategies vary to reflect different organisational environments and characteristics.[7]

However, an alternative school of thought exists that is difficult to reconcile with contingency theory. These are the systems theorists. Members of this school view organisations as systems made up of interdependent elements. They deduce that the benefits of planned change are greatest when changes to one part of a system reinforce changes to other parts. Thus effective planned change requires a number of interlinked actions, none of which is optional. The result is a standard change model that should be applicable to all organisational systems. Our aim in this chapter is to introduce contingency and systems theory and to see how they differ.

In the remaining sections of the chapter, we describe some of the better-known change tools. Many of these tools belong to a family tree whose lineage can be traced back to the classical change model of Kurt Lewin in the 1940s and the socio-technical systems theorists of the 1960s and 1970s. There are numerous branches of this family tree, including **organisation development**, **lean production**, TQM, best practice, the **learning organisation** and the **high-performance work organisation** (HPNO). The purpose of this section is to familiarise you with the broad principles of some well-known change tools.

The diverse pattern of change in Australia

Perhaps the most influential approach to planned organisational change in Australia grew out of the theory of 'flexible specialisation' first propounded in the United States in the mid-1980s. This theory predicted a paradigm shift in which organisations would abandon the **Taylorism**-based structures associated with mass production for what is called 'Post-Fordism'.[8] This theory was first popularised in Australia in John Mathews' book *Tools of Change*.[9] Mass markets had led to Taylorist production systems, which required bureaucracy, hierarchy and the 'de-skilling' of jobs by their subdivision into narrow, repetitive and meaningless tasks. Niche markets would lead to Post-Fordist production systems, which required flatter and more flexible organisational structures and multiskilled teams of employees. Figure 4.1 shows more fully the differences between the two organisational types.

Taylorism	Post-Fordism
Mass markets	Niche markets
Mass production	Flexible manufacturing
De-skilling of individuals	Multiskilled teams in a learning organisation
An employee resistance culture	A continuous improvement culture
Quality through inspection	Quality throughout the organisation
Imperative directives	Semi-autonomous structures
Bureaucratic organisation	Virtual organisation

FIGURE 4.1: Taylorist and Post-Fordist organisations

Throughout the 1990s, many Australian writers on organisational change anticipated a shift from Taylorism to Post-Fordism. Mathews puts the argument as follows:

> In the changed circumstances of the 1990s, when products have shorter life-cycles, and are developed with shorter lead times; when products are more closely attuned to customer and market demands; when product variety, diversity and quality are the determinants of competitive success — under these circumstances, it is firms which are prepared to adopt new production systems which gain a competitive edge. Such firms are prepared to experiment with non-authoritarian teamwork structures that dispense with traditional supervisory and surveillance systems; they are prepared to experiment with new programmable routines for switching products and services as market preferences change; they are prepared to enter into closer collaborative relations with both their customers and suppliers . . . Thus the organisational imperatives of the future will be for workplaces that maximise creativity, innovation and cooperation.[10]

Writing in 1990 as the Australian economy was opening up to global competition, Dunphy and Stace offered similar observations about the organisations of the future. They noted that business had lost faith in the large, centralised and inflexible organisational structures that once dominated the corporate landscape. Competition was forcing changes in organisational structure, culture and technology. In particular, 'Australia's leading edge organisations' demonstrated 'three complementary trends in restructuring': divisional structures, flatter organisations and radical devolution.[11]

Mathews, and Dunphy and Stace broadly agree on three major points. First, organisational change is expected to be widespread as a paradigm shift takes place. Second, this expectation is linked to economic change, including new and more intense forms of competition. Third, non-authoritarian teamwork structures are at the heart of the new production system and such teams depend on a skilled, flexible and cooperative workforce. Thus, the change histories of Australian organisations are largely scripted for them and broad economic forces (not organisational choice or the particular circumstances of each case) determine those trajectories.

Researchers agree that evidence shows some change towards Post-Fordism, but alongside is evidence of other trends. Taylorist forms of organisation also persist, sometimes intensified into Neo-Fordism, in which work effort is increased, career structures are truncated, surveillance is tightened and task control is surrendered to technology oversighted by managers.[12] Some organisations are devolving power to teams, but others are disempowering their workforce. The growing use of casual employees is widely considered a symptom of this counter-trend towards an un-skilled and disempowered workforce.

PERSPECTIVES

Casual workers — second class citizens?

The Post-Fordist vision sees employees as stable, multiskilled members of a work-team. Under Neo-Fordism they are much more likely to be second-class citizens employed on a casual basis and regarded by their employer as disposable. In 1990, casuals made up just 16 per cent of Australian workers. In 2004, they accounted for 27 per cent of the workforce. This trend goes hand-in-glove with the rapid growth of low-wage jobs. More than four-fifths of all jobs created in the 1990s paid less than $26,000 and almost half paid less than $15,600. Are employers opting for a cheap, throw-away workforce?

Peter Hendy, Chief Executive, Australian Chamber of Commerce and Industry said:

> The labour movement demonises casual employment for ideological reasons. But casual employment does not deserve it; it serves an important function in our

labour market ... most casual employees work in service industries such as retail, hospitality and clerical, and in industries with peaks and troughs such as agriculture and tourism. About 45% of casual employment is among the young and student workforce who are not looking for a long-term job commitment. More than 70% of casual workers want to remain in casual work.*

Greg Combet, Secretary, Australian Council of Trade Unions said:

> Economic growth has, unfortunately, gone hand-in-glove with inequality in Australia ... Nowhere is this phenomenon more evident than in the rapid

(continued)

growth of casual employment ... There are 2.2 million casual workers ... They have no access to basic entitlements, such as a holiday or a paid day off to care for a sick child. Because they are branded as credit risks, many casuals forgo the aspiration of owning their own home. With little incentive for employers to invest in training them, many casuals are trapped in low-skilled and insecure jobs.

In the short-term there may be savings from using casuals. But a long-term view — with its business imperatives of investment and better labour processes — suggests that cutting corners with casuals is not sustainable.**

Source: Adapted from David James 2004, (ed.) 'Comment', *Business Review Weekly, 27* May–2 June, pp. 56–7. *Reproduced with permission of Peter Hendy. **Reproduced with permission from Greg Combet.

Why do change paths differ? Theoretical explanations

Why do organisations take diverse change paths? One particular general theory provides an influential explanation for Australia: contingency theory. However, this approach needs to be contrasted with the equally influential systems theory of organisational change.

The contingency approach is said to require a 'reading of the firm's environment' to decide organisational structures. It appeals because 'the "if–then" formula constitutes a break with the "one-best-way" approach, whilst retaining powerful guidelines for what power-holders should actually do to sustain effective organisation'.[13] The leading Australian exponents of this approach are Dunphy and Stace. Whatever their views on the likely future structure of organisations, they subscribe to a fairly open view of the processes by which organisational structures change.[14]

Dunphy and Stace's contingency model of change has a number of parts. First is the notion that change programs require managers to make choices or confront dilemmas. Essentially, this is a rejection of the 'one right way' approach to change. Stace and Dunphy list five dilemmas of change which require a choice from the following options:[15]

1. adaptive or rational strategy development
2. cultural change or structural change
3. continuous improvement or radical transformation
4. empowerment or leadership and command
5. economic or social goals.

Stace and Dunphy's idea that change requires managers to confront dilemmas is an important one that runs through this book. We introduced it in chapter 2 and noted it again in chapters 3 and 6, where we discuss Stace and Dunphy's contingency model at length.

Central to the model is the idea that choices about the scale of change and the style of change management should 'fit' the environment. This 'fit' is sometimes labelled **external fit**, reflecting the match between the change strategy and the organisation's external environment. If product or capital markets are undergoing significant and rapid change, then managers need to choose a change strategy that is transformative in scale (a new mission, radical restructuring, culture change and so on) and directive in style (able to be directed quickly without room for uncertainty and delay). Conversely, stable technologies, product markets and capital markets allow businesses to rely on incremental adjustment (by continuous improvement), in which cooperation with internal stakeholders (through devolved decision-making structures) reinforces the change program. There also must be **internal fit** between the change strategy and internal organisational characteristics. Thus, Dunphy and Stace argue that key stakeholders' opposition to change may necessitate a directive or coercive style of change management, while their support for change may permit a cooperative or consultative style.[16]

The strength of Dunphy and Stace's contingency approach to change lies in its recognition of the importance of external or environmental fit — that is, that a change strategy must be selected to fit prevailing conditions. Dunphy and Stace are weaker in covering the systemic nature of change, or the need for integration of different elements of an organisational change program. This holistic approach to change is represented in Pettigrew and Whipp's framework for competitive success.[17]

Pettigrew and Whipp drew up their model on the basis of observations of firms in four British industries: automobile manufacture, book publishing, merchant banking and life insurance. A review of the characteristics of the higher performing organisations in these industries led Pettigrew and Whipp to identify five central factors (figure 4.2) for managing strategic and operational change.

Two aspects of the model require attention. First, it is a **holistic model** in which each factor of change must be linked to every other factor. This internal match between elements of the model relates to the notion of internal fit introduced earlier. Second, each factor is divided into 'primary conditioning features' and 'secondary mechanisms'. The primary conditioning features are catalysts or enabling factors, whose role is to facilitate change in the secondary or operational mechanisms. Clearly, businesses are not free to pick and choose what elements of the model to apply. Effective application of the 'secondary mechanisms' for change rests upon interlinked application of the 'primary conditioning' catalysts.

A debate persists in which contingency theorists criticise complex 'one best way' models of organisational change, given the likelihood of poor environmental 'fit'. Surely the turbulent realities of change in each organisation will force organisations

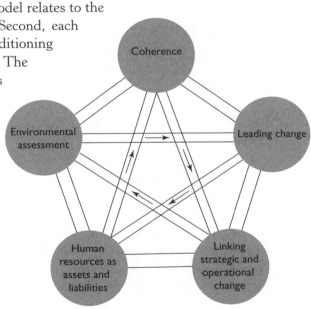

FIGURE 4.2: Framework for competitive success

Source: From Andrew Pettigrew & Richard Whipp, *Managing Change for Competitive Success*, Blackwell Business, Oxford, p. 104, © 1993.

away from planned change, dropping some elements of the formula for change and re-arranging others. In answer to this reaction the exponents of systemic or holistic change models argue that such indiscipline will be fatal to change. The success of the plan rests upon realising the synergies between the elements of the change plan. Any weak link in the chain of elements in the plan will cause the whole endeavour to fail.

Change tools

Change tools tend to be both analytical and prescriptive. Their analytical side is represented by general statements or theories about the actual causes, processes and consequences of organisational change. In the best examples, these theoretical statements are supported by sound empirical evidence. The prescriptive aspect of change tools takes the form of statements about how organisational change should happen.

The discussion of change tools in this chapter is intended to deal with mainly their analytical side, but a warning is useful: this terrain is littered with contributions that, without warning or explanation, abandon the hard ground of research and analysis for the swamp of prescription.

The plan for the section is to discuss the following change tools:

- Lewin's classical model
- socio-technical systems
- the organisation development school
- the learning organisation
- lean production
- TQM
- business process re-engineering
- best practice
- the high-performance work organisation.

Kurt Lewin's classical model

Most early writings on organisations are concerned with the maintenance of order or equilibrium rather than planned change. Kurt Lewin, a social psychologist widely accepted as the first significant writer on planned organisational change, shared this presumption that equilibrium was the normal state of organisations. Writing in the 1940s, he developed a model of change that could be used to guide organisations from one stable state to the next.

Lewin's approach to organisational change is grounded in a general system of ideas termed 'field theory'.[18] The theory owes something to his background as a Jewish refugee from Nazi Germany in the 1930s before he went on to work as an applied psychologist at MIT until his death in 1947. His interests spanned the major issues of his time — the position of Jewish minorities in society, the restoration of democratic values to post-war Germany, and racial and labour problems in the United States. His approach to these disparate problems was unified through his interest in group dynamics — that is, the fluid relationship between individuals and small groups. How can groups cohere and conflicts within them be resolved? Field theory concerns the socio-spatial relationship between individuals and groups; the psychological needs of individuals; and the 'field forces' that incline group dynamics towards movement or stability.[19] While Lewin's underlying purpose often was to suggest approaches to resolving group conflict, field theory is suitable for many other applications.

Among its uses, field theory can be applied to organisational change. The essence of the model is that organisations are constantly exposed to two sets of field forces: those that maintain stability and those that break it down. The normal state for most organisations is one of equilibrium in which the forces for stability are dominant. To achieve change, an organisation would need to reduce the forces for stability or increase the forces for change. An example of reducing a force for stability can be found in the Norske Skog Boyer mill case (case 3), which describes how change began in the 1980s with the revelations that the mill was losing money, the machinery was out of date and the plant was over-staffed. This information was used to destabilise the status quo by legitimising corrective action. In any particular change situation, a large number of such forces are likely to converge to weaken attachment to the past and drive acceptance of the new.

Lewin's change model involves three steps.

- *Unfreezing*. This step requires a reduction in the field forces that maintain an existing organisational culture and method of operation. Unfreezing often involves breaking psychological attachment to the past by using information that demonstrates the existence of problems. In the case of Norske Skog, unfreezing was associated with the revelation in the 1980s that the plant's inefficiency (as shown by benchmarking comparisons) threatened its future.
- *Moving*. This step entails the creation of cognitive recognition in the workforce of the need for change, and the establishment of new norms of behaviour around a particular set of new structures and processes. The 'moving' phase at Norske Skog involved the development of new team-based structures and processes for continuous improvement in quality, safety, output, cost control and the like. It also involved culture change to gain acceptance of new norms and values consistent with Norske Skog's aim to become 'best practice'.
- *Refreezing*. As soon as new values, structures and processes have been installed, cultural reinforcement is necessary to stabilise the system or restore equilibrium. Refreezing is apparent in the Norske Skog mill case through the enterprise bargaining process, which reaffirms the commitment of both management and unions to the structures and values of continuous improvement.

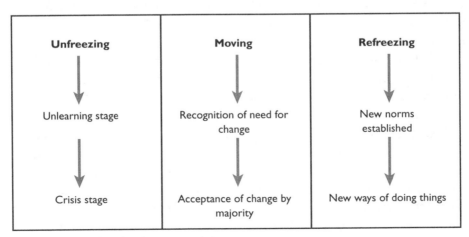

FIGURE 4.3: Lewin's classic change model

Figure 4.3 (page 115) is a diagrammatic representation of Lewin's classic change model. The most common criticism of this model is that the third step — refreezing — no longer applies to many organisations. Organisations now are encouraged to thrive on chaos and constant change — concepts that resonate with actual experience in which the period of time between phases of planned change has dwindled to zero. How can refreezing occur when a new phase of change is introduced before the last phase of movement is fully accomplished?

Socio-technical systems

In the early 1960s, critics began to question the assumption of organisational equilibrium inherent in Lewin's field theory of change. The study of organisations was transformed as theorists took account of both internal and external drivers of change. One example of the former is Blau and Scott's study, *Formal Organisations*, published in 1963.[20] From a systems perspective, it treated organisational change as a dialectical process originating largely in internal conflicts. This study typified the tendency of systems theorists to characterise conflict (and therefore change) as disruptive. This approach was challenged by social action theorists such as Silverman[21], who rejected the notion of equilibrium, portraying organisations instead as existing in a state of flux while changes in the participants' orientations and values re-shaped their interactions. Given that social orientations are shaped by the wider values of society, organisational change also had to be linked to the ferment of norms and values in the outside world. Thus, social action theorists inferred that hierarchical organisational cultures may change under assault from the social orientation towards 'direct democracy', which was prevalent during the late 1960s in the wider society of universities, protest politics and trade unionism.

Coinciding with this radical insight was the opening up of systems theories of organisation to environmental change. Open systems theory appeared in the 1960s in the writings of Katz and Kahn[22], Lawrence and Lorsch[23] and others seeking to break down the unrealistic assumption that organisations could be inert to changes in their environment. Among the most important open systems theorists were a number of writers seeking to factor the consequences of scientific and technological dynamism into organisation theory. This group includes Burns and Stalker.[24] Exploring how organisations respond to innovation, they distinguished two ideal types: the mechanistic model (a bureaucratic form) and the organic model (no clear hierarchy, fluid roles, *ad hoc* communication and a high-trust work culture). Burns and Stalker's organic model is a clear forerunner for the Post-Fordist ideas propounded in the 1980s and 1990s.

Perhaps the most influential open systems theorists were those belonging to the Tavistock Institute of Human Relations in London, especially Fred Emery and Eric Trist. Writing in 1965, they drew connections between different environmental conditions and organisational structures: in a 'placid randomised' environment, causal links with organisational structure are weak and small undifferentiated firms can survive; in a 'placid clustered' environment, only specialised and strategically focused organisations can compete; in a 'disturbed reactive' environment, differentiation strategies will not work and firms must either cooperate or risk head-to-head competition; and, finally, in 'turbulent fields' where the environment is in a state of flux, only highly adaptive, non-bureaucratic organisations can survive.[25] There are foundations here for open systems theory and the subsequent contingency approach of Dunphy and Stace. Our principal concern with Emery and Trist, however, is their membership of the socio-technical systems school.

Socio-technical systems theory originated among a group of organisational psychologists in the Tavistock Institute of Human Relations in London. It began as a rejection of technological determinism, or the idea that a given form of technology must necessarily produce a counterpart form of social organisation. In their classic study of British coal mining, Trist and Bamforth[26] discovered that social organisation related to technology in a different way. Their study dealt with the replacement of manual coal hewing by a mechanised system (the longwall system with a mechanical coal cutter and conveyor transportation). Manual coal hewing allowed miners to work with high autonomy in cohesive teams. The longwall system fragmented tasks into repetitive operations, broke up teams and increased the need for task coordination and close supervision. Miners accepted the technology but rejected the 'production line' social organisation, retaining their established team structure to both give their work meaning and maintain safety. The observations of Trist and Bamforth present the idea that work can be organised to both fit technology and achieve social satisfaction.

The central insight of socio-technical systems theory, according to Mathews, is that both the social and technical systems of work can be jointly optimised, in contrast to the Taylorist approach (which sought to optimise only the technical system) and the human relations approach (which aimed to optimise only the social system).[27] In other words, work organisation can be arranged both to provide for the increased productivity associated with mechanisation and to make work a meaningful social experience. In 1981, Trist codified the core elements of the socio-technical systems approach into seven principles.[28]

1. The work system, which comprised a set of activities that made up a functioning whole, is the basic unit rather than the single jobs into which it was decomposable.
2. Correspondingly, the work group, rather than the individual job holder, is central.
3. Internal regulation of the system by the group is rendered possible, rather than the external regulation of individuals by supervisors.
4. A design principle based on the redundancy of functions rather than the redundancy of parts, introduced by Emery, characterises the underlying organisational philosophy, which tends to develop multiple skills in the individual and immensely increase the repertoire of the group.
5. The discretionary, rather than the prescribed, part of work roles is valued.
6. The individual is treated as complementary to the machine rather than as an extension of it.
7. Variety is increased for the individual, rather than decreased as in the bureaucratic mode.

The socio-technical systems approach identified the semi-autonomous work group as a basic building block of work organisation. Multiskilled work teams rotate varied tasks among members, regulate internal group relations, and exercise discretion over aspects of work, including their relationship to technology. Through such structures, work could be humanised; further, in the right kind of environment (notably Emery and Trist's 'turbulent fields'), the chances of organisational survival would be improved.

The socio-technical systems approach has been extremely influential since the 1970s. It guided the practice of organisational consulting in the United States and Britain, where the Tavistock Institute functioned as a consulting business. Perhaps more significant was the impact of the socio-technical systems approach in Norway and Sweden, where it was to be incorporated into a number of successful innovations, including the well-known work reorganisation experiments at Volvo's Kalmar and Udevalla factories.[29] In the Netherlands, a variant known as the Dutch socio-technical school also became well known. The Dutch approach looks above the semi-autonomous work group to treat the whole organisation as the key system. Thus, socio-technical principles need to apply to all aspects of the business, including strategy, marketing, product development, supply chain operations, information systems and so on.[30] The outcome is a socio-technical approach that is better adapted to total business requirements but, arguably, less sensitive to the human issues of job satisfaction and social cohesion.[31]

The organisation development school

Parallel to the growth of the socio-technical systems approach in Britain and Europe, the organisation development school evolved in the United States. While current exponents of this approach claim that it derives from 'five major backgrounds or stems'[32], they do so by incorporating new ideas that dilute the original meaning of organisation development. A review of these five 'stems' demonstrates which are the original and essential parts of organisation development and which elements have been grafted on to maintain its practical relevance.

The first stem is the laboratory training of sensitivity training groups, or T-groups. Pioneered by Kurt Lewin from observations about race and community relations, T-groups are based on the insight that group members modify their behaviour if they are fed data about it. In an organisational context, the T-group can become a change mechanism. Small groups under the tutelage of an organisation development consultant or practitioner can learn to manage change better by taking account of interpersonal relations, personal growth, leadership and the like. T-group techniques are now called 'team building' and play an integral part in the change processes of many organisations.

The second stem is action research, which is discussed in chapter 10 as a tool for measuring and evaluating change. It also is a powerful change intervention tool. Again, it originates in the observations of Lewin and others who were interested in the use of research data in change interventions. Action research initially involved an extension of the data fed to T-group members to include survey research data. Social scientists skilled in data collection became integral participants in the process of organisational change.

The third stem is participative management, which is associated with the ideas of Douglas McGregor (Theory X) and Rensis Likert (System 4). McGregor[33] and Likert[34] both generated typologies of management style in which a participative approach was contrasted with authoritarian or autocratic alternatives. Participative management was incorporated into organisation development because it embraces the development of conflict resolution techniques as essential in persuading people to accommodate change. Inherent in this stem was a 'gradualist' or 'evolutionary' approach to change that is consistent with the word 'development'.[35]

The fourth stem is productivity and quality of work life. Waddell, Cummings and Worley associate this stem with the Tavistock Institute and socio-technical systems theorists such as Trist.[36] It reflects an adaptation of organisation development in the 1970s to incorporate job redesign activities under the joint supervision of management and unions. Australian interest in organisation development probably peaked in the 1970s after the Commonwealth Government established the Productivity Promotion Council to stimulate and promote organisation development innovations.[37] Although prominent organisations such as ICI, CSR and Philips Industries experimented with **semi-autonomous work groups**, the general take-up of such practices remained limited.[38]

The fifth and final stem is 'strategic change', which involves improving the alignment among an organisation's environment, strategy and organisation design. Strategic change accounts for both the growth of strategic management theory over the past 20 years and the emergence of strategy consulting as the lynchpin of consulting practice. Without accommodating this newcomer, the capacity of organisation development consultants to advise business on organisational change would be limited. The inclusion of strategy into the organisation development framework brings with it, however, the possibility of rapid transformational change to adjust to environmental shock. Consistent with the requirements of transformation, organisation development must be broadened — some would say diluted — to allow for non-participative organisational transformation.

The organisation development movement lives on in consulting practice. It has adjusted to changing business requirements by becoming a broad-based set of tools to facilitate organisational change. Undoubtedly, it has become more complex and sophisticated because it has developed over the decades. That sophistication is evident in the ethical codes governing practitioners and in their wide range of diagnostic and intervention tools. As organisation development has broadened to incorporate elements of **socio-technical systems** and strategic management, however, it has lost its distinctive character. Its identity is now blurred with other change tools such as best practice, high-performance work organisation and the like.

Organisation development retains strong appeal to business because team building and personal development have continuing relevance. It stands accused, however, of being 'ahistorical, acontextual and aprocessual' by those who argue that change tools should be moulded to the contingent characteristics of each organisation.[39]

The learning organisation

The concept of the 'learning organisation' was popularised in Australia in the early 1990s when the appearance of Peter Senge's book, *The Fifth Discipline*, coincided with an intensive policy drive by the Commonwealth Government to improve Australia's skill base.[40] The idea of organisational learning is much older. Argyris and Schon published *Organizational Learning: A Theory of Action Perspective* in 1978, using a multidisciplinary fusion of sociology, social psychology, information theory and other areas.[41] Organisational learning also draws on many older approaches to management and training. From organisation development, it takes the concept of 'participative management', asking what skills are needed to make it work. From various learning theories, it absorbs ideas about 'learning by observing' and reinforcement behaviour, and then asks how an organisation can become a learning environment. From systems theory, it takes the lesson that every aspect of an organisation is interconnected.

Models of organisational learning are built on two central assumptions. The first is that knowledge (skill) is an important resource that determines organisational effectiveness. The second assumption is that organisational knowledge can be improved by attention to the learning process. In particular, the learning process can be linked to organisational goals and reinforced by the proper use of feedback. Learning is conceptualised as a process of trial and error in which goal-setting and feedback are the critical variables. Field and Ford identify three types of organisational learning.[42]

1. **Haphazard learning.** The objectives of learning are unclear and there is no process to reinforce positive lessons. Consequently, organisational errors can be learned and perpetuated. Field and Ford give the example of a car service centre (CarCare) where the mechanics' routine includes replacing rather than repairing parts, ignoring complicated problems and ticking off routine checks that have not been performed. Customer complaints occur but go to the reception desk, not to the mechanic. Consequently, the mechanics receive no feedback about their work and are unaware of customer satisfaction as an organisational goal, or of the customer's role in a feedback process that guides their learning. What learning occurs may or may not be useful.

2. **Goal-based (single-loop) learning.** This introduces both goal-setting and simple internal feedback to reinforce lessons. The goals for CarCare may include a standard measure of 'right first time' quality reinforced by performance targets for each mechanic. Feedback can be business-wide quality data (conveyed on a noticeboard), a measure of team performance (passed on via team briefings) or individual performance information (communicated through performance appraisals). There is a single feedback step, so this process is called 'single-loop' learning.

3. **Double-loop learning.** In a dynamic environment, the messages conveyed by goal-based learning swiftly become out of date. The quality targets, for example, set one year will eventually fall behind competitors' performance and need to be revised. As customer expectations, market pressures, product ranges and standards keep shifting, people in the workplace can respond by questioning old goals through a process of critical questioning. This dynamic process may coincide with goal-based learning — the two processes each providing feedback to the individual or team. Thus, two feedback loops may exist, with one involving learning from the pursuit of established goals and the second involving learning by questioning those goals. Because there are two feedback loops, the expression 'double-loop learning' was coined. A learning organisation is one that engages in double-loop learning.

Waddell, Cummings and Worley argue that single-loop learning reinforces the status quo whereas double-loop learning challenges it.[43] For this reason, double-loop learning can lead to a model of organisational change. By itself, however, double-loop learning tells us little about the full agenda for organisational change in a learning organisation. What is the wider organisational context in which double-loop learning can function?

McGill, Slocum and Lei provide a conventional answer, identifying five characteristics of the learning organisation.[44] These include a flat organisational structure emphasising teamwork; two-way information systems based on benchmarking and continuous improvement measures; human resource practices that develop skills and cooperative attitudes; an organisational culture that promotes innovation and creativity; and a counselling or democratic leadership style. This formula has much in common with TQM, best practice and other generic change tools.

Field and Ford present the elements of a learning organisation through the device of the 'propeller' that drives organisational learning (figure 4.4). The four blades of the propeller represent aspects of the organisation that need to be integrated with the vision of a learning organisation, which they place at the hub of the propeller. The four blades are an enterprise-based employee relations strategy that promotes cooperation; a work organisation system that empowers semi-autonomous work teams to make full use of double-loop learning; a skill-forming, training and learning strategy that equips the workforce to implement double-loop learning fully; and a technology and information system with hardware, software and 'social software' that are consistent with the requirements of a learning organisation. The Field and Ford model of a learning organisation is essentially an organisation development intervention framework.

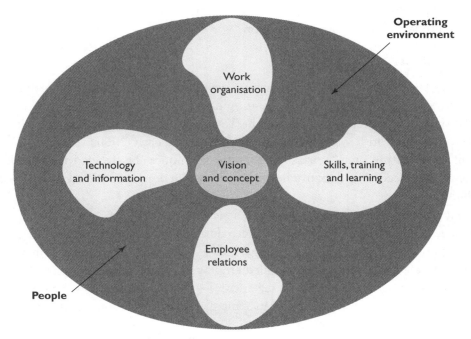

FIGURE 4.4: The organisational propeller

Source: Reproduced from L. Field & B. Ford 1995, *Managing Organisational Learning from Rhetoric to Reality,* © Pearson Education Australia, p. 23.

Senge's explanation of a 'learning organisation' model has an advantage in that it explicitly recognises how individual and team learning, culture and systems thinking contribute to organisational learning. Senge identifies five discrete processes (or disciplines, as he terms them) that combine to form a learning organisation.

- *Personal mastery* is the 'discipline of continually clarifying and deepening personal vision, of focusing energies, of developing patience, and of seeing reality objectively'.[45]
- *Shared vision* 'involves the skills of unearthing shared pictures of the future that foster genuine commitment and enrolment rather than compliance ... leaders learn the counterproductiveness of trying to dictate a vision, no matter how heartfelt'.[46]
- *Team learning* 'is the process of aligning and developing the capacity of a team to create the results its members truly desire. It builds on the disciplines of personal mastery and shared vision (for talented teams are made up of talented individuals) and involves mastering the practices of dialogue and discussion'.[47]
- *Mental models* are 'deeply ingrained assumptions, generalisations, or even pictures or images that influence how we understand the world and how we take action'.[48]
- *Systems thinking* is a 'conceptual framework, a body of knowledge and tools that has been developed over the last fifty years, to make patterns clearer, and to help us see how to change them effectively'.[49]

Senge's approach to organisational learning, like the others outlined earlier, owes much to related tools, including organisation development and socio-technical systems theory. Like organisation development, it is a normative construct with fairly weak foundations in positivist research. The consultants who endorse organisational learning would argue that it is an action-oriented tool that becomes fully understood only through application in a concrete situation.

Lean production

The socio-technical systems, organisation development and organisational learning approaches to change discussed earlier originated in Europe and the United States. Lean production, sometimes known as the Toyota system, comes from Japan. It is said to have originated in a visit by Sakichi Toyoda in the early 1950s to a Ford plant in Detroit.[50] Reflecting on US mass production techniques, he decided that a different approach was needed in Japan where shorter production runs dictated the need for flexibility.

What evolved at Toyota was a production system driven by the triple targets of zero defects, zero inventory and zero waste. Zero defects and waste were to be achieved by the integration of people and technology into a **kaizen**, or continuous improvement system, operated by teams of multiskilled employees. Zero inventory was to be gained from **just-in-time** supply chain management — a system that was extended to both internal inventory control (between departments and work stations) and external suppliers. Just-in-time is sometimes known as a 'pull' production system because downstream customers (internal or external) pull production through the system, with their orders determining production upstream. Rather than manufacture for stock buffers, the production system is at work only when there is an order (**kanban**) to be filled immediately. This method of inventory management is a high-risk system exposed to stop–start disruption of production. For this reason, it needs to be supported by a highly integrated production system staffed by highly trained and motivated employees who are embued with a philosophical commitment (or *kaizen* consciousness) to quality and waste reduction.[51] Indeed, just-in-time production can work only when integrated with other techniques in the Toyota system. The Toyota system offers obvious advantages.

- The costs of rectifying faults are reduced.
- Inventory costs are reduced.
- Labour costs are cut by the transfer of tasks from expensive core workers to suppliers.
- Close long-term supplier relationships facilitate improved design and quality.
- *Muda*, the Japanese term for waste, is eliminated.

Having spread through Japanese manufacturing, the Toyota system was enthusiastically embraced by US manufacturers eager to emulate the secrets of the Japanese to prevent their further encroachment into US markets. In 1985, the International Motor Vehicle Program (IVMP) was established at MIT to study Japanese methods in automotive manufacture. Findings from the project were published in 1990[52], popularising the Toyota system as a universal set of best practices that yield performance benefits 'regardless of context and environment' for manufacturers.[53] At the same time, the term 'lean production' was coined to emphasise that:

> ... it uses less of everything compared with mass production — half the human effort in the factory, half the manufacturing space, half the investment in tools, half the engineering hours to develop a new product in half the time. Also it requires keeping far less than half the needed inventory on site, results in many fewer defects, and produces a greater and ever-growing variety of products.[54]

Lean production is essentially the same as the Toyota system — a 'pull' production system associated with supplier integration and continuous improvement by teams towards the targets of zero defects, zero inventory and zero waste. This simple model has changed over time, however. One development widely found in Australia is **manufacturing resource planning** (MRP II). As a computerised order and material tracking system, MRP II has obvious applications to making just-in-time inventory management more accurate and reliable, but it can be applied to the much larger task of planning all aspects of an organisation's operations. MRP II integrates the following six core functions:[55]

- business planning, sales and operations planning (where monthly sales data drive production planning)
- master production scheduling (where broad monthly production plans become weekly individual end item needs)
- materials requirement planning (where the master production schedule is linked to an analysis of materials needs, inventory and orders)
- capacity requirements planning (where the master production schedule is linked to the available capacity of equipment and labour)

- shopfloor control (where shopfloor operatives interact with MRP II through outputs and inputs)
- financial integration (where MRP II data are translated from volumes to dollars to manage cash flow and financial forecasting).

Lean production has its critics. Some reject its claims to be a universal 'best way'. Like its proponents, they focus on automotive production. Berggren compared lean production in US automotive plants (still relying on assembly-line techniques) with the Swedish socio-technical systems model in Volvo plants (where teams assemble the whole car). Both systems use teams, but the Swedish approach allows them more authority and enriched work. Berggren concludes that the Volvo plants compared favourably with lean production in terms of worker dignity as well as efficiency.[56] Similarly, a US comparison of lean production (top management-driven quality processes in a Chrysler plant) and 'American team production' (self-directed work teams in GM's Saturn plant) found both performed well, but employee rights were much better safeguarded at Saturn.[57] Lastly, a comparative study of 71 automotive components plants in Europe, North America and Japan confirmed that some aspects of lean production (tight process control and integrated operations) are more productive, but others (teamwork organisation and human resource policies) are not associated with high performance.[58] Lean production may not be the only formula for success, even in automotive production where it originated.

Critics also question the human face of teamwork and work effort in lean production systems. Berggren found that: the pace of assembly-line work in lean US car plants was 'more inexorable'; demands for concentration increased; rigorous personal discipline was enforced on attendance, dress and the like; and teams had little discretion over production matters. He concludes that the lean production ideal of trust and a culture of reciprocity between workers and company did not match reality. He quotes one unionist as saying 'They talk a lot about flexibility, but it's a one way street. It's always the employees who are supposed to be flexible, never the company'.[59] Also, lean production systems have so little room for error that they often are policed by strict surveillance techniques, which create a system of 'management by stress'. Surveillance can be 'vertical' (electronic monitoring of individual effort) or 'horizontal' (peer group scrutiny).[60] Lean production is widely criticised because it does not empower employees; rather, it intensifies control over them.

Total quality management (TQM)

Closely related to the change tool of lean production is TQM. The two share many common characteristics and reached the Western world by a common path from Japan. TQM, however, like other tools of the quality movement, has its origins in the United States. It is one of a family of techniques or philosophies belonging to the 'quality movement'. This approach to organisations can be traced to the pioneering work of Walter Shewart of Bell Laboratories in 1924. He developed a series of statistical control charts to detect changes in the variability of production processes. His central idea, to diagnose faults in the production process *before* production rather than rectify product faults *after* production, remains a central plank in many quality programs. It is claimed to be less expensive to prevent faults than to rectify them.

Shewart's ideas were taken up in the United States by innovators such as W. Edwards Deming, Joseph Juran and Armand Feigenbaum, but were not widely practised in the United States or Europe for several decades. Post-war Japanese industry, on the other hand, proved a receptive audience. Deming travelled to Japan with the US occupation forces after 1945. He established links with Japanese managers planning to rebuild the devastated manufacturing base and introduced them to his ideas about quality control and improvement. From the 1950s, the Japanese Union of Scientists and Engineers (JUSE) promoted the ideas of Deming and Juran throughout Japanese industry, providing them with the loyal following they could not attract in America.

The global recession in 1980–81 forced many US producers to examine why they could no longer sell their products.[61] Companies such as Xerox came to realise that the Japanese had eroded their market share, asked how they had done it, and then sought to copy them. Quality management was discovered in America. Lester describes the return of the quality movement to the United States in the 1980s as follows:

> The story of how the quality movement re-entered the United States has an almost biblical cadence: a tiny group of octogenarian prophets (Deming and Juran), without honour in their own land, wandering in exile for decades before returning triumphant, at the head of mighty armies of low-cost, high-quality Japanese products.[62]

So, what 'model' do the leaders of quality management propose? Broadly defined as 'fitness for use', quality is about ensuring customer requirements are met. Beyond this common point of departure exists a number of different and sometimes conflicting models. Despite the influence of the 'quality movement', the ideas of that movement are difficult to pin down with precision. Nettle argues it is not a self-conscious group with a common creed or a precise and coherent set of principles; rather, the movement consists of a loose coalition of people with a broad interest in quality tools. He describes that movement in Australia as comprising 'networks of interest in leading edge companies, professional associations, government departments, consultancies and academia'.[63]

To show the diversity of opinion within the quality movement, it is possible to split ideas into the two camps of total quality control (TQC) and total quality management (TQM). TQC possesses the following elements:

- **statistical quality control** (SQC) — a set of techniques to measure and control variation and ensure consistency in a process. Random and predictable elements of variation are separated so the random (problematic) part can be eliminated.
- **quality assurance** (QA) — formal management structures for controlling quality. International (ISO9000 series) and Australian (AS3900) series of quality assurance standards exist. These prescribe formal structures, the allocation of responsibilities, standard tasks, measurement, feedback and recalibration processes. QA standards have a systemic or holistic character.
- **quality circles** (QC) — teams in which employees are trained in the use of SQC techniques, which they then apply to problem-solving and productivity improvement. Often called 'employee involvement teams', quality circles require flexible, decentralised, collective decision-making, or a participative management approach.

Like lean production, TQC techniques are intended to apply to the whole operational process, forming a fully integrated system focused on the elimination of random quality variance. The proponents of TQC also back the preservation of autonomous quality departments staffed by professional 'quality engineers'. In this idea, they differ from the advocates of TQM, who consider quality management to be less a specialised preserve of those with technical training and more a philosophy led by the chief executive officer and other top managers, and embraced by the whole organisation.

The philosophical character of TQM is conveyed in Deming's quality guidelines. Again, a biblical tone is present. Deming proclaimed 14 points, which included such maxims as 'create a constancy of purpose', 'eliminate empty slogans' and 'drive out fear'.

While Deming's quality guidelines illustrate the cultural attributes of TQM, they are imprecise in terms of its operational characteristics. Dawson, however, lists six features of TQM.[64]

- First, it is a *total management approach*, affecting task performance by every employee. It is not compartmentalised into a quality assurance department.
- Second, it emphasises *continuous improvement*, or incremental change. This element, known by the Japanese as *kaizen*, is shared with lean production systems.
- Third, it applies *appropriate quality control techniques*. While these may include SQC techniques, they are subordinated to the social process of continuous improvement.
- Fourth, and related, it applies *group problem-solving techniques* to improve processes. Among these tools is 'brainstorming', where teams interrogate quality data to find ways of improving processes.
- Fifth, it focuses on *internal and external customer and supplier relations*, or the value chain. Communication and teamwork along the chain are deemed essential to clarify and meet customer requirements.
- Sixth, it requires *high-trust relationships* and *eliminates adversarial industrial relations*. Open and participative management is necessary to engage the cooperation of teams in the process of continuous improvement. The divided loyalties characteristic of confrontational industrial relations may prove problematic.

The popularity of TQM was greatly enhanced by the development of national quality awards substantially based on TQM principles. Naturally, Japan has the 'Deming' award. In 1987, the US Congress established the Malcolm Baldrige National Quality Award (based on seven broad criteria: leadership, information and analysis, strategic planning, human resource management, process management, business results and customer focus). Initially popular, applications for the Baldrige award fell dramatically from 106 in 1991 to 29 in 1996. In Australia, the Australian Quality Council administers the Australian Quality Awards for Business Excellence. This national private-sector organisation formed in the late 1980s by bringing together several state-based groups that promote TQM.

There is considerable overlap in the content of TQM and lean production. They share a common emphasis on: the empowerment of teams to drive continuous improvement; the development of total management systems with appropriate structural and cultural characteristics; and the extension of continuous improvement throughout the supply chain. There are also differences; for example, TQM does not necessarily prescribe just-in-time supply chain management, is less focused on cost-reduction and has a stronger emphasis on cultural change.

TQM and lean production share a common criticism. To what extent does TQM live up to its claims to devolve decision-making to empowered teams? Kerfoot and Knights question whether quality teams do more than restore legitimacy for managerial 'privilege and authority'.[65] From an employee perspective, the experience of TQM may be quite different from the positive account that managers often give. In particular, the experience of 'empowerment' may be disappointing, failing to give employees much in the way of increased power and influence, not offering a great increase in the degree of discretion and often not winning workforce cooperation.

We encourage you to examine the Norske Skog mill case (case 3) to determine whether the changes in that organisation brought meaningful empowerment and commanded widespread employee support.

Business process re-engineering

Business process re-engineering first won global attention following the publication in 1993 of Hammer and Champy's bestseller, *Re-engineering the Corporation*, although it had been extensively practised in the United States in the preceding decade. Hammer and Champy were forceful salespersons. They proclaimed 'America's largest corporations — even the most successful and promising among them — must embrace and apply the principles of re-engineering, or they will be eclipsed by the greater success of those companies that do'.[66] US business seized on business process re-engineering and implemented it widely. In late 1994, *BusinessWeek* estimated that 83 per cent of the largest US corporations had re-engineered their workplaces.[67] While Australia has no comparable data, it is likely that Australian companies also used business process re-engineering extensively at this time.

The basic idea, as with many other change tools, is founded in a rejection of the segmented structures associated with Taylorism. As Lester puts it, 'instead of structuring a business enterprise around narrowly defined functions and tasks, it is better to organise around integrated business processes, sequences or agglomerations of tasks, which in combination deliver something of value to the customer'.[68]

Organisations that divide up tasks on functional lines must carry enormous costs in coordination and re-integration; they become rigid and wasteful, and much work is done pacifying internal customers rather than adding value to the end user. The re-engineering solution is to plot the essential elements in the flow of work, cutting across functional divisions and keeping only those steps in the process that add value to the end user. Everything else is wasteful and can be scrapped or outsourced to another organisation that can perform the task more efficiently.

Hammer and Champy express the key elements of re-engineering as follows:
- *fundamental* — question every aspect of why you do what you do, and how you do it, making no assumptions
- *radical* — get to the root of things and do not make superficial changes or simply modify existing structures

- *dramatic* — aim for quantum leaps in performance, not incremental changes, because re-engineering is the tool for 'heavy blasting', not chipping away at the coal face
- *process oriented* — focus re-engineering on business processes, not on tasks, people or structures. Re-engineering does not work on fragments of a business process; rather, the process must be attacked as a whole.

A number of factors combined to make business process re-engineering appealing in the 1990s.

1. It is a strategic tool that requires the analysis of core and secondary processes. In the 1990s, many diversified corporations divested their less profitable divisions and retreated to their core business. This approach to portfolio management resembles, at a strategic level, what business process re-engineering aims to do at the work process level. Such 'lean' corporate strategies sensitised many organisations to the savings available from this approach.

2. It arrived at a time when many organisations were introducing integrated information technology systems. These had such a pervasive effect on work flows that redesign or re-engineering was inevitable. In particular, information technology systems' automated information flows eliminated the need for the layers of middle managers who previously had acted as a transmission belt.[69]

3. It leads to downsizing, delayering and outsourcing. Re-engineered organisations usually have fewer workers and fewer layers of management, and retain fewer core activities by outsourcing information technology, maintenance, catering, security and other non-core activities. Stace and Dunphy observe that 'it is not uncommon for organisations to have shed or "downsized" up to 30 per cent or more of employees in the last decade using re-engineer techniques'.[70]

4. It is a radical tool, requiring that old structures and processes be torn up and new ones be designed to replace them. The 'clean sheet of paper' metaphor runs through Hammer and Champy's book. This radical approach held appeal for those who had become bogged in the complexity and slow progress associated with incremental change models.

5. It is a managerialist (or 'top–down') tool, not a participative one. Hammer and Champy vest primary responsibility for business process re-engineering in a 'leader' (the authorising executive), a 'process owner' (a manager with relevant responsibilities), a re-engineering team (including outsiders to break up vested interests), a steering committee (of senior managers) and a 're-engineering czar' (a coordinator and facilitator). The aim of business process re-engineering is to break down functional silos, so resistance is to be expected. It follows that strong leadership is demanded at the expense of participation. Resistance is not to be tolerated.

The popularity of business process re-engineering stemmed largely from its alignment with contemporary trends in corporate strategy, technology and human resources, rather than from inherent attractions. Viewed independently of these advantages, the approach promises great benefits but also can be difficult and disruptive. Business process re-engineering is so difficult that many firms claiming to be re-engineering were probably engaged in nothing more than downsizing or outsourcing. Champy told the story of one manager who admitted 'we don't really know how to do re-engineering in our company; so what we do is, we regularly downsize the company and leave it to the three people who are left to figure out how to do their work differently'.[71]

Figure 4.5 summarises the characteristics and the positive and negative features of business process re-engineering. They emphasise its ongoing nature: 'The mistake in re-engineering is to assume the task is ever completed. The business environment is unforgiving, and is particularly tough on those organisations which do not ensure their work organisation is constantly reviewed.'[72]

Typical intervention practices
- Analysis of core and secondary business(es)
- Downsizing to reduce absolute staff numbers, followed by rightsizing to match new structures and processes
- Value analysis to examine levels of approval, reporting methods, work processes and systems

Levels of intervention
- Association with major new strategic initiatives or a process of radical business refocus
- Re-engineering that cascades from the corporate level to the business and work unit levels, through the use of project or task teams

Typical gains
- Corporate survival
- The creation of customer orientation and the break-up of ossified structures
- Business strategies supported by process capability
- The elimination of unnecessary work

Typical risks
- Re-engineering may fail to meet excessive expectations
- A radical approach can destroy tacit knowledge essential for company operation, causing complete failure
- Re-engineering driven from too low in the organisation will lack authority and resources
- The process founders on endless consultation.

FIGURE 4.5: Re-engineering work processes

Business process re-engineering has critics. The evidence of problems is an alleged high incidence of failure or shortfall on potential delivery. Lester cites the case of Mutual Benefit Life, an early US re-engineering success that was declared insolvent. He also quotes a McKinsey study that found only a small fraction of 20 re-engineering projects had delivered benefits to bottom-line performance.[73] Such small-scale results abound in the literature. What do the founders of re-engineering believe? As late as 1996, Hammer claimed 'three out of four re-engineering efforts work'.[74] Champy, on the other hand, reported underperformance, arguing that:

> On the whole even substantial re-engineering payoffs appear to have fallen well short of their potential. Re-engineering the corporation set big goals: 70 per cent decreases in cycle time and 40 per cent decreases in costs; 40 per cent increases in customer satisfaction, quality and revenue; and 25 per cent growth in market share. Although the jury is still out on 71 per cent of the ongoing North American re-engineering efforts in our sample, overall, the study shows, participants failed to attain these benchmarks by as much as 30 per cent.[75]

It is hard to draw firm quantitative conclusions from these data about the overall effectiveness of business process re-engineering. Nevertheless, critical research consistently throws up one serious 'design flaw' in re-engineering. Lester calls this the 'troublesome paradox that lies at the heart of the re-engineering project itself'.[76] On one hand, business process re-engineering depends on the constructive input of teams of empowered employees; on the other hand, it almost inevitably entails massive disruption and job loss. How can support be won from a workforce for an activity that threatens them?

Jaffe and Scott endorse this criticism. They attribute the problem to technocratic assumptions about organisations and conclude that re-engineering needs to be redesigned to accommodate employee participation.[77] Similarly, Levine and Mohr claim that re-engineering encounters a 'threshold challenge' when attention shifts from 'technical system design' (business process/work flow/technology) to 'social system design' (roles/measures/structures). Fear and uncertainty arising from technical system design can be overcome only if social system design is given precedence; the people who do the work should be the ones engaged in redesigning both the technical and social systems.[78]

Best practice

Best practice is an abbreviation of 'world's best practice' — a term that conveys the challenge of global competition as much as corporate aspiration. As the 'Change management in action' example (Australian Federal Police) shows, the broad principles of best practice can be applied to any kind of organisation — even the police. However, the model originated in manufacturing. Like lean production, Americans exploring the Japanese competitive challenge to US manufacturing developed the concept of best practice. In 1986, the MIT Commission on Industrial Productivity was formed to address the decline in US industrial performance. Unlike the International Motor Vehicle Program, which examined lean automotive production in several countries, the Commission on Industrial Productivity confined itself to US manufacturers and their particular environment. It studied eight industries: automobiles, chemicals, commercial aircraft, consumer electronics, machine tools, microelectronics, steel and textiles. Interdisciplinary teams of researchers were asked to find out what had gone wrong in these industries and what could be done in response. The results were published in 1989 in *Made in America*.[79]

Two answers were provided for improving US manufacturing productivity. The first described national policies conducive to improved performance. Neglect of skills, technology and productive investment had to be dealt with at a national level. The United States needed better macro-economic, science, education and regulatory policies that would encourage industry.

The second answer was directed at business enterprises. What common factors seemed to explain the best practice success stories such as Motorola, Chapparal Steel, Hewlett-Packard, Boeing, Xerox and Levi Strauss? The MIT Commission's researchers claimed to observe 'six key similarities among the best practice firms'. These six similarities are principles of management resembling those found in lean production and TQM. They are:

- a focus on simultaneous improvement in cost, quality and delivery
- closer links to customers

- closer relationships with suppliers
- the effective use of technology for strategic advantage
- less hierarchical and less compartmentalised organisations for greater flexibility
- human resource policies that promote continuous learning, teamwork, participation and flexibility.[80]

CHANGE MANAGEMENT IN ACTION
Best practice in the Australian Federal Police

11 September 2001 was a memorable day for Australian Federal Police (AFP) Commissioner Mick Keelty, and not just because of terrorist attacks in the United States. It was also the day that he received results from the first comprehensive survey of AFP staff about HR issues. 'We got an 84% return from staff. We were blown away with that. We realised [the results] were too important to us as an executive not to listen to what our people were telling us.' In early 2003, the AFP did another survey and got a 91 per cent response rate. It now believes it taps into staff attitudes, and is treating its human resources seriously.

The HR revolution in the AFP was not of Keelty's making. It began in the mid-1990s before he became Commissioner (in early 2001). The AFP saw the challenge as breaking down the old hierarchical police culture with its bastions of rank, hours of work, overtime, and penalties and moving towards a new team-based system. Out went the old award and in came a new certified agreement. In a highly unionised industry, union support for change was critical. Keelty says he has that support. 'The union has been on board. There's been a common purpose with the union that this approach makes sense. It's about recognising the value of the individual. That's what a union should be about: getting good terms and conditions for the individual. And what we were putting forward were good terms and conditions.'

The staff survey opened management's eyes to many staff issues. These have been taken on board in the certified agreements, which have taken pay from penalty rates to a composite salary, and which have reduced the stress on staff of long working hours. The agreement has also built in greater flexibility and new rewards and supports the new system of a devolved management structure built around teamwork. About a third of police are uncomfortable with this, and would prefer everything in black and white with clear lines of authority. But the majority are adjusting well, and increasingly possess the education and skills to handle more autonomy. This devolved management approach fits the AFP well. It needs the professional skills of accountants, lawyers and diplomats to handle the challenges of high-tech fraud, narcotics crimes and people smuggling. Such professionals are accustomed to using their judgement. To stay abreast of developments in these fields, the AFP now forms partnerships with commercial organisations like Qantas, the Commonwealth Bank and Westfield, further dissolving its old insular culture.

With devolution comes accountability, both for the pay increases given to staff and for performance. The AFP has to justify its budget by proving results. To this end it employs some unusual performance measures such as the street value of confiscated drugs, and the recovery of past fraud losses. Now, like many other 'best practice' organisations, the AFP can measure the impact of devolved management and enriched HR practices on the bottom line.

Source: Adapted from Nicholas Way 2004, 'Feds democratic revolution', *BRW*, 2–8 September, pp. 56–7 and reproduced with permission.

What do these principles of best practice mean? First, most firms seek to improve in cost, quality or delivery, believing gains in one have to be traded off against the others; best practice firms aim to improve all three simultaneously. Second, traditional manufacturers were production driven, relying on scarcity to sell whatever they made; global market saturation requires best practice firms to be customer driven, basing production decisions on where there is a market need. Third, closer links with suppliers facilitate just-in-time production, which reduces inventory costs and can lead to cooperation and improvement on design and quality. Fourth, rather than implement technological innovation in products and production methods just because it is feasible, best practice firms do so only when it meets customer needs. Fifth, organisational structures that devolve decisions to functionally integrated business units and have fewer layers of hierarchy are more flexible and responsive to customers. Sixth, people need to have appropriate skills and attitudes to take the responsibility for customer value, which is the cornerstone of best practice.

The vital ingredient for best practice is not just in the six key similarities, but also in the way in which they are combined. The six elements were not used as 'independent solutions but rather as a coherent package of changes'.[81] Richard Lester, the project's Research Director, still emphasises the importance of synergies or complementarities among the six elements. Writing almost a decade later, he reflects:

> At that time we had been puzzled by the slowness of other companies to emulate the patterns of the successful companies. After all, most of these firms were well known, and the practices we had highlighted were not new even then. Our conclusion at the time was that what distinguished these companies was their ability to see these practices not as independent solutions but as part of a coherent system. They had understood the strength of the linkages between business elements that others saw as separable. Whereas most firms were taking a piecemeal approach to organisational change, focusing first on one thing and then another, our leading firms seem to have recognised the need for systemic change and the importance of aligning their organisational practices with each other.[82]

The holistic character of best practice is illustrated in figure 4.6. Improvements in efficiency, effectiveness and equity are the output of the system; they are accomplished by changes to operational practices. At the hub is process improvement undertaken by multiskilled and empowered teams (stemming from a flatter, less compartmentalised organisational structure). Those teams are guided through their closer relations with customers and suppliers, work in systems that use technology intelligently to support their customer focus and are moulded by human resource policies designed to equip teams and business units with the capabilities to make best practice work. Such system links can be observed in the Norkse Skog mill case (case 3) at the end of this book.

Two groups of enablers or catalysts facilitate best practice. They are not, of themselves, essential practices in a best practice operational system, but they are vital to the smooth operation of the core practices. First, cultural enablers — stable and diffused change leadership and an empowered workforce — create the 'frame of mind' in which best practice also becomes possible. Second, information enablers — internal workplace and team performance indicators linked to external benchmarks of best practice —

guide and reinforce change activities. The complexity of best practice also demands the articulation of clear goals or strategies concerning both conventional business objectives and the phasing in of best practice.

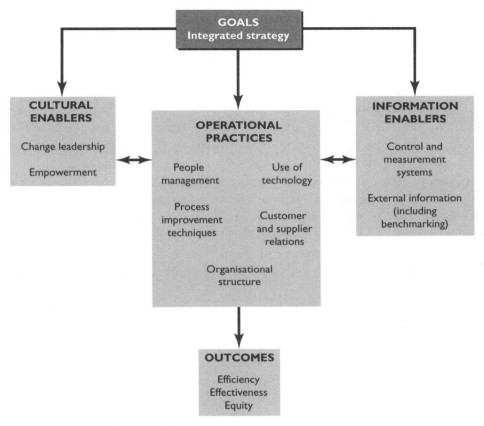

FIGURE 4.6: Best practice as a holistic system

Source: M. Rimmer, J. Macneil, R. Chenall, K. Langfield-Smith & L. Watts 1996, *Reinventing Competitiveness: Achieving Best Practice in Australia*, Pitman Publishing, Melbourne, © Commonwealth of Australia.

The best practice model has been influential in Australia. In mid-1991, a tripartite mission of Australian business, union and government leaders went to MIT and met members of the Commission on Industrial Productivity. The model of best practice identified in *Made in America* became the basis for an Australian version. Shortly after the tripartite mission returned to Australia, the Commonwealth Government's Australian Best Practice Demonstration Program began to offer project funding to assist firms to implement these new principles. A condition of funding was that firms be willing to open their doors to demonstrate to others how best practice worked. In 1991 and 1992, 43 businesses (mostly manufacturers) were selected to participate in the program. In 1994, an additional group (many of them small service organisations) also was selected. In 1996, the newly elected Coalition government terminated the program, but by then it had largely done its work. When the program began in 1991, best practice was perceived as new, revolutionary and difficult. By 1996, the core ideas were widely disseminated and well understood. Surveys in the mid-1990s demonstrated that 'continuous improvement by empowered work teams' was generally understood and extensively practised in Australian industry.[83]

The popularisation of best practice in Australia is not just a smooth process of learning to apply complex organisational principles. It also is the story of a battle for ownership of the label 'best practice'. Given that it is obviously good to be best practice, many interest groups have commandeered the appellation, giving the term a particular meaning to suit themselves. First among these groups was the Australian union movement, led by the powerful Australian Manufacturing Workers Union (AMWU). Fearing the further loss of members' jobs as Australian manufacturing became less competitive, the AMWU led a drive for union delegates and shopfloor workers to become more involved in production decision-making. If the managers could not save manufacturing, then rank-and-file unionists would show them what to do.

But if union policy supported best practice in the mid-1990s, that support extended to only a particular approach to best practice. Union support was contingent on the unions being able to partner management in decision-making from a position of strength. Also, there had to be payback for union support. In response to this union point of view, the Labor government of the day expanded the model of best practice prescribed by its Australian Best Practice Demonstration Program to include several union-friendly elements:

- a learning organisation committed to continuous improvement that manifests itself in a highly skilled and flexible workforce and recognises the value of all people in the organisation
- a cooperative industrial relations environment that incorporates effective consultation throughout the organisation and, where appropriate, means that relevant unions contribute to the process of change
- innovative human resource policies, including a commitment to occupational health and safety, and equal employment opportunity
- the integration of environmental management into all operations.

The inclusion of these elements effectively required best practice firms to take account of union policies on skill formation, industrial democracy, occupational health and safety, equal employment opportunity and the environment. Unions also expected that the productivity gains generated by best practice would be shared with their members through higher wages and more secure jobs.

There were countervailing pressures from the other side of the political spectrum, however. A loose coalition of interests, including the Australian Quality Council, business leaders, consultants and some academics, took a different view of best practice. Their version appeared in a report, *Leading the Way*, published in 1994 by the Australian Manufacturing Council.[84] This version added 'leadership' (which was to be shared between managers and work teams) to the list of essential elements, but made no mention of unions. Because the Labor government of the day was eager to placate business demands opposing union representation, this non-union approach gained endorsement. A third round of best practice grants were awarded in 1994, explicitly including a number of small, non-unionised workplaces. In the earlier rounds, union support and willingness to negotiate enterprise agreements had been essential conditions for inclusion in the program and therefore access to government funding.

The outcome was that best practice became a pawn in a political fight between those who wished to deepen union involvement in industrial democracy and those who wished to free managers from union interference. The two sides could not agree on the meaning of best practice when they differed so much on the basic issue of who should exercise power in the workplace. Following the election of a conservative government in 1996 and the termination of the best practice program, most unions began to lose interest in best practice. It was no longer seen as a means to accomplish industrial democracy; managers were left to run best practice projects as they chose and unions reserved the right to be uncooperative.

The Australian Best Practice Demonstration Program established and publicised role models of how continuous improvement by empowered teams led to more efficient and equitable workplaces. Its aim was to encourage extensive uptake of such work systems. Did this approach work? The most reliable data on this issue came from a 1995 survey of Australian workplaces, which found that almost half (47 per cent) of workplaces made use of work teams in their production systems.[85] While many of these workforces may have failed to live up to the full requirements of the best practice model, they do reveal the extent of its influence.

Two problems are attributed to best practice. First, it has been observed that best practice innovations may not be sustained to the point where they become the normal *modus operandi* of a business. We discuss this problem in chapter 11, which describes how the firms in the Australian Best Practice Demonstration Program often failed to implement vital parts of the holistic model of best practice, causing the system to under-perform, which created the risk that the investment would be discontinued. A case at the end of this book, describing best practice at the Norske Skog mill (case 3) shows that with additional time, however, best practice systems can become fully functional.

Study of these cases also suggests that the best practice cure may work but the patient can still die. Norske Skog can claim substantial gains from continuous improvement by empowered teams, but its operations are not trouble free and certainly not guaranteed to survive. The efficiency of the Norske Skog mill remains limited by outdated equipment. In a study of Australian manufacturers' strategies, Buxey concludes that best practice 'on its own cannot be expected to bring enough improvement in operations to overcome the various (cost) handicaps of the Australian business environment, compared to say China'.[86]

The first criticism that 'system failure' arises from partial implementation of best practice would be rejected by those who make the second criticism. They are opposed to the idea that best practice can be described as a system at all. They insist that the need for organisational fit prevents the construction of a general model of best practice that is applicable to all workplaces. Purcell presents a forceful case against a universal model of best practice.[87] A universal model of best practice must, he says, meet two tests. First, the model must identify components of best practice and how each policy reinforces the effectiveness of others (internal fit). Second, the effectiveness of the model needs to be demonstrated in terms of both diffusion and performance (external fit). Purcell notes that there is 'little agreement among researchers on quite what practices and policies do lead to better performances'.[88] Further, if a universal model is so beneficial, then why has it failed to spread? And, why does it not perform better than alternative models? The contemporary popularity of alternatives, including what Sisson calls the 'bleak house' approach (low-commitment, low-skill and low-trust work for a low-cost reward)[89] is well known.[90] Further, such firms can perform just as well as best practice firms.[91] How, then, is it possible to label any particular model as best practice?

Purcell does not conclude, however, that best practice models have no value or that a contingency approach is the only valid one. Rather, he steers a middle path between the best practice systems and contingency approaches, seeking to avoid the excessive simplicity of the former and the unmanageable complexity of the latter. On the one hand, he rejects what he calls the 'utopian cul-de-sac' that a 'universal bundle of best practice HRM is universally applicable'.[92] On the other hand, he is equally critical of the contingency/best-fit approach, which sets an impossible objective of 'modelling all the contingent variables, showing their interconnection, and the way in which changes in one variable have an impact on others'. Instead, he advocates an approach akin to the 'change path' perspective advocated at the beginning of this chapter. Best practice models are helpful 'not in defining a precise list of items, but in pointing to the architecture (broad design) of human resource processes which are translated to behaviour to suit the changing needs of the organisation'.[93]

High-performance work organisation

Closely related to best practice is 'high-performance work organisation' (HPWO) — an American expression that groups together a set of work practices used by US firms in the 1980s and 1990s to improve competitiveness. The work practices in question should be familiar already from the description of various practices earlier in this chapter. Osterman lists the following four practices: quality circles/off-line, problem-solving groups; job rotation; self-managed work teams; and TQM.[94]

In other words, the substance of HPWO is no more than a combination of TQM with off-line, problem-solving groups and elements of work enrichment and work group autonomy drawn from the socio-technical systems approach. There is now a large body of research on HPWO, which we discuss in chapter 10. In chapter 10, we also look at the argument that capital markets in the United States are averse to investment in intangibles such as workforce skills and commitment, and therefore tend to discourage the diffusion and sustainability of HPWO. We confine the discussion here to two definitional matters. First, what are the elements of HPWO? Second, can we distinguish different (perhaps complementary) approaches to HPWO that account for differences in definitions?

There is loose consensus that HPWO is typically about 'work being organised to permit front-line workers to participate in decisions that alter organisational routines'[95], but most authorities specify the operational details of HPWO in practice and diverge at this point. Becker and Gerhart demonstrated this divergence by comparing the operational definitions employed by five US authorities on the subject.[96] The writers in question belonged mainly to the same school of thought, so more consistency might be expected than was found. They prescribe the following practices:

- Kochan and Osterman (1994) — four practices, including self-directed work teams, job rotation, quality circles and TQM
- MacDuffie (1995) — ten practices, including the four listed by Kochan and Osterman plus suggestion schemes and human resource practices such as contingent pay and various hiring and training practices
- Huselid (1995) — 11 practices, confined to mainly human resource activities (job analysis, selection, training, contingent pay, information sharing, attitude surveys and performance appraisal) and excluding work teams and TQM
- Cutcher-Gershenfeld (1991) — four practices, including self-directed work teams, job rotation, feedback on production goals, and conflict resolution
- Arthur (1994) — 11 practices, including self-directed work teams and quality circles, but also additional elements such as job design, supervisory span of control and social events.

The five authorities fail to agree on a single one of the 27 practices in their combined list. On only two practices (self-directed work teams and quality circles) do four authorities agree, while agreement among three is confined to only a further two practices (contingent pay and post-induction training). Becker and Gerhart conclude from this lack of agreement that 'researchers have much to learn about what constitutes a high performance [human resource] strategy'.[97]

Although this apparent disagreement is disconcerting, recent authors on the subject are likely to see it as symptomatic of the diverse phenomena grouped together as HPWO. Osterman argues:

> The changes within American firms are not all of one piece. It is not accurate to speak of a single set of changes that are sweeping across the landscape. One obstacle to studying these questions systematically is that there is no unambiguous way of defining a high performance work system.[98]

Following Osterman, we can settle for the conclusion that HPWO is a loose term that imprecisely applies to a smorgasbord of practices. Diversity may not be quite so random, however. It is possible also to group a handful of dominant approaches to HPWO, which stem from the authors' different interests. The diversity of these approaches accounts for the lack of overlap in lists of practices. Three such approaches to HPWO are:

- *the human resource approach*. This is to be found in the work of authors such as Huselid (1995) who confine HPWO to a specific approach to the conventional range of human resource activities (including job analysis, selection, recruitment, training, remuneration, performance appraisal and so on). The HPWO approach to these activities emphasises an investment in human resources designed to motivate employees to offer maximum commitment discretionary effort. From this comes the term 'high-commitment' work practices or management, which is favoured by human resource management specialists such as Purcell.[99]
- *the industrial relations approach*. This approach is found in the work of authors who prescribe deals with unions as a means of building HPWO.[100] This approach is

exemplified by some as the 'mutual gains' trade-off, where the high commitment needed to deliver productivity gains is underpinned by employee benefits, including job security and gain sharing.[101] More traditional industrial relations scholars attack 'mutual gains' scholars for devoting too much attention to firm performance and too little to conventional negotiation and conflict.

- *the quality management approach.* The emphasis here is on TQM and its associated operational characteristics. Group problem-solving is linked to supply chain management and the elimination of random quality variation. Approaches to the human factor in HPWO can be crude, however. The creation of a 'quality first' culture, for example, may be left to management insistence and owe little to the sophisticated practices espoused in both the human resource management and industrial relations approaches.

HPWO continues to dominate debates among US industrial relations, human resource management and management academics, despite the lack of precision about the meaning of the term. This dominance is due to the rapid growth and importance of the cluster of HPWO practices. One question above all others continues to be debated: Does HPWO deliver better performance?[102]

Review

This chapter began with the opening case of a merger between IBM and PwC Consulting where a unique change path or trajectory evolved as the organisation combined the 'free spirits' of the consulting arm with the rigid rules of IBM. This case established a dominant theme of the chapter — that is, that the change path or trajectory encountered by an organisation will differ from any model or formula prescribed in a change-planning tool.

We developed this theme by looking at the pattern of change in Australia. Experiencing growing competition in capital and product markets in the 1980s, Australian businesses began to undergo a transformation in technology, organisational structure, work methods, skills and attitudes. One dominant theory of this transformation depicted Taylorist production systems being replaced by Post-Fordist systems. In niche markets where competitiveness demands speedy and flexible response, rigid bureaucracies must give way to flexible, decentralised and customer-oriented organisations. The evidence suggests, however, that organisations and industries fit poorly to the standard Post-Fordist template. Elements of Post-Fordism are widespread, but have blended with alternative strategies and structures because organisations have customised change paths to meet their particular needs.

We then explored the same theme at a theoretical level. First, we described a number of general change theories. We then undertook a detailed examination of the tension between contingency and holistic (systems) models of change. The dominant contingency model in Australia is that developed by Dunphy and Stace. Their model offers management a range of change paths, which are selected depending on the scale and style of change that fits organisational conditions (external fit). We contrasted this model with Pettigrew and Whipp's holistic 'framework for competitive success', in which change requires reinforcing links among the elements that make up the model (internal fit). A continuing and unresolved tension persists between the contingency and holistic approaches to change.

We described a number of influential change models or tools. Beginning with Lewin's classic model that dates back to the 1940s, our chronological review introduced the socio-technical systems approach and the organisation development school, which evolved through the 1960s and 1970s, and the organisational learning model, which appeared in the late 1970s. All three schools of thought have cast a long shadow, influencing both modern ideas and contemporary organisational practice.

In contrast, the next set of models owe more to the responses of Western business to the Japanese challenge of the early 1980s. Lean production and TQM owe much to Western ideas of quality control, but their modern influence grew only when they were re-imported in the 1980s. Both lean production and TQM appeared to succeed while overturning long-standing assumptions about the kind of operational systems that deliver best results in supply chain integration and quality production. Criticism is directed, however, at the social or cultural conditions necessary to support those operational systems. Cooperative work teams, which are seemingly unproblematic in Japan, have been portrayed as coercive when implanted in Western countries.

The final three models — business process re-engineering, best practice and HPWO, owe much to lean production and TQM, but have been heavily adapted to meet conditions in the United States and other countries. Of the three, business process re-engineering is the most radical because it has least to do with continuous improvement of existing processes and goes furthest in challenging organisations to identify and retain 'core' processes. Closely associated with outsourcing and downsizing, it fits with portfolio management strategies that urge businesses to 'stick to the knitting'. Business process re-engineering also requires, nevertheless, staff to rethink how work is done. Here lies what is seen as the 'design flaw' of re-engineering: staff are threatened with outsourcing and redundancy, yet are expected to show commitment to a radical re-think of their jobs. Is it realistic to expect high commitment from an intimidated workforce?

The politics of building workforce commitment permeate best practice and HPWO. These two models have much in common. Both emphasise the contribution of empowered teams committed to continuous improvement. They also prescribe similar conditions for such teamwork to flourish. There is a difference, however. Best practice is a model of a complete business system, encompassing all key processes such as strategy, design, marketing, supply, operations and human resources. Models of HPWO tend to focus on the human resource management and industrial relations policies, which support teamwork and have correspondingly little to say about operations and other business processes.

Our review of both best practice and HPWO models revealed considerable diversity. They generally agree on the core element of empowered teamwork, but the task of listing ancillary practices spawns rival approaches. This wide variety of theories and models appears to stem from the diversity of organisational practice. The 'one best way' view of organisational change does not match reality; instead, firms are doing many different things. Organisations craft individual change paths by selecting from a wide product range of tools and practices; by customising standard techniques to suit contingent requirements; and by modifying or abandoning tools as strategic, operational and political circumstances demand.

The change process is experienced by organisations as a search for the unknown. Like any other 'rite of passage', this process of discovery can exhibit consistent patterns. These are the generic models of change. The human element in change, however, resists being pigeonholed into particular models. Managers and employees are consciously involved in the change process. At times, some will lead and others will resist; always, they are forging their own change path, modifying standard tools to meet local conditions, seeking their own interests and interpreting the change experience through the lens of their values and norms.

Key terms

best practice. A holistic program for empowered teams to drive continuous improvement in all aspects of a business's operation, leading to world-class results in productivity and equity, (p. 108)

business process re-engineering. Fundamental re-evaluation and redesign of a business's processes, retaining and improving only those that add value to the end user, (p. 108)

change path (or **change trajectory**). The experience of change unique to an organisation arising from its particular configuration of personal, organisational and environmental influences, (p. 108)

change planning tool (or **change model**). A general recipe or formula for introducing change in all organisations, or a particular class of organisation, (p. 108)

contingency model. A model by which managers select change strategy to fit organisational requirements and environment, (p. 109)

double-loop learning. A form of organisational learning reinforced by two feedback loops. The first involves learning from the pursuit of existing goals. The second involves questioning and adjusting those goals to reflect new needs. (p. 120)

external fit. The alignment of change strategy to external environmental conditions, (p. 112)

goal-based (single-loop) learning. Adult learning reinforced by feedback that performance meets targets, (p. 120)

haphazard learning. Adult learning without clear objectives that is not reinforced by feedback, (p. 120)

high-performance work organisation (HPWO). A loosely defined group of practices relating to work organisation, human resources, industrial relations and quality management practices. Typically, these practices entail more cooperative production methods to increase productivity. (p. 110)

holistic model. A change model comprising interdependent elements, of which each is essential, (p. 113)

internal fit. The alignment of change strategy to internal organisational characteristics, (p. 113)

just-in-time. A 'pull' system of inventory management guided by the target of zero inventory, (p. 122)

kanban. An order that activates production in a just-in-time system, (p. 122)

kaizen. Team-based continuous improvement, (p. 122)

lean production. A continuous improvement and production system that minimises the use of inputs and inventory, (p. 110)

learning organisation. A cooperative system of work organisation in which semi-autonomous work teams, supported by appropriate technology and information systems, engage in double-loop learning, (p. 110)

manufacturing resource planning (MRP II). A computerised order and material tracking system used for inventory management, production planning, cost control and monitoring of shopfloor efficiency, (p. 123)

organisation development. A change intervention tool involving team-building exercises informed by action research activities and supported by participative management, (p. 110)

Post-Fordism. A production system requiring flatter and more flexible organisational structures and multiskilled/high-discretion work teams, catering for the customer requirements of a niche market, (p. 109)

quality assurance (QA). Formal management structures or systems to control quality. These systems allocate responsibility, designate tasks and prescribe measures. The elements of these systems are set down in Australian and international quality assurance standards. (p. 125)

quality circles (QC). Teams of employees that engage in continuous improvement to achieve zero quality defects, (p. 125)

semi-autonomous work group. Multiskilled work team that rotates tasks among members and exercises discretion over

matters normally decided by supervisors or lower management, (p. 119)

socio-technical systems. A theory of work organisation that gives equal weighting to social and technical influences, (p. 119)

statistical quality control (SQC). A set of techniques to measure and control variation and ensure consistency in a process, (p. 125)

Taylorism. A model of work organisation ascribed to F. W. Taylor involving the separation of mental and manual work, the design of simple and standardised manual tasks to eliminate scope for discretion, and the exercise of strict control over work effort, (p. 110)

total quality management (TQM). A holistic approach to quality improvement involving all parts of an organisation in the measurement, analysis and removal of quality problems, (p. 108)

Review questions

1. What role can change planning tools such as the 'ten commandments for implementing change' play in the development of an organisational change path or trajectory?
2. Why are the contingency and systems approaches to organisational change hard to reconcile?
3. Is Post-Fordism more influential than Neo-Fordism in contemporary Australia?
4. Should organisations follow Lewin's classical change prescription to 'refreeze' after the 'moving' stage?
5. How do the socio-technical systems and organisation development approaches to organisational change differ?
6. Can lean production or TQM work in Western business organisations?
7. Are the six key similarities identified in *Made in America* as the essence of best practice sufficient to guarantee organisational competitiveness?
8. Is there 'one best way' of achieving best practice?

Discussion questions

1. 'Business process re-engineering is no more than downsizing.' Discuss.
2. Is it essential to enact all the elements of best practice together to achieve any performance improvement? Discuss.
3. Are the many different approaches to high-performance work organisation a sign of its strength or weakness as a practical change intervention? Discuss.

Work assignment

Change tools

Describe the change history of your own organisation (or an organisation with which you are familiar) over the past three to five years, showing
1. how 'generic' change tools or solutions were applied; and
2. how they were modified or abandoned to suit organisational requirements.

Suggested further reading

Dunphy, D., Griffiths, A. & Benn, S. 2003, *Organisational Change for Corporate Sustainability*, Routledge, London.

Lester, R. K. 1998, *The Productive Edge: How US Industries Are Pointing the Way to a New Era of Economic Growth*, W. W. Norton & Company, New York.

Mathews, J. 1994, *Catching the Wave: Workplace Reform in Australia*, Allen & Unwin, Sydney.

Osterman, P. 1999, *Securing Prosperity: The American Labor Market: How It Has Changed and What to Do about It*, Princeton University Press, Princeton, New Jersey.

Rimmer, M., Macneil, J., Chenhall, R., Langfield-Smith, K. & Watts, L. 1996, *Reinventing Competitiveness: Achieving Best Practice in Australia*, Pitman Publishing, Melbourne.

Stace, D. & Dunphy, D. 2001, *Beyond the Boundaries: Leading and Recreating the Successful Enterprise*, 2nd edn, McGraw-Hill, Sydney.

End notes

1. A. A. Huczynski 1998, *Management Gurus: What Makes Them and How to Become One*, Routledge, London, p. 2; F. G. Hilmer & L. Donaldson 1996, *Management Redeemed, Debunking the Fads that Undermine Corporate Performance*, The Free Press, Sydney.
2. J. Kotter 1996, *Leading Change*, Harvard Business School Press, Boston.
3. R. M. Kanter 1985, *Change Masters: Corporate Entrepreneurs at Work*, Allen & Unwin, London.
4. R. M. Kanter, B. A. Stein and T. D. Jick 1992, *The Challenge of Organizational Change*, The Free Press, New York, p. 383.
5. V. J. Callan, G. Latemore & N. Paulsen 2004, 'The best-laid plans: Uncertainty, complexity and large scale organisational change', *Mt Eliza Business Review*, 7 (1), pp. 10–17.
6. S. Clegg, M. Kornberger & T. Pitsis 2005, *Management and Organisations*, Sage, London, p. 384.
7. D. Dunphy & D. Stace 1990, *Under New Management: Australian Organisations in Transition*, McGraw-Hill, Sydney.
8. M. Piore & C. Sabel 1984, *The Second Industrial Divide: Prospects for Prosperity*, Basic Books, New York.
9. J. Mathews 1989, *Tools of Change: New Technology and the Democratisation of Work*, Pluto Press, Sydney.
10. J. Mathews 1994, *Catching the Wave: Workplace Reform in Australia*, Allen & Unwin, Sydney, p. 3.
11. T. Bramble & D. Fieldes 1992, 'Post-Fordism: historical break or utopian fantasy?', *Journal of Industrial Relations*, 34(4), pp. 562–79.
12. Dunphy & Stace, op. cit., pp. 44–8.
13. P. Thompson & D. McHugh 1990, *Work Organisations: A Critical Introduction*, Macmillan, London, p. 95.
14. Dunphy & Stace, op. cit.
15. D. Stace & D. Dunphy 2001, *Beyond the Boundaries: Leading and Recreating the Successful Enterprise*, 2nd edn, McGraw-Hill, Sydney, p. 6.
16. Dunphy & Stace, op. cit., pp. 74–8.
17. A. Pettigrew & R. Whipp 1993, *Managing Change for Competitive Success*, Blackwell, Oxford, p. 104.

18. K. Lewin 1951, *Field Theory in Social Science*, Harper & Row, New York.
19. K. Lewin 1948, *Resolving Social Conflicts*, Harper & Row, New York.
20. P. M. Blau & R. W. Scott 1963, *Formal Organisations: A Comparative Approach*, Routledge & Kegan Paul, London.
21. D. Silverman 1970, *The Theory of Organisations*, Heinemann, London.
22. D. Katz & R. Kahn 1966, *The Social Psychology of Organizations*, John Wiley & Sons, New York.
23. P. Lawrence & J. Lorsch 1967, *Organization and Environment: Managing Differentiation and Integration*, Harvard University Press, Boston.
24. T. Burns & G. M. Stalker 1961, *The Management of Innovation*, Tavistock, London.
25. F. E. Emery & E. L. Trist 1965, 'The causal texture of organisational environments', *Human Relations*, 18, pp. 21–32.
26. E. L. Trist & K. Bamforth 1951, 'Some social and psychological consequences of the longwall method of coal getting', *Human Relations*, 4, pp. 3–38.
27. Mathews 1994, op. cit., p. 39.
28. E. L. Trist 1981, *The Evolution of Socio-Technical Systems: A Conceptual Framework and an Action Research Program*, Ontario Quality of Working Life Centre, Ottawa.
29. C. Berggren 1992, *Alternatives to Lean Production: Work Organization in the Swedish Auto Industry*, ILR Press, Ithaca, New York.
30. Mathews 1994, op. cit., p. 43.
31. F. van Eijnatten 1993, *The Paradigm that Changed the Workplace*, Van Gorcum Publishers, Assen Maastrict.
32. D. M. Waddell, T. G. Cummings & C. G. Worley 2000, *Organisation Development and Change*, Nelson, Melbourne, p. 6.
33. D. McGregor 1960, *The Human Side of Enterprise*, McGraw-Hill, New York.
34. R. Likert 1961, *New Patterns of Management*, McGraw-Hill, New York.
35. D. Dunphy 1981, *Organisational Change by Choice*, McGraw-Hill, Sydney, p. 45.
36. Waddell, Cummings & Worley, op. cit., p. 13.
37. H. Andreatta & B. Rumbold 1974, 'Organisation development in action: job design and development', *Personnel Practice Bulletin*, 30(4), pp. 342–56.
38. D. Dunphy, H. Andreatta & L. Timms 1976, 'Redesigning the work organisation at Philips', in *Australian Organisational Behaviour: Readings*, eds W. M. Ainsworth & Q. F. Willis, Macmillan, Melbourne.
39. A. Pettigrew 1985, *The Awakening Giant: Continuity and Change at Imperial Chemical Industries*, Blackwell, Oxford, p. 15.
40. P. Senge 1990, *The Fifth Discipline: The Art and Practice of the Learning Organization*, Doubleday, New York.
41. C. Argyris & D. Schon 1978, *Organizational Learning: A Theory of Action Perspective*, Addison-Wesley, Massachusetts.
42. L. Field with B. Ford 1995, *Managing Organizational Learning*, Longman, Melbourne.
43. Waddell, Cummings & Worley, op. cit., p. 448.
44. M. McGill, J. Slocum & D. Lei 1993, 'Management practices in learning organisations', *Organisational Dynamics*, Autumn, pp. 5–17.
45. Senge, op. cit., pp. 236–7.
46. ibid.
47. ibid.
48. ibid., p. 7.
49. ibid.
50. T. Clarke & S. Clegg 1998, *Changing Paradigms: The Transformation of Management Knowledge for the 21st Century*, Harper-Collins Business, London, p. 108.
51. A. Harrison 1994, 'Just-in-time manufacturing', in *New Wave Manufacturing Strategies*, ed. J. Storey, Paul Chapman Publishing, London, p. 181.
52. J. P. Womack, D. T. Jones & D. Roos 1990, *The Machine that Changed the World: The Story of Lean Production*, Harper-Perennial, New York, p. 34.
53. J. Lowe, R. Delbridge & N. Oliver 1997, 'High performance manufacturing: evidence from the automotive components industry', *Organizational Studies*, 18(5), pp. 783–98.
54. J. F. Krafcik & J. P. McDuffie 1989, *Explaining High Performance Manufacturing: The International Automobile Assembly Plant Study*, IMVP, MIT Press, Massachussetts.
55. A. Spreadbury 1994, 'Manufacturing resource planning', in *New Wave Manufacturing Strategies*, ed. J. Storey, Paul Chapman Publishing, London, p. 154.
56. Berggren, op. cit., p. 164.
57. H. Shaiken, S. Lopez & I. Mankita 1997, 'Two routes to team production: Saturn and Chrysler compared', *Industrial Relations*, 36(1), pp. 17–45.

58. Lowe, Delbridge & Oliver, op. cit., p. 796.
59. Berggren, op. cit., p. 6.
60. G. Sewell 1998, 'The discipline of teams: the control of team-based work through electronic and peer surveillance', *Administrative Science Quarterly*, 43, pp. 409–28.
61. R. E. Cole 1995, *The Death and Life of the American Quality Movement*, Oxford University Press, New York, p. 5.
62. R. Lester 1998, *The Productive Edge: How US Industries are Pointing the Way to a New Era of Economic Growth*, W. W. Norton & Co., New York, p. 203.
63. D. Nettle 1995, 'The quality movement in Australia', *Labour and Industry*, 6(3), pp. 27–40.
64. P. Dawson 1994, 'Total quality management', in *New Wave Manufacturing Strategies*, ed. J. Storey, Paul Chapman Publishing, London, pp. 106–9.
65. D. Kerfoot & D. Knights 1995, 'Empowering the quality worker? The seduction and contradiction of the total quality phenomenon', in *Making Quality Critical: New Perspectives on Organisational Change*, eds A. Wilkinson & H. Willmott, Routledge, London, p. 236.
66. M. Hammer & J. Champy 1993, *Re-engineering the Corporation: A Manifesto for Business Revolution*, HarperCollins, New York, p. 2.
67. *Business Week*, 7 November 1994.
68. Lester, op. cit., p. 208.
69. ibid., p. 210.
70. Stace & Dunphy, op. cit., p. 238.
71. J. Champy 1995, *Re-engineering Management: The Mandate for New Leadership*, HarperCollins, New York, p. 3.
72. Stace & Dunphy, op. cit., p. 240.
73. Lester, op. cit., p. 210.
74. ibid., p. 211.
75. Champy, op. cit.
76. Lester, op. cit., p. 211.
77. D. T. Jaffe & C. D. Scott 1998, 'Re-engineering practice. Where are the people? Where is the learning?', *Journal of Applied Behavioural Science*, 34(3), pp. 250–67.
78. L. Levine & B. J. Mohr 1998, 'Whole system design (WSD): the shifting focus of attention and the threshold challenge', *Journal of Applied Behavioural Science*, 34(3), pp. 305–26.
79. M. L. Dertouzos, R. K. Lester & R. M. Solow, 1989, *Made in America: Regaining the Productive Edge*, Harper Perennial, New York.
80. ibid., p. 18.
81. ibid., p. 26.
82. Lester, op. cit., pp. 246–7.
83. Australian Manufacturing Council (AMC) 1994, *Leading the Way: A Study of Best Manufacturing Practice in Australia and New Zealand*, Melbourne.
84. ibid.
85. A. Morehead, M. Steele, M. Alexander, K. Stephen & L. Duffin 1997, *Changes at Work: The 1995 Australian Workplace Industrial Relations Survey*, Longman, Melbourne, p. 507.
86. G. Buxey 2000, 'Strategies in an era of global competition', *International Journal of Operations and Production Management*, 20(9), p. 1014.
87. J. Purcell 1999, 'The search for best practice and best fit in human resource management: chimera or cul-de-sac?', *Human Resource Management Journal*, 9(3), pp. 26–41.
88. Purcell, op. cit., p. 27.
89. K. Sisson 1993, 'In search of HRM', *British Journal of Industrial Relations*, 31(2), pp. 201–10.
90. Australian Centre for Industrial Relations Research and Training (ACIRRT) 1998, *Australia at Work*, Prentice Hall, Sydney.
91. S. Wood & L. de Menezes 1998, 'High commitment management in the UK: evidence from the workplace industrial relations survey and employers' manpower and skills survey', *Human Relations*, 51(4), pp. 485–515.
92. Purcell, op. cit., p. 36.
93. ibid., p. 38.
94. P. Osterman 1999, *Rediscovering Prosperity: The American Labor Market: How It Has Changed and What to Do about It*, Princeton University Press, Princeton, New Jersey, p. 99.
95. E. Appelbaum, T. Bailey, P. Berg & A. L. Kalleberg 2000, *Manufacturing Advantage: Why High-Performance Work Systems Pay Off*, Cornell University Press, Ithaca, p. 7.
96. B. Becker & B. Gerhart 1996, 'The impact of human resource management on organizational performance: progress and prospects', *The Academy of Management Journal*, 39(4), p. 785.
97. ibid., p. 784.
98. Osterman, op. cit., pp. 94–8.
99. Purcell, op. cit., p. 37.

100. E. Cohen-Rosenthal 1995, *Unions Management and Quality: Opportunities for Innovation and Excellence*, Irwin Professional Publishers, Burr Ridge, Illinois.
101. T. A. Kochan & P. Osterman 1994, *The Mutual Gains Enterprise*, Harvard Business School Press, Boston.
102. P. B. Voos & H Kim 2001, 'High performance work systems in the US context', *Transfer*, 7(3), pp. 422–40.

5

NEW FORMS OF ORGANISING

In 1995, Gannett Corporation launched the USAToday.com online news service in response to concerns about the future growth of its *USA Today* newspaper, one of the most widely read national newspapers in the United States, in the face of declining newspaper readership, increasing competition from other media formats, and rising paper costs.

USAToday.com was set up as a 'skunk-works' operation independent of the traditional business. People were recruited from outside the organisation and a collaborative, entrepreneurial workplace culture evolved, with the focus on flexibility and speed of response and delivery.

However, while the new business was achieving a small profit by 1999, its growth rate was disappointing and it was contributing little to overall business performance. Tom Curley, company president, believed the key problem was USAToday.com's isolation from the print business: the unit was unable to tap into the main business's resources. In addition, some USAToday executives saw USAToday.com director Lorraine Cichowski as a competitor and made little effort to share their people or physical resources with her. As a result, the unit over time was starved of cash, staff morale dipped and many of its star recruits left.

Curley now believed that integration was the way forward. He argued that *USA Today* should adopt a 'network strategy' whereby news content would be shared across three platforms: newspaper, USAToday.com, and its 21 local television stations. In 2000, Cichowski was replaced and USAToday Direct, a newly created television operation, was launched. While these two organisations continue to operate separately from the newspaper, with their own distinctive processes, structures and cultures, Curley insisted that the senior leadership of all three businesses be tightly integrated. Daily editorial meetings among the heads of the different units are held to review stories and assignments, share ideas and identify potential synergies. While fostering cross-unit collaboration, the units remain physically and structurally independent with distinctive staffing models. Staff within the online news service are generally younger than their counterparts in the print media and operate in a more collegial manner, in an entrepreneurial, fast-paced environment. The reporters are still strongly independent, seeking to provide more in-depth coverage of stories than their television counterparts.

Curley also made changes at the organisational and senior management level that further confirmed his commitment to a network strategy. Firstly, he replaced senior executives who did not support his vision, thus ensuring the message delivered down the line was clear and consistent. Curley also introduced a range of new initiatives to promote and institutionalise cross-unit collaboration and information sharing. Unit-specific goals in the executive incentive program were replaced with a common bonus program tied to growth targets across all three media units. New human resource policies were also introduced to support the 'network' form of organising. Staff were encouraged to seek transfers between the different media units to broaden their skills and knowledge; and staff willingness to share stories and other news content was now an important staff remuneration and promotion criterion. Allied to this, the 'Friends of the Network' recognition program was set up to recognise and reward cross-unit achievements.

Introduction

It is clear from discussion in earlier chapters that we are experiencing a major paradigm shift in the nature and composition of organisations, not only in terms of the systems and structures that served so well in more benign and certain times, but also in terms of intra- and inter-organisational stakeholder relationships. We have argued that competing successfully in the new business environment requires an 'inside-out', wide-angle view of the world, coupled with go-to-market speed, flexibility and adaptability. This approach has necessitated a shift from the traditional hard, rational, quantitative approach to managing organisations to a softer, more qualitative, intuitive, people-focused approach, and an appreciation of the importance of considering both social and technical components in workplace design, as identified by the Tavistock group in the early 1960s (see chapter 4).

In a highly competitive, customer-driven, global marketplace, only organisations that are 'focused, fast, friendly and flexible' can hope to win.[1] Such organisations have a resolute commitment to continuous innovation and improvement. These are the building blocks of the 'learning organisation' in which organisational capabilities and knowledge creation rather than products and markets are the key source of competitive advantage.[2] In 'knowledge-rich' organisations[3], there is support and encouragement for employees 'to run "experiments in the margin", to continually explore new business and organisational opportunities that create potential new sources of growth'.[4] 'Experiments in the margin'[5] or 'successive adaptation' allows 'planned opportunism to occur'[6], organisations can expand their areas of interest and develop new capabilities and expertise, which in turn increases their flexibility and responsiveness to changing circumstances. This type of flexibility, in which a company is virtually reinventing itself and its business, is needed for long-term survival in the future.[7]

The 'Opening case', for example, illustrates the tensions between preservation and change at *USA Today* as it trials new organisational practices that will allow it to *explore* the future as it *exploits* the present.[8] *USA Today's* 'ambidextrous' form of organising, with its complementary independencies and interdependencies, has enabled the organisation to capture and exploit the synergies of cross-unit collaboration between its existing mature business and newly emerging businesses. As the two developing businesses independently explored new opportunities for growth, they were able to tap into the resources and know-how of the existing business. Correspondingly, as the mature business sought to take advantage of its existing capabilities to grow its profits, it was able to learn and draw information from the new technologies being explored in the emerging businesses, adding greater depth and new dimensions to the traditional print form.

The 'Opening case' also highlights the importance of addressing both social and technical components in workplace design. It was clear that if it were to survive, *USA Today* had to capture and exploit the new communications and media technologies and do so in a way that would enrich and complement, rather than threaten and undermine, the organisation's existing traditional print business. Initially, the new unit, USAToday.com, was set up as a completely separate entity from the main business, with no interaction between the two, but with the expectation that the developing unit would be able to call for assistance and support from the existing business when needed. Inevitably, with none of the senior managers in the existing business accountable for or involved in the new unit's operations, tensions surfaced and the emerging business was effectively sidelined and starved of resources. The resulting hostility and rivalry between the existing and emerging businesses highlight the problem of focusing on systems and structure at the expense of social and relational dimensions when redesigning organisations. The problems at *USA Today* were only resolved by managing the structurally independent units, with their own distinctive systems, processes, cultures, through a tightly integrated senior team that recognised and rewarded cross-unit collaboration and information sharing. The management implications of the issues identified in the 'Opening case' underline the need for sensitivity to the dualities of exploration and exploitation and greater understanding of how traditional and new organisational practices can be organised to strengthen and support each other.[9] These important issues are explored further in this chapter in the section 'Managing the dualities of organisation design' (page 163). We also explore the dynamics and complementarities that manifest in designing and developing different forms of organising, but which are often misunderstood or ignored. For example, both the *USA Today* and Unilever (see the 'Change management in action' case, page 153) experiences suggest that unless people processes and relational issues are addressed simultaneously alongside structural and boundary changes, an organisation is unlikely to realise significant performance improvement. We in fact argue in this chapter that *people* processes play an overarching role in the structures–processes–boundaries relationship that is central to designing organisations.

This chapter does not seek to study the history and development of organisation design over the past 50 or so years. Neither does it attempt to classify and define different structural forms (such as functional, divisional and matrix), although these are mentioned. The aim here is to investigate the emerging key themes in new forms of organising and the factors that are driving these changes. We deliberately talk about *organising* rather than *organisation* because the latter suggests a passive, reactive mindset implicit in the classic unfreeze–refreeze model of change, whereas *organising* conveys the 'dynamic, perpetual and simultaneous character'[10] of the change process. In the following section, we briefly look at the evolution of organisation design and the context in which this has occurred.

The section 'Organising for success' (page 154) investigates emerging themes for leading and managing organisations of the future. In particular, it considers the INNFORM Project on innovative forms of organising for the 21st century, an international project that was managed from Warwick Business School by Professor Andrew Pettigrew. The European component of the study collected comparative data from 450 large- and medium-sized Western European companies on the nature and degree of change across the three organisational design dimensions of *structure* (delayering, decentralising and project-based organising), *process* (investment in information technology, horizontal and vertical communications, and new human resource practices) and *boundaries* (downscoping, outsourcing and strategic alliances). We consider the findings within these three broad areas in some depth and discuss their implications. In the section 'Organising today for tomorrow' (page 171), we consider what the emerging key dimensions of new forms of organising signify for leading and managing in the 21st century.

Designing organisations

While we moved from the Industrial Age to the Information Age in the mid-1960s[11] as new service industries emerged and developments in information technology accelerated, the 1980s represented a watershed period and the beginning of true global competition as trade barriers crumbled, widespread deregulation occurred across industries, and the increased rate of technological change — with the convergence of computing, networks, the Internet and video technologies — reshaped the way in which business is conducted. The 1980s was the decade of 'delayering, downsizing and outsourcing'.[12] For knowledge-based companies in particular, the Taylorist model with its adherence to hierarchy, stability, uniformity and specialisation, specifically designed to exert authority and control over a largely uneducated workforce, becomes untenable in dealing with highly-skilled knowledge workers.[13] Moreover, these old-style 'corpocracies'[14] are proving to be totally ineffectual in responding quickly and decisively to the demands of a technology-driven, customer-focused and increasingly global, marketplace. As Scott Morton suggests, the development of the 'hierarchical mass production firm'[15] is merely a 'happenstance of a particular set of forces. ... There is nothing pre-ordained or inevitable about their existence or indeed, their continuance.'[16] Many organisations began experimenting with new organisation configurations and disman-tling the traditional pyramidal organisation model. The highly formalised, mechanistic nature of the functional configuration (figure 5.1a) with its focus on efficiency and work specialisation, excellent in a relatively stable environment, lacked flexibility and respon-siveness within the context of an increasingly volatile external environment. In an attempt to relax the rigid formalities of the functional structure, organisations gradu-ated to a divisional structure. A major shortcoming of the divisional structure (figure 5.1b) was the loss of efficiency, because resources tended to be duplicated within div-isions and the development of technical excellence through functional specialisation was diluted.[17]

The matrix configuration (figure 5.1c) was an attempt to combine the efficiencies of the functional configuration with the responsiveness of the divisional structure. How-ever, while matrix structures may achieve efficiencies, increase responsiveness and encourage the involvement of lower levels of management in decision-making, they also have many shortcomings. Particular problems are conflicting lines of responsibility and authority, and possible friction between central headquarters and divisions.[18] In an attempt to break down the barriers between divisions and improve synergies, many organisations began establishing smaller, 'networking' business units. Limerick and Cunnington describe this new paradigm as a 'loosely coupled system', 'simultaneously assert[ing] both autonomous distinctiveness and interdependence', which allows for 'differentiation' and 'integration' between business units.[19] Collaboration and com-munication *across* functional units form the ethos of the loosely coupled network organisation. In this environment, autonomous business units work both independently and collaboratively on projects, depending on the skills and resources needed to com-plete a task.

Birkinshaw describes networks as 'an emerging alternative to the traditional hierar-chical model of organisation'.[20] He refers to Baker's argument that all organisations are networks of relationships, ties and dependencies, whether classified as a bureaucracy or a network organisation. According to Baker, organisation *type*, however, 'depends on the particular pattern and characteristics of the network'.[21] A network characterised by high formalisation, vertical specialisation, centralised planning and control, and vertical communication represents what we would term a bureaucracy. On the other hand, a network characterised by flexibility, decentralisation, devolution of authority, and strong horizontal communication and linkages more closely fits the network organ-isation type.[22]

Research gathered on what capabilities a firm must develop to operate successfully as a network organisation identified *flexibility* as an overarching core capability that was integral to ensuring a firm's adaptiveness and responsiveness to environmental oppor-tunities and threats. At the grassroots level, essential capabilities were found to include: managing customer or supplier relationships, particularly the 'internal coordination' of information and resources to expedite the relationship; developing 'vicarious capa-bilities' to manage the interface with outsourcing partners (that is, how well a firm is able to identify and 'absorb' capabilities from its external environment, which the research suggests is closely tied to the firm's innovative capacity)[23]; developing a strong network of external contacts on whose expert knowledge and advice the firm can draw; and being able to identify internal best practice and then transfer and diffuse it through the organisation.[24]

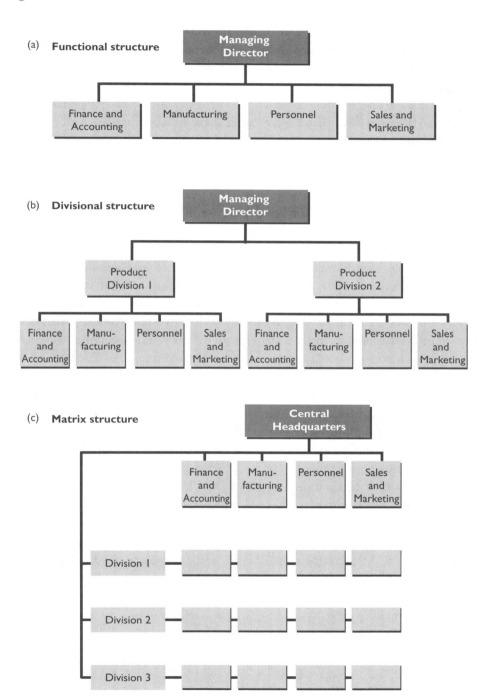

FIGURE 5.1: Functional, divisional and matrix structures

All this information suggests that success in the new global economy requires a paradigmatic shift from organisation as machine to organisation as a dynamic, interactive organism — a shift from a risk-averse, adversarial, control-oriented bureaucracy to an entrepreneurial, collaborative, flexible form. Ghoshal and Bartlett note that many large, diversified companies that prospered and grew through the post-war period from the 1950s to 1970s began to founder when the traditional management tools and techniques for successfully organising a large **multidivisional organisation** proved ineffectual against the environmental '**breakpoints**'[25] that heralded the post-industrial age, particularly economic globalisation, the development of the service sector, the technological revolution and the shift from the '**smokestack**'[26] to the 'knowledge' economy.[27] Ghoshal and Bartlett consider a number of companies (particularly General Electric and ABB) that successfully overcame these breakpoints by developing a new organisational model that focuses on a key set of management processes rather than on organisational structure.[28] They identify three core processes that underpin the new management approach: entrepreneurial (encouraging initiatives), integrative (linking and leveraging competence) and renewal (managing rationalisation and revitalisation).[29] These processes are discussed in further detail later in this chapter.

The success of ABB's (representing the merging of Swedish ASEA and Swiss Brown Boveri) 'global **matrix structure**' has made it a classic example of how to manage the dilemmas of being 'simultaneously global and local, big and small, centralised and decentralised'.[30] Between 1988 and 1993, ABB built its global matrix structure, comprising six business segments. International networks were established, significant decentralisation occurred (including all human resource responsibilities) and ABB subsidiaries were established as independent profit centres. The evolving organisational form underlined a strong country focus as the company sought to integrate its worldwide operations.

In 1998, problems inherent with matrix management along with the company's commitment to finding the most effective and innovative organisational form to manage its complex and diversified global operations, led ABB to evolve its global matrix structure to a '**network multidivisional form**'[31] It dissolved its regional management layer and established seven business segments which included 33 business areas. The business (or product) segments now became the primary focus. The aim of these changes from the traditional matrix form to the network multidivisional form at ABB was to emphasise and encourage horizontal communication; flexibility and boundary spanning; cross-divisional knowledge transfer and learning; and improve intra-organisational relationships and processes. At the same time, ABB's small corporate headquarters, based in Zurich, continued to play a powerful, central, strategic role, while business area managers in the different business segments maintained responsibility for worldwide product strategy-making.

In essence, ABB was endeavouring to create a 'strategically flexible organisation' that would allow it to manage its different divisions dynamically.[32] This approach entailed learning how to balance and integrate the dualities of old and new organisational practices, for example nurturing innovation alongside rigorous financial and operational systems; and balancing formalised, central controls and policies with decentralised decision-making that would support more flexible forms of organising.[33] We examine in further detail later in the chapter the 'bi-modal' work practices apparent in modern organisations as they seek to manage the tensions between managing flexibility and efficiency; networks and hierarchy; centralisation and decentralisation; and meeting both global and local needs.[34]

CHANGE MANAGEMENT IN ACTION

Organising for success at Unilever — changing structures, processes and boundaries

Created in 1930, Unilever is a manufacturer and marketer of branded consumer products, focusing on foods, detergents and personal products. In 2002, the company's operations were consolidated into two global divisions: Foods, and Home and Personal Care. Its main competitors are L'Oréal in home and personal products, Nestlé and Kraft in food, and P&G (formerly Procter & Gamble) over both groups.

Unilever unusually has two parent companies, which operate as a single unit: Unilever NV based in the Netherlands, and Unilever Plc based in London. At the head of each parent company is a 'chairman', who acts as chairman of the combined Unilever Group, not as CEO of one of the separate companies. The Unilever culture, significantly shaped by its two chairmen and executives, was conservative, risk-averse and collegial. Unilever's recruitment strategy and the set of business principles crafted and articulated by senior management provided the bonds that held the decentralised national and regional organisations together.

Through the 1960s and 1970s, Unilever pursued a strategy of **horizontal and vertical integration**. The company's tradition of decentralisation with little imposition or monitoring from headquarters resulted in brand proliferation. There were also numerous sole-supplier companies in the different regions, which were increasingly involved in the product development process. In response, product coordination groups were established, increasing from three in 1962 to ten by 1977. This led to the formation of product-based organisations in different regions all with different levels of central influence and significantly shifted the balance of power away from the national companies and the sole-supplier service companies.

Senior management recognised that there was a lack of strategic focus among the far-flung decentralised businesses. They now sought to impose greater strategic direction from the centre and focus the national and regional organisations on Unilever's core businesses of foods, detergent, personal products and chemicals. Between 1984 and 1988, Unilever sold £2 billion of non-performing brands and non-essential supply companies and purchased £4 billion of new businesses that were seen as value adding to the core businesses.

The Starfish program, launched in 1988, continued with the strategic refocus of the mid-1980s, paying particular attention to the different geographical areas and subcategories within the core businesses. The key question at this time was how to globalise beyond its traditional European base. This period was a time of gradual change. The organisation's structure — its three-man committee at the top, the powerful national operating companies, the board in the middle comprising individuals with international product coordination roles and regional responsibilities; processes governed by the principle of devolution; and the collegial managerial networks — remained relatively intact.

A review of strategy in 1992 identified emerging opportunities in Asia and Eastern Europe. The review underlined the importance of adopting a greater geographical focus and reiterated the need to remove underperforming businesses. Changes to *processes* were also implemented at this time to complement and support the *strategy* and *boundary*

(continued)

changes. There was increasing recognition of the 'economic and social value' of sharing information and experiences across the increasingly product-dominated form of organising and Perry (Unilever chairman at the time) supported and encouraged intra-organisational network building and knowledge transfer across countries and regions.

The next major period of change at Unilever took place under Niall Fitzgerald, Chairman from 1996 to September 2004. There was widespread concern that the organisation was experiencing 'performance drift' and 'organisational fatigue'. As one observer scathingly commented, Unilever comprised 'extra levels of complexity on an already convoluted structure with confused account-abilities, constipated decision making and frustrated de-motivated staff'.

Fitzgerald's vision for Unilever was a form of organising that would provide clear principles and a strategic framework within which people would have considerable freedom. Headquarters would only interfere if they moved outside the framework or failed to meet their plans. To achieve such a form of organising, the first priority of the 'Restructuring for Outstanding Performance' initiative launched in 1996 was to remove the confusion between product coordination groups with profit responsibility and local companies with operating responsibilities. The key advantages of the new structure included establishing a clear corporate focus, and separating profit and operating responsibilities from policy. As another outcome of the restructuring, Unilever established global ownership of key categories, brands and strategies without undermining its well-crafted decentralisation capabilities, which its rivals L'Oréal and P&G were unable to match.

Other changes were implemented in tandem with the restructure. The emphasis on organising around *process* as opposed to *function* underlined the innovation focus (that is, combining research and development and marketing as championed earlier by Perry) and enabled cross-border rational-isation, which also helped reduce the power of national operating companies.

The complementary sets of changes undertaken appear to be central to the company's improved business performance. From 1985 to 1999, Unilever's operating margins grew from below 6 per cent to above 11 per cent; return on capital more than doubled from less than 11 per cent to over 22 per cent and net cash flow from operating activities totalled over 50 billion euros. However, the organisation's underlying sales growth was below expectations and had failed to reach the same level as its main competitors, resulting in a drop in the share price in 1999. This disappointing result was the impetus for the 2000 launch of the 'Path to Growth' program. Fitzgerald stressed that 'a single initiative is not enough — it needs to be reinforced again and again, and each initiative needs to be part of an integrated whole'.

Source: Reprinted by permission of Sage Publications Ltd from Andrew M. Pettigrew & Richard Whittington 2003, 'Complementarities in Action: Organizational Change and Performance in Unilever 1985–2002', in *Innovative Forms of Organizing*, eds A. M. Pettigrew, R. Whittington, L. Melin, C. Sanchez-Runde, F. A. J. van den Bosch, W. Ruigrok, T. Numagami, © Sage Publications, London, chapter 8, pp. 173–207; www.unilever.com/company accessed on 9 November 2004.

Organising for success

Figure 5.2 provides an overview of the key themes and perspectives on organising for success in the 21st century that are discussed in this section. As suggested by figure 5.2, we argue that a holistic, systems approach is integral to managing the complexities and dualities inherent in innovative forms of organising. In the following discussion, we outline the three major interrelated themes from the new organisational forms literature, as identified by Fenton and Pettigrew, and consider Kanter's three key strategies for the post-entrepreneurial organisation. In 'Changing structures, processes and boundaries' (page 159), we discuss the nine indicators of organisational change encompassed in the three key design variables of structure, process and boundaries, and consider these within the framework of the INNFORM study referred to earlier as well as providing other examples.

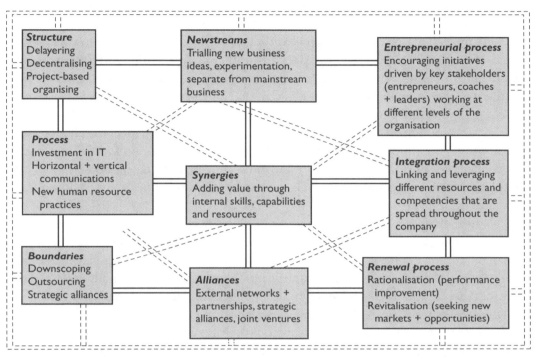

FIGURE 5.2: A 'systems view' of interrelationships within and among different perspectives on organising for success in the 21st century

To compete successfully in the new competitive landscape, described in the previous section, requires careful reappraisal of the traditional command and control system — in which a clearly defined, functionally specialised, hierarchical structure served as a buttress for stability and continuity — and experimentation with more flexible and agile organisational forms which support and encourage innovation, exploration and learning. The focus has shifted from organising around structure to organising around processes and social and relational dimensions. In their study of the nature of new organisational forms, Fenton and Pettigrew identify three major interrelated themes in the new organisational forms literature.[35]

The first theme concerns the changing boundaries of the globalising firm. In the highly competitive, technology-driven, global environment, changing consumer expectations have forced a shift of focus from 'economising to adding value'.[36] As noted in chapter 2, in an environment characterised by discontinuous change, one of the core strategic imperatives imposed on organisations of the future is the need to focus on portfolios. As a result, large, global companies are seeking to develop their core competencies by focusing on single industries rather than diversification, and outsourcing non-core activities. This focus has led to a re-evaluation of the relationships among structure, systems, people and processes, and a better understanding of the interchanges and inter-dependencies among these elements, which must be captured in organisational design.

The second theme concerns the knowledge firm in the knowledge economy. Developing a 'knowledge-rich' organisation demands a shift in focus from the hard, more tangible elements of work organisations (strategy, structure, systems) to the soft, intangible elements (skills, staff, leadership style, shared values), also discussed in chapter 2. Jackson argues that one of the principal and most costly errors made when considering organisation design is to focus on structure rather than on the 'soft processes and relationships'. As he comments, if an organisation is 'a collection of people working together to achieve a common purpose', then 'the role of organisation design is to facilitate the relationships between people so that purpose can be achieved'.[37] As with the first theme's requirement to develop a firm's core competencies to meet the challenges of globalisation and a highly competitive marketplace, the nurturing of a highly capable, multiskilled workforce also demands a holistic approach to organisation design so that the full spectrum of organisational skills, resources and capabilities are recognised, captured and exploited.

The third theme considers the emergence of 'network' organisations, which 'represent a shift away from *transactions* as the primary unit of analysis to *relationships* in the exchange [author's italics]'.[38] Inter- and intra-organisational interdependence and collaboration — and the synergies arising from the sharing of knowledge, human capital, resources and technology — form the building blocks of network organisations.

All three themes indicate that the boundaries within and between organisations must become more fluid and permeable if the focus is to shift successfully from a hard, rational content-oriented approach to a softer, process- and relationship-oriented approach. As we have seen in previous chapters (and also illustrated in the 'Opening case' and 'Change management in action' case), many companies have established team-based work groups and developed more open, flexible organisational forms by creating smaller business units, and promoting greater cross-functional interdependence (between marketing and supply, for example). In all cases, the aim was to push decision-making further down the line, to give more accountability and authority to each business unit or work team, and to overcome the traditional mindset that eschewed responsibility for problems that (historically) belonged elsewhere. The emergence of these new organisational forms recognises that survival in the new competitive landscape depends on nurturing an innovative, creative, thinking workforce that embraces the new working relationship of collaborative individualism at both an intra- and inter-organisational level. Kanter argues that to compete successfully in the post-entrepreneurial world, old-style 'corpocracies' must be dismantled in favour of leaner, flatter, more responsive forms.[39] Kanter identifies three key strategies for the post-entrepreneurial organisation: the development of synergies, alliances and newstreams (see figure 5.2). These are similar to the three core processes (to encourage initiatives; to link and leverage competence; and to manage rationalisation and revitalisation) noted earlier, which Ghoshal and Bartlett suggest are the building blocks of the new management model (see figure 5.2).[40]

- *Synergies*. Seeking synergies ties in with Samson's principles of *alignment, integration of effort* and *being up front* (see chapter 2). As with these three principles, developing synergies is about adding value by recognising, capturing, sharing and extending the full gamut of skills and resources that are available to the organisation. This approach recognises that only organisations that are flatter, less hierarchical, more interested in involving employees in their work, more open and more concerned about integration across functional departments can be responsive to a changing environment. As *USA Today* (see 'Opening case', page 146), for example, searched for more effective ways of organising its different interests, president Tom Curley realised that the business required greater integration, not separation, and set about implementing a 'network strategy' to enable cross-unit sharing of resources, skills and information.

- *Alliances.* The network organisation, emphasising the importance of developing partnerships and 'close working relationships' with other organisations, represents the core theme of Kanter's second post-entrepreneurial strategy. As noted in chapter 3, by developing strategic alliances, organisations are able to pool resources and achieve synergies that otherwise would have proved impossible or too costly to undertake independently. In an environment that demands a 'focused, fast, friendly and flexible' response, the post-entrepreneurial organisation is outsourcing non-core services and building close, cooperative relationships with suppliers.

- *Newstreams.* To provide the conditions and climate that encourage innovative thinking and allow the freedom to pursue new opportunities, the post-entrepreneurial organisation sets up official channels to ensure new ideas are not hijacked or ignored by its mainstream businesses. Newstreams, which work autonomously from the mainstream and pull together skills and resources from different areas of the organisation, allow organisations to run 'experiments in the margin', where new ventures can be trialled without risking existing mainstream projects.

Kanter pinpoints the following characteristics of the newly emerging form of organising: it is person- not position-centred, emphasising expertise and relationships rather than power and status (also illustrated in chapter 7); it is concerned with developing best practice through diversity, creativity and innovation, not specialisation and repetition; it is results- rather than rules-oriented, encouraging its people to experiment and take risks; it recognises and rewards individual and group endeavours, not rank or position; it operates and finds opportunities through its range of intra- and inter-organisational networks, rather than relying on formal structures and channels of communication (and, in this way, seeks to expand rather than restrict the flow of information); and it is renewal- rather than stability-oriented, continually seeking to leverage new opportunities and empower its workforce, rather than pursuing ownership and control. These characteristics are typical of trends in many firms today as they search for the most effective and innovative form of organising that is appropriate and relevant to their operations and market conditions.

Consider, for example, the flexible work arrangements at Gauld Tulloch Bove, a Sydney suburban accounting firm. By offering the option to work from home, the company has been able to attract and retain high-calibre, self-motivated staff. The company trialled different 'remote' work arrangements until it settled on a format that suited its staff and the type of work they had to perform. One early problem was the logistics of carrying cumbersome files between home and office. These sorts of initial hurdles were largely overcome through networked computers and paperless filing in computer storage, which also ensured reliable records and paper trails. It is now a requirement for all partners to work from home one day a week because they 'get so much more done'; and home-based workers are expected to spend half a day each week at the office as well as attend firm-wide functions so that they feel, and are seen as, part of the team. So far, the partners are very happy with the gains from the new work arrangements, citing increased productivity, excellent staff retention rates, job satisfaction, high morale and happy customers.[41]

These new themes for leading and managing organisations of the future presuppose a radically different organisational form. The shift to 'horizontal integration around processes allows the organisation to dismantle the hierarchy as well as functional compartmentalisation'[42], thus creating a much more flexible, fluid and inclusive form of organising where the emphasis is on coordination and collaboration across boundaries and where 'alterations in structural form [are] continuously shaped alongside movements in organisation process and boundaries'.[43] The importance of aligning and linking these three design variables — structure, process and boundaries — is considered in the following section.

Changing structures, processes and boundaries

As noted in the preceding discussion, organisational design traditionally was concerned predominantly with structure and form. The changing boundaries of the globalising firm, the growth of the knowledge firm in the knowledge economy, and the emergence of 'network' organisations as companies seek a more flexible and responsive form have instead emphasised (if not forced) the need to recognise and understand the interconnectivity of structure, systems, people and processes, and to capture the dynamics of these relationships in organisational design. The importance of adopting a holistic approach to organisational change is borne out by the findings of the INNFORM Project on innovative forms of organising for the 21st century. The purpose of the study was to 'map the contours of contemporary organisational innovation, to examine the management practices involved in the processes of innovation, and to test for the performance benefits of these changes'.[44] The study investigated organisational innovation in different geographic locations (Europe, Japan and the United States) and at two different time points (1992 and 1996).[45] This study provided comparative data on the nature and degree of change across the three organisational design dimensions of structure, process and boundaries. Key indicators of change within each dimension were:

- delayering, decentralising and project-based organising (indicating change in structure)
- investment in information technology, horizontal and vertical communications, and new human resource practices (indicating change in process)
- downscoping, outsourcing and strategic alliances (indicating change in boundaries).

We now consider the findings of the European study (based on responses collected from 450 large- and medium-sized Western European companies) in terms of these nine indicators of organisational change (within the three broad areas of structure, process and boundaries), and discuss their implications.

Changing structures

This section examines the three structural indicators of change: delayering, decentralising and project-based organising.

Delayering

Nearly 30 per cent of the companies indicated that they had decreased the number of layers between the chief executive officer and the lowest manager, so that between 1992 and 1996 'profit responsibility decreased from 3.5 to 3.2'.[46] Delayering was particularly prevalent among companies operating in more volatile, highly competitive environments. An anomalous finding was the 20 per cent of companies that reported an increase in management layers; this outcome tended, however, to be the result of high sales' growth rates, leading to a concomitant increase in organisational size and managerial complexity.[47]

Decentralisation

In tandem with delayering, decision-making authority was being devolved down through organisations. While 36 per cent of companies reported high levels of decentralisation of operating decisions in 1992, this level had risen to 61 per cent in 1996. Decentralisation of strategic decision-making was also occurring, although among fewer companies, with an increase from 12 per cent in 1992 to 18 per cent in 1996.

Project-based organising

Between 1992 and 1996, project-based organising rose dramatically — up 175 per cent. While functions were still deemed to be very important, the establishment of cross-functional teams, promoting collaboration and coordination across traditional business unit boundaries, was seen to be essential for creating a more competitive, more responsive and flexible organisation, attuned to the needs of the marketplace.

Changing processes

Underpinning the changes to structure, significant changes to internal processes were reported.[48] These changes included horizontal and vertical communications, investment in information technology, and new human resources practices.

Horizontal and vertical communication

While horizontal communications doubled between 1992 and 1996, vertical communications trebled. The dramatic increase in vertical communications indicates that while companies are keen to encourage the transfer and diffusion of knowledge across the organisation, delayering and decentralisation (two key structural change indicators) do not symbolise the demise of hierarchy. Paradoxically, the devolution of authority and responsibility has reinforced the importance of hierarchical lines of authority and accountability. Thompson and McHugh state that 'decentralisation of the form is accompanied by centralisation of the substance of power'. While large, unwieldy bureaucracies are flattening organisational structures and devolving authority and decision-making responsibility to smaller, semi-autonomous business units, Thompson and McHugh note that 'corporate headquarters now have much more sophisticated means of monitoring and regulating the management of subsidiaries'.[49] Dawson,

Drinkwater, Gunson and Atkins also refer to concerns about the application of electronic media for 'remote monitoring' of organisational members. The counterpoint they pose is that the Big Brother perspective of technology's role disregards the real benefits that arise from the ability to access information at incredible speed and disseminate it equally quickly to a very large audience working in different time zones and geographic locations.[50] The INNFORM study suggests that 'companies adopt a dual approach, simultaneously investing in hierarchies and networks, creating a new balance between centralisation and decentralisation'.[51] Investment in sophisticated information technology systems has been a critical factor in enabling the complementary development of both vertical and horizontal communication networks.

Investment in information technology

Between 1992 and 1996, investment in information technology increased fourfold, with 82 per cent of companies reporting increased investment in information technology infrastructures that would help them improve and extend vertical and horizontal integration. It became increasingly clear, however, that the gains sought from investment in information technology hardware would not be fully realised unless undertaken in conjunction with appropriate 'software' investment in new human resource practices. Dawson et al.'s examination of the implications of electronic communication technologies for the organisation and control of work appears to support the view that information technology investment should be undertaken only with a full appreciation of the effect on the social and political fabric of organisational life. They express concern over the 'tendency for processes of change to be technology driven' with scant regard for the impact on social and relational processes. When social innovation (new attitudes and forms of behaviour) takes place alongside technological innovation, however, new forms of organising are more likely to succeed, particularly because people now have the skills to understand the role of technology both as an empowering tool and a constraining mechanism.[52]

New human resources practices

Sixty-five per cent of companies in the European study reported increased use of new human resources practices. These included team-building, cross-company training events and workshops, and mission-building activities. These new initiatives were critical levers for enhancing the exchange of ideas and knowledge across boundaries, and encouraging the establishment of cross-functional teams. For these companies, the new human resources initiatives were the means to provide 'the skills and the glue to make the flatter and more horizontal organisational structures work'.[53] As emphasised in chapter 6, large-scale change must involve the simultaneous and continual management of the *behavioural* agenda as well the *intellectual* and *management* agendas. (Chapter 6 discusses the importance of integrating human resources management practices with corporate and business strategies.)

Changing external boundaries

In chapter 2, we argued that competitive advantage depends on an organisation's ability to focus on its distinctive skills and capabilities, and to develop and exploit these within a framework and culture of continuous improvement and innovation. We found that companies committed to developing and strengthening core competencies are focusing on single industries rather than diversification; seeking to outsource peripheral, non-core activities; and developing collaborative partnerships and alliances to share complementary skills and knowledge. These themes form the three components of external boundary changes outlined below.

Outsourcing

Sixty-three per cent of companies reported increases in outsourcing over the period 1992–1996. Outsourcing was regarded as a means of increasing flexibility and was more widely adopted by larger companies and in knowledge-intensive sectors.

Developing alliances

In tandem with outsourcing, 65 per cent of companies reported forming long-term strategic alliances as they sought to share complementary skills and expertise or secure skills, knowledge and resources no longer available in-house. To illustrate, Vivid Group, a Perth-based Web design and technology company, uses alliances expressly because they are 'very good for sharing knowledge'. (See more detailed examples given below of more current external boundary changes occurring in Australia.)

Downscoping

While the net shift from diversification was small — only 11 per cent of companies reported reductions in diversification between 1992 and 1996 — the most significant trend was the move from unrelated to related diversification. Closer to home, Woolworths and Australia Post, for example, indicate that the trend is to seek related growth through joint venture partnerships offshore that depend on the unique mix of skills, technical expertise and intellectual capital they are able to bring to the venture. (see 'Perspectives' case, 'Globalisation and growth through joint venture partnerships', page 166).

Examples of changing external boundaries

BRW's 2004 survey of Australia's *Fast 100* companies (the fastest growing small and medium-sized enterprises) indicated that 53 of these had established some form of partnership or alliance in order to gain or share skills and knowledge. Vivid Group, a Perth-based Web design and technology company (ranked 85 in the *Fast 100* listing) uses alliances because they are 'very good for sharing knowledge'. The company also outsources its Web hosting because this is not its area of expertise. Vivid Group's key alliances are with customers. Using one of its own products called MyCRC, a customer-relationship management tool for cooperative research centres, the company manages a CRC's relationship with industry. Similarly, Sydney-based Detech Building Services (ranked 88) draws on the building trades subcontracting system to build its alliances as it has neither the scope nor expertise to provide the various specialist services needed for property repairs and maintenance.[54]

Woolworths and Australia Post (see 'Perspectives' case, 'Globalisation and growth through joint venture partnerships', page 166) provide further illustration of changing external boundaries as they seek to extend their organisation's activities and look for growth opportunities outside Australia. These first steps into offshore partnerships by two major Australian organisations indicate that globalisation is not only essential to an organisation's future prosperity, it is also shaping a new and very different competitive landscape in which knowledge work and knowledge workers are the key to economic growth.[55]

Managing complementary changes

Of the 450 companies in the INNFORM study, 20 per cent were changing structural elements, 28 per cent were changing process elements and 50 per cent were redefining boundary elements. Within these groupings, 11.2 per cent were implementing structural and boundary changes, 10.3 per cent were implementing structural and process changes, and 14.3 per cent were implementing boundary and process changes. Only a very small number of companies (4.5 per cent) were implementing changes simultaneously within the three broad areas of structure, process and boundary (figure 5.3), yet performance improvement was greatest among these organisations that were innovating across the spectrum of change elements. For companies enjoying a 'performance premium of more than 60 per cent'[56], implementing organisation-wide programs of complementary changes clearly provided greater synergies. In contrast, undertaking a few isolated initiatives generally led to a worse performance.

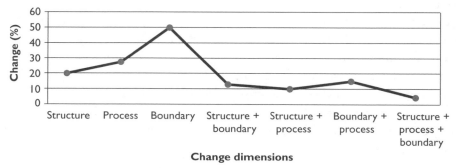

FIGURE 5.3: Managing complementary change: the percentage of change at 450 European companies, by area of change

In summary, the INNFORM findings indicate that the elements of structure, process and boundaries, while seemingly very different and unrelated on the surface, complement and nourish each other. If organisations implement change in one area without regard to the impact on changes in other elements, then negative performance will result. Delayering and decentralising without simultaneously committing resources to increasing horizontal communications and removing cross-structural boundaries, for example, would impact adversely on the transfer and diffusion of knowledge, ideas and skills through the organisation (as is highlighted in case 1, William Angliss Institute of TAFE, page 361). The unimpeded sharing of knowledge is fundamental to fostering organisational learning, which in turn depends on how well an organisation aligns and links the three design variables (see the discussion on organisational learning in chapter 3). This study confirms that an organisation's ability to recognise and exploit the interconnectivity of, and interaction among, all aspects of the three design variables — structure, process and boundaries — provides the key to long-term survival and success.

Managing the dualities of organisation design: integrating traditional and new forms of organising

We have talked about the seemingly contradictory dilemmas of change in earlier chapters and argued the importance of trying to understand the relationships and synergies between these rather than taking them at face value, or concluding we must make an 'either/or' choice. Stace and Dunphy, for example, refer to the five dilemmas of change (discussed in chapters 2, 3, 4 and 7) that managers must recognise and attend to when managing the change process. These include: adaptive or rational strategy development; cultural change or structural change; continuous improvement or radical transformation; empowerment or leadership and command; and economic or social goals.[57] Stace and Dunphy underline the need for a balanced perspective that encompasses both hard and soft issues (relationships and processes, as well as structures and systems), and recognises that seemingly opposing forces can complement and sustain each other.[58]

Reporting on the findings of the INNFORM Study, Sanchez-Runde and Pettigrew similarly refer to the series of dualities organisations must learn to manage as they seek higher performance through greater innovation and flexibility.[59] The high performing, innovating organisations identified in the INNFORM study are seen to be adopting 'ambidextrous' forms of organising as they simultaneously develop networks alongside hierarchies; support and encourage horizontal integration while promoting upwards performance accountability; and maintain central control of strategy-making as they decentralise operations.

The change experiences of *USA Today* (see 'Opening case', page 146) and Unilever ('Change management in action' case, page 153), as they explore and experiment with new forms of organising, appear to support the findings of a growing body of studies that indicate that while innovative forms of organising are emerging within organisations, neither hierarchies nor many other traditional organisational practices are being summarily removed. What appears to be happening is more a case of the 'new *supplementing* the old, rather than the new *supplanting* the old [author's italics]'.[60] Quinn, Anderson and Finkelstein, for example, argue that there is no universal form of 'network organisation'; rather, what are evolving are 'forms of organising, not forms of organisation', which are 'typically embedded in larger organisational structures that are still at least partly bureaucratic'.[61] Palmer and Dunford similarly note that the 'co-existence and integration of old and new practices is gaining greater attention in the field of organisational design'.[62] Their survey of new organisational practices (identified as delayering, empowerment, networks/alliances, outsourcing, disaggregation, flexible workgroups, short-term staffing, reduction of internal and external boundaries) in over 2000 firms operating in Australia found, for example, that the greater use of new organisational practices did not spell the demise of traditional practices such as formalisation or centralisation. In fact, they found that *higher* levels of formalisation were associated with the introduction of new organisational practices; moreover, the coordinating and direction-setting role of a corporate centre emerged as equally important and relevant for firms operating in a complex and uncertain environment. Palmer and Dunford's findings support Raynor and Bower's contention that 'responding effectively in uncertain markets often requires more — not less — direction from the center'. Based on their research into modern diversified companies, Raynor and Bower furthermore argue that the role of corporate headquarters 'in creating a strategically flexible organization has cascading effects on how executives manage other aspects of the company: whether divisions are clustered into groups, for example, and how compensation is structured'.[63]

Volberda also contends that specialised, programmatic routines are unsustainable when competing in complex and uncertain environments. What are needed in these conditions are flexible, dynamic capabilities.[64] In addition, to ensure an organisation's 'controllability' and 'responsiveness' 'management must cope with a constructive tension between developing capabilities and preserving organizational conditions [such as structure, culture, technology], which can be considered the building blocks of flexibility'.[65]

The message here for organisation leaders is to give careful consideration to the possible synergies and connections between their existing organisational practices and the proposed new arrangements before they discard all that has gone before. They need to examine the environmental conditions within which they are operating and use this as a starting point to calculate which of the traditional practices remain relevant and how best to integrate the old with the new.[66] Raynor and Bower, for example, acknowledge that conventional group or divisional structures are not 'wired' appropriately for operating in today's business environment as these forms of organising inhibit responsiveness, and cross-boundary collaboration and information-sharing. In their view 'a more flexible structure, coupled with tight financial controls, best serves a dynamic corporate strategy'.[67] By serving as the basic building blocks of organisational design, elements of traditional organisational structures, systems and processes can be used constructively to complement and enrich new work arrangements, thus ensuring both 'controllability' and 'responsiveness' (see, for example, 'Opening case', page 146). Senior managers therefore need to be sensitive to the dualities of *exploration* (trialling new routines and work arrangements) and *exploitation* (protecting and developing structures, capabilities, controls and rewards that are central to the success of existing operations); and develop greater understanding of how traditional and new organisational practices can be organised to strengthen and support each other.[68]

New forms of organising and the implications for people management

As we have argued, increasing an organisation's flexibility is not simply confined to changing structure. It is based on an integrated, systemic design approach that encompasses changes to hardware (structure and reward systems) and software (leadership, work practices, organisational culture and values). If, for example, we consider the nature and degree of change that has taken place at William Angliss Institute of TAFE (see end-of-book case 1, page 361) against the organisational design dimensions of structure, process and boundaries, the Institute's experience suggests that it is an organisation's ability to recognise and exploit the interconnectivity between all aspects of the three organising variables that provides the key to long-term survival and success. Underpinning this symbiotic relationship, *process* considerations, in particular communications and *people* processes, emerge as integral to effective structural and boundary changes because mutually reinforcing, complementary changes across the three design dimensions depend ultimately on the contribution and commitment organisation members are prepared to make. This outcome is further corroborated by INNFORM case study findings. Sanchez-Runde, Massini and Quintanilla make the point that

> At the end of the day, since it is people who get things done in the organization, the question of how individuals themselves are managed, through a given set of HRM practices, is of the utmost importance.[69]

At William Angliss Institute of TAFE, for example, the challenges of globalisation and an increasingly competitive marketplace have fuelled the need to nurture a highly capable, and empowered workforce. As it has explored new forms of organising around structures, processes and boundaries, processes, in particular communications and human resources practices, have emerged as the pivotal intermediary that will ensure the full spectrum of organisational skills, resources and capabilities are recognised and exploited.

If changes to an organisation's strategy and structure 'should be paralleled by changes in the way it manages its personnel'[70], successful process changes ultimately depend on sound leadership to give shape and meaning to the complementary changes required. Sanchez-Runde, Massini and Quintanilla are emphatic in this regard claiming that 'Leadership has so direct an influence on work dynamics that one can hardly separate innovative work organization from leadership patterns'.[71] As well as the critical part the 'framing' activities of senior management play in providing a 'coherent strategic direction', the INNFORM findings also indicate that leaders are 'highly dependent on actors within and outside the organization to translate these ideas and develop more detailed strategizing and organizing practices'.[72]

The William Angliss experience highlights the key role a leader plays in articulating and promoting the vision, values and beliefs that *frame* organisational behaviour and action. Its experience also suggests that if these attributes are to lead to meaningful, consistent system-wide behavioural change, the support of stakeholders at all levels of the organisation are required to provide the form and substance for the new work processes. Thus leadership can be described as a 'social process' that is 'enacted in an ongoing way through continuous processes of communication, inspiration and dialogue throughout the organization' and serves as the 'integrative essence through which culture and structure are realized, reinforced and changed'.[73] They play a key role in establishing an organisation's cultural, structural and processual framework, which will determine whether it can create a dynamic, 'strategically flexible' form. We noted earlier in the chapter that if an organisation is 'a collection of people working together to achieve a common purpose', then 'the role of organisation design is to facilitate the relationships between people so that purpose can be achieved'.[74] As depicted in figure 5.4 (page 166), processes serve as a conduit, linking and permeating the different elements of structures and boundaries. The challenge for organisation leaders is to recognise the complex overarching, 'multi-disciplinary' role that processes play in the structures-processes-boundaries relationship, and ensure that changes to structures and boundaries complement, and are formed alongside, changes to organisation processes. In addition, as highlighted in the William Angliss Institute of TAFE case, senior management plays a critical role in not only framing the new ways of organising and behaving, but also engaging other actors as supporters who are willing to translate these into meaningful action.

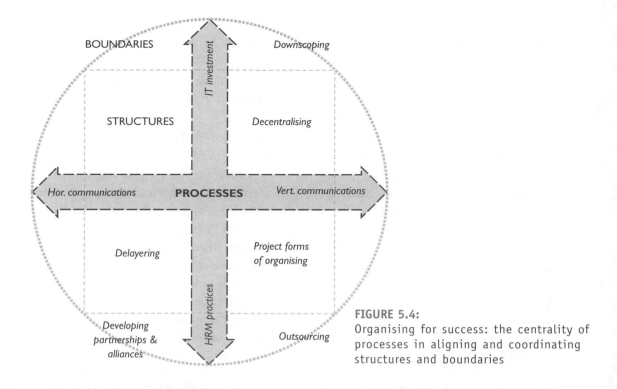

FIGURE 5.4:
Organising for success: the centrality of processes in aligning and coordinating structures and boundaries

---

Globalisation and growth through joint venture partnerships

Example 1: Planning for growth at Woolworths
With its accumulated expertise in IT and supply chain management, Woolworths, Australia's largest supermarket operator, is keen to expand its operations into developing Asian markets, in particular India and China, whose increasingly affluent middle classes make investing in these two countries very attractive. While Woolworths is always examining ways of growing the business and is looking for offshore partners, it does not want to rush into any joint venture arrangement without careful consideration of all the issues, which could take several years. Senior management stated that any such venture will be small and experimental in nature, most likely focusing on a niche market where they could effectively lever their intellectual property.

Example 2: Australia Post moves into China
Australia Post has formed a joint venture company with China Post to offer logistics in China. 'Sai Cheng', the joint venture company, is constructing a 20 000 square metre transport and logistics hub near Shanghai to deliver manufactured goods around the world. The company plans to construct another five logistics hubs across China.

Sai Cheng's operations are modelled on Australia Post and Qantas's Australian Air Express joint venture, which combines transport services with strategically positioned warehouses.

Graeme John, Australia Post Chief Executive Officer, believes Sai Cheng could become a $1 billion global business within seven to ten years. Such success would then lead to the joint venture business model being replicated in other countries to build a global logistics business.

Sources: Wendy Frew 2004, 'Overseas ventures high on Woolies' shopping list', *The Age*, Saturday, 27 November 2004, Business, p. 3; Stephen Dabkowski 2004, 'AustPost puts stamp on China,' *The Age*, Wednesday, September 15 2004, Business p. 1.

The virtual organisation: fact, fad, or fantasy?

The preceding discussion suggests that despite calls to flatten hierarchies, downsize, outsource, decentralise, and form alliances and networks, we are yet to witness the demise of traditional forms of organising. While organisations are exploring and experimenting with new work arrangements, these appear to be supplementing rather than supplanting existing work practices. While advances in information and communications technologies have played a significant part in challenging and reshaping the way in which people in organisations work and interact, they have also, somewhat ironically, facilitated the development of more flexible, adaptive work practices that complement and support traditional, yet ever relevant, work practices. The experiences of *USA Today* and Unilever attest to this (see 'Opening case', page 146 and 'Change management in action' case, page 153).

Carly Fiorina, former Chief Executive Officer of Hewlett-Packard, suggested that by 2005 the digital revolution had begun in earnest. Think of photography, once a 'physical, chemical, analogue process', now 'digital ... mobile, virtual and personal'. Fiorina argues that the same pattern of change is underway in every industry. She identifies three key issues that technology companies in particular will need to grapple with. First, is the need for simplicity. For consumers to recognise the benefits of going digital, the technology needs to be understandable and easy to use. Secondly, value will accrue increasingly through horizontal rather than vertical connections. This consideration is important because the digital age also brings with it a 'democratisation of information' as the traditional barriers of time, distance and wealth are largely removed. Thirdly, there will be little room for compromise. As technology becomes central to people's lives and businesses, businesses and consumers will expect technology to be affordable, reliable, secure, adaptable, innovative, compatible and easy to use.[75]

This suggests that the revolution in communications and digital technologies and the rise of the Internet as a means of doing business must inexorably drive changes to organisational structures, processes and boundaries.[76] But is the virtual organisation, like the once much-touted paperless office, reality or illusion? Chesbrough and Teece acknowledge that 'many large and cumbersome organizations have been outperformed by smaller "networked" competitors'. But for every success story, there are as many failures. In their view, the benefits of the virtual organisation have been oversold; they suggest that those businesses that pursue outsourcing and strategic alliances with little regard for the consequences on accumulated in-house knowledge and capabilities, may be jeopardising their own futures.[77] Adler similarly notes that the zeal with which many organisations have embarked on 'bureaucracy busting' through delayering and outsourcing has in many cases come back to haunt them as they discover too late that they have removed repositories of 'precious skills and experience' that were also very effective in 'diffusing lessons learned in one part of the organization to others'. Adler points out that some degree of hierarchy, formalisation and repository of knowledge and expertise are essential in large and complex organisations not only 'to avoid chaos and ensure that employees are not continually reinventing the wheel', but also for 'efficiency, conformance quality and timeliness'.[78] We highlighted this notion in the section on 'Managing the dualities of organisation design'. As we have attempted to highlight through this chapter, rather than following the latest fad, organisations need to examine the types of innovation they are pursuing and choose the most appropriate organisational configuration that will support and enhance their prospects for success. This may or may not include delayering, downsizing, outsourcing, or some aspects of virtual forms of organising. Increasingly, however, the route to success in a global economy appears to be through growth, rather than downsizing and cost reductions, and in developing, exploiting and protecting the organisation's intellectual capital.[79] (See examples in 'Perspectives: Globalisation and growth through joint venture partnerships', page 166.)

The preceding discussion suggests that there are degrees of virtuality. At Gauld Tulloch Bove, for example, staff have the option of working from home, but are expected to spend at least half a day each week in the office. Dawson et al. suggest that 'considerable interpretative flexibility' exists over 'what constitutes a virtual workplace as different individuals and groups shape the design, uptake and local configuration of this emerging technology'. They suggest, for example, that the form of organising at the Australian Taxation Office, which allows a proportion of staff a greater degree of time and space flexibility, cannot be compared to the 'virtual' arrangements of a small publishing firm whose 'members work from home and meet no more than once a month'.[80]

As with most innovative forms of organising, organising virtually does not eliminate the use of traditional work practices; however, the principal means of doing business is likely to rely to a large extent on sophisticated communications technology and over time the new forms of organising become more and more evident.[81] Nike serves as an example of a company that harnessed advanced communication and logistic technology 'to create a global network of organisations' comprising manufacturers, suppliers, retailers etc., to help them produce and distribute athletic shoes worldwide. These activities are taking place alongside Nike's other business operations where traditional work practices are more appropriate. However, centralised strategic planning, performance measurement and quality control systems increasingly use sophisticated software to monitor, coordinate, control and disseminate information. For firms operating in complex, dynamic and highly competitive markets, the need for planning (for example, to ensure conformance quality, efficiency and timeliness) needs to be weighed against the need for creativity and flexibility so that the optimum balance between old and new forms of organising is achieved.

Despite the heralding of a new era of business with the arrival of the Internet, there is little information on organisations that are benefiting from internetworking. Brews and Tucci use the term Internet-Generation Companies (IGCs) to refer to organisations that have successfully transformed into Internet-based infrastructures. In these companies, the 'Internet-based networks *are* the organizational structure, linking customers, suppliers, business partners, managers, and employees'. The basis of competitiveness of these IGCs is embedded in high-value-added services or solutions.[82] Overall, however, despite the potential for gains in internetworking, progress among firms is slow. The main reasons for this are cited as 'lack of resources and skills, customer resistance, an inability to develop standard processes for Internet enabling, and the scope and scale of the transformation'.[83] One exception is Cisco Systems, which

Brews and Tucci describe as 'the world's most deeply internet-worked company' which has achieved 'unparalleled efficiency and speed' through internetworking. As they explain, over 90 per cent of Cisco's orders are submitted online; these are then transmitted simultaneously to suppliers and partners; and Cisco customers can track the progress of their order online. In addition, more than 80 per cent of after-sales service inquiries are dealt with electronically using FAQ pages that lead users to the advice or instructions they are requesting. Brews and Tucci argue that 'internetworking is transforming the strategy, structure, and operations of Old Economy businesses. A superior organizational form that more efficiently delivers more complex and sophisticated products/services is emerging ... offering innovative and exciting products/services inconceivable before the appearance of the Internet, at levels of efficiency and precision unimaginable only a few years ago'.[84]

The Internet is also revolutionising the way teaching and learning is undertaken across the primary, secondary and higher education sectors. Consider, for example the application of e-learning in remote Aboriginal communities. The Australian Flexible Learning Framework (AFLF), a consortium of state and federal governments, is funding a trial e-learning program in remote Aboriginal communities to the tune of $800,000. According to AFLF chairman, Jim Davidson, 'The philosophy is if you have communities in remote areas, you can provide training with (their own) songs and images. You present materials in a different way, because it's an oral culture. They have created different (online) characters that convey different messages. It's a good and effective way of getting skills into the communities. It sure beats building lots of TAFE colleges across the place'. Davidson is referring here to MARVIN (Messaging Architecture for the Retrieval of Versatile Information and News), designed by J. Easterby-Wood, manager of interactive communities in the Northern Territory Department of Health and Community Services. With this software, animated characters represent real-life community role models. Koori teenagers armed with digital cameras were also involved in developing a customised life-saving substance abuse course drawing on 'their own mob's environment and language'. For Easterby-Wood, e-learning is not just about enriching lives but also saving them because the program was able to provide resources to support the Koori-developed course on substance abuse. 'We had two or three hundred people turn up instead of two or three. It's about oral-based training in their own language.' While distance was one major issue in reaching communities spread over 300,000 square kilometres, the number of languages to be found across these communities was another. To overcome this, the software was customised with the help of local Koori trainers in each community. Tiga Bayles, president of the Aboriginal and Islander Community School is adamant that by delivering training and education programs through e-learning to remote communities, the impact on success and retention rates will be significant as people no longer have to leave or travel great distances to benefit from these programs.[85]

Within the higher education sector the Internet revolution is seen as a means of 'providing alternative learning environments, knowledge repositories, communications facilities and pedagogic modes' to meet the needs of students who are unable for whatever reasons to attend a traditional on-campus course.[86] While 'faculty' in the traditional sense will be of little relevance to the newly emerging online university, the new online mode of learning and course delivery does not spell the end of bricks and mortar higher education institutions. 'There will always be a place for Oxbridge and the Ivy League. But they do not represent the future shape of global higher education.'[87]

For the moment, as the findings from the INNFORM study suggest, accessing and delivering education on line is not replacing existing modes of delivery, but is 'embedded within more conventional organisational structures'.[88] Within this conventional configuration, however, the implications of these new modes of working are profound because they demand new skills and competencies, and new ways of communicating with and relating to individuals and groups at both the intra- and inter-organisational level. Alderman refers to the development of online distance education as a revolution in teaching and learning that requires a 'completely new pedagogy'. The significant impact that virtual forms of working can have on the way in which organisational members communicate with and relate to each other, as well as to the organisation and outsiders, underscores the key points discussed in this chapter.

At the process level in particular, underpinning investment in information technology with supportive human resource practices is vital; it is important to teach people not only *how* to use the new technologies (the technical component), but also *what* existing routines and behaviours (the social component) must change if they wish to participate meaningfully in the new ways of working. As inferred earlier, progress is likely to be slow in this area unless significant investment is made to provide targeted resources, and appropriate skills training and education for both employees and customers to overcome resistance.

At the structural level, the establishment of virtual project-based teams may result in a shift from 'hierarchical structures of reporting and command relationships to self-regulatory teamwork arrangements'.[89] This shift leads to a flatter structure and the devolution of decision-making to team members.

At the boundary level, these virtual teams span functional boundaries and, in some cases, represent relationships with remote collaborators such as outside contractors and suppliers (as in the examples provided in the section 'Changing external boundaries', page 160). Stace and Dunphy suggest that managing change will increasingly 'centre around stabilising networks of subcontractors and joint ventures and ensuring that they are moving in a coordinated way to establish advanced work forms'.[90] Consequently, a key issue for remote collaboration and effective outsourcing is establishing sound interpersonal relationships with external partners or team members. A study of the Australian Commonwealth Scientific and Industrial Research Organisation (CSIRO), for example, found that there was 'a higher level of misunderstanding and communication problems' with remote collaborators if the partners never met face to face.[91] The types of problem that can be encountered in boundary spanning with remote collaborators underline the importance of linking the *what* with the *how* at the process level, and again recognising the interconnectivity of different aspects of the three design variables of structure, process and boundaries. Useem and Harder point to the need for effective 'lateral leadership' to manage these sorts of relationships whose expertise includes '*deal making*', creating a 'web of relations between outside vendors and inside operations', acting as negotiator and facilitator between the two parties; and '*partnership governing*', which involves building commitment and understanding, communicating regularly, and thereby forging an enduring, mutually satisfying relationship with joint venture or outsourcing partners.[92]

Organising today for tomorrow

Discussion so far confirms the introductory observation that we are experiencing a major paradigm shift in the nature and composition of organisations. While hierarchy may be alive and well, the philosophy underpinning new forms of organising sees hierarchy as one piece of a complex amalgam of interrelated design components that all have an equally important part to play. As organisations experiment with new forms of organising, the emphasis is no longer on structure and control, functional hierarchy, size and scale, costs and efficiencies, decision-making and planning, but on relationships and processes, collaboration and inclusion, flexibility and boundary spanning, creativity and change.

In 'Designing organisations' (page 149), we briefly referred to the three core processes (*entrepreneurial*: encouraging initiatives; *integrative*: linking and leveraging competence; and *renewal*: managing rationalisation and revitalisation) that Ghoshal and Bartlett believe underpin the new management paradigm. We now consider these processes and compare them with the new forms of organising already discussed, particularly the findings of the INNFORM study. (The links between these different perspectives also are illustrated in figure 5.2, page 155.)

The *entrepreneurial process* 'drives the opportunity-seeking, externally focused ability of the organisation to create new business'. This entrepreneurial mindset is not simply the prerogative of senior management, but is imbued in the firm's vision, beliefs and values, and guides all behaviour and action. Pivotal to the entrepreneurial model are three management roles. First, the *entrepreneurs* are the ideas people who work at the 'frontline', able to anticipate market trends. Their primary task is to 'create and pursue new growth opportunities'. Second, *coaches* at middle and senior management level play a key role in reviewing, developing and supporting entrepreneurial initiatives. Third, *leaders* at the highest levels of the organisation articulate the vision and set the direction that 'defines the boundary within which the entrepreneurial initiatives must be contained'. Key characteristics of the entrepreneurial process include: small, 'functionally incomplete', performance units that pool resources; a highly structured, rigorously implemented financial control system; a multistage resource allocation system to fund new business proposals; and a clearly articulated and well defined strategic mission.[93]

The three management roles that Ghoshal and Bartlett identify within the entrepreneurial process support the INNFORM study finding that hierarchy is alive and well within organisations, albeit hierarchy with a difference. The traditional organisational structure, with its rigid, hierarchical, top–down approach is no longer seen to be workable. Organisations are realising that internal flexibility and coordination are essential if they are to respond effectively to the demands of stakeholders and the dynamic, highly competitive, market-driven, customer-oriented environment. The traditional mechanistic, hierarchical structure that vested power and authority in senior management and enjoyed abundant one-way, vertical communication, but little information sharing across the organisation, is being refashioned into a much more dynamic, fluid form that simultaneously allows for differentiation and integration of different business segments. The key characteristics of the entrepreneurial process (as described above) and the dramatic rise (as reported in the INNFORM study) of project-based organising, delayering and decentralising confirm that, while the hierarchy of responsibility may still exist, the uni-directional, top–down chain of command has been replaced by influences from a variety of sources and levels in which *projects* rather than *positions* are central.[94] These characteristics typify the network organisation type. As the elements within and across each of the organisation design variables identified in the INNFORM study impinge on each other, so the three managerial roles within the entrepreneurial process are mutually reinforcing, combining to define and demonstrate a more collaborative, flexible and inclusive approach to doing business at all levels of the organisation. Support for, and commitment to, new initiatives communicated through the entrepreneurial process in turn depend on a synergistic connection with the integration process and renewal process.

The *integration process* enables management 'to link and leverage its dispersed resources and competencies to build a successful company'.[95] The integration process works in conjunction with the entrepreneurial process to identify and align the different resources and competencies required to pursue new opportunities. The success of an integrative approach depends on the willingness of organisation members to share knowledge and resources, and collaborate with each other. If the key function of the integration process is to link and align different parts of the organisation, then shared values — imparted through an appealing and meaningful vision articulated by senior leaders and cascaded down through the organisation — serve as a primary motivating mechanism. Within this context, the leaders at all levels of the organisation have a defining part to play, because it is their responsibility to locate and bring together (from across the organisation) the wide range of skills, knowledge, expertise, and technical and physical resources required to pursue new opportunities and projects.

The requirements of the integration process, to identify, strengthen and link internal resources, skills and competencies, are analogous to the internal process changes reported in the INNFORM study. As that study showed, changes to structure are underpinned by far-reaching changes to horizontal and vertical communications, investment in information technology, and new human resources practices. The central theme in both cases is on developing and leveraging a company's distinctive skills and capabilities, which demands a radical shift in focus from organising around structure to organising around processes and social and relational dimensions.

The *renewal process* is concerned with managing the dualities of rationalisation and revitalisation (the core components of the renewal process). Unfortunately, the risk is that organisations become victims of their own handiwork. They become absorbed by past successes, and inertia and complacency set in. Managers become hesitant to take risks and demonstrate an almost obsessive zeal in applying the outdated and unworkable routines and rituals that brought success in the past. As a result, innovation and creative thinking are stifled. An organisation that succeeds in balancing the seemingly conflicting needs of rationalisation and revitalisation is alert to shifts in its environment, ever ready to challenge the status quo, and actively seeks opportunities to grow new markets. At the same time, it recognises the need to strive for performance improvement in existing operations, often achieved through reducing costs, improving quality and service, reconfiguring systems and processes, and reducing development time.

As with Kanter's newstreams, the renewal process fuels the capacity for continuous improvement and learning, which are integral to building the knowledge-rich firm in the knowledge economy. The renewal process, with its focus on rationalisation and revitalisation, also is woven through the different themes of changing structures, process and boundaries (see figure 5.2), again underlining the symbiotic relationship between the tangible and intangible elements of work organisations, and the dangers of favouring structure and systems over the softer process and relational dimensions when designing organisations.

In chapter 2, we considered the set of fourteen principles (alignment, distributed leadership, integration of effort, being out front, being up front, resourcing the medium term, time based, bias for action, learning focus, enabling disciplines, measurement/ reporting and publication, customer value, capabilities creation, and micro to macro) that Samson identifies as guiding behaviour in the world's 'excellent' companies. The key themes of the new forms of organising (whether viewed as the three dimensions of changing structures, processes and boundaries, or as synergies, alliances and newstreams, or as entrepreneurial, integrative and renewal processes) are clearly diffused through these fourteen guiding management principles.

As with Samson's management principles, the key findings on new forms of organising underpin the need to move away from the traditional analytical approach to managing and organising, and to give more consideration to the process and relational dimensions. Earlier discussion on the need for sensitivity to organisational dualities, such as the need for controllability and responsiveness also underlines the importance of adhering to principles 10 and 11 (enabling disciplines, and measurement/reporting and publication). As these suggest, when experimenting with new forms of organising, organisation leaders must not abandon sound planning, analysis and decision-making in favour of *laissez-faire* management. Rather, organisations should seek to redress the imbalance that has existed historically between these two seemingly paradoxical views of organising and recognise that traditional and new organisational practices can be organised to complement and reinforce one another. For this to happen demands a holistic, whole-brained approach to managing organisations. Figure 5.2 gives an overview of the different perspectives on organising for the 21st century that we have discussed in this chapter. It shows the interrelationships and interdependencies of the different components *within* each perspective and also traces the similarities and overlaps *among* the different perspectives. By adopting a complementary, systemic approach, an organisation will be better equipped to manage the complexities and dualities inherent in innovative forms of organising.

Review

In this chapter, we examined different perspectives on new forms of organising and found common themes emerging for leading and managing in the 21st century. We also considered the confluence of external and internal factors that are compelling organisations to experiment with different forms of organising. Globalisation, deregulation, privatisation, increasingly sophisticated technology, and the transition from the Industrial Age to the Information Age have radically reshaped industries and have had a resounding impact on the structures, processes and boundaries that shape organisations. Increased competition at both the local and global levels calls for increased responsiveness and flexibility, and continuous improvement and innovation. More sophisticated and demanding customers expect high-quality, differentiated products and services, while well-educated, highly skilled employees demand commensurate rewards and quality of work life. Faced with these types of pressure, traditional machine bureaucracies and divisional structures lacked the flexibility and often the capability to respond swiftly and effectively to changes in the marketplace.

As organisations wrestled with developing an organisational form that would enable them to interact and compete successfully in this very different external environment, it became increasingly apparent that developing and nurturing internal capabilities would not be realised unless there was a stronger focus on the softer organisational processes. Organisations need to learn how to balance the traditional hard, rational, quantitative approach to managing organisations with a softer, more qualitative, intuitive, people-focused approach. This shift in emphasis has led to the devolution of decision-making power down through organisations, the development of a more participative management style within an open, learning environment, and the establishment of boundary spanning teams to encourage the cross-pollination of knowledge and ideas sideways across the organisation deck. In this regard, we also considered the series of dualities organisations must learn to juggle as they seek higher performance through greater innovation and flexibility. The growing evidence is that high performing, innovating organisations are not abandoning traditional work practices such as hierarchies, centralisation and formalisation, but rather are adopting 'ambidextrous' forms of organising. In this context, we explored the concept of the 'strategically flexible organisation' that incorporates both controllability and responsiveness, blending more formalised, traditional work practices with new flexible work arrangements. This entailed learning how to balance and integrate the dualities of old and new organisational practices, for example nurturing innovation alongside rigorous financial and operational systems; and balancing formalised, central controls and policies with decentralised decision-making that would support more flexible forms of organising.

Advances in information and communication technologies have played a key role in facilitating intra-organisational networking and collaboration as well as inter-organisational partnerships and alliances. The successful transfer and diffusion of knowledge within an organisation depends on trust and an understanding of the mutual benefits and synergies to be gained. Changes to structure (such as decentralising decision-making power and establishing project-based work groups within and across companies) cannot take place, therefore, without complementary changes to process (educating and training people to give them the skills and confidence to work in teams, share information and ideas, and use the new communication technologies; investment in appropriate information technology) and boundaries (establishing sound external partnerships and alliances).

Our examination of the various experiences of new forms of organising indicates that companies concentrating on only one of the key design variables (whether structure, process or boundaries) will not experience the same performance gains as found in those companies that undertake changes simultaneously across all three dimensions. This underlines the importance of recognising and understanding the interdependence and complementarities of the different design variables, and of adopting a systemic rather than piecemeal approach to organisational change. Our investigation of different studies of new forms of organising also highlights that organisations are not simply dismantling old structures, systems and processes in favour of the new. On the contrary, they are investing in both hierarchies (for performance measurement and accountability) and networks (horizontal collaboration and cooperation), in both centralisation (strategic decision-making) and decentralisation (operational decision-making), and in both empowerment and control. The challenge for senior management is to manage the resulting dualities present within the modern organisation and to 'integrate the different forms of organising into a coherent whole'.[96] Investment in sophisticated information technology infrastructure has been instrumental in enabling organisations to manage hierarchies and networks simultaneously.

Finally, the experiences of new forms of organising documented in this chapter demonstrate that organising is a perpetual, dynamic process. Leading and managing today for tomorrow involves synchronising continuity and change. An organisation cannot change the colour of its spots and adopt new behaviours overnight; a pattern emerges only as a result of experiential learning. Organisations need to combine 'bold strokes' with 'long marches'[97], experimenting and seeking new opportunities and new ways of doing business, while simultaneously managing and nurturing existing business operations.

Key terms

breakpoints. Radical, framebreaking change that triggers a fundamental review of organisational systems, processes, structure and design, (p. 152)

horizontal integration. Moving into activities that are competitive with or complementary to a firm's existing activities, (p. 153)

matrix structure. A combination of structures that can comprise either product and geographical divisions, or functional and divisional structures operating alongside each other in the one organisation, (p. 152)

multidivisional organisation. Subdivision of an organisation into autonomous/semi-autonomous business units (divisions) on the basis of products, services, geographic areas or the processes of the firm, (p. 152)

network multidivisional form. Similar to the multidivisional organisation, but the network form of organising depends on *cooperation* for success. Therefore, the network multidivisional form emphasises horizontal communication; flexibility and boundary spanning; cross-divisional knowledge transfer and learning; and intra-organisational relationships and processes. (p. 152)

smokestack. The industrial economy — a term that Stace and Dunphy attribute to Alvin Toffler[98], (p. 152)

vertical integration. When a company owns or is involved in both upstream and downstream value chain activities. For example, a brewery producing its own input (raw materials upstream) and owning the distribution centres, namely retail outlets such as pubs and liquor stores (downstream). (p. 153)

Review questions

1. What key factors are compelling organisations to experiment with new forms of organising?
2. Describe the Taylorist model of organisation design. Provide an example.
3. Distinguish between functional, divisional and matrix structures. Outline the advantages and disadvantages of each.
4. Identify and describe Kanter's three key strategies for the post-entrepreneurial organisation.
5. Identify the key indicators of change within the three organisational design dimensions of structures, processes and boundaries.
6. Explain the meaning of the term 'ambidextrous' forms of organising.

Discussion questions

1. Discuss the implications of new forms of organising for people management.
2. Identify and explain the relevance of Ghoshal and Bartlett's three core processes for organising for the 21st century.
3. It is argued that the Internet, and increasingly sophisticated communications and digital technologies are transforming the nature of work and traditional organisational forms. Discuss in relation to organisational structures, processes and boundaries.

Work assignment

William Angliss Institute of TAFE — challenges for change

Read the end-of-book case study (case 1, page 361) on William Angliss Institute of TAFE.

1. Identify the forces for and against change within the organisation.
2. Identify, as far as possible, what changes have occurred across all nine key indicators of change within the three organisational design dimensions of structures, processes and boundaries (use figure 5.4, page 166, to guide you through these).
3. Based on your response to question 2, identify the key challenges facing the organisation.
4. What recommendations would you make to the Institute to help resolve the challenges you have identified?

Suggested further reading

Birkinshaw, J. & Hagström, P. (eds) 2000, *The Flexible Firm: Capability Management in Network Organizations*, Oxford University Press, New York.

DiMaggio, Paul (ed.) 2001, *The Twenty-First Century Firm*, Princeton University Press, Princeton.

Pettigrew, A. M. & Fenton, E. M. (eds) 2000, *The Innovating Organization*, Sage Publications, London.

Pettigrew, A. M., Whittington, R., Melin, L., Sanchez-Runde, C., van den Bosch, F. A. J., Ruigrok, W. Numagami, T. (eds.) 2003, *Innovative Forms of Organizing*, Sage Publications, London.

End notes

1. R. M. Kanter 1996, 'Beyond the cowboy and the corpocrat', in *How Organizations Learn*, ed. K. Starkey, International Thomson Business Press, London, pp. 43–59.

2. Ikujiro Nonaka 1996, 'The knowledge-creating company', in *How Organizations Learn*, ed. K. Starkey, International Thomson Business Press, London, pp. 18–31; Y. Doz & H. Thanheiser 1993, 'A process of organisational renewal', in *Strategic Thinking: Leadership and the Management of Change*, eds J. Hendry & G. Johnson with J. Newton, John Wiley & Sons, Chichester, pp. 293–310.

3. 'Introduction', in *How Organizations Learn*, ed. K. Starkey, International Thomson Business Press, London, pp. 7–17.

4. P. M. Senge 1990, 'The leader's new work: building learning organizations, *Sloan Management Review*, Fall, pp. 7–23.

5. ibid., p. 7.

6. D. Ulrich & M. F. Wiersema 1989, 'Gaining strategic and organizational capability in a turbulent business environment', *The Academy of Management Executive*, 3(2), p. 118 of pp. 115–22.

7. T. Goss, R. Pascale & A. Athos 1993, 'The reinvention roller coaster: risking the present for a powerful future', *Harvard Business Review*, November–December, pp. 97–108.

8. Charles A. O'Reilly III & Michael L. Tushman 2004, 'The Ambidextrous Organization', *Harvard Business Review*, April 2004, pp. 74–81; H. W. Volberda 1998, *The Flexible Firm*, Oxford University Press, New York, p. 74.

9. Andrew M. Pettigrew & Richard Whittington 2003, 'Complementarities in action: organizational change and performance in BP and Unilever 1985–2002', in *Innovative Forms of Organizing*, eds A. M. Pettigrew, R. Whittington, L. Melin, C. Sanchez-Runde, F. A. J. van den Bosch, W. Ruigrok, T. Numagami, Sage Publications, London, chapter 8, p. 201; O'Reilly & Tushman 2004, op. cit.

10. A. Pettigrew 1999, 'Organising to improve company performance', *Hot Topics*, Warwick Business School, 1(5).

11. Phillip K. Ruthven 1999, 'Foreword', in *How Big Business Performs: Private Performance and Public Policy*, eds P. Dawkins, M. Harris & S. King, Allen & Unwin, St Leonards, New South Wales, pp. v–ix.

12. D. Jackson 2000, *Becoming Dynamic: Creating and Sustaining the Dynamic Organisation*, Macmillan Business, London.

13. Doz & Thanheiser, op. cit., p. 296.

14. Kanter, op. cit., p. 48.

15. M. Scott Morton 1995, 'Emerging organizational forms: work and organization in the 21st century', *European Management Journal*, 13(4), pp. 339–45.

16. ibid., p. 341.

17. D. Limerick & B. Cunnington 1993, *Managing The New Organisation*, Business & Professional Publishing, Sydney.

18. ibid., p. 43; G. Johnson & K. Scholes 1999, *Exploring Corporate Strategy: Text and Cases*, 5th edn, Prentice Hall, London, pp. 409–11.

19. ibid., pp. 38, 48.

20. J. Birkinshaw 2000, 'Network relationships inside and outside the firm, and the development of capabilities', in *The Flexible Firm: Capability Management in Network Organizations*, eds J. Birkinshaw & P. Hagström, Oxford University Press, New York, chapter 1, pp. 4–17.

21. W. E. Baker 1992, 'The network organization in theory and practice', in *Networks and Organizations*, eds N. Nohria and B. Eccles, Harvard Business School Press, Cambridge, Massachusetts.

22. Birkinshaw, op. cit., p. 7.

23. S. Jonsson 2000, 'Innovation in the networked firm: the need to develop new types of interface competence', in *The Flexible Firm: Capability Management in Network Organizations*, eds J. Birkinshaw & P. Hagström, Oxford University Press, New York, chapter 6, p. 110 of pp. 106–25.

24. Birkinshaw, op. cit., pp. 5–6.

25. D. Stace & D. Dunphy 2001, *Beyond the Boundaries: Leading and Recreating the Successful Enterprise*, 2nd edn, McGraw-Hill, Sydney, p. 20.

26. D. Stace & D. Dunphy 1996, *Beyond the Boundaries: Leading and Recreating the Successful Enterprise*, McGraw-Hill, Sydney, p. 32.

27. S. Ghoshal & C. A. Bartlett 1995a, 'Building the entrepreneurial corporation: new organizational processes, new

managerial tasks', *European Management Journal*, 13(2), pp. 139–55.

28. ibid., pp. 139, 145.
29. ibid., p. 145.
30. S. Ghoshal & C. A. Bartlett 1995b, 'Changing the role of top management: beyond structure to processes', *Harvard Business Review*, January–February, p. 86 of pp. 86–96.
31. W. Ruigrok, L. Achtenhagen, M. Wagner & J. Rüegg-Stürm 2000, 'ABB: beyond the global matrix towards the network multidivisional organization, in *The Innovating Organization*, eds A. M. Pettigrew & E. M. Fenton, Sage Publications, London, chapter 4, pp. 117–43. Ruigrok, Achtenhagen, Wagner and Rüegg-Stürm provide an in-depth analysis of the evolution of the ABB matrix organisation through the 1990s.
32. Michael E. Raynor & Joseph L. Bower 2001 'Lead from the center: how to manage divisions dynamically', *Harvard Business Review*, May, p. 94 of pp. 93–100.
33. Ian Palmer & Richard Dunford 2002, 'Out with the old and in with the new? The relationship between traditional and new organizational practices', *The International Journal of Organizational Analysis*, 10(3), p. 221 of pp. 209–225.
34. Carlos J. Sanchez-Runde & Andrew M. Pettigrew 2003, in Pettigrew, Whittington, Melin et al, op. cit., chapter 10, p. 244.
35. Fenton & Pettigrew, op. cit., p. 7.
36. ibid., p. 7.
37. Jackson, op. cit., p. 44.
38. Fenton & Pettigrew, op. cit., p. 7.
39. Kanter, op. cit.
40. Ghoshal & Bartlett 1995a, op. cit., p. 145.
41. Kath Walters 2004, 'Home, but not away', *BRW*, October 7–13, p. 70.
42. Fenton & Pettigrew, op. cit., p. 25.
43. Pettigrew, op. cit.
44. R. Whittington, A. Pettigrew, S. Peck, E. Fenton & M. Conyon 1999, 'Change and complementarities in the new competitive landscape: a European panel study, 1992–1996', *Organization Science*, 10(5), September–October, p. 588.
45. A. M. Pettigrew & E. M. Fenton 2000, 'Complexities and dualities in innovative forms of organizing', in *The Innovating Organization*, eds A. M. Pettigrew & E. M. Fenton, Sage Publications, London, chapter 10, pp. 279–300.

46. D. Shaw 1999, *Organising for the 21st Century*, PricewaterhouseCoopers, London, p. 5; W. Ruigrok, A. Pettigrew, S. Peck & R. Whittington 1999, 'Corporate restructuring and new forms of organizing: evidence from Europe', *Management International Review*, Special Issue 39(2), pp. 41–64; Pettigrew, op. cit., p. 2; Whittington et al., op. cit., p. 590.
47. Ruigrok, et al. 1999, op. cit., p. 50.
48. Pettigrew, op. cit.; Ruigrok et al. 1999, op. cit.; Shaw, op. cit.
49. P. Thompson & D. McHugh 1995, *Work Organisations: A Critical Introduction*, 2nd edn, Macmillan Business, London, p. 192.
50. P. Dawson, R. Drinkwater, N. Gunson & M. Atkins 2000, 'Computer-mediated communication and the virtual workplace: the social and political processes of change', *Labour and Industry*, 10(3), April, pp. 17–36.
51. Ruigrok et al. 1999, op. cit., p. 53.
52. Dawson et al., op. cit., pp. 30–2.
53. Whittington et al., op. cit., p. 591; Pettigrew, op. cit., p. 2; Ruigrok et al. 1999, op. cit., p. 55.
54. Tim Treadgold 2004, 'The Mating Game', *BRW*, October 14 – November 10, pp. 57—58.
55. R. Duane Ireland & Michael A. Hitt 1999, 'Achieving and maintaining strategic competitiveness in the 21st century: The role of strategic leadership', *Academy of Management*, 13(1), pp. 43–57.
56. Pettigrew, op. cit., p. 2.
57. Stace & Dunphy 2001, op. cit.
58. Whittington et al., op. cit., p. 588.
59. Carlos J. Sanchez-Runde & Andrew M. Pettigrew 2003, 'Managing dualities', in *Innovative Forms of Organizing*, eds A. M. Pettigrew, R. Whittington, L. Melin, C. Sanchez-Runde, F. A. J. van den Bosch, W. Ruigrok, T. Numagami, Sage Publications, London, chapter 10, pp. 243–250.
60. Fenton & Pettigrew, op. cit., p. 280 of pp. 279–300.
61. J. B. Quinn, P. Anderson & S. Finkelstein 1998, 'New forms of organizing', unpublished monograph in *Readings in the Strategy Process*, 2nd edn, eds H. Mintzberg & J. B. Quinn, Prentice Hall, New Jersey, p. 162 of pp. 162–74.
62. Palmer & Dunford 2002, op. cit., p. 220.
63. Raynor & Bower 2001, p. 94, op. cit.

64. Henk W. Volberda 1998, *Building The Flexible Firm*, Oxford University Press, Oxford, p. 107.
65. ibid., p. 103 and pp. 6–7.
66. ibid., p. 123; Palmer & Dunford 2002, op. cit., p. 221; Pettigrew, Whittington, Melin et al, op. cit.
67. Raynor & Bower 2001, op. cit., p. 100.
68. Andrew M. Pettigrew & Richard Whittington 2003, 'Complementarities in action: organizational change and performance in BP and Unilever 1985–2002', in *Innovative Forms of Organizing*, eds A. M. Pettigrew, R. Whittington, L. Melin, C. Sanchez-Runde, F. A. J. van den Bosch, W. Ruigrok, T. Numagami, Sage Publications, London, chapter 8, p. 201; O'Reilly & Tushman 2004, op. cit.
69. Carlos J. Sanchez-Runde, Silvia Massini & Javier Quintanilla 2003, 'People Management Dualities', chapter 11, p. 258 in Pettigrew, Whittington, Melin et al, op. cit.
70. ibid., p. 257.
71. ibid., p. 265.
72. Leona Achtenhagen, Leif Melin, Tomas Mullern & Thomas Ericson 2003, in Pettigrew, Whittington, Melin et al, op. cit., p. 55.
73. P. Bate, R. Kahn & A. Pye 2000, 'Towards a culturally sensitive approach to organization structuring', *Organization Science*, 11(2), March–April, pp. 197–211.
74. Jackson, op. cit., p. 44.
75. Carly Fiorina 2004, 'Totally digital', *The Economist* 'The World in 2005', p. 115.
76. *The Economist* 2000, 'The Dot Com imperative', *The World in 2000*, The Economist Publications, London, p. 104, cited in Stace & Dunphy 2001, op. cit., p. 31.
77. Henry W. Chesbrough & David J. Teece 2002, 'Organizing for innovation: when is virtual virtuous?', *The Innovative Enterprise, Harvard Business Review*, (BEST OF HBR 1996), August, pp. 127–35.
78. Paul S. Adler 1999, 'Building Better Bureaucracies', *Academy of Management Executive*, 13(4), pp. 36–47.
79. R. Duane Ireland & Michael A. Hitt 1999, 'Achieving and maintaining strategic competitiveness in the 21st century: the role of strategic leadership', *Academy of Management Executive*, 13(1), pp. 43–57.
80. Dawson et al., op. cit., p. 23.
81. Janice A. Black & Sandra Edwards 2000, 'Emergence of virtual or network organizations: fad or feature', *Journal of Organizational Change Management*, 13(6), pp. 567–76.
82. Peter J. Brews & Christopher L. Tucci 2003, 'Internetworking: building internet-generation companies', *Academy of Management Executive*, 17(4), p. 9 of pp. 8–22.
83. ibid., p. 14.
84. ibid., p. 22.
85. Eric Wilson 2004, 'Laying framework of life in the e-bush', *The Age*, 'Next' Issues section, November 23, p. 7, © Eric Wilson.
86. A. D. Gilbert 2001, 'Education readies for a virtual future', *The Age*, 'IT' section, 14 August, p. 9 (edited text from a speech delivered to The Manning Clark Symposium, July 2001).
87. G. Alderman 2002, 'Time to get ready for the online revolution', *Guardian Weekly*, 17–23 January, p. 23.
88. M. Atkins & P. Dawson 2000, 'Conceptualising the virtual organisation: emerging forms of work in virtual organisations', Paper presented at the 10th Annual BIT Conference, Manchester Metropolitan University, United Kingdom, 1–2 November.
89. Dawson et al., op. cit., p. 31.
90. Stace & Dunphy 2001, op. cit, p. 212.
91. I. McLoughlin, D. Preece & P. Dawson 2000, 'From Essex to cyberspace: virtual (organisational) reality and real (organisational) virtuality', Paper presented at the British Academy of Management Annual Conference, University of Edinburgh, 12–15 September.
92. Michael Useem and Joseph Harder 2000, 'Leading laterally in company outsourcing', *Sloan Management Review*, Winter, pp. 25–36.
93. Ghoshal & Bartlett 1995a, op. cit., pp. 145–8.
94. R. M. Kanter, B. A. Stein & T. D. Jick 1992, *The Challenge of Organizational Change*, The Free Press, New York, pp. 12 and 13; C. Hampden-Turner 1995, *Corporate Culture: How to Generate Organisational Strength and Lasting Commercial Advantage*, Piatkus, London, p. 168.
95. Ghoshal & Bartlett 1995a, op. cit., p. 145.
96. Quinn, Anderson & Finkelstein, op. cit., p. 162.
97. Kanter et al., op. cit., p. 492.
98. A. Toffler 1990, Powershift: Knowledge, *Wealth and Violence at the Edge of the 21st Century*, Bantam Books, New York.

6

HUMAN RESOURCE MANAGEMENT AND ORGANISATIONAL CHANGE

Holden, the Australian subsidiary of General Motors, underwent wide ranging organisational change over three years from 2001 to 2003 to ensure that it remained competitive in a very dynamic industry. Andrea Grant, the executive Director, Human Resources, who joined Holden in November 2000, was the first woman to take a seat on Holden's board of directors. When she joined the company, Grant described it as highly successful with innovative, high-tech products, but with a very traditional and bureaucratic culture. Since then, Grant has helped to transform Holden's Human Resources (HR) from a traditional, personnel function primarily to one where HR is considered a strategic business partner, and helped to create organisational capability and a culture to enable Holden to meet its future business challenges.

Grant's first initiative was to create a vision for the HR department. After collaboration and consultation with HR employees and customers in the business, she developed the first Holden HR strategy using the organisation's strategic plan to identify the key objectives for the department. She created an HR structure that would support the business and its strategy. This new structure is a matrix of customer support roles and centres of expertise including 'organisational capability (encompassing leadership development, employee development and organisational development), employee relations (work/life, diversity, employee relations and industrial relations) and HR shared services (recruitment, compensation and benefits, workforce planning, HR processes and systems as well as an HR transaction service centre)'. The new structure created many opportunities for HR talent, both existing and new, and people were matched with roles to ensure a highly competent HR team. Subsequently, with input from almost every HR employee and a cross-functional team of 60 senior Holden managers the HR strategy was reviewed and an HR Balanced Scorecard with an integrated set of strategies and scorecards was developed.

While the Holden board of management had significant plans for growing the business, if its business goals were to be met, the capability and some aspects of the company's culture needed to change. It required a 'high performance' culture where levels of communication and employee involvement are high, and employees are empowered, and able to take risks.

Working with the then chairman and managing director, Peter Hanenberger, Grant started at the top to create a diverse and talented board of directors — changing its age, gender, competency and values demographics. They implemented an 18-month program focused on developing a top executive team, including defining the role and purpose and processes of the board, accountabilities of the directors, and individual and team development. The result has been a more effective and focused board with improved team and business leadership capability.

A new set of values: 'aspirational values', 'dreams come true', 'game changing', 'boundary less', 'engage' and 'trust' were created. Grant says these values describe the culture needed to achieve Holden's vision and business strategy, and are being integrated with all HR processes and the behaviours of Holden's top 150 managers.

The strategies also included the development of leadership competencies, which form the basis of all leadership development, progression, succession and recruitment decisions regarding present and future leaders. These behaviours and actions are aligned with the company's values, which in turn reinforce the desired culture.

To address some of the soft skills needed to get harmony and productivity in their complex and diverse management teams, HR instigated workshops and training modules based on Daniel Goleman's 'emotional intelligence'. Other initiatives implemented in the organisation included new maternity leave guidelines to address the retention of women in the business.

Grant sees organisational change as a journey, and its effects on people must be fully considered and managed. She believes that it has to be a series of changes that are integrated and consistent with an overall strategy. To help employees understand and cope with the impact of structural and cultural change, appropriate consultation and communication prior to and during the change is essential. And time. Grant estimates these changes will take about five years at Holden.

Source: Adapted from C. Donaldson 2004, 'Beholden to HR', *Human Resources*, 54, 19 April, pp. 10–11; C. Fox 2004, 'Shifting gears' *Boss Magazine*, 13 August 2004; D. Goleman 1995, *Emotional Intelligence*, Bantam Books, New York; C. Nader 2002, 'Holden sets new industry standard', *The Age*, 9 October.

Introduction

Worldwide changes such as global competition, advances in technology, changing customer expectations and employee demands for the right to participate in workplace decisions and have an appropriate work–life balance are altering the manner in which organisations compete and the type of work to be done. Coupled with this development is the recognition of the importance of an organisation's human capital and people management in organisational success.[1] The adoption of a strategic orientation to managing people and of 'high-performance' or 'high-commitment' practices have been argued to have a positive impact on the performance of firms.[2] These practices are supported by the human resource management (HRM) systems and processes, including comprehensive employee recruitment and selection procedures, retention policies, incentive-based compensation and reward systems, **performance management systems** and extensive employee involvement, training and development.

From the 'Opening case' of Holden, we can observe that awareness of changes in its external environment (including local and global competition, and technological innovation) and the need to realign the organisation's capabilities, its internal environment, and culture with its strategic directions for growth, impelled the company to consider the HR strategies to leverage the desired changes. We also see the roles that management and the HR function played in analysing the need for change, and in designing and implementing appropriate and consistent HR strategies to address this need. The purpose of this chapter is to examine the roles of the human resource function, human resource professionals and all those responsible for people management in organisation change, and the devolution of responsibility for aspects of change throughout the organisation. We also explore the importance of an interactive relationship between corporate and business strategy, change strategy and HRM strategy. We delve deeper to illustrate how specific HRM strategies can be employed as key interventions to leverage organisation change, and to see why it is important to measure and evaluate their impact on organisational performance.

The nature of human resource management

What is human resource management (HRM)? On the face of it, this looks like a simple question. And it can be answered simply. Broadly defined, human resource management is the set of policies, practices and systems that influence employees' behaviour, attitudes and performance.

Michael Armstrong defines HRM as

> . . . a strategic and coherent approach to the management of an organisation's most valued assets — the people working there who individually and collectively contribute to the achievement of its objectives.[3]

Strategic human resource management (SHRM)

> . . . deals with the macro-concerns about structure, values, culture, quality, commitment, matching resources to future needs, performance, competence, knowledge management and human resource development, and creating a positive climate of employee relations.[4]

There are various theoretical perspectives of human resource management. For example the 'behavioural perspectives' identify the behaviours necessary for the achievement of the organisation's strategic objectives and 'the resource-based perspective' sees people as a key resource capable of providing a competitive advantage. Both of these perspectives are based on the notion that HR has at its core a set of strategies aligned with the longer-term vision, mission and strategic intentions of the organisation.

The integration of HRM with corporate and business strategies

Effective delivery of organisational change requires an alignment between the organisation's corporate and business strategies, its change strategies and its HRM strategy. In earlier chapters on strategy and high-performance approaches, we saw that a reciprocal interdependence exists between an organisation's strategies (both deliberate and emergent) and strategic HRM. This goal of strategic integration is central to Guest's 1997 model of HRM.[5]

Guest's approach to strategic human resource management is based on the view that a core set of integrated HRM practices aligned with the organisation's strategic plans can achieve superior individual and organisational performance. This framework focuses attention on the relationships between valued outcomes in HRM, that is, high commitment, including the internalisation of the importance of human resources by line management, high quality, and task flexibility, the alignment of the set of the policy choices that should deliver these outcomes, and their contribution to the achievement of organisational success.[6] The Guest model has six components: an HRM strategy, a set of HRM policies, a set of HRM outcomes, behavioural outcomes, performance outcomes and financial outcomes.[7] They are designed as a whole package and each is necessary to ensure superior performance (see Table 6.1).

TABLE 6.1	Linking HRM and performance				
HRM strategy	HRM practices	HRM outcomes	Behaviour outcomes	Performance outcomes	Financial outcomes
Differentiation (Innovation)	Selection		Effort/ Motivation	High: Productivity	Profits
	Training	Commitment		Quality Innovation	
Focus (Quality)	Appraisal		Cooperation		
Cost (Cost-reduction)	Rewards	Quality	Involvement	Low: Absence	ROI
	Job design			Labour turnover Conflict	
	Involvement	Flexibility	Organisational citizenship	Customer complaints	
	Status and Security				

Source: Reproduced from 'Linking HRM and performance' by David E. Guest, p. 270, *International Journal of Human Resource Management*, Vol. 8, 1997, © Taylor and Francis Ltd.

Many writers note, however, the complexity of the notion of 'fit' or 'alignment' and suggest this goal is too simplistic.[8] Mabey, Salaman and Storey contend that this relationship between human resource and corporate strategies assumes a rational, consensual, explicit and unilinear process of strategic decision-making. However, strategies may not always be easy to discern, and the processes of decision-making may be implicit, incremental, negotiated and compromised.[9] Other factors — such as power structures, the presence or absence of unions, legal regulation and the competence to make HRM strategy — may also need to be considered.

Other views of the link between organisational strategy and strategic HRM suggest mutual integration and support, but also that a resource-based perspective may be more appropriate. The 'resource-based view' of the firm argues that unique bundles of tangible and intangible resources, rather than the product-market combinations, lie at the heart of a firm's competitive advantage and suggest that human resource decisions, integrated in a human resource system, have an important influence on the development of organisational capabilities and on the firm's performance.[10] Three general types of resource can be sources of competitive advantage: physical capital (for example, plant, equipment and finances), organisational capital (for example, structure, planning and systems) and human capital (for example, skills, judgement and adaptability). In relation to HRM, organisational strategies may be chosen to exploit the competitive advantage in existing human resource strengths, organisational capabilities and **core competencies**.[11] According to Collis and Montgomery[12], the resource-based view (RBV) of the firm

> ... sees companies as very different collections of physical and intangible assets and capabilities. No two companies are alike because no two companies have had the same set of experiences, acquired the same assets and skills, or built the same organizational cultures. These assets and capabilities determine how efficiently and effectively a company performs its functional activities. Following this logic, a company will be positioned to succeed if it has the best and most appropriate stocks of resources for its business and strategy. . . . Superior performance will therefore be based on developing a *competitively distinct* set of resources and deploying them in a well-conceived strategy.[13]

Thus the RBV combines the internal analysis with the external analysis to ensure that it capitalises on the strengths of the firm, the firm's skills, and capabilities and characteristics that competitors find themselves unable to imitate.[14] For example, organisational strategies might be chosen to exploit the competitive advantage in existing human resource strengths, core competencies and organisational capabilities. Thus the strategic value of the workforce and workplace learning are key issues.[15]

Prahalad suggests that any large-scale change involves the simultaneous and continual management of three main agendas. Each agenda requires a strategic orientation towards HRM:

> The first [is] ... *the intellectual agenda*: the vision, 'strategic intent' and business strategy positioning of an organisation. The intellectual agenda stretches the limits of thinking about the value the organisation is able to add for stakeholders, customers and society as a whole. The second is the *management agenda*: this is concerned with building appropriate structures and networks, introducing appropriate technologies and systems, and having the courage to shift resources between competing needs. The

third is the *behavioural agenda*: this focuses on creating corporate values and ethics, developing appropriate leadership styles, learning systems, competencies and skills, reinforcement and rewards for appropriate employee behaviours.[16]

Consistent with these views, Gratton et al. suggest that for the HRM system to work effectively to leverage change, the organisation also must ensure more than an external fit (vertical link) and an internal fit (horizontal link); it also requires a temporal link.[17] Short-term performance must be balanced with long-term success, because 'the time cycles for people resources are considerably longer than those for financial or technological resources'.[18] As the short-term aims of the business strategy are achieved, lessons from the process provide a foundation on which to develop and implement the next stage of human resource policies and processes, and to take the organisation further towards its stated longer term goals and direction. This was evident at Holden in the decision to introduce a program of 'soft skills' through 'emotional intelligence' workshops for its V6 group to get them on track and performing as an integrated team. This approach is consistent with the notion of emergent strategies discussed in previous chapters, where organisations account for those unplanned business needs arising from the myriad of unforeseen events that can affect their business.

Matching strategic choice with HRM initiatives

The notion of alignment between organisation and business strategies and HRM policy and practices are reflected in the contingency models of strategic HRM. While we have seen that there are a variety of perspectives on the relationship between organisational strategy and HRM strategies[19], these models are useful in illustrating how the choice of specific HRM policies and practices can be used to achieve desired business and change objectives.

Kochan and Barocci — matching human resource activities at stages of the organisation or business unit life cycle

In their model, Kochan and Barocci argue that different aspects of the human resource system — such as recruitment, selection and staffing, compensation and benefits, training and development, and labour employee relations policies and practices — need to be used to support the particular life cycle stage of the organisation or business unit. These stages are the *start-up*, *growth*, *maturity* and *decline*.[20]

At the start-up stage, the human resource emphasis will be on attracting and retaining highly motivated staff to fit the desired culture of the new organisation. This approach may involve rapid development of skills and paying above market rates to retain the currency of these skills. At the growth stage, employee training and development should be introduced and used to mould an effective management team through management and organisational development. In the mature stage, training and development practices need to maintain the flexibility and skills of the workforce — both young and older workers. An illustration of this can be seen in Coles Myer's **human resource development** strategy, which has various aspects including formal business education programs. This strategy illustrates an attempt to maintain flexibility and develop the capability of its staff to meet competitive challenges.[21] Linda Heron, Coles Myer's General Manager, Learning and Development, introduced the concept of a corporate university at Coles supermarkets.[22] This concept, The Coles Myer Institute, has now been operationalised throughout Coles Myer businesses, where 4000 of its employees are now completing retail diplomas and many more are completing degree and postgraduate studies.[23] These include a wide variety of learning delivery modes including distance learning, face-to-face and fast-track, intensive residential programs. The objective of this initiative is to provide an integrated, holistic and strategic approach to the company's education and business needs, and to develop its competitive advantage through life-long learning and skills enhancement.

We should note, though, that the complexity of multiple demands at any given time means that parts of organisation may be in the decline stage, and human resource practices are needed to reinforce the change in focus (that is, to emphasise restructuring, retraining, career consulting and possibly outplacement services), while other parts of the organisation undertake appropriate HR activities to support growth and change strategies to reorient the business to competitiveness.

Schuler and Jackson — matching business strategy and HRM policy and practices

Schuler and Jackson propose a widely cited model of HRM choices associated with particular business strategies.[24] The model is based on Porter's 1985 generic strategies for achieving competitive advantage under different industry conditions[25] and is consistent with David Guest's model presented earlier. Schuler and Jackson argue for a best-fit approach, whereby different types of business strategy — *innovation*, *quality enhancement* and *cost reduction* — are associated with particular employee role behaviours and distinct HRM policies and practices.

The emphasis of an *innovation* strategy is on producing goods and services that are different from those of competitors. It is about changing the way in which people work. Organisations pursuing this type of strategy, such as Microsoft Australia, emphasise values such as self-directed teamwork, information sharing, risk-taking, experimentation and tolerance of non-critical mistakes, tolerance of ambiguity and uncertainty as the tasks change rapidly, and a strong orientation towards the marketplace and clients. These organisations need to rely on internal and external technical and professional training to maintain the currency of their highly skilled workforce. Performance management systems focus on process, the development of **competencies** that support the organisational strategy of innovation, and recognition and rewards that are linked to critical behaviours and competencies (risk-taking, such as teamwork and information sharing, organisational learning) in addition to outputs.[26]

A *quality enhancement* approach has an intermediate or more long-term focus, and emphasises enhancing the product and/or service. It requires employees to demonstrate relatively repetitive and predictable behaviours to ensure quality of output. Commitment to the goals of the organisation also is important. To achieve this focus, organisations emphasise cooperative behaviour and teamwork, and have a modest concern for the quantity of output. They also have a high concern for process and undertake few risk-taking activities. HRM policies and practices used to underpin this strategy include relatively fixed and explicit job descriptions, high levels of employee participation in decisions relevant to immediate work conditions, and extensive and continual job-related training and development. Performance appraisal uses a mix of individual and group criteria that are mostly short term and results oriented. Employee–management relations are viewed as cooperative, with a relatively egalitarian treatment of employees with some guarantees of employment security with narrow career paths.

By contrast, the primary focus of a *cost reduction* strategy is on increasing productivity and being the lowest-cost producer. This can mean a reduction in the number of employees and/or a reduction in wage levels. Cost reduction also can be pursued through labour flexibility, such as the use of part-time employees or subcontractors, casual labour and work simplification and the use of control mechanisms such as measurement procedures.[27] A cost-reduction strategy is suited to a more mechanistic form of organisation, with highly formalised systems and a command-and-control orientation. The workforce is characterised by higher need for structure and stability, and relatively lower need for autonomy and challenge. Strong emphasis often is placed on values such as conformity, predictability, authority, productivity and careful innovation in processes rather than products. Strategy usually is determined at the top, with technical specialists and accountants providing input into control system design. Training is used to skill people, to instil predictability into their behaviour, and to reinforce the corporate values and norms. Appraisal and remuneration systems tend to be highly structured and linked to market pay levels. While organisations pursuing this type of strategy traditionally have offered 'jobs for life', with slow and steady promotion through the hierarchy, and attractive superannuation and benefit schemes[28], this approach is no longer the case; instead, a marked trend towards flexibility and casualisation of the workforce is the norm.

Once again we should point out that these categories are not discrete and organisations often pursue more than one competitive strategy at a time. For example, companies such as Holden, ANZ and Coles-Myer focus on aspects of cost, innovation and quality strategies for different areas of their businesses. This strategy presents the organisations with the challenge of stimulating and rewarding different behaviours and outputs, while at the same time trying to manage the tensions that may arise as a consequence.[29]

Miles and Snow — matching business strategies and HRM systems

Miles and Snow propose an alternative human resource strategic choice or matching model.[30] Their framework identifies modes of strategic orientation and associated human resource practices. They argue that for an organisation to be superior, there must be a clear and direct match between its mission and values, the organisation's strategy, and its set of functional strategies including HRM. These authors identify the following modes of strategic orientation — *defenders*, *prospectors*, *analysers* and *reactors*.

- *Defender* companies generally have small niche markets or a limited product line, and a focus on stability and efficiency. Employees enter at junior levels and are skilled through extensive on-the-job training, progressing through functional career paths. Performance appraisal is based on production or output targets. Rewards are linked to the position in the company hierarchy. This is a common approach for staff in the highly competitive fast food sector.
- *Prospector* companies are opportunists who operate within a very narrow product or service range. They are constantly looking for new opportunities and ways of responding to emerging market trends and tend to move in and out of markets to take advantage of opportunities. They focus on innovation and flexibility and adapt well to change and uncertainty. They primarily recruit talent and competencies rather than develop them, because the skills are required quickly. Rewards are high and linked to performance and incentives. Commitment on both sides is relatively low. Career opportunities are limited and employee turnover is high. Software development and information technology companies often follow this type of strategy.
- *Analyser* companies operate in at least two product areas, and usually adopt a combination of cautious innovation and stable, efficient production systems. Such companies look for opportunities to open up and then follow them. They employ a congruent combination of recruitment, training and career development, and performance and reward management strategies to support the particular approach.
- *Reactor* companies are trying to survive and might have tried to adopt the other strategies but failed to implement them effectively. They usually lack a consistent strategy–structure–culture relationship and, as a result, usually have a poor performance record. This approach is really a non-strategic orientation.

High-performance work system

Another approach to organisational change that notes the integration between organisational strategy and the HRM system is the high-performance work system. As noted in earlier chapters, there is no one clear definition of this perspective. It is founded upon a resource-based view, is related to best practice, and has considerable overlap with the practices of 'high commitment management'[31] and 'high commitment practices'[32]. The high-performance work system is a general description of an integrated set of system-wide practices to achieve organisation-wide goals. Some of the main features are:

- flatter organisation structures, with wide spans of control encouraging autonomy, empowerment and delegation of responsibility to individuals and teams
- job design involving multiskilling, the optimising of the technical system, work processes that encourage maximum interaction and flexibility among team members, and employee participation in planning changes in work equipment or design
- wide scale use of semi-autonomous or self-managed teams, with the objective of improving quality and competitiveness
- comprehensive employee recruitment and selection procedures
- extensive use of ongoing training and development
- employee participation in selection processes
- performance management systems

- skill-based or knowledge-based rewards systems, with pay for performance and profit- or gain-sharing systems linked to organisational goals.[33]

Regardless of the HRM paradigm adopted, the intention of a change initiative is to influence the performance of individuals in some way — that is, to 'alter the way organisational members think, behave, interact, communicate, make decisions, reward, monitor, praise and coach' so that these are consistent with the new strategic directions.[34] Supporting this intention are the HRM strategies designed to deliver it. So before we start our examination of how HRM strategies, policies and practices can help to translate the organisation's vision into behaviours that deliver desired changes in the workplace, it is important to explore who carries the responsibility for the various aspects of employing human resource management as change levers at various levels in the organisation.

HRM roles

Much of the HR function's role in organisational change is in creating alignment, by developing HR strategies, policies and practices that support the process by which the organisation adapts to its environment and meets its objectives. However, the practice of human resource management is no longer 'owned' by the human resource function — nor should it be. Increasingly, as HRM takes on a more strategic focus and central place in organisational change, accountability for adding value through people is being devolved throughout the organisation. This has required a redefinition and sharing of the HRM roles and activities by employees, line managers, senior executives and human resource professionals — by helping to plan for, design and implement initiatives that communicate, select, teach, coach, measure and reward the behaviour that is expected, and makes a major contribution to guiding the organisation and its members into a new shape and new ways of behaving.[35]

A number of writers have attempted to classify the various HRM roles and activities, and argue for a new set of HR competencies.[36] Ulrich suggests that there are four key human resource roles and competency sets that add value in an increasingly complex environment. These four roles are described as **strategic partner**, **administrative expert**, **employee champion,** and **change agent**.[37] The human resource roles proposed by Ulrich also have significant overlap with those proposed by Dunphy and Stace[38], which require competency in *human resource strategy, systems, line accountability* and *change consultancy*. Further research found evidence of two additional competency domains — *culture management* and *personal credibility* — and argues strongly for one other — *strategic performance management*.[39] In recent research, using the resource-based perspective, Lengnick-Hall and Lengnick-Hall state that HR needs to move away from its traditional operational and bureaucratic focus towards the strategic imperatives of building capability, expanding boundaries and managing new roles. They propose four roles that are appropriate for HR management in the knowledge economy: (1) human capital steward, (2) knowledge facilitator, (3) relationship builder, and (4) rapid deployment specialist.[40] While none of these categories is discrete (for example, significant overlap exists between the strategic and the change activities), Ulrich's roles provide useful frameworks, because the responsibility for HRM and various aspects of change management at both a strategic and operational level is embedded across these roles, and employees, line management, human resource professionals and senior management have involvement in various aspects.

Partners in strategy

The *strategic partner* (or human resource strategy) role focuses on aligning human resource strategies and practices with the business strategy and its execution. This demands a high level of human resource and business competence. Human resource professionals must be fully conversant with, and have a broad understanding of, the economic, technological and human aspects that make up the organisation's core capabilities that drive successful strategy implementation in their organisations, as well as understanding how the various human resource functions affect those capabilities.[41] Senior human resource professionals, with the support of management must become 'intrapreneurial' — that is, innovate on behalf of the organisation and create an organisational climate and culture that encourages, facilitates and rewards innovation.[42] To accomplish this orientation, they need to understand how the organisation's **human capital**, which goes beyond traditional knowledge, skills, and abilities to encompass capabilities not directly related to task performance, including experiences and social skills, as well as values, beliefs and attitudes, can contribute to its competitive advantage.[43] To gain this level of understanding, they need up-to-date intelligence of the configuration of their employees and their particular strengths and weaknesses, including skills, knowledge, culture and values. So line managers are key players in this information-collection strategy, too. Together they must be able to determine how best to use these capabilities, identify what gaps exist between the present configuration and the future skills, knowledge, work behaviours, values and attitudes that employees will need to deliver future goals, and which specific human resource strategies will bridge those gaps.

This shift in the roles of human resource professionals — with a move away from purely administrative roles towards the provision of specialist consultancy and strategic support to management — has been noted in the past decade in the United States, Europe and Australia.[44] We have seen this for example, in the Holden example, where the human resource function was restructured to allow human resource professionals to operate as strategic partners, change agents and champions, and HR consultants on all strategic human resource matters.[45] Not every organisation, however, has structured its human resource function to allow it to operate strategically. The level of human resource input into the planning, formulation and implementation of organisational strategy differs widely across organisations and often between different business units within the same organisation. A recent US study by Lawler and Mohrman from the University of Southern California, found that board representation by HR is relatively low and that there has been little change over the last five years in actual HR practices and the way HR spends its time. However, they reinforce the need for HR to have a structure to ensure that it has the competencies to participate in strategy development and implementation, change management and organisational effectiveness.[46] Australian research supports this. A study by *HR Magazine* found that while not one of the top 100 Australian stock exchange listed companies had an HR executive on its board, almost half these companies have HR representation at the executive level.[47] But Australian boards operate under different governance models from the United States. There are more non-executive directors on Australian boards. While it helped having HR representation at board level, Shane Freeman, Group General Manager of Human Capital at ANZ, suggested that it was more important to get HR issues on the board agenda for discussion and decision-making.[48]

However, more recent research supports the evolving strategic role of HR. A report by Accenture — based on interviews with 200 senior executives in the United States, Europe and Australia — found that these executives listed workforce-related issues as four of their top five strategic priorities. And perhaps equally encouraging for HR professionals and managers (and employees), 74 per cent of the executives in this study said that people-related issues are more important to a company's success now than they were a year ago.[49]

Systems role

The *administrative expert* (or human resource systems) role represents the traditional role of efficiently designing and delivering human resource processes while maintaining quality. These roles have significance at both strategic and operational levels and aspects of these are shared by line managers and HR professionals. The roles include designing, implementing, maintaining and evaluating appropriate human resource and organisational systems, such as HRD systems, and performance management and reward systems, and human resource information systems, that help to leverage, support and sustain the new business objectives. For example, Lawler and Morhmon argue that in the knowledge economy an opportunity exists for HR to add value by employing information technology for much of the transactional tasks, thereby allowing HR more time for the key strategic and specialist HR roles or to analyse the data to evaluate various HR approaches. But these tools are also important strategically given the need to measure and evaluate complex aspects of the individual and organisation's performance. Coles Myer Ltd, Australia's largest corporate employer with around 170 000 employees, has reinvented the way they recruit by implementing a centralised on-line recruitment function for all its businesses and brands.[50] The new system is an end-to-end, on-line recruitment function, which captures the process from requisition to induction and incorporates candidate management and tracking. It allows the company to provide a more strategic recruiting function and make cost savings through immediate communication, improved reporting, the collection of accurate information, improve processes, build recruitment pools in advance of needs, and increase public awareness of careers at Coles Myer.[51]

Line accountability role

While much of the *employee champion* (or human resource line accountability) role deals with the operational, day-to-day issues, concerns and needs of individual employees and the representation of these concerns to management, there is also a strategic element to this approach. The strategic aspect includes building individual capability, which enables the employee to contribute to his or her best ability. At the strategic level, human resource specialists have designed integrated HR strategies linked to the business goals, while the responsibility for the implementation and management for achieving these goals has been devolved to line managers. These responsibilities include recruiting and selecting employees for specific parts of the organisation, identifying the need for and enabling appropriate training, development and career management, coaching and managing their performance, ensuring they are equitably rewarded for their work efforts to engender motivation, commitment and job satisfaction.[52] This approach requires line managers to become more efficient in people management as they are responsible for bringing these policies to life. Their approach to leadership can make all the difference to the success of an organisation's change agenda.[53] In a research study involving a number of companies Purcell found that

> ... the way in which managers brought these HR policies to life and exercised leadership was strongly related to positive employee views on such areas as involvement, worker-management relations, communication, openness, coaching and guidance, performance appraisal, reward and recognition, training, job influence and quality control. All of these practices are heavily influenced by the behaviour of line managers.[54]

Agents and facilitators of change

In previous chapters we noted that change interventions can affect both the level of change and the type of change.[55] The level of change (breadth) can range from whole organisation or system-wide change through to individual and personal change. The type of change (depth) can range from hard interventions, such as mergers and/or acquisitions, strategic repositioning/restructuring and technical and systems change, to soft interventions such as work redesign, human system design (such as performance management and reward systems) and cultural change (figure 6.1). Stace and Dunphy argue that it is critical to consider the interrelationship between these two dimensions and ensure a blending between the depth and breadth of change so the change effort is sustained.[56]

Organisational change encompasses two key roles: change consultant and change agency, which overlap. These roles have both strategic and operational components, and can be shared by many of the organisation's key constituents. The *change consultant* role helps the organisation build a capacity for change by facilitating the creation, development, implementation, reinforcement and evaluation of human resource strategies for transforming the organisation. The change consultant role demands competence in understanding this interaction and the use of the appropriate interventions.

The second aspect of this competency is the *change agent* role — that is, the individual or the group who is responsible for driving change in the organisation. This role can be undertaken by the leader of the company, a senior manager who has been given the task of leading an aspect of the change, the head of the human resource function or other human resource professional, or external corporate consulting firms. The core responsibility of the change agent is to lead the change, blend the breadth and depth of change interventions, and ensure the change efforts are sustained.[57] (The role of change

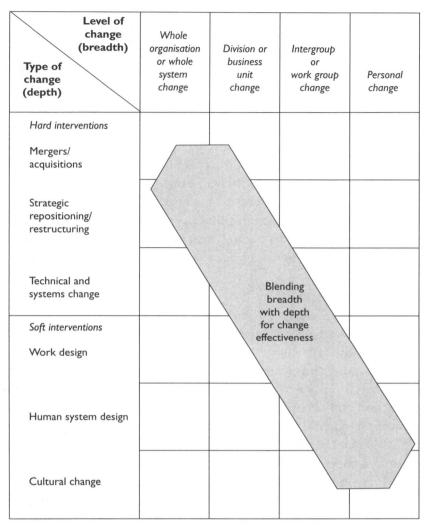

Level of change (breadth) → Type of change (depth) ↓	Whole organisation or whole system change	Division or business unit change	Intergroup or work group change	Personal change
Hard interventions Mergers/ acquisitions				
Strategic repositioning/ restructuring				
Technical and systems change		Blending breadth with depth for change effectiveness		
Soft interventions Work design				
Human system design				
Cultural change				

FIGURE 6.1: Change intervention analysis

Source: From D. Stace & D. Dunphy 2001, *Beyond the Boundaries: Leading and Recreating the Successful Enterprise,* 2nd edn, McGraw-Hill, Sydney, p. 226, © 2001 McGraw-Hill Australia.

leadership is discussed in more detail in chapter 7.) This role demands a wide knowledge of the organisation and the broader business context. It also requires well-developed skills in leadership, negotiation, persuasion and influence. Andrea Grant was acting as one of the key change agents at Holden with the restructure of the HR function work redesign and role redefinition, supported by the new accountabilities, values and behaviours needed to achieve the business objectives. These changes allowed the HR function to offer change consultancy services to the business. Similarly with the restructure of the board of directors at Holden. To assist in the transition towards a focus on growth and to reinforce the change towards a more responsive, high-performance culture, Hanenberger and Grant recruited new members for the board that addressed the need for diverse representation, including age and gender diversity, and a broad range of competencies that would assist in leading and managing change. So creating new organisational agents for change.[58] Change agency in operation was also evident from the approach to reorient the values of the board of directors at National Australia Bank (NAB) where Lynne Peacock (seconded from the group's European operations) assisted the new CEO, John Stewart, to develop change strategies that would facilitate and reinvigorate the bank's culture across the whole organisation. This involved rebuilding and extending its senior management team.[59] In many organisations, managing opposition to change is also a key challenge and needs to be anticipated with well thought out strategies to manage it effectively. For example, to break down the resistance to the new culture, NAB recruited new board members and senior management, with a mix of technical, practical and strategic skills and terminated the employment of others.[60] The interaction between these changes and the new behaviours and values of its change agents operated as a powerful mechanism for 'unfreezing' the current ways of working. It sent powerful messages to create a readiness for change, as well as helping to sustain the changes throughout the company.

Change competence

Leading change, devolving responsibility for leading change, or implementing human resource policies to leverage change demands that the organisation has core competence in change management. The change process is complex and while the management of change is an exhilarating and challenging responsibility, it may be fraught with pressure and stress.[61] Apart from having sound reasons for the change, putting the change strategy into action and making the changes a reality requires devolution of responsibility predicated on individual, managerial, functional competencies and organisational capability.[62] It also makes a number of critical assumptions. It assumes a high level of human resource competence and strategic partnering with the business to provide expert advice. It assumes that managers at all levels in the organisation have developed the prerequisite communication, negotiation, change leadership and management skills, shared values and mindset, and that there is organisational support in terms of appropriate human resource development strategies to help them acquire the skills necessary to implement, manage and sustain the change program. It also assumes consistency within stated priorities, including time to carry out the activities involved in managing people. Underpinning these assumption are the notions of workplace equity, including employee empowerment and participation. Finally, devolution of responsibility assumes that power relationships, conflict and resistance to changes from employees, or any other groups (such as unions or professional associations) that may affect the implementation of human resource policies and practices are addressed to the satisfaction of all key stakeholders.[63] In fulfilling these roles, care should also be taken to provide better balance between employers and employee interests at work.[64] The change effort can be diminished if any one of these assumptions is not met.

In the next section, we take a closer look at the various human resource initiatives and activities, including organisational restructure and work design, recruitment and selection, training and development, performance management and reward management, and explore how they operate change levers.

Organisational structure and work design

Any attempt to change the organisation, either incrementally or on a large scale, requires an examination of the fit between the organisation's strategic intentions and its structure. The choice of an appropriate structure is a necessary, although not sufficient, condition for the success of an organisation's change efforts.[65] As shown in the previous chapter, different structures carry implications for the organisation's culture (including its values/attitudes/beliefs, power relationships, **job design**, work content and skill levels), for learning and development and career opportunities, and for employee commitment and job satisfaction.[66] Through the design of the structure, the organisation establishes expectations of what individual employees and groups will do to achieve its purposes, and allows for the flow of communication and learning throughout the organisation. The structural design also helps to build the organisation's capacity to embrace and capitalise on change by ensuring the organisation has the ability to be flexible and adaptable to the changing external context.

Changing the organisation's structure may take place at many levels throughout the organisation. An organisation may introduce strategic business units to enhance business priorities and strategic networks such as the centralisation of HR at Coles Myer to eliminate the competition between its various businesses, or to induce flexibility through horizontal or cross-functional teams. It may restructure a function such as HR to ensure that it is value-adding to the business. Such was the case at Holden to move the human resources function from a traditional administrative HR function to a strategic business unit, to allow human resource support for change initiatives at strategic and operational levels as the first step in changing the culture of the company. Other examples of changes in organisational structures included the complete restructure and reporting relationships in NAB. National Australia Bank appointed a new executive team. Among the key changes included placing the risk management unit under the control of Michael Ullmer, chief financial officer.[67] Strategic outsourcing — such as outsourcing non-core aspects of HR including payroll — are also common in changes employed by companies in searching for efficiencies.

One area in which organisational change is most evident is the way in which work is performed. Buchanan argues that the objectives of work design have a strategic focus, with the main concerns being 'the need for quality, flexibility and responsiveness in meeting customer requirements in an increasingly competitive climate'.[68] These objectives are consistent with the shift to a high-performance/high-commitment philosophy discussed earlier. Changes to organisational structure and work design need not be permanent. Temporary structures, teams and work assignments may be used to suit the organisation's change agenda and serve a specific purpose in the change process.

Changing the form of an organisation requires complementary job design at the individual and group level. To ensure the appropriate changes are being made for congruence and interactivity between other human resource initiatives this should be founded upon a sound **job analysis**. The process of job analysis and design (or job redesign) requires specifying (1) the content of the job, (2) the methods of performing the work, and (3) the reporting relationships to meet the objectives of the organisation and the needs of the employee.[69] There is general consensus on the aspects of a job that influence a person's responses. These are issues concerning autonomy, control and skill, the roles of managers, and the impact of technology. Similarly, there are shared concerns for psychological outcomes and for performance.[70] Job design is considered to be more effective when both the motivational and mechanistic aspects are considered.[71]

Effective job analysis lies at the heart of planning and implementing change. It is also integral to the effective conduct of many other human resource processes, such as recruitment and selection, training and development, and performance and reward management, and ultimately to the achievement of organisational goals. Envisaging and designing the types of jobs that an organisation requires is a crucial first step in delivering the first stages of a 'turnaround' strategy.

Job redesign must be supported with other strategies that allow greater depth in interpersonal and behavioural change. Many industries are now using competency-based frameworks — that is, identifying the set of behaviour patterns, attitudes and values needed to perform the tasks and functions of a role to the required level of performance, setting out clear reporting accountabilities, and establishing the key performance indicators required to achieve business objectives.[72] Holden started on this part of its change-management path with a two-pronged approach. It analysed the needed roles and competencies in the HR function and at board of management level. The human resource levers for change included a complete restructure and redesign of work practices in both the human resource function and at the board level. The redefinition of roles for human resource professionals in line with the new HR competencies supported the new accountabilities and behaviours needed to achieve the business objectives. This approach was also evident at NAB. The roles and responsibilities of its board of management have been redefined, with an emphasis on a new set of management values, behaviours and competencies. It is also being used at Coles Myer Ltd. (See 'Change management in action: Corporate university'.)

CHANGE MANAGEMENT IN ACTION

Corporate university

As part of its major cultural change strategy, and restructure and centralisation of its HR function, Coles Myer Ltd (CML), introduced the notion of a 'corporate university' — the Coles Myer Institute (CMI) — to ensure a strategic orientation to its strategic human resource development by aligning training and development with business strategies to help the organisation build the capabilities to meet current and future demands.

The Coles Myer Institute (CMI) and its 120 employees are the primary source of all Learning and Development solutions for all Coles Myer employees. The foundation of this approach is the Coles Myer Learning Framework, which is the tool that employees use to understand how their own broad development needs are met. This competency framework is based on quality standards from the Australian Qualification Training Framework (AQTF), the Australian National Training Authority (ANTA). These standards, which range from vocational education and training (for example, AQF2 'Self Leadership') to higher education (for example, AQF8 'Strategic Leadership'), plus a standard training needs analysis process and centralised management of administrative processes, ensure that the CMI delivers optimal learning experiences for its participants.

The CMI has strong internal capability to provide learning and development solutions for induction, technical training, and frontline retail management — AQF levels 2, 3 and 4. It complemented these capabilities by engaging external partners to provide a broader view and experience of management and leadership practices beyond Coles Myer for middle and executive management — AQF levels 5, 6, 7 and 8.

The CMI formed a strategic alliance with Deakin University to provide a valued qualification framework. This alliance assisted the CMI in its creation of a learning culture, in attracting and retaining high-value staff, and for employees to view the CMI as an opportunity for them to gain greater access to integrated, innovative and high quality education and development programs to further their chosen careers.

Deakin's award framework, and flexible delivery methods provided the company with the ability to integrate individual learning pathways. This framework covers accredited and professional development programs, including traditional knowledge-based undergraduate and postgraduate programs, competency-based Vocational Education and Training programs, and customised management and leadership programs. The alliance embraces a wide range of learning (that is, technical and professional as well as business management), and utilises blended learning approaches (combining e-learning with face-to-face approaches, mentoring, and action learning). In 2005, the CMI, in partnership with DeakinPrime, the corporate arm of Deakin University, was awarded the prestigious Corporate University Xchange (CUX) Alliance Award for this corporate institute learning and development model.

Source: Based on address given by Linda Heron to Deakin MBA Deakin University, Waurn Ponds, Victoria, 15 March 2005. Reproduced with permission from Linda Heron.

Staffing the organisation

An organisation's ability to implement change and successfully derive competitive advantage depends largely on the quality of its workforce, because it is people who commit to the organisation or otherwise, learn and innovate, lead and manage, make decisions, design, develop and produce new products, penetrate new markets and serve customers more efficiently.[73] The organisation must ensure it attracts qualified applicants, has mechanisms to identify the best candidates to fill its jobs, and has the appropriate strategies in place to motivate them to perform, and to satisfy and retain them. It also has to have legal and equitable exit strategies where downsizing or retrenchments are necessary but unavoidable elements of the change initiatives. (We return to this issue later in the chapter.)

To ensure recruitment and selection policies and processes operate to leverage the desired changes, managers and HR professionals designing and implementing these policies need a clear understanding of the organisation's vision, mission and values, and its goals for change. They also require sound knowledge of the business, the industry and the wider social context, and insight into the kind of people needed to fill these jobs, and the work behaviours and values to be demonstrated. Maund, using a competency perspective, suggests that key activities are required in developing a recruitment strategy.[74] These key activities include the identification of the organisation's required competency profile; an assessment of the organisation's existing competency profile (that is, the gap analysis); the design of staff and management development programs (to close the gap between existing and required competency profiles); and the design and implementation of an organisation-wide policy on staff selection, career development and staff retrenchment if applicable.

One of the critical staffing decisions often concerns whether to recruit and select candidates from inside or outside the organisation. The organisation may wish to change an entrenched culture that operates as a barrier to change. For example, when long-standing employees have become so embedded in the old culture and ways of working that they are resistant to the proposed changes and even may not be capable of acquiring the new skills, competencies or work values and attitudes, external recruitment is an option.[75] (Resistance to change and approaches to managing these issues are examined in more detail in later chapters.) Recruiting externally can act as a mechanism to change unwanted work attitudes and behaviours, and communicate to current employees the need to change. This was NAB's approach when it recruited 'new blood' from outside the organisation for the board of directors and its senior executive ranks. As the board and senior executives are key change leaders in any organisation, ensuring that not only the structure of the board, but its collective competencies and values reinforce the desired culture and set the organisational climate is critical.

Some organisations use staffing to leverage change by employing new selection criteria linked to redesigned jobs and the competencies required to fill them. This way internal candidates who meet the new competency criteria are retained and new recruits are also brought from outside the organisation. This strategy may also be supported by a focus on 'person–organisation fit'. It is a values-driven approach. Proponents of this approach argue that benefits can accrue to both the individual and their employing organisation when there is congruence between their core values.[76] These benefits include a positive impact on work adjustment and increased levels of job satisfaction, career success[77] and communication among employees.[78] In addition, the approach can result in higher levels of organisational performance, employee commitment, loyalty and employee involvement in decision-making.[79] New selection criteria, based on redesigned roles and state of the art HR competencies were employed at Holden to ensure that the HR function could add value to the organisation and help it achieve its strategic objectives. We should note, however, that external recruitment as a change mechanism can also carry some risks, especially when the positions are low in power. To avoid the risk of newly hired employees trying to operate outside the dominant entrenched culture and facing possible resistance or rejection, or taking on the characteristics of the culture they were recruited to change, organisations need to ensure they hire external recruits in sufficient numbers to allow them to 'become a powerful constituency for change'[80] and ensure that other mechanisms to reinforce the new culture such as the performance management and reward system are in alignment.

Recruitment and selection strategies are also used to change the staffing mix to gain more organisational flexibility and diversity. The organisation may wish to take advantage of opportunities in the market, responding rapidly or using its diverse capabilities, or to avoid a threat in its environment or unanticipated and adverse environmental change.[81] Alternatively, the organisation may wish to change its configuration of full-time versus part-time, casual or contract employees, or working time so as to meet its changing business demands or to provide more job satisfaction by allowing its employees to balance work and life issues.

Or, the organisation may wish to attract a more diverse group of employees, such as workers of a different gender, age or ethnicity. It may wish to ensure equal representation of these groups in senior roles and in roles in which they traditionally have not been employed or are underrepresented, to meet legislative responsibilities, redress inequalities or proactively tap into a wider talent pool to gain up-to-date knowledge or fresh attitudes and values. As part of its platform for change, many companies have recognised that it is critical to attract and promote employees with the potential to deliver the organisation's goals such as quality, and customer service. Contrary to the recent dominant trend towards casualisation of the workforce, along with the downside of the 'flexible firm' (where casual workers can be vulnerable and manipulated), other firms such as Autoliv Australia are providing their casual workforce a pathway to permanent employment.[82]

Social trends also indicate that, if not addressed, declining growth in the labour force will result in labour shortages, lower levels of participation in training and development for workers as they age, increasing competition for younger workers.[83] Many organisations have recognised that a diverse workforce, including mature aged workers, can be a key aspect of its human capital advantage and are now specifically designing policies to change their age profile and attract and retain mature aged workers. Coles Supermarkets have implemented a diversity strategy to attract a range of employees, including people from the different ethnic groups representing its broad customer base, people with disabilities, older workers and those with varying education qualifications, from school leavers to university graduates. This staffing strategy also links with the company's aim to grow and develop the business and to compete by delivering quality service through a more committed and satisfied workforce. Autoliv Australia, which employs approximately 850 people from a wide range of ethnic backgrounds, has instigated a range of work–life balance measures to attract and retain its predominantly female workforce including early finish on a Friday, a prayer room[84], modified hours to accommodate specific start and finish needs, leave without pay for up to six weeks for emergencies, access to all sick leave as carer's leave, options to purchase extra leave, and access to long service leave after seven years.[85]

It is also clear that older workers will become critical to the survival and success of Australia's organisations as the population ages. This effect will require organisations to re-examine their attraction and retention, and learning and development strategies, and determine how best to utilise the talent in their entire workforce to ensure the continued motivation and reward of mature-age staff.[86] This approach will require the introduction of a number of practices for combating ageism including commitment from the top for diversity management, that is, work restructure and design to accommodate employees' needs for flexibility, training workforces to enhance the organisational skill set and training managers in understanding all aspects of workplace discrimination and its elimination.[87] Many Australian companies have recognised this need and introduced strategies to attract and retain older workers. These organisations include Centrelink, which has introduced a Mature Age Worker Strategy, retailer David Jones where 35 per cent of its employees are over 45, and Westpac which is on its way to achieve its target of hiring 900 mature-age workers for its call centres within three years.[88]

Downsizing

Changing the organisation may necessitate the separation of some of its current workforce as a proactive and deliberate strategy to increase productivity and effectiveness, to improve profits and share price, to gain competitive advantage, or to influence work processes leading to work redesign.[89] Often, at the same time that firms are retrenching some employees they are hiring new staff, presumably with the skills and potential to execute new strategies.

Downsizing — the reduction of workforce numbers to improve the bottom line — has been widely used in Australia, the United States and Britain. It involves the termination of a number of employees for commercial reasons.[90] It can often be about reducing costs or taking protective action.[91] The need to cut workforce numbers may be precipitated by a combination of factors, such as mergers or acquisitions, major or minor restructuring and redesign of the organisation, the introduction of new technologies, or an internal crisis. Alternatively, downsizing may be due to external factors, such as a downturn in the economic environment, a loss of business confidence, the changing value of the currency, or an external crisis of some kind. Recent trends in downsizing indicate that a large percentage of Australian organisations have employed this strategy on more than one occasion.[92] Between 1993 and 1995, 57 per cent of Australian and 48 per cent of New Zealand organisations cut their workforce numbers.[93] The use of downsizing in Australia increased in the late 1990s, with 62 per cent of organisations reporting downsizing during 1997–1998. Some 36 per cent of these organisations had downsized once, 30 per cent had done so on two occasions, and 34 per cent had done so three or more times.[94] Moreover, of all employees who held a job in the three years to 30 June 1997, an estimated 7 per cent (or 685,400) employees had been retrenched or made redundant on one or more occasions during this period.[95] A marked relationship has been found between downsizing and deskilling — it disadvantages specific groups of vulnerable workers such as older employees, supporting the proposition that downsizing leads to a loss of skills and knowledge within organisations.[96]

Approaches to downsizing

Organisations may adopt a variety of methods to reduce the number of their employees. Cameron has identified three types of downsizing strategy: **workforce reduction**, **work redesign** and **systematic change**.[97]

Workforce reduction usually is adopted as the first choice. It is a short-term directional strategy aimed at cutting the number of employees through transfers, attrition, early retirement or voluntary severance packages, lay-offs and terminations. While some of these approaches permit a relatively quick workforce reduction, they often are used indiscriminately, and the impact and benefits often are short term. The danger is that the organisation may lose core competencies and valuable human capital. To operate effectively, this strategy needs sound human resource planning and needs analyses as a basis for the reductions.[98]

Work redesign is a medium-term strategy that focuses on reducing the work through work design and work processes, rather than cutting the number of employees. It requires an assessment of whether specific functions, hierarchical levels, departments or divisions, products or services could be changed or eliminated. This strategy often is used in tandem with workforce reduction. It too requires sound human resource planning and takes time to implement. It avoids, however, the problem of the organisation simply carrying on with fewer employees (as well as the attendant problems of employee dissatisfaction and possible work overload).

Systematic change is a long-term strategy requiring considerable human and financial commitment. It includes widespread and deep organisational cultural change and transformation, right down to the levels of values and attitudes. This strategy takes considerable time to implement and its main focus is continuous improvement. It is dependent upon a skilled and empowered workforce assuming responsibility for continually searching for improved methods and practices while the organisation maintains work processes that are meaningful and satisfying. It is also consistent with the human resource philosophies of high-commitment, high-performance organisations and best practice.

There is a large body of evidence that many downsizing efforts have failed to meet organisational objectives and bring the expected benefits.[99] The reasons for failure include: poor preparation and poor management of downsizing projects; lack of understanding of downsizing issues such as employee resentment and concern, loss of morale, lack of innovation and creation[100]; the inability of organisations to look beyond a traditional approach to management[101]; failure to foresee or manage the extent of resistance to change and its impact on productivity, efficiency and competitiveness[102]; a reduction in productivity and quality of work, and lost business opportunities as a result of the lack of resources to take on new work[103]; and the increased mobility of the workforce due to broken psychological contracts.[104] Research in the United States indicates some benefits from the use of downsizing or lay-offs in high-performance work systems over time, such as increased overall employment level, reduced employment of managers and reduced use of contingent workers. The focus of this research, however, was on firm performance, and the promised 'mutual gains' in employee rewards were not evident.[105]

In light of the research that demonstrates the long-term impact of downsizing on the organisation, its employees and other stakeholders, alternatives should always be thoroughly examined before an organisation adopts this strategy. Top management must plan the downsizing activities with the human resource function addressing such issues as the desired outcomes, the targeted workforce, redundancy or severance packages, the processes for the transition, and redeployment systems.[106] In addition, as we have argued throughout this book, leading and managing the change effort is a critical component. In the event of downsizing, the organisation's leaders must be visible and provide direction and overall vision. They also have clear and open, honest and timely communication strategies, communicating the reasons for the downsizing to all members of the organisation and its stakeholders.[107] An example of this openness can be seen in the announcement by the US photographic company, Kodak, that it was going to close its Melbourne manufacturing plant in nine months, and cut its workforce by more than 600 staff as a result of the worldwide introduction and rapid adoption of digital cameras and the decline in the use of film.[108]

Finally, the organisation must ensure that it manages all its workers appropriately through the downsizing and change process. The organisation must make sure that those who are to leave the organisation are provided with guidance and outplacement advice as well as being treated with respect and dignity, while at the same providing support and communication on the future for the survivors.[109] Many of these notions, and more, are encapsulated in advice on thinking strategically and humanely on downsizing from Wayne Cascio in the 'Perspectives' box.[110]

Human resource development (HRD)

To meet the demands for change the organisation must put in place human resource development (HRD) strategies to ensure individual, team and **organisational learning**.[111] HRD is the broad set of activities operating across all levels of the organisation, concerned with investment in learning and improving the performance of its human resources as a whole. HRD activities include education, training and development, career management and planning, and organisational learning.[112] A critical focus of an HRD strategy is to make certain the initiatives support and deliver the organisation's change objectives. Drawing upon the SHRM and HRD research to reinforce this view, Mabey and Iles argue that

'... HRD has become increasing linked with strategy formulation, implementation and change ... this strategic integration operates externally (Mabey and Iles, 1993) at a number of different levels — first-order corporate decisions; second-order organisational structure and operating procedure decisions; and third-order functional decisions (Purcell, 1989) — and internally across the range of HR levers'(Mabey and Iles, 1993).'[113]

A learning strategy as a key lever for change has been part of the broad-based change management program at Coles Myer.[114] HRD initiatives demonstrate the organisation's commitment to diversity and talent management to ensure competitiveness in the retail sector. These initiatives include programs to prepare women for senior management by identifying the skills, experience and learning they need.'[115] Holden introduced its program on emotional intelligence to enhance its manager's capability to use their soft skills as well as their technical skills. To address more specific learning needs in the dynamic knowledge and information industry, the Reuters news agency has changed the way it delivers training to its employees (see 'Change management in action').[116]

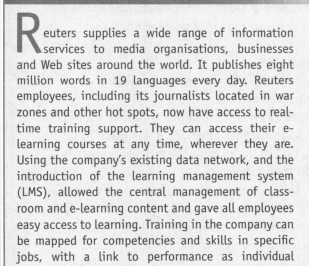

CHANGE MANAGEMENT IN ACTION
Reuters — from carrier pigeons to e-learning

Reuters supplies a wide range of information services to media organisations, businesses and Web sites around the world. It publishes eight million words in 19 languages every day. Reuters employees, including its journalists located in war zones and other hot spots, now have access to real-time training support. They can access their e-learning courses at any time, wherever they are. Using the company's existing data network, and the introduction of the learning management system (LMS), allowed the central management of classroom and e-learning content and gave all employees easy access to learning. Training in the company can be mapped for competencies and skills in specific jobs, with a link to performance as individual development and organisational and personal skill gaps can be tracked. The e-learning courses available to staff and managers range from company product and job-specific skills training to employee induction, business and management skills, technical and compliance training. The e-learning modules typically include pre-course assessment, discrete self-paced learning, study guides, interactive screens, quizzes and, finally, employee certification. This strategy has resulted in an increase in the breadth of the training and development offerings and a significant reduction in training and development costs for the company.

Source: Adapted from S. Faulkner 2004, 'Reuters: the inside story', *HRMonthly*, September, pp. 34–5.

Organisational learning

Knowledge creation and continual learning (for the organisation as well as the individual and the team) in changing business environments is widely articulated as a key sources of sustainable competitive advantage.[117] While many organisations have explicitly or implicitly adopted an organisational learning focus as part of its HRD strategy[118], there is no agreed definition of, and a great deal of confusion over, organisational learning. There are numerous models of organisational learning.[119] Many are based on the work of Argyris and Schon who have proposed two major types of learning.[120] The first is single-loop, adaptive level learning, which involves detecting and correcting performance gaps to achieve what the company intended. These organisations define the 'governing variables' — that is, their goals, plans, values, assumptions etc. — and act to achieve them. The second is double-loop learning, which refers to higher-level learning or generative learning. It is an active learning process and allows the organisations to question their assumptions and behaviour. These organisations then re-examine their 'governing variables' and alter them in light of what they have learned. Double-loop learning is necessary to keep up with changing environments and underpins organisational learning.

Organisational learning requires the adoption of a proactive learning process where the company makes a continuous effort to strive for perfection. It is premised on having organisation-wide systems and processes in place that allow the exploration and sharing of mental models (which are the values and assumptions that underpin how people view and interact with the world, and also allow the acquisition of new knowledge).[121] It requires specific integrated characteristics, including appropriate organisational structures, a culture that encourages innovation and learning from mistakes, and reinforces continual learning and sharing of knowledge.[122] These processes help employees to shed outdated knowledge, techniques and beliefs, as well as learn and deploy new ones, thus helping firms to deliver particular strategies successfully.[123] The organisation is also required to reflect on successes and failures; and apply and disseminate (1) the insights gained, and (2) have appropriate systems to measure and evaluate the extent of the learning.

Characteristics of organisational learning

An organisation that is employing an organisational learning model to leverage change has systems that are underpinned by the following elements:[124]

- a clear picture of where the organisation wants to be and a vision for how it should operate, strategic objectives that defines the learning that must occur for them to be achieved, and a strategic planning process that is about 'learning' as well as 'doing'. It helps key people to learn, change their mindsets and develop a future focus.
- a communication policy and approach that keep learning as a primary and visible objective.
- a clear understanding by employees at all levels of the importance of both learning and doing, knowing that learning how to learn is an important part of the process.
- understanding that learning can be derived from successes and failures, and used to shape future behaviour.
- understanding that learning is a continuous process and at its most powerful when it becomes habitualised and internalised.
- learning from both the internal and external environment at all levels of the organisation, and a premium is placed on sharing knowledge across organisational boundaries.
- a system of rewards that encourages all employees to ask questions and challenge the current ways of working. It encourages entrepreneurial and innovative behaviour. Bonuses and incentives are balanced across rewarding current performance, innovation, courage and risk.
- performance reviews and career development programs that are both action- and learning-oriented, and that reinforce the organisation's stated values. Multidirectional personal feedback on performance, both positive and negative, is frequently sought and given.
- unlearning and the reconstruction and adaptation of an organisation's knowledge base is a key managerial task.

- feedback systems that guarantee ongoing system-wide communication about what has been done and what has been learned. Improvement is as important as results. Information systems are designed to support this balance between learning and doing. Information on both lessons and results is widely available.
- training and education programs that support the change strategies and the value on learning and which maximise the balance between learning and doing.

An illustration of these elements in action is evident in the findings of Australian educational researchers who conducted a project involving 96 secondary schools, over 5000 students and 3700 teachers and their principals.[125] Consistent with the principles of organisational learning, high schools operating as learning organisations are characterised by four dimensions: a trusting and collaborative environment; the capacity for organisational learning is increased when members of the organisation are encouraged and supported to take initiatives and risks and are open to change; the school's mission and goals are monitored and reviewed for continual development of shared understandings, values and practices; and continual learning, feedback and opportunities is employed to improve knowledge and skills.[126]

The concept of organisational learning is, however, not without its critics and its problems. Many theorists warn that organisational learning may be no more than an idealised construct rather than a practical working model.[127] The conditions for organisational learning may not exist. There may be a lack of employee commitment, the ability of employees to manage their own continuous learning and development, organisational mechanisms to support and share mutual learning, an appropriate culture that supports openness, and experimentation, independent thinking, authority based on expert knowledge rather than status and a pluralist ideology[128], and trust in learning leadership.[129] Others warn of the dangers of pursuing organisational learning non-strategically through getting so immersed in the process of organisational learning that it absorbs more energy and resources than necessary and detracts from core business activities by pursuing change simply for the sake of change.[130] Nevertheless we cannot dismiss the importance of the whole notion of organisational learning. While it may not be appropriate for organisations operating in less turbulent environments, and for those who do not wish to or cannot change their environment[131], much of its philosophy and elements for success underpin high performance organisations and has influenced organisational practices throughout the United Kingdom, United States and Australia.

Management development and careers

Management development, and career planning and management are major vehicles for harnessing human effort to help the meet the need for change. In every type of organisation, from royal houses, religious organisations, sports teams, and public and private enterprises, succession planning is an important consideration to guarantee that they have leaders to manage their affairs. This involves the identification, tracking and development of 'high-potential employees' that the company believes are capable of being successful in senior positions. This talented group usually has to be seen by top management as fitting into the company's culture and values, and having the personality characteristics needed to successfully represent the company.

As noted in our earlier discussion, management and human resource professionals have diverse strategic and operational roles in employing HRD interventions that have been designed as mechanisms for change.[132] Senior managers influence the development of the strategy. Line managers implement the strategies. It also assumes that appropriate systems such as management development initiatives, career and succession planning supporting the future envisioned needs are in place. In conjunction with the HR function, all managers help to facilitate the change process by developing talent. All these employees must also have the necessary competencies to assist in doing their part in communicating, reinforcing and institutionalising the new behaviours, attitudes and values, by providing appropriate advice, tools, processes, education, training and career development opportunities. A lack of strategic thinking in management development and career and succession planning can create gaps in the key leadership positions and lead to the loss of valued employee talent. It can also result in career stagnation for the individual, low productivity, low levels of motivation and increased absenteeism — matters that are costly for the organisation and the individual employee by inhibiting the ability of both to meet change challenges head on.

A wide range of Australian organisations, as part of their change management strategies, are tailoring management development initiatives to meet their respective business and personal growth needs. A great deal of this strategic thinking in relation to management development, career and succession planning integrated with performance management is evident in the approach adopted by Coles Myer Ltd (refer to 'Change management in action: Corporate university', page 196).

Performance management

Performance in the form of employee behaviour is at the heart of every organisation and at the heart of virtually every organisational change. To deliver the organisation's change agenda, the organisation must have internally consistent approaches for measuring, appraising and providing feedback on both the individuals' and the organisation's progress towards desired objectives. This is necessary to check the validity of these objectives, to assess whether they are being successfully communicated throughout the organisation, to discover the extent to which they are being achieved and doing what they intended, to take action where necessary to improve performance, and to ensure appropriate rewards and benefits reinforce the behaviours and the outcomes required to deliver the changes.

Armstrong defined performance management as 'a strategic and integrated approach to delivering sustained success to organisations by improving the performance of the people who work in them and by developing the capabilities of teams and individual contributors'.[133] Performance management systems focus on the process (or set of processes) designed to manage the performance of the individual, the group and the organisation against its objectives. Research indicates that organisations with a well-developed performance management system tend to outperform organisations without such a system.[134] Apart from improving business results by optimising the performance of employees, increasing motivation and making the employee more accountable,[135] the performance management process may also drive and reinforce organisational change more specifically — for example, by determining development needs consistent with new behaviours, and by allocating rewards such as pay and promotion for desired outputs.[136]

A model of performance management

While we cannot tap into a universal model of performance management, most models depict it as a cyclical process with a common set of elements.[137] These elements (figure 6.2) include:

- setting clear performance objectives derived from the organisation's strategy and the department or business unit's purpose
- conducting informal and ongoing management of performance, using a range of appropriate management styles such as mentoring, coaching, directing and providing feedback
- formally monitoring, measuring and reviewing outcomes and providing feedback on results to employees, often using a performance appraisal and management system
- identifying training and development needs, and rewards linked to individual or team outcomes, to reinforce new behaviours.
- setting new objectives and activities
- feedback loop into the strategic and change objectives.

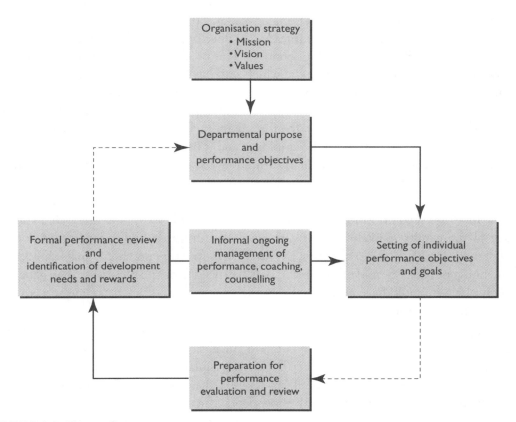

FIGURE 6.2: The performance management process

To ensure a performance management system operates effectively to leverage a desired change, its objectives should be clearly communicated. Effective performance management requires total commitment from senior management from its development through to implementation and use of the system. To engender ownership of the system, all levels of the organisation should have input into the planning, design and implementation. Acceptance of any performance management system is more likely when employees understand the need for its introduction, participate in its development and are aware of how it will affect them, and are trained in its use. It is important that employees representing a variety of functions, including HRM professionals, legal representatives, union representatives, senior and line management and system users, are involved so the essential strategic and operational issues are addressed. These issues may include the business strategy, employee involvement and equity, workplace technology and work design. Furthermore, the performance management system must suit the culture of the organisation. It is not possible to design 'a one size fits all' system, especially in larger and more complex organisations. Different solutions are required for different groups of employees and must be integrated with the way in which employees actually work, the way in which work is managed and the value that those employees produce.

Performance appraisal

The appraisal of individual performance is a central component of the performance management process. **Performance appraisal** is the assessment or review of an individual's past performance, usually against set objectives, and the setting of future performance objectives. It should include the identification of development/training needs. It may be used as a basis to determine rewards or bonuses. This process usually involves conducting appraisal interviews on a regular basis, at which staff have the opportunity to discuss their performance ratings and related issues (such as training or career development needs) with their immediate line manager.[138] To enhance both ownership of the system and the employees' commitment to its goals, the formal appraisal interview or review should be a participative process, with both the employee and the employer involved in appraising performance and setting future goals. Information on performance needs to be accurate so employees can determine whether their performance is above or below set targets. Furthermore, the performance measures and decisions need to be accepted by the people who use them, to assist commitment to the system. Locke and his colleagues assert that knowledge of the results is likely to motivate employees towards higher performance and acceptance of goals.[139] To ensure they retain their motivation potential, goals should be challenging but realistic and achievable. Goals also need to be specific rather than general, and employees should have access to the appropriate resources (such as time and equipment) and the appropriate context in which to achieve the goals.[140]

When a performance management system is operating effectively, communication regarding performance is an ongoing component of day-to-day management. Informal individual performance feedback should occur on a regular basis where necessary, and contingencies affecting performance should be addressed as they arise, through counselling, coaching or other communication with supervisors. Further, when performance feedback is continual, the discussions of performance levels and achievement in the formal part of the appraisal or review process should present no surprises for either the appraiser or the appraisee. The success of these activities will depend on the commitment and competency of the manager to handle the range of complex issues involved in people management.

Traditionally, performance appraisal and the review process have involved one-to-one communication between the subordinate and their superior. Apart from the errors that can occur when one person rates another, many researchers comment on the tension between the manager's role in judging the employee's contribution, value, capability and potential, and providing counselling and support for developmental purposes.[141] A move towards a participative discussion based on the employee's self-review has the advantage of enhancing the counselling component and reducing the judgemental aspect of the appraisal.[142] This approach can help to deliver behavioural and cultural change where the desire is to create a more open and trusting and committed workforce. But these systems must be implemented and managed appropriately. The quality of the management is an important variable in the success of their operation. Purcell argues that doing appraisals badly is much worse than having no appraisal system at all.[143] And without acceptance of the system, the change objectives for the system are dissipated. As levels of employee autonomy and discretion increase, however, there has been a rise in the use of performance appraisal as a control mechanism.[144] A number of researchers warn against an excessive focus on control or manipulation of the use of the system to reinforce power over employees.[145] (This issue of the use of power and control is addressed in later chapters.)

Some organisations have introduced new approaches to complement the measurement and evaluation of performance to alleviate the criticisms of perceived negative feedback and possible bias as well as providing depth of information. These include a balanced scorecard approach to measuring the performance of human resources, **360-degree feedback**, used at the Victorian Department of Justice and for senior management at Coles Myer, and the open approach used by Sinclair Knight Merz Group (illustrated in the 'Perspectives' box, page 210).[146]

360-degree feedback

Multirater or 360-degree feedback is based on multisource feedback on the perceptions of a person's behaviour and the impact of that behaviour. This feedback can be gleaned from subordinates, peers, supervisors, internal and external customers, and the employees themselves. These systems can be used as a tool in leveraging participation and involvement in a move towards high performance and other behavioural change efforts. This approach is premised on the view that the challenges facing today's employees and organisations can be better met through more complete feedback from a wide range of people who interact with the employee. It can lead to higher quality personal and professional development, enhanced learning and personal behavioural change. In addition, multirater systems are intended to help change the culture of the organisation, achieve goals, clarify requisite behaviour, enhance team effectiveness and provide assessment beyond the normal hierarchical relationship.[147] Successful use of 360-degree feedback requires an open, participative and supportive environment, however, rather than a command-and-control environment.[148] Many Australian companies use this approach as part of their performance management systems and to support their human resource development and succession planning objectives.[149] Other organisations use the process with a much more specific change agenda. Following a merger with Caltex, Ampol introduced a 360-degree feedback system as one of several steps to reinforce organisational core values and develop a new 'one company' culture.[150] As with other appraisal systems, 360-degree feedback is not without its critics. Some writers warn that these systems should be used for feedback for development and motivation purposes only, not for making judgements for rewards such as pay.[151]

Finally, it is vital that a pilot test and evaluation of any new system, employing feedback from all users, regardless of its type, is conducted before it is fully adopted or amended. Training in the use of the performance management system and its components, for both appraisers and appraisees, also is essential. Furthermore its use must be consistently monitored to ensure its relevance, to ascertain that there is a balance between the costs and the benefits of the system, that results are fair, accurate and related to performance — that is, to ensure the system is achieving its stated objectives for change.[152]

PERSPECTIVES — Performance by instinct

Sinclair Knight Merz Group is a professional services consulting firm with 4500 employees, and offices in Australasia, Asia, the Pacific, Europe and South America. It provides services in areas such as engineering, scientific studies, geotechnical engineering, planning, economics, logistics, project management, spatial information and architecture. The company has an innovative management philosophy based on 'natural' ways to manage the organisation and its people by accommodating 'basic instincts'. This includes a values-based culture; an organisational structure based on 'families' and 'tribes', an organisational learning and development orientation, stable leadership, and an open approach to performance management.

The key elements of the system are:

- *Language.* As language is very important to humans, the appraisal system is based on 'Dialogues'. This term has a positive meaning and reflects the company's intentions of conducting an adult-to-adult conversation.
- *Significant topics.* In keeping with the principle that people do their best work in a secure and supportive environment, the Dialogue is designed for open discussion on subjects important to the employee and manager. Topics include job objectives, performance, career goals, learning and development needs, and work–life balance. A close relationship, and communication between managers and staff is encouraged, which is seen as the biggest driver of employee satisfaction and retention.

- *Employee-driven.* The Dialogue is driven by the employee, while managers are encouraged to create the environment for a constructive communication. Being employee-driven reduces the appraisal system's orientation as a management power or control tool.
- *No ratings.* The system at SKM does not have performance ratings as these distract from the discussion and may contribute to the exercise of inappropriate power. It is designed to allow discussion of the employee's contribution and identify relative strengths and development opportunities to ensure they can then make their best contribution. This discussion happens in a supportive environment to encourage and motivate performance and also ensure satisfaction with the process.
- *No copies.* While managers and staff retain a copy of the Dialogue, these are not reported to higher, 'corporate' levels of management. This way staff and managers ensure openness and freedom of discussion.
- *Closing the loop.* Staff record the completion of their Dialogue and their degree of satisfaction with the discussion. In the three years since the new system was introduced, the completion rate is 70–80 per cent with satisfaction levels around 4.5 out of 5.

Source: Reproduced with permission from Paul Dougas and Andrew O'Keefe 2004, 'Basic instinct', *HRMonthly*, February, pp. 38–40.

Rewarding performance

Rewarding performance is one of the most important roles and functions for both human resource professionals and managers within organisations. **Reward management systems** are directly concerned with eliciting and reinforcing desired behaviours and work outcomes and are commonly used to generate and leverage change.[153] Any reward initiative should support both the needs and considerations of the organisation — that is, its business and change objectives, desired organisational culture, and control costs — and an individual's concerns — including equity, purchasing power and the satisfaction of personal needs such as recognition, appreciation, influence and participation, skills development, opportunities for learning and new challenges, and career development.[154] Like the other key human resource processes we have discussed, an organisation's reward strategy is not developed in isolation, but is influenced by the organisation's culture, its mission, the values of its managers, power coalitions in the organisation, business strategy and the broader human resource strategy.

Financial rewards — remuneration and benefits — are a major determinant of the quality of people drawn to an organisation, the level of employee performance at work and whether that performance complements the goals of the organisation. Apart from encouraging employees with the appropriate skills and knowledge to join and remain with the organisation, they also operate as a mechanism for change by rewarding specific outputs, behaviours and values required to deliver the organisation's strategy, promoting the desired culture, and motivating employees to embrace change.

The design and operation of any reward system requires a strong understanding of performance and the application of motivation theory, particularly goal-setting theory[155] and expectancy theory, which suggests that a person's motivation to perform a task is a result of the value that the person places on the likely outcome (such as the reward) and the probability of that outcome.[156] There must be a clear link between the effort required by the employee and the level of performance, and between the performance and rewards; that is, there must be a strong likelihood that if the employee expends the effort, the desired performance will result and that performance will result in the rewards. These connections also must be understood by managers, particularly line managers and employees, because they need to know what work behaviours, attitudes and outputs are expected, how the performance will be measured, and how that performance will be recognised with appropriate rewards.

Part of this is an awareness of the differing motivations and needs of employee groups in the specific industry and workplace. They must determine the particular motivations of their workforce — which relates back to understanding the business, as discussed earlier — and address these to meet employee needs more effectively. There is great variation in the value that people place on specific rewards. For some employees, money is a primary motivator, although organisations frequently overestimate the value to employees of financial rewards. For other groups, different aspects of the employment relationship — such as quality of work life, increased responsibility or power, new challenges and opportunities to learn — may provide the primary motivation. Managers must be conversant with both financial and non-financial aspects of rewards, using them in the most effective combination for every organisational situation and individual employee to meet the organisation's objectives and sustain particular organisational change efforts. The criteria for the effectiveness of a reward system are similar to those of performance appraisal, because these two systems are interconnected. It is essential to have employee consultation during both the design and implementation phases.[157] Lockyer warns that reward systems must be easy for employees to understand and consideration must be given to the cost and time spent in administering these systems, because these may be considered to be excessive and influence the success of the systems.[158]

The traditional approach to reward management is being replaced by other approaches of variable pay and benefits. Many companies now include salary packaging as a common tool used to meet the diverse needs of the workforce. These systems include **performance-related pay** (which is probably most compatible with expectancy theory predictions), or incentive compensation pay (which is linked to individual, team, business unit or company performance) for particular skills and competencies (as measured by the achievement of goals and objectives set through performance management systems) and other **employee benefits**. Kessler identifies three types of pay-for-performance systems: individual merit and performance-related systems based on indicators such as traits, skills, competencies or objectives; individual bonuses based on output such as production levels, targets or sales; and collective bonuses linked to the performance of the group, section, department or organisation.[159] Individual pay for performance has been used to reinforce a number of organisational change initiatives.[160] It can be employed to send powerful messages about the type of employees whom the organisation wishes to attract and retain — for example, where a shortage of skills exists. This is one of the strategies adopted by companies such as Motorola who applied a 'hot skills' model in Australia and the Asia–Pacific.[161] The company considers *internal drivers,* that is, the strategic importance of the skills to their business strategy, and *external* or *market drivers*, which assesses which skills are hot, the premium that other organisations pay to attract and retain these skills, and how this premium is being delivered, before finally deciding on a premium. This approach aligns the reward skills strategy with business needs, not only to ensure a strategic fit but also allow an organisation to adapt and change readily. This way, the organisation can administer the premium according to the strategic importance of the skill internally and to enhance employee satisfaction. The variable component can be withdrawn when the skill is no longer in such high demand, whereas fixed pay cannot.[162]

Other organisations, particularly those with reduced promotion opportunities, employ pay for performance as part of their motivation and retention strategies and also provide a notion of 'fairness' in rewards for the high performer. Further, companies may use performance-based pay to facilitate changes in organisational culture and values.[163] For example, John Fletcher, the CEO at Coles Myer, embarked on a massive change agenda that included increase in profits and share price. His base reward package comprised base compensation, which was set when he first came into the job, and the annual bonus, which is based on performance and share price improvement.[164] NAB had to pay 'record sign-on bonuses and market-leading pay' to entice Ahmed Fahour, the former CEO of Citibank Australasia, to fill its newly created position as

Australian CEO, where his key role is to integrate the structure and the culture of the Australian operations and create value, and also to recruit Michael Ullmer, its new chief financial officer.[165] Performance-based pay can be employed also to increase the levels of employee commitment to the organisation by setting individual goals and objectives, to increase communication between managers and employees, to encourage managers to take responsibility for making and defending pay decisions, and to contain costs. This reward approach also has been pursued as a means to weaken competing interests such as the influence of trade unions and to undermine collective bargaining as the determinant of pay.[166]

Non-financial benefits are the other key component of the reward system. The choice of these benefits should relate to the business objectives, the desired culture and values of the organisation, and the needs of employees. If recruitment policies are targeting a previously neglected group (such as women returning to work) to help change the culture and work practices in an organisation, then the organisation may need to offer a range of benefits and rewards that are attractive to this group. These could include child-care facilities on site, to reduce travelling time, anxiety and the costs for working parents. Alternatively, the organisation could offer flexibility in start and finish times to accommodate those with responsibilities for school-age children, or family-friendly arrangements such as job sharing, home-based work, parental leave, carer's leave and breaks. These arrangements also could include work-at-home options, flexible hours, job sharing or salary sacrificing of child-care costs. In its endeavour to become an 'employer of choice' for women Autoliv Australia has introduced a set of integrated HR strategies in Equal Employment Opportunities for Women (EEOW), staffing, retention, development and reward management, which has brought benefits for both employer and employees. Apart from the increase of women in executive and line management roles and an increase in engineering educational qualifications related to the workplace, benefits to the company range from a staff turnover level below 0.5 per cent, absenteeism below 4 per cent, and an increase in sales.[167]

Some organisations offer benefits relevant to the business — for example, discounted air travel for airline employees and their families, and low-interest home loans for employees of financial service organisations. Some organisations are introducing staff share plans, as at the ANZ where all employees are entitled to share in the success of the organisation, and in retail operations where employees are entitled to a staff discount card for use in the company's stores. Others are providing opportunities for further education and career development as specific rewards.

Results of a 2003 survey indicate that Australian organisations are adopting a wide range of mechanisms for rewarding staff and reinforcing its change and performance objectives. It found that only 20 per cent of Australian employees would receive a cash bonus that year, but that was up five percentage points from a survey conducted three years previously.[168] Alternative rewards range from the Christmas hampers, a leisure and lifestyle program that includes vouchers for fast food and shopping along with petrol and roadside assistance discounts to encourage a work life balance, a T-shirt bearing the firm's new advertising strategy, a photo frame and photo album with company's logo on an inside page, to movie tickets. But cash still features as a reward.

Companies such as Mallesons Stephen Jaques, ANZ and Westpac are using performance incentives to reward staff throughout the year. Australian Fitness Network gave its staff a mid-year bonus of $500 after running a successful convention — and only a two-hour time frame to spend it on something personal. However, 50 per cent of the survey respondents said that a financial bonus would generate more loyalty towards their employers.[169] The real value of these rewards and benefits can be assessed only by the people receiving them. Ultimately, it is their perception of the value that provides the motivational stimulus, so organisational understanding of the needs of their workforce and communication with the reward recipients must be open, honest and continual to optimise these levers for change.

Evaluating the contribution of human resource activities to organisational change

A final, and vital, part of the equation in using HR levers for change is demonstrating what they have delivered in relation to the organisation's performance. The organisation must be able to measure these activities, evaluate the progress and contribution they have made to the organisation, and communicate the value that has been added as a result of the change efforts, and assess whether recalibration of the change levers is needed. Also, this process is an opportunity for reflection, re-analysis and reappraisal before fine-tuning the course of change, as evaluation provides useful qualitative and quantitative data to review past performance and plan for future change management. This evaluation applies to human resource activities as much as to any other change endeavour, as we will see in more detail in chapter 9.

Evaluating a human resource program requires gathering data about organisational or individual outcomes related to its change strategies, interpreting the data, and reaching a conclusion about the quality or standard of the measured outcome. Traditional individual and team performance measures may include, individual or team output, absenteeism, turnover, resignations, lost time through injury, grievances, perceptions of managerial practices, employee attitudes on satisfaction, commitment etc. Organisational performance measures include labour productivity, product and service quality, unit cost ratios, revenue productivity, profits, market share and return on investment (ROI).[170] But appropriate multiple measures rather than single indicators are necessary and should be used with caution to ensure meaningful data.

Other approaches use benchmarking, that is, measuring not only progress against the results of the change, but also the implementation of the HRM practices, through the use of metrics such as cost–benefit analysis, opinion surveys and any other procedure that checks outcomes against goals (such as the information gleaned in the performance management process). Using industry benchmarks across a range of workforce performance productivity measures, for example, can help managers to understand how their workforce shapes up against other parts of the organisation, how it is doing in relation to its past performance, and against similar companies or industries. It can also indicate how they can target improvement efforts to become more financially and operationally competitive.

One of the newer tools available to ensure that the HR strategies and the efforts of the employees are aligned with specific, long-term business objectives is the 'HR score-card', which is based on Kaplan and Norton's balanced scorecard.[171] Becker et al. recommend that change leaders take a systematic approach in assessing the strengths and weaknesses of the current change process, and also measure its progress by using a 'change checklist' approach. They recommend specific areas to measure. These are: leading change; creating a shared need; shaping a vision; mobilising commitment; building enabling systems; monitoring and demonstrating progress; and making it last. They also support this approach with guiding questions for change sponsors and guidelines for implementation. (See chapter 9 for a detailed description of this model.)

More recently, out there on the horizon, there has been a great deal of discussion regarding a different approach to measuring the impact of HR and change endeavours: human capital management (HCM). As we have stated earlier, human capital is the sum of the total workforce's skills, knowledge and experience, values and attitudes, and motivation and commitment. It is formally defined by Bontis et al. as follows:[172]

> Human capital represents the human factor in the organisation; the combined intelligence, skills and expertise that gives the organisation its distinctive character. The human elements of the organisation are those that are capable of learning, changing, innovating and providing the creative thrust which if properly motivated can ensure the long-term survival of the organisation.

Human Capital Management is a movement away from some of traditional methods of measuring HR activities towards assessing the value of the human contribution and allowing management to maximise that value by aligning employee's skills and capabilities to the strategic direction of the business.[173] It looks at the direct links between outcomes of the initiatives (for example, specific change levers) and the profits, productivity, market share, share price etc. It requires breaking down the boundaries between the functional areas in the organisation — for example, between finance, knowledge management and all aspects of HR — and integrating reporting mechanisms. A great deal of controversy and debate still occurs on this approach and the specific metrics to be used — as these will be firm-specific and no one set of numbers or accounting formula is appropriate to all types of organisations.[174] However, the approach is being taken seriously in many quarters and is being proposed as an approach for organisational reporting in the United Kingdom.[175] As part of a UK government task force, the Chartered Institute of Personnel and Development (CIPD) has developed a draft framework to help UK firms to measure and communicate the value of their people policies. This framework is based on the principles that reporting on human capital requires multiple indicators: that the information should be of value to those receiving it; that it reports on factors relevant to the future performance of the company — including narrative and qualitative and quantitative information; and that it should contain information on barriers to the effective use of its human capital. The task force proposed five categories or activity areas of human capital management information that could be collected. These activity areas are: human capital strategy; acquisition and retention; learning and development; management; and performance.[176] Table 6.2 (page 216) illustrates one of the activity areas (performance), and the primary and secondary indicators.

TABLE 6.2	Human capital performance indicators: performance		
Activity area	Narrative — near-term and long-term	Primary indicators	Secondary indicators
Performance	The value created by human capital. Indications of the strategy for the collection and retention of knowledge. Criteria used to determine individual and team performance. Levels of current success and improvement trends.	Market capitalisation per employee. Revenue per employee. Profit per employee. Value-added per employee. Sales per employee.	Adjusted profit/employee. Unit productivity/employee. Measures of customer satisfaction. Measures of employee satisfaction and loyalty.
Management and leadership	Value created by management and leadership. Development of firm capabilities. Durability of management strategy.	Percentage flow of human capital in and out of the organisation.	Employee perceptions of management.

Source: This material is taken from *Human capital: external reporting framework* by CIPD, 2003, with the permission of the publisher, the Chartered Institute of Personnel and Development, London.

Regardless of which measurement approach is employed, the results of these evaluations must be communicated by appropriate means to the appropriate stakeholders so that the organisation can determine whether to (1) take steps to change the practices that are preventing the achievement of its objectives or (2) accelerate their change efforts, or (3) maintain the status quo.

Review

In this chapter, we sought to explore the use of HRM policies and practices as levers to generate, implement and sustain individual and organisational change. We noted that the HRM function has evolved over the past decade from an administrative and operational role to one that has developed much more of a strategic orientation. Simultaneous, with this development has been the devolution of responsibility for organisational change, through the exercise of people management across the organisation. The human resource function, the human resource specialist, senior and line management all must carry specific responsibilities for aspects of the change process.

We explored the importance of the interactive relationship between corporate and business strategy, change strategy and HRM strategy and planning, investigating a number of theoretical models (while recognising that there are multiple perspectives) on HRM. We noted that HRM strategy often needs to be fluid to address organisation strategies that may emerge from contingencies and a changing external environment.

We delved further to explore the means by which various human resource practices can operate as specific mechanisms to generate change. We saw how the first of these practices, job design and analysis, supports organisational restructuring and human resource planning, and includes the establishment of appropriate job designs to represent new work arrangements. We examined methods of influencing cultural change efforts by recruiting and selecting employees who will fit the organisation's changing needs and adding to its capability, and comparing the various uses, benefits and downside of internal and external recruitment as change tools. The use of downsizing as a directional strategy also was explored and noted the lessons from the research on the importance of leadership, planning, communication and management of the downsizing process. These lessons we saw, help to make sure that respect for the rights of all individuals involved, both those who are exiting the organisation and those who remain, are addressed and maintained, to manage resistance and maintain morale, high levels of motivation and job satisfaction; and to assist the achievement of the desired organisational outcomes.

The organisation must determine the core human capabilities that it requires, including the skills, knowledge, attitudes and values that support the new directions of the business. It is then required to formulate and implement appropriately designed education, training and development initiatives; strategies for succession planning, including managing and developing careers; and encourage and reinforce a culture of organisational learning to develop capabilities for its present and future needs.

Managing individual performance is a critical tool in delivering an organisation's change strategy. We noted the widespread movement towards the use of holistic performance management systems and examined the key steps in the process. To be effective, performance management requires both the appraiser and appraisee to have input into the performance appraisal and review processes. We remarked that new approaches that use feedback from a number of sources — for example, 360-degree feedback — are gaining popularity. Some writers recommend, however, that these approaches should be used guardedly, that is, for development purposes and not as a mechanism for administering rewards.

We explored the notion that rewards are one of the most important change levers that organisations can employ. We examined various ways in which reward management strategies can be used to attract and retain employees, and to measure, reinforce and motivate the desired values, attitudes and behaviours, and outcomes to generate and sustain change. We discussed the growing use of performance-based reward systems across many industry sectors.

Finally, we raised the issue of the need to measure and evaluate the whole range of human resource initiatives as change interventions. We looked at traditional HR measures and a number of newer approaches including benchmarking, HR scorecards, and human capital management and noted the need to communicate the results to ensure the change effort delivers its objectives.

Key terms

360-degree feedback (or appraisal). The process of obtaining feedback from multiple sources, such as subordinates, peers, supervisors, customers and the employees themselves, (p. 209)

administrative expert. The traditional human resource role, which is concerned with designing and delivering human resource processes efficiently while maintaining quality, (p. 189)

change agent. The role of helping the organisation build a capacity for change, (p. 189)

competencies. The behaviour patterns that an employee must have to perform their tasks and functions with competence. These are set as the criteria against which applicants can be measured and assessed. (p. 186)

core competencies. The capacity of a firm's human resources to perform its key tasks or activities, (p. 184)

downsizing. The reduction of workforce numbers to improve the organisation's bottom line, (p. 200)

employee benefits. Elements of rewards given in addition to various forms of cash pay — for example, child-care facilities or a health club membership, (p. 212)

employee champion. The role of dealing with the day-to-day problems, concerns and needs of individual employees, and representing these concerns to management. It includes helping to increase the employee's commitment to the organisation and their ability to deliver results. (p. 189)

human capital. The sum of the employees' knowledge, skills, and abilities and encompasses capabilities not directly related to task performance, including experiences and social skills, as well as values, beliefs, and attitudes, (p. 190)

human resource development. The broad set of activities concerned with the organisation's investment in learning and improving the performance of its human resources as a whole. It includes education, training and development, as well as career management and planning, and organisational learning. (p. 185)

job analysis. The process of recording and describing the purpose, characteristics and duties of a given job. The results are used for a variety of human resource activities. (p. 195)

job design. The structuring of the specific content, methods and relationships in a job to ensure it satisfies its role and function within the organisation, (p. 195)

organisational learning. A process whereby the organisation and its employees continually learn and apply what they have learned to improve the way in which the organisation functions, (p. 202)

performance appraisal. The assessment of an individual's past performance, usually against set objectives, and the setting of future performance objectives. It may include the identification of development or training needs, and the determination of rewards or bonuses. (p. 208)

performance management systems. The process (or set of processes) designed to manage the performance of the individual, the group and the organisation against objectives. It includes the development of competencies that support the organisational strategy, and of recognition and rewards that are linked to critical behaviours and competencies (for example, teamwork and information sharing) as well as outputs. (p. 182)

performance-related pay. Financial reward linked to individual, team, business unit or company performance. It also can be pay for particular skills and competencies, measured by the achievement of goals and objectives set through performance management systems, (p. 212)

reward management systems. Systems designed to manage all forms of remuneration and non-financial benefits that employees receive as part of an employment relationship, (p. 211)

strategic human resource management. The design and implementation of internally consistent policies and practices, which are aligned with the organisation's strategy, to ensure employees contribute to the achievement of business objectives, (p. 182)

strategic partner. The role of aligning the organisation's HR strategies and practices with business strategy and its execution, (p. 189)

systematic change. A long-term strategy requiring considerable human and financial commitment. It includes widespread organisational cultural change, right down to the levels of values and attitudes, (p. 200)

workforce reduction. A short-term directional strategy aimed at cutting the number of employees through transfers, attrition, early retirement or voluntary severance packages, lay-offs and terminations, (p. 200)

work redesign. A medium-term strategy aimed at reducing the work through changes to work design and processes, rather than cutting the number of employees, (p. 200)

Review questions

1. Briefly describe the multiple HRM roles that help to facilitate organisational change. Why are these dispersed across the organisation?
2. What overlap is evident across the models posited by Kochan and Barocci, Schuler and Jackson, and Miles and Snow? How do they differ in approach?
3. Why is effective job analysis and job design central to most organisational change efforts?
4. What organisational knowledge is required by those who are responsible for staffing the organisation (recruitment, selection and downsizing) to meet its change goals?
5. Why is HRD a key component of most organisational change efforts?
6. How do performance management and reward systems operate to leverage change in employee behaviour?
7. Why is it necessary to measure the contribution human resource activities make to any organisational change effort?

Discussion question

Why is it necessary to adopt a strategic approach to HRM when an organisation is changing its strategic orientation?

Work assignments

HRM and change at Holden

1. Using the facts of the 'Opening case: HRM and change at Holden' (page 180), identify the internal and external forces for organisational change at Holden. What forces were operating to constrain change?
2. Using the facts of the Holden case as a basis for your decision, try to identify the type of generic strategies being adopted.
3. From your identification of the change in strategic orientation, comment on the appropriateness of the use of the human resource policies and practices that were employed to leverage that change. To what extent do you think these are aligned with the organisation's strategic intentions?
4. What measures were put in place to evaluate the success of the change effort?

HRM and change at an organisation you know

1. Using one of the strategic choice models, examine the links between your own organisation's global strategies, business strategies and the HRM strategies. To what extent are these integrated?
2. Demonstrate how initiatives in the following human resource activities (where relevant) have contributed to organisational change.
   (a) job analysis and design
   (b) recruitment and selection
   (c) downsizing
   (d) training and development
   (e) performance appraisal
   (f) reward management.
3. Identify the measures that your organisation uses to evaluate the contribution of human resource initiatives to the effective implementation of its organisational change agenda.

Suggested further reading

Armstrong, M. & Baron, A. 2002, *Strategic HRM The Key to Improved Business Performance*, Chartered Institute of Personnel and Development, UK.

Becker, B. E., Huselid, M. A. & Ulrich, D. 2001, *The HR Scorecard: Linking People, Strategy and Performance*, Harvard Business School Press, Boston, Massachusetts.

Lawler III, E. E. & Mohrman, S. A. 2003, 'HR as a strategic partner: what does it take to make it happen?' *Human Resource Planning*; 26(3), pp. 15–29.

Lengnick-Hall, M.L. & Lengnick-Hall, C.A. 2002, *Human Resource Management in the Knowledge Economy: New Challenges, New Roles, New Capabilities*, Berrett-Koehler, San Francisco, CA.

Purcell, J. 2003, 'Inside the black box', *People Management*, May 15, pp. 30–33.

Ulrich, D. & Smallwood, N. 2004, 'Capitalizing on capabilities', *Harvard Business Review*, June, pp. 119–27.

End notes

1. See, for example, B. Becker & B. Gerhart 1996, 'The impact of human resource management on organizational performance: progress and prospects', *The Academy of Management Journal*, August, pp. 779–801; C. Mabey, G. Salaman & J. Storey 1998a, *Human Resource Management: A Strategic Introduction*, Blackwell, Oxford; B. E. Becker, M. A. Huselid, P. S. Pickus & M. F. Spratt 1997, 'HR as a source of shareholder value: research and recommendations', *Human Resource Management*, Spring, pp. 39–47; M. A. Huselid, S. E. Jackson & R. S. Schuler 1997, 'Technical and strategic human management effectiveness as determinants of firm performance', *The Academy Of Management Journal*, 40(1), pp. 171–88.

2. M. Huselid 1995, 'The impact of human resource management practices on turnover, productivity and corporate financial performance', in 1998b *Strategic Human Resource Management: A Reader*, eds C. Mabey, G. Salaman & J. Storey, Blackwell, Oxford, pp. 128–43. For a discussion on the positive associations between the use of high-involvement work practices and employee retention and firm productivity,

see J. P. Guthrie 2001, 'High-involvement work practices, turnover and productivity: evidence from New Zealand', *The Academy of Management Journal*, 44(1), pp. 180–91.

3. M. Armstrong & A. Baron 2002, *Strategic HRM The Key to Improved Business Performance*, Chartered Institute of Personnel and Development, UK, p. 3.

4. ibid., p. 42.

5. D.E. Guest 1997, 'Human resource management and performance: a review and research agenda', *The International Journal of Human Resource Management*, 8(3), June, pp. 263–76; K. Legge 1995, *Human Resource Management, Rhetorics and Realities*, Macmillan, Basingstoke.

6. Legge, op. cit.

7. Guest 1997, op. cit., p. 270.

8. See Mabey, Salaman & Storey 1998a, op. cit.; P. Boxall & J. Purcell 2000, 'Strategic human resource management: where have we come from and where should we be going?' *International Journal of Management Reviews*, 2(2), p. 185.

9. Mabey, Salaman & Storey 1998a, op. cit., p. 74.

10. J. Barney 1991, 'Firm resources and sustained competitive advantage', *Journal of Management*, 17(1), pp. 99–120.

11. C. Hendry & A. Pettigrew 1986, 'The practice of strategic human resource management', *Personnel Review*, 15(5), pp. 3–8; A. Pettigrew & R. Whipp 1993, *Managing Change for Competitive Success*, Blackwell, Oxford; K. Kamoche 1996, 'Strategic human resource management within a resource-capability view of the firm', *Journal of Management Studies*, pp. 213–31; C. K. Prahalad & G. Hamel 1990, 'The core competences of the corporation', *Harvard Business Review*, May–June, pp. 79–91.

12. D. Collis & C. Montgomery 1995, 'Competing on resources: strategy in the 1990s', *Harvard Business Review*, July–August, pp. 119–28.

13. ibid., pp. 119–20.

14. ibid.

15. Barney, 1991, op. cit; P. Boxall & Purcell, J. 2003, *Strategy and Human Resource Management*, Palgrave Macmillan, Houndsmills, Hampshire.

16. C. K. Prahalad 1998, presentation at a Harvard Change Colloquium, 'Breaking the code of change', Boston, August, cited in D. Stace & D. Dunphy 2001, *Beyond the Boundaries: Leading and Recreating the Successful Enterprise*, 2nd edn, McGraw-Hill, Sydney, pp. 63–4.

17. L. Gratton, V. Hope-Hailey, P. Stiles & C. Truss (eds) 1999, *Strategic Human Resource Management: Corporate Rhetoric and Human Reality*, Oxford University Press, Oxford, pp. 172–3. See also J. Balogun & V. Hope-Hailey 1999, *Exploring Strategic Change*, Prentice Hall, Hertfordshire, United Kingdom, p. 197.

18. Gratton et al., op. cit., p. 173.

19. For a thorough discussion of strategic HRM and the various models and their limitations, see Boxall & Purcell, 2003 op. cit.; J. Bratton & J. Gold 2003, *Human Resource Management: Theory and Practice*, 3rd edn, Palgrave, Macmillan Houndsmills; T. A. Kochan & T. A. Barocci 1985, *Human Resource Management and Industrial Relations*, Little Brown, Boston, Massachusetts; Mabey, Salaman & Storey 1998a, op. cit., p. 65.

20. Kochan & Barocci, op. cit.

21. J. Cherrington 2004, 'ANTA adds HR experience', *HRMonthly*, September, pp. 44–5.

22. N. Nairn 1999, 'Training by degree', *HRMonthly*, May, pp. 40–3. This included a strategic alliance with Deakin University to deliver some of the undergraduate and postgraduate programs.

23. Cherrington, op. cit.

24. R. S. Schuler & S. E. Jackson 1987, 'Linking competitive strategies with human resource management practices', *The Academy of Management Executive*, 1(3), pp. 207–19.

25. M. E. Porter 1995, *Competitive Advantage*, Free Press, New York.

26. Schuler & Jackson 1987, op. cit., pp. 209–13; R. R. Collins 1987, 'The strategic contributions of the human resource function', *Human Resource Management*, 25(3), pp. 5–20.

27. Schuler & Jackson 1987, op. cit., p. 211.

28. Collins 1987, op. cit.

29. Schuler & Jackson 1987, op. cit., p. 216.

30. R. Miles & C. Snow 1984, 'Designing strategic human resource systems', *Organizational Dynamics*, Summer, pp. 36–52.

31. S. Wood & M.T. Albanese 1995, 'Can we speak of a high commitment management on the shop floor?', *Journal of Management Studies*, March, 32 (2), pp. 215–247.

32. Huselid 1995, op. cit.

33. G. Betcherman 1997, 'Changing workplace strategies: achieving better outcomes for enterprises, workers and society', Government of Canada and OECD, Ottawa; Guthrie, 2001, op. cit.; Huselid, 1995, op. cit.; E. E. Lawler 1992, *The Ultimate Advantage: Creating the High Involvement Organization*, Jossey-Bass, San Francisco; J. A. Neal, C. L. Tromley, E. Lopez & J. Russell 1995, 'From incremental change to retrofit: Creating high performance', *The Academy of Management Executive*, 9(1), pp. 42–51.

34. Mabey, Salaman & Storey 1998a, op. cit., pp. 408–9.

35. D. Ulrich 1998, 'A new mandate for human resources', *Harvard Business Review*, January–February, pp. 125–34; D. Dunphy & D. Stace 1990, *Under New Management: Australian Organisations in Transition*, McGraw-Hill, Sydney; J. Storey 1992, *Developments in the Management of Human Resources*, Blackwell, Oxford; C. Fisher & P. Dowling 1999, 'Support for an HR approach in Australia: the perspective of senior HR managers', *Asia Pacific Journal of Human Resources*, 37(1) pp. 1–19.

36. See, for example, J. Purcell 2004, 'The HRM-performance link: why, how and when does people management impact on organisational performance', John Lovett Memorial Lecture, University of Limerick, www.bath.ac.uk/werc/publications; Ulrich 1998, op. cit.; Dunphy & Stace, op. cit., pp. 178–99; W. G. Dyer 1999, 'Training HR champions for the twenty-first century', *Human Resource Management*, 38, pp. 119–24; Fisher & Dowling, op. cit.

37. Ulrich D. 1997, *Human Resource Champions: The Next Agenda for Adding Value and Delivering Results*, Harvard Business School Press, Boston, Massachusetts.

38. Dunphy & Stace, op. cit., pp. 178–99.

39. B. E. Becker, M. A. Huselid & D. Ulrich 2001, *The HR Scorecard: Linking People, Strategy and Performance*, Harvard Business School Press, Boston, Massachusetts, pp. 158–74.

40. M. L. Lengnick-Hall & C. A. Lengnick-Hall 2002, *Human resource management in the knowledge economy: new challenges, new roles, new capabilities*, Berrett-Koehler, San Francisco, CA.

41. Becker, Huselid & Ulrich op. cit.; E. E. Lawler & S. A. Mohrman 2000, *Creating a Strategic Human Resources Organization*, Center for Effective Organizations, Los Angeles.

42. A. Travaglione & V. Marshall 2000, *Human Resource Strategies: An Applied Approach*, McGraw-Hill, Sydney, pp. 165–6.

43. Lengnick-Hall & Lengnick-Hall, op. cit.

44. C. Fisher & P. Dowling, op. cit.; Becker, Huselid & Ulrich, op. cit.; R. Kramar 1999, 'Policies for managing people in Australia: what has changed in the 1990s?', *Asia Pacific Journal of Human Resources*, 37(2), pp. 24–31; E. E. Lawler III & S. A. Mohrman, 2003, 'HR as a strategic partner: what does it take to make it happen?', *Human Resource Planning*, 26(3), pp. 15–29.

45. Donaldson, 2004 op. cit.

46. Lawler III & Mohrman, op. cit.

47. C. Donaldson 2003, 'Top Australian boards snub HR', *Human Resources*, September 10, 40, pp. 1, 9.

48. ibid.

49. S. J. Wells 2003, 'From HR to the top', *HR Magazine*, Alexandria, USA, June, 48 (6), p. 46.

50. Lawler III & Mohrman, op. cit.

51. Anonymous 2003, 'On line recruitment — Coles Myer', *HRMonthly*, December, p. 38.

52. D. E. Guest 1987, 'Human resource management and industrial relations', *Journal of Management Studies*, 24(5), pp. 503–21; See Purcell, 2004, op. cit for a model outlining the key elements in this process.

53. J. Purcell 2003, 'Inside the black box', *People Management*, May 15, pp. 30–3.

54. ibid., p. 33.

55. D. Stace & D. Dunphy 2001, *Beyond the Boundaries: Leading and Recreating the Successful Enterprise*, 2nd edn, McGraw-Hill, Sydney, pp. 224–31.

56. ibid.

57. ibid., p. 229. For a detailed discussion of change leadership types, see Stace & Dunphy 2001, op. cit., pp. 164–94; chapter 7.

58. Donaldson 2004, op. cit.

59. D. Hughes 2004a, 'NAB maps out cultural revolution', *The Age*, 21 August, John Fairfax Holdings Limited.

60. D. Hughes 2004b, 'New directors for NAB', *The Age*, 14 August, John Fairfax Holdings Limited.

61. D. Buchanan, T. Claydon & M. Doyle 1999, 'Organization development and change: the legacy of the nineties', *Human Resource Management Journal*, 9(2), pp. 20–37.

62. D. Ulrich and N. Smallwood 2004, 'Capitalizing on Capabilities', *Harvard Business Review,* June, pp. 119–127.

63. P. McGovern 1999, 'HRM policies and management practices', in *Strategic Human Resource Management: Corporate Rhetoric and Human Reality,* eds L. Gratton, V. Hope-Hailey, P. Stiles & C. Truss 1999, Oxford University Press, Oxford, pp. 133–52.

64. T. Kochan, 2004, 'Restoring Trust in the Human Resource Management Profession', *Asia Pacific Journal of Human Resources,* 42(2), pp. 132–146.

65. G. Johnson & K. Scholes 1999, *Exploring Corporate Strategy,* 5th edn, Prentice Hall, London.

66. Mabey, Salaman & Storey 1998a, op. cit., p. 234.

67. D. Hughes 2004a, op. cit.

68. D. A. Buchanan 1994, 'Principles and practices of work design', in *Personnel Management: A Comprehensive Guide to Theory and Practice in Britain,* ed. K. Sisson, Blackwell Business, Cambridge, Massachusetts, p. 100.

69. L. E. Davis 1996, 'The design of jobs', *Industrial Relations,* 6(1) pp. 21–45. For an excellent discussion of a range of job design approaches, see Buchanan, op. cit.

70. D. Holman, C. Clegg and P. Waterson 2002, 'Navigating the territory of job design', *Applied Ergonomics,* May, pp. 197–205. These authors present a detailed review of job design from three perspectives: functionalism, interpretivism and critical theory.

71. F. P. Morgeson, M. A. Campion 2002, '*Minimizing tradeoffs when redesigning work: evidence from a longitudinal quasi experiment', Personnel Psychology* Autumn, 55(3), pp. 589–612.

72. E. E. Lawler III 1994, 'From *job-based* to *competency-based* organizations, *Journal of Organizational Behavior,* January 15(1), pp. 3–15. See also R. Boyatzis 1982, *The Competent Manager,* John Wiley & Sons, New York; G. Roberts 1997, *Recruitment and Selection: A Competency Approach,* Institute of Personnel and Development, London (for examples of lists of competencies).

73. J. W. Walker 1992, *Human Resource Strategy,* McGraw-Hill International Edition, Singapore, p. 9.

74. L. Maund 2001, *An Introduction to Human Resource Management: Theory and Practice,* Palgrave, Hampshire, p. 171.

75. D. A. Nadler & M. B. Nadler 1998, *Champions of Change: How CEOs and their Companies Are Mastering the Skills of Radical Change,* Jossey-Bass, San Francisco, p. 245.

76. J. A. Chatman 1991, 'Matching people and organizations: selection and socialising in public accounting firms', *Administrative Science Quarterly,* 36, pp. 459–84; A. Lawrence 1998, 'Individual–organisational value congruence in human resource practitioners', in *Management Theory and Practice: Moving to a New Era,* ed. G. Griffen, Macmillan, Melbourne, pp. 158–74; R. K. Lester 1998, *The Productive Edge: How US Industries Are Pointing the Way to a New Era of Economic Growth,* W. W. Norton & Company, New York, p. 244.

77. R. D. Bretz & T. A. Judge 1994, 'Person organization fit and the theory of work adjustment: implications for satisfaction, tenure and career success', *Journal of Vocational Behavior,* 44(1), pp. 32–54.

78. P. Karathanos, D. M. Pettypool & M. D. Troutt 1994, 'Sudden lost meaning: a catastrophe?', *Management Decision,* 32, pp. 15–19.

79. Chatman, op. cit.; Lawrence, op. cit.

80. Nadler & Nadler, op. cit., p. 247.

81. H. Bahrami 1998, 'The emerging flexible organisation', in 1998b, *Strategic Human Resource Management: A Reader,* eds C. Mabey, G. Salaman & J. Storey, Blackwell, Oxford, p. 187.

82. Long, C. 2004, 'Casually speaking', *The Sydney Morning Herald,* 14 August.

83. L. Rolland 2004, 'Rock of Ages', *HRMonthly,* April, pp. 28–9.

84. Franklin, R., personal communication, November, 2004.

85. Australian Government Equal Opportunity for Women in the Workplace Agency, EEWA BAA Winner 2003 Case Study: Autoliv, pp. 1–3, www.eowa.gov.au/Case_Studies

86. C. Rance 2004, 'Does Diversity Pay?' *HRMonthly,* April, pp. 20–6.

87. Hatton, A. 2004, *The Aging Population: Implications for the Australian Workforce. Report by Hudson Australasia,* cited in 'Age discrimination the new sexism', *Human Resources,* 63, 25 August, pp. 1, 9.

88. P. Vincent 2004, 'Age shall not weary them', *Sydney Morning Herald,* 28 August, John Fairfax Holdings Ltd.

89. K. Cameron 1994a, 'Strategies for successful organizational downsizing', *Human Resource Management*, 33, pp. 189–211; F. Gandolfi & P. A. Neck 2003, 'Organisational downsizing: a review of the background, its developments and current status', *Australasian Journal of Business and Social Inquiry*, 1(1) November, pp. 16–29.

90. Gandolfi & Neck, op. cit.

91. W. Cascio 2003, cited in Picket, L., 'Cutbacks threaten innovation', *HRMonthly*, February, pp. 14–15, 19.

92. R. D. Iverson & J. A. Pullman 2000, 'Determinants of voluntary turnover and layoffs in an environment of repeated downsizing following a merger: an event history analysis', *Journal of Management*, 26(5), pp. 977–1004.

93. C. R. Littler, R. Dunford, T. Bramble & A. Hede 1997, 'The dynamics of downsizing in Australia and New Zealand', *Asia Pacific Journal of Human Resources*, 35(1), pp. 65–82.

94. P. Dawkins, C. R. Littler, M. R. Valenzuela & B. Jensen 1999, 'The contours of restructuring and downsizing in Australia', Melbourne Institute of Applied Economics and Social Research, University of Melbourne, Melbourne.

95. Australian Bureau of Statistics 1998, *Retrenchment and Redundancy, Australia*, cat. no. 6266.0, AGPS, Canberra.

96. P. Dawkins and C.R. Littler 2001, 'Downsizing? Is it working for Australia?', Published by the Melbourne Institute in association with CEDA and The Myer Foundation, July.

97. K. Cameron 1994a, 'Strategies for successful organizational downsizing', *Human Resource Management*, 33, pp. 189–211.

98. T. H. Wagar 1998, 'Exploring the consequences of workforce reduction', *Canadian Journal of Administrative Sciences*, 15(4), pp. 300–9.

99. S. H. Appelbaum, A. Everard & L. T. S. Hung 1999, 'Strategic downsizing: critical success factors', *Management Decision*, 37(7), pp. 535–52; K. Cameron 1994b, 'Investigating organizational downsizing: fundamental issues', *Human Resource Management*, 33, pp. 183–8; W. Cascio 1994, 'Downsizing? What do we know? What have we learned?', *Personnel Review*, 23(4), p. 53; Dawkins & Littler, op. cit.

100. D. Dougherty & E. H. Bowman 1995, 'The effects of organizational downsizing on product innovation', *California Management Review*, 37(4), pp. 28–44; S. J. Freeman 1994, 'Organizational downsizing as convergence or reorientation: implications for human resource management', *Human Resource Management*, 33(2), pp. 213–38; Cameron 1994a, op. cit.

101. Cascio, 1994 op. cit.

102. Cameron 1994a, op. cit.

103. A. Mabert & R. W. Schmenner 1997, 'Assessing the roller coaster of downsizing', *Business Horizons*, 40(4), p. 46.

104. W. McKinley, C. M. Sanchez & A. G. Schick 1995, 'Organizational downsizing: constraining, cloning, learning', *The Academy of Management Executive*, 9(3), pp. 32–43.

105. P. Osterman 2000, 'Work reorganization in an era of restructuring: trends in diffusion and effects on employee welfare', *Industrial & Labor Relations Review*, 3(2), p. 188.

106. Mabert & Schmenner, op. cit.

107. F. Lamb 2003, 'Communicating the big picture', *HRMonthly*, July, pp. 37, 39.

108. B. Speedy 2004, 'Digital death for Kodak plant', *The Australian*, 17 September.

109. ibid.; K. P. De Meuse, P. A. Vanderheiden & T. J. Bergmann 1994, 'Announced layoffs: their effect on corporate financial performance', *Human Resource Management*, 33(4), pp. 509–30.

110. Cascio cited in Picket, 2003, op. cit.

111. M. Armstrong 2000, *Strategic Human Resource Management: A guide to action*. Kogan Page, London.

112. R. Harrison 1997, *Employee Development*, Institute of Personnel and Development, London, p. 7.

113. C. Mabey & P. Iles 1993, 'The strategic integration of assessment and development practices: succession planning and new manager development', *Human Resource Management Journal*, 3(4), pp. 16–34, cited in Thornhill, A., Lewis, P., Millmore, M. & Saunders, M. 2000, *Managing Change: A Human Resource Strategy Approach*, Pearson Education Limited, Harlow, UK, p. 163.

114. Nairn, op. cit.

115. ibid., p. 45.

116. S. Faulkner 2004, 'Reuters: the inside story', *HRMonthly*, September, pp. 34–5.

117. A. P. de Geus 1988, 'Planning as learning', *Harvard Business Review*, March–April, pp. 70–4; A. P. de Geus 1997, 'The living company', *Harvard Business Review*, 75(2), pp. 51–9; P. M. Senge 1993, 'Transforming the practice of management', *Human Resource Development Quarterly*, 4(1), pp. 5–32.

118. M. Pedlar, J. Burgoyne & T. Boydell, 1991, *The Learning Company*, McGraw-Hill, Maidenhead.

119. L.K. Lim & C.A. Chan 2004, 'Development and application of an organisational learning matrix', *International Journal of Management* 21(1), pp. 100–7. This article provides a useful review of some of the other models of organisational learning.

120. C. Argyris & D. Schön 1978, *Organizational learning: A theory of action perspective*, Addison, Reading, MA. See also C. Argyris 1995, 'Action science and organizational learning', *Journal of Managerial Psychology*, 10(6), 20–6; C. M. Fiol & M.A. Lyles 1985, 'Organizational learning', *Academy of Management Review*, 10(4), 803–13; J. Swieringa & A. Wierdsma 1992, *Becoming a Learning Organization: Beyond the Learning Curve*, Addison-Wesley Publishing Co., Wokingham; G. Probst & B. Buchel 1997, *Organisational Learning: the competitive advantage for the future*. Prentice Hall Europe, Hemel Hempstead; P.M. Senge 1992, *The Fifth Discipline: The Art and Practice of the Learning Organization*, Random House, Milsons Point, NSW.

121. P. M. Senge 1994, 'Learning to alter mental models', *Executive Excellence*, 11(3), pp. 16–17.

122. T. G. Cummings & C. G. Worley, 1997, *Organization Development and Change,* 6th edn, South Western College Publishing, Cincinnati, p. 503. There are many different approaches to organisational learning and few organisations can be seen to conform to any specific organisation model. In addition, questions have been raised about its sustainability. See J. Woodall & D. Winstanley 1998, *Management Development: Strategy and Practice*, Blackwell Business, Oxford.

123. Pettigrew & Whipp, op. cit., p. 238.

124. R. Beckhard & W. Pritchard 1992, *Changing the Essence: The Art of Creating and Leading Fundamental Change in Organizations*, Jossey-Bass, San Francisco, pp. 22–3; O. Lundy & A. Cowling 1996, *Strategic Human Resource Management*, Routledge, London; Mabey, Salaman & Storey 1998a, op. cit., p. 308; Pettigrew & Whipp 1993, op. cit.; P.M. Senge 1999, 'Creative tension', *Executive Excellence*, 16(1), pp. 12–13; J. Storey & K. Sisson 1993, *Managing Human Resources and Industrial Relations*, Open University Press, Buckingham; Thornhill et al, op. cit., p. 173. The message behind many of these elements as change levers is unitarist and that there would be incongruity of values. In such circumstances, learning may occur but not necessarily in a way that furthers the strategic goals of the enterprise.

125. H. Silins & B. Mulford 2002, 'Schools as learning organisations: the case for system, teacher and student learning', *Journal of Educational Administration*, 40 (4/5), pp. 425–46.

126. ibid., p. 442.

127. Thornhill et al, op. cit., p. 173; Storey & Sisson 1993, op.cit.

128. Thornhill et al, op. cit., p. 175.

129. S. H. Appelbaum, D. Hebert & S. Leroux. 1999, 'Empowerment: power, culture and leadership — a strategy or fad for the millennium', *Journal of Workplace Learning*, 11(7), pp. 233–54; L. Ellinor & G. Gerard 1998, *Dialogue: Rediscover the Transforming Power of Conversation*, John Wiley & Sons, New York, NY; M. R. Fairholm & G. Fairholm 2000, 'Leadership amid the constraints of trust', *Leadership & Organization Development Journal*, 21(2), pp. 102–9; I. Palmer & C. Hardy 2000, 'Managing organizational learning: has the time come or gone?', *Thinking About Management*, Sage Publications, London, pp. 197–227. See R. W. Cooksey 2003, '"Learnership" in complex organisational textures', *Leadership & Organization Development Journal*, 24 (4), pp. 204–13, for an in-depth discussion of the notions of leadership and learnership in the context of organisational learning.

130. Palmer & Hardy, op. cit.; E. Shapiro 1995, *Fad Surfing in the Boardroom: Reclaiming the Courage to Manage in the Age of Instant Answers*, Harper Collins, Sydney, cited in Cooksey, op. cit.

131. B. Burnes, C. Cooper & P. West 2003, 'Organisational learning: the new management paradigm?', *Management Decision*, London, 41(5/6), pp. 452–64; S. Henderson 1997, 'Black Swans do not fly double loop: the limits of the learning organization', *The Learning Organization*, 4(3), 99–105; A. Mumford 1998, 'Managing learning and developing management', *Human Resource Development International: Enhancing Performance, Learning and Integrity*, 1(1), 113–18; Thornhill et al, op. cit., p. 175.

132. Ulrich 1998, op. cit.; A. Lawrence & F. Graetz 1999, 'The HRD practitioner's role as a change agent', in *Human Resource Development: Roles, Perceptions and Practice Choices*, ed. F. Sofo, Woodslane, Warriewood, New South Wales, pp. 93–111.

133. Armstrong, 2000, op. cit., p. 214.

134. D. McDonald & A. Smith 1995, 'A proven connection: performance management and business results', *Compensation and Benefits Review*, 27, pp. 59–64.

135. B. Townley 1989, 'Selection and appraisal: reconstituting "social relations"', in *New Perspectives on Human Resource Management*, ed. J. Storey, Routledge, London.

136. A. Saunier & M. Mavis 1998, 'Fixing a broken system', *HR Focus*, March, pp. 1–4.

137. Mabey, Salaman & Storey 1998a, op. cit., pp. 126–7; M. Armstrong 1994, *Human Resource Management*, Kogan Page, London, p. 162.

138. G. Anderson 1996, 'Performance appraisal', in *The Handbook of Human Resource Management*, 2nd edn, ed. B. Towers, Blackwood Publishers, London, p. 198.

139. E. Locke, R. Shaw, L. Saari & G. Latham 1981, 'Goal setting and task performance: 1969–1980', *Psychological Bulletin*, 97, pp. 125–52.

140. Cummings & Worley, op. cit., p. 380; Locke et al., op. cit., pp. 125–52.

141. D. McGregor 1957, 'An uneasy look at performance appraisal', *Harvard Business Review*, 35, pp. 89–94: Bratton & Gold, op. cit., p. 270.

142. H. H. Meyer 1991, 'A solution to the performance appraisal feedback enigma', *The Academy of Management Executive*, 5, pp. 68–76.

143. J. Purcell 2004, 'The HRM-performance link: why, how and when does people management impact on organisational performance', John Lovett Memorial Lecture, University of Limerick, www.bath.ac.uk/werc/publications

144. Townley, op. cit.; T. Newton & P. Findlay, 1998, 'Playing god: the performance appraisal', in eds C. Mabey, G. Salaman & J. Storey, *Strategic Human Resource Management: A Reader*. 1998b, pp. 128–43.

145. Harrison, op. cit., p. 234; Townley, op. cit.

146. A. O' Keefe & P. Douglas 2004, 'Basic instinct', *HRMonthly*, February, pp. 38–40.

147. R. Lepsinger & A. D. Lucia 1997, *The Art and Science of 360 Degree Feedback*, Jossey-Bass, San Francisco.

148. R. Wood, J. Allen, T. Pillinger & N. Kohn 2000, '360 degree feedback: theory, research and practice', in *Human Resource Strategies: An Applied Approach*, eds A. Travaglione & V. Marshall, McGraw-Hill, Sydney, p. 214.

149. S. Kearney 2004, 'Leading by example', *HRMonthly*, February, pp. 30–1.

150. Wood et al, op. cit.

151. T. N. Garavan, M. Morley & M. Flynn 1997, '360 degree feedback: its role in employee development', *Journal of Management Development*, 16(2) pp. 134–47. For a discussion of the methodological issues, see Wood et al., op. cit., pp. 209–30.

152. A. R. Nankervis & P. Leece 1997, 'Performance appraisal: two steps forward, one step back?', *Asia Pacific Journal of Human Resources*, 35(2), p. 83.

153. Cummings & Worley, op. cit., p. 370.

154. R. Rudman 1995, *Performance Planning and Review: Making Performance Appraisals Work*, Pearson Professional, Melbourne, Australia, p. 173.

155. Locke et al., op. cit.

156. V. Vroom 1964, *Work and Motivation*, John Wiley & Sons, New York. For a discussion of the application of these motivation theories and the core issues that must be addressed in designing a performance management system, see Mabey, Salaman & Storey 1998a, op. cit., pp. 125–52.

157. A. Bowey, R. Thorpe, F. Mitchell, G. Nicholls, D. Gosnold, L. Savery & P. Hellier 1982, 'Effects of incentive payments systems, United Kingdom 1977–80',

Research Paper no. 36, Department of Employment, London, p. 32.

158. Lockyer, op. cit., pp. 283–305.

159. I. Kessler 1994, 'Performance pay', in *Personnel Management: A Comprehensive Guide to Theory and Practice in Britain*, 2nd edn, ed. K. Sisson, Blackwell Business, Cambridge, Massachusetts, p. 466. See also J. Storey & K. Sisson 1998b, 'Performance related pay', in *Strategic Human Resource Management: A Reader*, eds. C. Mabey, G. Salaman & J. Storey, Blackwell, Oxford, pp. 144–51.

160. Kessler, op. cit., pp. 476–81; Bowey et al., op. cit.

161. M. De La Salle & J. Ashworth 2001, 'Climate change — handling hot skills', *HRMonthly*, March, p. 44.

162. ibid.

163. E. Schein 1992, *Organizational Culture and Leadership*, 2nd edn, Jossey-Bass, San Francisco.

164. A. Kohler 2004, 'Department stores are not extinct: Fletcher', *Inside Business*, ABC TV, September, p. 26.

165. D. Hughes 2004, 'NAB maps out cultural revolution', *The Age*, 21 August. John Fairfax Holdings Limited; A. Kohler 2004, 'NAB announces star signings', *Inside Business*, ABC TV, August 15.

166. Kessler, op. cit., p. 478.

167. Australian Government Equal Opportunity for Women in the Workplace Agency, EEWA BAA Winner 2003 Case Study: Autoliv, pp. 1–3. www.eowa.gov.au/Case_Studies/.

168. F. Tyndall 2003, 'Sorry about the bonus, here's a picture of the boss', *Australian Financial Review*, December 20.

169. ibid.

170. J. & J. Gold 2003, *Human Resource Management Theory and Practice*, 3rd edn, Palgrave Macmillan, Houndsmills, Hampshire.

171. Becker, Huselid, Ulrich, op. cit.; R.S. Kaplan & D.P. Norton 1996, *The Balanced Scorecard: Translating Strategy into Action*, Harvard Business School Press, Boston, Massachusetts.

172. N. Bontis, N.C. Dragonetti, K. Jacobsen & G. Roos 1999, 'The knowledge toolbox: a review of the tools available to measure and manage intangible resources', *European Management Journal*, 17(4), pp. 391–402.

173. Anonymous 2003, 'Building a human capital strategy' *Strategic HR Review*, May/June 2(4), pp. 12–16.

174. See for example metrics proposed by B. N. Pfau & S. A. Cohen 2003, 'Aligning human capital practices and employee behavior with shareholder value', *Consulting Psychology Journal*, 55(3) pp. June 1; J. Fitz-enz 2001, 'Four steps to find the impact of human capital' *Corporate University Review*; March/April 9(2), pp. 23–4.

175. D. Brown & A. Baron, 'A capital idea', 2003, *People Management*, June 26, (9)13, pp. 42–5.

176. ibid., p. 42. See pp. 44–5 of this article for the range of metrics of each of the five criteria.

7 LEADERSHIP FOR CHANGE

'What kind of business leader do we want and need to run the 21st century organisation?' This was one of the key questions considered by a panel convened to discuss contemporary leadership issues and review nominees for the *AFR BOSS* 2004 True Leaders List. Criteria used to assess 'true leaders' were 'success in business and in organisation, an ability to inspire and nurture staff, and an interest in meeting community needs'. It seems the heroic or charismatic leader model is well and truly passé, with the need for a more realistic and human leadership style and a focus on social responsibility. The sorts of qualities the panellists saw as hallmarks of great leaders include:

- the ability to rally people behind clearly and simply defined goals
- acting as guardians of the organisation's culture — able to explain its core values
- the ability to make connections with people inside and outside the organisation
- self-awareness, emotional control and empathy towards their people
- passion and personal investment in the job
- recognition that senior management does not have the monopoly on good ideas
- ability to see people as the 'precious commodity', the core of the organisation.

Profile 1

Michael Hawker, CEO, Insurance Australia Group, thinks that management structure doesn't matter so long as an organisation's values are constant and upheld, and communication is clear and open. Efficiency is therefore critical. 'It breeds responsibility, accountability, focus and competitiveness, which should ensure the long-term future of the company and, most important, the jobs of the people within it.' Experience has also taught him that a CEO needs to concentrate on the big picture and avoid getting bogged down in the detail.

Profile 2

Theresa Gattung, CEO, Telecom New Zealand, says she is very open about her mistakes and vulnerabilities. She believes this non-defensive approach has worked well in encouraging and accepting feedback among her predominantly male senior management team. For Gattung, leadership is about authenticity and character. She believes that the leaders who gain the respect of their followers are true to themselves. They are 'passionate about what they are doing, communicating that in a heartfelt way that touches hearts. If you pretend to be something you are not, it is very hard to convey that depth of character that marks leadership as successful over a period of time.'

Profile 3

Robert Franklin, CEO, Autoliv Australia, a car restraint manufacturer, believes passionately in nurturing a diverse and flexible workforce. When he joined Autoliv Australia, it contained all the hallmarks of a traditional manufacturing business. By redesigning training programs, introducing new promotion criteria and workplace practices aimed at improving work–life balance and fostering diversity, the achievements of the company's female workers and those from a range of ethnic backgrounds became more widely recognised and rewarded. His core values are 'about fundamental issues of fairness — behaving ethically and honestly, treating people as you expect to be treated and recognising that we are all different. We should encourage and enjoy that.'

Profile 4

For Tony Howarth, Chairman of Alinta, a rapidly expanding national energy corporation, the key attributes to strong leadership and effective management are financial literacy; the ability to invest in people; trust, integrity; commonsense and empathy. Financial literacy is important because it enables senior management to understand the financial drivers of the industry they are operating in. Leadership is also about 'having vision, being able to engender confidence and bring others with you in an environment of loyalty and trust'. Critical to this approach is recognising that people are the backbone of the business and investing in them.

Sources: Adapted from Catherine Fox 2004, 'Just keep it simple, keep it real', *AFR BOSS*, 5(8), pp. 52–3; James Hall 2004, 'Our Top 25 Leaders: Profiles', *AFR BOSS*, 5(8), pp. 58–70; Majella Corrigan 2004, 'Tony Howarth's Alinta Formula: invest in staff', *Management Today*, October, pp. 6–11. See also end-of-book case 2 'Autloliv Australia'.

Introduction

Against a backdrop of increasing globalisation, deregulation, the rapid pace of technological innovation, shifting social and demographic trends, and the growing knowledge workforce, few would dispute that the primary task of management today is the leadership of organisational change.[1] Key words in the lexicon of the newly emerging organisational model include 'novelty', 'quality', 'flexibility', 'adaptability', 'speed' and 'experimentation'. In view of these requirements, the traditional organisational structure, with its hierarchical, top–down approach, centralised control and historically entrenched values of stability and security, is an anachronism. As we saw in chapter 5, the impetus now is towards flatter, more 'flexible and agile organisational forms'[2] in which the boundaries are 'fluid and permeable'.[3] Management is recognising the need to dismantle the traditional barriers between different business areas, encourage cross-functional information sharing and involve able employees at all levels of the organisation in the planning and decision-making processes.

These changes have triggered a radical shift in the role of senior managers from the traditional authoritarian (often remote) command-and-control style to a more open, participative management style. With the emphasis now on cooperation, collaboration and communication, as illustrated in the 'Opening case' profiles, managers need to hone a completely different range of leadership skills. Traditionally, as presaged by the classical themes of planning, directing and controlling, managers focused on the technical or operational dimension of management — for example, budgeting, increasing efficiency, and improving quality and productivity. To be effective leaders in an environment of change and flux, however, an interpersonal dimension, which underpins a strategic focus, becomes critical. [4]

Within this framework of organisational flux and renewal, this chapter explores the differences between managing and leading, and why understanding these differences is relevant to the change process. It then seeks to investigate the various dimensions of change leadership, which include: the function of leadership; the different change leadership roles; and the key characteristics, skills and attributes required for leading change effectively. The final section considers the importance of adopting different leadership styles and approaches over time as changing circumstances impact on the type of change required.

Managing versus leading

There has been considerable debate in the literature over the difference between leadership and management. Are they mutually exclusive or can they be complementary? To lead means to show the way, to influence or guide others. [5] It conjures up the image of someone who is willing to go first and steer followers into uncharted territory, even someone who is willing to do things differently and challenge the status quo. The verb 'to manage' stems from the Latin word *manus*, meaning 'hand'. It is about exercising control or domination over others. These definitions suggest that the critical difference between managing and leading is 'the difference between what it means to handle things and what it means to go places'. [6] The managerial mindset is concerned with rationality and control, focusing on problem solving and getting things done as efficiently and effectively as possible. While managers seek to limit options and risk-taking, leaders actively seek out novel ideas and approaches to issues. [7] According to Zaleznik, managing doesn't require genius or heroism, but 'persistence, toughmindedness, hard work, intelligence, analytical ability, and perhaps most important, tolerance and goodwill'. [8] Generally, the understanding is that leaders 'do the right things' while managers 'do things right':

> [W]hen you think about doing things right, you think about control mechanisms. You think about how-to. Leaders ask the what and why question, not the how question. Leaders think about empowerment, not control. And the best definition of empowerment is that you don't steal responsibility from people. [9]

At Coca Cola Amatil (CCA), for example, CEO Terry Davis, is a strong advocate of leadership as empowerment rather than control. For Davis, leadership is about constantly challenging the status quo and thinking constantly about 'what are we doing wrong?' rather than 'what we do right'. He is more concerned about 'creating passion' and providing a vision of where the business is headed and what it can become. This attitude has been instrumental in encouraging a culture of continuous improvement down to the smallest level of detail at CCA.[10] (See 'Change management in action' case 'Setting the direction at Coca-Cola Amatil', page 242.)

Does this mean *managing* should be abandoned in favour of *leading*? Kotter argues that while management and leadership are obviously different and require particular skills and attributes, we should not adopt one over the other. Rather, he argues, 'leadership and management are two distinctive and complementary systems of action. Each has its own function and characteristic activities. Both are necessary for success in an increasingly complex and volatile business environment.'[11] The findings of the Australian Business Leadership Survey[12] suggest that Australian business managers clearly understand the distinction between leading and managing. They defined management as being concerned with day-to-day operations; maintaining efficient and effective systems and procedures; and overseeing financial management and ongoing monitoring of the workplace. Leadership was defined as both a strategic and people-related activity that required creating a vision for the business; setting the direction; motivating people; ensuring the professional development of workers; and leading by example.

Today's increasingly complex and unpredictable environment suggests that success will come only to those organisations that are capable of continually reinventing themselves, of anticipating and responding to challenges on all fronts. This responsiveness requires a significant shift in management focus from operational to strategic issues that inevitably involve coping with change. Figure 7.1 outlines Kotter's analysis of the shift from operational tasks to leading change.

Management	Leadership
Planning and budgeting	**Establishing direction**
Establishing detailed steps and timetables for achieving needed results and then allocating the resources necessary to make them happen	Developing a vision of the future, often the distant future, and strategies for producing the changes needed
Organising and staffing	**Aligning people**
Establishing some structure for accomplishing plan requirements, staffing the structure with individuals, delegating responsibility and authority for carrying out the plan, providing policies and procedures to help guide people, and creating methods or systems to monitor implementation	Communicating the direction by words and deeds to all those whose cooperation may be needed, so as to influence the creation of teams and coalitions that understand the vision and strategies, and accept their validity
Controlling and problem-solving	**Motivating and inspiring**
Monitoring results versus planning in some detail, identifying deviations, and then planning and organising to solve these problems	Energising people to overcome major political, bureaucratic and resource barriers to change by satisfying very basic, but often unfulfilled, human needs
Produces a degree of predictability and order, and has the potential to produce consistently the key results expected by various stakeholders (for example, always being on time for customers; always being within budget for stockholders).	**Produces change,** often to a dramatic degree, and has the potential to produce extremely useful change (for example, new products that customers want; new approaches to labour relations that help make a firm more competitive).

FIGURE 7.1: Comparing management and leadership roles

Source: Extract from p. 155 of *Beyond the Boundaries: Leading and Recreating the Successful Enterprise,* 2nd edn by D. Dunphy et al., © McGraw-Hill Australia. Adapted with the permission of The Free Press, a division of Simon & Schuster Adult Publishing Group, from *A Force for Change: How Leadership Differs from Management* by John P. Kotter, Inc. All rights reserved.

As we can see from Kotter's summary of the role of leadership compared with management (figure 7.1), the management approach views an organisation like a machine whose smooth running depends on establishing tight controls, detailed planning and streamlined procedures to ensure stability and uniformity. On the other hand, the corresponding leadership functions reveal a very different way of working. Instead of planning and budgeting, for example, leadership is more concerned with developing a vision and setting a direction for the future. Flexibility and adaptability are key modes of the leadership approach, so as to align people, build commitment and be responsive to changes in the environment.

Kotter's leadership model suggests that strong interpersonal skills — not technical and analytical know-how — are a key contributing factor to effective change leadership. Bennis also argues that in the post-bureaucratic organisation a new and very different kind of relationship is required between leaders and followers, involving a far more subtle and indirect form of influence based on cooperation and inclusion.[13] Goleman states that while effective leaders differ in many ways, the one quality that distinguishes outstanding leaders from also-rans is a high degree of emotional intelligence.[14] The definitions and hallmarks of the five components of emotional intelligence identified by Goleman represent a range of interpersonal skills that delineate the ability to work with others.

- *Self-awareness* comes from a clear and realistic understanding of oneself — one's strengths, weaknesses, ambitions and needs. Self-aware people are honest with themselves and with others and, as a result, their opinions are respected and sought.
- *Self-regulation* implies self-control, where a person is in charge of their emotions and does not act on impulse, but considers a situation calmly and logically before taking action.
- *Motivation* refers to the drive to achieve and seems to be one trait that all effective leaders possess. Highly motivated people are motivated by intrinsic rather than extrinsic factors. They exude a passion and enthusiasm for their work, and have high expectations of themselves and others.
- *Empathy* does not imply a desire to please everyone and be seen as the popular 'Mr Nice Guy'. Rather, it refers to the ability to consider and acknowledge employees' needs and opinions, and weigh these against other relevant factors before making sensible decisions. Goleman suggests that empathy is particularly important in light of the increasing use of cross-functional, team-based work groups, globalisation and the need to develop and retain talented people.[15]
- *Social skill*, along with empathy, refers to a person's ability to relate to, and work effectively with, other people. Leaders with a high degree of social skill develop a strong rapport with their employees. They know what makes them tick and, consequently, how to motivate them. Goleman describes social skill as 'friendliness with a purpose: moving people in the direction you desire'.[16]

These issues are analysed further in the following section, which looks at the various dimensions of the leadership function.

Dimensions of leadership

In this section, we discuss three dimensions of leadership in the context of change within an organisation: function, role and attributes.

The leadership function

The notion that 'leadership and management are two distinctive and complementary systems of action'[17] suggests that the key to leading change is learning how to balance and conciliate what appear to be conflicting dilemmas. It is about finding a balance between continuity and change, short- and long-term actions, accountability and freedom, and planning and flexibility.[18] These contingencies reflect the conciliating behaviour and actions required to fulfil the 14 guiding principles (discussed in chapter 2) for leading and managing organisations in an environment characterised by flux and uncertainty. As noted in chapter 2, to reconcile these paradoxes requires a systemic, 'big picture' approach to leading change (see also the 'Opening case' profiles (page 228) where different leaders express a similar view).[19] Change leaders need to view the organisation as a complex and dynamic system of interdependent parts that influence and impinge on each other. Mant argues that 'the *sine qua non* of leadership lies in the capacity to change and shift systems', which itself depends on a person's capacity to exercise good judgement.[20] In his view, successful leaders have **'broadband' intelligence**, with capabilities 'across the entire repertoire of multiple intelligences' coupled with a capacity for systems thinking (see end note 21 for further explanation of multiple intelligences).[21] This versatility is reflected in their work, through the connections it allows them to make; and in their ability to relate to and understand all kinds of people. People with 'broadband' intelligence are able to draw on one, all, or combinations, of these intelligences as the situation demands. Mant gives the example of Bob Clifford, boat builder extraordinaire, who founded Incat (International Catamarans). He not only knew how to build and work on continuously improving the speed and design of his catamaran ferries, he also recognised the need to look beyond the technical side and understand something about the behaviour and thinking of passengers and ferry operators. In addition, he also made the connection that rather than concentrating simply on design, he could create value and possibly a niche market by focusing on the logistics of construction, and thus become a leader in this newly emerging field.[22]

Intelligent leaders, drawing on their broadband versatility and their systems thinking capability, recognise that an organisation is more than just a sum of its parts, and that the involvement and engagement of the human component is crucial to building commitment to the change process.[23] Leaders of **systemic change** must practise 'the art of inclusion'.[24] This means breaking down the traditional barriers between functional areas, involving able employees at all levels of the organisation in the planning and decision-making processes, and encouraging the cross-fertilisation and sharing of ideas among different business areas.[25] Leaders help others to look to the future in a holistic manner. They motivate the rest of the organisation and help it grow. Leaders create the opportunities for the future of the organisation.

With the emphasis now on consultation, cooperation and collaboration and a participative, open management style, what is happening to the traditional notions of power and authority vested in leaders? Boulding identifies three sources of personal power:
- *authority* power, as in the power of threat or 'power over'
- *economic* power, as in the power to exchange or 'power to'
- *integrative* power, as in inclusive, accepting or 'power with'.[26]

Integrative power represents ultimate power because it is inclusive; it involves and energises others to action. This approach does not mean that leaders do not or should not exercise authority power (for example, acting responsibly and authoritatively on behalf of an organisation as its leader and figurehead is very different from self-interested **authoritarianism**); rather, leaders should appreciate the need to blend these powers according to the situational context.[27] It may be difficult, however, for many senior business leaders to break the habits of a lifetime (especially those who have relied heavily on authority power to dominate and control), because their position and status would now seem vulnerable. It is not that authority and control are no longer impor-tant, or that what senior managers do has changed significantly. Rather, the change must be in the way in which senior managers perform their tasks, their behaviours and their actions, and the beliefs and values that underpin them.[28] The proactive, context-based style of leadership that is now required reinforces the view that the traditional management model with its reliance on coercion and control, and its rigid adherence to rules and regulations is more likely to hamper an organisation's ability to move forward. Freas, Goldsmith and Lyons suggest that 'corporate success is now intimately related to the way in which individual executives think, act, and interact on a daily basis. They must now do the right thing, not simply the written thing. It is not enough to take prob-lems to others and await a response. The competition will not stand back and wait'.[29]

The leader profiles documented in the 'Opening case' reinforce the view that the tra-ditional management metaphor is no longer enough. Leadership for change is about inspiring rather than directing; partnering and involving rather than dividing and con-trolling; and encouraging diversity and challenging conventional wisdom, rather than conforming to the status quo. Above all, it is about engaging people's trust and commit-ment by recognising their contribution and communicating honestly, openly and often. The concepts of trust, openness, equity and fairness are common themes running through the different 'Perspectives' and cases presented in this chapter. In other chap-ters, we have also noted that a trust-based culture defines the essence and values of the learning organisation and is critical to its success because reciprocated trust encourages a collective identity that facilitates the transfer and diffusion of knowledge across busi-ness units (see, for example, chapter 3).

As highlighted by the comparison between management and leadership roles in figure 7.1 (page 231), to be effective and credible, senior managers must shift their focus from managing operational tasks (planning and budgeting, organising and staffing, and con-trolling and problem-solving) to confronting the challenges involved in leading change (setting a direction and articulating a compelling vision, and aligning, motivating and inspiring people). As leaders rather than managers, personal attributes and abilities — not position and status — will be the foundation of their power source. In chapter 6, we argue that if senior human resource professionals are to add value in an increasingly complex and dynamic environment, then they need to fulfil the four key roles of strategic partner, administrative expert, employee champion and change agent. Successful execu-tion of these multiple roles demands a range of complex skills and high emotional intelligence. Leadership therefore is not about abdicating power and control, but about recognising that 'increasingly leadership will be about gaining more responsibility and power by delegating more responsibility and power'.[30] As this description suggests, empowerment involves valuing and trusting people; it does not imply abandonment. The core values and operations of high-performing organisations are premised on a profound belief and trust in the individual. In these organisations, focus, direction and excellence in performance are achieved 'by embedding a sense of discipline in the ongoing routines and the everyday behaviours of individuals'.[31] Similarly, Collins argues that good-to-great organisations are built on a culture of discipline, which gives people both freedom and responsibility within a consistent and clearly defined framework. Collins observes that the good-to-great companies in his study 'hired self-disciplined people who didn't need to be managed, and then managed the system, not the people'.[32] Boulding notes that while authority in the guise of threat power is more likely to succeed when it is combined with integrative power, the irony is that 'threat often destroys integrative power and hence destroys its own power'.[33] The implication here is that a leader who relies on threat as a means of control may initially gain compliance, but the resulting alienation, cynicism and distrust will slowly erode the leader's credibility and authority, and thus their major source of influence and power.

These points appear to support the view that to win over and sustain commitment to the change process, leading change must be as a 'reciprocal' rather than 'one-way relationship' — one that encourages two-way learning and development.[34] To move from an autocratic, telling style to an integrative, involving approach clearly requires leaders endowed with high emotional intelligence (particularly self-awareness, empathy and social skills) who are able to build rapport and communicate and relate easily with others. Professor John Sarros from Monash University, who led the Australian Business Leadership Survey (ABLS) referred to earlier, identified *flexibility* (being open-minded, adaptable, alert to change, able to delegate); *professional development* (open to new experiences and learning); *a people-oriented* focus (involving, including, facilitating); *forward thinking* (ongoing liaison and communication with markets, businesses and governments, identifying core competences, managing information and strategic planning); and *open communication* (disseminating information honestly and freely, fostering teamwork, listening and talking to staff), as fundamental leadership strategies for confronting the challenges of today's business environment.[35]

The results of a global succession management company survey reveal a vacuum in leadership training and development in Australian companies at the middle management level, a cause for serious concern given the importance of identifying and nurturing a company's future business leaders. According to the survey, conducted by Development Dimensions International, Australia's middle managers lack the basic skills required to take on senior leadership positions in their organisations. The study included 140 human resources managers in Australia, New Zealand and the Asia–Pacific at companies with at least 500 staff. Survey results for this region showed only 14.5 per cent of respondents felt confident about the leadership skills of middle managers, compared to 43 per cent in a global survey. Nearly 75 per cent of Australian respondents believed that leadership training and development for Australian middle managers was totally inadequate, yet their responsibilities had multiplied over the last five years.[36]

The need to include succession planning as a key item on an organisation's strategic planning agenda is debated further in the later 'Perspectives' case on succession planning in Australia (page 239).

Who leads whom?

The dominant themes in the change literature tend to emphasise that transformational change will not occur without strong leadership and know-how from the top.[37] More importantly, leadership at the top must be 'personalised', because it provides the 'soft glue' — a sense of shared values and purpose — that holds the organisational community together.[38] Handy argues

> The glue is a sense of common identity, linked to a common purpose and fed by an infectious energy and urgency. Mere words cannot create this glue; it has to be lived.[39]

The need for strong, personal leadership from the top that provides a clear overarching vision and focus seems particularly critical as organisations discard their traditional, hierarchical organisational structures in favour of leaner, flatter, boundary-less forms comprising smaller, autonomous networking units.[40] The autonomy and elasticity implicit in the design and working relationships of these 'organisations without walls' mean the line between **loosely coupled** and **decoupled** is easily overstepped.[41] Organisations most successful in managing the dynamics of loose–tight working relationships meld strong 'personalised' leadership at the top with 'distributed' leadership. Distributed leadership is represented by a group of influential, experienced and trusted individuals in both formal and informal positions of authority operating at different levels of the organisation.[42] Pearce also points to the changing role of leaders with the shift to team-based knowledge work. This shift, he argues, is a result of top-down pressures (an increasingly competitive, global environment) and bottom-up pressures (the changing expectations and nature of the workforce). In this environment, the traditional 'vertical' leadership model with one person firmly in charge is no longer appropriate. Pearce argues that 'as the complexity of knowledge work increases, the need for shared leadership also increases'.[43] In an increasingly complex and fluid business environment, one person alone cannot consider and resolve the myriad routine and complex issues that must be dealt with each day.[44] The days when all the answers could be made at the top are gone and 'must now give way to integrated thinking and acting at all levels'.[45]

In the 'Opening case' (page 228), we noted the key criteria used by the judging panel for the *AFR BOSS* 2004 True Leaders List. These criteria would appear to support the view that 'broadband' and systems thinking capabilities are prerequisites for today's business leaders. The importance of these capabilities is reflected in the different leader profiles outlined in the 'Opening case'. They emphasise inclusiveness and openness; authenticity and character; devolving responsibility and accountability; honest two-way communication; trust and integrity. These 'true leaders' recognise above all that people are the core of the business and thereby demonstrate their capacity to balance personalised leadership with distributed leadership. Similarly, the 'Perspectives' case on succession planning in Australia highlights the need to ensure enabling systems and processes are in place to 'institutionalise leadership behaviour down the line'.[46] The investment in leadership training and development at all levels of the organisation by the companies profiled here indicate that when a company believes that 'leadership must be plural and systemic', very different possibilities and opportunities become available.[47]

Change leaders therefore must work hard to 'breed a team of disciples'[48] who, as champions of the cause, will ensure the vision cascades down through the organisation. Kotter (as noted in chapter 2) found that companies successful in this regard actively sought to develop leadership qualities in young employees.[49] Senior executives in these companies observed that the process of decentralising to smaller business units itself devolved responsibility to less senior staff and created a more challenging work environment. As the leader profiles in the 'Opening case' and the different perspectives on succession planning in Australia suggest, the way forwards is clearly through the use of integrated power, rather than authority or economic power.

John Sculley, former chief executive officer of Apple Computers and Pepsi, explains that the most effective chief executive officers believe in the 'beehive principle', or 'swarm theory', where the hive is smarter than any individual bee: 'The best CEOs are the ones who realise they don't have all the answers ... The worst CEOs are poor listeners who talk out to people with one-way communication'. He believes that being a good mentor requires functional competencies and the ability to work with a team.[50] Sculley's views on the role of leadership align with the findings of Pasternack, Williams and Anderson. Drawing on the results of a survey and interviews they conducted with thousands of executives as part of the World Economic Forum's Strategic Leadership Project, Pasternack, Williams and Anderson concluded that 'successful leadership need not be a solo act ... Rather than an aria, leadership can be a chorus of diverse voices singing in unison'.[51] If, however, leadership is to become 'everyone's business'[52], then the focus of leadership must shift from the individual to the institution.[53] Pasternack, Williams and Anderson express concern with the cult of the charismatic chief executive officer that pervades the media, with organisations being portrayed as 'reflections of the personalities who head them'[54] rather than of the management systems, practices and culture that underpin their success. They point out that behind many personalised corporate success stories is a strong decentralised leadership model in which key leadership tasks are grounded in organisational systems, practices and cultures.[55] Jack Welch, General Electric's (GE) legendary boss and often portrayed as the classic charismatic leader, worked to build a strong leadership cadre throughout the company, to ensure the company's continuing evolution and growth on his retirement after 20 years at the helm. Without a strong succession planning process in place, companies often stumble when a strong leader departs and leaves behind a leadership vacuum. This point is echoed in some of the leaders' comments reported in the 'Perspectives' case on succession planning in Australian companies. From his early days as chief executive officer in the 1980s, Welch demonstrated that he clearly understood the importance of succession planning and leadership development. When interviewed in 1993, Welch commented that while CEO succession was still a long way off, he thought about it every day.[56] Over the years, he showed a remarkable ability for recognising talent, and actively encouraged and supported promising managers. The priority placed on management training programs is seen as one of the key factors for GE's phenomenal success. John Sidgmore, a former manager at GE who later became Vice-Chairman of WorldCom, claims he honed his leadership skills at GE: 'It is a great place to work. You learn to manage people and evaluate them. The culture of running all these superfit businesses within one company creates leaders.'[57]

It is worth looking briefly at the succession planning process at GE. The search for a new chief executive officer at GE began well before Jack Welch stepped down in September 2001. Over a seven-year period, dozens of GE managers were interviewed. After a thorough investigation of their achievements with the company, which included interviewing colleagues for their opinions, the list of candidates was reduced to six. These six finalists were then assigned demanding new jobs within the company and underwent another round of tough tests. The group was whittled down to three, who were appointed vice-chairmen and given two more years to prove their leadership calibre. At the end of the two-year stint as vice-chairmen, each candidate had to submit an assessment of his performance. In November 2000, Jeffrey Immelt, who began his career with GE in 1982, was named as Welch's successor, almost a year before Welch retired from the position he had held for over 20 years.[58]

Noel Tichy, a professor of organisation at the University of Michigan, co-authored the book *Control Your Destiny or Someone Else Will*, which documents the first ten years of Welch's tenure as chief executive officer at GE. He commented when interviewed in September 2000 that Welch, in planning for his successor, did not try to clone himself: 'It needs someone who can take a fresh look at GE and architect GE for tomorrow. It is not going to be the Jack Welch era any more'.[59] The key to effective succession planning is a future orientation, being able to look forward and anticipate the sorts of skills and expertise that will be needed in three to five years, not just the present, and putting in place a system of 'capability development'.[60] The 'Perspectives' case on succession planning in Australian companies suggests there is increasing awareness of the importance of implementing management training programs to help identify, support and encourage talented employees at all levels of the organisation, not just at executive level.

Succession planning responsibility: the role of leaders

The three perspectives that follow (see the 'Perspectives' box) provide some insight into the views of senior leaders on the value of succession planning in relation to their company. They point to the importance of implementing management training programs to help identify, support and encourage talented employees. Greg Martin, Chief Executive of AGL, believes that increasingly companies are beginning 'to think about people, performance and succession as strategically important issues for long-term success'.[61] This approach means identifying people with talent and potential within a company and creating opportunities for them to learn and develop. Martin believes that the tendency to 'pick winners' is a high-risk strategy. Karen Morley, of the Melbourne Business School agrees. Her research showed that some organisations worked on the assumption that 'you simply picked a few people who might go into senior positions later'.[62] The problem here is that as organisations and the environments in which they operate undergo change, different leadership styles are required, not simply clones of yesterday's CEO. General Electric (GE), for example, recognised that the company needed a successor who would 'architect GE for tomorrow', not simply follow in Welch's footsteps. Similarly, the profile below on Wesfarmers (perspective 3) notes positively that Chaney's successor will bring a different leadership style to the top job. Key factors for effective succession planning that emerge from the different perspectives presented below are: starting the process early; ensuring that succession planning is built into the company's strategic planning process; promoting and grooming potential from *within* the company; and implementing management training programs to help identify, support and encourage talented employees throughout the organisation, not just at senior level.

PERSPECTIVES — Succession planning in Australian companies

Perspective 1

Julian Tertini, Managing Director, Fantastic Holdings, believes that companies are failing in their duty if they do not take a long-term view to develop leadership from within. If a company has a strong and healthy corporate culture, the danger of bringing in a star from outside the organisation is that they are likely to want to put their stamp on the organisation. His aim is to appoint from within the company's own body of highly competent people who understand and are deeply committed to the business and know where it is going. Neither does he see company leadership as restricted to the chief executive. Leaders are needed in many different parts of the organisation and if appointments are made from within, it gives people something to strive for.

Source: Adapted from Andrew Heathcote 2004, 'A good succession plan', *BRW*, 19–25 August, p. 66.

Perspective 2

Soheil Abedian, Joint Managing Director, Sunland Group, says his company is very focused on succession planning and has made it one of its priorities. Sunland believes in promoting from within its own ranks and expends considerable resources in training and encouraging its own people. As we saw at Fantastic Holdings, Sunland would never contemplate head-hunting a person from another culture for a senior position in the company. Because of the specialised operations of the company, which is structured around segmented areas of land, housing, hotels and high-rise developments, Abedian views the accumulated knowledge and expertise of Sunland's own people as critical to Sunland's success as it is these factors that differentiate it from other property companies, which cannot be bought or hired from outside the company.

Source: Adapted from Andrew Heathcote 2004, 'A good succession plan', *BRW*, 19–25 August, p. 66.

Perspective 3

Michael Chaney, CEO of Wesfarmers for 12 years and named on the *AFR BOSS* True Leaders List for four years in a row, stepped down from the job in July 2005. Richard Goyder, a senior colleague at Wesfarmers, had been named as his successor. The succession planning process gets underway early at Wesfarmers. The company conducts regular 'best practice conferences' where 'emerging talent' is given the opportunity to talk to senior management about challenges confronting the company. By 'dovetailing' leadership development with succession planning in this way, the company is able to track and nurture a number of talented people coming up through the organisation. The search for Chaney's successor began in earnest in May 2000 at the company's annual planning conference, of which two days are always devoted to succession planning. A group of potential successors, including Goyder, were shortlisted for the top job. From this point, it was seen as critical to keep the shortlisted group within the company and ensure healthy competition between them. According to Chaney, any of his senior colleagues could run Wesfarmers, thanks to the company's 'ingrained and gradual succession planning' that ensures a successor who will bring a new perspective and fresh ideas, and is not simply a leadership clone.

Source: Adapted from James Hall 2004, 'Michael Chaney, CEO, Wesfarmers', *AFR BOSS*, 5(8), p. 63.

Critical change leadership roles

While there is no single recipe for success, what emerges as the principal, immutable ingredient is the need for strong leaders who perform a number of critical roles. These roles include:

- energising and mobilising the workforce into a state of readiness for change
- envisioning the future ideal and defining the direction in a way that appeals to, and inspires, all stakeholders on a personal level
- demonstrating personal commitment and involvement by consistently and relentlessly communicating and modelling the new behaviours
- providing enabling systems and structures that will sustain the momentum for change.[63]

These key components of change leadership are explained and examined in the following sections against the actions taken by business leaders in different organisations, some of which we have profiled through this chapter.

Energising and instilling a readiness for change

A perusal of the change literature makes it clear that senior leaders, before they can begin the complex task of implementing organisation-wide change, need to create a sense of urgency, or a felt need for change, to gain employees' support and commitment. As mentioned before, leaders at the top need to start with a 'big picture' approach that involves an analysis of the organisation's strengths and weakness against trends in its external environment. This diagnostic process allows people to see what is wrong with the organisation and helps to stimulate unrest and dissatisfaction with the status quo.[64] The problem for many organisations is that success tends to generate complacency and consequently danger signals on the organisation's periphery are either dismissed or ignored. To make change tangible and real, leaders must link the change process 'to key business processes and performance measures'.[65] (See also chapter 3 for discussion on the importance of developing an organisation's peripheral vision.) Effective strategies for creating a sense of urgency are to seek outside opinion and to benchmark against successful companies. Reger et al. suggest that taking a closer look at the competition can be a particularly potent energiser if current business operations seem to be running satisfactorily and there appears to be no apparent reason for change.[66] This closer look at the competition often serves to highlight the seriousness of the situation to the workforce, or at least the gap between where the organisation is currently and where it could be. By explaining the change process to staff members at all levels of the organisation, highlighting both the opportunities and challenges that exist and, in particular, involving them in deciding on and implementing the mechanisms for change, they are less likely to resist or block the new ways of working.[67]

The change literature also notes that the appointment of a new leader provides a powerful catalyst for change. For example, a major research study of the Fortune 1000 in 1986 found that strategic redirection, when it occurred, was preceded by leadership change (specifically, an outsider replacing an insider).[68] This new blood, not burdened by the old values, beliefs and attitudes, brings new energy and vision, which are essential ingredients to initiating and executing change. The National Australia Bank (NAB), for example, appointed John Stewart in February 2004 as its new CEO. Originally with the NAB in Europe, Stewart has the formidable task of turning around public perceptions, and winning back consumer and shareholder confidence in NAB Australia, severely damaged after the foreign exchange scandal. Stewart believes that if the Bank's problems are to be resolved, the Bank's bureaucratic top–down culture, which has bred arrogance and mismanagement, must first change. He has moved swiftly and decisively to show this is no mere rhetoric, instigating a number of sweeping changes in the short time since his appointment in February 2004. By October 2004, he had replaced 80 per cent of the senior executive, there was a 70 per cent turnover among the Board of Directors, and a new charter of values was in place.[69]

Creating a vision and setting the direction

A primary role of change leadership is to inspire a **shared vision**. Jackson[70] argues that as more and more companies devolve decision-making, which simultaneously removes several layers of management and increases the span of control and responsibility, shared visions and values become increasingly important to ensure a committed and involved workforce. A vision is necessary to give meaning and structure to the change efforts. It provides a focus and a sense of direction, which, while offering a challenge, must be realistic and acceptable to the majority of the workforce. In addition, for the majority of stakeholders to commit to this vision, it is critical that as many as possible have had meaningful input into its substance. Kotter points to under-communication of the vision by a factor of 10 (or 100 or even 1000) and permitting obstacles to block the new vision as two key factors that lead to the derailment of change efforts.[71] 'Blockers' might come in the guise of people, or emanate from new or existing organisational systems and structures that do nothing to recognise or reward the new ways of working. To help change the culture at NAB, for example, John Stewart recognised that he needed a supportive team of executives who shared his vision and would live by the new charter of values. In addition, the existing autocratic, command and control bureaucracy, with its attendant silos and rivalries, clearly posed a threat to major culture change. To remove this impediment, NAB has restructured its core domestic operations (retail banking, wealth management, corporate and institutional lending) into one division. The new charter of values, the reformed team of senior executives, and the structural changes instigated at NAB all indicate that Stewart has recognised and removed major roadblocks to culture change and set the direction and purpose for change.

Leadership commitment and involvement

The involvement of senior management is seen as fundamental to the success of the transformation process. It is their role to define the direction, set performance goals and gain the support of other key stakeholders who, as champions of the cause, will promote and sustain the change agenda and help cascade the vision down through the organisation.[72] The last point underlines the recurring theme that one all-powerful individual, no matter how *charismatic* his or her personality, cannot sustain effective change leadership. On the contrary, successful change leaders recognise that leadership must be everyone's business and work hard to inspire others with their honesty, enthusiasm and personal commitment.[73]

Terry Davis, Managing Director of Coca-Cola Amatil (see 'Change management in action' case, 'Setting the direction at Coca-Cola Amatil'), underlines the pivotal role that top management plays in providing a vision that acts as a road map for the way forward and gives purpose and meaning to the change agenda. Davis actively created a 'passion' and climate for change by bringing in key new senior people committed to his vision, introducing new remuneration incentives to reward high performers, and setting clear, transparent targets aimed at growing the business. He recognised there was hitherto untapped talent in the workforce which he sought to challenge and energise through his vision and the support of key people brought into the organisation (his powerful guiding coalition) to help him cascade the message across and down through the organisation.[74]

Communication by top management is a powerful lever in gaining commitment and building consensus to required change. Successful implementation occurs in companies where executives 'walk the talk', teaching new behaviours by example.[75] In our various profiles on the views and leadership styles of different leaders, the ability to 'make connections' with people inside and outside the organisation emerges as pivotal to business success. These leaders refer to the need for a more open and inclusive leadership style in which honest and open communication plays a major role, helping to build trust and engender enthusiasm and confidence.

Communication, therefore, is about informing and involving people at all levels of the organisation in the change process, and providing access to meaningful information about company performance. As Jackson points out, if continuous improvement is the key to competitive success, then people need access to data that will help them plan improvements.[76] At Coca-Cola Amatil, for example, Davis has pursued a more innovative and performance-oriented approach, instilling a passion for excellence in customer service; setting clear financial targets; and expecting his people to take a 'multi-disciplinary' approach by sharing information and expertise across functional business units.

CHANGE MANAGEMENT IN ACTION
Setting the direction at Coca-Cola Amatil

When Terry Davis became Managing Director of Coca-Cola Amatil (CCA) in December 2001, he set down a number of challenging financial targets, which he expected the business to meet over the first three years of his tenure. It was a take-no-prisoners strategy that gave focus and direction to organisation members. The unequivocal message Davis conveyed to organisation members was that unless they lifted their game poor performers had no future with CCA.

While CCA was seen as a brand leader, Davis quickly discovered that the company was not achieving a satisfactory return on capital. Davis believed CCA needed to take immediate steps to look for opportunities to grow its business much more aggressively. He found that there were skills gaps at senior management level which he filled by bringing in new blood from outside the organisation, people with no stake in CCA's past who would help him implement his vision to grow the company.

Two years after his appointment as Managing Director, CCA Amatil's ongoing businesses recorded total profit growth of 39 per cent and an improvement of 34 per cent in return on capital employed. At the end of June 2004, the company recorded its fifth consecutive half-year double-digit earnings growth, increasing its net profit by 16.6 per cent to $127.7 million.

According to Davis, there are many highly able and talented people in the company who just needed to be 'energised'. A strong believer in linking remuneration to shareholder performance, he scrapped the existing option schemes and replaced them with a share scheme. He introduced public financial targets aimed at improving return on capital and linked senior executive remuneration with shareholder returns. Davis has worked tirelessly to encourage product innovation and growth, instilling a more performance-oriented approach with a strong customer-first focus. Processes and facilities have been radically streamlined allowing more people to be 'on the ground and in the field' getting close to the customer and understanding their needs. Consequently, corporate headquarters has been halved and now works primarily as a value-adding centre that different parts of the business can call on for specialist advice and expertise. In his view, the company needed to become 'more relevant to our customers, not just our consumers'. In his first year as Managing Director, CCA introduced Vanilla Coke to the Australian market, the first new flavour in 18 years. The company has since launched another 28 new products and also expanded into the non-carbonated beverage sector.

As leader, Davis emphasises the importance of direct, face-to-face communication, which encourages openness, transparency and honesty. He conducts yearly performance reviews with the top 50 people in the company outlining his expectations and listening to their views and issues. Davis also recognises the depth of knowledge and expertise that resides among talented people at all levels of the company and expects and encourages the different business units to share information and expertise.

Source: Adapted from Richard Jones 2004, 'CCA — the flavour of the month', *Management Today*, November/December, pp. 7–11; James Hall 2004, 'The real thing', *AFR BOSS*, June, accessed at www.afrboss.com.au/print-magazine.asp?doc_id=23484 on 19 October 2004.

Reinforcing the message and institutionalising the new behaviours

To ensure the success of organisational change over the long-term, change leaders need to implement mechanisms that will reinforce and institutionalise change. Integral to this approach is the establishment of new organisational systems and structures that represent the new work arrangements and reporting requirements.[77] The move to team-based work groups, for example, may necessitate a redefinition of the roles and responsibilities of group members, retraining and reskilling of staff, the merging and renaming of business divisions, and the reallocation of office space.

In this respect, management has considerable discretionary power to drive organisational change through the strategic use of symbolic and substantive actions. Ironically, the power of such mechanisms — for example, the role of recognition, and performance and reward measures — is often undervalued.[78] Other substantive actions include changing a company logo, removing executive perks (such as the executive-only dining room, special parking areas or a large office suite), holding special ceremonies to recognise and reward outstanding achievements among staff members, and tying bonuses to improvements in staff performance. As Bertsch and Williams note, 'what gets rewarded, gets repeated'.[79] In addition, the language and behaviour of change agents, particularly those in positions of power and authority, have proved to be powerful symbols in signalling an organisation's commitment to new ways of working.[80]

Historically, senior managers in Australian companies have tended to underestimate the power of symbolic and substantive actions as a catalyst for changing behaviours and attitudes.[81] This traditional reluctance to recognise and reward individual excellence has been found to adversely affect employee commitment and performance potential. Based on his study, Johnson observes that management need to be more alert to the significance of signals and symbols in effecting strategic change.[82] In his example of a menswear retail store, the effect of having to wear the clothes sold in the shop (rather than written plans or words from management) finally gave meaning to the changes. Clearly, Terry Davis, Managing Director of Coca-Cola Amatil had no qualms about challenging the status quo and rewarding those who were willing and able to match his energy and enthusiasm. Similarly, Roger Corbett, CEO and Managing Director of Woolworths (see 'Change management in action' case, 'Corbett's leadership formula at Woolworths'), sought to instil an egalitarian and team-focused culture through his own behaviour and actions, adhering to the principle 'treat other people as you like to be treated yourself'. Leading by example, Corbett wears a name badge, as he expects all his staff to, and does so with pride. Offices at Woolworths are simple and there are few extra privileges for senior organisation members.

To successfully fulfil the different critical roles outlined above, effective change leaders obviously require certain characteristics, skills and attributes. All these are explored in the following section.

CHANGE MANAGEMENT IN ACTION
Corbett's leadership formula at Woolworths

When Roger Corbett was appointed divisional head of Big W in 1990, he embarked on a study tour of Wal-Mart's operations in the United States and returned convinced that the Wal-Mart business model, in particular its highly successful 'every day low prices' strategy was what was needed to revitalise the ailing Big W. When he took over the Big W business in 1990, it was barely breaking even. By 1991, it was back in the black and by 1995 reaped a net profit of $40 million on sales of $1.5 billion.

When Corbett took over as CEO and Managing Director of Woolworths Limited in 1999, he was keen to introduce Big W's everyday low pricing policy into Woolworths Supermarkets. He recognised that this needed to be part of an overall organisational change strategy aimed at reducing business costs. Project Refresh, a five-year business improvement program based on the Wal-Mart business model was launched in 1999. The first step in Project Refresh was to restructure the state-based business platform into a unified national shared services platform, providing immediate scale and efficiency benefits. In half-yearly results to January 2004, Project Refresh initiatives and improved operational efficiencies had achieved costs savings of 3.28 per cent, or $1574 million since 1999. The second stage of Project Refresh is already underway and the aim is to reduce business costs by another one per cent of sales. The estimated cumulative savings over the next five years as sales continue to climb are expected to reach $6.9 billion. Despite the large-scale restructuring and focus on improving operations from the ground up, only a handful of people were retrenched, generally older workers who were at the end of their working life. Corbett took the view that they were in the business of giving people jobs and so those people who were not happy in their new positions as a result of the restructuring were given the opportunity 'to work into other jobs'.

What are the principles and characteristics that govern Corbett's leadership style and underpin his success as a leader? Corbett adheres to the principle 'treat other people as you like to be treated yourself'. For Corbett, integrity of purpose and example, and of lifestyle and attitude are fundamental contributions a leader can make to the cultural health of a business. If leaders claim to uphold certain standards of behaviour, but then conduct themselves according to very different standards, their integrity is undermined and cynicism takes over. In contrast, if leaders model the high standards they espouse and show by doing in their work and personal life, this sets the bar for the rest of the organisation. Organisation members have the right to expect their leadership has integrity and is focused on creating an environment that protects them, and supports and values their contribution at every level. In line with this guiding philosophy, Corbett describes the Woolworths culture as egalitarian. Everyone, including Corbett, wears a name badge. Offices are simple; there are few extra privileges for senior organisation members; everyone uses the same toilets and lunchroom. These fundamental values are embedded in the company's human resources policies and Corbett endeavours to lead by example.

Corbett also believes passionately that everyone in the organisation has to be a team player. In fact, he argues, it is the 'only platform' on which an organisation the size of Woolworths (with around 150,000 employees and 1500 stores) can operate. Corbett interacts with different groups of colleagues on a daily basis and the attributes he identifies as critical in operating as an effective team player include the ability to delegate, thereby acknowledging and supporting the skills and knowledge of others; and integrity of behaviour and action that is essential to building trust among team members.

Corbett strongly believes that if an organisation is to continue to grow and be successful, there has to be 'constant stretch'. In his view, 'if you are not stretching yourself and the business to a point where the effort actually hurts and creates demands at all levels, you can be sure that you are not stretching the business against your competitors'.

Sources: Adapted from *Management Today* August 2004, 'Leading by example: Roger Corbett's formula', pp. 6–11; Sue Mitchell October 2003, 'Roger Corbett's other big W', *AFR BOSS*, accessed at www.afrboss.com.au/printmagazine.asp?doc_id=22447 on 3 September 2004; *AFR BOSS* CLUB Transcript, Roger Corbett, CEO of Woolworths, Speaker at the AFR BOSS Club Seminar on Wednesday, 4 June 2003, accessed at www.afr boss.com.au/events/transcript.asp?eventid=371 on 6 October 2004.

Leadership skills, characteristics and attributes

We already have noted that effective change leadership requires strong interpersonal skills and a high degree of emotional intelligence.[83] Are these the qualities that employees themselves look for in their leaders? In a longitudinal survey of business and government executives undertaken between the early 1980s and 1995, Kouzes and Posner asked the following question: 'What values (personal attributes or characteristics) do you look for and admire in your superiors?'[84] The 225 characteristics identified by managers were reduced to the 20 characteristics.

At the top of this list were honesty (88 per cent); forward looking (75 per cent); inspiring (68 per cent); competent (63 per cent); and supportive (41 per cent). Over the years, the most admired characteristics have changed very little. In a study undertaken in the late 1990s in the UK subsidiary of a major multinational, staff identified similar leadership characteristics when asked what they felt were essential attributes of a 'good people manager'.[85] The eight attributes they identified as essential were honesty; good communicator; people person; available and approachable; professional; inspiring and motivating; supportive; decisive; team player; and good listener.

These characteristics and attributes support the argument discussed earlier that strong, inspiring, personalised leadership, which provides a clearly articulated vision and defines the future direction, is an imperative in times of change and uncertainty. An analysis of all the characteristics and attributes described in figure 7.2 also reveals that the role of leadership has moved from 'telling' to 'involving'. The focus now is on two-way communication, collaboration and cooperation, which entail 'developing and maintaining effective relationships with people'[86] at all levels of the organisation. These characteristics and attributes are reflected in, and further reinforce the findings of, the Australian Business Leadership Survey (ABLS), referred to in earlier discussion on the leadership function, which identified flexibility; professional development; people-oriented focus; and open, honest communication as fundamental leadership strategies for confronting the challenges of today's business environment.[87] An effective leader no longer dictates the terms and conditions that followers simply enact, but views leadership as a team effort and inspires others to take responsibility.[88] This approach requires someone with excellent communication, listening and influencing skills, who is sensitive to subordinates' needs and able to motivate, energise and encourage creativity.[89] The critical attributes for superior executive leadership (summarised in figure 7.2) are reported in a number of sources quoted here (particularly Handy and Javidan) and represent an amalgam of these findings. They are similar to many of the definitions and hallmarks of emotional intelligence discussed in chapter 3. While strong self-image or self-confidence is critical, for example, this attribute will not work if combined with arrogance and disregard for the feelings of others. On the contrary, self-confidence needs to be grounded in humility; it must reflect an understanding of one's own strengths and weaknesses, and a belief in the ability of others. Kets de Vries, for example, refers to the 4 Hs of effective leadership: hope, humanity, humility and humour. As noted in the 'Opening case', (see Profile 4 on Tony Howarth, Chairman of Alinta, page 229), leaders need to be able to control their egos and possess empathy and courage. Similarly, Terry Davis at Coca-Cola Amatil believes that by focusing as much energy on factors the company doesn't do well as on those it does do well 'creates a healthy modesty about what we do'.

Figure 7.2 also underlines that excellent interpersonal, communication and listening skills need to be combined with high energy levels and a passion for the job. Again, these themes are reiterated in the leader profiles we have examined through this chapter. A key force for this energy is to build networks and alliances, inspiring, motivating and involving as many people as possible in the change process. Figure 7.2 also notes that change leaders' energy and focus need to be 'combined with awareness of other worlds'.

This means they must understand the importance of external as well as internal alliances, and be skilled in reading trends and sensing changes in the environment and how these can be transformed into opportunities for the future.[90] If we refer to the 'Opening case', we find that this capacity for 'awareness of other worlds' aligns with a number of the qualities the 2004 True Leaders panellists identified as hallmarks of great leaders, in particular the ability to make connections with people inside and outside the organisation; and the capacity for self-awareness and emotional control.

Strong self-image, belief in oneself
Self-confidence: willingness to step into unknown (needs to be combined with humility, capacity to listen)
Ability to draw others to a vision
Ability to take decisive action
Awareness of own strengths and weaknesses

High energy levels
A passion for the job
Energy and focus, combined with an awareness of other worlds and moving outside the circle
Contagious enthusiasm and commitment

A love of people
Belief in, and sensitivity to, followers
Genuine interest in followers' needs, concerns and views
Behave as a friend
Theory Y leaders: subordinates who are capable and willing to work to their potential and take on responsibilities
A capacity for 'aloneness', the ability to walk alone and gain satisfaction from others' achievements

Functional competence
Knowledge, experience and credibility that are key factors in gaining support and commitment of others for the change effort

Knowledge of the organisation
An understanding of the operational context: the organisation's culture and history, including the background and personalities of key individuals who may help or hinder the change process

Strong drive
Ambition; desire to make an impact
Challenge status quo: strong sense of self-control, purpose and competence

FIGURE 7.2: Key attributes for effective change leadership

Sources: Adapted from M. Javidan 1995, 'Leading a high commitment, high performance organisation', in *Strategic Change: Building a High-Performance Organisation*, ed. P. Sadler, Elsevier Science, Oxford, pp. 44–5; C. Handy 1997, 'New language of organising', *Executive Excellence*, May, p. 14.

Another key quality noted in figure 7.2 is a sound knowledge of the history and workings of the organisation, and of the personalities that have contributed to its identity. These insights can be invaluable in identifying forces for and against change, where allies and resistors are most likely to be stationed.

Summary of dimensions of change leadership

The critical change leadership roles all underline that a change leader needs to demonstrate extraordinary levels of energy and drive to sustain the momentum for change. Essentially, the change leadership role encompasses a 'charismatic' dimension that is crucial for *envisioning*, *empowering* and *energising* followers. Kets de Vries states that 'energising' is the key word in describing successful leaders.[91] Whipp and Pettigrew also suggest that to fully understand the dynamics of change, we need to 'appreciate the role of energy within the process; its source, means of generation and how it is sustained or dissipated . . . leadership is one key way of creating and redirecting energy within the change process'.[92] Figure 7.3 describes the charismatic dimensions of the change leadership role. 'Envisioning' involves providing a clear and compelling vision of the future that can create energy and commitment across the organisation. 'Energising' refers to a leader's personal demonstration of confidence in, commitment to and enthusiasm for the project. 'Empowering' or 'enabling' concerns both the physical and mental support given to followers through both symbolic and substantive actions. It is important to recognise that while Nadler and Tushman coin the term 'charismatic', they do not depict charismatic leaders as mystical, omniscient individuals, but rather as people with strong interpersonal skills who are able to communicate and relate with others easily, and articulate a clear and compelling vision to which key stakeholders are willing to commit. In addition, leaders' energy, enthusiasm and personal commitment, coupled with a strong belief in the abilities of others, serve to engage, motivate and energise a critical mass of followers. As noted in the 'Opening case', the 'heroic' leadership model is being supplanted by a more realistic and human leadership style that includes a strong focus on social responsibility. Kets de Vries himself argues that good leadership is about hope, humanity, humility and humour, but it also takes guts and a dose of narcissism to make the tough decisions. In his view, the best leaders are not too charismatic and are able above all to put the interests of the organisation before their own self-interests.[93]

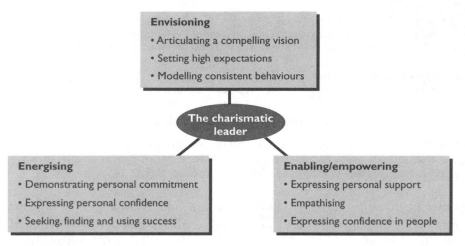

FIGURE 7.3: The charismatic leader

Source: From D. A. Nadler & M. L. Tushman 1990, 'Beyond the charismatic leader: leadership and organizational change', © 1990 by The Regents of the University of California. Reprinted from *California Management Review*, 32(2). By permission of The Regents.

As we have emphasised, however, if change is to be successful over the long-term, then leadership cannot be vested in a single individual. It is not possible for one person, no matter how driven and committed, to maintain indefinitely the energy and enthusiasm of an entire workforce. Effective change leaders need to have the support of key constituents, working in both formal and informal positions of influence and authority at different levels of the organisation, who help to build widespread commitment and involvement. In addition, the charismatic role not only has to be shared through its empowering and energising dimensions; it also needs to be combined with what Kets de Vries and Nadler and Tushman term 'instrumental leadership'.[94] As we have noted, one of the critical leadership roles is to put in place mechanisms that will reinforce and institutionalise change. The social skills component of emotional intelligence, for example, refers to leadership competence in building and leading teams.

Other dimensions of the instrumental role include: explaining and showing the new values and behaviours; and implementing new systems and structures, including reward and punishment measures that are consistent with the new ways of working. The key elements of instrumental leadership, therefore, are organisational design, control and reward, which 'involves managing environments to create conditions that motivate desired behaviour'[95] — that is, putting in place the enabling mechanisms that reinforce the required new values and behaviours.

Charismatic role	Key attributes	Instrumental role
Change leadership mindset	Honesty/integrity/trustworthiness	Management mindset
Strategic focus	Inspiring	Operational/technical focus
Systemic/big picture focus	Competent	Business unit focus
Envisioning, energising	High degree of emotional intelligence	Planning and control
Concern for shared values, attitudes, motivating staff	Strong interpersonal skills	Concern for systems, structures and resource (human and physical) improvement

FIGURE 7.4: Summary of change leadership roles

Figure 7.4 attempts to encapsulate the different aspects of the charismatic and instrumental roles. The charismatic role focuses on the key change leadership dimensions, similar to Kotter's leadership roles. The instrumental role focuses on the functions of Kotter's management role. While the two roles perform distinctive functions, they complement and strengthen each other. The ability to conciliate and balance the two roles depends on whether a leader possesses the key attributes required for effective change leadership. These attributes (captured in figure 7.2), which demarcate strong interpersonal skills as a key binding ingredient, provide the nexus between the charismatic and instrumental roles (as illustrated in figure 7.4). These attributes also point to the importance of 'broadband' intelligence as they involve capabilities 'across the entire repertoire of multiple intelligences'.[96]

In chapter 2, we considered Samson's argument that 14 guiding principles (see table 7.1) underpin the culture, systems, action and behaviour of high-performing organisations. Samson's findings indicated that high-performing organisations that embrace and live out these guiding principles develop powerful, distinctive organisational capabilities because they are able to balance and integrate both the hard (principles 1, 4, 6, 7, 10, 11 and 12) and soft (principles 2, 3, 4, 5, 8, 9, 13 and 14) issues. (Note that principle 4 is common to both.) Recognition of, and support for, the distinct but complementary elements of the 14 guiding principles, along with the necessary interplay between their tangible and intangible elements, require leaders who possess the attributes to capture effectively the synergies that evolve from networking and blending the similarly distinctive but complementary charismatic and instrumental elements of the two leadership roles.

TABLE 7.1	Fourteen guiding management principles	
'Hard skill' principles		**'Soft skill' principles**
Alignment (1)		Distributed leadership (2)
Being out front (4)		Integration of effort (3)
Resourcing the medium term (6)		Being out front (4)
Time based (7)		Being up front (5)
Enabling disciplines (10)		Bias for action (8)
Measurement/reporting and publication (11)		Learning focus (9)
Customer value (12)		Capabilities creation (13)
		Micro to macro (14)

Complementing leadership style with differing forms of change

Whipp and Pettigrew claim that the 'key to understanding the process of leading change is to link that process to its contexts'.[97] Large-scale organisational change takes time and occurs against a backdrop of the vicissitudes of organisational life. New contexts, new opportunities and threats demand strategic and operational flexibility and adaptability if an organisation is to take advantage of unanticipated developments in its different environments. In turn, changes in situational context may require a different style of leadership approach, if not different leaders. From this point of view, the function of leadership is a process, enacted over a length of time during which periods of ongoing **incremental change** may be punctuated by radical, **discontinuous change** as environmental shifts occur.[98]

In attempting to reach a better understanding of what is meant by corporate transformation, Blumenthal and Haspeslagh argue that change is transformational only if it triggers organisation-wide behavioural change. They identify three forms of corporate transformation: operational improvements; strategic transformation; and corporate self-renewal. Operational improvements focus on 'a quantum improvement in the firm's efficiency, often by reducing costs, improving quality and service, and reducing development time'. Operational efficiencies take place within the existing organisational framework and culture; they may involve redesigning work processes and changing the roles and responsibilities of employees from management to the shopfloor. Strategic transformation, the next stage in the continuum, 'seeks to regain a sustainable competitive advantage by redefining business objectives, creating new competences, and harnessing these capabilities to meet market opportunities'. Compared with operations improvement, the strategic transformation process takes longer, is less clear-cut and has less apparent chances of success. Although Blumenthal and Haspeslagh distinguish between the two corporate transformation processes of operational improvements and strategic transformation, they do, nevertheless, seem inextricably linked; the mere process of reviewing work processes, systems and structures must inevitably lead a firm to reassess its existing competences and ponder what new skills and competences it must develop to meet its changing environment. A distinctive feature of the strategic transformation process is more clearly reflected, however, in the deeply entrenched, programmatic nature of the behaviours that it seeks to unlock. In particular, Blumenthal and Haspeslagh found that many managers demonstrate an almost obsessive zeal in applying the outdated and unworkable routines and rituals that brought success in the past, and that a lot of time and energy must be expended in training and helping managers to understand and accept new business theory.[99]

Ghoshal and Bartlett similarly note that the most common 'cause of failure is success'. When ambitions are exceeded and targets are fulfilled, the danger is that not only the passion but also the capacity for continuous improvement and learning are diminished.[100] To prevent this 'ossification', high performing organisations empower their people to constantly challenge existing policies and procedures and question senior management decisions without fear or favour.

The problems that surface in the strategic transformation process indicate a need for corporate self-renewal — the final stage in Blumenthal and Haspeslagh's transformation continuum. Corporate self-renewal 'creates the ability for a firm to anticipate and cope with change so that strategic and operational gaps do not develop'. This definition suggests that an organisation that succeeds in corporate self-renewal is alert to shifts in its environment and proactively seeks to change behaviours and develop new ways of doing things to remain competitive.[101]

In applying the three components of corporate transformation to particular cases of organisational change (see for example, the end-of-book case 1, the William Angliss Institute of TAFE, and other cases in this book), the question arises of whether it is possible for improving operations and strategic transformation to occur independently. Any firm that decides to embark on organisation-wide change is doing so in the light of shifts in its external environment for which existing systems, structures, processes and competences are no longer appropriate. As these cases appear to indicate, improving operations is only the first link in the chain. Redesigning work processes and changing roles and responsibilities almost inevitably lead an organisation to reconsider its existing business objectives, skills and competencies (the key elements of Blumenthal and Haspeslagh's strategic transformation process). In addition, operational improvements need not end before strategic transformation begins; the two processes may be under way simultaneously. Improvements to operations become an ongoing process as an organisation moves towards viewing change as a permanent item on the agenda.

Drawing on their extensive studies of organisational change in Australia, Stace and Dunphy categorise four forms of change that they observed in successful corporate transformations (see figure 7.5). They also note that each form of change requires a different leadership style. The first two forms of change, developmental and task-focused, represent incremental change. Incremental changes are made within the context, or frame, of the current set of organisational strategies and components (corresponding to Blumenthal and Haspeslagh's notion of operational improvements). This is **framebending** rather than **framebreaking** change, where change is managed as a series of small, gradual steps. In this context, an organisation's strategy is in alignment with its environment, and the aims are to maintain the existing culture, values and beliefs, and ensure stability and continuity. The use of a standard set of organisational procedures breaks down, however, in the face of crises or events outside the experience of the existing routines. In this context, strategic drift occurs and the organisation is no longer in alignment with its environment. Under these circumstances, *transformational* or *turnaround* change is required. Transformations and turnarounds represent framebreaking, systemic change, which entails 'new ways of perceiving the environment, the organisation and the relationship between the two'[102] (as in Blumenthal and Haspeslagh's concept of strategic transformation and corporate self-renewal). The four forms of change outlined by Stace and Dunphy, and the distinctive leadership styles adopted to manage these, are illustrated in figure 7.5.

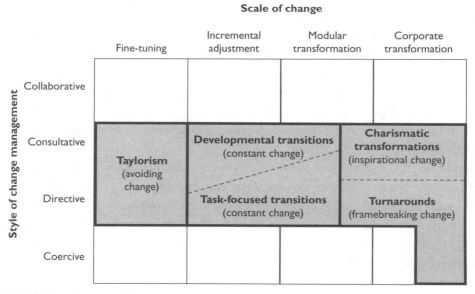

FIGURE 7.5: Four forms of change

Source: D. Stace & D. Dunphy 2001, *Beyond the Boundaries: Leading and Recreating the Successful Enterprise*, 2nd edn, McGraw-Hill, Sydney, p. 109. © 2001 McGraw-Hill Australia.

1. *Developmental transitions* (constant change). This approach is used by organisations implementing framebending (rather than framebreaking) change that does not involve a radical departure from existing strategy. The key to this approach is

ensuring the idea of continuous change is inculcated into the culture of the organisation. This approach is characteristic of smaller organisations operating in the service industries, whose focus is on responding flexibly, quickly and innovatively to customer needs.

Coaches[103], whose approach is hands on, people-centred, consultative and informal best lead developmental transitions. The workplace culture tends to be highly cohesive and collegial, with the emphasis on interdependence, teamwork and collaboration. Coaches show a strong interest and belief in their followers, have excellent communication and listening skills, and have high expectations of themselves and others.

2. *Task-focused transitions* (constant change). Like developmental transitions, the task-focused approach is incremental in orientation. The leadership style is directive, however, with senior management framing and driving the agenda. The focus of this approach is on compliance and conformity, with the aim of increasing productivity, efficiency and, above all, profits.

Task-focused transitions require **captains** as leaders. The directive, authoritative leadership style of task-focused transitions is compatible with the action and behaviour of business unit leaders in areas of technical expertise (law, engineering and accounting, for example) where the emphasis is on rationality and consistency rather than charisma. This style of leadership is successful when the followers are in favour of change and the group mindset accepts a directive approach. Captains at senior management level also act directively and decisively, although they encourage consultative leadership at the business unit level (but within a tightly controlled framework).

3. *Charismatic transformations* (inspirational change). This approach calls for radical transformation when the organisation is out of strategic alignment with its environment and action must be taken swiftly and decisively, thus precluding participation in the decision-making process by all but the senior executive. A critical component of this approach is the **charismatic leader** who is able to rally support with their inspirational style and thus create a readiness for change. A second critical component is that key constituents communicate the need for change clearly and constantly, to ensure staff understands not only *what* must change but also *how* to change. As these critical components indicate, a downside to this strategy is the reliance on the personality of the charismatic leader.

As highlighted in our earlier discussion on the importance of leadership training programs and succession planning, if a leader, whose strong personality and visible commitment and involvement have been the driving inspiration for change, departs without installing a successor with the same views and management style, then all the good work can unravel very quickly.

4. *Turnarounds* (framebreaking change). This form of change is also revolutionary in nature, taken when the organisation is out of strategic alignment with its environment and swift, decisive action is necessary for the organisation's survival. Unlike charismatic transformations, however, there is no support for this type of radical change. The **commander** approach used in turnarounds is top–down directive and, at its most extreme, coercive in gaining compliance rather than commitment. It is a tough, hard-nosed strategy aimed at breaking out of the old frame of reference by

creating new structures, getting rid of excess staff and obsolete systems, and often setting up a new dominant coalition. Its focus is on making strategic gains first before tackling attitudinal or behavioural change across the organisation.[104]

Overall, Stace and Dunphy's study of how organisations manage organisational change found that the most successful organisations deliberately use a mix of change management styles and move from transformational to incremental scales of change depending on context and organisational needs. Their research indicates that if organisations take an exclusively hard-nosed transformational, framebreaking approach under directive or coercive leadership, then the result is a cynical, distrustful, demotivated workforce. Whipp and Pettigrew's research also supports the need for a 'variation in leadership styles to match changing circumstances' — all the more so given that leading change is likely to involve several leaders operating at various levels of the organisation.[105]

A classic example of the deliberate mixing of leadership styles is the corporate revolution that took place during the 1980s at GE. When Jack Welch first began the revolutionary transformation of the company, he adopted a directive or coercive leadership approach to initiate radical, paradigmatic change. Faced with massive resistance, he believed framebreaking, turnaround change was the only viable option. He argued that 'you've got to be hard to be soft'.[106] As his comment suggests, however, if transformational change is to be successful in the long-term, it needs to involve 'a healthy mix of both **normative [change]** and **coercive change** tactics'.[107] At GE, the initial delayering, restructuring, hiring and firing was followed by grassroots programs and innovations aimed at expediting and consolidating the new organisational design and working relationships.

Increasingly, organisations must seek a balance between the two forms of change. The coercive approach may suit radical, paradigmatic change in the short-term but, while it may win compliance, it does not win commitment. As Welch realised, he had to revert to the normative approach to win trust and achieve 'buy-in' through all levels of the organisation.

Kanter et al. assert that for large-scale organisational change to be successful, change leaders need to combine 'bold strokes' with 'long marches', instigating swift, short-term control measures to confront crisis (which are often necessarily top–down mandates, as in Stace and Dunphy's charismatic transformations and turnarounds), followed by long-term, organisation-wide initiatives that must win the commitment and support of all stakeholders if they are to succeed.[108] The importance of adopting different leadership styles to manage different situations underpins the need for leaders who are adept at both charismatic and instrumental leadership roles. Charisma alone, or the power of an individual personality, is not enough to ensure lasting systemic change. Effective change leaders use the envisioning dimension of the charismatic role to energise and enable others operating at different levels of the organisation to become involved in, and meaningfully contribute to, the change process. They also must create a nexus between the traditional technical or operational dimension of management and the strategic, interpersonal, dimension (refer to figure 7.3, page 248, and figure 7.4, page 249). By melding charisma and widespread involvement with instrumental factors that focus on developing roles, responsibilities, structures, systems and rewards, a leader sets in place the critical building blocks for driving organisation-wide change and establishing strong management principles that guide an organisation's values, actions and behaviour.

The need for different leadership approaches across time and context also underlines the importance of leadership skills in balancing integrative power with authority and economic power. In a crisis situation, when the survival of the organisation is at stake, for example, critical decisions have to be made urgently with no time for inclusion or widespread involvement. As illustrated in the key leadership characteristics and attributes listed in figure 7.2 (page 247), senior executives must be able to — indeed, are expected to — act decisively and courageously. They also need to have a capacity for 'aloneness'; they must make the hard decisions knowing that their actions may not be popular but are in the best interests of the long-term future of the business. As in the case of Welch at GE, once the crisis is over and the long march begins, integrative power, matched with interpersonal skills, is essential to win over what is likely to be a hostile and suspicious workforce.

Review

This chapter explored key dimensions of change leadership. We considered whether leadership differs from management and, if so, whether the functions of management are relevant to leading change. We found that management and leadership are different and require distinctive skills and attributes, but that one should not be abandoned in favour of the other. Each has its own part to play and the challenge for change leadership is to learn to draw on the different dimensions of both roles, depending on context and situation.

We then explored the different dimensions of leadership and the possibility of distinguishing features such as typical characteristics and attributes. In the section on the function of leadership, we considered the concept of power and authority, and who should lead change. Sponsorship at the highest level was found to be pivotal in promoting and sustaining the change agenda. If, however, the new behaviours are to be instilled throughout the organisation, change leadership cannot be the sole prerogative of senior managers. Senior managers must build a network of change agents at all levels of the organisation — agents who act as examplars of the new behaviours and help cascade the vision down the organisation.

While there is no guaranteed recipe for successful change leadership, effective change leaders appear to perform a number of critical roles, including:
- challenging the status quo and creating a readiness for change
- inspiring a shared vision and personally communicating the future direction with clear and honest answers to the 'what', 'why' and 'how' questions
- enabling others to act by energising, empowering, building teams and providing tangible support with appropriate resources
- creating additional sponsors at different levels of the organisation, involving as many people as possible to build commitment
- taking symbolic and substantive actions, including: using rewards and recognition to gain support; recognising short-term gains or success stories to emphasise recognition of the new behaviours; and taking decisive action to identify and address resistance

- modelling the way, by enacting the new behaviours in deed as well as in words, and personally demonstrating senior management involvement and commitment
- with the help of key stakeholders, communicating the message repeatedly up, down and across the organisation, to ensure the momentum and enthusiasm for change is not diminished over time.

We then considered the characteristics and attributes required to perform these critical leadership roles effectively. The characteristics most sought after in leaders are honesty, trust and integrity — someone who is forward looking, inspiring, decisive, competent, supportive, fair minded and a good communicator and listener. The critical attributes for effective leadership include: a high degree of self-confidence and empathy; a strong drive and seemingly inexhaustible supplies of energy; high levels of self-discipline and control; and functional competence. In addition, trust, openness, equity and fairness are recurring themes in the leader profiles presented in this chapter, underlining the central role these values play in building and communicating a collective organisational identity that facilitates trust and knowledge sharing.

In the final section on styles of change leadership, we considered the need for flexibility and adaptability in a leader when dealing with different forms of organisational change. This calls for leaders with strong interpersonal skills who are able to adopt different communication styles depending on both whom they are dealing with and the situational context. We discussed different forms of incremental and transformational change, referring to the Stace and Dunphy model and the types of leadership style appropriate to each. We concluded that systemic organisational change demands a long-term, strategic approach, which blends operational improvements (the instrumental role which reflects the traditional managerial functions) with charismatic change leadership (with its focus on strategic transformation and corporate self-renewal).

Key terms

authoritarianism. Demanding strict obedience and adherence to person or persons in positions of authority and power, (p. 234)

broadband intelligence. Exhibited by people whose intelligence has been allowed to develop in a balanced way, stimulated by a wide variety of influences and activities. Leaders with broadband intelligence are able to draw on and make connections between the seven distinctive forms of intelligence: linguistic; logical mathematical; spatial; musical; bodily kinaesthetic; interpersonal; and intrapersonal. (See also related endnote 21.) (p. 233)

captains. Leaders who exhibit a directive, authoritative leadership style. This style of leadership is successful when the followers are in favour of change and the group mindset accepts a directive approach. (p. 253)

charismatic leaders. Leaders who, through their personal attributes and strong interpersonal skills, are able to inspire and enthuse others to commit to their vision for the future, (p. 253)

coaches. Leaders who exhibit a hands-on, people-centred, consultative and informal leadership style. Coaches show a strong interest and belief in their followers, have excellent communication and listening skills, and have high expectations of themselves and others. (p. 253)

coercive change. Top–down, mandated change that involves little or no consultation with subordinates, (p. 254)

commanders. Leaders who exhibit a top–down, directive leadership style. At its most extreme, this leadership style can be coercive, gaining compliance rather than commitment. (p. 253)

decoupled. Where a lack of coordination and control mechanisms results in the organisation's loss of focus and direction, (p. 236)

discontinuous change. Rapid, turbulent, unpredictable change, forcing a radical departure from the familiar, (p. 250)

framebending. Change that focuses on individual organisational components/subsystems rather than the entire organisation, and that takes place within the existing organisational framework and culture, (p. 252)

framebreaking. Systemic, organisation-wide change that challenges the status quo and involves fundamental changes to strategy, structure, systems and culture, and leads to new ways of perceiving the environment, the organisation and the relationship between the two, (p. 252)

incremental change. Predictable, familiar change that is managed as a series of small, gradual steps within the context, or frame, of the current set of organisational strategies, structures and systems, (p. 250)

loosely coupled. Where there is both integration and differentiation between an organisation's component parts — that is, where the business units or functional areas of an organisation assert both autonomy and interdependence, (p. 236)

normative change. A change process that is inclusive and seeks the participation and involvement of all organisational members, (p. 254)

shared vision. A vision that gives meaning and structure to the change efforts. It provides a focus and a sense of direction that, while offering a challenge, must be realistic and acceptable to the majority of the workforce. In addition, if the majority of stakeholders is to commit to this vision, then as many as possible must have had meaningful input into its substance. (p. 241)

systemic change. Holistic, organisation-wide change that recognises the interconnectivity of an organisation's component parts, (p. 233)

Review questions

1. Distinguish between the traditional model of leadership and the sorts of skills and attributes required for leading the 21st century organisation.
2. Explain the distinction between leadership and management.
3. Define emotional intelligence and its five components.
4. Explain the meaning of 'personalised' leadership as opposed to 'distributed' leadership.
5. List the key factors for effective succession planning.
6. Describe task-focused transitions. When would it be most appropriate to adopt this form of change?
7. Explain the similarities and differences between charismatic transformations and turnarounds.
8. How does charismatic change leadership differ from the commander approach? Can you think of examples of these two leadership styles (stories you have read about in the media, for example)?

Discussion questions

1. Define broadband intelligence. Identify the correspondence between broadband intelligence and emotional intelligence. Which of these concepts do you think has the greater scope and scale?
2. What do you understand by Mant's claim that the *sine qua non* of leadership 'lies in the capacity to change and shift systems' and how is this relevant to change leadership?

3. Discuss the difference between charismatic and instrumental leadership roles.
4. Pearce argues that 'as the complexity of knowledge work increases, the need for shared leadership also increases'. Discuss.

Work assignment

Leadership roles and analysing change

Draw on the critical change leadership roles discussed in the chapter to analyse the change process at your own organisation or the William Angliss Institute of TAFE (see the end-of-book case 1).

Suggested further reading

Collins, Jim 2001, *Good to Great: Why Some Companies Make the Leap. . .and Others Don't*, HarperBusiness, New York.

Goleman, D. 1998, 'What makes a leader?', *Harvard Business Review*, November–December, pp. 93–102.

Jackson, D. 2000, *Becoming Dynamic: Creating and Sustaining the Dynamic Organisation*, Macmillan Business, London.

Mant, Alistair 1999, *Intelligent Leadership*, Allen & Unwin, St. Leonards, NSW.

Pearce, Craig L. 2004, 'The future of leadership: combining vertical and shared leadership to transform knowledge work', *The Academy of Management Executive*, pp. 47–57.

Stace, D. & Dunphy, D. 2001, *Beyond the Boundaries: Leading and Recreating the Successful Enterprise*, 2nd edn, McGraw-Hill, Sydney.

End notes

1. See D. Jackson 1997, *Dynamic Organisations: The Challenge of Change*, Macmillan Business, London; D. Stace & D. Dunphy 2001, *Beyond the Boundaries: Leading and Recreating the Successful Enterprise*, 2nd edn, McGraw-Hill, Sydney; R. M. Kanter, B. A. Stein & T. D. Jick 1992, *The Challenge of Organizational Change*, The Free Press, New York; D. Limerick & B. Cunnington 1993, *Managing the New Organisation*, Business and Professional Publishing, Sydney; J. Naisbitt & P. Aburdene 1990, *Megatrends 2000: Ten New Directions For the 1990s*, Avon Books, New York; D. Ulrich & M. F. Wiersema 1989, 'Gaining strategic and organizational capability in a turbulent business environment', *The Academy of Management Executive*, III(2), pp. 115–22.

2. H. Bahrami 1992, 'The emerging flexible organization: perspectives from Silicon Valley', *California Management Review*, 34(4), p. 33.

3. M. Useem & T. A. Kochan 1992, 'Creating the learning organization', in *Transforming Organizations*, eds T. A. Kochan & M. Useem Oxford University Press, New York, pp. 398–9; Kanter, Stein & Jick, op. cit., p. 12.

4. M. Javidan 1995, 'Leading a high commitment, high performance organisation', in *Strategic Change: Building a High Performance Organisation*, ed. Phillip Sadler, Elsevier Science, Oxford, p. 34.

5. See, for example, the 1991 *Concise Collins Dictionary*.

6. J. M. Kouzes & B. Z. Posner 1995, *The Leadership Challenge*, Jossey-Bass, San Francisco.

7. Abraham Zaleznik 2004, 'Managers and leaders: are they different?' *Harvard Business Review*, January, pp. 74–81.

8. ibid.

9. W. Bennis & R. Townsend, 1995, *Reinventing Leadership: Strategies to Achieve a New Style of Leadership and Empower Your Organisation*, Piatkus, London.

10. James Hall 2004, 'The real thing', *AFR BOSS*, June, accessed at www.afr-boss.com.au/printmagazine.asp?doc_id=23484 on 19 October 2004.
11. J. P. Kotter 1990, 'What leaders really do', *Harvard Business Review*, May–June, p. 103.
12. Australian Business Leadership Survey Results reported in *Management Today* 2004, 'Business wants ... hands off policy', March, pp. 30–2. Based on analysis of 511 survey respondents and interviews with a further 129 executives in Phase Two of the three-year Australian Business Leadership Survey (ABLS) carried out by the Leadership Research Unit, Department of Management, Monash University, and the Australian Institute of Management.
13. W. Bennis 1999, 'The end of leadership', *Organizational Dynamics*, 28(1), pp. 71–9.
14. D. Goleman 1998, 'What makes a leader?', *Harvard Business Review*, November–December, p. 94 of pp. 93–102.
15. ibid., p. 100.
16. ibid., p. 101.
17. Kotter, op. cit., p. 103.
18. J. O'Toole 1999, 'Lead change effectively', *Executive Excellence*, April, p. 18.
19. Jackson, op. cit., p. 99; J. Laabs 1998, 'Show them where you're headed', *Workforce*, November, p. 46; R. Stata 1992, 'A CEO's perspective', in *Transforming Organizations*, eds T. A. Kochan & M. Useem, Oxford University Press, New York, pp. 377–80; Useem & Kochan, op. cit., pp. 391–406.
20. Alistair Mant 1999, *Intelligent Leadership*, Allen & Unwin, St Leonards, NSW, p. 51.
21. ibid., pp. 40–1, 160–1. Alistair Mant refers to Howard Gardner's work on the nature of intelligence. Gardner believed that at least seven forms of intelligence existed. These comprised: *linguistic* (the ability to manipulate language effectively); *logical mathematical* (the ability to manipulate symbols, like the scientist); *spatial* (the ability to process information continuously in three dimensions); *musical* (the ability to manipulate sound in a complex way); *bodily kinaesthetic* (the ability for physical coordination); *interpersonal* (the ability to know what is happening between people and to mobilise it); and *intrapersonal* (the ability for self understanding without which all the others may be distorted in use). People with 'broadband' intelligence are able to draw on one, all or combinations of these intelligences as the situation demands.
22. ibid., pp. 42–3; p. 65.
23. H. Mintzberg 1998, 'Covert leadership: notes on managing professionals', *Harvard Business Review*, November–December, pp. 140–7; Laabs, op. cit.; Jackson, op. cit.; Kouzes & Posner, op. cit.
24. O'Toole, op. cit., p. 18.
25. J. B. Rieley 1994, 'The circular organisation: how leadership can optimise organisational effectiveness', *National Productivity Review*, Winter, p. 11.
26. K. E. Boulding 1989, *Three Faces of Power*, Sage Publications, Newbury Park, California, pp. 79–123.
27. C. M. Avery 1999, 'All power to you: collaborative leadership works', *Journal for Quality and Participation*, March–April, p. 37. Avery refers to the work of Boulding, op cit.; Jackson, op. cit.
28. Jackson, op. cit., p. 91.
29. A. Freas, M. Goldsmith & L. Lyons 2000, 'Management is dead ...', *People Management*, 26 October, pp. 60–4.
30. Jackson, op. cit., p. 98.
31. Sumantra Ghoshal & Christopher A. Bartlett 1997, *The Individualized Corporation*, HarperCollins, New York, pp. 52–3.
32. Jim Collins 2001, *Good to Great: Why Some Companies Make the Leap . . . and Others Don't*, HarperCollins, New York, p. 125.
33. Boulding, op. cit., p. 142.
34. R. Whipp & A. Pettigrew 1993, 'Leading change and the management of competition', in *Strategic Thinking: Leadership and the Management of Change*, eds J. Hendry & G. Johnson with J. Newton, John Wiley & Sons, Chichester, p. 203 of pp. 199–228.
35. James Sarros 2004, quoted in *Management Today* in a report on Australian Business Leadership Survey Results, March, pp. 30–2.
36. Gabrielle Costa 2004, 'Our middle managers not up to it: HR experts', *The Age*, Wednesday, April 14, 'Business' section, p. 5.
37. See Stace & Dunphy, op. cit., p. 154; J. P. Kotter 1995, 'Leading change: why transformation efforts fail', *Harvard Business Review*, May–June, pp. 59–67; B. Bertsch & R. Williams 1994, 'How multinational CEOs make change programmes stick', *Long Range Planning*, 27(5), pp. 12–24; B. Blumenthal & P. Haspeslagh 1994, 'Toward a definition of corporate transformation',

Sloan Management Review, Spring, pp. 101–6; Stata, op. cit., p. 379; Kanter, Stein & Jick, op. cit.; D. A. Nadler, R. B. Shaw & A. E. Walton 1995, *Discontinuous Change: Leading Organizational Transformation*, Jossey-Bass, San Francisco.

38. C. Handy 1997, 'New language of organising', *Executive Excellence*, May, pp. 13–14.
39. ibid., p. 14.
40. Jackson, op. cit., p. 94; C. A. Bartlett & S. Ghoshal 1995, 'Changing the role of top management: beyond structure to processes', *Harvard Business Review*, January–February, pp. 86–96; T. Eccles 1993, 'The deceptive allure of empowerment', *Long Range Planning*, 26(6), pp. 13–21; Limerick & Cunnington, op. cit., p. 145.
41. Bahrami, op. cit., pp. 33–52; L. Hirschhorn & T. Gilmore 1992, 'The new boundaries of the "boundary-less" company', *Harvard Business Review*, May–June, pp. 104–15.
42. R. J. Butler, D. H. R. Price, P. D. Coates & R. H. Pike 1998, 'Organising for innovation: loose or tight control?', *Long Range Planning*, 31(5), pp. 775–82; Handy, op. cit., p. 16; Jackson, op. cit., p. 100; Whipp & Pettigrew, op. cit., p. 210.
43. Craig L. Pearce 2004, 'The future of leadership: combining vertical and shared leadership to transform knowledge work', *The Academy of Management Executive*, 18(1), pp. 47–57.
44. Whipp & Pettigrew, op. cit.; Kotter 1995, op. cit.; D. Nadler & M.L. Tushman 1989, 'Organizational frame bending: principles for managing reorientation', *The Academy of Management Executive*, III(3), pp. 194–204.
45. P. M. Senge 1990, 'The leader's new work: building learning organizations', *Sloan Management Review*, Fall, p. 7.
46. B. A. Pasternack, T. D. Williams & P. F. Anderson 2001, 'Beyond the cult of the CEO: building institutional leadership', *Strategy + Business*, 22, p. 3. Available from www.strategy-business.com.
47. ibid., p. 7.
48. F. Desmarescaux 1998, 'The leadership imperative', *Asian Business*, August, p. 14 of pp. 14–16.
49. Kotter 1990, op. cit., p. 111.
50. D. Cafaro 2001, 'Championing change from the vantage of a CEO's perch', *Workspan*, 44(6), pp. 42–8.
51. Pasternack, Williams & Anderson, op. cit., p. 3.

52. Kouzes & Posner 1995, op. cit., p. 16; Whipp & Pettigrew, op. cit., p. 210.
53. Pasternack, Williams & Anderson, op. cit.
54. ibid., p. 4.
55. ibid.
56. Anonymous 1993, 'Jack Welch's lessons for success', *Fortune*, 25 January, pp. 86–94.
57. John Sidgmore quoted in report by G. Alexander 2000, 'GE heirs step forward to try on shoes of a legend', *Sunday Times*, 24 September, 'Business' section, p. 7.
58. G. Alexander, op. cit.; Anonymous 1993, 'Jack Welch's lessons for success', *Fortune*, 25 January, pp. 86–94.
59. Noel Tichy quoted in Alexander, op. cit., p. 7.
60. These represent the views of Don Smith, executive career management specialist of Harris Smith and Associates, which appear in N. Tabakoff 1999, 'Replacing the boss in a holistic way', *Business Review Weekly*, 10 September, pp. 76–82.
61. James Hall 2004, 'Your life after me', *AFR BOSS*, 5(8), p. 62.
62. ibid., p. 62.
63. Kouzes & Posner, op. cit.; Kotter 1995, op. cit., p. 60; Stata, op. cit., pp. 377–8; N. M. Tichy & M. A. Devanna 1990, *The Transformational Leader*, John Wiley & Sons, New York; M. Beer & E. Walton 1990, 'Developing the competitive organization: interventions and strategies', *American Psychologist*, 45(2), p. 159 of pp. 154–216.
64. Beer & Walton, op. cit.; Bertsch & Williams, op. cit.; Kotter 1995, op. cit.; Nadler & Tushman, op. cit.; B. A. Spector 1989, 'From bogged down to fired up: inspiring organizational change', *Sloan Management Review*, Summer, pp. 29–34.
65. See D. M. Schneider & C. Goldwasser 1998, 'Be a model leader of change', *Management Review*, p. 43 of pp. 41–5.
66. R. K. Reger, J. V. Mullane, L. T. Gustafson & S. M. DeMarie 1994, 'Creating earthquakes to change organizational mindsets', *The Academy of Management Executive*, 8(4), pp. 31–46; Schneider & Goldwasser, op. cit., p. 43.
67. J. Macneil, J. Testi, J. Cupples & M. Rimmer 1993, *Benchmarking Australia: Linking Enterprises to World Best Practice*, Longman, Melbourne, p. 87.
68. Kotter 1995, op. cit.; Bertsch & Williams, op. cit.; G. Lewis 1993, 'Managing strategic change', in *Australian Strategic Management: Concepts, Context and*

Cases, eds G. Lewis, A. Morkel & G. Hubbard, Prentice Hall, Sydney, pp. 249–271.

69. Adele Ferguson 2004, 'National Emergency', *BRW*, October 7–13, pp. 38–43.

70. Jackson, op. cit., p. 94.

71. John P. Kotter 1996, *Leading Change*, Harvard Business School Press, Boston, Massachusetts, pp. 9–11.

72. Avery, op. cit.; Kouzes & Posner, op. cit.; Kotter 1995, op. cit.; Bertsch & Williams, op. cit.; Blumenthal & Haspeslagh, op. cit.; Rieley, op. cit.; Kanter, Stein & Jick, op. cit.; O. Harari 1999, 'The spirit of leadership', *Management Review*, April, pp. 33–6; R. A. Heifetz & D. L Laurie 1998, 'Adaptive strategy', *Executive Excellence*, December, pp. 14–15; B. Trahant & W. Burke 1998, 'Leadershift', *Executive Excellence*, August, pp. 13–14.

73. Whipp & Pettigrew, op. cit.; Kouzes & Posner, op. cit.; D. A. Nadler & M. L. Tushman 1990, 'Beyond the charismatic leader: leadership and organizational change', *California Management Review*, Winter, pp. 77–97.

74. For more details, see R. W. Beatty & D. O. Ulrich 1991, 'Re-energizing the mature organization', *Organizational Dynamics*, 20(1), pp. 16–30; Kotter 1990, op. cit.; Nadler & Tushman, op. cit.

75. For more details, see Kouzes & Posner, op. cit.; Kotter 1995, op. cit., p. 63; Kanter, Stein & Jick, op. cit., p. 384; D. C. Hambrick & A. A. Cannella 1989, 'Strategy implementation as substance and selling', *The Academy of Management Executive*, 3(4), pp. 278–85.

76. D. Jackson 2000, *Becoming Dynamic: Creating and Sustaining the Dynamic Organisation*, Macmillan Business, London, pp. 153–4.

77. See Kanter, Stein & Jick, op. cit., p. 384; M. F. R. Kets de Vries 1994, 'The leadership mystique', *The Academy of Management Executive*, 8(3), p. 75 of pp. 73–89.

78. Jackson 1997, op. cit.; Useem & Kochan, op. cit.; Kotter 1995, op. cit.; Bertsch & Williams, op. cit.; Kanter, Stein & Jick, op. cit.; G. Johnson 1992, 'Managing strategic change: strategy, culture and action', *Long Range Planning*, 25(1), pp. 28–36; G. Johnson 1990, 'Managing strategic change; the role of symbolic action', *British Journal of Management*, 1, pp. 183–200.

79. Bertsch & Williams, op. cit., p. 18.

80. Javidan, op. cit., pp. 38–9; Bertsch & Williams, op. cit., p. 17; Johnson 1990, op. cit., pp. 187–8.

81. L. Gettler 1999, 'Australian bosses lack people skills: study', *The Age*, 27 November, 'Business' section, p. 5.

82. Johnson 1992, op. cit., p. 35.

83. Goleman, op. cit.; Kotter 1995, op. cit.

84. Kouzes & Posner, op. cit., p. 20.

85. Jackson 1997, op. cit., p. 87.

86. B. Adams & C. Adams 1997, 'Power of paradox', *Executive Excellence*, September, p. 19.

87. James Sarros 2004, quoted in *Management Today* in a report on Australian Business Leadership Survey Results, March, pp. 30–32.

88. See, for example, Jackson 1997, op. cit., pp. 97–8 on fostering teamwork.

89. Handy, op. cit., p. 14; Javidan, op. cit., p. 44; Laabs, op. cit., p. 46; R. L. Ackoff 1999, 'Transformational leadership', *Strategy and Leadership*, January–February, p. 21 of pp. 20–5.

90. See Harari, op. cit., pp. 33–6. In the section 'Inventing the future', Harari uses the term 'strategic trend-sniffing' and quotes Steve Jobs: 'The best way to predict the future is to invent it'.

91. Kets de Vries, op. cit., p. 75.

92. Whipp & Pettigrew, op. cit., p. 208.

93. Manfred Kets de Vries 2001, *The Leadership Mystique*, Pearson Education, United Kingdom; Catherine Fox 2003, 'Manfred Kets de Vries on Leadership', *AFR BOSS*, May, accessed at www.afrboss.com.au/printmagazine.asp?doc?id=19040 on 24 October 2004.

94. The authors Kets de Vries and Nadler & Tushman argue that successful change leaders fulfil two roles: charismatic and instrumental. Charismatic leadership depends largely on the personality and dynamism of one individual. As we have seen, however, one person alone cannot sustain complex, systemic organisational change. These authors argue, therefore, that change leaders also must perform an instrumental role. The combination of these two roles is seen to create a powerful force for change as the 'charismatic part of leadership becomes more concrete and focused, and the instrumental part becomes more flexible and human' (Kets de Vries, op. cit., p. 76), thus melding hard issues (strategy, systems and structure) with the softer, people-centred issues.

95. Nadler & Tushman 1990, op. cit., p. 85.
96. Mant, op. cit.
97. See Whipp & Pettigrew, op. cit., p. 209. They argue that 'the analytical judgements and resulting action from strategic decisions cannot remain separate from the circumstances in which they are taken. . . . it is the tension between these forces that impels the process of change. This relationship demands careful attention in understanding the problems of leading change.'
98. Whipp & Pettigrew, op. cit., p. 208; Nadler & Tushman 1988, 'What makes for magic leadership?', *Fortune*, 6 June, pp. 115–16.
99. Blumenthal & Haspeslagh, op. cit., pp. 101–6.
100. Ghoshal & Bartlett 1997, op. cit., p. 63.
101. Blumenthal & Haspeslagh, op. cit., pp. 101–6.
102. Lewis, op. cit., p. 252.
103. See Stace & Dunphy, op. cit., pp. 164–89 for a detailed description of the role of coaches in leading developmental transitions. They argue that the four forms of change demand a different style of change leadership, a different communication strategy and also a distinctive approach to rebuilding corporate culture.
104. For further details on the four different approaches to leading change, see Stace & Dunphy, op. cit., pp. 164–89: the role of captains in leading task-focused transitions is discussed on pp. 171–8; the role of charismatics in leading charismatic transformations is discussed on pp. 178–82; the role of commanders in leading organisational turnarounds is discussed on pp. 182–8.
105. Whipp & Pettigrew, op. cit., p. 210.
106. Fortune 1993, 'Jack Welch's lessons for success', Fortune Book Excerpt, 25 January. This article comprises excerpts of interviews with Jack Welch recorded in N. M. Tichy & S. Sherman 1993, *Control Your Destiny or Someone Else Will*, Doubleday Publishing, New York. The book documents the corporate revolution that took place at General Electric over a number of years.
107. See Limerick & Cunnington, op. cit., pp. 217–18, for a description of the 'freeze–thaw' approach to change. Welch's actions at General Electric are used as an example of the deliberate strategy to 'sequence normative and coercive techniques of change'.
108. Kanter & Stein, op. cit., p. 492.

OPENING CASE
Power and Change: Soccer in Australia

With more than 350,000 registered players, soccer in Australia is recognised as one the highest participatory sports. Until September 2003, the national body representing organised soccer in Australia was known as Soccer Australia (SA). However, culminating in 2002, SA was operating under the burden of significant financial difficulties, with members' equity at negative $2.6 million as at 30 June 2002. Furthermore, political infighting between SA and state federations, reduced staffing levels, deficient strategic planning and direction, and mixed results in international competition have since been identified as some of the significant issues facing SA at the time.

On 9 August 2002, in the midst of this 'crisis', the Federal Minister for the Arts and Sport announced that an independent review would be undertaken into SA. The aim of the independent review was to critically assess the governance, management and structure of soccer in Australia, to make recommendations for the establishment of a best practice structure for the management and governance of soccer in Australia, and to provide a change management plan for delivering these recommendations.

The review culminated in a report, released on 7 April 2003, which subsequently has become known as the Crawford Report. The report called for a 'truly' independent board to develop both policy and strategy to lead Australian soccer into the future, requiring a new constitution to be drawn. Key to the implementation of its recommendations was the report's insistence that the existing board stand down immediately, and be replaced by an interim six-member board to be headed by Australia's second-richest man Frank Lowy.

Legal advice received by the review committee suggested that an interim board could be installed if first, the current board resigned and, second, if the current board was unwilling to resign, current members of SA could replace the existing directors. The Lowy team formally indicated that they would be prepared to be involved in an interim board for SA to drive the changes outlined in the Crawford Report, provided that the stakeholders of soccer in Australia decided to wholeheartedly support the proposed changes and his involvement.

On 10 April 2003, the SA board announced a decision to clear the way for the appointment of an interim board to implement the Crawford reforms, a move welcomed by the review chairman. However, it was to take months of political manoeuvring and delays before the board was to step down.

The conclusion of the power struggle between the remaining SA board and the Crawford Inquiry team, did not herald the end of the change process for soccer in Australia. Indeed, the change management program recommended by the Crawford Report had only begun, with far reaching transformations still to be implemented across all levels of the sport. The first major change was to be the dissolution of SA in September 2003, making way for the new company, the Australian Soccer Association Limited (ASA) and then, in 2005, the Football Federation Australia.

Source: Adapted from D. Crawford. 2003, *Report of the Independent Soccer Review Committee into the Structure, Governance and Management of Soccer in Australia,* Australian Sports Commission, ACT. (Report can be downloaded at www.soccerinquiry.org.au/report2003.htm)

Introduction

What is **resistance** if not resistance to control? And what is **power** if not the application of control? Power and control, therefore, are at the heart of understanding responses to change, particularly the confrontations and pain associated with overcoming, bypassing or removing the barriers that frustrate change efforts. These barriers may be described as resistances to change. The resistance to change described in the 'Opening case' is a demonstration of power exercised in open conflict, and where change and overcoming resistance are direct functions of who yields the greatest power. In the case of Soccer Australia, the real power was with the government, which provided the lion's share of funding to the organisation. The government's insistence on instituting an independent inquiry and following the Crawford Report recommendations brought about radical change in the organisation. In the 'Opening case', power could be seen as a function of the control of resources.

At its most bland, change may be defined as the movement away from a present state towards a future state.[1] This statement, however, conceals the fact that overcoming resistance to change is rarely easy or painless. At the same time, the capacity to conquer resistance smoothly and implement change to successfully meet environmental challenges is essential for organisational survival.[2] Nevertheless, the right techniques for surmounting resistance have become obscured by cautious researchers who frequently do not get beyond describing the complexity of change, and zealous business consultants who discard theoretical discussion in favour of simplistic but authoritative solutions. The change mantra is chanted enthusiastically by business 'gurus' such as Kotter, Huber and Glick, and Kanter[3], who have championed ideas such as vision, strategy, flexibility and responsiveness. 'Serious' researchers such as Pettigrew,

Laughlin, and Greenwood and Hinings[4] propose sophisticated diagnoses for confronting resistance and for understanding and effecting change. The difficulties for management practitioners are further clouded by the variety of concepts, practices and tools that can be used to manage resistance, and the manipulation of power and control are firmly embedded in these practical interventions.

This chapter explains resistances to change. The first section focuses on the application of power and its impact on resistance to change. Specifically, we explore the nature of power and its dimensions, thereby leading to a review of the techniques for dispersing and modifying power relationships to minimise resistance. This 'road' leads to the second section of the chapter, which examines the nature of empowerment as a technique for managing resistance. The third section of this chapter concentrates on the broader nature of responses to change. We examine the role of change theory and organisational culture, concluding with an examination of methods for overcoming resistance.

Power, politics and control

According to Lee, power 'resists explanation in terms of a single theory', and definitions of power seem to reflect a lack of consensus that undermines its capacity to be conceptualised.[5] Typically, however, the concept of power has emerged from social theory[6] and is viewed as the ability of one party to get another to do something that they would not do otherwise, despite any form of resistance. In other words, power generally is characterised as a set of behaviours intended to change another set of behaviours.[7] Buchanan and Badham take an even simpler view, arguing that power should be seen as the ability of individuals to achieve desired outcomes.[8] Their definition begins to reveal the relationship between power and resistance.

Power is associated with influence, the allocation and mobilisation of resources, the ability to manipulate situations, the capacity to affect systems and processes, the fulfilment of needs and the achievement of objectives. But, ultimately, it can be encapsulated in its capacity to overcome resistance.[9] Power, therefore, is the chief vehicle through which resistance is tackled or avoided. Foil noted that power in organisations is reflected both in overt decisions and behaviours, and in the empty spaces of non-decision and non-behaviour.[10] With this reflection in mind, we can see why organisational culture — those embedded values, beliefs and norms that collectively reside within an organisation — remains such an influential element in the use of power to overcome resistance.

Given that power is a reflection of the cultural boundaries of an organisation, it can be experienced at an individual level, within interpersonal relationships or within broader, more formalised systems, structures and procedures.[11] The power relationships within Soccer Australia (now the Football Federation Australia), for example, are a reflection of that organisation's values. Organisational culture is therefore a form of hidden power that influences employees whether they realise it or not.

Power also is linked to **politics** and control. Pfeffer defines politics by using power as the pivotal reference: 'Those activities within organisations to acquire, develop and use power and other resources to obtain one's preferred outcomes in a situation where there is dissension or uncertainty about choices'.[12] The application of power to overcome resistance and ambiguity is fundamental to Pfeffer's view of politics. Politics has been concerned mostly with the use of power to champion particular interests and acquire scarce resources.[13] Politics can be described as a process where disparate concerns clash, creating inevitable partisan interests.[14] Power, generally, is perceived in a 'political' light based on the interests and goals of the person perceiving it. Machiavellian practices (named for Niccolo Machiavelli, a 16th century Italian writer who described a particularly cynical and ruthless approach to politics and all human affairs) for example, are distinguished as political because a specific approach to power is used to achieve an objective — in this case, ruthless activities. Power does not necessarily have to mean something negative. Vince, for instance, suggests that power is not necessarily a constraint, but a natural feature of organising. He advises, however, to acknowledge the importance of politics, and the ways in which information is directly mediated by power relations.[15] Organisational change remains a politicised process because decisions must be made in the face of uncertainty. In other words, politics will fill the gaps left by formal structures.

Whilst politics has traditionally been cast in a negative light and something to be avoided in organisation settings, recent thinking suggests that politics may be utilised as a positive force.[16] Political skill has been re-framed recently, as an interpersonal style that can help managers to facilitate change.[17] Butcher and Clarke suggest that politically able managers are those who understand that their role is one of continuous management of change.[18] In fact, they suggest that the political manoeuvring of managers facilitates implementing change such as establishing the interests of individuals that match the change plan, networking and seeking stakeholder support. Politics is never more apparent than during planned change management programs[19], perhaps because it is a time where power relationships themselves are 'unstable and inconsistent'.[20]

Perspectives on power

The foundational work on power emanates from two distinct disciplines — social theory and organisation theory — each providing an essential cornerstone of the present research and practice. Sociological commentators driven by the foundational work of Marx and Weber focus on how power becomes embedded in structures, while organisation theorists such as Narayanan and Fahey concentrate on how power is acquired and wielded outside of established structures, largely taking the distribution of power in formal structures for granted.[21]

Sociological theory perspectives on power

Durkheim saw the trend towards power in organisations being controlled by professional management as the chief vehicle for individual self-interest to be withheld in favour of the needs of the community and the society.[22] Similarly, Mannheim developed the thesis that power within the boundaries of 'free-enterprise', industrial, capitalist nations is becoming less attached to class identification and more associated with the bonds of common education and professionalism.[23] This viewpoint stood in opposition to the doctrine of Marxism, which argued that power is fixed within the confines of a class society, irrespective of autonomy or detachment from any pre-existing social group. Marx argued that power is defined by the categories of ownership of the means of production.[24] He proposed that capitalist societies unjustly remove the wealth from the workers who produce it. Marx viewed power in terms of mistreatment and the ongoing exploitation of workers who remain powerless in the capitalist class structure.[25] He famously observed that within the capitalist system, all the methods for increasing the productiveness of labour are applied at the cost of the individual worker and that these methods 'mutilate the worker into a fragment of a human being, degrade him to become a mere appurtenance of the machine, make his work such a torment that its essential meaning is destroyed … they transform his whole life into working time, and drag his wife and children beneath the Juggernaut wheels of capital's care'.[26]

Marx, obviously not a fan of capitalism, saw the power that the system gives to certain individuals and organisations as inequitable. Most important, from the manager's viewpoint, is Marx's assumption about the exploitation of those who perform the work. Managers have the delicate task of maximising productivity without abusing the power with which Marx claims the capitalist system endows them.

Weber acknowledged that power is derived from controlling the means of production, but he took an additional step in maintaining that power also can be derived as much from knowledge of operations as from ownership.[27] This view presupposes that all organisational members possess the agency to use power, although Weber accepted that this was not necessarily equal for all members. In many ways, Weber provided the first commentary on empowerment, which has become an essential ingredient in managing resistance to change.

Dahl determined that power was the ability of one element to influence another in a manner that would not have occurred under natural circumstances.[28] He acknowledged that power is a raw intervention for attempting to control resistance. Dahl aimed to identify the **sources of power** in decision-making processes.[29] Like Marx and Weber before him, he assumed that the implementation of power occurs only in the context of observable conflict and resolution.[30] This assumes that individuals are aware of their grievances and use influence to act on them.

Although groundbreaking in developing the concept of power in organisations, social explanations of power are limited by their assumption that employers and employees are insightful about their abundance or lack of power. In contrast, today's organisation theorists seek to explore power from a multidimensional viewpoint, beginning with the formal structures and relationships noted by sociologists and moving into the hidden, ambiguous and even unconscious applications of power.

Organisational theory perspectives on power

The early organisation studies used social theory as a springboard for their conceptualisation of power.[31] While they began with a common definition of power — that is, the ability to get an individual or group to behave in a way that they otherwise would not (what Buchanan and Badham identified as episodic power)[32] — they subsequently focused on identifying sources of power, initially believing that power exists only in decisions where conflict is observable. Organisation theorists later began to challenge the existing models of decision-making, counselling that power could be employed covertly or without confrontation.[33] This observation marked a turning point, which proved the catalyst for serious investigation of the bases and sources of power. It also yielded a greater appreciation of the limitations of the existing change management theory, which emphasised overcoming resistance through hard, direct and confrontational interventions. Organisation theory perspectives on power are related to the second and third dimensions of power explained shortly. In these dimensions, power is used to suppress opposition, sometimes through new policies and systems. It has long been assumed that power is used like a stick to beat the less powerful, but more and more evidence suggests that power is more complex and subtle. Power is sometimes more like giving a lollipop to a screaming child.

Bases of power

French and Raven proposed five **bases of power** in organisational resources that have withstood the test of time, only recently having been further developed.[34] Here, we explore their bases of power and the implicit approach to overcoming change that each assumes.

- **Reward power** is based on the belief that the change initiator has access to valued rewards that will be dispensed in return for compliance. Reward power is based on the hope that an extrinsic reward will compensate for a loss of autonomy or for the political danger of supporting a change. *It is commonly used to overcome resistance to change by 'purchasing' support and loyalty.* It typically comes in the form of remuneration, awards, compliments, gestures of praise and social recognition.

- **Coercive power** is based on the belief that the change initiator can administer unwelcome penalties or sanctions. Coercive power is grounded in fear. *It is used to overcome resistance by associating a lack of compliance with suffering of some kind.* It may involve demotion, physical or psychological injury, unwanted transfer, withholding of needed resources, loss of overtime bonuses, humiliation in front of peers, threat of plant closure or even redundancy or sacking.

- **Referent power** is based on the belief that the change driver has desirable abilities and personality traits that should be copied. Referent power depends on people's need for leadership, inspiration and acceptance. *It can be used to overcome resistance to change by manipulating personal loyalties and friendship.* It may take the form of personal charisma, 'reciprocal identification' (friendship), common values, mutual interests, collective perspectives and IOUs.

- **Legitimate power** is based on the belief that the change initiator has the authority to give instructions as a direct consequence of their formal position or rank within the organisation. Legitimate power relies on hierarchy and the assumption that an individual's place in the organisational structure bestows certain power privileges. *It can be used to overcome resistance by presenting change as a necessary condition for success that can be decided only by the senior personnel of the organisation.* It may take the form of new activities, procedures, policies, systems or strategies imposed on the organisation.

- **Expert power** is based on the belief that the change driver has superior knowledge relevant to the situation and the challenges presented to the organisation. Expert power is based in perceived knowledge and information. *It can be used to overcome resistance via claims that specialist knowledge is needed to appreciate the relevance and appropriateness of change attempts, and that decisions should be left to these experts.* It may involve the use of external consultants, internal specialists or a select group of well-informed, senior managers.

French and Raven's power bases take a relational perspective. In the words of Buchanan and Badham: 'Power is not merely the property of the individual, to be acquired and accumulated. Power is a relational construct.'[35] These bases depend on the beliefs of others. Change initiators can manipulate rewards and penalties, make friends, covet information and demand change, but if others do not believe in their bases of power, then they may be unwilling to comply. According to Hardy and Leiba-O'Sullivan, this model revolves around resource dependency because it links power to the control of scarce resources such as information, expertise, credibility, prestige, money, rewards and penalties.[36] The association with resource possession also opens this grouping of power bases to a political interpretation; for example, managers scramble for control of resources to bolster their power base.

Benfari, Wilkinson and Orth built upon French and Raven's bases of power, appending three additional elements: information power, affiliation power and group power.[37] *Information* relates to the ability to access non-public knowledge through personal connections and can exist at all levels from secretaries to senior executives. Not dissimilar to referent power, informational power can be used to overcome resistance when knowledge, particularly foreknowledge, can effect a change effort. Forewarning of a union strike in response to a change initiative, for example, may provide an opportunity to prevent the action. In some cases, informational power can foreshadow undesirable reactions to change intercession before they occur. *Affiliation* relates to power 'borrowed' from a more 'genuine' authority source by association, such as the power of the chief executive officer's personal assistant. Affiliation power can be used to overcome resistance by implicitly or explicitly threatening the direct involvement of the associated authority. *Group* power comes about as an outcome of solidarity. It can be driven by group problem-solving and collective resolutions, such as in industrial action or cartel behaviour. Group power can be used to overcome resistance when the critical mass of employees accepts a change, or for when employees resist a change.

Additional bases of power observed by other researchers include: *technological* power, which asserts that the assembly line of the mid-20th century controlled workers by determining task specification, speed of work and isolation[38]; *bureaucratic* power, which provides control over decision-making and information accessibility[39]; and *philosophical* power, which revolves around the power associated with inculcated values and world views. While clearly an overlap exists with some of French and Raven's bases, it is also clear that a change initiator may use a substantial range of power-based mechanisms for introducing change. When describing the personal power characteristics of an individual, researchers usually refer to power sources.

In January 2002, the National Australia Bank (NAB) announced plans for a corporate restructure, which aimed to build the company around regionalised financial services teams. The new structure included the creation of three regional business units in Australia, New Zealand and Great Britain/Ireland. The then National Managing Director and Chief Executive Officer (CEO), Frank Cicutto, indicated that the new structure would help to ensure that management in geographically distant regions (especially Great Britain and Ireland) could concentrate on the strategic issues of that region.

However, in February 2004, Cicutto resigned as CEO of the NAB in the wake of the $360 million currency trading loss. Despite the significant media attention covering the trading losses, it was NAB's venture into international banking that had stimulated a greater financial burden. In 2001, NAB suffered $4 billion losses on the US mortgage-writing subsidiary, HomeSide.

With board approval, Frank Cicutto appointed PricewaterhouseCoopers (PwC) to conduct an inquiry into how the $360 million trading disaster occurred. However, the extensive existing relationships between PwC and NAB meant that significant controversy ensued, questioning the independence of the report. NAB's management of the PwC report was further compromised when Frank Cicutto and Chairman Charles Allen resigned before the release of findings. This controversy occurred at a time when independent, non-executive director Cathy Walters was reportedly raising concerns about the inquiry with fellow directors. Media accounts suggested that Walters alleged the PwC inquiry (which led to her sacking as the audit committee chair) was improperly influenced by Mr Kraehe, who was then head of the risk committee and had been on the board at the time of the HomeSide disaster. The situation worsened when the board elected to appoint Graham Kraehe as Chairman.

The financial industry regulator, the Australian Prudential and Regulation Authority (APRA), also conducted an investigation into the losses, releasing a report in March 2004. Both reports criticised the NAB for management flaws, systemic flaws in currency trading, and board inaction in response to increasing losses. APRA also highlighted a careless approach to trading risk management, stating that a warning letter sent to chairman Charles Allen a year before the currency scandal was exposed, identifying problems with risk management and governance, had not been brought to the board's attention. However, APRA's Chairman, Dr John Laker, reported that although the problems identified in the report were serious, they did not threaten the viability of the NAB or its capacity to meet its obligations.

By this time, the boardroom 'brawl' had seen the loss of shareholder value, a chairman, two chief executives and several senior managers; the board left with only three original board members still sitting. New CEO, John Stewart, (recruited from the Bank's British division in early February 2004, but before the shock waves of the scandal had dissipated), was faced with the challenge of reconstructing the NAB board, and overseeing his executives' implementation of the widespread systematic and cultural changes demanded in the inquiry reports.

Sources of power

The bases of power provide a neat explanation of the factors that managers and workers may control. The limitation of this explanation, however, and as the 'Change management in action' illustrates, is that it does not illuminate the political process associated with the acquisition of these power bases. In response, the notion of sources of power has been conceived, which takes the 'latent property' approach that power is something that someone possesses. Hardy and Clegg expand on this notion by asserting that a person's power base depends on available resources and prevailing circumstances, making the 'list' of potential power bases infinite.[40] Bases for power may be considered those factors that an individual controls, while sources of power are the political instruments through which these bases are obtained.[41]

The distinction is not a pedantic one, even from a practical, managerial perspective. Change programs encounter barriers and change initiators assert their power to overcome those obstacles. An understanding of the base of their power is pivotal. A department's new manager, for example, may seek to use his or her legitimate power to champion a new initiative, but might encounter resistance from other department heads. If the resistance proves severe then the new manager may become involved in a fight for more power. Put simply, many change attempts fail because the likely resistance is not anticipated or the expected resistance is not met with the most appropriate discharge of power. In some cases, the essential political process of gathering the prerequisite sources of power is not undertaken. It is often assumed that a structurally based form of power is sufficient.

Power is not inherently positive or negative. It is tightly bound up with the perceptions of organisational members. While the notion of overcoming resistance implies that the obstacles to change, human or otherwise, must be overwhelmed with force, the successful use of power is allied to the context of the resistance. Sometimes this context necessitates finding some additional sources of power by political means. As we discuss later in this chapter, some effective methods for managing resistance revolve around redistributing power and gathering sufficient information about organisational culture to reveal the systems that will enable change most readily. The former approach may prevent, or at least diffuse, resistance while the latter may minimise resistance. Before we present these approaches, however, it is necessary to establish a framework for refocusing power and resistance, to shed light on organisational change attempts.

Dimensions of power

Lukes' three dimensions of power provide the basic framework on which we build our examination of the relationships between power and change.[42] The **first dimension of power** is exercised in open conflict or debate. Change and, in particular, overcoming overt resistance in this dimension are direct functions of who wields the greatest power. The approach is about overpowering openly displayed resistance, like a military officer who issues a 'direct' order to a reluctant soldier. The **second dimension of power** is exercised to suppress conflict or debate. Resistance is a limited issue because open conflict and debate are avoided in favour of maintaining the status quo. The manager who communicates policy and instructions to staff via memos and emails rather than face-to-face meetings and forums may be operating in this second dimension. The **third dimension of power** is a reflection of the institutional norms and procedures that bind the domain and direction of conflict and its resolution. Power is embedded in this dimension in collective meaning — what organisation theorists would term 'culture'. The degree to which change is accepted is an expression of the organisation's culture. In other words, power is accepted in ways in which it has been accepted in the past. When

Australian cricket selectors choose the national team, they are exercising power in the third dimension, even though they may encounter resistance from the team captain. Each dimension of power and its association with change is described and interpreted in the following section.

Change in the first dimension of power

The exercise of power in the first dimension occurs where observable conflict exists and is resolved during the decision-making process.[43] This view links power to the control of scarce resources on which others depend, and represents the practical application of the bases and sources of power described earlier. In other words, when power from one of the bases is exercised, it may be categorised as a first dimension use. Fiol, and Hardy and Leiba-O'Sullivan[44] claim that the first dimension stems from the sociological understanding that power is employed to influence the outcome of decision-making, wherein power is defined as the ability of one party to get another party to do something, even against their will if necessary.[45] This first dimension is both behavioural and functionalist in that it highlights the overt exercise of power in decision-making (behavioural) and the outcome of that decision-making (functional). Change management interventions that use power in the first dimension seek to overcome explicit resistance by overpowering it. The expression 'resistance to change' was originally conceived from this orientation. Resistance from this viewpoint is a threat to the existing power-holders and challenges their right to make changes (bases of power). The outcome can be a battle between those who hold the bases of power and those who do not, but seek to acquire the bases of power such as two staff clambering for the same promotion.

Change in the second dimension of power

While the focus of management in the first dimension is on the political use of resources and the assumption that the most powerful party will emerge with those coveted resources, the second dimension does not presuppose that political contests are open to all participants. Put simply, resistance to change is not necessarily overt because some organisational members will always remain powerless. Lack of political confrontation does not equal lack of resistance. The primary orientation of power when used in the second dimension is the suppression of conflict. Power is used to ensure harmony, at least on the surface. This outcome is achieved by determining what may or may not be brought out into the open in the first place. Opportunities for resistance and dissension are withdrawn. Resistance to change is avoided because power is cleverly used to ensure the changes that are introduced do not upset the existing but concealed conflict. Rather than confronting the opponents to change, they are sidelined, or simply eliminated from the decision-making loop. As Bacharach and Baratz caution, this dimension is often associated with 'non decision-making'.[46] The second dimension of power still assumes, as does the first, that power is embedded in opposition and discord. The remedy, however, is not to overpower resistance, but to bypass it through political activity. Naturally, the difficulty is that such an application of power is inherently volatile. The effect of this potential volatility in organisations is that change programs may never really gain any momentum.

Three forms of non-decision-making have been noted.[47] First, the more powerful individuals deal with grievances by dismissing them as minor or irrelevant, or by undertaking endless and typically inconclusive examination by committees. Second, anticipating the first non-decision-making technique, less powerful individuals do not even bother to raise grievances. Third, the more powerful individuals control which matters are 'legitimate' and the mechanisms through which they are raised, thereby circumventing any confrontations. Despite the cynical nature of power as used in the second dimension, some evidence suggests that power can still be used without manipulation or coercion in 'empowered' organisations. We explore this idea later in the chapter.

Change in the third dimension of power

Lukes' third dimension acknowledges that power may be used to prevent conflict from occurring in the first place, even avoiding the need for non-decisions to be made to bypass conflict. Lukes believes that power can be used to manipulate people's 'perceptions, cognitions and preferences in such a way that they accept their role in the existing order of things, either because they can see or imagine no alternative to it, or because they view it as natural and unchangeable, or because they value it as divinely ordained or beneficial'.[48] This dimension is substantially different from the preceding two in its assumptions about power and conflict, because power is used not only to resolve or repress conflict but, also, to preclude it from emerging.[49]

Power in this dimension is not only economic and structural, but also ideological.[50] Through the construction of everyday beliefs and practices, power is used to produce consensus, replacing overt systems with covert forms of domination. Power is intrinsically hidden in the existing cultural status quo.[51] It can be exposed only by a revelation of the deep cultural significance of activities and behaviours. In this way, when the use of power aligns with the third dimension, it represents an approach described in critical theory as well as in the Marxist concept of mistreatment.[52] Although this form of power use exploits the powerless, it also can be employed by subordinates as a form of resistance[53]; the cultural structures that entrench the powerful also can institutionalise some practices and activities that are likely to prevent other changes from being easily introduced. A change policy that is designed to prevent employees from arriving late to work, for example, may backfire when the same employees collectively decide to leave on time as well, eliminating any overtime normally assumed.

A fourth dimension of power

Hardy and Leiba-O'Sullivan nominate a **fourth dimension of power**[54] to build on Lukes' model, derived from developments in the study of power, particularly by Foucault.[55] The fourth dimension is concerned with the limits of power. Hardy and Leiba-O'Sullivan suggest that the first two dimensions deal with the surface of power via the mobilisation of resources and the control of decision-making processes. They further note that the third dimension addresses a deeper level of power, because it is applied by manipulating the meanings that shape the lives of organisational members.

The fourth dimension is deeper again; here, power is embedded in the very fabric of the system, constraining what is thought, what is seen, how it is seen and what limits the capacity for resistance.

According to Hardy and Leiba-O'Sullivan, there is no such thing as freedom from power. Power is inescapable; it cannot be eliminated, only redistributed. The fourth dimension assumes that some participants may enjoy the advantages of the power relations embedded in the system, but that 'they can neither control nor escape them'.[56] Power is used in the fourth dimension with the assumption that power relations cannot be controlled because they are seamlessly entwined in the system. Change management approaches, therefore, should acknowledge the inability of change initiators to dissolve power structures. The elimination of one structure will, by definition, lead to its replacement by another. The best approach to overcoming resistance to change is to accept that the power structures do not necessarily best facilitate the implementation of necessary change. In such cases, it may be best to consider the redistribution of power relations — what researchers have come to describe as **empowerment**. If genuine empowerment means freedom from power, then the concept is not achievable, so we must conceptualise empowerment as a re-distribution of power. We discuss this important realisation in the next section. Table 8.1 summarises the dimensions of power.

TABLE 8.1	The dimensions of power			
	First dimension: conflict outcome	**Second dimension: conflict suppression**	**Third dimension: meaning-making**	**Fourth dimension: systemic**
Power mechanism	Power exercised through open conflict and debate	Power exercised to suppress conflict and open debate	Power embedded in collective meaning; power exercised to suppress awareness of potential conflict	Power embedded in the system; power redistributed to achieve organisational goals
	Control of resources	Control of processes	Control of meaning	Control of system
Seat of power	Those who control resources	Those who determine legitimacy of conflict	Those who control meaning-making and culture	Organisational system
Empowerment mechanism	Transfer of resources to employees to influence decision-making; the number and type of resources transferred are limited	Transfer of decision-making process to employees; management sets the parameters of decision-making	Political consciousness heightened so how meaning is managed is understood; meaning is managed to legitimise organisational goals and influence behaviour covertly	System re-engineered to change power brokers and those empowered
	Relational	Relational	Motivational	Systemic

Empowerment

Although the concepts of power and empowerment are both logically and practically linked, much of the work on empowerment in research and popular business literature avoids any discussion of power.[57] This lack of a substantive connection between power and empowerment stems from the relative associations that the two terms elicit. Power has traditionally been coupled with exploitation, while empowerment has enjoyed, particularly in recent times, a favourable position in change management discussion. Empowerment or participation in decision-making has been part of management since the beginnings of industrial democracy.[58] Foegen argues that empowerment is little more than a fine-tuning of the managerial task of delegation.[59] Empowerment may be understood simply as the redistribution of decision-making to involve employee or worker participation.

Worker participation is a central issue in change management.[60] Companies have responded by introducing a gamut of organisational structures, including worker-owned structures (employee share participation programs), matrix structures, feminist structures, local economies, managed cooperatives and alternative trade organisations. A critical action learning approach, for instance, suggests that empowering processes are those that focus on workers developing their own capacities, facilitating their own learning, advocating for their own wants and developing the power of self-determination.[61] While each program has its own nuances, the common ingredients revolve around being 'more knowledge intensive, radically decentralised, participative, adaptive, flexible, efficient, and responsive to rapid change'.[62] These characteristics are effectively an attempt by organisations to disseminate power in the hope that collective decisions will facilitate essential changes without provoking resistance or conflict. Empowerment undermines resistance by giving ownership of change-related decisions to those who could oppose them. It is an inside-out approach to change management.

Given that power can never be eliminated (remember the fourth dimension), however, empowerment may be viewed as an attempt to redistribute power or create a more equitable balance of power so organisational objectives can be achieved and employee satisfaction can be increased simultaneously. True freedom from power is not attainable, so change initiators must explore the best ways of redistributing it.

The popular rationale for empowerment

Empowerment has been preached as a solution to change resistance because it is designed to liberate employees, improve financial performance, enhance customer relations and increase job satisfaction.[63] It has even been proposed as a prerequisite for organisations to flourish in the global environment.[64] Some commentators, such as Sante and Bakke, believe that empowerment is not primarily about strategic sense, but about community, contributing to society and 'improving the world'.[65] While some empowerment advocates insist that it is a kind of management panacea, others are more cynical, observing that senior managers have instrumental reasons for implementing empowerment programs.[66] Such programs are rarely introduced to enhance morale or demonstrate equitability; rather, their usual aim is to improve productivity, lower costs, raise customer satisfaction or dissolve unending resistance. Although empowerment may be a worthwhile end, in practice it remains another vehicle for increasing productivity.

From a theoretical perspective at least, cynical approaches to empowerment may miss a vital point. 'Sincere' empowerment revolves around the recognition that organisational members possess vast quantities of knowledge and motivation. From this perspective, empowerment is not so much about giving power away, but about assuming that people already have it.[67] Barner gives a slightly different spin to this idea, suggesting that if power is transferred, then it subsequently must be enabled.[68] This process of 'enablement' assists people in developing the competencies necessary to manage their own empowerment. Either way, the outcome of empowerment can mean unleashing a wealth of knowledge and the desire to use it to improve organisational performance.

Principles of empowerment

Empowerment works in two ways: the **relational approach** and the **motivational approach**.[69] The relational approach aims to redistribute power to employees within specified guidelines, using decentralisation and team-based structures. It is a 'hard', formal management solution. The motivational approach aims to reduce feelings of powerlessness by creating a sense of ownership and capability, using cooperative goal-setting and positive reinforcement. The motivational approach is a 'softer' alternative, which recognises that formal structures are not the only mechanisms of power.

Relational approach to empowerment

This method aims to reduce dependencies that make task performance difficult by delegating power and authority. Typically, this outcome is achieved via the development of some form of team or sub-structure that can bypass standard organisational arrangements and bureaucratic power configurations. Self-managing teams, for example, which set performance standards, monitor performance, select equipment, participate in recruitment decisions, schedule work and deal with discipline and absenteeism, are common in this approach. Advocates believe the approach improves organisational effectiveness because employees will mobilise the power delegated to them, take risks and go beyond the set standards.

The relational approach to empowerment involves significant change particularly that associated with the formal decentralisation of power. Characteristically, however, boundaries are set so employees are permitted to make decisions only within specific areas imposed by management, to ensure the increased power of the employee is not used to pursue personal objectives at the expense of the organisation. In other words, employees are empowered to make only decisions that the perennial power-holders are comfortable with, and that do not challenge the newly modified structural boundaries. It is a kind of selective empowerment that cynical observers may consider to be merely another management initiative to improve performance while simultaneously avoiding the resistances to change interventions. If organisational members remain unconvinced that the empowerment program is sincere and not just another management device to manipulate performance, then management will be forced to confront resistance to the empowerment program.

Motivational approach to empowerment

The motivational approach involves less structural delegation of power, but emphasises open communication and cooperative goal-setting designed to increase commitment and involvement. Other common strategies involve role modelling, organisational learning and positive encouragement to offset stress or anxiety and persuade individuals that they are capable and worthy.[70] The primary aim is to encourage feelings of responsibility. Perhaps the best way in which to understand the motivational approach is to see it as an attempt to foster employees' perceived custody of performance. The principal intention is to counteract feelings of powerlessness, which are viewed as the major impediment to performance. Achieving this objective may not have a direct implication for the delegation of power and authority.

It has been suggested that motivational empowerment can be an important ingredient in creating an organisation that acts as a complex adaptive system; in other words as an organisation where adaptive change emerges naturally out of the system, rather than being imposed from the top down.[71] Smith and Rupp suggest that managers who allow employees to interact autonomously, without central control, also allow emergent structures and creativity to flourish.[72]

The strength of the motivational approach to empowerment is that it is sensitive to the negative psychological and emotional experiences that employees endure when subjected to powerlessness. The difficulty is that this approach does not provide a substantial physical demonstration of management's intentions or sincerity in introducing empowerment. It also relies on senior and middle management's willingness and skills to practise motivational empowerment. There remains the danger that either employees or managers (or both) will consider the practices to be too 'touchy feely'. In addition, employees may interpret the method as a lack of management commitment to introducing more physical, structural empowerment. The motivational approach can, however, pave the way for more radical relational empowerment at a later stage.

Empowerment practices for managers

Although a complex undertaking, empowerment may be introduced into an organisation within the broad guidelines outlined in table 8.2.[73]

TABLE 8.2	Activities for empowerment
Activity	**Implementation**
Information sharing	Including sensitive information, to develop, trust and enable the mobilisation of knowledge capital
Gradual structural reorganisation	• Developing a vision statement by all levels of the organisation • Setting goals cooperatively • Setting guidelines to decision-making • Appraising performance through cooperative effort, not supervision • Training to learn skills of empowerment

(continued)

TABLE 8.2 (cont'd)

Activity	Implementation
Cultural fit	• Working to ensure the structure and culture of the organisation support empowerment by creating an 'empowerment ecosystem' • Dismantling hierarchy in favour of small teams • Decentralising functions and eliminating groups of functional specialists • Setting up free and frequent information flow • Establishing a system of accountability for decision-making • Hiring new employees based on 'cultural fit'
Leadership	Leaders become: • advisers • guardians of principles • accountability managers • encouragers[74]
Employees	Employees become: • decision-makers • strategic planners • capital allocators.

Resistance to empowerment

Despite the intuitive and popular appeal of empowerment, there is evidence that the technique is not meeting the expectations of employers or employees.[75] Lee goes so far as to propose that empowerment is a 'symbol of oppression'.[76] Suffice to say that empowerment may not deliver the anticipated outcomes. Foegen suggests that managers may resist a changed role (with less 'power') and that employees may not want to be empowered as a result of perceived condescension from management, increased workload, responsibility and risk.[77] Some people simply do not want the 'power' to make decisions if it means accepting accountability for the outcomes. Furthermore, employees may be cynical about empowerment because they recognise the essential truth about humans: power and hierarchy are forever. As the cliché suggests, nature abhors a vacuum, and a power vacuum is the fastest to fill.

Kirkman, Jones and Shapiro studied the circumstances under which employees resist teams, which are a fundamental element in empowerment structures.[78] They note that employee resistance revolves around perceived unfairness, increases in workloads, unclear role definitions, uncertain managerial support and a lack of team member social support. Their research underpins the notion that empowerment programs can lead to employee concerns about trust. We consider this element in change programs, along with the psychological adjustments necessary for change to occur, in chapter 10.

Like many management practices, empowerment has not gone as planned for some organisations. Sometimes, empowerment is given little more than lip service[79], where employees are told they are empowered but know better because they are 'second-guessed' by managers or left out of decision-making on matters of importance. The fact that empowerment may be resisted highlights the fact that it does not create a power-free environment, as described by Hardy and Leiba-O'Sullivan's fourth dimension. Empowerment, therefore, presents a paradox.

The paradox of empowerment

The shortcomings of empowerment and the motivations for resistance highlight what Stohl and Cheney label as the paradox of workplace democracy.[80] Empowerment can be viewed as disguising control within the rhetoric of freedom and therefore putting a more 'humanistic' face on manipulation — that is, 'clothing the fist of power in a velvet glove'.[81] Empowerment initiatives may become the instruments of control from which they are proposed to liberate.[82] By using power to create the perception that organisational and employee interests converge, some empowerment programs reduce the need to apply more overt and coercive forms of power to meet organisational goals and counter resistance.

The important message here is that 'true' empowerment programs either are rare or do not exist. That is not to say that business empowerment practices could not result in some positive experiences and outcomes for both employees and organisations. Hardy and Leiba-O'Sullivan note that some practices of empowerment, such as 'those that grant autonomy, provide variety and challenge, relax formal controls, enhance the opportunity for personal initiative, generate an emotional attachment to collective goals', may constitute substantial improvements in work practices and result in employees 'who believe themselves more highly valued, who feel more excitement and passion in their work, and who derive a more rewarding work experience'.[83] Employees may enjoy being empowered, although introducing an empowerment program smoothly and convincing employees that it will be to their benefit are not necessarily straightforward processes.

While empowerment inevitably contains a risk of exploitation, it also offers changes that can be advantageous to the working life of some employees. Again, we return to the fundamental assumptions about management and change theory. Mainstream management researchers, for example, tend to see power and empowerment as tools that can be used variously to improve performance, sometimes in ways that positively influence employees and sometimes not. In contrast, critical theorists see power through a lens of exploitation, considering empowerment to be nothing but a means of conquering resistance. The difference is that organisational theorists see empowerment as a *response to resistance*, while critical theorists see it as a *mechanism for overcoming resistance*.

Perhaps one way of explaining the disappointing results of empowerment programs is that some organisations may be disinclined to examine the link between power and empowerment. An empowerment program must attend to all three (possibly four) dimensions of power. There is little to be gained by doling out resources and decision-making authority if employees have no conception of their powerlessness in the first place. Further, nothing will come of resistance to the existing power relationships or of any newly developed change initiatives unless employees can take control of those same resources and the authority to use them.

Responses to organisational change

Almost all change management attempts are met with some type of barrier or resistance. As we see in this chapter and throughout this book, there can be many explanations for this resistance, including organisational politics, the inappropriate use of power, challenges to cultural norms and institutionalised practices, lack of understanding, inopportune timing, inadequate resources, incorrect information and even just employee suspicion of honourable management intentions.[84] The literature and research on resistance exhibit consensus on the view that managing resistance is a prerequisite of successful change management, but tend to deal with acceptance or commitment to change separately from rejection of change (what we have been calling resistance). Resistance may be any structural, systemic or human barrier that impedes both deliberately introduced and externally pressured change. The purpose of this section is to draw together the issues associated with fostering acceptance of change and to examine the avenues for overcoming resistance. We consider the role of change theory and assumptions in dealing with change responses, both positive and negative, as well as the impact on resistance of conventional change management strategies. We also consider the importance of identifying impediments to change and the role of organisational culture.

Resistance and commitment

The acceptance or rejection of change may be conceptualised as a continuum that stretches from commitment to resistance. The study of these responses to change has tended towards one extreme or the other.[85] Commitment and resistance, therefore, may be discussed separately and give the false impression that they are unrelated change management issues, when they may be better understood as polar extremes of the single issue — that is, response to change. As Dent and Goldberg argue, there is probably a case for retiring the phrase 'resistance to change'.[86]

Recent literature has emphasised the potentially positive or at least benign nature of resistance.[87] Resistance to change can serve positive purposes, such as forcing change initiators to reconsider hasty plans or marshalling employees' support for a new vision. De Val and Fuentes highlight that resistance is equivalent to inertia, in that it aims to keep the status quo, and is therefore not generally a negative notion since change itself may not be inherently beneficial to organisations.[88] Resistance has, in fact, been re-framed by some as both a positive and necessary force that can inform change efforts through providing alternative ideas, harnessing people into the problem-solving process and aiding the consideration of alternatives.[89] From this perspective there is utility within resistance that can be harnessed through a problem-solving approach to change.[90]

However, management ordinarily views resistance as an unwelcome force. This feeling by management is primarily because resistance can occur irrespective of the value of the change effort being proposed. It is also worth noting that resistance may manifest in a variety of forms, ranging from active resistance (where change is aggressively challenged) to passive resistance (where change is indirectly undermined). Somewhere between resistance and acceptance is apathy to change. Although people might have been informed about imminent changes, they greet the new proposals with indifference and passive resignation. Piderit demonstrates that understanding the nature of ambivalence in employee responses to change is useful in anticipating the mechanisms through which they may communicate their responses to change agents.[91] She remarks that humour, for example, is a common conduit for delivering change responses.

The acceptance of change may range, like resistance, from weak to strong. Lawler proposes that the chief determinants of commitment are information, knowledge, power and rewards.[92] Coetsee adds the notion of shared vision as another essential element.[93] The most comprehensive analysis of commitment has been undertaken by Ulrich, who highlights the management tools necessary for developing commitment: communication, challenging work, training and development, control, collaboration and teamwork, shared gains, a work culture, shared strategy and vision, concern for people, and technology to aid in work efficiency.[94] The important implication of work programs to elicit commitment to change is their link with empowerment.[95] Empowerment provides the contemporary management solution for cultivating commitment to change.

Mode and level of change

Change, or the intention to change, precedes resistance. The nature of change and change processes within an organisation are likely to have an impact on the responses of organisational members to that change. In addition, the underpinning theories to which a change driver may consciously or unconsciously subscribe will influence the response to resistance. Therefore, considering the relationship between change theory and responses to change is essential.

Change theorists have developed a range of sophisticated conceptual models to explain the nature of change within both industries and organisations. For the purpose of exploring the link between these theories and change responses, we consider two dimensions of change — mode and level — as proposed by Meyer, Goes and Brooks.[96] 'Mode' refers to the size and rapidity of the change, while 'level' describes whether the change is proceeding within a specific organisation (internal) or as part of a broader, sector-wide reform (external). To describe the relationship in the simplest possible terms, change may be large or small and may occur inside an organisation or within an industrial sector. The resulting categories are reproduced in figure 8.1.

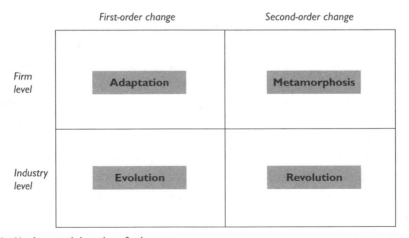

FIGURE 8.1: Modes and levels of change

Incremental or 'first-order' changes within organisations may be categorised under the banner of adaptation theories, which assume that organisations adjust and respond to their changing environments constantly and deliberately. In other words, the mode of change is small and gradual. Any events outside the organisation are irrelevant; successful change is firmly in the hands of managers. The level of change is perceived to be within the organisation alone (internal). Implicit in this perspective is the assumption that resistance to change can be overcome by the selection of the correct approach to deal with it. Resistance is merely another strategic challenge that managers face. Management may, for example, use human resource practices to leverage change, such as employee attitude surveys, which provide information on performance along critical dimensions. Such data are used to bolster cultural change at an individual level and identify where commitment or resistance to change may be found. The consequence of this internal approach is that unsuccessful change, along with the resistance and dissatisfaction it produces, also is the responsibility of managers.

While adaptation theorists are concerned with gradual, internal change, metamorphosis theories concentrate on radical change within organisations. In other words, while the level of change is internal in both theories, the mode differs; it is rapid in the latter theory. The metamorphosis theory suggests that organisations tend to be stable and inert, but occasionally undergo substantial transformation, like Telstra following the telecommunications deregulation. The transformations are sometimes stimulated by progressive maturity through life-cycle stages[97] or by severe shifts in structure, strategy or technology.[98] The important assumption is that change comes rapidly and sometimes without warning. Resistance can be significant because organisational members may be expected to modify their assumptions and practices substantially, with little time to acclimatise. Telstra, for example, was forced to examine its customer service quality when it began to compete for the first time in a market with other telecommunications providers.

A third category of change theory can be identified as evolutionary in orientation. It focuses on incremental change (slow) within industries rather than individual organisations (external). The key to this theoretical standpoint is that organisations are coerced into change by pressures from within their institutional environment, but that they tend to be able to respond gradually, which can allow the natural resistance to be more sensitively approached. The banking sector, for example, has recently undergone substantial downsizing as a result of increased competition and sector-wide pressure to reform. The process for most banks has been slow, undertaken over the course of several years.

Revolutionary change theory emphasises second-order or radical change within industries. The implication of these assumptions about the nature of change is that generally there is no resistance to change because there is no change to be resisted. When change is imposed on an organisation, however, it hits with such ferocity that resistance is either futile or too late. The airline industry in Australia always has been characterised by this form of change where new companies like Compass and Impulse have entered the market unexpectedly, made a big impact and then departed just as quickly.

Relationships between the mode and level of change

A common starting point for observing and conceptualising change is to establish its underpinning force — what we have called the level.[99] This is important in shaping the response to change that organisational members display; for example, a change that is imposed on the organisation by an outside force such as a regulatory agency may be resisted less (or, more importantly, resistance may be directed away from the organisation) than a change enforced internally.

As described earlier, the mode for change may be monumental or subtle. In each case, however, the mode can act as an impetus for change. This 'impetus' or 'catalyst' can be classified according to its source. Thus, an internally driven change, such as a re-engineering initiative by management, can be contrasted to involuntary change made by an organisation as a result of a radical change, such as in trade practices legislation. Some researchers call a radical external change an external 'jolt'.[100] In other words, change can be categorised on the basis of whether it is planned or unplanned.[101] Planned or premeditated changes may display certain characteristics that are uncommon in planned changes. Similarly, planned resistance may differ significantly from spontaneous resistance. In addition, the magnitude of the planned or unplanned change can have a considerable impact on resistance.

The rapidity with which an organisation should be capable of responding to the need for change is the subject of some debate. Laughlin demonstrates that external disturbances can be so large that the organisation, unless it responds immediately and profoundly, may be permanently incapacitated or worse.[102] In contrast, Fox-Wolfgramm, Boal and Hunt insist that short of life and death, all change is incremental and should be implemented gradually.[103] Kanter, Stein and Jick point out that successful change comes from both swift action and prolonged efforts.[104] To complicate matters further, management has to contend with another dimension: organisational response to change.

Separating out change levels and modes, their magnitude and organisational responses is an extremely complex task. First, the change impetus may be significant or weak in magnitude. Second, it may originate from inside the organisation, the immediate organisational environment or the industrial sector. Finally, an organisation may be differentiated based on its response to the change imperative. Responses may vary from complete disinterest to strategic proactivity. Whatever the stimulus, the change may proceed irrespective of the desires and actions of management because the barriers to change are too engrained.

Strebel synthesises the relationship between the force of resistance and the mode for change succinctly.[105] He notes four possible outcomes when the two elements interact. First, when the resistance force is strong and the mode for change is weak (or slow), no change will occur. Second, when resistance is weak and the mode for change is also weak (or slow), change may occur sporadically. Third, when the change mode is strong (or fast) but encounters strong resistance, change may occur discontinuously. Finally, when the mode of change is strong (or fast) and the resistance to change is weak, change may be continuous.

The Meyer, Goes and Brooks matrix shows the relationships between levels and modes of change. Figure 8.2 illustrates the change arena, in a similar way to Strebel's description. Visualising this model is an effective way of conceptualising the ways in which change can arise. As represented in figure 8.2, when a minor change mode or force meets resistance, there is no change, just inertia. On the other hand, as the diagonal arrow highlights, when strong, radical change forces meet little resistance, organisational reinvention can proceed. When the response to change is positive and committed, change may occur incrementally to allow minor organisational revision. Fitful change in the form of organisational renewal can occur when strong change forces are met with resistance.

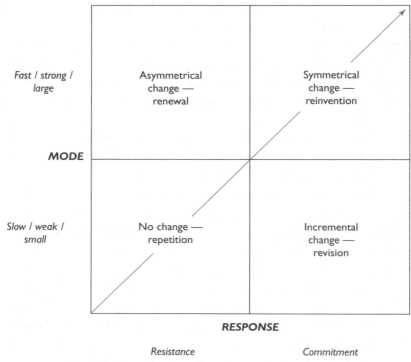

Fast / strong / large	Asymmetrical change — renewal	Symmetrical change — reinvention
Slow / weak / small	No change — repetition	Incremental change — revision

MODE

RESPONSE

Resistance   Commitment

FIGURE 8.2: Mode and response to change

Resistance to change

Although the meaning of 'resistance to change' is intuitively clear, how resistance translates into practical change dissension is unclear. Agocs explains that resistance can include a wide range of behaviours, including refusal to engage in joint problem-solving, refusal to seek common ground, the silencing of advocates for change, sabotage, the use of sanctions and a general lack of cooperation.[106] While researchers have interpreted the term 'resistance to change' in various ways, four views predominate. First, resistance to change is a psychological concept, suggesting that individuals by nature challenge any type of change.[107] Second, resistance to change is a systems concept, reflecting organisational members' discomfort with process modifications that are likely to disadvantage them.[108] Third, the **institutionalised resistance** perspective suggests that organisational members resist change when they do not believe it is necessary. Finally, the **organisational culture** view suggests that members resist change that is contrary to their dominant attitudes and beliefs. The main distinction across the schools of thought is illustrated in their respective assumptions about the causes of resistance.

The psychological model of resistance

Advocates of the psychological model specify a range of causes that stimulate resistance to change. Typical causes include uncertainty, lack of tolerance, differences of opinion concerning the need for change and threatened self-importance. The general themes are fear and anxiety; organisational members fear change because they automatically associate it with some form of personal trauma. They may fear loss of status, privilege or the unknown, or lack trust in the proposed strategy.[109] In an evaluation of nine organisations implementing change programs, Bovey and Hede[110] found that resistance was the result of emotions, which in turn were produced by irrational ideas about the impact of change. They found a high correlation between irrational thinking and behaviour such as blaming, avoidance and being under external control. Psychological model experts recommend a number of methods for overcoming this negative but in-built human reaction, including empowerment, participation, education, facilitation, negotiation, manipulation and coercion[111] — what we understood earlier in this chapter to be the application of power. Lee tells us, 'For the most part, people not organizations resist change'.[112] He likens the change-maker to a foreign material in an organism, subject to combat with a natural self-healing system that constantly seeks to return to normal. Individuals are analogous to anti-bodies fighting an unwelcome change virus. The psychological transition that individuals are faced with is so important that we discuss it further in chapter 10.

The systems model of resistance

In contrast, researchers such as Dent and Goldberg prefer the systems model view-point, and reject the notion that people resist change.[113] They argue that people do not resist change but, instead, resist losing something they like, such as status, money or comfort. The problem, according to Dent and Goldberg, is that the change process is complicated when decision-makers believe that all change will be resisted. These decision-makers assume that the obstacles are created by individual anxiety rather than by the systems they work within and the resources they control. Kotter's studies reinforce the validity of this observation.[114] He concludes that individuals seldom delib-erately sabotage the change process; rather, they usually are forced by the existing performance appraisal system to choose between the new vision and their self-interest. It has also been observed that the size of a firm, rather than its individual participants, may predispose an organisation towards resisting change, given the differing natures of the systems that they constitute and operate within.[115]

Dent and Goldberg, and Kotter also lean towards the strategic choice approach to change, arguing that change can be successfully instituted as long as the correct infor-mation about any given system is available. Researchers who tend towards new institutionalism (such as Post and Altman)[116], however, suggest that it is almost impossible to determine all the elements in a system necessary to make change predict-able. They caution that barriers to change may arise on a macro level, rather than always on an intra-organisational level, and that individual organisations cannot easily manipulate or control these barriers. In their research, for instance, Marci, Tagliaventi and Bertolotti[117] found that resistance to change could be understood as the result of interdependence between the economic environment, the wider industry, the patterning of behaviours within the organisations networks, and the dispositions of individuals.

Institutionalised resistance to change

The systems perspective of change appears to share parallels with the concept of institu-tionalised resistance. When resistance becomes institutionalised, these behaviours have become embedded in an organisation's legitimate structures, decision-making processes and resource allocation. In other words, it can be argued that the behaviours are predetermined within the system. An organisation's formal systems do not, however, necessarily obstruct change. Institutionalised resistance occurs as a result of informal systems and unspoken expectations within an organisation. In other words, change can be resisted not because it is impractical within the existing structures and systems, but because it threatens changes to the ways in which things have been done in the past. Agocs highlights several ways in which institutionalised resistance is introduced.[118]

First, the need for change is denied, which may involve attacks on the change drivers and the importance of the change message. Labianca, Gray and Brass demonstrate through their research that employees' resistance to change may stem as much from difficulties in adapting to new organisational 'schemas' — the cognitive frameworks that give form and meaning to experience — as from purposeful, self-interested behaviour.[119] These schemas sometimes are so entrenched that organisational members deny that any sort of change is necessary. These schemas can be so powerful that they reinforce institutionalised resistances and behaviours.

Second, responsibility for dealing with the change issue is refused altogether. Ironically, empowerment programs may fail because institutionalised resistance prevents employees from accepting a redistribution of power. Research by Folger and Starlicki[120] illuminates the importance of perceived unfairness of change; for example, employees may reject any responsibility for change because they either consciously or unconsciously assume that it will be unjust.

Third, change that has already been agreed is refused at the time of implementation. Organisational members simply decline cooperation. This form of resistance can lead to repressive acts to dismantle the change that already has occurred.

Implicit in Agocs'[121] ideas regarding institutionalised resistance is the idea that resistance occurs because people perceive power in resistance. From this perspective power and resistance to change are, at least in some circumstances, blood relatives. In other words the simple ability to resist and, in so doing, to delay, alter, amend and even halt the change process, may in itself be a form of power. In these circumstances, the continuum is not power versus resistance, but rather, power versus power.

A minor political party, for instance, may resist government proposed legislation of any persuasion, even though the legislation may, in some part, agree with its own espoused political agenda. The model of resistance as power does not yet have much empirical support to confirm its existence. However, Sun Tzu, a Chinese general, who lived more than 2400 years ago, understood power and how it may be sought through opposition or resistance. His famous document *The Art of War*, translated into numerous languages provides insight into how resistance of this kind may be managed.[122] If resistance arises because it senses the opportunity to wield power, the logic of that resistance will differ from the models of resistance previously outlined. Under normal circumstances, the negotiation process states the problem, identifies the underlying cause(s) and offers, within acceptable guidelines and boundaries, several alternatives that go someway towards solving that which those opposing the change perceive as the cause of the problem. The final solution may not fully satisfy any one party, yet it may be acceptable to all parties.

However, opposing change as a form of power dismisses conventional logic and adopts pseudo-logic of its own. In the workplace, the conventional wisdom of using the tools of empowerment, participation, education, facilitation and negotiation against what we term 'opposition inspired power' is of doubtful value. Instead, we must employ tactics of a more considered nature. Sun Tzu offers several suggestions. Consider his strategies of war. He points out that 'To win one hundred battles is not the acme of skill. To subdue the enemy without fighting is the supreme excellence.'[123] To achieve this outcome, Sun Tzu advises not to engage in protracted campaigns, but to take pre-emptive action where possible and to seek quick decisions. For Sun Tzu, what was of supreme importance in war was to upset the enemy's strategic plans. When facing an opposition with power, Sun Tzu suggested that the key to victory was not necessarily in the battlefield, but in devising apt strategies. Such strategies, he stated might include moving swiftly and attacking in places where you were least expected, acting craftily, and using initiative to wrong-foot the opposition. Sun Tzu attached great importance to employing politics, diplomacy and strategic considerations for the purpose of subduing an enemy. In an organisation that seeks change, opposition to that change may be seen as an enemy to that change.

As can be seen from the previous discussion, combating institutionalised resistance revolves around applying power in ways that simultaneously empower organisational members and begin to deconstruct the dysfunctional schemas that dominate the interpretation of the meaning and value of change programs. For managers to achieve this, they need to understand the relationship between resistance and culture. Myriad management techniques have been used to introduce change and replace undesirable schemas with more positive ones.

Organisational culture and resistance

Although culture can be a slippery concept, its impact on organisational behaviour is well established.[124] Just as nations have cultures that dictate how its citizens act towards each other and outsiders, organisations have cultures that govern how their members behave. Culture conveys assumptions, norms and values, which have an impact on activities, practices and goals, thus orchestrating how employees undertake their work and what they view as significant within the workplace. While organisational culture has been defined in a variety of ways, it has a number of recurring themes: first, culture is intrinsically inflexible; second, it is determined by the members of an organisation; third, it is shared by members of an organisation; and finally, while its influence on behaviour can be profound, its core assumptions frequently are hidden from most organisational members.[125] Organisational culture, therefore, can be viewed as a pattern of beliefs and expectations that are common to members of a social unit and subsequently set the behavioural standards or norms for all new employees.[126]

Despite a diversity of research methods, terms and assumptions, researchers' conclusions about culture and the resistances that it can create for change have been remarkably similar. Researchers have variously noted that all organisations possess cultures, that some cultures are stronger than others and, perhaps most importantly, that these cultures can exert a powerful influence on individual behaviour and organisational outcomes.[127] Culture has been related to performance and excellence in the marketplace,[128] as well as to employee commitment, cooperation, efficiency, job performance and decision-making.[129] Organisational culture has proven a significant tool in unravelling the conundrum of organisational behaviour. Unfortunately, while the concept of culture may be enormously useful for understanding the mechanisms governing change, the precise activities for introducing culturally sensitive change remain ambiguous.

Resistance as a socially constructed reality

According to Ford, Ford and McNamara, resistance is not something to be found within individual people, but within the constructed realities that those individuals operate within.[130] In other words, challenges to an individual's worldview stimulate resistance. Ford, Ford and McNamara criticise traditional models of resistance for taking a modernist perspective that presumes all people share a reality, and therefore view a change initiative in the same way. The weakness of this approach, they suggest, is that different responses to change are viewed as misunderstandings of or barriers to that change, requiring the change agent to merely identify the source of resistance in the individual and, subsequently, to apply appropriate strategies to overcome it. Instead, they suggest that 'resistance is a systemic and public phenomenon found in the conversations (interactions) in which people engage'.[131] This view is shared by Butcher and Atkinson[132] who emphasise the importance of language in shaping organisational phenomena, perceptions of reality and, importantly, revealing and legitimising bottom-up or emerging models of change. Although not overtly explored by these authors, this perspective can be seen to coalesce with the organisational culture perspective, given that it defines language as 'in part the external expression of internal mindsets that define an organisation'.[133] Ford, Ford and NcNamara claim that as a socially constructed reality, resistance is formed through the three different 'background' conversations of resignation, complacency and cynicism. Managing resistance therefore requires bringing these background conversations into the foreground for examination, and working through them.

Sources of resistance

The four perspectives of resistance, which have been outlined (the psychological, systems, institutional and organisational culture models), provide differing theoretical models that conceptualise the causes of resistance. However, it can be difficult to operationalise exactly how these causes may manifest in an organisational environment. The work of de Val and Fuentes[134] can be viewed as an attempt to provide a method for recognising a resistance issue by identifying its more observable symptoms. Hence, while the *macro causes* of resistance may be described by using the four paradigms previously outlined, the *micro sources* of resistance are usefully summarised by de Val and Fuentes. Building on the work of Rumelt[135], they suggest that the sources of resistance can be grouped into five categories: first, distorted perceptions of the need for change, including barriers to interpretation and vague strategic priorities; second, low motivation for change; third, a deficient creative response; fourth, political and cultural deadlocks; and, finally, a miscellaneous category. A more comprehensive picture of these sources of resistance can be found in table 8.3.

TABLE 8.3	**Sources of resistance**	
Stage of change	**Source of resistance**	**Examples/manifestations of the resistance**
Formulation	1. Distorted perceptions of change need, barriers to interpretation and vague strategic priorities	Myopia — difficulty projecting into the future with clarity Denial/refusal — to accept contradictory information Perpetuation of ideas — not adjusting ideas to changed situation Implicit assumptions — which distort reality Communication barriers — which distort information Organisational silence — limiting information flow
	2. Low motivation for change	Direct costs of change Cannibalisation of costs — sacrificing losses for gains Cross subsidy comforts — where the status quo offers benefits as well as disadvantages Past failures Different interests — between employees and employers
	3. Lack of creative response	Fast and complex change — prohibiting an effective situation analysis Resignation to change Inadequate strategic vision or commitment of top management
Implementation	4. Political and cultural deadlocks	Departmental politics Incommensurable beliefs — disagreement about the nature of the problem & proposed solutions Deep rooted values & loyalty Lack of awareness of the social dimension of change
	5. Other	Leadership inaction Embedded routines Problems with collective action Lack of necessary capabilities Cynicism

Source: Adapted from M. P. de Val & C. M. Fuentes 2003, 'Resistance to change: a literature review and empirical study', *Management Decision,* 41(2), pp. 148–55. Republished with permission, Emerald Group Publishing Limited, www.emeraldinsight.com

As can be seen, de Val and Fuentes' typology crosses the boundaries of the four theoretical models of resistance that we have previously identified. For example, 'departmental politics' as a source of inertia is arguably an expression of institutionalised resistance, whilst 'lack of motivation' due to past failures is potentially an expression of psychological resistance. This crossing of boundaries can also be identified in the work of other authors, such as Trader-Leigh[136], who have taken a similar approach to de Val and Fuentes. It can also be seen that the examples/manifestations of resistance in the third column are reflective of the nature of the form of resistance, where for example political manoeuvring can commence to block the implementation of a new policy.

It is here that the main limitation of the *sources of resistance* approach as a tool for managing change becomes evident: the sources of resistance approach forces the practitioner to address symptoms rather than underlying causes. How would a practitioner, for instance, treat the problem of 'cynicism' if this had been identified as a source of inertia? This challenge would be difficult without further theoretical understanding, such as how organisational culture and psychology may contribute to the development of cynicism. As a result, in the forthcoming section where we discuss overcoming resistance to change, we will return once again to the four major models of resistance.

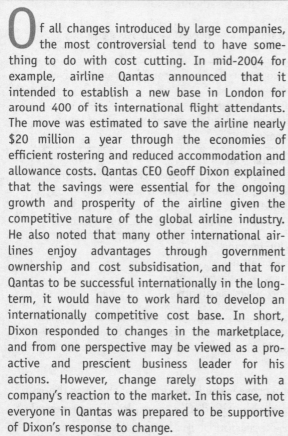

CHANGE MANAGEMENT IN ACTION
Qantas — company response to market change

Of all changes introduced by large companies, the most controversial tend to have something to do with cost cutting. In mid-2004 for example, airline Qantas announced that it intended to establish a new base in London for around 400 of its international flight attendants. The move was estimated to save the airline nearly $20 million a year through the economies of efficient rostering and reduced accommodation and allowance costs. Qantas CEO Geoff Dixon explained that the savings were essential for the ongoing growth and prosperity of the airline given the competitive nature of the global airline industry. He also noted that many other international airlines enjoy advantages through government ownership and cost subsidisation, and that for Qantas to be successful internationally in the long-term, it would have to work hard to develop an internationally competitive cost base. In short, Dixon responded to changes in the marketplace, and from one perspective may be viewed as a pro-active and prescient business leader for his actions. However, change rarely stops with a company's reaction to the market. In this case, not everyone in Qantas was prepared to be supportive of Dixon's response to change.

In large Australian companies, some forms of resistance to change are institutionalised and highly organised. These resistances to change are typically championed by unions representing employees. When Dixon announced his intention to move local jobs offshore, his guarantee that no jobs would be lost as a result was inadequate to prevent unions from immediately threatening industrial action if the proposed plan were to be implemented. The Flight Attendants Association, for example, indicated that they would fight the move, their greatest fear being that the move would herald the arrival of a trend towards international outsourcing where maintenance, call centres, booking and pilots would all eventually be subject to re-location in the name of economic efficiency. Union organised meetings around the country shortly after Dixon's announcement concluded that industrial action was inevitable if Qantas did not change the plan. Qantas, however, continued to argue that industrial action was not justified as the company was offering all new jobs to existing Australian staff first.

While the resolution of this dispute may be decided within the parameters of industrial relations, negotiation and arbitration, it is clear that the initial change was brought about through a response to an external change. This external change, however, also stimulated resistance by the employees and representative unions who would be disadvantaged as a consequence.

Overcoming resistance to change

Cost cutting is rarely a happy exercise. The Qantas example exemplifies one of the most sobering lessons of change management: change introduced towards the best interests of the company and its shareholders is not necessarily also in the best interests of those who are charged with the operation of its core business. Resistance to change is endemic and unavoidable because environmental change is endemic and unavoidable. The point is not whether Dixon is right or wrong to move staff offshore, but rather that the management of change is sensitive, requiring the flexing of senior management muscle at times, and acquiescence at others, in order to navigate around the collision of power.

Consumers, who sometimes resist change, also wield power. In 2003, McDonald's Australia led the way with the introduction of its 'Salads Plus' menu, which featured a range of low-fat alternatives to the traditional high-fat offerings. But this new menu has not shielded McDonald's Australia from the fallout caused by the 2004 film *Super Size Me*, an internationally successful documentary focusing on the negative health effects of McDonald's food, which drew attention to the company's US policy of offering super-sized meals.[137]

Super Size Me filmmaker Morgan Spurlock interviewed experts around the United States about the health impacts of McDonald's food, but drew audiences to his film through the novelty of recording the impact of eating nothing but McDonald's food, three meals a day, for a month. During the period Spurlock gained 11.25 kilograms and suffered from diminished libido, depression and kidney dysfunction.

McDonald's Australia CEO Guy Russo argued that the company has never suggested that customers should eat every meal in the restaurant and that Spurlock had deliberately doubled his caloric intake while avoiding exercise. More unusually, though, Russo produced and fronted a series of television advertisements in which he refuted the claims made in *Super Size Me*. Russo's response to change had originally been to introduce new products to satisfy a market with changing taste. But in the midst of media controversy, he attempted to overcome resistance by making a rapid and direct change.

From a theoretical view we have noted the rift between those who favour incremental approaches to change and those who advocate rapid change. The argument is not about whether attempts at organisational change are usually successful; both views accept that change attempts fail at least as often as they succeed.[138] Beer, Eisenstat and Spector discovered in one-third of the change cases they studied that the outcome of the program was worse than the situation before its implementation.[139] Similarly, Porras and Robertson note that less than 40 per cent of change efforts reported in literature produced a positive result in the dependent variable of concern.[140] Molinski concludes that the change process itself is the culprit.[141]

The paradox of this argument is that change programs can preclude effective change outcomes by their very nature. The difference of opinion is not about whether change attempts often fail or even whether every organisation possesses implicit barriers to change, but about what can be done to overcome those barriers that commonly lead to failure. New institutionalists argue that the likelihood of overcoming the barriers to change is linked to the power of external forces or jolts. In other words, traumatic or overwhelming environmental change will stimulate internal change, because it moves the onus of change from the organisation to an 'outside' force. In contrast, strategic choice advocates believe that the obstacles to change can be purposefully deconstructed, independent of the size of the external force. The question that remains is how the obstacles to change can be overcome.

Greenwood and Hinings developed a useful theoretical framework for charting how organisations typically go about the change process.[142] Their model helps to explain why certain change processes can meet with significant resistance and why others proceed comparatively smoothly. They note that organisational structures and systems can be conceptualised best as archetypes or patterns that govern all organisational processes, and that they are underpinned by the collective values and beliefs of organisational members. Whenever an organisation attempts to divorce itself from its core archetype, the results are revealed as 'tracks', which act as beacons signalling change. The greater the attempted shift away from the core archetype, the heavier is the subsequent resistance. Radical change and change inconsistent with the flow of the archetype are more likely to fail than incremental change, which does not challenge the fundamental nature of the organisation in one step.

Irrespective of the nature of change, a general consensus can be seen among writers that change involves having to overcome some form of organisational inertia.[143] As a result, change management is about challenging conventional wisdom and designing new paradigms while finding the difficult balance between stability and dynamism. This elusive equilibrium should be seen in a match between an organisation and its context or environment. To find success, an organisation must have a 'fit' between its primary products/services and the needs of the marketplace. Also clear is that every organisation possesses 'core' constituents — whether systems, processes, values, behaviours or communication channels — that are especially important. If change efforts focus on these elements of the organisation, then change may be more easily introduced. Unfortunately, tackling these elements may also mean higher levels of resistance. Understanding which cultural elements are 'elastic' and can withstand some intervention, and which will 'snap' under modest pressure, therefore, is essential. Table 8.4 summarises the types of resistance, their cause and common solutions.

TABLE 8.4	Summary of resistance types	
Resistance type	**Resistance cause**	**Management solution**
Psychological	Employees feel anxiety or fear about the change and its personal implications.	Alleviate anxiety and fear through consultative and empowering activities.
Systemic	The current methods prevent new ways of thinking or working.	Redesign systems to support new changes — for example, re-engineering and total quality management.
Institutionalised	The need for change is denied.	Demonstrate the value of the proposed change or the urgency of change for organisational prosperity or survival.
Cultural	The proposed changes challenge the beliefs and values of organisational members.	Introduce activities and policies to replace obstructive values.

Sometimes, resistance to change emerges from areas or individuals not within the company but from those having a direct financial interest in it: from investors. Take, for example, the situation with News Corporation. It announced its intention to relocate its corporate headquarters from Adelaide to Delaware in the United States sometime before the end of calendar year 2004. This relocation, they advised, involved moving News Corporation's primary listing to the New York Stock Exchange while remaining listed on the Australian Stock Exchange (ASX). News Corporation believed that there were substantial benefits to be obtained by the change including increased liquidity, a lower cost of capital and an increased demand for shares.

Under the proposed change, existing Australian shareholders would swap existing ordinary and preferred shares into equivalent voting and non-voting shares in the new company. Initially, Australian investors reacted positively sending the News Corporation share price significantly upwards. For the change to be successful, regulatory, tax, court and shareholder approvals need to be obtained.

The first three approvals are relatively minor. Peter Costello, the Federal Treasurer, announced that under the *Foreign Acquisitions and Takeovers Act 1975*, he has decided to raise no objections under the Government's foreign investment policy to News Corporation's proposal. News Corporation already receives 80 per cent of its earnings outside Australia, so tax problems are minimised and there should be no problem from the courts unless and until shareholders start creating problems.

The major difficulty was in convincing Australian shareholders of the advantages of having News Corporation based in America. Provided there is dual listing — on the New York Stock Exchange and the ASX — most shareholders seemed likely to indicate their approval to the relocation. Unfortunately, the initial reaction to the dual listing from Standard and Poor's, which runs the S&P 500 in the United States, was that a company could not simultaneously be a member of the Australian ASX 50 blue-chip index and the S&P 500 index in the United States due to 'double counting'. Consequently, if the shareholders vote to approve the relocation to the United States, then after listing on the S&P 500 in the United States, News Corporation will disappear from the Australian indices. This would cause the Australian market to lose billions of dollars in annual share trading activity, and would seemingly disadvantage Australian investors.

In response to S&P's decision, the Australian Stock Exchange proposed a complicated new index to keep News Corporation in the Australian listings. While S&P rejected the ASX plan as setting an unacceptable precedent, it agreed to a delay in the transfer of News Corporation to the S&P 500. However, Rupert Murdoch was able to push through approval by shareholders, which meant that by December 2004 the first 25 per cent of shares were being shifted to the United States. The remainder was shifted in three-monthly intervals over nine months in 2005.

Review

This chapter considered two elements of organisational life that have a profound influence on attempts at change management: power and resistance to change. We noted that the two concepts are irrevocably intertwined, in that the application of power in one form or another must be used to overcome resistance. Power is fundamentally defined as the ability to get an individual or group to behave in a way they otherwise would not, whereas resistance is defined as the structural, systemic or human barriers that impede change, whether deliberately introduced or externally pressured.

Initially, we explored perspectives of power. We observed that social theory perceives power as a combative mechanism that can be used to overpower resistance and even exploit workers. In contrast, organisation theorists consider power to be a more complex, multidimensional concept, which can begin with the formal structures and relationships noted by sociologists, but also includes the hidden, ambiguous and even unconscious applications of power. Next, we identified the bases of power: reward, coercive, legitimate, referent and expert. Bases for power are those factors that an individual controls, in contrast to sources of power, which are the political instruments through which these bases are obtained. In making this distinction, we identified the relationship between power and politics.

We also explored the theory that power can be applied in three escalating dimensions. In the first dimension, power is exercised in open conflict or debate. In the second dimension, power is exercised to suppress conflict or debate. In the third dimension, power is a reflection of the institutional norms and procedures that bind and constrain the domain and direction of conflict and its resolution. In this last dimension, power is linked to culture, which is a critical concept associated with resistance.

Finally, we emphasised the importance of understanding the notion and practice of empowerment, which revolves around the redistribution of power from higher in the organisational hierarchy to lower. We cautioned, however, that the use of empowerment as a tool to dampen resistance to change is sometimes met by heightened resistance and cynicism from the newly empowered members of the organisation.

The second section of this chapter concentrated on the broader nature of resistances to change. The acceptance or rejection of change may be conceptualised as a continuum that stretches from commitment to resistance. We used the typology proposed by Meyer, Goes and Brooks as a way of understanding the complexities of change theory and how they relate to resistance. In this model, we considered two dimensions of change: mode (the size and rapidity of the change) and level (whether the change is proceeding within a specific organisation or as part of a broader, sector-wide reform). Change may be large or small, and may occur inside an organisation or within an industrial sector.

We observed that resistance can be overcome by using a variety of techniques, including empowerment, participation, education, facilitation, negotiation, manipulation and coercion, which we noted was the application of power. We determined that organisational members may resist change for four principal reasons: First, because they fear change and are anxious (the psychological model); second, because they see change as impractical given the existing systems (the systems model); and third, because they see no need for change (the institutionalised model) or fourth, they wish to correct any imbalances that have affected the status quo (the cultural model). We also observed that the *sources of resistance* perspective may be helpful in recognising resistance in an organisational environment, by identifying its observable symptoms.

Key terms

bases of power. Those factors that provide an individual with a foundation for exercising power, (p. 268)

coercive power. Power based on the belief that the change driver can administer unwelcome penalties or sanctions, (p. 268)

empowerment. The redistribution of decision-making to involve employee or worker participation, (p. 274)

expert power. Power based on the belief that the change driver has superior knowledge relevant to the situation and the challenges presented to the organisation, (p. 269)

first dimension of power. When power is exercised in open conflict or debate, (p. 271)

fourth dimension of power. When power is embedded in the very fabric of the system, constraining what is thought, what is seen and how it is seen, and providing the means of limiting the capacity for resistance, (p. 273)

institutionalised resistance. When resistance behaviours are embedded in an organisation's legitimate structures, decision-making processes and resource allocation, and lead members to believe that there is no need for change, (p. 284)

legitimate power. Power based on the belief that the change driver has the authority to give instructions as a direct consequence of their formal position or rank within the organisation, (p. 268)

motivational approach (to empowerment). A way of understanding and practising empowerment that emphasises open communication and cooperative goal-setting designed to increase commitment and involvement, (p. 276)

organisational culture. The pattern of beliefs and expectations that is common to members of a social unit and subsequently sets the behavioural standards or norms for all new employees, (p. 284)

politics. Those activities within organisations to acquire, develop and use power and other resources to obtain one's preferred outcomes when there is dissension or uncertainty about choices, (p. 265)

power. The ability to get an individual or group to behave in a way they otherwise would not, or the ability of individuals to achieve desired outcomes, (p. 264)

referent power. Power based on the belief that the change driver has desirable abilities and personality traits that should be copied, (p. 268)

relational approach (to empowerment). A way of understanding and practising empowerment that includes significant structural change, particularly associated with the formal decentralisation of power, (p. 276)

resistance. Any structural, systemic or human barriers that impede both deliberately introduced and externally pressured change, (p. 264)

reward power. Power based on the belief that the change driver has access to valued rewards that will be dispensed in return for compliance, (p. 268)

second dimension of power. When power is exercised to suppress conflict or debate, (p. 271)

sources of power. The political instruments through which bases of power are obtained, (p. 267)

third dimension of power. When power is a reflection of the institutional norms and procedures that constrain the domain and direction of conflict and its resolution, (p. 271)

Review questions

1. What are the differences between power, politics and control?

2. Explain how the concepts of *bases of power* and *sources of power* are different.

3. Identify each of the five *bases of power* identified by French and Raven. In the context of implementing a change management program, what are the strengths and weaknesses of each base of power?

4. What is meant by the term the *first dimension of power*? How does this differ from the *second, third* and *fourth dimensions of power*?

5. Explain the features of an empowerment program that are likely to contribute to success. What features should be avoided when designing an empowerment program?
   (a) What are the pros and cons of empowerment programs?
   (b) Explain how power and empowerment are linked. How does the link between power and empowerment contribute to *paradox* of empowerment suggested by Stohl and Cheney?
6. Explain the situations in which resistance to change may arise in organisations.
   (a) What are the four main perspectives that explain the reasons for resistance to change arising in an organisation?
   (b) Explain each perspective.
7. Explain the difference between the *sources* and *causes* of resistance to change.
8. How might resistance to change be perceived as a positive force?
9. Explain the difference between the *relational* and the *motivational* approach to empowerment.

Discussion questions

1. How are power and change related in organisations? Discuss with reference to the four dimensions of power.
2. 'Empowerment leads to better results for everybody in an organisation.' Discuss, identifying the positive and negative features of empowerment programs.
3. Are *resistance* to change and *commitment* to change unrelated issues, or are they the extremes of a continuum representing responses to change? Explain your answer, and discuss how your perspective changes the way in which resistance is understood.

Work assignments

Power issues at the Australian Soccer Association (Football Federation Australia)

Total time

30–50 minutes of discussion

Imagine you are charged with the responsibility of implementing the changes outlined in the Crawford Report at the Australian Soccer Association (Football Federation Australia — refer to the 'Opening case', page 263, and the Crawford Report itself found at: www.soccerinquiry.org.au/report2003.htm).

   Identify five principles that you have learned in the chapter to help you understand the potential power relationships that may need to be managed. Describe how each power principle you have identified would influence how you would implement the change management program. Discuss your ideas in groups when they are documented.

Developing an empowerment policy

Total time

30–50 minutes of discussion

Imagine you are charged with the responsibility of introducing an empowerment program into the NAB following the crisis outlined in 'Change management in action', (page 270). As the case study implies, given the nature of the industry it would be inappropriate for all controls and regulation to be transferred to employees. In other words, an empowerment program would need to strike a balance between top–down control and the enablement of employees. What would be some aspects of the organisation that may need to be controlled centrally, by management? Discuss whether a *relational* or *motivational* approach to empowerment may be more appropriate for this organisation. Make sure you identify what new activities and responsibilities employees might assume and the benefits they might enjoy as a result. Discuss your policy in groups when they are documented.

Suggested further reading

Butcher, D. & Clarke, M. 2003, 'Redefining managerial work: smart politics', *Management Decision*, 41(5), pp. 477–87.

Ford, J. D., Ford, L. W. & McNamara, R. T. 2002, 'Resistance and the background conversations of change', *Journal of Organizational Change*, 15(2), pp. 105–21.

Garrety, K., Badham, R., Morrigan, V. , Rifkin, W. & Zanko, M. 2003, 'The use of personality typing in organizational change: discourse, emotions and the reflexive subject', *Human Relations*, 56(2), pp. 211–35.

de Val, M.P. & Fuentes, C.M. 2003, 'Resistance to change: a literature review and empirical study', *Management Decision*, 41(2), 148–55.

Stohl, C. & Cheney, G. 2001, 'Participatory processes/paradoxical practices', *Management Communication Quarterly*, 14 (3), pp. 349–407.

End notes

1. J. George & G. Jones 1995, *Understanding and Managing Organizational Behavior*, Addison-Wesley, Massachusetts.

2. C. Handy 1994, *The Empty Raincoat*, Hutchinson, London; T. Peters 1993, *Liberation Management*, Pan Books, London; P. M. Senge 1990, *The Fifth Discipline: The Art and Practice of the Learning Organization*, Doubleday/Currency, New York.

3. J. Kotter 1990, *A Force for Change*, The Free Press, New York; G. Huber & W. Glick (eds) 1995, *Organizational Change and Redesign: Ideas and Insights for Improving Performance*, Oxford University Press, New York; R. M. Kanter, B. A. Stein & T. D. Jick 1992, *The Challenge of Organizational Change*, The Free Press, New York.

4. A. Pettigrew 1985, *Awakening the Giant*, Prentice Hall, New York; R. C. Laughlin 1991, 'Environmental disturbances and organisational transitions and transformations: some alternative models', *Organizational Studies*, 12, pp. 209–32; R. Greenwood & C. Hinings 1993, 'Understanding strategic change: the contribution of archetypes', *The Academy of Management Journal*, 36, pp. 1052–81.

5. M. Lee 1999, 'The lie of power: empowerment as impotence', *Human Relations*, 5, pp. 34–7.

6. R. A. Dahl 1957, 'The concept of power', *Behavioral Science*, 2, pp. 201–15; M. Weber 1978, *Economy and Society: an Outline of Interpretive Sociology*, 2 vols,

eds G. Roth & C. Wittich, University of California Press, Berkeley, California.

7. C. M. Foil 1991, 'Seeing empty spaces: towards a more complex understanding of the meaning of power in organizations', *Organizational Studies*, 12(4), pp. 547–66.

8. D. Buchanan & R. Badham 1999, *Power, Politics and Organisational Change: Winning the Turf Game*, Sage Publications, London, p. 47.

9. C. Stohl & G. Cheney 2001, 'Participatory processes/paradoxical practices', *Management Communication Quarterly*, 14(3), p. 384.

10. Foil, op. cit., p. 547.

11. Buchanan & Badham, op. cit., p. 6.

12. J. Pfeffer 1981, *Power in Organizations*, Ballinger, Cambridge, Massachusetts, p. 10.

13. H. S. Baum 1989, *Organizational Politics Against Culture*, Harcourt Brace, California.

14. D. Butcher & M. Clarke 2003, 'Redefining managerial work: smart politics', *Management Decision*, 41(5), pp. 477–87.

15. R. Vince 2001, 'Power and emotion in organizational learning', *Human Relations*, 54(10), pp. 1325–51.

16. D. Butcher & M. Clarke 2003, op cit; P. Perrewe, G. Ferris, D. Frink & W. Anthony 2000, 'Political skill: an antidote to workplace stressors', *Academy of Management Executive*, 14(3), pp. 115–25.

17. P. Perrewe, et al. 2000, op. cit.

18. D. Butcher & M. Clarke 2003, op cit.

19. D. Buchanan & D. Boddy 1992, *The Expertise of the Change Agent: Public Performance and Backstage Activity*, Prentice Hall, London.

20. K. Garrety, R. Badham, V. Morrigan, W. Rifkin & M. Zanko 2003, 'The use of personality typing in organizational change: discourse, emotions and the reflexive subject', *Human Relations*, 56(2), pp. 211–35.

21. C. Hardy & C. S. Clegg, 1996, 'Some dare call it power', in *Handbook of Organisational Studies*, eds S. Clegg, C. Hardy & W. Nord, Sage Publications, London, p. 623.

22. E. Durkheim 1957, *Professional Ethics and Civic Morals*, Routledge & Kegan Paul, London.

23. K. Mannheim 1936, *Ideology and Utopia*, Harcourt Brace & World, Florida, pp. 155–6.

24. K. Marx 1976, *Capital*, Penguin, Harmondsworth, United Kingdom.

25. J. M. Jermier 1998, 'Introduction: critical perspectives on organizational control', *Administrative Science Quarterly*, 43, p. 236.

26. Cited in Jermier, op. cit., pp. 236–7.

27. M. Weber 1947, *The Theory of Social and Economic Organization*, The Free Press, New York.

28. Dahl, op. cit.

29. ibid.

30. C. Hardy & S. Leiba-O'Sullivan 1998, 'The power behind empowerment: implications for research and practice', *Human Relations*, 54(4), pp. 451–83.

31. J. D. Thompson 1956, 'Authority and power in identical organizations', *American Journal of Sociology*, 62, pp. 290–301; D. Mechanic 1962, 'Sources of power of lower participants in complex organizations', *Administrative Science Quarterly*, 7(3), pp. 349–64; M. Crozier 1964, *The Bureaucratic Phenomenon*, University of Chicago Press, Chicago.

32. Buchanan & Badham, op. cit.

33. For information on the early organisation theorists, see A. M. Pettigrew 1973, *The Politics of Organizational Decision Making*, Tavistock, London; I. C. MacMillan 1978, *Strategy Formulation: Political Concepts*, West, St Pauls, Minnesota; J. Pfeffer 1992, 'Understanding power in organizations', *California Management Review*, 35, pp. 29–50; V. K. Narayanan & L. Fahey 1982, 'The micropolitics of strategy formulation', *The Academy of Management Review*, 7(1), pp. 25–34; B. Gray & S. Ariss 1985, 'Politics and strategic change across organizational life cycles', *The Academy of Management Review*, 10(4), pp. 707–23; C. R. Schwenk 1989, 'Linking cognitive, organizational and political factors in explaining strategic change', *Journal of Management Studies*, 26(2), pp. 177–88.

34. J. French & B. Raven 1958, 'The bases of social power', in *Studies in Social Power*, ed. D. Cartwright, Institute for Social Research, Ann Arbor, Michigan.

35. Buchanan & Badham, op. cit., p. 49.

36. Hardy & Leiba-O'Sullivan, op. cit., pp. 453–4.

37. R. C. Benfari, H. E. Wilkinson & C. D. Orth 1986, 'The effective use of power', *Business Horizons*, May–June, pp. 12–16.

38. R. Edwards 1979, *Contested Terrain*, Basic Books, New York.

39. Jermier, op. cit., p. 246.
40. Hardy & Clegg, op. cit.; C. Hardy 1985 'The nature of unobtrusive power', *Journal of Management Studies*, 22(4), pp. 384–99.
41. S. B. Bacharach & E. J. Lawler 1981, *Power and Politics in Organizations: The Social Psychology of Conflict, Coalitions, and Bargaining*, Jossey-Bass, San Francisco, p. 34.
42. S. Lukes 1974, *Power: A Radical View*, Macmillan, London.
43. Hardy & Leiba-O'Sullivan, op. cit., p. 453.
44. C.M. Fiol 1991, 'Managing culture as a competitive resource: an identity-based view of sustainable competitive advantage', *Journal of Management* 17, pp. 191-211; Hardy & Leiba-O'Sullivan, op. cit.
45. Dahl, op. cit.; N. W. Polsby 1963, *Community Power and Political Theory*, Yale University Press, New Haven.
46. P. Bacharach & M. S. Baratz 1962, 'The two faces of power', *American Political Science Review*, 56, pp. 947–52; Hardy & Leiba-O'Sullivan, op. cit., p. 455.
47. S. R. Clegg 1989, *Frameworks of Power*, Sage Publications, London, p. 77.
48. Lukes, op. cit., p. 24.
49. S. Ranson, C. R. Hinings & R. Greenwood 1980, 'The structuring of organizational structure', *Administrative Science Quarterly*, 25(1), pp. 1–14.
50. D. C. Hoy 1986, 'Power, repression, progress: Foucault, Lukes, and the Frankfurt School', in *Foucault: A Critical Reader*, ed. D. C. Hoy, Basil & Blackwell, Oxford. pp. 123–47.
51. Clegg, op. cit.
52. Jermier, op. cit.
53. Clegg, op. cit.; A. Giddens 1979, *Central Problems in Social Theory*, Macmillan, London; Hardy & Leiba-O'Sullivan, op. cit.
54. Hardy & Leiba-O'Sullivan, op. cit.
55. M. Foucault 1980, *Power/Knowledge*, Pantheon, New York; C. Hardy 1994, 'Understanding interorganizational domains: the case of the refugee systems', *Journal of Applied Behavioral Science*, 30(3), pp. 278–96; D. Knights & H. Willmott 1992, 'Conceptualizing leadership processes: a study of senior managers in a financial services company', *Journal of Management Studies*, 29(6), pp. 761–82.
56. Hardy & Leiba-O'Sullivan, op. cit., p. 461.
57. ibid., p. 451.
58. M. Hancock, J. Logue & B. Schiller 1991, *Managing Modern Capitalism: Industrial Renewal and Workplace Democracy in the United States and Western Europe*, Praeger, New York; N. Lichtenstein & J. Howell 1993, *Industrial Democracy in America*, Cambridge University Press, Cambridge.
59. J. H. Foegen 1999, 'Why not empowerment', *Business and Economic Review*, April–June, p. 31.
60. C. Stohl & G. Cheney 2001, 'Participatory processes/paradoxical practices', *Management Communication Quarterly*, 14(3), pp. 349–407.
61. T. J. Fenwick 2003, 'Emancipatory potential of action learning: a critical analysis', *Journal of Organizational Change Management*, 16(6), pp. 619–32.
62. Stohl & Cheney, op. cit., p. 350.
63. D. Bowen & E. Lawler 1992, 'The empowerment of service workers: what, why, how, and when', *Sloan Management Review*, 33(3), pp. 31–9; R. Ford & M. Fottler 1995, 'Empowerment: matter of degree', *The Academy of Management Executive*, 9(3), 21–31.
64. Stohl & Cheney, op. cit.; C. Stohl 2001, 'Globalizing organizational communication', in *The New Handbook of Organizational Communication*, eds F. M. Jablin & L. L. Putnam, Sage Publications, California, pp. 323–75.
65. S. Wetlaufer 1999, 'Organizing for empowerment: an interview with AES's Roger Sante and Dennis Bakke', *Harvard Business Review*, January–February, pp. 120–1.
66. T. Eccles 1993, 'The deceptive allure of empowerment', *Long Range Planning*, 26(6), pp. 13–21.
67. K. Blanchard, J. Carlos & W. Randolph 1995, *Empowerment Takes More than a Minute*, Jossey-Bass, San Francisco.
68. R. Barner 1994, 'Enablement: the key to empowerment', *Training and Development*, 48(6), pp. 72–86.
69. Hardy & Leiba-O'Sullivan, op. cit., p. 463.
70. R. M. Bokeno 2003, 'Introduction: appraisals of organizational learning as emancipatory change', *Journal of Organizational Change*, 16(6), pp. 603–18.
71. A. D. Smith & W. T. Rupp 2003, 'An examination of emerging strategy and sales performance: motivation, chaotic

change and organizational structure', *Marketing Intelligence & Planning*, 21(3), pp. 156–67.

72. A. D. Smith & W. T. Rupp 2003, op. cit.

73. Blanchard, Carlos & Randolph, op. cit.

74. Wetlaufer, op. cit.

75. See Hardy & Leiba-O'Sullivan 1998, op. cit., p. 452.

76. M. Lee 1999, 'The lie of power: empowerment as impotence', *Human Relations*, pp. 23–45.

77. J. H. Foegen 1999, 'Why not empowerment', *Business and Economic Review*, April–June, p. 32.

78. B. Kirkman, R. Jones & D. Shapiro 2000, 'Why do employees resist teams? Examining the "resistance barrier" to work team effectiveness', *International Journal of Conflict Management*, 11(1), pp. 74–92.

79. Wetlaufer, op. cit.

80. Stohl & Cheney, op. cit.

81. Jermier, op. cit., p. 235.

82. Fenwick, op. cit.

83. Hardy & Leiba-O'Sullivan, op. cit., p. 467.

84. E. Schein 1985, *Organizational Culture and Leadership*, Jossey-Bass, San Francisco; J. Pfeffer 1981, *Power in Organizations*, Ballinger, Cambridge, Massachusetts, p. 10.

85. For commitment, refer to M. Beer & B. Spector 1990, 'Why change programs don't produce change', *Harvard University Business Review*, November–December, pp. 158–66; D. Nadler & M. Tushman 1989, 'Organizational frame bending: principles for managing reorganization', *The Academy of Management Executive*, 3(3), pp. 194–204; for resistance, refer to J. Kotter & L. Schlesinger 1979, 'Choosing strategies for change', *Harvard Business Review*, March–April, pp. 106–14.

86. E. Dent & S. Goldberg 1999, 'Challenging resistance to change', *Journal of Applied Behavioral Science*, 35, pp. 25–42.

87. M. P. de Val & C. M. Fuentes 2003, 'Resistance to change: a literature review and empirical study', *Management Decision*, 41(2), 148–55.

88. de Val & Fuentes, op. cit.

89. V. J. Mabin, S. Forgeson & L. Green 2001, 'Harnessing resistance: using the theory of constraints to assist change management', *Journal of European Industrial Training*, 25(2), pp. 168–91.

90. V. J. Mabin, S. Forgeson & L. Green 2001, op. cit.

91. S. Piderit 2000, 'Rethinking resistance and recognizing ambivalence: a multidimensional view of attitudes towards organizational change', *The Academy of Management Review*, 25(4), pp. 783–94.

92. E. Lawler 1992, *The Ultimate Advantage: Creating the High Involvement Organization*, Jossey-Bass, San Francisco.

93. L. Coetsee 1999, 'From resistance to commitment', *PAQ*, Summer, pp. 204–22.

94. D. Ulrich 1998, 'Intellectual capital-competence — commitment', *Sloan Management Review*, Winter, pp. 15–26.

95. D. Harvey & D. Brown 1996, *An Experiential Approach to Organizational Development*, 5th edn, Prentice Hall, Englewood Cliffs, New Jersey.

96. A. Meyer, J. Goes & G. Brooks 1993, 'Organizations reacting to hyperturbulence', in *Organizational Change and Redesign: Ideas and Insights for Improving Performance*, eds G. P. Huber & W. H. Glick, Oxford University Press, New York, pp. 66–111.

97. J. Kimberly & R. Miles 1980, *The Organizational Life-Cycle*, Jossey-Bass, San Francisco.

98. Laughlin, op. cit.; R. E. Miles & C. C. Snow 1984, 'Fit, failure and the hall of fame', *California Management Review*, 26(3), pp. 10–28; D. Miller & R. Frieson 1984, *Organizations: A Quantum View*, Prentice Hall, Englewood Cliffs, New Jersey; M. L. Tushman & E. Romaneli 1985, 'Organization evolution: a metamorphosis model of convergence and reorientation', in *Research in Organizational Behavior: Volume 7*, eds L. L. Cummings & M. Staw, JAI Press, Greenwich, pp. 171–222.

99. J. Greenberg & R. Barron 1995, *Behavior in Organizations*, 5th edn, Prentice Hall, Englewood Cliffs, New Jersey.

100. A. Ginsberg 1988, 'Measuring and modelling changes in strategy: theoretical foundations and empirical directions', *Strategic Management Journal*, 9, p. 559–75; Laughlin, op. cit.; J. Skinner, B. Stewart & A. Edwards 1998, 'Amateurism to professionalism: modelling organisational change in sporting organisations', *Sport Management Review*, 2(2), pp. 173–92.

101. S. L. Brown & K. M. Eisenhardt 1997, 'The art of continuous change: linking

complexity theory and time-paced evolution in relentlessly shifting organizations', *Administrative Science Quarterly*, 42, pp. 1–34.

102. Laughlin, op. cit.

103. S. J. Fox-Wolfgramm, K. B. Boal & J. G. Hunt 1998, 'Organizational adaptation to institutional change: a comparative study of first-order change in prospector and defender banks', *Administrative Science Quarterly*, 43, pp. 87–126.

104. R. Kanter 1989, *When Giants Learn How to Dance*, Simon & Schuster, New York.

105. P. Strebel 1994, 'Choosing the right change path', *California Management Review*, Winter, pp. 29–31.

106. C. Agocs 1997, 'Institutionalized resistance to organizational change: denial, inaction and repression', *Journal of Business Ethics*, 16, pp. 917–31.

107. R. Kreitner 1992, *Management*, Houghton Mifflin, Boston; A. Dubrin & A. Ireland 1993, *Management and Organization*, South-Western Publishing, Cincinnati, Ohio.

108. K. Lewin 1947, 'Frontiers in group dynamics: I. Concept, method and reality in social sciences: social equilibria and social change', *Human Relations*, 1, pp. 5–41; E. Dent & S. Goldberg 1999, 'Challenging resistance to change', *Journal of Applied Behavioral Science*, 35, pp. 25–42.

109. C. Gray 2002, 'Entrepreneurship, resistance to change and growth in small firms', *Journal of Small Business and Enterprise Development*, 9(1), pp. 61–72.

110. W.H Bovey & A. Hede 2001, 'Resistance to organizational change: the role of cognitive and affective processes', *Leadership and Organization Development Journal*, 22(8), pp. 372–82.

111. R. Aldag & T. Stearns 1991, *Management*, South-Western Publishing, Cincinnati, Ohio; J. Schermerhorn 1989, *Management for Productivity*, John Wiley & Sons, New York; S. Friedman 2004, 'Learning to make more effective decisions: changing beliefs as a prelude to action', *The Learning Organization*, 11(2), pp. 110–28.

112. R. Lee 1995, 'Appreciating resistances,' in *Managing in the Age of Change*, eds R. Ritvo, A. Litwin & L. Butler, Irwin Professional Publishing, Illinois, pp. 67–73.

113. Dent & Goldberg, op. cit.

114. J. P. Kotter 1995, 'Leading change: why transformation efforts fail', *Harvard Business Review*, 73(2), pp. 59–67.

115. C. Gray 2002, 'Entrepreneurship, resistance to change and growth in small firms', *Journal of Small Business and Enterprise Development*, 9(1), pp. 61–72.

116. J. Post & B. Altman 1994, 'Managing the environmental change process: barriers and opportunities', *Journal of Organizational Change Management*, 7(4), pp. 64–81.

117. D.M. Marci, M.R. Tagliaventi & F. Bertolotti 2002, 'A grounded theory for resistance to change in a small organization, *Journal of Organizational Change*, 15(3), pp. 292–310.

118. Agocs, op. cit.

119. G. Labianca, B. Gray & D. Brass 2000, 'A grounded model of organizational schema change during empowerment', *Organization Science*, 11(2), pp. 235–57.

120. R. Folger & D. Starlicki 1999, 'Unfairness and resistance to change: hardship as mistreatment', *Journal of Organizational Change Management*, 12(1), pp. 35–50.

121. Agocs, op. cit.

122. Hanzhang, General Tao, 1993, *Sun Tzu: The Art of War*, Wordsworth Editions Ltd., Ware, Hertfordshire, UK.

123. ibid.

124. T. Deal & A. Kennedy 1982, *Corporate Cultures: The Rites and Rituals of Corporate Life*, Addison-Wesley, Massachusetts; W. G. Ouchi 1981, *Theory Z*, Addison-Wesley, Massachusetts; T. Peters & R. Waterman 1982, *In Search of Excellence*, Harper & Row, New York, pp. 74–9 and 318–21.

125. Schein, op. cit.

126. H. Schwartz & S. M. Davis 1981, 'Matching corporate culture and business strategy', *Organizational Dynamics*, Summer, pp. 30–8.

127. J. P. Kotter & J. L. Heskett 1992, *Corporate Culture and Performance*, The Free Press, New York.

128. Peters & Waterman, op. cit.

129. R. A. Cooke & J. L. Szumal 1993, 'Measuring normative beliefs and shared behavioural expectations in organisations: the reliability and validity of the organisational culture inventory', *Psychological Reports*, 72, pp. 1290–330; A. L. Wilkins & W. G. Ouchi 1983, 'Efficient cultures exploring the relationship between culture and organizational

performance', *Administrative Science Quarterly.* 28(3), pp. 468–81.

130. J.D. Ford, L.W. Ford & R.T. McNamara 2002, 'Resistance and the background conversations of change', *Journal of Organizational Change*, 15(2), pp. 105–21.

131. Ford, Ford & McNamara, op. cit., pp. 106–7.

132. D. Butcher & S. Atkinson 2001, 'Stealth, secrecy and subversion: the language of change', *Journal of Organizational Change Management*, 14(6), pp. 554–69.

133. Butcher & Atkinson, op. cit., p. 555.

134. de Val & Fuentes, op. cit.

135. R.P. Rumelt 1995, 'Inertia and transformation', in *Resource-based and Evolutionary Theories of the Firm*, ed. C.A. Montgomery, Kluwer Academic Publishers, MA, pp. 101–32.

136. K.E. Trader-Leigh, 2002, 'Case study: identifying resistance in managing change', *Journal of Organizational Change*, 15(2), pp. 138–55.

137. Information on the documentary is available from www.supersizeme.com

138. M. Beer & N. Nohira 2000, 'Cracking the code of change', *Harvard Business Review*, 78(3), 133–41; P. Senge, A. Kleiner, C. Roberts, R. Ross, G. Roth & B. Smith 1999, 'The dance of change: a fifth discipline resource', Nicholas Brealey, London.

139. M. Beer, R. A. Eisenstat & B. Spector 1990, 'Why change programs don't produce change', *Harvard Business Review*, 68(6), pp. 158–66.

140. J. Porras & P. Robertson 1983, 'Organization development: theory, practice and research', in *The Handbook of Industrial and Organizational Psychology*, eds M. Dunnette & L. Hough, Consulting Psychologists Press, Palo Alto, California, pp. 719–822.

141. A. Molinski 1999, 'Sanding down the edges', *Journal of Applied Behavioral Science*, 35(1), pp. 8–26.

142. R. Greenwood & C. Hinings 1993, 'Understanding strategic change: the contribution of archetypes', *The Academy of Management Journal*, 36, pp. 1052–81.

143. C. Oliver 1992, 'The antecedents of deinstitutionalisation', *Organizational Studies*, 13, pp. 563–88.

Suncorp Metway was created in 1996 by a merger between Suncorp insurance group, Queensland Industry Development Corporation, and Metway Bank. In 2001, GIO general insurance operations was added. Today the finance conglomerate offers a range of financial services including home loans, managed funds and general insurance.

John Mulcahy has been CEO since the start of 2003. His vision is to create value in a broad portfolio of financial services — a challenge that other banks have attempted without success. On his arrival, Mulcahy looked at the organisational structure at Suncorp Metway and discovered weaknesses. Those who managed the 1996 merger had decided to build a common culture by putting together all the functions divided between the pre-merger organisations — distribution, design/product management, operations and so on. The downside of this merger-approach was an organisation confused in structure and lacking clear authority and accountability. Throughout 2003, Suncorp Metway went through a complete restructure, re-designing the roles of all its 8000 staff. The job was huge. Every job in all six levels of the organisation was examined, each level taking six weeks to complete. The outcome was a system of 'high-performance work teams' designed to deliver organisational accountability and better results in both mono-line divisions and wider group performance.

Judging from financial metrics, Suncorp Metway is doing a good job under Mulcahy's leadership. Full-year earnings rose 61 per cent to $618 million in 2003–2004. Profitability rose strongly across the board, pre-tax profit doubling in insurance, and rising from $318 million to $371 million in banking. Cost-cutting targets were met. Lastly, the group paid a 33 per cent increase in dividends, which caused a 41-cent rise in the share price bringing it up to $14.81, a two and a half year high.

However, Mulcahy is not content to rely on such measures. He believes staff are motivated by a view of where Suncorp Metway is headed. Without that broader context, employees will not understand how to perform in their re-designed jobs. So how can he know if employees have engaged with his vision? By asking them and measuring the responses. Suncorp Metway is big on metrics. The company reviews product quality and design by surveying other people's customers as well as its own. Suncorp Metway also surveys its employees every year to measure their engagement, job satisfaction, and their understanding of accountability, responsibility and the group perspective. The results provide feedback at team level. But they can also be compared with international benchmarks to check if the organisation as a whole is on track.

Mulcahy has described himself saying 'I am a catalyst and a driver, but I don't replace local leadership'.[1] If Mulcahy is to succeed in his role, he has to know how his local leaders are performing in theirs. That is the attribute that Suncorp Metway measures.

Source: Adapted from Andrew Cornell 2004, 'Sorting Suncorp', *AFR BOSS*, October, pp. 48–51.

Introduction

There is a saying: 'If you can't measure it, you can't manage it.' But how do managers measure and evaluate organisational change? As we shall see, managers can always find data to measure change. But is that data good enough to show whether their change program has worked? That result from data is a much greater challenge.

Measuring change

Managers measure change using many different statistics. By monitoring performance for a range of variables critical to the business, the Suncorp Metway case shows this point clearly. At the top of the list are organisation-wide financial measures such as earnings, pre-tax profits, dividends and share prices. There are also product division measures such as profits and cost reduction targets. Accountability is monitored closely at all levels of the organisation, with performance measures cascading right down to the basic level of the team. Suncorp Metway also measures staff attitudes. In a context of rapid change, it is essential for employee attitudes to be aligned with the organisation's vision. From team level to organisation level, Suncorp Metway measures the 'intangible asset' of employee engagement with its vision and mission.

Evaluating the effects of change programs

Managers find it difficult to demonstrate what results their change programs deliver. The Suncorp Metway case indicates where the problem lies. In 2003–2004, the business enjoyed strong performance on all its financial measures. But how far was this performance attributable to a change program in which 8000 jobs were re-designed to create high-performance work teams? Suncorp Metway's financial success cannot be proven to be a performance outcome of high-performance work teams because the impact of that change cannot be isolated from the effects of other changes occurring at the same time. Throughout 2003–2004, Suncorp Metway overhauled many aspects of the business including marketing and product design as well as job design and teamwork. So much change took place that the organisation was transformed, bearing little resemblance to the situation just three or four years earlier. In such a context, it is hard to separate those gains caused by high-performance teams from gains produced by other causes. Not least, did improved performance simply reflect improved market conditions? These questions are tough to answer.

This is the 'causality problem'. Managers, unlike many natural scientists, cannot perform a control experiment in which they identify the effects on performance of a single variable (the change program) by repeating the experiment while holding all other variables constant. In the real world, everything changes simultaneously and experiments cannot be repeated and controlled under laboratory conditions. Managers are unable to separate and measure the effects of the many 'input' or 'causal' variables that influence performance, or to quantify the gains due only to the change program.

If managers can measure overall 'change' easily, then why should they worry about estimating the separate contribution of the change programs? Why not just be content to evaluate whether the business as a whole is improving or deteriorating? If objective data show that a business makes a good **return on equity** or is benchmarked 'best in class', does it matter what part a change program played in that overall success?

Measuring the effects of particular change interventions, though, is important because only some succeed. The research by Ashkenas in the United States shows that only 25–30 per cent of change efforts succeed.[2] Similarly, Champy claims that business process re-engineering succeeds in only 25–33 per cent of cases.[3] Change interventions are not guaranteed to succeed, partly because there is a human dimension to managing change. Human fallibility gives rise to the one-eighth rule, which says that:

- one-half of the people will not believe the connection between the way in which business manages people and profit
- one-half of those who do believe will try a single, one-shot solution rather than a systemic approach
- one-half of firms that do make systemic changes will persist long enough to see the difference.

Given that $\frac{1}{2} \times \frac{1}{2} \times \frac{1}{2} = \frac{1}{8}$, this element is known as the 'one-eighth rule'.

If a change program is not working, then it is consuming financial and human resources for no purpose. Circumstances can exist in which a change program causes a business to perform worse. A study of benchmarking **total quality management (TQM)** in the United States found it worked best in firms already performing well, had no effect on mid-level firms and had a deleterious effect on poor performing firms.[4] Managers need hard evidence of the impact of their change program. It is possible that the change intervention, with some rectification, can be made to work better for the overall good of the business. Managers need to measure, recognise and act on the difference between an effective change intervention and an ineffective one.

The objective of this chapter is to introduce a range of approaches to both the measurement of change and the evaluation of change interventions. We look first at how conventional measures, strategy-driven measures and **benchmarking** can be used to measure change. Second, we cover a number of approaches to the measurement and evaluation of change interventions. We review the causality problem outlined above.

Then we look at some existing and proposed tools used by management to evaluate change interventions: TQM analytical tools, the **human resources (HR) scorecard** and **action research**. In this chapter, we refer to the Norske Skog Boyer mill case (end-of-book case 3, page 383), which is about an Australian operation that illustrates several of these approaches (notably, strategy-driven measurement and benchmarking).

Measures of change

Here, we look at three ways in which managers can quantify change. Most common are financial indicators of performance. In most cases, measures of financial performance look backwards, linking the present to the past. Second are strategy-driven measures. These measures may be non-financial (for example, quantifying customer satisfaction or safety performance) and may look forwards, evaluating present performance in relation to future targets. Third are benchmarks, which measure the changing gap between an organisation's performance and world best practice.

Conventional financial measures

In the past, managers have assessed change mainly by examining financial indicators of performance. Dollar-based indicators or ratios are the basic building block or standard from which measures of business activity or performance are derived. Such financial measures can be used to evaluate whether an organisation is benefiting from change. Before describing some common financial indicators of change, we need to make three cautionary points.

First, long-term financial data are needed to measure and evaluate change, not just a comparison of the current and preceding years. Analysis of trends over three to five years reduces the influence of atypical events. Current results also may be a poor indicator of the future because they still carry the legacy of past successes in innovation or investment that are running down, or the effects of data manipulation by management. Conversely, current results may fail to indicate that current investments or change initiatives are about to bear fruit.

Second, financial measures will not help the analyst distinguish performance results arising from an effective change program from those caused by changes in the state of the economy, the industry environment or the quality of organisational strategy. They reveal what is happening, but not necessarily why it is happening.

Third, to understand the processes behind particular financial results, analysts today frequently look at techniques to integrate non-financial measures of 'activities' or 'processes' with measures of financial performance. Sole reliance on financial measures is often thought to be inadequate. Examples of non-financial measures include both simple quantity data relating to numbers of product faults, safety incidents and the like, and attitudinal data on customer satisfaction and employee attitudes, for example.

Despite these cautions, financial measures remain vital when assessing how an organisation is changing. Included in the list below are ways of measuring financial or economic performance that can be used to evaluate change. For simplicity, we have excluded several commonly used financial ratios (including asset use, liquidity and capital structure ratios), which relate more to capital market behaviour than to operational performance. You should be aware, however, that a complete assessment of change cannot occur without incorporating measures of the efficient use of capital. The following are financial measures of change.

- *Share price performance.* Shareholders must receive a reasonable return on investment, so they are stakeholders in successful change. Share price performance is one measure relevant to them. Frequently, this financial measure is assessed by comparison with trends in share prices for other firms listed on a particular exchange. This measure is not applicable to all organisations. It can be used only for listed firms, which make up a minority of all businesses. Further, it mainly indicates expectations of future performance in earnings and dividends, and is a very indirect measure of the past record of change.

- *Market share.* Customers too are stakeholders in successful change. One way of measuring their response to organisation change is whether that business's market share is growing or declining. This element is not always easy to measure. Reliable data on some markets may not be available. Further, multiproduct businesses may find performance varies across their portfolio of markets. Also, better measures of customer response other than market share may be possible. Surveys of customer satisfaction, for example, often give more direct and relevant information about customer reactions to organisational change. Such surveys can identify varying degrees of satisfaction among different groups of customers. They also can discriminate among attitudes to different factors in customer value such as cost, quality and timely delivery.

- *Overall performance measures.* These financial measures include return on equity (profit after tax divided by shareholder's funds); return on total assets (earnings before interest and tax divided by total assets); and sales growth (current year's sales divided by previous year's sales). Return on equity is the most widely used ratio, showing overall performance.[5] In recent years, many firms have adopted economic value added as a financial metric in which net accounting income is adjusted to remove a capital charge. Businesses that cannot cover their risk-adjusted cost of capital are deemed to 'destroy shareholder value' as opposed to 'creating shareholder value'.[6] For the purpose of evaluating organisational change, these ratios must be plotted over several years.

- *Profitability measures.* These ratios include net profit/sales (opening profit before tax divided by sales); profit after tax/sales; and expenses/sales. The first two profit/sales ratios may be published, but often are a poor indicator of management quality. Conversely, changes in expenses/sales ratios over time may be a good indicator of the effective management of change, but such data (although collected internally) may not be released externally. Like overall performance measures, profitability needs to be assessed by the trend over time.

- *Cash flow.* This financial measure is an absolute figure trended over time, rather than a ratio. Ability to generate improved cash flow is an important indicator of good management performance, but data need to be treated cautiously to allow for abnormal borrowings for investment.

- *Internal targets or budgets.* Unlike the measures outlined above, this financial measure can be used to evaluate change at the devolved level of a department or work section within an organisation. If budgets are set appropriately to incorporate expected inputs and outputs of the change program, then meeting those targets can be a useful indicator of performance.

One difficulty with the financial measures of performance outlined above is that they may not agree. Performance according to different measures can diverge if those measures reflect the separate needs of various stakeholders such as the organisation's shareholders and customers. One example is when increasing market share (and customer satisfaction) requires lower prices, which reduce profitability and return on equity (and shareholder satisfaction). The inclusion of employees and suppliers as other stakeholder groups can exacerbate such tensions, although conventional accounting performance measures do not test for their satisfaction. How can an holistic assessment of performance be achieved, integrating the different available measures into a single coherent picture? One solution is to link performance measures to clearly defined strategic goals.

Strategy-driven measures

The relationship between strategic planning and change was discussed in chapter 2. We encourage you to revisit that chapter to refresh your understanding of different approaches to strategic planning. Our purpose here is only to outline how strategic planning is linked to measures of change.

One approach by businesses to measuring change stems from what was called the 'rational' or 'cookbook' approach to strategic planning. A simplified version of this approach reduces strategic planning to four elements: vision, mission, strategy and implementation.[7] The business's vision (optimal potential position) determines its mission (a summary statement of product/market thrust for stakeholders), which governs its strategy (specific targets). Implementation activities are then derived from the strategy. This process entails making concrete decisions and allocating resources under real-world constraints. In the implementation process, the business sets targets for what it seeks to achieve. A simple diagram of this model of strategy is given in figure 9.1.

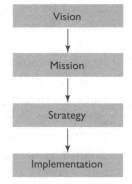

FIGURE 9.1: A simple model of rational strategic planning

How are measures of change developed in this model? They are derived from targets set in the implementation part of the planning process and they should coincide with an organisation's 'core processes' or **critical success factors (CSFs)** (the things that a business must get right to succeed).

In a market-driven organisation, CSFs usually concern the elements of customer value, such as cost, quality and timely delivery. Increasingly, however, these CSFs are supplemented by additional factors associated with good corporate citizenship, such as safety and environmental sustainability. A business ordinarily identifies only a handful of CSFs, if it is to concentrate effectively on them. An example is given in the case on the Norske Skog Boyer mill (end-of-book case 3, page 383). The mill developed six CSFs with its parent corporation in the mid-1990s, Fletcher Challenge:

- responsiveness
- resource management
- product management
- customer satisfaction
- environmental responsibility
- safety performance.

Selecting appropriate CSFs is a difficult process. There are usually many contenders, each backed by a determined lobby group within the organisation. Only a handful can be chosen, and these must be correct for the business as a whole, not for sectional interests.

Cascading from the CSFs are performance measures. These commonly are called **key performance indicators (KPIs)**, although terminology varies. The Norske Skog Boyer mill had three kinds of measurable target. First were six mill-wide key result areas, which mostly related to cost, quality and delivery, or to 'corporate citizenship objectives' such as accidents and environmental incidents. The key result areas were:

- mill gate cash cost (total variable cost and fixed cash cost divided by production)
- working capital (money tied up in inventory to run the business)
- first-grade production (total accepted production classified as first grade)
- on-time dispatch (percentage compliance with delivery schedules)
- environmental excursions (incidents in excess of regulated limits and licence conditions)
- accident moving frequency rate (actual accident rate against improvement target).

Because these measures applied to the mill as a whole, they did not directly reflect performance in the various processes carried out in different parts of the operation (forest management, pulp mill, paper mill, finishing, customer relations, project engineering, stores, product development and so on). Consequently, a second set of measures (also known as key result areas) was derived from the mill-wide key result areas for the 15 business units within the plant. One such subdivision is the Pulp and Services Business Unit, whose performance is measured on safety and environmental incidents, money tied in inventory, the cost of pulp ingredients, tear and tensile pulp quality, paper machine stoppages caused by pulp shortage, and other measures of cost, quality and delivery. Third, the business units comprised approximately 50 work teams that also had measures (called key performance indicators (KPIs)) that cascaded out of the business unit key result areas. Most teams had only a couple of KPIs; for example, the Process and Product Support Group was assessed on the number of 'housekeeping' and safety audits completed on time. Such indicators serve a dual purpose of monitoring and motivating performance at the work team level.

The discussion above shows how performance measures can be developed from a simple rational model of strategic planning, but limitations to this model are evident. We examine three of these limitations.

1. *How do the many KPIs that cascade from strategy feed into a measure of 'bottom-line' financial performance?* All the parts of the strategy may be on track, but is it making

money? **Value-based strategic management** is one technique that enables the conversion of disaggregated performance data into a single measure of shareholder value. Value-based management requires that 'cost and value drivers' (or CSFs) be determined for the operational parts of the organisation. Measures of these are developed in the form of KPIs, which are then converted into dollars. The model then incorporates financial data on working capital and asset performance to yield return-on-investment and return-on-equity figures. If properly executed, the model allows shopfloor employees to see how their performance helps determine shareholder value.

2. *How can the strategic 'big picture' be drawn, pulling together various measures of stakeholder-based interests?* We observed above that measures of change reflecting divergent stakeholder interests can move in different directions. An increasingly popular solution to this problem is Kaplan and Norton's balanced scorecard.[8] We discussed this strategic approach to performance measurement at length in chapter 2. We encourage you to read that section again to renew your understanding of how strategy and measurement must balance four perspectives: the customer perspective, the internal perspective, the innovation and learning perspective and the financial perspective. By integrating these four perspectives, the balanced scorecard helps management understand the holistic nature of change and prevents a suboptimal focus on the needs of any single stakeholder. The balanced scorecard approach to strategy and measurement lends itself to new applications. Later in this chapter, we discuss one such development: the HR scorecard, which is an adaptation of the balanced scorecard to the special problem of evaluating human resources management (HRM) activities. We also look at Kaplan and Norton's recent ideas about using their scorecard to measure those 'intangibles' such as skill and culture that are so important in making change programs succeed.

3. *How appropriate for the management of 'discontinuous change' are the measures or KPIs likely to be derived from a rational strategic planning model?* The foundation of the rational planning model lies in management's capacity to envision the future — an assumption that must be discarded for discontinuous change (described in chapter 2). What are the implications for such measures as KPIs that cascade from CSFs, which are themselves governed by a rationally determined vision and strategy? The problem here is captured in what Stacey calls the 'paradox of control'. Discontinuous change requires flexible or opportunistic decision-making and control systems.[9] What does this factor mean for the measurement of change? Perhaps the maintenance of organisational flexibility is a more important critical success factor, with its own measures or KPIs, than the conventional measures that cascade out of rational strategy.

Benchmarking

Benchmarking is a third approach used by managers to measure change. The American Productivity and Quality Center, a leading consulting and research organisation, defines the term as:

> ... the process of continuously comparing and measuring an organisation with business leaders anywhere in the world to gain information which will help the organisation to take action to improve its performance.[10]

This definition endows benchmarking with two essential features. First, data are used to compare an organisation with others recognised as being 'best practice'. Second, lessons are drawn from those best practice organisations to drive improved performance. Benchmarking is thus relevant to organisational change as both a technique for measuring change (how is the organisation's measured distance from best practice organisations trending over time?) and as a technique for learning how to change (what lessons can be learned from best practice organisations?).

As a formal technique for organisational improvement, benchmarking originated in the Xerox corporation in the United States in the early 1980s.[11] Following Xerox's success with the technique, in 1991 it was made a requirement of the prestigious Baldrige National Quality Awards in North America. From this springboard, it was swiftly adopted by a majority of the US Fortune 1000 firms as a mainstream business process.

Benchmarking was soon taken up in Australia. In the early 1990s, the Australian Quality Awards and the Commonwealth Government's Australian Best Practice Demonstration Program endorsed it. Growing interest in quality accreditation, especially the international ISO 9000 standard, also helped spawn interest in benchmarking. As more businesses insisted their suppliers conform to the best practice processes required for quality accreditation, interest in benchmarking surged. By 1992, 70 per cent of Australia's top 500 businesses either were benchmarking or were intending to do so.[12] Benchmarking of some kind is now used by almost all large Australian businesses.

Distinguishing three different types of benchmarking on the basis of the benchmarking partners is customary.

- *Internal benchmarking*. This method involves comparisons among different parts of the same organisation. Internal benchmarking is sometimes criticised because the highest standards within a corporation may fall short of world best practice, causing comparisons and emulation to focus on uncompetitive models. It is sometimes justified, however, as a method of learning how to benchmark made easy by the ready access to benchmarking partners. Where big businesses operate internally competitive 'global sourcing' strategies (allowing different subsidiaries to bid for each other's markets), internal benchmarking can be used to feed information into strategic decision-making about which operations perform best and should be extended, and which should be wound up.

- *Industry or competitive benchmarking*. This method means benchmarking against other firms in the same industry. A common difficulty facing industry benchmarking is that these firms frequently are competitors and therefore are reluctant to divulge benchmark data that may reveal the secret to their competitive advantage. One advantage of industry benchmarking is that firms in the same industry are likely to share the same technology and business processes, and therefore find benchmarking comparisons easy to make. An example of this advantage is given in the Norske Skog Boyer mill case (end-of-book case 3, page 383). The Canadian Pulp and Paper Association collects benchmark data for paper mills around the world, allowing comparison on standard efficiency measures such as machine speed, employee hours per tonne of product, and so on. Norske Skog also can compare mill gate cash cost (the leading critical success factor) with best practice overseas.

- *Process or generic benchmarking.* This method involves comparisons among businesses that share the same broad processes. These often are established 'core' processes, such as supplier management (in which Toyota's supplier program makes it a leader), order receipt and dispatch (Domino's pizza), standardised customer service (McDonald's) and so on. Almost any process, however, can be benchmarked. Many companies have, like Norske Skog Boyer, benchmarked continuous improvement programs around Australia. Many firms have even benchmarked Xerox's benchmarking process. Process benchmarking has many advantages. Because benchmark partners are unlikely to be competitors, gaining access without arousing suspicions can be easier. This method also can generate the biggest gains, especially when firms seeking to improve a 'peripheral' process unlock the secrets of best practice from businesses for which it is a 'core' process. Xerox, which makes copying machines, learned from mail-order retail firms about improving their distribution. Process benchmarking encounters problems, however. Beginners find especially problematic the diagnostic tasks of analysing and evaluating internal processes (deciding what to benchmark) and the detective work in searching for external best practice (finding benchmark partners).[13]

Many models of the benchmarking process exist. The best known remain those developed by US firms that pioneered the technique — namely, Xerox, Westinghouse and Motorola. All models share common features. First is an internal phase (deciding what CSFs to benchmark, selecting a benchmarking team and collecting internal benchmark metrics data). Second is an external phase (choosing, approaching and visiting partners, and gathering external metrics data). Third is another internal phase (comparing external and internal data, analysing performance gaps, and recommending, implementing and monitoring improvements). The simple seven-step model in figure 9.2 was developed for the Australian Best Practice Demonstration Program and is a typical example of the benchmarking process.

Step 1	Identify the process to benchmark.
Step 2	Define the project. Choose a team.
Step 3	Collect internal information.
Step 4	Research and choose benchmark partners. Determine a data collection method.
Step 5	Collect information from partners.
Step 6	Analyse gaps, make recommendations and implement.
Step 7	Monitor and continuously improve.

FIGURE 9.2: Seven steps for benchmarking

In practice, not all benchmarking exercises follow these steps. One reason relates to the existence of different styles of benchmarking, some of which discard parts of the above process. Macneil, Rimmer and Testi distinguish the following five main styles.[14]

- Process-driven benchmarking occurs when the steps of a model are followed in a strict sequence. While such an approach is likely to be disciplined and thorough, it risks failing to take account of organisational culture, and adjust to employee and customer inputs.
- Data-driven benchmarking exercises can omit the organisational learning parts of the benchmarking process. Databases are consulted to compare a business with relevant comparators. Performance gaps are measured and then adjusted to remove that part of the gap stemming from what might be termed 'acts of god' (differences that are environmentally determined rather than internally manageable). An example of this 'data normalisation' process is the benchmarking between Asian telecommunication organisations. The 'act of god' in this case was the obligation upon Telecommunikasi Indonesia to provide line services to poor communities across an enormous archipelago of islands, unlike its Singapore counterpart, which had to construct infrastructure for only a small, highly developed island. Significant non-manageable differences in benchmark performance stemmed from this single exogenous factor.
- People-driven benchmarking puts benchmarking teams first (often a vertical slice of the business from top management to shopfloor employees), allowing them to shape the process. High involvement can be won but at the expense of structure and discipline in the process.
- Strategy-driven benchmarking is strong in its analysis of CSFs but often weak in terms of the involvement of teams, who have to learn what causes a performance gap and apply solutions to closing it.
- A hybrid or mixed style can yield a positive balance, producing a benchmarking project with a disciplined approach to process, thorough data analysis, team involvement in learning and implementation, and a strategic focus on the right CSFs.

Until 1996, the Commonwealth Government promoted people-driven benchmarking in Australia as a tool for organisational learning and continuous improvement. This style of benchmarking has since fallen into disuse, to be replaced in many organisations by data-driven benchmarking. Most large Australian businesses now purchase benchmark data from consulting firms and industry associations that gather and market such data for their specialised fields of operation. One example of a consulting firm supplying benchmark data is KPMG, which publishes an annual benchmarking report on Australia's finance sector. The report presents data for banks and insurance companies on critical measures such as credit quality (loan write-off/average receivables), growth (increase in total assets) and efficiency (operating expenses/operating income).[15]

While benchmarking has become a common business technique over the past decade, it does encounter criticism. One widely held view is that benchmarking deters innovation that will make a firm best in class; rather, it encourages copying, which locks businesses permanently into second place.[16] The basic reason is that benchmarking shows a performance gap at a point in time. Inevitably, a lag exists while the low-performing firm analyses reasons for the gap and takes action to close it, by which time the best-in-class firms will have further raised their performance. Figure 9.3 shows the dynamics of measuring and closing a performance gap.

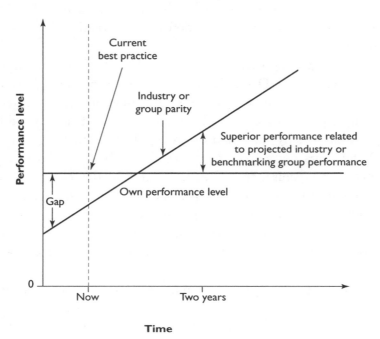

Time

FIGURE 9.3: Upward movement of best practice

Source: J. Macneil, J. Testi, J. Cupples & M. Rimmer 1993, *Benchmarking in Australia*, Longman, Melbourne, p. 191. Reproduced with permission of Malcolm Rimmer.

Plausible though it seems, this criticism is more likely to apply to internal or industry benchmarking (where the scope for comparison is limited) than to process benchmarking (which can stimulate innovation in unpredictable and highly productive ways).

A second criticism of benchmarking concerns the difficulty of transferring best practice between benchmark partners. As an improvement tool, benchmarking assumes that the reasons for a performance gap can be easily understood and the causes can be rectified. Research shows these assumptions may be untrue where the causes of competitive advantage lie in **tacit knowledge** held in the best practice firm.[17] Tacit knowledge refers to the unique combination of skills and cooperative social arrangements that sometimes underpin outstanding performance. Its significance as a source of competitive advantage often is unrecognised within a firm and does not lend itself to diagnosis and emulation through benchmarking. Research suggests that this is a significant obstacle to the transfer of best practice, even within firms. Tacit knowledge cannot be easily identified or absorbed by the recipient, while the communications necessary for an effective exchange relationship in this area often overburden the donor firm.[18]

Benchmarking the triple bottom line

A new application for benchmarking has been found in corporate citizenship. The huge growth of 'socially responsible' investment funds has created an incentive for businesses to present themselves as socially and environmentally responsible. Firms do this by reporting a **triple bottom line** (TBL) that shows social and environmental performance as well as their financial results. By 2002, 45 per cent of the 250 largest global businesses published reports on their TBL. In France, listed companies are required to disclose their social and environmental performance, while half of Britain's top 100 detailed their TBL credentials and 72 per cent of Japan's top 100 companies produced sustainability reports. Australian business is going this way too. In 2001, two major federal government superannuation schemes with $3 billion of investment in Australia appointed Westpac Investment Management as primary governance adviser. As the scheme's CEO, Steve Gibbs, said: 'The move is not about ethics or even hugging trees, it is about managing risk.' Poor social and environmental credentials are a risk investors are becoming unwilling to take.

Businesses benchmark the TBL by measuring their performance against international standards. Four international frameworks set standards for TBL reporting. These are the Global Reporting Initiative (GRI), Accountability 1000, Social Accountability 8000, and the United Nations Global Compact. All are available free on line to businesses willing to benchmark against their standards. The United Nations Global Compact prescribes ten principles:

'Human Rights
- *Principle 1:* Businesses should support and respect the protection of internationally proclaimed human rights; and
- *Principle 2:* make sure that they are not complicit in human rights abuses.

Labour Standards
- *Principle 3:* Businesses should uphold the freedom of association and the effective recognition of the right to collective bargaining;
- *Principle 4:* the elimination of all forms of forced and compulsory labour;
- *Principle 5:* the effective abolition of child labour; and
- *Principle 6:* the elimination of discrimination in respect of employment and occupation.

Environment
- *Principle 7:* Businesses should support a precautionary approach to environmental challenges;
- *Principle 8:* undertake initiatives to promote greater environmental responsibility; and
- *Principle 9:* encourage the development and diffusion of environmentally friendly technologies.

Anti-corruption
- *Principle 10:* Businesses should work against all forms of corruption, including extortion and bribery.'

Source: Adapted from Julie Macken 2002, 'Trick or Treat', *AFR BOSS*, October, pp. 36–9; UN Global Compact, www.unglobalcompact.org. Reproduced with permission from the Global Compact Office of the United Nations.

Measuring and evaluating change interventions: the causality problem reconsidered

So far, we have examined three approaches to measuring change in an organisation. The three approaches ask, respectively, how trends in an organisation's performance are to be judged (a) financially, (b) against strategic targets and (c) against benchmarks of best practice.

We noted that such information can tell managers how the organisation as a whole is changing, but cannot isolate the effect on overall performance of a specific change program or intervention. It is difficult, we argued, for managers to measure the performance outcomes of a change program because they cannot conduct control experiments in a real-world situation where everything is in a state of flux. This 'causality problem' makes it difficult to evaluate change interventions.

We also noted in the introduction to this chapter that change programs fail sufficiently often for managers to need to consider what they can do to measure and evaluate them. Many steps can be taken to solve or alleviate this problem. First, it is helpful to consider some simple ideas about research methods to determine the most fruitful approach to the problem. You may be familiar with a basic distinction in social science research method between the **positivist research** (or quantitative) approach and the **phenomenological research** (or qualitative) approach.[19] Some features of these two contrasting approaches are shown in table 9.1.

TABLE 9.1	Characteristics of positivist and phenomenological research methods	
Characteristic	**Positivist method**	**Phenomenological method**
1. Nature of reality	Objective and apart from researcher	Subjective, as seen by participants in the study
2. Relationship of researcher to subject	Independent	Interactive
3. Role of values	Value free	Value laden
4. Research process	Deductive Showing cause and effect Context free Predictive generalisation	Inductive Showing interaction of factors Context bound Situational theory

The positivist method is in the tradition of the natural sciences. The researcher is independent from the research subject and seeks to validate objective and context-free propositions about 'cause and effect', which should have the status of predictive generalisations. Phenomenological research is based on the proposition that social sciences differ from natural sciences because researchers' values necessarily shape their interaction with research subjects in the inductive process of developing context-bound explanations of situational phenomena.

The causality problem here is the difficulty of proving a cause-and-effect relationship between a change program and performance outcomes. It is very much a problem in the positivist tradition. Given that experiments cannot be replicated in business situations, a control experiment cannot be conducted to isolate the effect of a change program. As a result, positivist proof of the 'cause–effect' relationship between a planned change and a performance outcome is generally beyond reach. However, there are two 'near enough is good enough' approaches to establishing within the positivist tradition the impact of a change program. The first positivist approach was outlined above in discussing strategy-driven targets. It involves the logical cascading of strategic targets into CSFs and KPIs. If those KPIs are developed properly they will allow change to be monitored and plausible conclusions to be reached about the success of planned change. The second positivist approach involves the application of a set of analytical or diagnostic tools often used in TQM exercises. Developed mainly by production engineers interested in quality, these tools are intended to prove cause-and-effect relationships so quality problems can be traced to a source. The significance of these tools for organisational change lies in many managers' reliance on them to assist continuous improvement activities by work teams. It follows that these tools often are used in a localised or workplace context to show particular cause-and-effect relationships in operational processes. Such TQM analytical tools can be used to show the results of change interventions.

Notwithstanding the attractions of developing 'hard' or objective proof that a change intervention has succeeded, the practising manager is not a positivist researcher detached from the study subject. For this reason, the phenomenological approach is highly relevant to the measurement and evaluation of change programs. Managers use phenomenological methods to test the impact of change activities for several reasons.

The first advantage of phenomenological method is the important contribution that tacit knowledge (the unique combination of skill and workplace cooperation) makes to competitive advantage. By its nature, tacit knowledge tends to be complex, intangible and unquantifiable — qualities that make it elusive to the positivist researcher but not to the phenomenologist.

The second advantage is the widespread use of the action research method in change interventions. The term 'action research' describes a specific phenomenological technique in which the researcher attempts to simultaneously bring about a change and monitor its results. Many business change interventions take this form, conducted by change leaders whose purpose is to both introduce and validate change. Many action research projects have the underlying aim to improve tacit knowledge. Such action projects are likely to be found where a consultant is hired to improve 'culturally sensitive behaviour' in areas such as communications, team problem-solving, leadership and quality consciousness.

In the remainder of this chapter, we examine both positivist and phenomenological approaches to the measurement and evaluation of change programs. First, we consider some 'data driven' positivist approaches to the problem. How can strategy-driven measures be designed to capture cause and effect in planned change? Can TQM analytical tools prove that continuous improvement yields gains? And, what does the balanced HR scorecard reveal? Second, we look at action research, which is the leading phenomenological approach to evaluating change activities.

Monitoring change through strategy-driven measures

We have already described above the basic principles used in designing strategy driven measures. Such measures can be employed not only to track change, but also to isolate the effects of a change program. They will rarely deliver a scientific proof of the 'control experiment' kind, but they can provide reasonably persuasive data to satisfy managers about whether their policies are succeeding or failing. We have already examined in the

Norske Skog Boyermill case (end-of-book case 3, page 383) an example of the creative use of KPIs to track the effective implementation of business strategy at team level. Examples are now multiplying to show how creative minds can adapt this basic model of the strategy driven measure to apply to a very wide range of change situations.

One example of such innovative measurement concerns the performance of boards of directors as they respond to demands for improved corporate accountability. Epstein and Roy have developed a comprehensive set of board metrics, which, if applied and acted on, will prevent slipshod corporate governance and discourage collapses like Enron.[20] They propose a system of metrics to monitor board vigilance. Their scheme comprises 54 different metrics divided into four groups — inputs (11 metrics), processes (27), outputs (12) and outcomes (4). One input metric is the percentage of independent board members. Process metrics include the percentage of meetings without the CEO, and the percentage of meeting time allocated to opposing points of view. Amongst the output measures are complaints from customers, employees and the community, and the percentage of failed projects. Lastly, outcomes are tracked by measuring EVA, stock price, return on investment, and earnings. Clearly, measures such as these can facilitate monitoring a particular kind of change — the transformation of a corporate board from a toothless cipher to a vigilant and tough watchdog.

Another creative approach to performance measurement has been developed for research organisations. Most research organisations draw wholly or in part upon public funding. As a result, change has been forced upon them both to survive upon leaner funding, and to be more accountable to governments and other stakeholders. However, improved accountability is difficult to accomplish using conventional cost-based accounting, which undervalues resources and assets (primarily skill) and also outputs (knowledge). However, research on German and Australian research organisations reveals how creative approaches to measuring such 'intellectual capital' can solve the problem.[21] The measures reported are shown in figure 9.4.

Intellectual capital
- Human capital (the ratio, stability, training and experience of scientific staff)
- Structural capital (IT expenditure per employee and teleworking)
- Relational capital (foreign assignments, visits and employment in teaching)

Key processes
- Government funded research as a percentage of total income
- Percentage of new contracts with inter-institute cooperation
- Projects for foreign customers

Results
- Financial
- Intangible
  - Research oriented (publications, prestigious grants)
  - Economy oriented (patent applications and licence income)
  - Society oriented (Internet site hits by external users)

FIGURE 9.4: Performance measurement in scientific organisations

Source: Adapted from Appendix A in K. H Leitner & C. Warden 2001, 'Managing and reporting knowledge-based resources and processes in research organisations: specifics, lessons learned and perspectives', *Management Accounting Research*, 15 (1), pp. 47–8, with permission from Elsevier.

The systems of metrics described above were designed to plot the impact of particular types of change initiative. Indeed, these examples illustrate how a creative approach to measurement can yield metrics suitable for monitoring change in almost any situation. Over the past decade, managers have applied their imagination to this challenge, and business has witnessed a huge increase in the creative development of metrics to measure change. However, researchers today are now reporting a backlash against the measurement craze.

One example of a reaction against measurement comes from the Canadian province of Alberta.[22] In 1993, a new government was elected with a mission to cut its deficit by reforming the public sector and making it more accountable. Across the board cuts were imposed. But in addition, a more searching exercise was introduced in which missions, goals and strategies were defined flowing to every unit of government administration. Performance measures were then cascaded down to monitor accomplishments. The Treasury officials driving this exercise insisted that all activities be measured, arguing 'if you can't measure it, it is not worth doing'. To begin with, managers supported the new goals and measures, believing that the data would inform reasoned justification for their aims and activities. They expected the new measurement system to support reasoned argument. Experience taught them otherwise. Measures were imposed from above that blocked entrepreneurialism and initiative and were used to justify arbitrary rationalisation plans. This approach to measuring change became counterproductive because it made government administration less responsive to and thoughtful about real needs, and bred resistance amongst the middle managers whose expertise was marginalised. Despite the apparent 'rationality' of business planning, such 'strategy-driven measures' cannot be scientifically independent or positivist tools to measure change; they will always retain a 'subjective' character that is shaped by the political processes governing their design and implementation.

TQM analytical tools

The positivist (or scientific) techniques most widely used to measure and evaluate change activities are TQM analytical tools. (We gave an account of the origins and characteristics of TQM in chapter 4.) It is a common tool employed to implement organisational change.[23] By 1995, 37 per cent of all Australian workplaces with 20 or more employees claimed to have TQM in place.[24] Managers are attracted to TQM for many reasons. Its techniques are simple and can be applied by most employees, yet they also make rigorous use of hard statistical data. In addition, TQM offers practical remedies to real quality problems.

TQM is usually described as a philosophy rather than a technique. It has a number of defining features, including the following:
- an aim to improve quality, which is defined by customer needs
- the use of systematic measurement and analysis of processes to reveal the origins of quality problems
- the involvement of employees in process improvement
- an 'holistic' approach to quality improvement, including all employees, all aspects of operations, and external parties (including customers and suppliers).

TQM requires small teams of workers (referred to by a variety of titles, including quality circles and productivity or process improvement groups) to make use of a number of tools or techniques that enable them to identify and measure faulty processes that cause abnormal variance in quality. These tools include:

- brainstorming
- statistical process control (SPC)
- flowcharts and workflow diagrams
- Pareto analysis (the 80:20 rule)
- **cause-and-effect charts** (Ishikawa diagrams).

We have no space here for a thorough description of TQM techniques, but a brief discussion of Pareto analysis and cause-and-effect charts can illustrate how the use of data and the analysis of causation characterise TQM. Pareto analysis is based on the **Pareto principle** that a few of the causes account for most of the effect (the 80:20 rule). A Pareto chart is a bar chart that represents this point graphically. Its use in TQM is to present data to prioritise the most significant causes of deviation from quality standards. Each column in the bar chart represents an individual cause of quality variance. At a glance, the user can identify from the highest columns the two or three factors that cause most quality problems, allowing those factors to be prioritised for analysis and action.

Cause-and-effect analysis is sometimes used following Pareto analysis to identify the causes of quality problems that have been prioritised and to point the way to specific improvements. Many teams develop Ishikawa or 'fishbone' diagrams to assist this process. Typically, a team constructs such a diagram by first identifying a quality problem and then working backwards to isolate the major causes, minor causes, subcauses and subsets of causes. Quality teams often use brainstorming meetings to construct the diagram. They may then gather data to verify it. As soon as the causes of a problem are tracked down in this way, the team usually has little difficulty finding a solution. After the solution is implemented, measuring improvements over time is a simple matter.

Can TQM techniques prove that change interventions deliver results? Yes, but usually in a fragmentary way. The typical claims from TQM analysis relate to specific process improvements at the team level. A stores team may record improvements in the percentage of stock returned, a production team may record improvements in its quality 'non-conformance' rates, and an administration team may record improvements in the percentage of non-scheduled cheque runs. Such data are valuable in many ways. First, a high validity in the link between cause (change action) and effect (performance gain) usually exists. Second, the team directly involved experiences motivational benefits.

Such fragmentary evidence is difficult to aggregate into a big picture. It is hard to tell, for example, what is the overall impact of TQM on the corporate bottom line. As a result, organisations sometimes lose track of the net effect of TQM and fail to recognise when excessive enthusiasm for micro gains conceals a macro cost. Hilmer and Donaldson tell the story of Florida Power and Light — a US utility and TQM success story: 'At one time during the TQM implementation, Florida Power and Light had about 1900 teams working with the guidance, direction and support of eighty-five full-time staffers on TQM projects. Literally thousands of processes, ranging from the replacement of light bulbs to the paying of small accounts, were being methodically analysed by teams trained in statistical and process flow analysis. Form and bureaucracy began to drive out substance to the point where the eighty-five strong staff contingent had to be disbanded. Once line managers again started to work on the application of specific ideas to lower costs or speed up responses to customers, rather than on filling in forms, success was assured.'[25]

The problems in this example are not uncommon. In the absence of effective company-wide measurement and evaluation, TQM projects can run out of control, applying low-return processes and building up unnecessary overhead costs and counter-productive formalities.

The HR scorecard

A third positivist approach to measuring and evaluating change programs is the HR scorecard. In our discussion of strategy and change in chapter 2, we introduced Kaplan and Norton's notion of a balanced scorecard to measure strategic performance. The HR scorecard was adapted from Kaplan and Norton's work by Becker, Huselid and Ulrich.[26] These human resources experts also are interested in measuring strategic performance. Their challenge is to measure the contribution made by human resources to strategic performance. This challenge stems, first, from the appreciation that human resources can be the key to competitive advantage and, second, from corporations' failure to measure and value the contribution of their intangible human resources asset. As Norton puts it, the worst grades (for executives) are reserved for their understanding of strategies for developing human capital.[27] Becker, Huselid and Ulrich propose three stages of activity to fill this gap:

- a seven-step process to clarify links between business strategy and human resources and associated measures of human resources performance
- an HR scorecard made up of four dimensions: (1) key human resources 'deliverables' (ways in which human resources affect CSFs) that will leverage HRM's role in the overall business strategy; (2) the high-performance work system that supplies these deliverables; (3) the alignment of the high-performance work system with business strategy; and (4) the efficiency with which these 'deliverables' are generated
- a measurement system, derived from the four elements of the HR scorecard, that balances cost control and value creation. Typically, measures of the fourth ingredient (efficiency in generating deliverables) show cost control. These measures include absenteeism and accident rates, cost per hire, cost per trainee hour, the percentage of employee development plans completed and so on. Conversely, measures of the second ingredient, the high-performance work system, show value creation. These measures include the number and quality of cross-functional teams, the back-up talent ratio and the number of employee suggestions generated and implemented.

The HR scorecard can be used directly to measure the human resources contribution to business strategy and therefore to change in the organisation as a whole. We are more concerned here, however, with the problem of how to isolate and evaluate the specific impact of a change program or intervention. Becker and colleagues do not neglect this question.

- First, they recognise that the HR scorecard is a change program itself.
- Second, they concede that the HR scorecard, like all change programs, risks failure.

- Third, to minimise this risk, they identify a **change checklist** (table 9.2) — seven key success factors that managers can monitor to evaluate this (or any other) change process.
- Fourth, they develop a rating system to measure performance on these seven factors.

TABLE 9.2 The change checklist — key success factors for change	
Key success factors for change	**Questions for assessing and accomplishing change**
1. Leading change (who is responsible)	Do we have a leader: who owns and champions the change? who demonstrates public commitment to making it happen? who will garner resources to sustain it? who will invest personal time and attention to following it through?
2. Creating a shared need (why do it)	Do employees: see the reason for the change? understand why the change is important? see how it will help them and/or the business in the short term and long term?
3. Shaping a vision (what it will look like when finished)	Do employees: see the outcomes of the change in behavioural terms — that is, what they will do differently as a result of the change? get excited about these outcomes? understand how the change will benefit customers and other stakeholders?
4. Mobilising commitment (who else needs to be involved)	Do the sponsors of the change: recognise who else needs to be committed to the change for it to happen? know how to build a coalition of support for the change? have the ability to enlist the support of key individuals in the organisation? have the ability to build a responsibility matrix to make the change happen?
5. Building enabling systems (how it will be institutionalised)	Do the sponsors of the change: understand how to sustain the change by modifying human resource systems (such as staffing, training, appraisal, rewards, structure, communication)? recognise the technology investment required to implement the change? have access to financial resources to sustain the change?
6. Monitoring and demonstrating progress (how it will be measured)	Do the sponsors of the change: have a means of measuring the success of the change? plan to benchmark progress on both the results of the change and the implementation process?
7. Making it last (how it will be initiated and sustained)	Do the sponsors of the change: recognise the first steps needed to get started?

Source: Reprinted by permission of Harvard Business School Press from *The HR Scorecard: Linking People, Strategy & Performance* by B. Becker et al., Boston, MA, 2001, © 2001 by the Harvard Business School Publishing Corporation. All rights reserved.

The rating system for the change checklist requires simple subjective assessment by change leaders of performance on each of the seven key success factors for change. Scoring on a range of 0–100 for each factor, change managers can graph an overall profile. Figure 9.5 shows a fairly typical profile for the early stages of a change program where highly motivated change leaders have a strong vision but little success mobilising wider commitment, building enabling systems and demonstrating progress.

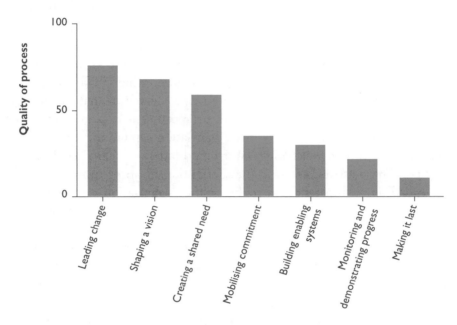

Key success factors in the change process

FIGURE 9.5: Profiling the change process

Becker, Huselid and Ulrich seek to apply a positivist or scientific approach, raising the standards of human resources measurement towards those achieved in finance and operations. They aspire to a positivist method, for example when they aim to prove with hard data a causal relationship between human resources inputs and strategic performance outputs. The value judgements of the researcher and the research subject permeate human resources, however. Is it possible to maintain objectivity when prioritising human resources variables and developing operational measures?

It is especially doubtful whether Becker, Huselid and Ulrich succeed in sustaining such positivist 'principles of good measurement' (as they call them) for their change checklist, which relies on subjective evaluation and makes no pretence of showing causal links. The checklist nevertheless remains a useful analytical tool to assist the measurement and evaluation of change programs.

The challenge of measuring 'change' has been taken up again by Kaplan and Norton in their latest work upon measuring 'intangibles'.[28] 'Learning and growth' was one of the four 'perspectives' they identified in their original work on the balanced scorecard.

In their latest work they revisit this perspective, dividing it into three components — 'human capital', 'information capital' and 'organisation capital'. Human capital relates to what they call 'strategic job readiness' — an organisation's capacity to fully deploy employee skills and capabilities to deliver customer value. Information capital concerns the 'strategic IT portfolio' — a blend of systems and skills so that IT is fully functional. Lastly, organisation capital concerns an organisation's readiness for change.

Kaplan and Norton call these assets 'intangibles' to contrast them with financial and physical assets, which can be ascribed a cash value. However, they should not be dismissed because they do not lend themselves easily to measurement. Kaplan and Norton claim that 'intangible assets' are worth far more than tangible assets to many organisations, and measuring them is the 'holy grail' of accounting.[29] Have they discovered the 'holy grail'? They claim so, the discovery being located in that quadrant of their 'strategy map' where the 'learning and growth perspective' is broken down into its constituent measurables. One of these — the 'organisation capital' intangible — concerns an organisation's readiness for change. Four broad 'attributes' are listed under organisation capital. These attributes are *culture* (adoption of an organisation's vision and mission); *leadership* (competency to mobilise the organisation's strategy); *alignment* (staff share awareness of the organisation's strategy and are motivated by incentives to pursue it); and *teamwork* (to share 'best practices'). These attributes can be measured in many different ways, the precise design of the measures depending on the characteristics of each organisation. Like the HR Scorecard, a scoring system can be developed in which actual performance is rated against a target score. The target score might be between (say) 20 per cent and 100 per cent, depending on a subjective assessment by management of the importance of an attribute. Similarly, the actual score will be a subjective evaluation by management. As with the HR Scorecard, 'hard numbers' will rest on a 'soft' value judgement.

Action research

Action research is a phenomenological technique widely employed by consultants when implementing change programs. Its status as a phenomenological method stems from the researcher's integral part in shaping change without seeking to maintain objective distance. French and Bell define action research as:

> The process of systematically collecting research data about an ongoing system relative to some objective, goal or need of that system; feeding those data back into the system; taking actions by altering selected variables within the system based both on the data and on hypotheses; and evaluating the results of actions by collecting more data.[30]

The psychologist Kurt Lewin and colleagues pioneered action research in the 1940s. Lewin is associated with a top–down or planned model of organisational change (see chapter 4) in which managers intervene in the dynamic between those systemic forces maintaining the status quo and other systemic forces for change. Understanding those forces would allow managers to plan the successive stages of 'unfreezing' an organisation, 'movement' and 'refreezing'. Lewin also came to see research or enquiry as part of a cycle of 'planning, acting, observing and reflecting' in the change process. He thus established how a close nexus between research and action assisted organisation members in managing change. Figure 9.6 shows a step-by-step model of the typical action research process.

Step 1	Organisational stakeholders identify the need for change.
Step 2	A behavioural science consultant is introduced to the organisation.
Step 3	The consultant conducts data gathering and analysis.
Step 4	Research findings are fed back to stakeholders.
Step 5	The consultant and stakeholders analyse research and plan change.
Step 6	Action is taken to implement change.
Step 7	Data are collected and analysed to monitor change.
Step 8	All parties review data and adjust change.

FIGURE 9.6: Action research model

Action research grew in popularity in the 1970s through its use by 'participative management' or 'organisation development' researchers and consultants.[31] Their approach to action research reflected the belief that effective change required joint decision-making by managers and employees. It followed that broad-based constituencies also had to be involved in the action research process. This approach came to be called 'participatory action research' or 'action learning'[32], and has led to a number of applied techniques for organisational research such as the 'search conference'.

From a positivist standpoint, critics frequently ask whether action research constitutes bona fide research or whether it should be properly classified as consultancy or journalism.[33] In response to such criticism, the advocates of this approach coined the term 'action science', which Gummesson describes in the following manner.[34]

- Action science always involves two goals: to solve a problem for the client and to contribute to science.
- The researcher and the client should learn from each other and develop their competencies.
- The researcher must investigate the whole, complex problem, but make it simple enough to be understood by everyone.
- Cooperation between the researcher and the client, feedback to the parties involved, and continuous adjustment to new information and new events is essential.
- Action science is primarily applicable to the understanding and planning of change in social systems, so it is a suitable research and consulting strategy for business organisations.
- The corporate environment and the conditions of business must be understood before the research starts.
- The method should be judged not solely by the criteria used for the positivistic paradigm, but by criteria more appropriate for this particular method.

Whatever its scientific merits, action research can yield a highly persuasive demonstration of the link between a change program and performance results. That proof is likely to be accepted most readily by those who participated in the action research — both consultants and organisation members. 'Seeing is believing', and those who participate directly in change interventions are easily inclined to accept the cause-and-effect relationships developed during action research.

Conversely, acceptance of action research will be lower among outsiders who do not experience or understand the 'subjective perception of reality' that is accessible to research participants and is the basic building block of phenomenological research. Does it matter whether outsiders do not believe in the claimed 'findings' of action research? From the standpoint of business, maybe not. What matters to organisation members often is their subjective opinion that the change intervention succeeded (although they may regret that head office, share market analysts and other external members of the business community do not hold the same faith in the validity of action research). From the standpoint of the research community, the answer may be different. How can researchers add findings from action research to the body of publicly accepted knowledge when it is private knowledge? The following paradox thus arises: many organisations 'know' that change interventions work, yet they can give no 'objective' proof to counter the scepticism of the research community.

Review

We began this chapter by observing the importance to managers of measurement and evaluation. We then distinguished the task of measuring change (which all businesses do) from that of measuring and evaluating change programs or interventions (which is more difficult).

First, we examined a number of ways in which to measure change. These were classed as conventional financial measures, strategy-driven measures or benchmarking. Within each broad type, several specific approaches exist — each with its own strengths and weaknesses. Large organisations today typically monitor change using all three types of measure, because financial reporting requirements are supplemented by the needs to monitor performance against strategic targets and to benchmark performance against best practice.

Second, we described several ways of measuring and evaluating the performance of change programs. We observed that such exercises are important because many change interventions fail and because managers need to recognise how their change activities are performing and act on that knowledge. This process requires research.

We distinguished between positivist and phenomenological approaches to research. Managers often prefer a positivist or 'scientific' proof that a change program improves performance, but the impossibility of conducting control experiments in business is a serious problem for the positivist approach. We then looked at several approaches to measuring the effects of change programs.

- Strategy-driven metrics or KPIs are a common and persuasive way to measure the impact of change initiatives. They can lay claim to rationality because of the logical way they cascade from business strategy. They are also highly flexible. With imagination, managers can develop metrics to measure almost any change initiative. However, their scientific independence is open to challenge. Because the design and application of this measure of change initiatives has a subjective aspect to it, such metrics are sometimes found to be politically controversial.

- TQM analytical tools are used widely to establish cause and effect in underperforming work processes. While simple and effective in the hands of a work team engaged in continuous improvement, they are less suited to the overall evaluation of a change program.
- The HR scorecard is a recent innovation to assist managers to develop positivist measures and analysis for human resources activities — traditionally an area of business that has defied quantification. The human resources scorecard is accompanied by a checklist of key success factors in the change process — each of which can be subjectively rated to give an overall evaluation of change.
- Action research is the principal phenomenological approach to measuring and evaluating change programs. The approach is widely employed by consultants who simultaneously research and participate in organisational change. Such methods can yield a persuasive demonstration to 'insiders' involved in the change process, but may be less easily understood and accepted by sceptical 'outsiders'.

Key terms

action research. Research in which the subject (often an organisation) both influences and is influenced by the researcher and the research process, (p. 306)

benchmarking. The search among comparable organisations for best practices that lead to superior performance, (p. 305)

cause-and-effect chart. Also termed an Ishikawa or 'fishbone' diagram, a device used by quality circles or work teams to identify a hierarchy of causes affecting quality ranging from major causes to minor ones, (p. 320)

change checklist. Key success factors that managers can monitor to gather systematic data to evaluate the change process, (p. 322)

critical success factors (CSFs). Variables, often related to cost, quality and delivery, that must be managed effectively for a business strategy to succeed, (p. 308)

human resources (HR) scorecard. An adaptation of the balanced scorecard to evaluate the contribution of human resources to strategic performance. It is a measurement system involving four dimensions: (1) human resource deliverables, (2) high-performance work systems, (3) alignment of the high-performance work system

with strategy, and (4) efficiency in generating deliverables. (p. 306)

key performance indicators (KPIs). Measures of critical success factors (CSFs) that may relate to the organisation as a whole or to its parts (including work teams), (p. 309)

Pareto principle. Also known as the 80:20 rule, the principal that a few of the causes usually account for most of the effect, (p. 320)

phenomenological research. Research based on the assumption that the researcher's values shape interaction with research subjects and, therefore, that valid findings must be situational or context bound, and reached through qualitative methods, (p. 316)

positivist research. Research based on the assumption that the researcher is independent of the subject, is objective and can validate predictive generalisations about cause-and-effect relationships, (p. 316)

return on equity. A financial ratio calculated by dividing the declared accounting profit of an organisation by accounting investment. It is a widely used financial measure of changes to performance. (p. 305) tacit knowledge. The unique combination of skills and cooperative social arrangements that influences organisational performance, (p. 314)

total quality management (TQM). An holistic approach to quality improvement involving all parts of an organisation in the measurement, analysis and rectification of quality problems, (p. 305)

triple bottom line (TBL). Corporate reporting of social, environmental, and financial performance, (p. 315)

value-based strategic management. A technique to convert disaggregated performance data into a single, organisation-wide measure of shareholder value, (p. 310)

Review questions

1. Can managers prove a causal link between a change program and performance outcomes?
2. Why should managers measure the results of a change program?
3. What are the differences between positivist and phenomenological approaches to research, and why is this important for the evaluation of change programs?
4. Show how measures of change can cascade out of a rational strategic planning process. Are such measures 'value free'?
5. Outline the main strengths and weaknesses of benchmarking as a measurement and learning tool.
6. Can TQM measurement techniques prove the causes of quality problems and the effects of solutions?
7. Describe Becker, Huselid and Ulrich's framework for profiling and evaluating the change process. Does it allow an objective assessment of change?
8. What are the defining features of action research? Is it a valid method to evaluate organisational change?

Discussion questions

1. 'If you cannot measure it, it is not worth doing.' Discuss this statement in relation to change management.
2. 'The only measures that matter are financial ones.' Discuss the 'pros' and 'cons' of this point of view.

Work assignment

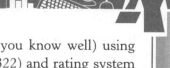

Evaluating a change intervention

Evaluate a change program in your own organisation (or one you know well) using Becker, Huselid and Ulrich's change checklist (table 9.2, page 322) and rating system (figure 9.5, page 323). What does the overall profile you derive tell you about the effectiveness of change management in this case?

Suggested further reading

Becker, B. E., Huselid, M. A. & Ulrich, D. 2001, *The HR Scorecard: Linking People, Strategy and Performance*, Harvard Business School Press, Boston.

Dunphy, D., Griffiths, A. & Benn. S. 2003, *Organisational Change for Corporate Sustainability*, Routledge, London.

Hussey, J. & Hussey, R. 1997, *Business Research: A Practical Guide for Undergraduate and Postgraduate Students*, Macmillan Business, London.

Kaplan, R. S. & Norton, D. P. 2001, *The Strategy Focused Organization: How Balanced Scorecard Companies Thrive in the New Business Environment*, Harvard Business School Press, Boston.

Macneil, J., Testi, J., Cupples, J. & Rimmer, M. 1994, *Benchmarking Australia: Linking Enterprises to World's Best Practice*, Longman Business and Professional, Melbourne.

End notes

1. V. J. Callan, G. Latemore & N. Paulsen 2004, 'The best-laid plans: uncertainty, complexity and large-scale organisational change', *Mt Eliza Business Review*, 7 (1), p. 15.

2. R. Ashkenas 1994, 'Beyond the fads: how leaders drive change with results', *Human Resource Planning*, 17(2), pp. 25–44.

3. J. Champy 1995, *Reengineering Management: The New Mandate for Leadership*, Harper Business, New York.

4. Ernst & Young and the American Quality Foundation 1992, 'The International Quality Study Best Practices Report: An Analysis of Management Practices that Impact Performance', Ernst & Young, Cleveland, Ohio.

5. G. Hubbard, G. Pocknee & G. A. Taylor 1996, *Practical Australian Strategy*, Prentice Hall, Sydney.

6. R. S. Kaplan & D. P. Norton 2001, *The Strategy Focused Organization: How Balanced Scorecard Companies Thrive in the New Business Environment*, Harvard Business School Press, Boston.

7. B. Houlden 1996, *Understanding Company Strategy*, 2nd edn, Blackwell Business, Oxford.

8. R. S. Kaplan & D. P. Norton 1996, *The Balanced Scorecard: Translating Strategy into Action*, Harvard Business School Press, Boston.

9. R. D. Stacey 1993, *Strategic Management and Organisational Dynamics*, Pitman Publishing, London.

10. American Productivity and Quality Center (APQC) 1993, *The Benchmarking Management Guide*, Productivity Press, Cambridge, Massachusetts, p. 4.

11. R. C. Camp 1989, *Benchmarking — the Search for Industry Best Practices that Leads to Superior Performance*, ASQ Quality Press, Milwaukee.

12. J. Macneil, M. Rimmer & J. Testi 1993, *Raising the Standards — Benchmarking and Best Practice in Australia; Progress in the Top 500 Enterprises*, Monash University, Melbourne.

13. J. Macneil, J. Testi, J. Cupples & M. Rimmer 1994, *Benchmarking Australia: Linking Enterprises to World's Best Practice*, Longman Business and Professional, Melbourne.

14. Macneil, Rimmer & Testi, op. cit., p. 22.

15. See, for example, KPMG 2000, *Financial Institutions Performance Survey* (Annual Report), Melbourne.

16. F. G. Hilmer & L. Donaldson 1996, *Management Redeemed: Debunking the Fads that Undermine Corporate Performance*, The Free Press, Sydney, p. 106.

17. B. Kogut & U. Zander 1992, 'Knowledge of the firm, combinative capabilities and the replication of technology', *Organization Science*, 3(3), pp. 383–97.

18. G. Szulanski 1996, 'Exploring internal stickiness: impediments to the transfer of best practice within the firm', *Strategic Management Journal*, 17, pp. 27–47; G. Martin & P. Beaumont 1998, 'Diffusing "best practice" in multinational firms: prospects, practice and contestation', *International Journal of Human Resource Management*, 9(4), pp. 671–95.

19. J. Hussey & R. Hussey 1997, *Business Research — A Practical Guide for Undergraduate and Postgraduate Students*, Macmillan Business, London, p. 47.

20. M. J. Epstein and M. J. Roy 2004, 'Improving the performance of corporate boards: identifying and measuring the key drivers of success', *Journal of General Management*, 29(3), pp. 1–22.

21. K. H. Leitner & C. Warden 2004, 'Managing and reporting knowledge-based resources and processes in research organisations: specifics, lessons learned and perspectives', *Management Accounting Research*, 15 (1), pp. 33–51.

22. B. Townley, D. J. Cooper & L. Oakes (2003), 'Performance measures and the rationalisation of organizations', *Organization Studies*, 24 (7), pp. 1045–71.

23. T. Kochan & P. Osterman 1995, *The Mutual Gains Enterprise*, Harvard Business School Press, Boston.

24. A. Morehead, M. Steele, M. Alexander, K. Stephen & L. Duffin 1997, *Changes at Work: The 1995 Australian Workplace Industrial Relations Survey*, Longman, Melbourne, p. 188.

25. Hilmer & Donaldson, op. cit., p. 99.

26. B. E. Becker, M. A. Huselid & D. Ulrich 2001, *The HR Scorecard: Linking People, Strategy and Performance*, Harvard Business School Press, Boston.

27. D. Norton, cited in Becker, Huselid & Ulrich, op. cit., p. ix.

28. R. S. Kaplan and D. P. Norton 2004, 'Measuring the strategic readiness of intangible assets', *Harvard Business Review*, February, pp. 52–63.

29. ibid., p. 52.

30. W. H. French & C. H. Bell 1984, *Organization Development: Behavioral Science Interventions for Organizational Improvement*, 3rd edn, Prentice Hall, Englewood Cliffs, New Jersey.

31. D. Dunphy 1981, *Organisational Change by Choice*, McGraw-Hill, Sydney.

32. D. M. Waddell, T. G. Cummings & C. G. Worley 2000, *Organisation Development and Change*, Nelson Thomson Learning, Melbourne, p. 30.

33. E. Gummesson 1991, *Qualitative Methods in Management Research*, Sage Publications, California, p. 102.

34. ibid., p. 102.

THE PROBLEMS OF HUMAN ADJUSTMENT AND ECONOMIC SUSTAINABILITY

OPENING CASE
Jalco — a manufacturing success

Barry Smorgon worked in the family business, Smorgon Consolidated Industries, until it broke up in 1994. Looking for a new challenge, within a year he bought 80 per cent of JC Allan, a small manufacturing company in western Sydney. Working with John Tisdale, managing director for 17 years, and owner of the remaining 20 per cent, they enlarged their manufacturing business through a process of acquisition and diversification. Renamed Jalco, the firm has grown to operate on six sites with 450 employees. Its range of manufactures has expanded from health, cosmetic and personal care products to include automotive products and food. It also has part-ownership of a plastics business and a 50:50 logistics joint venture with Patrick Corporation. Between 1996 and 2002 its sales expanded from $18.5 million to $84 million.

The basis for Jalco's growth has been contract manufacturing, making products that other manufacturers have decided to outsource. Typically these products are near the end of their life cycle and production is due to be phased out. Because outsourcing is so popular, this kind of contract manufacturing has turned into a growth industry. Jalco is doing well at it, and has the confidence to expand its own production capacity. It has just acquired an extra 3400 square metres of factory space for food production relying on the maxim 'if you build it, they will come'.

Jalco's clients include manufacturers like Avon, Unilever and Colgate, who set up Australian operations 20 or 30 years ago. These clients have now decided that their strength lies in brand management, marketing and distribution and have outsourced production to Jalco. For example, Jalco has a contract with Colgate to manufacture Ajax powdered cleanser in a cardboard canister — a product line that Colgate no longer wishes to make but plans to retain in its product portfolio. Jalco acquired some specialised manufacturing equipment from Colgate, and simply included Ajax powder in its own product range.

Contract manufacturing faces its own special challenges. Business depends on the whims chiefly of US executives of multinationals who make most of the outsourcing decisions. No special favours get done for an Australian contract manufacturer, especially when the Australian dollar is rising and competitors in China and South-East Asia offer so many advantages. Jalco lost 35 per cent of its business in 2003, including its two largest contracts, and must constantly renew its customer base even to stand still. The logistics of operations and production are dizzying for an organisation that manufactured 4500 separate products in 2003. Equipment and staff must be flexible in a business where manufacturing lines may change three or four times a day. Working this way would be fatal for any manufacturer of the old school used to being cushioned by steady customers and products, but these are the conditions under which Jalco flourishes.

Source: Adapted from Deborah Tarrant 2004, 'Top entrepreneurs — Barry Smorgon', *AFR BOSS*, April, pp. 70–1.

Introduction

The Jalco case is an extreme example of an organisation that has built its entire *modus operandi* around the uncertainties of change. The company expects its customers to turn over, and its product lines to be in constant flux. Its workers are accustomed to switching from one product to the next, operating new equipment, customising old plant and, yet, still meeting the demanding quality specifications of their customers. Jalco confronts on a daily basis the challenges of change that other manufacturers take years to accommodate.

Jalco is an unusual manufacturer. Contrast it with a more typical example — Hardie Irrigation (see the 'Change management in action' box below). The Hardie's case exposes quite different change dynamics. First, unlike Jalco where change is constant, Hardie's shows how the trajectory of a change program over time can be uncertain and slow. Seven years and two management teams were needed before a hierarchical and inefficient operation finally turned into one where teams participated in continuous improvement to deliver quality. Hardie Irrigation shows how change programs can be messy and unpredictable, rarely delivering results to a dependable timetable. In comparison Jalco's capacity to manage constant change means it can promise reliable delivery and quality to build the reputation on which it can secure customers.

Second, the Hardie Irrigation case shows that slow and unreliable change may be connected with the difficulty managers and employees encounter in developing new attitudes to go with teamwork and a new production system. Contrast this possibility with the Jalco culture, in which everyone shares the attitude that yesterday will be different from today. However, the Jalco culture is unusual for manufacturing. Most often, problems of human adjustment will accompany any change intervention. Such personal adjustments to change are sometimes called **transitions**.[1] They involve fundamental change in behaviour, attitude and belief so that people can come to terms with a new work situation. Transitions are a central part of the dynamic of organisational change.

Third, the Hardie Irrigation case shows how economic factors can both drive change and then cause it to be abandoned. Initially, these factors compelled Hardie Irrigation to explore new ways of making local manufacturing competitive against imports. But eventually economic realities intruded and it decided to cease manufacturing and import its product lines. The Hardie Irrigation scenario is a common one for manufacturers seeking long-term survival in a narrow market sector. In contrast, Jalco stands this economic challenge on its head, seeking long-term profitability by opportunistically grabbing short-term production opportunities for a wide range of products. However, the Hardie Irrigation situation is more typical for manufacturing. Change programs in such firms have to pass economic **cost–benefit analysis** tests if they are to be sustained in the long run. Those tests pose two questions. (1) Is the change program delivering a net benefit? and (2) Is that benefit sufficient to ensure competitiveness? (We discussed how organisations make these economic evaluations of change in chapter 9.) This calculus also has been linked by Kochan and Osterman to a 'sustainability problem' to explain the apparent preference of US managers for short-term change programs, which downsize, rather than long-term ones, which build teamwork, high commitment, or a **mutual gains enterprise**.[2] The **sustainability** problem occurs when firms terminate slow-maturing investments in 'people-centred' change because financial markets impatiently demand quick results.

In this chapter, we examine how change programs perform over time. The discussion concentrates upon two questions. (1) Can people adjust to change to make it succeed? and (2) Does change deliver sustained economic benefits to justify investment in people?

CHANGE MANAGEMENT IN ACTION
Hardie Irrigation abandons manufacturing

Hardie Irrigation was the trading name for an Australian manufacturing and distribution subsidiary of the US-owned James Hardie Industries. Its business was manufacturing and selling sprinklers and other irrigation products. In 1997 another US-owned corporation, Toro, acquired the Australian business and closed manufacturing plants in New South Wales and Victoria. However, it tried to continue manufacturing at its 'best practice' factory in Murray Bridge in South Australia.

The Murray Bridge factory was seven years into an organisational change program to restore competitiveness when Toro acquired it. In 1990 Hardie Irrigation was a typical under-capitalised and inefficient manufacturer under threat from cheap imports. In 1991, a new management team had

been hired with a brief to turn the Murray Bridge plant around. They designed a change program that included:

- introducing teamwork (cellular manufacturing)
- redesigning production flows in the factory and reducing inventory
- building a customer focus and gaining quality accreditation
- training staff in quality, communications and conflict resolution.

Murray Bridge became a showcase for change of this kind. However, research in 1994 found that reform had only partly succeeded.[3] Some 'one off' gains were realised by redesigning the factory and introducing MRP II to cut inventory. But teamwork failed to deliver continuous improvement. Cellular manufacturing had failed. The mindset was unchanged. Management remained autocratic and employees unmotivated. Lacking measurable targets, the cells degenerated into what one manager called 'industrial communism' guided only by their own whims.

In 1997, Toro installed a new management team that revived the change program. A quality manager was installed who appointed new team leaders equipped with measurable targets and a directive style. Measurable targets relating to productivity, quality, safety and scrap guided continuous improvement. Researchers in 1998 found these changes were working. But they were not sufficient to save the plant. Toro had inherited equipment that was 15 years out of date. Although initially committed to investing in new equipment, Toro delayed. In 2000, it announced the abandonment of manufacturing. In future it would import all its product lines and make nothing in Australia. The change program had taken too long, had only partly succeeded, and was insufficient to guarantee the plant's future in Toro's strategy.

Human adjustment to change: transitions and stress

Researchers say that unless transition occurs, change will not work. Transitions are a process of personal psychological adjustment to change. Failure to make such adjustments is associated with pathological consequences, including stress and ill-health. To deal with these issues, we divide the discussion of adjustment to change into three parts.

- What are the changes to which people must adjust?
- What is the transition process? We examine how psychologists map the stages through which people pass in making a transition.
- What is the relationship between change in the workplace, stress and ill-health?

Economic benefits and sustainability

The sustainability problem occurs when financial 'short termism' causes a change program to be discontinued before it has time to work. In discussing sustainability, we look at three issues:

- **capital market 'short termism'** — does the demand for quick financial results cause firms to terminate investment in change prematurely?
- incomplete change — do **holistic change** programs fail when essential parts of an 'integrated design' are neglected at the first attempt?
- **core values** — is the key to sustainable long-term change found in an appropriate alignment between the core ideology (or 'core values') of a business and its organisational structure and operations?

Aspects of human adjustment and economic sustainability are likely to be intertwined. One possible scenario is that positive attitudes are associated with economic effectiveness in a virtuous circle where 'success breeds success'. Is it necessary, however, for management to 'win the hearts and minds' of the workforce for a change program to deliver on the bottom line? In the closing section of this chapter, we confront new evidence on this issue. This evidence casts doubt on whether change necessarily requires 'mutuality' (a compact or psychological contract) between management and the workforce that helps employees adopt a new mindset to adjust to change.

Change at work

Transitions are a process of personal adjustment to change at work. This process must be understood in the context of the changes that people encounter at work. What is the backdrop of change against which we can see and understand transitions?

The existence of a revolution at work was mentioned in chapter 2, in which we noted how neo-liberal economic policies, combined with the growing intensity of global competition, ended old certainties about work and introduced discontinuous change that is fast, traumatic and revolutionary. A close look at the contemporary employment situation exposes how vulnerable many people are; making them fearful of change that threatens their livelihood.

This vulnerability was revealed in March 2005 after Prime Minister Howard announced that the creation of 2.25 million jobs in 12 years had cut unemployment to 5.1%, the lowest figure since the 1970s, and that the scarcity of skills was choking economic growth. At the same time, the Australian Bureau of Statistics released data showing that two million Australian who wanted full-time work could not get it.[4] This number included:

- 578,000 under-employed part-time workers, 70 per cent of whom wanted full-time work.
  - 16,000 of these part-timers could not get full-time work because employers considered them too old
  - 110,000 part-timers complained full-time jobs in their line of work were not available.
- 570,000 workers were officially unemployed and, in addition:
  - 27,000 discouraged job seekers had stopped looking because they were considered too old.
- 323,000 workers had left the workforce after being retrenched or dismissed from their last job.

These data contradict the claim that work exists for all who want it. To the contrary, many workers are unable to get the work they want because of lack of skills, age, health problems, regional location, or the experience of constant rejection by employers. Change has adversely affected employees in other ways too:

- Research shows that many 'middle managers' have become unemployed or under-employed as downsizing has spread to all layers of organisations. Forced 'labour churning' (voluntary and involuntary turnover) has been estimated to affect as high as 25 per cent of all managers in Australia.[5]
- Working time has increased for a substantial minority of Australians after falling steadily throughout the 20th century. As many as 1.7 million workers in Australia (almost 20 per cent of the workforce) have been found to work extra hours as unpaid overtime.
- Working harder is also a common experience for many employees. The most recent national survey of Australian employees in 1995 found that in the previous 12 months 59 per cent of employees had found their work effort had increased while 46 per cent found the pace of the job was faster.[6]

- By 2004, casual workers made up 27 per cent of the Australian workforce — twice the level in 1982. Many of these would like permanent work because of the insecurity of casual employment.

What is the total impact of all these changes? Beck's analysis of such changes in the labour markets of Western economies presents a bleak picture of the future of work.[7] The proportion of the workforce who are unemployed, in precarious work or in bad jobs is multiplying at such a rate that the workforce in advanced industrial economies is coming to resemble that in the Third World. Beck calls this the 'Brazilianisation of the West', taking for his model a Latin American economy in which only a minority of economically active people are in full-time work, mostly because no better jobs are available. Combining the growing insecurities of work with the decline in State-funded social security, Beck draws a future scenario of a 'risk society' in which most individuals will be deprived of the normal benefits of secure citizenship.

The prevailing view is that change is affecting people's jobs in epidemic proportions. It also is likely that most people find change alarming because they are fearful of the risks of being displaced in the labour market or obliged to accept adverse changes to their job.

A conflicting view of the labour market questions the pessimistic view of authorities such as Beck. Wooden, for example, challenges whether changes in the Australian labour market have made employees worse off or simply are unacceptable to them. He shows that job security has not declined; using labour market statistics to demonstrate that the duration of jobs has remained stable. He also sees the growth of casual and part-time jobs as compatible with employee preferences for flexibility and leisure, rather than a tyrannical imposition by management.[8]

While researchers generally agree on the ways in which work is changing, controversy exists over the causes of that change and whether people's working and non-working lives are worse as a result. Do demand factors (the jobs that employers wish to offer) or supply factors (the jobs that employees wish to accept) have most influence in shaping change in the workforce? Are employment conditions (the net benefits that attract people to work) improving or getting worse? While opinion is divided on such questions, less disagreement exists about change at work speeding up and that personal adjustment to change is usually difficult.

Making transitions

According to Carlopio, Andrewartha and Armstrong, 'All organisational change requires personal change in an organisational setting. This means that every individual in an organisation, from the Chief Executive onwards, must be both willing and able to grow, learn and adapt.'[9] They observe that such change takes place at three levels: the organisation, the group or team, and the individual. In discussing transitions, we are concerned more with personal adjustment to change than with change at the organisational level, but it is helpful to start by looking at how teams handle or adjust to change. Some teams accommodate change better than others — a fact that often can be observed within a single workplace. This difference has important consequences for change at the individual and organisational levels.

The Hardie Irrigation case illustrates the problem of team adjustment to change. The Murray Bridge plant had mixed success with teamwork. A pilot cell formed in 1992, which was positively endorsed by management, caused shopfloor jealousies among workers. In an effort to address this effect, management formed a second pilot cell and, shortly after, rushed the extension of cellular manufacturing throughout the whole workplace. What results followed? First, the pilot cell, although successful, did not function as an example. Second, the other cells were poorly implemented and functioned badly. Everyone initially wanted to be in teams and then no-one wanted anything to do with them. Despite initial success, management concluded the cells were not working and reached a consensus that cellular manufacturing was wrong for the workplace. As the linchpin for change in the organisation, cells had failed both the organisation and the individuals.

The dynamics of team adaption to change can go sour and emerge as dysfunctional behaviour. Sinclair describes the negative side of team centred change as follows:

> The team ideology tyrannises because, under the banner of benefits to all, teams are frequently used to camouflage coercion with the appearance of cohesion, conceal conflict with the appearance of consensus, convert conformity into an appearance of creativity, to give unilateral decisions a co-determinist seal of approval, to delay action in the supposed interests of consultation, to legitimate lack of leadership, and to disguise expedient arguments and personal agendas.[10]

Many things can go wrong with teams, including their use for inappropriate tasks, ineffective leadership, and difficult team members. Another way to look at much the same phenomena, however, is as part of a developmental process. The following are taken from the many models of team development.

- Tuckman describes four generic stages in the team development process: forming (establishing roles, relationships, tasks and expectations), conforming (adjusting to the team), storming (resolving conflicts within the team) and performing (task performance and team maintenance).[11]

- Stace and Dunphy take a contingency approach, linking team skills to different levels of team functioning. Technical skill sets are linked to the goal of achieving flexible technical competence throughout the team; supervisory skills to the goal of flexible self-supervision; and managerial skills to the goal of self-management. The level of skill and team development required depends on environmental conditions and operational requirements.[12]

- Bishop and Graham developed a step-by-step guide to team development based on their experience of team implementation at the ANM Boyer mill (now Norske Skog).[13] Their five steps are:

   1. start-up, where the organisation is committed to work teams but structural and cultural change are yet to occur
   2. state of confusion, where the organisation structure is in transition between old and new arrangements, causing confusion and anxiety

3. leader-centred teams, where teams ask strong individuals to become team leaders, recreating old and comfortable supervisory styles

4. tightly formed teams, where work teams are properly structured and members' roles are developed and accepted

5. self-directed teams, where old structures are gone and new teams are fully functional at a high level of self-directed activity.

Whether teams help or hinder change at the organisational and personal levels depends on a number of factors. High in importance is management's understanding of the development process required for teamwork, and its political success in navigating teams through the stages. Judging progress through these stages is not easy. Ultimate success and failure are easily recognised, but managers and team members in the intermediate stages of development will be prey to fears that teamwork is inappropriate for their workplace. Rather than confront and resolve problems, they will retreat from the team-based approach to change. The Hardie Irrigation case illustrates this pitfall.

Vital to all organisational and team adaption to change is personal or individual adaption. Bridges labels this process of personal adaption 'transition' and distinguishes it from 'change' in the following way:

> It isn't the changes that do you in, it's the transitions. Change is not the same as transition. Change is situational: the new site, the new boss, the new team roles, the new policy. Transition is the psychological process people go through to come to terms with the new situation. Change is external, transition is internal.[14]

Bridges describes three stages in the process of transition: **endings**, the **neutral zone** and **new beginnings**. In reality, they do not occur as separate stages with clear boundaries; they tend to overlap.

Endings

This first stage of transition involves identifying what will be lost in the change process and accepting that loss. Bridges argues that 'the failure to identify and be ready for the endings and losses that change produces is the largest single problem that organisations in transition encounter'.[15] Managing endings is likely to be a complex process with a number of steps, including the following.

- *Identifying who's losing what.* This process requires a careful and thorough description of what will actually change (in processes, materials, personal and so on), followed by the identification of all people whose familiar way of doing things will be affected. Everyone who is affected must go into this inventory of loss, including not only those whose income or job security is at risk but also those whose values or sense of 'mission' is threatened.

- *Accepting the reality and importance of subjective loss.* Bridges argues that subjective perceptions of loss should be accommodated, not contested. If people are to be eased willingly through a transition, dismissing their feared losses as 'inaccurate', 'paranoid' or 'exaggerated' is unhelpful.

- *Not being surprised at overreaction.* People react to their subjective perception of change. There is no objective position from which overreactions can be gauged and dismissed. Also, seemingly small 'losses' may trigger reactions originating in past experience. Managing such responses at a rational level may be difficult. Fears of job loss, for example, can be sparked by apparently trivial and unrelated acts by management, such as calling a budget meeting or simply arranging a performance appraisal out of schedule.

- *Acknowledging losses openly and sympathetically.* As is normal in counselling, open and honest acknowledgement of pain and loss is deemed to be essential to closure.
- *Expecting and accepting signs of grieving.* Denial, anger, ambit claims, anxiety, sadness and depression are normal and cannot be avoided. These should not be mistaken for low morale or other warning signals of a poor work culture.
- *Compensating for losses.* Consider ways in which to make up for losses. Generous redundancy payments, for example, can help survivors in a workforce retrenchment accept the loss of colleagues and friends and, thus, make their own transition.
- *Giving people information.* Open, free and continual communication assists transition by minimising uncertainties or exaggerated 'fears of the worst'.
- *Marking the endings.* Symbolic closure with the past clarifies what is lost and what is not. New letterhead, job titles and the like, for example, have value partly in their symbolic clarification of loss to assist people through transition.
- *Treating the past with respect.* Failure to do so de-motivates survivors of change and breeds resistance.
- *Showing how endings ensure continuity of what really matters.* Core organisation values such as commitment to innovation or quality often persist while the organisation changes around them. Keeping such continuities minimises loss while reducing the risk of conflict over values.

The neutral zone

The neutral zone is the second stage of transition. External or situational change can be swift but psychological change requires an intermediate stage that is neither the old nor the new. It is a period when old patterns of habits, behaviours, attitudes and beliefs are extinguished for being no longer appropriate and new patterns are learned, practised and adjusted to by organisational members. Bridges describes this zone as a 'kind of emotional wilderness, a time when it wasn't clear who you were or what was real'.[16] It is a period of discomfort and discontinuity when anxieties are high, motivation is problematic and productivity may suffer. On the other hand, it also is a period when opportunity exists for creativity. It usually is not possible to fast track through the neutral zone or to escape it without compromising the whole transition process. Accepting that it must be passed through, Bridges suggests the neutral zone be managed in the following way.

- *Normalise the neutral zone.* Bring into the open and discuss reactions and feelings that people experience during this stage.
- *Find a positive metaphor.* A metaphor can give meaning to the stage, putting a positive spin on an otherwise difficult phase by communicating a sense of journey or experimentation. The metaphor should not conceal, repress or invalidate problems at this stage.

- *Create temporary systems for the neutral zone*. These may include communication systems to monitor morale, but also brainstorming or problem-solving groups to capitalise on the opportunity for creativity.
- *Strengthen intra-group connections*. Feelings of isolation are common. Connection with others allows problems to be pooled, normalised and resolved.
- *Use a transition monitoring team*. This is essentially for two-way communication, bringing change planners and workplace opinion or the 'grapevine' into closer touch.

New beginnings

The third and final stage of transition can occur only if people first have made an ending and second have spent some time in the neutral zone. While it is the last step in the change process, many organisations mistake it for the first. Like the previous two stages, it is psychological rather than situational. Unlike the other two stages, it is open ended, with no particular timetable that can be managed. The following are among the issues to consider in managing beginnings.

- *Ambivalence towards beginnings*. Internalising new commitments can be uncomfortable for many people, despite whatever progress they have made in handling losses. The response to beginnings can be fear as much as relief that the uncertainties of the neutral zone are passed.
- *The timing of new beginnings*. Because beginnings are reached internally through a process of adjustment, they can be only encouraged or supported. Managers have no power to force or demand new beginnings. Individuals will keep to their own timetables in starting over, and these often will not synchronise.
- *Clarification and communication of the purpose*. Reinforcing awareness of what change is supposed to accomplish, what might have happened otherwise and what problems might have bred in the absence of change is helpful. The lessons of change need to be kept in the public eye to sustain belief in the new beginnings.

To reinforce beginnings, Bridges also suggests four rules: (1) be consistent; (2) ensure quick successes; (3) symbolise the new identity; and (4) celebrate the successes.

Other approaches to transition

Bridges' three-stage model of transitions resembles many other models of psychological adaption to change. Lewin's planned model of change, for example, involves the three steps of unfreezing, moving and refreezing, which resemble Bridges' endings, the neutral zone and beginnings.[17] Lewin's model is directive, however, identifying the actions that managers must take to instruct personal change, whereas Bridges' model is facilitative, reminding managers that they can only guide or help people through transitions that are essentially their own responsibility.

Carlopio, Andrewartha and Armstrong's model of personal change builds on Lewin's work. It distinguishes four steps in the change process: unlearning, changing, relearning and institutionalising change.[18]

- *Unlearning* involves establishing a felt need for change and managing resistance.
- *Changing* requires establishing new learned and instinctive ways of thinking and behaving.

- *Relearning* entails processes of reinforcing, evaluating and modifying desired ideas and behaviour.
- *Institutionalising change* involves using human resource processes such as performance review to reinforce continual personal improvement that is consistent with desired change outcomes.

A first strength of this model is that it provides explicitly for continual feedback. As soon as the fourth stage of the process (institutionalising change) is complete, it feeds back into the first stage (unlearning) for the cycle to start again. This process captures the reality of continuous change in modern organisations. Most managers today would question whether Lewin's third stage of refreezing can occur when a new round of changes is likely to begin before the last round is complete.

A second strength of Carlopio, Andrewartha and Armstrong's model is the inclusion of a fourth step — that is, institutionalising change. They consider that those institutional forces reinforce personal change by means of personal development programs resembling 'continuous improvement for individuals'. The programs involve mainly making a habit out of personal improvement. Many modern organisations employ psychologists to run such personal development programs for managers. These programs are considered essential both as a method for developing managers' interpersonal skills and as a tool to prevent 'burn-out', thus protecting the organisation's investment in managerial human resources.

We have described Bridges' model of transitions and Carlopio, Andrewartha and Armstrong's model of personal change. What are the strengths of these models? One positive feature is that managers find them to be powerful tools for understanding change and facilitating change interventions. Part of that strength derives from the incorporation of practical insights and understanding gleaned from consulting and action research. That strength also derives from the applicability of the transitions model to change in all aspects of personal and work life — a characteristic that makes the model easy for individuals to understand and apply.

These models also have weaknesses, however. First, they are unashamedly normative, which is a disadvantage for those who want to know how people adapt to change, not how they *should* adapt. Second, and related to the previous point, they receive little support from hard positivist research that confirms people behave as the transitions model supposes they do. Third, they neglect the impact of social factors on personal psychological adjustment to change; in particular, they neglect the way in which the unequal distribution of power within organisations creates different experiences of change for those who are directing change and for those who are being directed.

Does it matter whether psychologists such as Bridges leave power out of their models of personal change? From one perspective, the answer is no. All people, whether they hold power or not, experience change and adapt to it with varying degrees of success. Power holders must internalise change as much as the powerless must do so. Transitions are a challenge for everyone who encounters change. This maxim may be true, but it also may be trivial, given the importance of 'subjective loss' in Bridges' model of transitions. In the model, psychological recognition of loss and the response to it are key ingredients in the transition process. But are all losses equal? To Bridges, all losses are subjective, so we cannot compare them. We cannot, conclude, therefore, that a male employee forced to retire ten years early experiences a greater loss than a manager who is relocated to an open-plan office. Objectively, however, it is reasonable to compare the two losses. In the 'social setting' of the workplace, people do make such comparisons. Further, they often make a social judgement that the manager adjusting to the open-plan office faces a lesser adjustment than that of the employee who has lost ten years earnings. Such social judgements influence how people actually adjust to change just as does the personal process of transition. The inability of Bridges' model to incorporate the 'social' responses to change associated with the unequal distribution of power is what renders it trivial.

A psychological account of 'transition' or personal change in the workplace is problematic because it is incomplete, neglecting important social variables that influence psychological states or adjustments. These social variables are discussed at length in chapter 7, in which we deal with power and resistance to change. A central point to be learned from that chapter is that a realistic account of change recognises that it may be contested. It is misleading to represent the contest as 'grieving behaviour' (as Bridges' model does) because that incorrectly denies the legitimacy of conflict and categorises contesting behaviour as a personal problem that needs to be treated, rather than as the expression of a legitimate interest that may need to be accommodated between social groups.

Change and its effect on stress and health

Notwithstanding their shortcomings, models of transition or personal adjustment to change help us understand why the change process can take so long and why change interventions often fail. The successive stages of endings and the neutral zone necessarily take time before new beginnings can occur, so planned change has to make allowance for that time.

The possibility exists for managers to mismanage transitions by failing to recognise the nature of the process and act effectively on that knowledge. What are the consequences if they neglect to assist transitions? An obvious consequence is that people will not adjust to new work demands or systems, leading them to perform poorly. A second consequence is that the enlarged gap between job expectations and performance will cause **stress**. Work-related stress is one of a number of health problems that may form part of the 'down side' of change.

Quinlan and Bohle define stress in terms of the 'discrepancy between the demands placed on the person and their skills and resources to deal with them'.[19] This view is called a 'transactional approach' to stress, because it perceives stress as arising from the interaction between a person and their environment. Stress is not a fixed attribute of either the individual or the environment. Jobs, therefore, are not inherently stressful; some people will find a job causes stress while others will not. Equally, people do not experience stress without encountering stressful conditions. The factors that have an impact on people to cause stress are called 'stressors'. They may be social, psychological and/or physiological. In chronic cases, stress can lead to many serious problems, including heart disease, mental breakdown and the dissolution of relationships.

While stress can occur in any activity, it is increasingly associated with work-related factors. A number of organisational variables have been identified as potential stressors.[20] Cooper groups them in the following six categories.

- *Factors intrinsic to the job*, including physical characteristics such as arduousness and danger. Unpleasant tasks can be stressors.
- *Relationships at work*, including interpersonal relationships within teams or between managers and other employees. Positive relationships lower job stress.
- *Organisational role*. Stress is associated with characteristics of individuals' roles such as role ambiguity, role conflict and responsibility for others.
- *Career development*. A lack of congruence between status and skill is associated with stress.
- *Organisational structure and climate*. Lack of autonomy and insufficient participation in decisions are associated with stress.
- *The home–work interface*. Conflict between domestic and work roles and expectations is linked to stress.

One effect of organisational change may be to increase the likelihood that individuals will experience work-related stress for one or more of these six reasons. A second effect may be to intensify stress to the point that individuals cannot cope with it, causing health problems and work-performance problems. People can respond to stress in both positive and negative ways. The range of responses to stress is depicted in figure 10.1. In the absence of normal levels of stress, people will experience 'rust-out' and be bored or unmotivated. Some level of stress or tension is necessary to provide positive motivation. Excessive stress, however, will cause distress and lead to 'burn-out'.

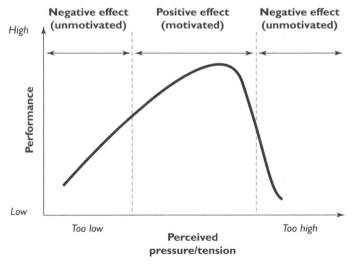

FIGURE 10.1: Responses to different levels of stress

Source: Reproduced from J. Carlopio, G. Andrewartha & H. Armstrong 2001, *Developing Management Skills 2nd edn*, © Pearson Education Australia, p. 110.

A growing body of evidence connects organisational change with ill health, including chronic stress-related illnesses. One landmark project is the Whitehall II study that took place in the United Kingdom in the late 1980s and early 1990s.[21] It examined the health effects of insecurity, retrenchment and privatisation on 10,308 civil servants employed in 20 London-based departments. Research subjects ranged from the high-paid permanent secretary level to the lowest paid office support staff. Baseline data were gathered for all participants via an initial clinical examination (which recorded physiological variables such as blood pressure, heartbeat and cholesterol level) and a questionnaire (which established socio-demographic data on health status, health behaviour and work characteristics). Longitudinal data were gathered from further questionnaires and clinical screening over a five-year period to 1993. The study captured changes to health as employees went through an employment transition process, involving movement from an initial secure state through a (possibly lengthy) period of rumour, insecurity and anticipation, to a final phase of certainty.

The study contrasted two groups of employees (those anticipating change and those experiencing it) with control groups undergoing no change. Changes were monitored for both self-reported health status and clinical measures of physiological condition. While men vulnerable to change were more inclined than women to self-report evidence of declining health status, both groups reported changes associated with morbidity: increased smoking and heavy drinking among women, disturbed sleep patterns among men, and anxiety and depression among both women and men. Clinical tests found that those vulnerable to change were likely to have higher stress-related indicators, including cholesterol levels, blood pressure, obstructed blood flow and increased body mass index. Perhaps most interesting, health indicators improved after change had passed. The Whitehall II study concluded that job insecurity associated with change harms the health of both men and women, although sometimes in different ways.

Researchers also claim that change at work is increasing stress levels in Australia. One study asserts that:

> In the 1990s stress appears to have become intimately linked with work. If you are unemployed, then labour market experiences like job searching and receiving knock-backs can cause immense stress. If you are either underemployed, working casually or working reluctantly part-time, then worrying about living on a low income can produce chronic stress. Finally, even if you're in a 'normal' job, day-to-day stress is never far away.[22]

The 1995 Australian Workplace Industrial Relations Survey (AWIRS) reported that 50 per cent of all surveyed employees claimed an increase in stress on the job in the previous 12 months, 42 per cent said there had been no change, and only 7 per cent said work stress had declined. Not all groups of workers were equally likely to claim increased stress.

- Only 33 per cent of young workers aged 15–20 years old reported higher stress, compared with 54 per cent in the 40–49-year-old age bracket.[23]
- Full-time workers (54 per cent) were more likely than part-time workers (38 per cent) to have a rising incidence of stress.
- Public employees (58 per cent) were more likely than private sector employees (46 per cent) to report higher stress.

- Casual workers (27 per cent) were only half as likely as permanent workers to claim higher stress.
- A greater share of high-paid workers (59 per cent) than of low-paid workers (46 per cent) recorded increased stress.
- Managers and professionals (both 62 per cent) were more likely than clerks (51 per cent), salespeople (42 per cent) and labourers (40 per cent) to experience increased stress.

Peterson tested whether employees in the AWIRS study reporting higher stress also were experiencing more changes in their job.[24] The strongest links were between reporting stress and having less say in decisions, less job satisfaction and poorer opportunities for promotion. Higher stress also was correlated with increased pace and effort in the job, longer work time and changing management practices. Those who experienced only changes in task content or method reported less stress.

Workplace bullying

Change and stress often go together, especially where employee security is threatened. We also know that chronic stress causes ill health. People often experience stress and its related health problems as personal difficulties that they must handle themselves. Occasionally, however, change-induced stress surfaces as antisocial acts performed by others, often with serious consequences for employee health. Workplace **bullying** is one example. Business awareness of workplace bullying as a health hazard is growing because organisations such as WorkSafe Victoria have publicised the problem.

Research suggests a link between organisational change and workplace bullying.[25] Interviews in 1995 with 64 predominantly white-collar Queensland workers who had experienced restructuring found evidence that managers may be the bullies.[26] The study reported that 'managerial styles in restructuring are predominantly seen as coercive' and that 'evidence of managerial behaviours transcending coercion into the realms of sadism was manifested in the majority of interviews'.[27] Managers were revealed to be doing the following:

- . . . shaking the fist and saying 'you will do it or else' . . . I felt assaulted every day of the week — they were sadistic
- . . . sacked 30 people in one week saying 'we don't need you any more'
- management has gone out and advertised a person's job while he was still in the position and told him to not apply
- she threw a phone at me, swore and called me a filthy bitch.

A survey of 373 Queensland employees who had experienced restructuring showed that such behaviour was not isolated or rare. While only three per cent of respondents had observed managers assaulting employees, 25 per cent had observed verbal threats, 32 per cent had encountered verbal abuse and 37 per cent had witnessed threats to dismiss people. Perceived reasons for bullying included poor management communication skills, and attempts to gain power. In one-third of cases, the victims of bullying sought counselling or medical attention, or took time off work.

Research in other countries confirms that bullying can be widespread[28], that managers are often the perpetrators[29], and that bullying often coincides with major changes such as budget cuts, changes in management and major internal restructuring.[30] The evidence on workplace bullying is of such concern that all Australian State governments are now examining ways in which to raise business and community awareness of the problem to prevent it at its source.[31]

In the chapter, so far we have been concerned with the human element in the dynamic of organisational change. Are changes at work making people more insecure? What is the process of psychological adjustment through which people must go to deal with change? Are they harmed by stress, bullying and other health problems? Our reason for looking at these issues is to understand why the processes of organisational change can be so slow and uncertain. The evidence that we have reviewed certainly shows that the human element in the change process is fallible. In particular, one dynamic of change that we observed takes the form of a 'vicious circle', which inhibits successful adjustment to change. In such cases, organisational change causes insecurity and stress, which management handle poorly, blocking the proper 'transition' to new attitudes and values needed for the change to succeed. The case of Hardie Irrigation (refer to the 'Change management in action' case, page 333) illustrates this dynamic and its outcome, which is a stalled and ineffective change program.

To avoid this vicious circle, the design of change programs or interventions needs to make allowance for personal adjustment. Such people-centred change programs are likely to give a high priority to the human resources function, as we discuss in chapter 6. Resources need to be devoted to consultation, training, counselling and conflict management. Will businesses sustain such investments in human resources? We examine this question in the next section.

Capital markets and sustainability

One particular people-centred model of change is the mutual gains enterprise outlined by Kochan and Osterman[32] and mentioned in chapter 4. It is a specific kind of change intervention designed to lead business towards productivity improvement by treating human resources as a source of competitive advantage. The need for mutual gains enterprises exists because insufficient investment in human resources reduces productivity for both the enterprise and the nation. At the centre of the mutual gains model are a number of workplace innovations, including teams, job rotation, total quality management (TQM) and quality circles. The purpose of these innovations is to harness employee skill, creativity and effort to the continuous improvement of productivity.

Supporting these innovations are necessary conditions, which include top management support. By itself, such support is not enough. To be successful, the mutual gains enterprise also needs to guarantee employee job security (to minimise fears of change) and offer performance-related pay incentives (as an incentive to accommodate change). The model thus requires an exchange in which management offers security and high remuneration, and employees reciprocate with high productivity.

US researchers surveying workplaces in 1992 found workplace innovations to be reasonably widespread, as might have been expected in view of the publicity given to successes at Xerox, Hewlett-Packard and Motorola. Few firms, however, appeared to have a deep and enduring commitment to these practices. More than half of the surveyed firms had adopted one of Kochan and Osterman's five workplace innovations, yet only 14.2 per cent had adopted three or more.[33] At the same time, an international study of TQM in four major industries discovered that employee coverage in the United States was only 12 per cent — the same as in Canada, but less than half the level in Japan (28 per cent).[34] Finally, research in Canada found that one-third of the workplace innovations found in 1986 were no longer present in 1992.[35] By the mid-1990s, the US quality movement with which these innovations were associated appeared to be receding, judging by the collapse in applications for the prestigious US Baldrige quality awards. The North American experience of workplace innovations often was of isolated innovations covering a few employees and only for a short time. Why were diffusion and sustainability so problematic when the benefits of mutual gains seemed so obvious?

Kochan and Osterman's explanation is that capital market 'short termism' caused analysts and investors to prefer businesses that cut short-term costs by downsizing over business that increased human resource investments to build a mutual gains approach. They argue that:

> Corporate executives are agents of and are held accountable to their shareholders. This means that top executives are accountable not to the average shareholder but to the Wall Street analysts and advisers who shape the opinion of investors and have the greatest incentive to encourage firms to maximise short-term gains because their jobs depend on squeezing maximum gains out of the portfolios they manage before their account is up for its next review ... American financial institutions bias managers towards short time horizons that lead them to avoid "intangible" investments, i.e. projects that have clear, visible short-term costs and only long-term, and somewhat invisible if not uncertain, benefits. Investments in training and human resource innovations clearly fit this description.[36]

Kochan and Osterman must be asked why stock analysts and shareholders cannot see human resources investments in the long-term being in their self-interest. Surely it is economically irrational to manage investments that forgo the greater earnings and share values ultimately said to be available from mutual gains? The answer that Kochan and Osterman offer is the **asymmetry of information** available to insiders (within an organisation) and outsiders (such as analysts and shareholders). Compared to 'insiders' who can fully assess the value of intangibles, outsiders (especially institutional investors) have available to them only 'asymmetric' or unequal information on which to base their valuation. On that limited information, they are less likely to approve investment in such assets. Kochan and Osterman quote Michael Jacobs' explanation of the problem:

> This [information asymmetries and under-investment] is a particular problem for intangible investments that fail to show up on the balance sheet. Research and development, employee training and other expenditures that are not capitalised as assets according to today's accounting norms are important investments in the long-term health and competitiveness of a company; yet they are immediately charged to earnings. Absent a way to communicate the merits of these expenses to shareholders, corporations would tend to minimise the amount of funds allocated to intangibles. This becomes a greater concern as shareholders place increasing emphasis on reported earnings, and disproportionately penalise companies that invest heavily in training and research.[37]

Not all firms suffer equally from this problem. Those that finance expansion through share release are more exposed than family companies, those that reinvest from earnings or those that finance directly from banks with which they may have a long-term relationship. Nations such as Japan and Germany, where businesses depend less on share markets for capital, are said to be better equipped than the United States, where corporations borrow from Wall Street. In the same way, US corporations with little external debt (such as Hewlett-Packard) have been better able to sustain long-term investments in human resources. If this diagnosis is correct, then the mutual gains change model will be difficult to sustain.

One response has been to invent ways in which to make intangible human resources investments more tangible.[38] Becker, Huselid and Ulrich's 'human resources scorecard' (described in chapter 9) was developed for this reason. Another response has been to change accounting practice to find ways for intangibles to be fully valued. There is now a vigorous debate among accountants about measuring intangibles.[39] On the one hand it is thought that intangibles have become the key to competitiveness in the new know-ledge economy; it is therefore essential they be fully recognised. On the other hand there are fears that, by their nature, they are too slippery to measure and full recognition will lead to lax accounting standards; in a post Enron/HIH environment corporate regu-lators fear such a development. Moves are afoot for several countries (the International Accounting Standards Board (IASB) countries) to adopt a uniform way of treating intangibles. Amongst these countries are Australia, Canada, France, Germany, Japan, New Zealand, and the United Kingdom. Several of these countries were committed to adopt new standards in January 2005. At the time of writing, all that remained to be decided was the nature of the new standards.[40]

The problem of justifying short-term costs for the long-term and uncertain benefits of organisational change was observed in firms participating in the Australian Best Practice Demonstration Program.[41] Many **best practice** firms kept hard 'cost' infor-mation. The greatest costs (excluding new capital equipment that may have been purchased anyway) were for training, benchmarking, quality programs and surveys of customers, employees and competitors. Collective expenditure for these items was high and steady for three to four years after commencement of a best practice change project. Given that the need for these activities is likely to be ongoing, costs were assumed to remain at this plateau in the future.

Conversely, few benefits could be proven until best practice was fully operational and had become accepted as the organisation's normal way of working. Estimates of benefits tended to be subjective. Most managers thought that initial windfall gains were fol-lowed after a year by falling performance as novelty interest passed. Subsequently, successful firms began to enjoy sustained improvements as a culture of continuous improvement was securely established and productivity rose towards full technical efficiency (the theoretical optimum productivity that can be extracted from a given stock of capital and labour).

The cost–benefit trade-off over time is shown in figure 10.2. Managers believed that a problem period existed when hypothesised gains fell below known costs. This position is shown as the line between the points A and B. Being uncertain that any recovery in the net balance would occur, managers might have asked change leaders during this period to cut costs on training, benchmarking and other continuous improvement activities, causing the change initiative to be terminated before it had time to deliver.

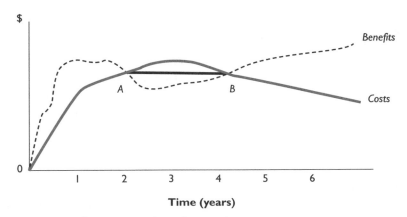

FIGURE 10.2: Best practice — cost–benefit trends

Source: From M. Rimmer, J. Macneil, R. Chenall, K. Langfield-Smith & L. Watts 1996, *Reinventing Competitiveness: Achieving Best Practice in Australia*, p. 218. © Commonwealth of Australia.

This study of Australian best practice firms also perceived capital market 'short termism' as a problem for the sustainability of best practice investments. In most cases, however, the problem took a different form from that described by Kochan and Osterman. The issue was not whether investment in best practice would cause share prices to fall, but whether the investment would be reflected in asset valuation if a corporation divested the operation. This problem became apparent because the 42 participants in the Australian Best Practice Demonstration Program were mainly divisions of larger corporations. As such, they were not directly listed on the stock market and were unlikely to influence greatly the share price of parent corporations, which were either based overseas (as were 22 of the 42 businesses) or very much larger than the best practice division.

More important than share prices were changes in corporate control. Between 1985 and 1995, no fewer than 28 of the 42 operations changed owners, were threatened by a take-over or experienced a change in majority ownership.[42] Such changes in corporate control do not necessarily cause the termination of long-term best practice investments because new owners are frequently attracted to such innovations, regarding them as evidence of good or progressive management. The threat of a takeover, however, can upset a change program in a different way. Such threats often create extra insecurity. Our discussion of transitions and stress showed that it is normal for fears and adjustment problems to threaten change. If the ordinary problems of human adjustment to change are compounded by the instability associated with changes in corporate control, then people may suffer 'change fatigue' and fail to make the necessary psychological transitions.

To summarise, businesses in Australia, as in the United States, may fail to sustain people-centred change programs because they take a short-term view of the human resource investments they require. In doing so, they may exacerbate the problem of personal adjustment to change — a factor that managers usually are inclined to neglect.

Incomplete change and sustainability

Our discussion of the sustainability problem in the previous section treats it as an *ex post* occurrence; that is, difficulties arise *after* those responsible for financial management cut the existing cost of intangibles because they cannot place a return on the balance sheet. Equally, the problem can arise as an *ex ante* obstacle when financial managers trim the costs of a change program *before* it has really begun. The reasons for cutting expenditure on future human resource investments are the same as for cutting back on past investments, but the result is different. The change program will begin with an inadequate budget, leading the organisation to defer or forgo essential activities.

Given that change programs often combine elements in a holistic or integrated way, the omission of key elements will cause the change program to under-perform. In the long-term, when a change intervention underperforms, those managers who cut costs at the beginning (thus tipping the odds in favour of program failure) will claim to have rightly done so. They then will feel justified in terminating those changes. What they will have proven, however, is not that the change program was always doomed to fail, but that an under-resourced and half-hearted version could not succeed. What they will have accomplished is the organisational equivalent of trying to run a car engine without oil or engine bearings.

Firms in the Australian Best Practice Demonstration Program experienced incomplete change. The 42 firms that entered the program in 1991–1992 and still were actively involved in 1994 were studied to see which elements of best practice they had mastered and which elements they were least likely to have implemented.

Chapter 4 explains this best practice model of change. Almost all had an integrated strategy linking best practice plans to business objectives. Benchmarking (mainly as a learning technique rather than for hard measurement) also was popular. In addition, most of the core operational practices had received attention. Organisations were undertaking process or continuous improvement in flattened organisational structures supported by better-trained employees and guided by customers and suppliers.

Other elements had not been successfully implemented in most firms. These elements were the cultural and information enablers — lubricants that are essential for the smooth running of best practice. The following three enablers or catalysts had been mastered in less than one-third of the firms.

- **Change leadership**. There were two measures of change leadership: first, stability and, second, diffusion through all levels of the organisation. Most program firms depended on one or two 'change champions', who often were senior managers or high-profile advisers to senior management. Successful change champions tended to be promoted out of the role while the failures exited the organisation. Few stayed in this 'pressure cooker' role long enough to firmly implement best practice.
- **Empowerment**. Empowerment was about the degree to which direct employees controlled their daily work and the scope for their involvement in the development of strategy. Most managers still distrusted their employees and resisted empowerment.
- **Control and measurement systems**. These involved the development of key performance indicators at the level of the team or cell. Most program firms had relegated this task to a later stage in best practice.

Three explanations were given for the omission of these pieces of the best practice jigsaw. The first is cost. Best practice programs claim scarce resources. Most firms scheduled expenditure on the elements of best practice by prioritising some elements over others. While this practice accounts for the backward development of measurement systems, it does not explain deficiencies in change leadership and empowerment, which do not depend on specific expenditures and activity but tend to reflect the overall effectiveness of the best practice package.

The second explanation is a contingency argument — that is, do all firms need all elements of best practice? As shown in chapter 4, the contingency argument applies more to whether the best practice package fits a firm's strategic or environmental conditions. The elements of best practice fit together in a holistic model, so it is difficult to detach any individual elements because they fit poorly to a particular firm. It is a poor explanation, therefore, of the incomplete implementation of best practice elements. Contingency factors are especially ill suited to explaining weaknesses in change leadership, empowerment and performance measurement. It is arguable that the residue left after such omissions is not sufficient to constitute best practice.

Third, learning best practice takes time. Observable gaps in 1994 reflect that many firms had commenced the holistic change package just three years earlier. Some changes cannot be accomplished in such a short period of time. This argument is especially relevant to the two cultural enablers of change management and empowerment. The Norske Skog Boyer mill case (end-of-book case 3, page 383) illustrates how much improvement could be gained in these elements over an extra four years (see 'Change management in action').

CHANGE MANAGEMENT IN ACTION
Cultural change at the Norske Skog Boyer mill, 1994–2004

Best practice began at the Boyer mill in the late 1980s, accelerating between 1991 and 1994 when the firm participated in the Australian Best Practice Demonstration Program. The top–down approach to a TQM-style program did not win acceptance, however. Researchers in 1994 found that change leadership extended no further than a small team of managers and employees empowered to control their daily jobs: 'many people had yet to buy into the process'.[43]

Four years later, the Boyer mill rated strongly in both areas. A stable management team had sustained its commitment to best practice by enacting Fletcher Challenge's 'Way We Work' principles to 'make decisions where knowledge is greatest'.[44] Clear signs were apparent that responsibility for best practice had spread to most managers and team leaders. Employee empowerment too had developed as teams took over new responsibilities for labour scheduling, production and monitoring performance against key performance indicators. Union delegates reported that workers 'had more pride in their jobs' and 'took more interest than they used to'.[45] An Employee Attitude Survey discovered that a 'majority of males tend towards the belief that they have a considerable amount of say in decisions'. Between 1994 and 1998, the company had succeeded in changing the mindsets of both managers and employees, making progress in both change leadership and empowerment. Subsequent events showed how durable this new culture had become. In 2000, the mill was sold to Norske Skog, a Norwegian multinational paper business. Despite the

What effect does uneven or incomplete development have on holistic change programs that depend on synergies among all their interdependent parts? This question is difficult to answer from the evidence from the Australian Best Practice Program firms because they were missing the measurement systems needed to provide relevant data. The subjective opinion of managers is that essential parts of a change program cannot be overlooked without affecting results. This approach may lead to a sustainability problem in the long-term — that is, the change intervention will be discontinued as a result of underperformance. How then can we explain the behaviour of organisations, such as the Norske Skog Boyer mill, that persist with changes through the difficult times when the change program is not in place properly and is not having the desired effect?

Sustaining change

Throughout this chapter, we have confronted a number of problems that can block planned change, including the ability of people to make transitions and the failure of organisations to resource and implement change. How, then, can we explain successful change management?

The role of core values

How do we explain the success of some businesses in managing change to remain best practice? This question has a magnetic appeal because unlocking the answer means also unlocking the secrets to business success. Richard Lester from the MIT Industrial Performance Center has been preoccupied with this question since the mid-1980s. In 1989, he was a co-author of *Made in America*[46], which sought to isolate the significant common characteristics of best practice firms. For the following decade, he continued to monitor those firms for what explained their ability to sustain best practice. Lester notes:

> Not all of the companies that were identified in 1989 in *Made in America* as paragons of best practice have continued to fare well. Some that did not, such as IBM, have struggled for reasons we might have anticipated based on our own analysis (we didn't unfortunately); others because of more contingent factors — poor business judgements or just plain bad luck. But most of these companies — firms like Motorola, Hewlett-Packard, Levi Strauss, Nucor, Chaparral Steel, Milliken — are still doing quite well; in some cases very well indeed. To what do they attribute their more recent successes?[47]

The first part of the answer to Lester's question is that the firms were doing what made them successful a decade before; they remained committed to continuous improvement in cost, quality and delivery, closer customer and supplier relations, flatter and less compart-mentalised organisational structures, new technology to improve customer value, training, multiskilling and teamwork. The second part of the answer is that these firms continued to understand the synergies that came from applying all these practices in a package, rather than tackling change in a piecemeal fashion. Nevertheless, Lester believes these two factors are an incomplete explanation. The best practice firms shared another characteristic.

Lester terms the missing ingredient 'listening to inner voices' — a phrase selected to contrast the approach with that of 'listening to the customer'. Lester does not mean that the best practice firms in his study were out of touch with customers and competitors, but that their strategies were shaped also by a 'core belief' in what they were doing. He con-cludes that 'these companies appear to be distinguished not only by the diligence with which they were pursuing a particular set of organisational practices, but also by the strength of their internal convictions'.[48] These internal convictions are referred to also as the 'core ideology' or 'core values' of a business — a set of beliefs that remains unchanged over a long period and that 'mobilises and inspires people at all levels of the organisation'.[49]

To illustrate his meaning, Lester points to Boeing — a firm distinguished for taking investment risks of 'bet the company' dimensions. Boeing's record of successful risk taking has never rested on matching the opposition, because no other company has been prepared to pioneer concepts such as the world's first commercial wide-bodied jet. Why did Boeing take the risk? Because it has had a sense of itself as an aviation pioneer, as a firm that 'pushes the envelope of aeronautical technology'.[50]

Lester's explanation of sustained success is supported by Collins and Porras's study of 'visionary' companies.[51] These 'visionary' companies were selected for their excep-tional stock market performance between 1926 and 1990 compared with comparable organisations. Methodologically, Collins and Porras's search for the secrets of success is distinguished by their rigorous comparison of the visionary firms (such as 3M, Amer-ican Express, Boeing and Citicorp) with comparison companies (such as Norton, Wells Fargo, McDonnell Douglas and Chase Manhattan). They also followed fluctuating for-tunes over 50 or more years to iron out short-term effects. Collins and Porras conclude that the visionary firms were distinguished by the following four factors.

- *The primacy of organisation.* The visionary firms maintained a focus on sustaining effective organisational structures and values.
- *A core ideology or values.* The visionary firms maintained a commitment to strong simple values, such as Boeing's belief in 'staying at the cutting edge of technology'.
- *Relentless drive for progress.* While the core values remained constant, every other aspect of the organisation changed in the drive for progress, including products, strategy, competencies, organisational structure, reward systems and so on.
- *An aligned organisation.* The visionary companies required alignment (or 'fit') between their core values and their strategies, processes and practices. 'A visionary company creates a total environment that envelops employees, bombarding them with a set of signals so consistent and mutually reinforcing that it's virtually imposs-ible to misunderstand the company's ideology and ambitions.'[52]

Core values can invite controversy. There is room for debate and controversy about these values.

Do people really matter?

Throughout this chapter we emphasise the human element in change. How can change initiatives be sustained to the point at which they become effective unless people adopt new mindsets and new ways of working? Some of the arguments we discuss in this chapter claim that the inability of people to adjust their thinking goes a long way towards explaining the slow diffusion and ephemeral nature of people-centred change interventions. A vicious circle can arise whereby human failure to adjust to change causes underperformance, which then reinforces negativity to change. Pinpointing the problem as one of personal adjustment prompts the identification of relevant solutions. For Bridges, the answer lies in healthy psychological adjustment. For Kochan and Osterman, the mutual gains enterprise requires a negotiated exchange in which management provide job security and pay incentives as a trade-off to win employee involvement in continuous improvement.

Recent research by Osterman raises doubts about this view of the sustainability problem.[53] First, do we need to explain a 'diffusion and sustainability' problem in the first place? His earlier research with Kochan had concluded that US business had failed to adopt and persevere with high-performance work practices such as TQM or self-managed teams. Also, they claimed this failure was caused by the way in which capital markets discouraged the adoption and retention of human resource investments related to people-centred change. In 1997, Osterman replicated a survey of US workplaces to determine whether the incidence of high-performance work practices had changed in the previous five years. The findings are shown in table 10.1. With the exception of self-managed work teams, the incidence of these practices had doubled. Further, the proportion of firms using a package of three or more practices had grown from 14.2 per cent to 39.5 per cent. Comprehensive programs were replacing piecemeal ones, and the retention of these practices was no longer a problem. Osterman found that more than 80 per cent of workplaces with a high-performance system in 1992 still had one in place in 1997, leading him to conclude that 'the capacity of employers to sustain these systems is quite high'.[54] These findings were the first surprise; perhaps there is no sustainability problem.

TABLE 10.1	**Proportion of US establishments with high-performance work practices involving at least half of core employees — a comparison across a five-year period**	
	1992	**1997**
Quality circles/off-line problem-solving groups	27.4%	57.4%
Job rotation	26.6%	55.5%
Self-managed work teams	40.5%	38.4%
Total quality management	24.5%	57.2%
Two or more practices	26.0%	70.7%
Three or more practices	14.2%	39.5%

Source: P. Osterman 1999, *Securing Prosperity: The American Labor Market, How It Has Changed and What to Do about It*, © 1999 The Century Foundation. Published by Princeton University Press, Princeton, New Jersey, p. 99. Reprinted by permission of Princeton University Press.

Osterman's second surprise concerned the conditions needed for high-performance work organisation. Previously, he and Kochan had argued that job security and pay incentives were essential to win employee involvement. The 1997 survey showed this assumption to be wrong. Of those firms that sustained best practice, 28 per cent had experienced layoffs (compared with 27 per cent of firms without high-performance practices). He concludes that 'both new adoptions and sustaining previous efforts seem quite possible even in the face of layoffs and organisational tumult'.[55] Firms with high-performance work systems revealed other surprises. Outsourcing and the use of temporary or 'contingent' workers were endemic, again attacking the notion that job security is part of the high-performance package. Also, the productivity gains from these work practices had not been shared with employees. High-performance workplaces were no more likely than the others to grant a pay increase. It is not necessary, it seems, for managers to guarantee jobs and share gains to persuade employees to devote themselves to continuous improvement. The word 'mutual' can be removed from 'mutual gains enterprise'.

What do employees think of such high-performance practices? A number of US studies report positive employee responses to teamwork and greater responsibility. Freeman and Rogers' survey of non-supervisory workers and lower managers in 'employee involvement' systems found that around 79 per cent 'report having personally benefited from their involvement in the program by getting more influence on how their job is done'.[56] A more informative picture comes from Batt's study of lower level telecommunications staff in the United States, which found that 68 per cent were satisfied with their participation in such systems, yet only 19 per cent were satisfied with the firm's level of consideration of employees.[57] Employees seem to have an ambivalent attitude towards changes that require more commitment and responsibility from them. On the one hand, they tend to respond well to their new role because it is more challenging and interesting; on the other hand, they are critical of managers, especially when change increases their fears of job insecurity.

Osterman concludes that employees are ambivalent to such changes. Employees do find high-commitment work systems attractive and their acceptance is part of the explanation for the growing use of such systems. Their cooperation is offered in a climate of fear, however, where downsizing, outsourcing, casualisation of work, and slow wages growth demonstrate 'power imbalances in the workplace'.[58] One consequence of this power imbalance is that employees are expected to offer increased commitment to their jobs at a time when the firm is reducing its commitment to them. More and more evidence is coming in to support the ambiguous benefits of high performance work systems. On the one hand the productivity benefits have been proven again and again. For example the influential study by Black and Lynch shows that 'high commitment practices' (together with new information technology) have created since 1995 a productivity miracle in the United States reversing a 25-year slump in growth and raising average annual productivity growth from 1.7 per cent to 3.0 per cent.[59] However, the success of 'high commitment work practices' may have damaged the trust between managers and employees. In particular, HR managers have lost the confidence of employees. As their role has become driven by strategic business priorities, they have ceased to protect workers by championing 'the social contract between managers and employees'. No longer do they balance the interests of the firm with those of the work-force. As a result, they can no longer broker trust between managers and workers, and are regarded poorly by both. Workplaces may have become more efficient, but at a cost in terms of social cohesion.[60]

Review

This chapter's opening case illustrated three problems with the performance of change programs over time. First, the process of change is often slow and uncertain. Second, change may require personal adjustment or transitions that are difficult to cultivate. Third, change programs can fall victim to premature expectations of an economic pay-off.

Change at work now assumes epidemic proportions, creating an ever-increasing demand for people to adjust. A widespread view is that change engenders heightened fears or a sense of risk among people. Change at work is thus identified with its negative aspects such as retrenchment and unemployment, longer working hours, precarious jobs and demands for extra effort. This perception places an increased responsibility on management and employees to progress through a process of transition, during which loss is accommodated, new attitudes and habits are learned, and 'new beginnings' are achieved.

While transitions may be an important aspect of the dynamic of change, they are only a part of the adjustment process. In addition to this psychological facet of change, a social dimension also influences attitudes and actions. In the social world, we find inequalities of power, and perceptions that change affects some people more than others. In other words, people differ in their influence over change and its impact on them. They also differ in their responses to change. Transitions are one response in which the individual comes to accept change at a personal level. Another response is for groups to express conflicting views about change and to negotiate the accommodation of their legitimate interests. A growing body of evidence showing that management and employee failure to accomplish transitions may be associated with excessive work-related stress (which is linked to health problems) supports the need for such social protection against change. It seems there is a pathological side to human adjustment to change, where organisations fail to take their people with them, and individuals suffer from occupational health problems.

Organisational change programs also may face a cost–benefit problem. This potential outcome arises in two ways. First, people-centred change can fall victim to capital market 'short termism'. Shareholders and their representatives will seek to cut the short-term human resource costs of change because the nature of any long-term benefit is intangible and uncertain. In the United States, researchers observe that firms that downsize enjoy an increase in share prices, while those that invest in skills suffer a fall in share prices. In Australia, the problem may take a different form at the 'product division' level. The issue here is whether changes in corporate control destabilise long-term change programs.

The second cost–benefit problem arises when organisations fail to complete all the elements of an holistic change program. Australian evidence suggests this non-completion is common, with the typical areas for neglect being measurement systems, change leadership and employee empowerment. Among the reasons for incomplete change are (1) the need to ration scarce resources in scheduling change and (2) the slow pace of human adjustment to the requirements of change leadership and empowerment. Incomplete change programs may under-perform and be discontinued. In some organisations, repetition of this behaviour creates a cycle in which impatient managers rush through a sequence of so-called 'fads', rejecting each before they have time to work.

Despite the problems associated with human adjustment to change and cost–benefit trade-offs, many organisations persist with change programs. One explanation identifies corporate core values as the vital ingredient to sustain the human activities and investments that make up effective change. According to this view, what distinguishes the true successes in business is a consistent and strong set of core values.

Do core values matter? New research on mutual gains and best practice enterprises suggests that values matter relatively little. Sustained use of high-performance work systems in the United States and Australia is increasing, but without the key ingredient of a compact or mutual understanding with employees. In the modern labour market, it seems to be sufficient for managers to demand behaviour that complies with change, irrespective of whether new attitudes or values underpin that behaviour.

Key terms

asymmetry of information. Unequal knowledge of organisational 'insiders' and 'outsiders' concerning the performance of investment in 'intangibles', (p. 347)

best practice. A holistic program for empowered teams to drive continuous improvement in all aspects of a business's operation, leading to world-class results in productivity and equity, (p. 348)

bullying. Workplace behaviour that involves tyranny over the weak, sometimes leading to adverse social and health outcomes, (p. 345)

capital market 'short termism'. The tendency for organisations to be influenced by capital market valuations to focus investments and activities on yielding short-term rather than long-term performance gains, (p. 334)

change leadership. The assumption of responsibility by managers or other employees for planning, monitoring and reinforcing change, (p. 350)

control and measurement systems. Reporting systems involving the collection, analysis and use of data to evaluate all aspects of performance, including the accomplishment of change to achieve best practice, (p. 350)

core values. The enduring values of an organisation that guide strategies and practices, and influence employee values to align with the company's ideology and ambitions, (p. 334)

cost–benefit analysis. Evaluation of the relative economic value of the inputs and outputs of organisational change, (p. 333)

empowerment. The redistribution of decision-making to involve employee or worker participation, (p. 350)

endings. A stage in psychological adjustment to change that involves the identification and acceptance of loss, (p. 338)

holistic change. Change to multiple parts of an organisational system where the benefits of change arise from synergies among changes in different parts of the system, (p. 334)

mutual gains enterprise. A form of best practice in which employee commitment to change is based on sharing the benefits of productivity improvement, usually by the award of guaranteed job security and higher pay, (p. 333)

neutral zone. A confused intermediate stage in psychological adjustment to change that is characterised by discomfort, anxiety, problematic motivation and low productivity, (p. 338)

new beginnings. The final step in psychological adjustment to change that involves the internalisation or acceptance of new values, beliefs, actions and habits, (p. 338)

stress. A psychological problem, sometimes manifested through physical health problems, arising from an excessive discrepancy between the demands placed on people and their skills and resources to deal with them, (p. 342)

sustainability. The maintenance of a change program to the point that it becomes accepted as prescribing a normal way of working and meets expectations of improved productivity performance, (p. 333)

transitions. A process of personal, psychological adjustment to change, often distinguished from situational (objective) change, (p. 332)

Review questions

1. List the most important changes taking place in work and evaluate how people may adjust to them.
2. How can teams help or hinder adjustment to change?
3. Is Ulrich Beck's vision of the 'risk society' applicable to Australia?
4. Can Bridges' model of 'transitions' at work explain why employees resist change?
5. Why does change lead to bullying, and what can managers do about this problem?
6. Do Australian businesses find it difficult to sustain change programs that require investment in human resources?
7. Is capital market 'short termism' an obstacle to sustained investment to help people adjust to change?
8. Critically review Lester's argument that best practice is sustained by 'listening to inner voices'.

Discussion questions

1. How do cost–benefit problems prevent organisations from sustaining people-centred change programs?
2. How can employees be persuaded to commit to high-performance work systems? You may base your answer upon the Norske Skog Boyer mill case study (end-of-book case 3, page 383) or upon knowledge of your own workplace.

Work assignment

Psychological adjustment to change

Describe a major change that has affected your workplace or another workplace with which you are familiar. List the main losses and evaluate how well the endings were handled. How strong are the new beginnings?

Suggested further reading

Beck, U. 2000, *The Brave New World of Work*, Polity Press, Cambridge.

Bridges, W. 1995, *Managing Transitions: Making the Most of Change*, Addison-Wesley, Massachusetts.

Dunphy, D., Griffiths, A. & Benn, S. 2003, *Organisational Change for Corporate Sustainability*, Routledge, London.

Osterman, P., Kochan, T., Locke, M. & Piore, M. 2001, *Working in America: A Blueprint for the New Labour Market*, Massachusetts Institute of Technology, Boston.

Rimmer, M., Macneil, J., Chenhall, R., Langfield-Smith, K. & Watts, L. 1996, *Reinventing Competitiveness: Achieving Best Practice in Australia*, Pitman, Melbourne.

End notes

1. W. Bridges 1995, *Managing Transitions: Making the Most of Change*, Addison-Wesley, Massachusetts.
2. Tom Kochan & Paul Osterman 1994, *The Mutual Gains Enterprise*, Harvard Business School Press, Boston.
3. V. Blewett 1996, 'Hardie Irrigation Best Practice Program', *The Best Practice Experience*, vol. 3, Pitman, Melbourne.
4. Editorial, *The Age*, 17 March 2005.
5. C. Littler & P. Innes 2004, 'The paradox of managerial downsizing', *Organization Studies*, 27 (7), 1159–84.
6. A. Morehead, M. Steele, M. Alexander, K. Stephen & L. Duffin 1997, *Changes at Work: The 1995 Australian Workplace Industrial Relations Survey*, Longman, Melbourne, p. 566.
7. U. Beck 2000, *The Brave New World of Work*, Polity Press, Cambridge.
8. M. Wooden 2000, *The Transformation of Australian Industrial Relations*, Federation Press, Sydney.
9. J. Carlopio, G. Andrewartha & H. Armstrong 1997, *Developing Management Skills in Australia*, Addison-Wesley Longman, Melbourne, p. 520.
10. A. Sinclair 1989, *The Tyranny of the Team*, Working paper no. 4, University of Melbourne Graduate School of Management, Melbourne.
11. B. W. Tuckman 1965, 'Developmental sequence in small groups', *Psychological Bulletin*, 63, pp. 384–99.
12. D. Stace & D. Dunphy 1994, *Beyond the Boundaries: Leading and Recreating Successful Enterprise*, McGraw-Hill, Sydney.
13. C. Bishop & C. Graham 1991, 'Self-directed work teams: the search for a better way', *Training and Development in Australia*, 18(1) pp. 23–8.
14. Bridges, op. cit., p. 3.
15. ibid., p. 5.
16. ibid.
17. K. Lewin 1951, *Field Theory in Social Science*, Harper, New York.
18. Carlopio, Andrewartha & Armstrong, op. cit., p. 524.
19. M. Quinlan & P. Bohle 1991, *Managing Occupational Health and Safety in Australia*, Macmillan, Melbourne, p. 155.
20. C. L. Cooper 1983, 'Identifying stressors at work: recent research developments', *Journal of Psychosomatic Research*, 27(5), pp. 369–76.
21. J. E. Ferrie 1999, 'Health consequences of job insecurity', in *Labour Market Changes and Job Insecurity: A Challenge for Social Welfare and Health Promotion*, eds J. E. Ferrie, M. G. Marmot, J. Griffiths & E. Ziglio, World Health Organisation, Copenhagen.
22. Australian Centre for Industrial Relations Research and Training (ACIRRT) 1999, *Australia at Work*, Prentice Hall, Sydney, p. 3.
23. Morehead et al., op. cit., pp. 566–7.
24. C. L. Peterson 1999, *Stress at Work: A Sociological Perspective*, Baywood, Amityville.
25. Denise Salin 2003, 'Ways of explaining workplace bullying: a review of enabling, motivating and precipitating structures and processes in the work environment', *Human Relations*, 56(10), pp. 1213–22.
26. P. McCarthy, M. Sheehan & D. Kearns 1995, *Managerial Styles and Their Effects on Employees' Health and Well-being in*

Organisations Undergoing Restructuring, Griffith University, Brisbane.

27. ibid., pp. 26–7.

28. Irish Taskforce on the Prevention of Workplace Bullying 2001, *Dignity at Work — The Challenge of Workplace Bullying*, The Stationery Office, Dublin.

29. A. Ishmael 1999, *Harassment, Bullying and Violence at Work: A Practical Guide to Combating Employee Abuse*, The Industrial Society, London.

30. H. Hoel & C. L. Cooper 2000, *Destructive Conflict and Bullying at Work*, Manchester School of Business, Manchester.

31. Queensland Workplace Bullying Taskforce 2001, Workplace Bullying: Issues Paper, Department of Industrial Relations, Brisbane.

32. Kochan & Osterman, op. cit., pp. 17–18.

33. P. Osterman 1994, 'How common is workplace transformation and who adopts it?', *Industrial and Labor Relations Review*, 47, pp. 173–88.

34. Kochan & Osterman, op. cit., p. 87.

35. G. Betcherman & A. Verma 1993, 'Follow-up to the New Technology Survey', Canadian Industrial Relations Research Association, June.

36. Kochan & Osterman, op. cit., pp. 9–10.

37. M. T. Jacobs 1991, *Short-Term America: The Causes and Cures of Our Business Myopia*, Harvard Business School Press, Boston, p. 36.

38. R. Kaplan and D. Norton 2004, 'Measuring the Strategic Readiness of Intangible Assets', *Harvard Business Review*, February, pp. 52–61.

39. J. Mouritsen 2003, 'Intellectual capital and the capital market: the circulability of intellectual capital', *Accounting, Auditing and Accountability Journal*, 16 (1), pp. 18–29.

40. S. Powell 2003, 'Accounting for intangible assets: current requirements, key players, and future directions', *European Accounting Review*, 12 (4), pp. 797–811.

41. M. Rimmer, J. Macneil, R. Chenhall, K. Langfield-Smith & L. Watts 1996, *Reinventing Competitiveness: Achieving Best Practice in Australia*, Pitman, Melbourne, pp. 217–18.

42. Rimmer et al., op. cit., p. 220.

43. D. Challis & D. Samson 1996, 'Australian Newsprint Mills Best Practice Programs',

The Best Practice Experience, vol. 3, Pitman, Melbourne, p. 90.

44. M. Rimmer and P. Derbyshire 2003, 'Norske Skog Boyer mill in Tasmania', case 3, in F. Graetz, M. Rimmer, A. Lawrence & A. Smith 2005, *Managing Organisational Change*, 2nd edn, John Wiley & Sons, Brisbane.

45. ibid.

46. M. Dertouzos, R. Lester & R. Solow 1989, *Made in America: Regaining the Productive Edge*, Harper Perennial, New York.

47. R. K. Lester 1998, *The Productive Edge, How US Industries Are Pointing the Way to a New Era of Economic Growth*, Norton, New York, p. 244.

48. ibid., p. 247.

49. ibid., p. 255.

50. ibid., p. 247.

51. J. C. Collins & J. I. Porras 1994, *Built to Last: Successful Habits of Visionary Companies*, HarperCollins, New York.

52. ibid., p. 201.

53. P. Osterman 1999, *Securing Prosperity: The American Labor Market, How It Has Changed and What to Do about It*, Princeton University Press, New Jersey.

54. ibid., p. 99.

55. ibid., p. 101.

56. R. Freeman & J. Rogers 1995, 'Worker Representation and Participation Survey: First report of findings', *Proceedings of the Forty-Seventh Annual Meeting*, ed. Industrial Relations Research Association, Washington, p. 340.

57. R. Batt 1996, 'From bureaucracy to enterprise? The changing jobs and careers of managers in telecommunications service', in *Broken Ladders*, ed. P. Osterman, Oxford University Press, New York, pp. 55–80.

58. Osterman 1999, op. cit., p. 107.

59. S. Black and L. Lynch 2004, 'What's driving the new economy? The benefits of workplace innovation', *The Economic Journal*, 114 (February), pp. 97–116.

60. T. Kochan 2004, 'Restoring trust in the human resource management profession', *Asia Pacific Journal of Human Resources*, 42 (2), August, pp.132–46.

CASE 1

William Angliss Institute of TAFE: changing structures, processes and boundaries

Prepared by

Fiona Graetz[1]

Background

William Angliss Institute of TAFE (WAIT) is the longest-running, single-purpose TAFE Institute in Victoria and serves the hospitality, food and tourism industries. It is a relatively small TAFE Institute with 318 staff members comprising 179 teaching (128 full-time and 51 part-time) and 139 non-teaching (113 full-time and 26 part-time) staff. Its revenue for the year ended 31 December 2004 was $34.78 million, of which the government contribution was around $18.47 million. This revenue compares to $22 million turnover in 1998, of which the government contract was around $14.5 million. As these figures indicate, the significant growth in funding did not emanate from government but other sources, and the prime contributor was the Institute's international sector.

The early years

William Angliss Institute of TAFE was founded in September 1940 as William Angliss Food Trades School, named after its benefactor, Sir William Angliss, a prominent Melbourne industrialist of the time who had gained a worldwide reputation as Australia's 'meat king'. In its early days as Food Trades School, the training focus was pastry cooking; retail butchery and smallgoods; bread making and baking; cooking and waiting. During the Second World War, the School's prime role was the training of defence force personnel as cooks. This focus continued in the post-war years, providing training for ex-servicemen and women. Through the 1950s, there was slow, but growing recognition of the need to incorporate formal 'institutionalised' training with the existing apprenticeship training programs. It was felt that this would not only raise the quality and consistency of standards within the catering industry, but also heighten its professional standing and give recognition to the craftsmanship and skills required.[2]

1960s to 1980s

In the 1960s, the Institute expanded its role and began training courses in the hospitality industry. 1971 saw the first intake for the School's Business Studies. The 1980s saw further developments as the Australian tourism and hospitality industry flourished. The Institute recognised the need to tailor courses to meet the diverse functions of different industry sectors. In addition to developing industry-specific courses such as sales and marketing courses for the travel and tourism industry, WAIT also provided in-house training to corporate clients.

From 1990

Until the late 1980s, WAIT was the only TAFE serving the food, hospitality and tourism industries in Victoria. In terms of the delivery and quality of courses provided, it was regarded as market leader. By 1992, however, there were 22 other public sector TAFE colleges competing directly for a share of the same market. In addition, both State and Federal Governments, keenly aware of the opportunities within these growth industries, were actively encouraging private companies to set up in competition with the publicly funded sector and offer courses for delivery nationally and internationally. Consequently, WAIT faced increasingly stiff domestic and international competition for a share of not only the fee-paying student market, but also the lucrative commercial contracts for on-site training, project management and consultancy. Initially, WAIT did not seek to enter the international fee-paying market that others started to pursue from the mid-1980s. By 1994, however, in an attempt to claw back market share from its competitors, WAIT embarked on an aggressive strategic marketing program to promote its education, training and consultancy expertise to this burgeoning market. This approach included attracting international students to study at the Institute, and offering courses offshore. From a modest intake of four international students in 1994, this figure had grown to 760 full fee paying international students ($8 million) in 2003, with students drawn from over 40 different countries.

Traditionally, TAFE Institutes in Victoria were guaranteed full funding from the State. However, government funding changes in the early 1990s focused on increasing efficiency and effectiveness in the TAFE sector by granting funds based on the ability of colleges to deliver their contracted amount of student contact hours and on driving the sector to higher levels of self-funding. As part of this drive to increase efficiency and effectiveness in the TAFE sector, TAFE colleges were also under enormous pressure to merge. WAIT vigorously resisted these pressures. By 1996, cutbacks to funding, industry rationalisation, increasing competition and decreasing student demand in traditional courses threatened the Institute's continuing viability as a small, standalone single-purpose TAFE college.

In 1997, its position came under further scrutiny when the newly elected Victorian Labor Government initiated a review of local government sectors. Under the terms of reference of the Kirby Review, the notion of 'critical mass' was applied. According to this model, a public sector enterprise needed to be a certain size, based on revenue, in order to exist. As this figure represented around $70 million, WAIT, with a turnover at that time of only $22–23 million, appeared unlikely to survive as a standalone entity. The Institute, however, bolstered by strong industry support, argued forcefully that it should be retained as a specialist-focused TAFE serving the hospitality and tourism industries. The Institute and its industry protagonists won the day and, at the end of 1997, while many other TAFEs were amalgamated, it was agreed that the Institute would remain standalone.

Changing structures, processes and boundaries: 1993 to 2004

This section explores changes across the organisational design dimensions of *structures* (delayering, decentralising, project-based organising), *processes* (communications, IT, and HR practices such as team building) and *boundaries* (outsourcing, strategic alliances, downscoping) over the period 1993 to 2004.

Changes to structures

In 1993, when Director, Ray Way (who had been at WAIT since the early 1960s) retired, the William Angliss Council appointed Christine French, who had been Director of a Queensland TAFE. As the first external appointment and first female director, this appointment symbolised a significant change in direction for the Institute.

One of the first initiatives of the new director was to dismantle the Institute's traditional hierarchical structure and move to a flatter team-based structure with a much wider span of control at the

top. Eleven people now reported to the director rather than just two as under the previous structure. A marked change to the original system was the shift to a program- instead of department-based structure, with areas grouped together according to industry links. All teaching programs were allocated to three newly formed schools: Hospitality Management, Retail Foods and Food Technology, and Tourism (see figure C1.1). It was felt a program-based structure linked to industry groups would ensure the development of a curriculum in line with the needs and expectations of industry and, therefore, be more attractive to potential students. As part of the restructure, a Commercial Services Division was established as a company and a CEO recruited externally. The primary function of this new division was to actively seek out and coordinate the provision of training and consultancy services to the Institute's expanding base of corporate clients, and to specialise in the delivery of labour market programs. A Quality Unit was also introduced led by Client Services Manager, John Barnes, who was recruited from outside the organisation.

This structure remained in place until 1998 when David Weston succeeded Christine French as Chief Executive Officer (CEO) of the Institute. For Weston, the creation of a Corporate Strategy Division was a key priority and he lobbied Council vigorously for this. This represented an enormous challenge for Council members because, at the time, the Institute was struggling to break even and the new division would require expenditure of $350,000 a year recurrent into the future. In the end, Council demonstrated its faith in Weston's vision and the Division was established at the end of 1998 with John Barnes appointed as General Manager.

> It has been the most fundamental decision that we've taken because it means as CEO I can delegate the responsibility to monitor and measure performance. I came to a very quick understanding that staff here didn't see our contract with the government as a customer provider relationship; they saw them as the enemy. In their view, the government was always putting these new constraints on us and changing the funding rate. So the General Manager's job principally is to manage that relationship with the government and make sure it is comfortable that we are performing. (Weston)

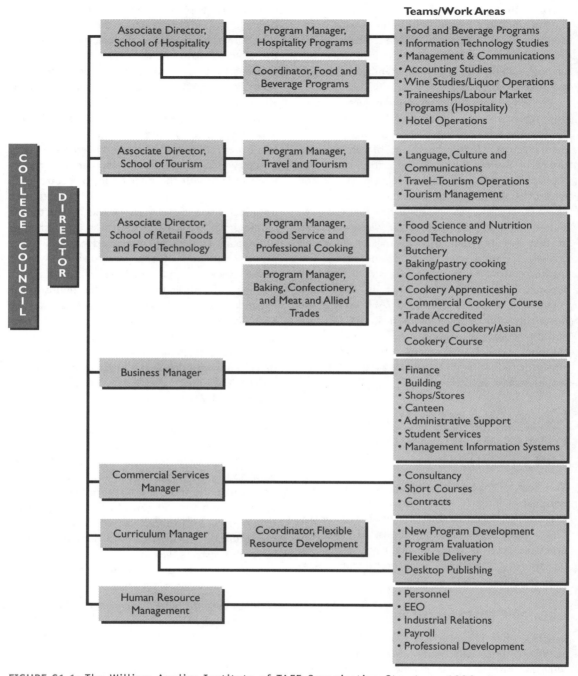

Teams/Work Areas

FIGURE C1.1: The William Angliss Institute of TAFE Organisation Structure, 1996
Source: William Angliss Institute of TAFE, *Annual Report 1996*. Reproduced with permission from the William Angliss Institute of TAFE and David Weston.

Further fine-tuning took place at the end of 2001. Instead of 11 direct line reports to the Institute's CEO, there are now seven (see figure C1.2). The Corporate Strategy and Business Services Divisions represent the internal service providers to the Institute's four profit centres. The four profit centre divisions — International, Student Education & Training, Industry Training, and Angliss Consulting — are based around clearly defined market segments and how these can be best served.

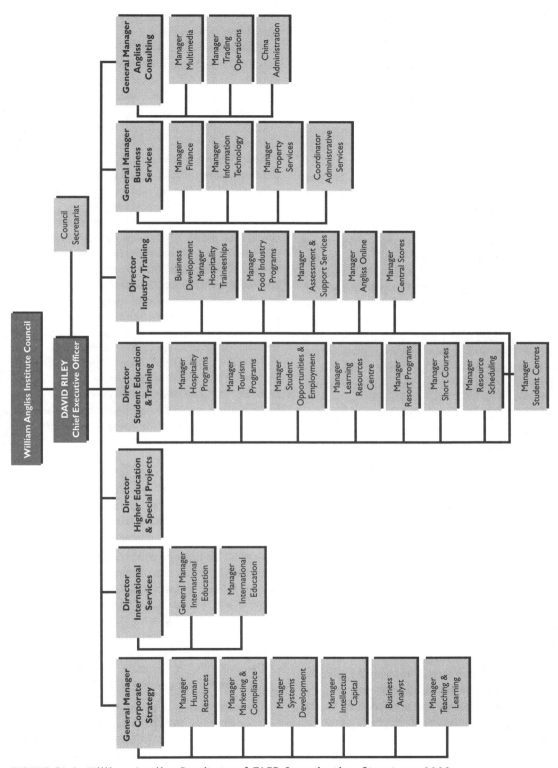

FIGURE C1.2: William Angliss Institute of TAFE Organisation Structure, 2003

Source: William Angliss Institute of TAFE, *Annual Report 2003*, accessed 1 April 2005, www.angliss.vic.edu.au. Reproduced with permission from the William Angliss Institute of TAFE and David Weston.

The establishment of a separate International Division reflects the increasing significance of this market segment to the Institute. This Division is responsible not only for international students but also international projects. By 2001, the Institute's international market had grown from less than $1 million in 1996 to a $6.5 million a year business, and is projected to grow beyond $8 million by 2005. Furthermore, partnerships recently forged with Shanghai University and Jinling Institute of Hotel Management in Nanjing, China, to offer a Diploma and an Advanced Diploma of International Hospitality Management underscore the Institute's strategy to position itself as a global player in the provision of specialist training within the tourism, hospitality and culinary arts sectors. Currently, 123 students at Shanghai University and 27 at the Jinling Institute are enrolled in these courses. The Institute's focus on strengthening international links was further demonstrated with the appointment of a Director with the responsibility of Director — China Operations and Chief Representative — Australia Angliss Consulting Shanghai Representative Office. The Institute is keen to expand its delivery of formal courses in WAIT campuses offshore. The Institute recognises that this expansion poses both challenges and opportunities for staff. While it will provide staff with the opportunity to work overseas and deliver courses to a new client group, they will need the capabilities and willingness to adapt to different learning styles and cultures, different living and working conditions, as well as different food and climate.

Human Resources is now incorporated in the new Corporate Strategy Division; and the Commercial Services Division, established under Christine French, has had its component parts distributed to different areas. Short courses, for example, are now managed within the Student Education Division. Weston, recognising that his own expertise and experience lay in managing the marketing and customer relations side of a business, delegated responsibility for academic matters to the Director, Student Education and Training. This Division is responsible for courses in which students enrol through VTAC (the Victorian Tertiary Admissions Commission) to undertake generic programs that will gain them employment in their chosen field when they have completed their training.

The Industry Training Division, on the other hand, deals with industry clients already working in their chosen field (either individuals or corporations) who require specific training and accreditation. This Division took the entrepreneurial, commercial component of the old Commercial Services Division that dealt with industry clients and matched it up with the traditional apprenticeship-training component that used to sit in the School of Retail Foods and Food Technology. By combining these once discrete areas, the aim was to blend the Institute's traditional mode of training delivery with more innovative, industry-responsive practices. Management recognises that if the Institute is to continue to compete successfully in both the national and international marketplace, it must satisfy the increasing demand and expectation in the Hospitality, Tourism and Food Industries for training programs specifically tailored to meet individual client needs. These might be delivered on-site, at the Institute, or involve a combination of both. This new direction and way of working has, however, proved challenging, particularly for staff who have taught for many years in the traditional trades areas at WAIT.

Angliss Consulting, the fourth part of the profit-centre arm, is a subsidiary company that existed previously as the Commercial Services Division, but which has since been completely remade. Its main business is the development of multimedia training products.

Angliss Consulting doesn't do any direct training, which is the rationale for having this as a subsidiary company; its brief is to go out there and exploit all of the developments in new, leading edge technology. Even though we've got some modest real targets in terms of revenue growth, there is massive potential in this area. This is the brave new world; who knows where it is going to lead. (Barnes)

Given the Institute's branding as a Centre of Excellence (see WAIT's mission statement in figure C1.3), the quality of its online program delivery is critically important. With the commitment to differentiate itself on the basis of quality of product, a new unit, Angliss Online, was set up in 2002 under the Industry Training Division to look specifically at how Information and Communication Technologies (ICT) can fit into online learning.

MISSION STATEMENT

Gain global recognition as the Specialist Centre of Excellence in vocational training and education for the Hospitality, Tourism and Culinary Arts sectors, by meeting the current and emerging needs of the Institute's key stakeholders.

Key strategies that drive the Institute's mission include:

- enhancing the Institute's position as Victoria's Specialist Centre and 'First Choice' for training in Hospitality, Tourism and Culinary Arts
- strengthening the Institute's position as a global player, providing national and international training and education opportunities
- focusing on quality
- continually improving the quality of service to students
- Innovating and leading, through the introduction of new products
- Partnering with industry.

FIGURE C1.3: William Angliss Institute of TAFE Mission Statement and key strategies

Source: Adapted from William Angliss Institute of TAFE, *Annual Review/Report 2003*. Reproduced with permission from the William Angliss Institute of TAFE and David Weston.

Changes to processes

With the appointment of Christine French as Director in 1993 and her brief to bring about change and introduce new ways of thinking and doing business at WAIT, a seismic shake-up within the Institute seemed inevitable. She made a series of appointments at senior management level (Client Services Manager, Project Manager and three new Heads of School). Christine French was concerned that there appeared to be no strategic plan, no clear set of systems and procedures in place, no vision, no sense of the Institute's role in the wider community and how it should prepare for the future.

It was clear that urgent consideration needed to be given to the Institute's strategies for managing the systems changes advocated by government; its strategies for increasing its market share in a highly competitive industry sector; its neglect of international market opportunities; and the need to consider other modes of course delivery. To this end, a number of new systems and processes were introduced during Christine French's tenure. These included: performance management systems, budgetary and accountability systems, and a quality management process that was designed to incorporate strategic planning. The structural changes that were implemented, with the focus on programs and working in teams, were designed to encourage cooperation and aid in the transfer and diffusion of new work practices among individuals in different areas of the organisation. Collaboration within and across program areas was recognised as essential if the Institute was to compete successfully for commercial contracts that called on a diverse range of skills and expertise. There was, however, increasing frustration among senior management at the rate and pace of change within the Institute. This effect was aggravated by reductions in government funding and meeting the productivity dividends demanded by government.

When David Weston was appointed CEO in July 1998, the Institute faced serious cash flow problems. By October 1998, the Institute had to ask the government for assistance to pay the salaries for the next month.

> *I'll tell you how financially viable it was. When I got here in July I asked if there were any skeletons in the closet that I hadn't been told about. By October I didn't have enough money to pay the wages one week. And under our Act we are not allowed to borrow. The Minister said we put you in there because you were going to clean it up. And I said, well sometimes there is a little delay in when these things can happen. Today I could lend him three times or five times what he loaned me and it wouldn't impact and I paid the money back in four months. But it was an organisation on the brink, not because of anything my predecessors did, but because they didn't know how to adapt to the changing market circumstances at the time. (Weston)*

Weston's appointment brought a new business focus to the Institute. Unlike his predecessors whose experience lay solely in the education sector, Weston had extensive management experience in both public and private sector organisations. He had also run his own consultancy business for ten years, specialising in the tourism and hospitality industries.

> I have tried to make things accountable and measurable and therefore easier to manage and easier to communicate to the staff what their contribution to the overall whole meant; and secondly, relieved them from having to feel obligated about the overall whole. (Weston)

As part of the government review, which began in 1997 and was still underway at the time of Weston's appointment, the Institute applied for an Australian Business Excellence Framework Award. The overall assessment of the Institute was that it did not have proper trending, planning, measurement or proper practices in place. This provided the impetus Weston needed to put in place a performance management framework.

To this end, John Barnes, General Manager of the new Corporate Strategy Division, was given primary responsibility for developing and implementing a corporate governance system. As the peak operating system, this included the development of a three-year strategic plan, which underpinned four key elements: a three-year marketing plan, three-year workforce management plan; a two-year risk management program; and the budget.

The workforce management plan looks at the Institute's staffing profile, such as how many numbers of staff are needed as a percentage of revenue; it also looks at a whole range of critical cross-organisational issues such as culture, enterprise bargaining agreements, teaching loads, succession planning, staff morale. 'It then drills down to each of the profit and cost centres in the place to actually look at what their aspirations are for the next three years and how they are going to be met—this is full of numbers and targets for different things' (Barnes). Under the 1-year profit centre plans, there are also individual performance plans for each staff member. The individual performance planning process has six-monthly objectives, at the end of which progress is reviewed and new objectives are set.

The Marketing Plan is 'driven by a guiding principle of customer relationship management and not many people know how to do it well' (Weston). When Weston came to the Institute, he found databases existed 'all over the place and nobody knew who was who'. The Institute now uses an off-the-shelf product called Maximiser. The database now has over 6127 contacts listed of which just under half are companies and the rest are individuals. All managers and supervisory level staff are expected to use the system and it is mandatory that they log every form of communication, whether it is a phone call, letter, email or meeting. It is the data's currency and level of detail that makes it so valuable.

> With this system, if we want to send an email out, we can send an email to all our restaurateurs, to all our customers in the bread industry etc., all those employee apprentices with us. When we mail out our quarterly newsletter it goes to that list. Data like this is very volatile, [we] have to keep using it, updating it. For an outside competitor to steal that list, it would be worth half a million dollars — not because of the list, but because it is not just a name and address. I can tell you who barracks for what football team so that when we host people to the MCG, we take them to their home teams. We know which women clients don't like football but like coming to our great chefs night. (Weston)

There has, however, been huge resistance to using the system, in particular with the concept of sharing client information that many viewed as 'personal property'. As Weston acknowledged

> You might be the best solo performer, but if you are not helping other people in other parts of the organisation; if you have a star performer in your team and somewhere else in the organisation desperately needs that person, you lose points by putting your arm around that person and saying no, they belong to me; they are part of my success, they are not part of the organisation's success. One of my failings is that there are still silos here. (Weston)

To try and overcome this, statistics on how many times a person has logged an item were broadcast monthly and Weston always made sure his name was at the top of the list.

As well as developing performance measurement processes, Weston also understood the importance of documenting procedures — 'we had virtually nothing documented and there was no standard format to it'. This became the first task for the Manager, Intellectual Capital, a newly created area in the Corporate Strategy Division.

His second task was to manage the data collected from across the organisation on the Institute's customer groups 'because again you can't grow your business unless you know what industry wants from you and you've got to be constantly sucking in information about who are the decision-makers in those companies' (Weston).

Other key areas that Weston established within the Corporate Strategy Division were Systems Development and the Council Secretariat. When Weston was first appointed, the Institute's IT budget was less than $300,000 a year and staff were sharing computers. The brief given to the Systems Development Manager was to 'find IT solutions for everything'. IT systems now in place include a Human Resources Management System; a new student management system; a finance and purchasing system; and a resource scheduling system. The Institute adopted a policy that no hardware would be more than three years old and this was achieved within the four years of Weston's tenure.

The role of the Council Secretariat is to coordinate and control the format and distribution of Council papers. In the past, the Directors used to write all the Council papers. Under Weston, members of the executive team now undertook this task. Weston also instituted a standard format and colour coding for all Council papers: key recommendations are highlighted; the key financial and policy implications are set out upfront. To ensure the financial section of the papers are easy to understand, John Barnes, General Manager, Corporate Strategy, developed a scorecard where all key performance indicators are changed on a monthly basis:

> *A star means we are ahead of budget; a target means we are on target; a downward graph means we are on a downward trend; and an alarm clock means, better look at this because we are in serious difficulty. (Weston)*

When Weston commenced as CEO of the Institute, he found that progressive government funding cuts had left many staff feeling scared, powerless and beleaguered. Indeed, one of the first tasks Council wanted him to undertake was to look at outsourcing and downsizing. Weston asked for more time and became convinced that 'the alternative to cutting was in fact to grow the business, and then if you do have surplus or wastage in the organisation, you will be able to take up the surplus into the new growth of the business'. For example, long-term employees that thought their careers at WAIT had come to an end filled the managerial positions in the newly created areas within the Corporate Strategy Division.

One of the very first decisions Weston made was to put all of the contracted teachers after 12 months on to permanent tenure. This move has brought both advantages and disadvantages: it has made the costs of delivery higher, but other new revenue sources (particularly through its international ventures) have allowed the Institute to fund this. Sessional staff delivers currently only 15 per cent of the Institute's government-funded teaching. The key advantage of this move has been the sense of certainty it has brought to staff, which in turn has led to increased loyalty and commitment to the Institute as reflected in the latest staff satisfaction surveys. As Weston shared his vision to 'grow the business', staff morale rose dramatically because they came to see that this approach was not just rhetoric. A staff satisfaction survey conducted in September 2000 (benchmarked against a number of other TAFEs and training providers) reported a 7.5 per cent increase in staff satisfaction in the one survey period. The 2001 staff satisfaction survey not only held the 7.5 per cent gain, it increased it by a further 1.5 per cent. As staff farewelled David Weston in 2002 and a new CEO came on board, there was a slight drop from 75.9 per cent to 74.1 per cent.

John Barnes, General Manager, Corporate Strategy Division, acknowledges that there is still a long way to go.

> *All the staff surveys indicate very high satisfaction at Council level — management of where the organisation is going and how it is measured and how people are held accountable. Mixed message from middle management — some good, some of them bad; and then much more mixed message when we get down to the actual delivery areas which means we've got a bit of inconsistency about getting the message through, and what do people need to do to achieve the big picture, the targets. That's the next real challenge for us — helping them understand where they fit; what numbers do they really need to follow. (Barnes)*

Given the level of anxiety and uncertainty that prevailed among staff in WAIT, Weston also set about changing the vocabulary and style of communication that was used. He stressed the concept of the Institute as a community that looked after and cared for its people.

> I likened us to a small country town with 300 people in the population and I said to people things like: In a small country town of 300 people there are some people who are at their physical peak and some people in their declining physical years and some who have not yet reached their peak. In a small country town of 300 people, there are people at that particular time of their life who are emotionally strong and there are those who are emotionally weak. There are those people who are intellectually gifted and those who are not. We, like a community, have all those attributes. And in a small country town they don't say because you are no longer at your physical peak we send you out of town; because you are finding it difficult emotionally at the moment, we don't abandon you. Those were the kinds of things we talked about here because what I discovered in the people elements of this organisation was a lot of pain and hurt and uncertainty. (Weston)

To this end, Weston instituted quarterly staff communication meetings that focused on celebrating individual and group achievements towards the target of growing the business and achieving excellence. Weston would invite individual staff members to come forward and inform others of their successes. When 300 people attended the first of these voluntary communication meetings in 2002, there was a strong sense that staff members were moving forward and embracing the new ways of working.

Weston also introduced staff length-of-service awards. Weston found there were many staff members with over 25 years of service who had never received any form of recognition. So he introduced very simple awards: plaques for ten years; a couple of Waterford crystal champagne flutes for 15 years; crystal decanter and whisky glasses for 20 years; and a canteen of good quality cutlery for 25 years. While Weston recognised that 'all the theory tells you those old fashioned

ten-year and 25-year pins can be negative, in this instance, for some reason or other, it worked'.

Changes to boundaries

Delivery of customised training programs to different industry groups is seen increasingly as the Institute's core business and primary revenue stream. By the mid-1990s WAIT was actively seeking joint venture arrangements with offshore and local institutions. One such affiliation, which is still in place, was with RMIT University, and the Australian Centre for Tourism and Hospitality was established through this link; another was with Drake International. By 2002, while the Institute was involved in a number of partnerships with other educational providers such as The Australian Alpine Institute, part of La Trobe University, with whom the Institute developed the Diploma of Alpine Resort Management for delivery at the Mt Buller Campus, its particular interest was in developing partnerships with industry. These include Angliss Hospitality Compliance, an initiative between the Institute, the Australian Hotels and Hospitality Association and Clubs Victoria through which WAIT delivers all compliance training to Association members (mandatory courses for responsible service of alcohol, gambling, hygiene for food handlers etc.); a major strategic alliance with the confectionery industry to set up a global training partnership; WAIT's role, forged in 2003, as national training coordinator for Stamford Hotels and Resorts; and the establishment in November 2002 of Australia's first Coffee Academy at WAIT in partnership with Dutch coffee company Douwe Egberts. Based on the success of its existing national partnership models, in 2004 Gloria Jean's Coffees approached WAIT to provide a customised training program that would be delivered to all Gloria Jean's staff in its 200-plus outlets located throughout Australia. WAIT's nationally accredited course in Retail (Operations) was tailored to meet Gloria Jean's specific needs and is now running in New South Wales, Victoria and South Australia, and will be rolled out to the remaining States and territories during 2005. In addition, in order to improve accessibility and responsiveness to its rapidly expanding interstate clientele base, WAIT opened a Sydney office in September 2004. This complements its South Australian office, established in 2003.

On the international front, in 2002 the Institute established a campus in China in partnership with Shanghai University to deliver dual award certification programs in Hospitality and Tourism Management. June 2004 saw the first cohort of 50 student graduates in China with Australian qualifications in hospitality management. The success of the education cooperation programs between WAIT and its Chinese partners, Shanghai University and Jinling Institute of Hotel Management, is reflected in the increasing number of students enrolling in the Australian accredited hospitality management courses, with over 300 students enrolled in September 2004, the start of the Chinese academic year.

A further example of the Institute's international reach is its collaborative partnership with the Australian Wheat Board (AWB) to provide formal training programs to the baking industry in Vietnam. In a quest to improve local baking skills, the AWB, which has been exporting wheat to Vietnam for around 50 years, sponsored the establishment of a Centre of Excellence for professional development in Ho Chi Minh City. The Centre of Excellence, a modern training bakery with state-of–the-art equipment, ovens and appliances, was opened in Vietnam in October 2004. The programs were developed jointly by WAIT and RMIT Vietnam and are aimed at industry professionals and new entrants to both bakeries and retail outlets. The Australian nationally accredited programs to be offered in 2005 include Certificates in Food Processing and Hospitality, and Diplomas in Food Technology and Confectionery Manufacturing. A number of short courses will also be offered, with businesses in Vietnam expressing an interest in areas such as workplace training and assessment; and food hygiene and safety courses.[3]

Looking to the future

David Riley, the Institute's current CEO, is only the seventh CEO in the Institute's proud history. He is a former deputy CEO of Tourism Victoria, and brings over 20 years of experience in the hospitality and tourism industries to the top job. Heralded as the Institute's 'guiding light', Riley views the Victorian Government's Ministerial Statement on Knowledge and Skills for the Innovation Economy, which advocates the establishment of

TAFE institutes as specialist centres of innovation, as a significant 'springboard' for the Institute. As the longest running specialist training provider to the hospitality and tourism industries, WAIT is therefore well positioned to be the model of best practice to other TAFE institutes.

In October 2002, the Victorian State Government formally recognised WAIT as the Specialist Centre for Hospitality, Tourism and the Culinary Arts, reinforcing its reputation and standing as the industry benchmark. This acknowledgement aligns with Riley's vision to develop WAIT as a centre of lifelong learning. Riley believes the Institute's future depends on it relationship with industry, and central to this direction are four key themes: what it means to be a specialist centre; financial viability; globalisation; and the opportunity for TAFEs to develop degree courses in niche areas as prescribed by the Ministerial Statement on Knowledge and Skills for the Innovation Economy. These four themes underpin the Institute's current Strategic Business Plan, which Riley designed to replace the previous broad-based strategic plan developed under Weston.

I have always talked about William Angliss since the day I arrived as being divided into the world at William Angliss and the world of William Angliss. The world at William Angliss is about building a new kitchen, a lecture theatre, the new coffee academy. The world of William Angliss is about where is our influence, where are we trying to go, what are we trying to do and the complexities of answering that question leads to a change in the way the Strategic Business Plan is presented and what it tries to cover and how it tells the story. When I talk about the world of William Angliss I talk about trying to make history. (Riley, 2004)

Themes for the future

The sorts of issues the Institute must grapple with in relation to the four key themes discussed above that underpin its future direction are discussed in the following sections.

Positioning as a Specialist Centre

The Victorian Government's endorsement of WAIT as the Specialist Centre for Hospitality, Tourism and the Culinary Arts, and the allocation of $1.15 million in funding in 2003 alone, establishes the parameters for the Institute's strategic agenda into the future. The Institute needs to determine how to make creative and innovative use of its specialist centre endorsement as it seeks out opportunities to position itself as a truly global player. Riley sees the need to develop more research and development (R&D) capacity as a key priority for the Institute if it is to realise the opportunities of Specialist Centre endorsement and be the 'First Choice' for training in hospitality, tourism and the culinary arts. Greater R&D capacity is already enabling the Institute to identify opportunities and trends (such as the growth in eco-tourism and the growing level of interest in event management) and pinpoint skills gaps. This approach has seen the development of a number of innovative, specialist courses including a Diploma in Dive Resort Management, a full fee paying, two-year course ($22,000) that involves partnerships in Cairns, the Gold Coast and Perth; and a Diploma in Eco-Tourism in partnership with the University of Ballarat located in regional Victoria offering specialist training with a focus on nature-based tourism. Through these partnerships, students gain training and experience in specialist areas not available in the Melbourne CBD. The Dive Resort Management program won the 2003 Victorian Tourism Award in the Tourism Education and Training category. In 2004, the Institute's Diploma of Resort Management, which encompasses the Dive, Spa and Marine Resort Management programs, again won the coveted Victorian Tourism Award in the same category.

Financial viability

Major revenue growth over the next few years is predicted to come from international projects and fee-for-service programs. Currently, 45 per cent of the Institute's revenue is generated from industry and 50 per cent is derived from government. This dependence on industry for higher levels of revenue, however, brings greater risk and exposure as economic downturns, political conflict, epidemics such as SARS, or the collapse of major organisations (for example, Ansett and HIH) impact on the Institute's ability not only to maintain existing partnerships or programs, but also to develop new ones. Riley, however, points out that financial viability is not the only measure of success. He points to student employment outcomes, with the latest National Centre of Education Research (NCVER) student outcomes'

survey showing that WAIT has one of the highest employment rates of all Victorian TAFEs. Success depends significantly on how the Institute nurtures its relationships with key stakeholders (for example, government, industry, students, staff and community) who have a significant influence over its strategic direction. With additional funding in 2003 of $250,000 (one-off) from the Office of Training and Tertiary Education for the development of an Alumni Plan, the Institute launched the Angliss Global Network, 'a professional development and networking association for industry professionals, graduates and current students of the Institute and other TAFEs'. Riley also recognises that the success of the Institute as a specialist centre depends ultimately on the accumulated knowledge, skills, talents and commitment of staff. Thus it is incumbent on the Institute to support and encourage its ongoing professional development and training.

Globalisation

WAIT is keen to establish itself as a global player in the provision of training and expertise in hospitality, tourism and the culinary arts. In the education sector, WAIT is not only looking to increase the number of international students studying at the Institute in Melbourne, but is also looking to forge partnerships with overseas universities and institutes and establish joint campuses offshore that act as feeder institutes where international students complete a diploma and then come to WAIT to complete a degree. As well as its partnership with Shanghai University, the Institute has delivered programs in Indonesia, Vietnam and Laos. The Institute's international division is responsible for identifying and developing new market opportunities offshore. To this end, the Institute has established a strong relationship with International Training Australia (ITA) and works closely with them to source, manage and deliver major international projects. WAIT is currently acting as the lead agent through ITA in the development of a major hospitality-training project in the Asia–Pacific Region.

Developing degree courses

The Ministerial Statement on Knowledge and Skills for the Innovation Economy provides TAFEs with the opportunity to offer degree courses for the first time in 'niche' areas not served by the Higher

Education Sector. These would be full fee paying degree courses that the Institute would need to demonstrate would be financially viable over the long-term. In addition to developing its own degree course, the Institute could also license an existing degree, take its name (for example Cornell University), and pay the body a licensing fee and a fee per student to do so. The homegrown and licensed degrees could then run in parallel.

The key strategies that drive the Institute's mission (refer to figure C1.3, page 367) underline its intent to become a global player and industry partner of choice. A comparison of its current mission statement and objectives with those of 1996 (see figure C1.4) highlights not only the radical boundary changes that have taken place, but also the critical structural and process changes that were implemented to take the Institute from an organisation on the brink to its current position as Victoria's Specialist Centre for Hospitality, Tourism and the Culinary Arts with a global outreach, and strong industry partnerships.

MISSION STATEMENT

William Angliss Institute exists to provide quality education and business services for the benefit of students and clients in the tourism, hospitality, food, and associated industries.

The Institute's Goals

1. Common Direction

Objective: To instil commitment to a common sense of direction amongst the people associated with the Institute.

2. Funding Base

Objective: To become more independent of Government funding sources by offering a range of commercial programs and services to external clients.

3. Employee Relations

Objective: To build employee commitment to change through active participation and flexible industrial agreements.

4. Diversification

Objective: To provide a wider, mobile, more flexible range of educational and business activities to meet the needs of present and potential clients.

5. Infrastructure

Objective: To develop an integrated set of facilities, procedures, and systems that will support our expansion.

6. Communication

Objective: To develop an effective Institute decision making structure that provides opportunities for wider input and contribution to common goals.

FIGURE C1.4: William Angliss Institute of TAFE Mission Statement 1996

Source: Reproduced with permission from the William Angliss Institute of TAFE and David Weston.

QUESTIONS

1. Drawing on figure 1.1 (page 23), identify and explain the impact of culture, context, knowledge and technology (the 'affectors') on the change process at WAIT.

2. According to the INNFORM findings, if changes to structures are to succeed, there must be *simultaneous* and *complementary* changes to processes and boundaries.

   (a) Analyse the changes at WAIT across all nine key indicators of change within the organisational design dimensions of structures, processes and boundaries and

   (b) Assess the extent to which the changes at WAIT appear to be systemic and complementary.

3. Does your assessment suggest key issues or indicators that WAIT needs to address in organising its structure, processes and boundaries?

END NOTES

1. This case study was undertaken with the generous support of David Riley, current CEO; past CEO David Weston; and John Barnes, General Manager, Corporate Strategy at WAIT. Material for this case study was collected from interviews conducted on-site; from journal articles; documentation available from the Institute's Web site; and in-house and published company documents made available to the author. Reproduced with permission from the William Angliss Institute of TAFE and David Weston.

2. Kathy Nunn 1990, *William Angliss College: the First Fifty Years*, Hargreen Publishing Company, Melbourne; Pauline Hagel & Fiona Graetz 1996, 'Learning and the Knowledge-Based Organisation: Theory and Practice in a Public Sector Organisation', paper presented at ANZAM '96 Conference.

3. *Anglissnews*, edition 13, summer 2004/2005, p. 1.

CASE 2

Autoliv Australia

Prepared by
Ann Lawrence[1]

Background

Worldwide changes such as global competition in all industry sectors, advances in technology, and changing customer and employee expectations have altered the way in which organisations compete and work is organised. The adoption of a strategic orientation to managing people, supported by appropriate human resource management (HRM) systems and processes, has been argued to have a positive impact on the performance of firms.[2]

Autoliv Inc, a Swedish multinational organisation, has adopted such a strategic orientation. With one million people killed globally in motor traffic accidents every year, improved automotive safety is a key priority. The company is the world's number one producer of car safety equipment. It produces a wide range of automotive components including airbags, seat belts, anti-whiplash systems, safety electronics, rollover-protection systems, steering wheels (with airbags), and child seats. Its customers include all major carmakers. Autoliv Inc. has 20 crash-test tracks, nine technical centres, 80 subsidiary manufacturing plants and joint ventures in 30 countries around the world, with 37,000 employees. With its successful growth strategy, Autoliv has become the global leader in the $15 billion automobile occupant restraint market. Frontal airbags account for 36 per cent of that market, side airbags for 14 per cent, seat belts for 29 per cent and electronics for 21 per cent. In 2004 it recorded sales of US$5.3 billion and is listed as a Fortune 100 company.[3]

Autoliv's strategy is reflected in its vision, mission and values in figure C2.1.

Our Vision:

To substantially reduce traffic accidents, fatalities and injuries.

Our Mission:

To create, manufacture and sell state-of-the-art automotive safety systems.

Our Values are:

- **Life.** We have a passion for saving lives.
- **Customers.** We are dedicated to creating satisfaction for our customers and value for the driving public.
- **Employees.** We are committed to the development of people's skills, knowledge and potential.
- **Innovation.** We are driven for innovation and continuous improvement.
- **Ethics.** We adhere to the highest level of ethical and social behavior.
- **Culture** We are founded on global thinking and local actions.

FIGURE C2.1: Autoliv — Vision, mission, and values

Source: L. Westerberg 2005, 'Autoliv — Human Values and Social Responsibilities', accessed 7 April, www.autoliv.com. Reproduced with permission from Autoliv Australia.

Autoliv Australia

Consistent with Autoliv's manufacturing strategy, assembly plants are located close to the customers and final products are typically delivered 'Just-in-time' (JIT), sometimes several times a day, to a vehicle manufacturer's plants. The Australian subsidiary, Autoliv Australia Proprietary Limited, which is situated in the northern Melbourne suburb of Campbellfield and has been operating since 1988, employs lean manufacturing approaches and JIT inventory systems to produce safety occupant restraint systems — including car seat belts, airbags and child restraints. It is a supplier of these products for the major car manufacturers in Australia — Ford, Holden, Toyota and Mitsubishi, and also exports to Korea and other South East Asian countries.

The growth and associated organisational change at Autoliv Australia has been a medium to long-term approach with a number of discrete steps. In the late 1980s and early 1990s, the company faced many operating problems and its continued survival was under threat. This scenario has been turned around. The first part of the recent change process began in 1997, under the guidance of the newly appointed Chief Executive Officer, Robert (Bob) Franklin and his executive team. Autoliv Australia has significantly changed the work practices of the traditional engineering and manufacturing business to a state-of-the-art business that recognises the diversity and value of its human capital. This approach has meant a focus on shared values and on integrated human resource management strategies that support the business objectives. The company now exhibits strong productivity growth and before tax profits, and is viewed as an 'employer of choice'.[4] Since 1997, with 260 employees, the company has grown in turnover from $50 million to $260 million a year — a growth of 20 per cent every year. Autoliv Australia is listed at number 817 on the BRW top 1000 index.[5] It now employs approximately 850 people and approximately 70 per cent of the employees work on the shopfloor — that is, directly involved in the manufacturing process; 75 per cent of its employees are women; 74 per cent of its employees are from non-English speaking backgrounds and represent 57 countries, speaking 50 different languages.[6]

The vision, strategies and values of Autoliv Australia are consistent with that of its parent company. The core values are global and they guide the way the business is managed — they are applied and executed locally through sound, value-based leadership practices including involvement and leading by example, strategic planning and involving everyone in the company's future, ensuring the growth and developing the potential of all its employees, utilising information and knowledge management approaches, uncompromising customer service, and continuous improvement.[7] Its business strategies and objectives are explicit in the following statement: 'Through skilled and educated people, we develop, produce and sell the most reliable, high quality, cost effective, innovative and environmentally friendly automotive safety systems.'[8]

Culture

Autoliv Australia has endeavoured to achieve its objectives by establishing a company culture reinforced by strong corporate values and ethics. Much of this achievement has been facilitated through the practice of a shared-values approach. The company's values are founded on 'high-performance' values such as trust, openness, integrity, teamwork, equity and fairness, equal opportunity, participation, consultation, communication and accountability.[9] These values and the associated behaviours are highly congruent with those of the CEO's inclusive and open leadership style and those of his management team including the HR Director. These have provided a catalyst for many of the initiatives for the diversity strategies and to enhance the quality of life for its employees, community and partners.[10]

This value-based leadership approach at Autoliv is evident in the communication and consultative decision-making processes in place, including face-to-face briefings with employees, the use of continuous improvement teams, and a hands-on approach to management. For example, a consultative committee has been implemented with three management representatives and 14 employees, of whom four are drawn from the National Union of Workers (NUW) and the Australian Manufacturing Workers Union (AMWU). This committee deals with issues as diverse as assisting in implementing the Enterprise Agreement, production improvements, changes to work schedules and conditions, equal opportunity and affirmative action programs, and the introduction of major changes in organisation, production, program, and technology that is likely to have significant effects on employees.[11] These practices all encourage an open and frank communication exchange throughout the company, and facilitate organisational learning.

Aligning HR practices to organisational strategies

Effective delivery of organisational change requires an alignment between the organisation's corporate and business strategies, its change strategies and its HRM strategy. To facilitate the delivery of its corporate objectives, Autoliv has designed and implemented an integrated set of HR strategies to leverage organisational change. These changes have been driven by business imperatives and have made good business sense. These new directions underpin the recognition of the need to develop employee, managerial and leadership talent and develop organisational capability for change through organisational learning.

The HR function

An important aspect of strategic HRM in organisational change is developing HR strategies, policies and practices that support the process by which the organisation adapts to its environment and meets its objectives. Putting the change strategy into action and making the changes a reality requires devolution of responsibility predicated on commitment from the top of the organisation, and on individual, managerial, and functional competencies, and organisational capability. The HR function at Autoliv has a strategic role in assisting the organisation to achieve its goals for change. Both the CEO and the Director of Human Resources have key roles in leveraging HR as a strategic partner and as agents for change.

Performance management

Autoliv Australia applies an integrated performance management model. Its company objectives of sustainable growth, customer focus, employer of choice, world class manufacturing, and social responsibility are directly linked to its Human Resource Management objectives and outcomes. Key performance indicators have been implemented for each of these objectives, which are cascaded down to job level. Specific job competencies have been clearly defined and every employee is informed of the skills required to do a job or to be promoted into a job. Autoliv also employs two tests to ensure its work practices and decisions are on track. First: Is the intended practice or action in agreement with the business objectives? And, secondly: Is it in line with the company's values and behaviours? This proactive self-assessment approach provides a large measure of consistency and it limits the potential for misunderstandings that can result in unwelcome and costly industrial disputes.[12] Other measures guarantee alignment with HR and organisational objectives. For example HR benchmarks all training initiatives in both hours and expenditure, with a minimum of two days per employee per year in Australia being the standard. HR also endeavours to benchmark practices across industries and globally to give the company a clearer insight on how it compares against others as a means of performance improvement.

Work design

One area in which organisational change is most evident is the way in which work is performed. Work design must have a strategic focus, with the attention to quality, flexibility and a customer focus. Autoliv has accomplished this by arranging its production cells into customer groups, for example, one for Ford, one for Toyota etc., with the customer's name prominently displayed for all to see. In addition, the team leaders maintain close contact with each customer, and performance measures are clearly shown for each customer grouping.[13] Underpinning its recruitment, development, performance management and review, promotion and succession planning, are key HR practices — training needs analyses and competency profiling. Understanding the business down to role competency level is seen as critical at the company for recruitment and selection, and ensuring that people are developed and placed into jobs that match their talents. Autoliv's competency profiles are based on a set of well-defined competencies for all positions, selection criteria of the person with the key competencies required for that position, and open communication and ownership of the processes to ensure objectivity in the selection decisions. These methods are integrated with human resource development, career planning and diversity, and occupational health and safety strategies.

Staffing the organisation

The organisation must ensure it attracts qualified applicants, has mechanisms to identify the best candidates to fill its jobs, and has the appropriate strategies in place to motivate employees to perform, and to satisfy and retain them. Autoliv has a policy of recruiting permanent employees. However, like many other companies, Autoliv Australia employs casual workers to cater for fluctuations in customer demand. However, it provides its casual workforce with a route to permanent employment. Autoliv initially uses a labour hire company to bring on all of its new casual recruits and then promotes to permanency as opportunities arise. The performance of its casual employees is reviewed at least every three months and where positions arise preference is given to casual employees. More than 300 of its workforce have moved to permanent positions in recent years.[14] By demonstrating employer commitment to a permanent workforce, this policy also assists in building employee commitment by providing employees with better job security, training opportunities and career choices. This approach also ensured that Autoliv is making sound staffing decisions based on demonstrated shared values and behaviours.

Education, training and development

A critical focus of an HRD strategy is to make certain the initiatives support and deliver the organisation's business and change objectives. Autoliv has recognised that attracting, retaining, developing and promoting employees with perceived potential to deliver the organisation's goals is a critical component of its success. Consistent with this approach is the commitment to valuing and developing the skills, knowledge and creative potential of its workforce. A key lever for the success in the organisation has been the development and implementation of an integrated training and development strategy underpinned by a continuous improvement philosophy. The foundation of these activities are training needs analyses and resultant competency profiles, the corporate plan, business priorities and performance development reviews. For example, the company has redesigned its training and career policies and programs to facilitate the movement of its staff, including women, to move into management. The strategy starts at the bottom — from the shopfloor up — to develop and promote women up through the organisation as supervisors and to management levels.

A wide variety of training and development programs from induction and orientation training through to technical and managerial skill development are offered internally and by accredited private providers. Training approaches range from short courses, Technical and Further Education (TAFE) programs, traineeships, on-the-job training, and internal workshops, to scholarships and study assistance. Examples include its Engineering Production Certificate, Train Small Groups, Assessor Training, Frontline Management Program, and Team Leaders Conference. The company also offers entry-level traineeships in transport, manufacturing, business and information technology.

Career development and succession planning

Career development and succession planning is seen as a critical component in reinforcing the values and the behaviours in action. The training and development initiatives are also integrated with the provision of structured career pathways. For example, production operators are encouraged to complete a Certificate II in Manufacturing. The design of this training is based on Autoliv systems and procedures and is delivered on site by trainers from educational providers such as TAFE colleges and involves relevant expert staff from Autoliv as guest speakers. This training is also complemented by action-learning projects and on-the-job learning through appropriate roles in the organisation, which enhances the knowledge base and promotion potential of the employees. Other development opportunities linked to career management and planning include a corporate training program, study leave, a mentoring program, developmental projects/responsibilities, and overseas appointments.

A key development tool is the company's new global leadership program that links preferred leadership behaviours to the company's performance management system and business key performance indicators.[15] These objectives and associated leadership behaviours listed in figure C2.2 are the foundation of its global leadership program for the senior executives of the company worldwide.

- demonstrate accountability
- exhibit integrity
- display enthusiasm
- promote teamwork
- encourage innovation
- be results oriented
- provide clarity & direction
- support diversity
- grow people
- supporting work life balance
- support global strategies

FIGURE C2.2: Global leadership behaviours

Source: Woollard, C. HR Director, Autoliv Australia, presentation to Deakin MBA, Geelong, 14 February 2005.

Reward and recognition

Rewarding performance is one of the most important functions within organisations because it is directly concerned with leveraging change through eliciting and reinforcing desired behaviours and outcomes. Rewards — remuneration and benefits — are a major determinant of the quality of people drawn to an organisation and the level of employee performance at work. Autoliv's reward strategy is not developed in isolation, but is influenced by the organisation's culture, its mission, values, business strategy and the broader human resource strategy. In relation to remuneration, Autoliv is comparable with industry standards. It has an Enterprise Agreement in place and the Metal, Engineering and Associated Industries Award, 1998, covers the employees. Their career paths are directly linked to remuneration. However, the company's use of 'non-financial' benefits to attract, retain and motivate its workforce sets it apart from many other organisations.

Equal opportunity and work life balance

All reward initiatives should support both the needs and considerations of the organisation and an individual's concerns. Autoliv provides equity and access and opportunity for all. These benefit both female and male members of staff. In its endeavour to become an 'employer of choice' for women, the company has implemented a suite of reward and work–life balance initiatives as part of its equal employment opportunity, staffing, retention, development and reward strategies. Autoliv has also recognised the diversity of needs of its employees for various rewards and benefits that suit their particular personal circumstances and obligations and has implemented a wide variety of initiatives to address them.

These initiatives include

- flexible hours, which allow employees the opportunity to attend to personal appointments during the day, when necessary; and modified hours to accommodate specific start and finish needs.
- early finish on Fridays.
- rostered day off (RDO) once a month.
- employees with 12 months to three years continuous service are entitled to ten weeks' paid maternity leave, while those with three years or more are entitled to 14 weeks. These employees can return to their previous or another mutually agreed position in the company. In its support for working mothers Autoliv has also provided a lactation room and facilities.
- paternity leave of one week is also available to those employees with 12 months' or more continuous service.
- availability of part-time work when returning from maternity leave, to meet family commitments, and when approaching retirement. In its endeavour to enhance quality of work life in circumstances such as family matters, taking or returning from maternity leave, as a step towards retirement, or returning from serious illness, an employee has the option of part-time work subject to consultation and agreement with the company.
- leave without pay for up to six weeks for emergencies.
- access to all sick leave as carer's leave.
- option to purchase two weeks' extra annual leave. Employees can purchase two weeks' extra annual leave by taking the 52/50 pay-rate option. This way, employees can balance out their personal requirements.
- option to save and purchase a year's paid leave. By working for four years on 80 per cent of normal pay, employees are then entitled to a year off.
- long service leave flexible options. Long service leave can be accessed after seven years and there is the ability to take this as double time at half pay.
- 100 per cent two-year income protection for all employees.
- access to an Employee Assistance Program to assist with personal problems.
- a prayer room to meet the religious practice needs of its Muslim employees.
- payout of 50 per cent of total accrued sick leave on termination of employment except in circumstances of summary dismissal or termination for misconduct, or 50 per cent sick leave paid out on employment date anniversary.

Equity is also demonstrated at Autoliv through applying the same working practices for all employees including management and the MD such as clocking on, rostered days off, informal corporate uniform, and delegating up — that is, by filling in for absenteeism by having the employee's boss perform the work of the missing staff member.

Results

Among the results of these actions at Autoliv since 2000, the number of women in management roles has increased by 15 per cent in four years, women in executive management has increased by 10 per cent, and women in engineering has increased by 20 per cent. Further results include an increase of women in industry-based learning programs from 20 per cent in 2001, to 60 per cent in 2004. Other benefits to the company range from increased retention with a staff turnover level below 0.5 per cent, a reduction in absenteeism with figures for 2003 below 4 per cent, no time lost due to industrial disputes, high levels of employee satisfaction, and an increase in sales.[16]

Both the CEO and the HR Director have indicated that while many of the policy changes including the work–life balance, equal opportunity, and diversity that at first impression might seem to be expensive, are in fact either highly cost effective or cost neutral because they significantly reduce the issues with unplanned absenteeism, low productivity and loss of key skills. They have brought other positive benefits to the company including enhancing Autoliv's ability to attract the best candidates, a dedicated and skilled workforce, a culture of pride of the company, high employee satisfaction, no industrial disputes, and wide community recognition for innovative and progressive practices. In recognition for the work on diversity and equal opportunity, and its progressive policies and practices, the company has been the recipient of multiple awards, and is a member of the 'National Diversity Think Tank' and various Government and Industry Advisory Boards. Autoliv's awards include:

- Employer of Choice for Women 2001–2005
- Organisation of the Year for the Advancement of Women — 2002
- Bob Franklin — Leading CEO of the Year for the Advancement of Women — 2002
- Outstanding Achievement for EEO Practice — 2003
- Victorian Workplace Excellence Award for Work–life Balance — 2003
- Society of Automotive Engineers Australasia — Advancement of Women into Engineering and Manufacturing Management — 2003
- Inducted into the Victorian Manufacturing Hall of Fame, June 2002. This recognises the recipients as creators of world-class Victorian made products.

- Victorian Government Award for Safety Map 2000
- Ford Manufacturing Excellence Award 2000
- FCAI Supplier of the Year to Automotive Industry — 1994, 1995
- Toyota Supplier Assessment TSA Silver Award — Supplier of the Year — 1996 and 2001
- Toyota Presidents Award — Components Supply — 2001
- Toyota Top 3 Components Supplier — 1996
- General Motors Worldwide Supplier of the Year for Seat Belts — 1994–1999.

Conclusion

As part of its strategy for success over the past seven years, Autoliv has adopted a strategic orientation to managing people. The company has supported its business strategies with innovative human resource management (HRM) systems and processes that align behaviours and actions with its values. As well as achieving its business growth objectives, the results also include creating an organisational culture that recognises and values learning, diversity, and enhances the work–life balance of its committed and motivated workforce.

Having achieved such success, Autoliv like all companies in the manufacturing sector in Australia, is mindful of the dynamic global environmental conditions that influence its ability to succeed or otherwise, particularly in relation to the costs of doing business. A flexible and change ready organisation, with a strategic orientation to its people management, underpinned by strong values of high trust and high performance, knowledge management, innovation and creativity, are well positioned to meet the challenges head on.

QUESTIONS

1. Using Porter's model of competitive strategies and De Cieri's directional strategies discussed in chapter 6, and the facts of this case study, categorise Autoliv Australia's business strategies.

2. Using Schuler and Jackson's framework, outline the key HR policies, practices and initiatives that Autoliv has introduced to facilitate the delivery of its intended changes. In your answer you should address the notion of the job design,

recruitment and selection approaches, training and development, performance management, and reward strategies.

In your opinion what extent are these strategies aligned with those of the organisation and capable of delivering its strategic intentions.

3. Many theorists argue that the scope and leadership style of change management are important considerations and that different organisational personnel carry responsibility for aspects of change management.

(a) Who is responsible for designing and implementing these changes at Autoliv?

(b) Analyse the scope of the changes at Autoliv and the various leadership and management approaches being employed.

END NOTES

1. I would like to acknowledge with sincere gratitude the generosity of Mr Bob Franklin, CEO, and Ms Cheryl Woollard, HR Director, Autoliv Australia in providing material for this case study. This was collected from presentations given to Deakin University MBA students and personal discussions with Mr Bob Franklin, CEO, and Ms Cheryl Woollard, HR Director, Autoliv Australia. Other material was collected from documentation available from the Autoliv Inc Web site, and other published materials and articles on the company. Reproduced with permission from Autoliv Australia.

2. C. Mabey, G. Salaman & J. Storey 1998a, *Human Resource Management: A Strategic Introduction*, Blackwell, Oxford; M. A. Huselid, S. E. Jackson & R. S. Schuler 1997, 'Technical and strategic human management effectiveness as determinants of firm performance', *The Academy Of Management Journal*, 40(1), pp. 171–88.

3. Autoliv, accessed 3 February 2005, www.autoliv.com

4. 'Autoliv — the company whose only dummies are for crash testing', 2003, *Australian Continuous Improvement Group: Best Practice*, May, www.acig.com.au

5. John Fairfax Holdings Limited 2004, 'Who is where — BRW 1000 index', *Business Review Weekly*, 11 November.

6. R. Franklin, CEO, 2004 Autoliv Australia, presentation to Deakin MBA, Geelong and Personal communication, 16 November; C. Woollard, HR Director, 2005, Autoliv Australia, presentation to Deakin MBA, Geelong, 14 February.

7. A. Banks 2002, 'Training and Diversity at Autoliv', presentation to ANTA Equity Conference, 2–3 September, Melbourne.

8. Autoliv Australia Pty Ltd Enterprise Agreement 2003, Australian Industrial Relations Commission, AG831333 PR942348, Melbourne, 23 December, p. 6.

9. C. Fox 2004, 'Our top leaders', *AFRBoss*, 13 August, John Fairfax Holdings Limited, p. 61.

10. R. Franklin 2004, personal communication, November.

11. Autoliv Australia Pty Ltd Enterprise Agreement 2003, Australian Industrial Relations Commission, AG831333 PR942348, Melbourne, 23 December, p. 8.

12. Australian Continuous Improvement Group, www.acig.com.au, op.cit.

13. ibid.

14. C. Long 2004, 'Casually speaking', *The Sydney Morning Herald*, 14 August.

15. A. Banks 2004, Organisational Development Manager, Autoliv Australia, in 'Investment in Training Pays Off', Northern Contact Issue, 18 July, www.northernacc.com/article

16. C. Woollard 2005, presentation to MBA, Deakin University, Waurn Ponds, Victoria, Monday 14 March.

CASE 3

Norske Skog Boyer mill, Tasmania

Prepared by

Malcolm Rimmer
and Penny Derbyshire

Overview

This case study shows how change management evolves over time. It does so by describing the implementation between 1991 and 2004 of 'best practice' at the Norske Skog paper mill at Boyer in Tasmania (previously the Australian Newsprint Mill or ANM). First, the case study records the serious problems threatening the mill in the 1980s and early 1990s. It then tracks changes from 1994 (when researchers undertook the first case study)[1], to October 1998 (when the research was replicated). Finally, the story is updated to 2004. The first case study took place at the conclusion of a project funded between November 1991 and April 1994 by the Commonwealth Government's Australian Best Practice Demonstration Program. The aim of subsequent research has been to track how well the implementation of best practice principles have fared over the decade since the project ended.

The Boyer mill in Tasmania is one of three in Australasia operated by Norske Skog, a Norwegian pulp and paper conglomerate. The second largest global producer of publication paper, in 2004 Norske Skog had 11,000 employees in 23 paper mills distributed throughout 15 countries in Europe, North America, Latin America, Australasia and Asia. Throughout the 1990s Norske Skog divested several non-paper businesses to concentrate on building assets in publication paper. This approach culminated in 2000 in the acquisition from Fletcher Challenge Paper of plants in Canada, Latin America and Asia as well as the three Australasian paper mills — Tasman (in New Zealand), the Albury mill (in New South Wales) and Boyer (in Tasmania). These three mills hold 100 per cent of the Australian and New Zealand newsprint markets. In 2000, long-term (10-year) contracts were renewed with the three major Australian newspaper producers — News Limited, John Fairfax and West Australian Newspapers. The Boyer mill is an old one, producing its first newsprint in 1941. It is an integrated operation, with its core processes comprising forestry management, pulp-making, paper-making, finishing, research and customer relations. Most of its product is newsprint, although some finer papers are also made on paper machine 2. A small proportion of the plant's feedstock is now imported, while most of its product is shipped to the mainland. In 2004, production was about 290,000 tonnes of newsprint, or about 40 per cent of Australian consumption.

Before its acquisition by Norske Skog, the Boyer mill was 100 per cent owned by Fletcher Challenge Paper — a New Zealand based corporation with global interests in pulp and paper. Fletcher Challenge performed poorly in the late 1990s suffering from low pulp prices, major losses from a 10 month strike in its Canadian mill in 1997/98, and the write-off in 1998 of GBP 275 million on the sale of the loss-making UK Paper. These troubles followed earlier instability and underperformance in the industry that had caused News Limited to offload to Fletcher Challenge in 1997 its 50 per cent stake in the Boyer mill, claiming it wished to 'to get out at the top of a peaking industry'. No-one, it seemed, was doing well out of newsprint. Nor has the position improved much since 2000. Yet, despite tough market conditions, the Boyer mill and the Albury and Tasman mills have a reputation as strongly performing assets and are valued by the parent company for their market share and long-term contracts. In 2000, Norske Skog CEO, Jan Reinas said he was very pleased the new ten-year contracts were in place so soon after the purchase of Fletcher Challenge Paper. 'The Australasian business is very important to us ... the new contracts secure the profitability of the business.'[2]

Norske Skog seeks to make profits through efficiency and high-value customer service and support. In early 2002, speaking on the brink of a downturn in the industry, Jan Reinas foreshadowed at the Annual General Meeting a program to maintain Norske Skog's long-term strength. He described how the Opportunities for Improvement (OPI) initiative 'aims at enlisting the total support of all employees at a mill to achieve productivity and efficiency improvements. This creates powerful, open and a learning organisation'.[3] This worldwide program for all Norske Skog mills is firmly in the tradition of the 'best practice' management approach that has been evolving at the Boyer mill for almost two decades. Both OPI and 'best practice' are associated at the Boyer mill with a culture of continuous improvement through a mill-wide, team-based structure.

The principles and policies that drive best practice at the Boyer mill have been taking shape since a recession in the early 1980s exposed the mill as being antiquated and uncompetitive. Inefficient machinery, product quality problems, overstaffing, poor communications, a hierarchical organisational structure and antagonistic industrial relations were among the problems reported at that time. The mill also was losing money, forcing management to take corrective actions.

Benchmarking in 1984–1985 revealed seven critical performance gaps:

- paper machines were narrow
- the three paper machines were slow, producing between 400 and 765 metres per minute compared with best practice at that time of 1100 metres.
- paper quality was low
- the mill was overstaffed using 12 worker hours per tonne of product compared with best practice of four hours per tonne
- the volume of non-labour inputs (wood, energy and transport) was high
- the mill had a poor safety record
- the mill had a poor environmental record.

The change program to close these performance gaps began in the mid-1980s, focusing initially on the following activities.

- *Investment in upgraded technology* approximated $400 million between 1985 and 1995. New machine drives were installed to increase paper machine speed on machines 2 and 3, while the machines were rebuilt to support the new speeds and improve quality. New facilities for treating effluent were built and other areas of the plant were upgraded.
- *Plant operations were rationalised* to focus on core activities and to simplify plant operation. This move led to the closure of paper machine 1, the eucalypt groundwood mill, the old growth eucalypt woodmill and the caustic chlorine plant.
- *Employment was reduced* from almost 1400 in 1986 to just over 450 in 1994.
- *New safety and environmental performance programs were introduced.*

In addition, changes were introduced in the following two areas.

- *New product development was undertaken* because the long-term viability of newsprint production at Boyer was considered uncertain. The mill began to manufacture two specialty papers — Image and Alabaster — developed on site.
- *A number of related management and workforce changes were introduced* under the umbrella of 'best practice'.

Between 1991 and 1994, best practice at the Boyer mill was supported by a project grant from the Australian Best Practice Demonstration Program. The objectives of this project were four-fold:

1. to improve innovative practices in work organisation and job design, as developed and implemented at the mill
2. to extend workplace training and education through open learning and computer-based information systems
3. to develop and extend quality management philosophies and practices
4. to evaluate and improve the mill's benchmarking.

This best practice project raised the momentum of workplace reforms that had begun in the mid-1980s, and laid foundations for the future. Since the project ended in mid-1994, best practice has continued to evolve in many ways. If the pursuit of best practice at Boyer can be depicted as an evolutionary process, then in what direction (and with what results) did best practice develop between 1994 and 2004? This case study seeks to answer this question. It falls into four parts. The following section looks at best practice in 1994, describing the elements that had been introduced and their part in the wider change program, and evaluating their contribution to mill performance. The next section updates the picture to 1998, reviewing the implementation of the different elements of best practice and giving special attention to three common problem areas: change leadership, employee empowerment and performance measurement. The third section provides a further snapshot of the mill in 2004. The final section looks at developments between 1994, 1998 and 2004 to see how best practice has evolved, and the role it has played in improving the performance of the mill.

The Boyer mill in 1994: introducing best practice

Best practice was defined as follows for the purposes of the Australian Best Practice Demonstration Program:

> *A holistic, comprehensive, integrated and cooperative approach to the continuous improvement of all aspects of an organisation's operations — including leadership, planning, people, customers, suppliers, the production and supply of products and services, and the use of benchmarking as a learning tool.*[4]

Organisations that perform in this way should achieve sustainable world-class outcomes in cost, quality, delivery and innovation for the benefit of all stakeholders, including customers, shareholders, managers and employees. Further refinement of this definition of best practice distinguishes nine constituent elements and requires that they all be applied in a mutually supportive or holistic fashion.[5] Which of these elements of best practice had the Boyer mill implemented in 1994?

Table C3.1 reports the stage of development of the Boyer mill in 1994 on eight of the nine elements (the exception being change leadership, on which there was insufficient information).

TABLE C3.1		Best practice at the Boyer mill, 1994	
Strategy 1. Simple strategy driven by a single factor. 2. Formal strategy not integrating change. 3. Business strategy integrated with change plan.	2*	**People management** 1. An ad hoc approach with no guiding philosophy. 2. Human resources approach. 3. Industrial relations approach. 4. Integrated human resources/industrial relations approach.	2*
Team structure 1. No active encouragement of teams. 2. No permanent teams, but team ethos actively encouraged. 3. Permanent teams for direct employees only. 4. Permanent teams for direct and indirect employees.	3*	**External relations** 1. Occasional or mandatory external relations. 2. Driven by competitive considerations. 3. Driven by rational opportunism.	2*
Technology 1. No significant investment in technology in previous ten years. 2. Significant investment in previous five to ten years. 3. Significant investment in previous five years, or planned within a year.	3*	**Change leadership** 1. No obvious change leadership. 2. Change leadership erratic or turbulent. 3. Steady change leadership by one or a few change champions. 4. Steady change leadership demonstrated at many levels of the enterprise.	
Process improvement 1. Primarily driven by a 'top down' framework or concept. 2. Primarily driven by special teams or groups of people. 3. Guided by the concept and the people.	1*	**Employee empowerment** 1. Direct employees have limited control over daily work. 2. Direct employees have substantial or full control over daily work. 3. Direct employees control own work and are involved in strategic decision making.	1*
Measurement and control 1. Limited mainly to macro accounting and financial data. 2. Macro data supplemented by measures for specific purposes. 3. An integrated, devolved and comprehensive measurement system.	2*		

* The level achieved at the Boyer mill.

The results reported in table C3.1 arise from the following findings.

- *Strategy.* The mill was deemed to have a 'formal strategy not integrated with change' in 1994. While a clear formal planning process was in place, this process did not integrate the best practice project into the business plan. Rather the two plans sat alongside each other. The dominant elements of the business plan relied on investment, rationalisation and downsizing to improve productivity and cut costs. Management in 1994 considered that 'change was driven by getting staff down and investment up'. While management planned for 'continuous improvement through teamwork', this approach was not deemed to be delivering results in 1994 and was not factored into plans or expectations.

- *Team structure.* By 1994, ANM had established permanent work teams for direct employees in most areas of the plant, but the work teams were clearly new and not fully operational.

- *Technology.* Between 1985 and 1995, $400 million was invested in upgrading mill technology — a large investment by Boyer's standards. A pessimistic evaluation of employee skills influenced the choice of a technology that was 'easier to understand, operate and maintain'.[6]

- *Process improvement.* In 1994, the Boyer mill's approach to process improvement was deemed to be framework or concept driven. While the mill devoted considerable resources to process improvement, its approach imposed a 'top–down' total quality management (TQM) approach rather than build a 'bottom–up' partnership involving staff in continuous improvement. Amongst the resources devoted to planning continuous improvement were a new consultative committee, an overseas study mission, a cross-functional design team, and a number of key individuals working together to design the work team system for continuous improvement. All that remained was to actually 'do' continuous improvement.

- *Measurement and control systems.* By 1994, the Boyer mill had progressed beyond simple management accounting and financial data to using some macro performance measures such as the benchmarks against international best practice derived from the mid-1980s from the

Canadian Pulp and Paper Association. These industry standards applied to the plant as a whole, and were not — at that time — broken down into work team targets (or key performance indicators, KPIs). This prompted the criticism that 'many of the measures available are too coarse and relate more to business performance than to organisational performance'.[7]

- *People management.* By 1994, a highly sophisticated human resource management (HRM) function had evolved which was proactive in integrating human resource issues such as work design, training, consultation, safety and motivation into production imperatives. Evidence of HRM effectiveness existed in several areas, including: the development of new training for the skilled electronics and instrument fitters' jobs demanded by the upgraded paper machine technology; management of the Best Practice Project, including the study mission; dispute-free management of downsizing; the introduction of advanced HRM software; and other training innovations such as Open Learning. Perhaps most important from the standpoint of best practice was the new structured entry-level training, which aimed to raise the skills of process workers to enable them to handle quality concepts, business analysis and team-building. Also important were the provision of structured training for team leaders and the use of computer-assisted learning on occupational health and safety and other matters. Finally, although enterprise bargaining was conducted at the Boyer mill before 1994, it was not clear that it was used to support the best practice initiatives, or that unions actively supported best practice at that time.

- *External relations.* This area concerns interactions with those outside the plant — government, unions, industry or employer bodies, consultants, educational bodies and so on — who can impart information, advice or funding to help advance best practice. In 1994, people from the Boyer mill were accustomed to dealing with outsiders, mainly in the competitive context of their industry. This profile was most evident in the data-driven benchmarking of the early 1980s (through the Canadian Pulp and Paper Association) and the benchmarking study mission in the early 1990s (visiting nine other manufacturing companies). This competitive 'industry' focus began to broaden during the 1991–1994 period as demonstration activities brought visitors, educators, consultants and others to the plant.

• *Employee empowerment.* This category was rated in 1994 to extend no further than limited control over the employees' daily work. This approach signified the novelty of the team-based structure; the persistence of hierarchy (six levels of management with a planned reduction to three); the dysfunctional nature of the consultative committee (described by management as a forum for 'passing on information and for people grandstanding on industrial relations'); and limited employee acceptance of best practice ('many people had yet to buy into the process').[8] This finding does not signify failure at that time to communicate the vision of best practice (which employees were alleged to understand) or to improve management/employee relationships (with the gap between 'us and them' claimed to be closing).[9] The vision of best practice, however, had yet to be enacted by giving employees responsibility to make decisions about how they work.

Several judgements can be made about the stage of development reached by best practice in 1994. First, it remained in the very early stages of application, despite a history of piecemeal innovation going back more than five years. Best practice was not integrated into strategy and operations; top–down processes governed continuous improvement; teamwork was new and untested; cultural acceptance of employee empowerment was limited; and devolved decision-making and authority were not matched to decentralised performance measures. Second, the most significant areas of change at the plant before 1994 were investment, rationalisation and downsizing — which combined to deliver a major improvement in performance between 1986 and 1994. Table C3.2 shows improvements over this period in five plant-wide performance indicators — production, employee hours per tonne (labour productivity), employee numbers, average machine speeds (for paper machines 2 and 3), and safety (measured by lost time injuries and accident moving frequency rate). The data show what gains were accomplished before best practice was operational.

TABLE C3.2	Boyer mill performance, 1986–1994	
	Annual average change 1986–1991 (%)	Annual average change 1991–1994 (%)
Production (48.8 gsm equivalent tonnes)	2.4	3.5
Labour productivity (employee hours per tonne)	7.2	15.4
Employee numbers	−6.25	−12.2
Machine speeds Paper machine 3 Paper machine 2	5.3 13.5	0.0 7.4
Safety Lost time injuries Accident moving frequency rate	15.6 13.5	11.7 0.0

Source: Data compiled from D. Challis & D. Sampson 1996, 'Australian Newsprint Mills', in *The Best Practice Experience*, vol. 3, ed. Australian Best Practice Demonstration Program, Pitman Publishing, Melbourne, pp. 61–90.

Third, by 1994 the Boyer mill was prepared for best practice. A wide array of preparatory activities had been undertaken, positioning the mill to make effective use of best practice methods in the future. These moves included using benchmarking as a learning tool; organisational redesign based on teamwork and de-layering; on- and off-site certified training that spanned technical and organisational skills; communication about the need for change and the nature of best practice; and computerisation of any tasks that put new technology into the hands of work teams to support continuous improvement. Although best practice was not operational and integrated into mill operations, the groundwork had been laid for future success.

The Boyer mill in 1998: making best practice work

Table C3.3 summarises observations in 1998 about the implementation of best practice.

TABLE C3.3		Best practice at the Boyer mill, 1998	
Strategy 1. Simple strategy driven by a single factor. 2. Formal strategy not integrating change. 3. Business strategy integrated with change plan.	3*	**People management** 1. An ad hoc approach with no guiding philosophy. 2. Human resources approach. 3. Industrial relations approach. 4. Integrated human resources/industrial relations approach.	4*
Team structure 1. No active encouragement of team ethos. 2. No permanent teams, but team ethos actively encouraged. 3. Permanent teams for direct employees only. 4. Permanent teams for direct and indirect employees.	4*	**External relations** 1. Occasional or mandatory external relations. 2. Driven by competitive considerations. 3. Driven by rational opportunism.	2*
Technology 1. No significant investment in technology in previous ten years. 2. Significant investment in previous five to ten years. 3. Significant investment in previous five years, or planned within a year.	2*	**Change leadership** 1. No obvious change leadership. 2. Change leadership erratic or turbulent. 3. Steady change leadership by one or a few change champions. 4. Steady change leadership demonstrated at many levels of the enterprise.	4*
Process improvement 1. Primarily driven by a 'top down' framework or concept. 2. Primarily driven by special teams or groups of people. 3. Guided by the concept and the people.	3*	**Employee empowerment** 1. Direct employees have limited control over daily work. 2. Direct employees have substantial or full control over daily work. 3. Direct employees control own work and are involved in strategic decision making.	2*
Measurement and control 1. Limited mainly to macro accounting and financial data. 2. Macro data supplemented by measures for specific purposes. 3. An integrated, devolved, and comprehensive measurement system.	3*		

* The level of performance achieved at the Boyer mill.

Over the previous four years, a number of important developments had taken place. A rating of the key developments is given in table C3.3.

- *Strategy.* In 1998, a draft vision was developed — 'to secure and grow our future by being the best paper business we can be'. Despite the improvements of the past decade, the Boyer mill still performed in the lower quartile of world producers, reflecting two fundamental long-term problems: lack of capital and a high cost structure. The first was due to structural difficulties in the paper industry such as chronic low returns. The second derived from the high costs of fibre supply, distribution and operations for a relatively old paper mill situated in Tasmania. These constraints appeared permanent. In particular, winning investment funds from the embattled Fletcher Challenge Group to further upgrade the plant was not an apparent prospect. This scenario left cost reduction as the only strategy for meeting competitive pressures (especially in the run up to renegotiating supply contracts with the newspapers). Boyer mill management believed in 1998 that to hold these contracts when they were next negotiated it would need to be more competitive on price than in the past.

  Mill management translated this competitive imperative into a concrete target to reduce mill gate cash cost by 21 per cent. Mill gate cash cost is a measure of total variable and fixed cash costs divided by output. The way to achieve this cost reduction target was based on achieving efficiencies by continuous improvement through teamwork. Best practice was integral to strategy in 1998 in a way it was not in 1994 when competitiveness depended on greater investment and downsizing.

- *Teamwork.* This category had grown to become integral to Boyer mill operations and strategy in 1998. About 50 teams existed covering all core processes — forest management, pulp mill, paper mill, finishing and customer relations, mill site support, project engineering and technical services, supply, mill services, general services and maintenance, general support, process and product development, human resources, information systems, administration and management. This team structure was formed in 1996 with strong inputs from

trade unions. The 1996 blueprint was to develop teams up through seven levels of responsibility beginning at 'supervisor decision-making' (step 1) rising to 'full team autonomy' (step 7). Key performance indicators guide each team.

Controversy existed between management and some employees in 1998 about the degree of autonomy that teams could exercise in setting KPIs. The management view was that they must dovetail into wider organisational targets while unions thought this an undue restriction on the employees' autonomy. Some variability in team performance was also apparent. Despite these controversies, the teamwork system appeared to be a robust method of decision-making and communication in which continuous improvement efforts were focused by relevant KPIs.

- *Process improvement.* This category had a bottom–up aspect in 1998 that benefited from the initiative contributed by work teams. There was also a top–down aspect in which the Boyer Improvement Council guided continuous improvement throughout the mill. This group was a decision-making body made up of senior mill managers, union officials and delegates, and representatives from different areas of the mill. The Boyer Improvement Council replaced a Consultative Committee that had been operating since 1987 and generally was agreed to have failed in its purpose of consultation, degenerating into a forum for industrial claims and formal communication. In 1995, a retreat was held to review consultation. This move led to establishment of the Boyer Improvement Team (later a council) and a strict delineation between on-line matters (consultation on continuous improvement) and off-line matters (negotiable union matters). In practice, the Boyer Improvement Council seemed to pull together the threads of continuous improvement within the mill, reviewing performance on the mill's six key result areas (mill-wide performance objectives), evaluating team performance (against KPIs), implementing suggestions and initiatives, and bringing management and unions to share a common purpose.

- *Performance measurement.* This element of best practice showed more change than any other.

In 1994, there existed conventional financial measures, some industry benchmarks and half a dozen mill-wide indicators of business performance. By 1998, three additional types of measure had been developed. First were six corporate critical success factors in the areas of responsiveness, resource management, product management, customer satisfaction, environmental responsibility, safety performance. These factors cascaded logically into eight mill-wide key result areas (KRAs), which in turn guided team KPIs. The KRAs were:

- mill gate cash cost (total variable cost and fixed cash costs divided by production)
- mill site working capital (money tied up in inventory to run the business)
- first-grade production (total accepted production classified as first grade)
- on-time dispatch (percentage compliance with delivery schedules)
- environmental care excursions (sum total of environmental excursions in excess of regulated limits and mill licence conditions)
- accident moving frequency rate (actual improvement in accidents against target improvement)
- customer satisfaction: press room running breaks (customer measurement)
- 'Way We Work' scorecard (cultural improvements in focus, accountability, involvement and response).

In 1998, these measures were reported monthly and discussed both at the business reviews (joint management/employee forums) and the Boyer Improvement Council. The business reviews, which were implemented with the assistance of a business coach from RLG International, discussed results from the performance areas about their KPIs. One example, was the Pulp and Services area, which reported data relevant to that area: safety and environmental incidents, money tied up in inventory, the cost of pulp ingredients, total pulp cost for each type of paper, tear and tensile pulp quality measures, and paper machine stoppages due to lack of available pulp. Similar detailed measures were presented for each performance and support area. In addition to the monthly area business reviews, the mill held a three-monthly mill-wide business review.

Feeding into the business area KPIs were team KPIs, which were operational targets for all employee groups. One example was the 'Safety and Housekeeping Audit' for the Process and Product Support Group, which recorded a moving tally of the number of audits completed on time measured against a rising target. This team also reported to the business review on safety problems identified for future action through the audit process.

By 1998, the Boyer mill was guided by performance measures that informed continuous improvement at the team level while driving performance management through mill-wide and business area indicators. Measurable targets ensured sharp accountability for mill, business unit and team performance. Management saw these performance measures as the key driver for continuous improvement. They ensured that teamwork delivered results.

- *People management.* In 1994 the HRM function was already highly developed to support teamwork, job redesign, skill formation, improved safety, and quality consciousness. Between 1994 and 1998, unions became more firmly integrated into best practice. This outcome was demonstrated at a number of levels. First, enterprise bargaining supported key changes to work practices to facilitate best practice. Important here was the introduction of annualised salaries. Wage rates were increased in 1995 to absorb average overtime earnings, and teams were entrusted to manage rosters for 'call in' and other aspects of work scheduling. Strong union alignment supported this arrangement (despite reduced earnings for some individuals) because union delegates and work teams assumed a stronger role in work scheduling and production. No longer was overtime allocated and paid to the 'foreman's favourites'. Nor did employees hold back task completion so jobs continued into 'penalty rate time'. These changes removed a lot of rigidities, allowing multiskilled work teams to function. Unions became better integrated in best practice in other ways. All four unions (the Australian Manufacturing Workers Union (AMWU), the Construction, Forestry, Mining and Energy Workers Union (CFMEU), the Communication, Electrical, Electronic, Energy, Information, Postal, Plumbing and Allied Services Union

(CEPU) and the Electrical Trades Union (ETU)) participated on the Boyer Improvement Council, where they had open access to business review meetings and to management in general. Union officials and delegates accepted the need for continuous improvement, supported teamwork, accepted operational responsibilities and believed that best practice changes helped save the mill. Underpinning acceptance of best practice was the belief that 'workers know better than managers how best to do the job' and that best practice lifts employees' 'pride in their work'.

While complete consensus remained elusive in the turbulent world of mill politics, the robust working relationship between management and unions did not seem threatened by the periodic disagreements at that time.

- *Change leadership.* This category was difficult to assess in 1994. In 1998, however, it was possible to evaluate the salient characteristics — the extent of top management support, the stability of change leaders, and the depth and spread of change leadership into work teams. On all three counts, the Boyer mill rated strongly.
  - The mill had implemented the Fletcher Challenge's 'Way We Work' principles, such as 'Decisions are made where knowledge is greatest' and 'Drive knowledge sharing and networking'. These principles were formulated at Boyer to fit best practice principles.
  - The mill manager at Boyer was a strong personal advocate of continuous improvement through teamwork and of an open management style.
  - Fletcher Challenge developed an employee capabilities statement (applicable to staff employees), shifting position requirements away from just technical competence towards coaching, teamwork and people skills.
  - A new management matrix structure was introduced, consistent with the removal of hierarchy and the application of the capabilities policy. This left only one level of management between the production teams and the mill manager.
  - Stability existed among senior mill management personnel. The mill manager joined Boyer in 1985, the chair of the Boyer

Improvement Council joined in 1993 and the human resources manager (previously, best practice coordinator and training and development manager) joined in 1986.
  - Responsibility for best practice was accepted by most managers and among many team leaders, team members and union delegates.

Despite these signs of strong, stable change leadership, developments in 1998 suggested incomplete acceptance of best practice by management. In 1997, a business coach from Ryberg Levey International was hired with a brief to (1) 'turn bosses into coaches', and (2) 'tune teams to business excellence'. Despite the development of teams, it was believed that many managers did not accept them, that they 'bossed rather than coached' and that the teams functioned as 'an end in themselves with no business outcomes'. Several steps were taken in 1997 to counter these criticisms, including the adoption of the 'Way We Work' principles, the development of a new Boyer vision and goals statement (embracing the new management capabilities), restructuring the management team into a new matrix structure, the introduction of a coaching skills program and the realignment of team KPIs to focus on mill key result areas (especially mill gate cash cost). Following these actions, it can be concluded that the Boyer mill possessed strong change leadership.

- *Employee empowerment.* This category was much stronger in 1998 than in 1994. Several developments were significant.
  - Team development after 1996 'empowered' teams to determine KPIs, manage some aspects of labour scheduling ('call in' and some minor outsourcing decisions) and handle some operational decisions.
  - At a higher level, employees were 'empowered' to participate in a number of decision-making forums, including the Boyer Improvement Council and the business reviews. The latter were an open forum for all employees to attend, review team performance and have input into decision-making.
  - Union delegates noted that employees 'had more pride in their jobs' and 'took more interest than they used to'. However, it was

felt that the opportunities for empowerment exceeded the willingness of some employees to become involved. This observation about the limited impact of best practice on employees was contradicted by a 1998 Employee Attitude Survey which found that 'a majority of employees hold the belief that they have a considerable amount of say in decisions' while 'employees who have been with the mill for 6–15 years expressed the view that teams did give some improvement to their day'.

In most respects, the Boyer mill's implementation of best practice had improved between 1994 and 1998. Best practice was more firmly integrated into strategy and operations; continuous improvement through teams (not investment and downsizing) was driving performance gains; team empowerment was the basis for employee acceptance of best practice; and managers were won over by an overhaul of management policies (to spread a coaching style) and the use of key result areas to measure business improvement objectives.

Was best practice delivering productivity gains? This question is a matter for debate. On the one hand, productivity growth had slacked since the dramatic improvements of the early 1990s when new technology and redundancies had boosted labour productivity, machine speed and safety. Labour productivity stabilised at just over three employee hours per tonne between 1994 and 1997. Also, paper machine speeds had stabilised their optimal technical performance by 1998. However, the focus on reduced costs (mill gate cash cost) was paying off. Between 1996 and 1998 mill gate cash cost fell by 12 per cent from $747 per tonne to $658 per tonne, a saving made possible largely by 'best practice'.

Under new owners: the Boyer mill in 2004

In the late 1990s, confidence in the future of the Boyer mill was precarious because of its ageing capital equipment, the inability of Fletcher Challenge to reinvest, and the disadvantages of its Tasmanian location — a sea journey away from its main suppliers and customers. Then, in 2000 Norske Skog acquired the mill, along with Fletcher Challenge's other pulp and paper assets.

Norske Skog is not afraid to close down underperforming assets. In 2004, it cut jobs when it shut down one of the three paper machines at the Tasman mill in New Zealand. However, operations and staffing at the Boyer mill remain untouched. The Boyer mill still has 450 employees, the same as a decade before; the two paper machines remain fully operational; the leaders of the management and union teams (including the mill manager, the head of human resources, and the local union leaders) still provide steady change leadership; and the workforce remains the same long-serving employees who learned best practice in the 1990s.

The social organisation of production within the mill also shows little sign of change. In 2002, a new enterprise agreement was certified. This re-affirmed a decade old commitment to the principles of best practice:

- The Boyer Improvement Council remained as a forum to 'discuss matters affecting efficiency ... and to inform and discuss with employees matters and issues affecting them'.[10]
- The objectives of the agreement were to secure the future of the mill by delivering on a vision that included 'an organisational structure that encourages employees to participate in the decision making process' and 'in which multi/disciplinary teams are product/process focused'.

Although the agreement was the product of tough bargaining, the bilateral commitment of management and unions to best practice remained strong. In certifying the agreement, Deputy President Leary of the Australian Industrial Relations Commission remarked 'the relationship with the unions and the company up there is a unique one ... a very good one'.

In several respects, this cooperative relationship has been strengthened by the new Norwegian owners and the principles and practices they carry into managing overseas operations. Amongst these are:

- core values of 'openness, honesty and cooperation'
- a 'corporate conduct policy' that prescribes high standards of conduct to and by employees
- corporate governance regulated by Norwegian law provides for employee directors (three of the eight board members) and for a contingent

of employee representatives and observers on the Corporate Assembly of the company.

- a requirement in the company's 'key capabilities' statement 'to build and participate in effective teams ... understanding the importance of collaboration and shared values in creating a high-performance environment ... understanding teams are to drive for better results and enhanced performance'
- an employee shareholding scheme (opened to Australian employees in March 2004)
- a corporate commitment to respect 'basic human rights and fundamental ILO conventions on the protection of employee rights'.

The last point has special significance for Norske Skog's operations in Australia. It commits Norske Skog to collective bargaining with trade unions rather than anti-union practices such as 'individual contracting' or the use of non-union collective agreements. In June 2002, just after the enterprise agreement was certified, this commitment was underwritten by a corporation wide agreement made between Norske Skog and ICEM (the International Federation of Chemical, Energy, Mine and General Workers' Union). Although the Norwegian United Federation of Trade Unions initiated the agreement, it applies to Norske Skog mills in five continents (including Australia). It guarantees basic employment conditions (including a sufficient basic wage, permanent employment and equal opportunity) as well as the right to belong to a union and to be represented by it in collective bargaining. Describing the agreement, the CEO Jan Reinas remarked that it committed the company to observing basic human rights and to guaranteeing good working and cooperation conditions. 'This is what we do at Norske Skog, and it is an absolute requirement for our entire global organisation'.[11] What Norske Skog brought to its Fletcher Challenge acquisitions (including the Boyer mill) was a commitment to cooperation with trade unions. This commitment underpinned the first experiments with best practice in the early 1990s, and continues to do so today.

Dealing with Norwegian owners appears to have sustained cultural or attitudinal commitments to best practice. But this commitment may not be enough to ensure the long-term survival of the Boyer mill. Since the acquisition, no new investment has been made at Boyer. In 2004,

Norske Skog made A$160 million available to the Albury mill (to rebuild the paper machine) and to the Tasman mill (to upgrade paper machines 2 and 3 following the closure of paper machine 1). These investments suggest a long-term commitment to newsprint production in New South Wales and New Zealand. The same may be untrue for the ageing paper machines at Boyer.

Sustaining best practice

It is now almost 20 years since a commercial crisis compelled the Boyer mill to undertake a major program of change. Beginning with new investment, rationalisation and downsizing, that program has evolved since the late 1980s to depend on continuous improvement through teamwork or best practice. Between 1991 and 1994, a Commonwealth Government-funded project speeded up preparation for best practice through benchmarking, training and experimental work teams. Between 1994 and 1998 best practice was turned from an idea with potential to a successful way of working. Between 1998 and 2004 best practice principles have survived a change of ownership, and remains the Boyer way of doing things. Although the Boyer mill still faces competitive threats, capital scarcity and other difficulties inherent in its location, it has used continuous improvement through teamwork to achieve planned cost reduction targets and other objectives. Survival of the mill has depended on the use of best practice methods to deliver results.

Those aspects of best practice that were untried in 1994 tended to function smoothly in 1998. This result was true for strategic planning (which was linked to change processes and to the key result areas designed to guide team operation); for teamwork (which pervaded all mill tasks and showed that continuous improvement could deliver results); for process improvement techniques (which were a major source of cost reduction and other improvements); and for HRM (where enterprise bargaining and changed employment conditions provided a basis for union and employee cooperation with best practice principles).

Other studies suggest that sustaining best practice is difficult where essential ingredients of a complex change program are neglected.[12] Particular deficiencies are considered likely in the three areas of (1) measurement and control systems suited to best practice, (2) stable and devolved change leadership, and (3) effective employee empowerment. Weaknesses in these three enablers of best practice make it likely to fail to show results, causing investment in best practice to be cut and the experiment curtailed.

The success of best practice at the Boyer mill can be partly explained by strong performance in these three areas since 1994. First, measurement and control systems were developed to guide and motivate teams, and synchronise their KPIs with mill-wide key result areas. Focused quantitative targets were used to 'pull' performance improvement. Second, stable and devolved change leadership was a characteristic of the mill. For the most part, the key managers had a record of extended service, their management style emphasised coaching and people skills relative to technical ones, and the machinery for management decision-making rested on inputs from below (teams and unions) as well as above. This ethos is strongly supported by Norske Skog today. Third is employee empowerment. The Boyer mill's record in this area is more difficult to assess. On the one hand, evidence that a proportion of the workforce remained unenthusiastic about teamwork and continuous improvement exists. On the other hand, teams exercised control over important production and employment issues, and employees had an input into decision-making at a reasonably high level. Union delegates pointed to concrete issues on which unions or teams exercised control.

Political support for best practice often depends on a delicate balance of opinion within the workplace. As in political life generally, that balance of opinion shifts over time in response to a vast array of influences. Perhaps one of the most significant facts about the Boyer mill has been the stable support of both management and unions for teamwork and cooperation over production. This consensus has been embodied in a series of local enterprise agreement, and now is upheld by an international labour agreement.

Literature on the sustainability of best practice emphasises the risk that capital market pressures can compel managers to adopt authoritarian short-term measures that are inconsistent with, and destructive of, best practice principles.[13] In an organisation such as the Boyer mill, these pressures would be manifested through the decisions of a corporate head office regarding either the conduct of the business or its divestment. News Corporation's sale of its share of the Boyer mill in 1997 had no apparent adverse consequences on the conduct of best practice, chiefly because Fletcher Challenge substantially embraced those principles. Nor did the subsequent sale to Norske Skog in 2000 upset the culture of teamwork and cooperation within the mill, not least because these values and methods matched those of the new owners. This case illustrates the importance of corporate support in ensuring the sustainability of best practice principles over 20 years. This longevity reflects an element of good management on the part of the Boyer managers and unions, and also an element of good luck — in the values of Norske Skog.

QUESTIONS

1. What contribution have best practice principles made to keeping the Boyer mill competitive?

2. In what respects had the Boyer mill achieved best practice by 1998, and what remained to be done?

3. How has the Boyer mill established and retained a culture the supports continuous improvement by teams?

END NOTES

1. D. Challis & D. Samson 1996, 'Australian Newsprint Mills', in *The Best Practice Experience*, vol. 3, ed. Australian Best Practice Demonstration Program, Pitman Publishing, Melbourne, pp. 61–90.
2. Norske Skog 2000, *Press Release*, 20 September.
3. CEO, Jan Reinas 2002, *Address to Annual General Meeting*, Oslo, 29 April.
4. M. Rimmer, J. Macneil, R. Chenhall, K. Langfield-Smith & L. Watts 1996, *Reinventing Competitiveness: Achieving Best Practice in Australia*, Pitman Publishing, Melbourne, p. 20.
5. Rimmer et al., op. cit., pp. 47–8.
6. Challis & Samson, op. cit., p. 70.
7. ibid., p. 88.
8. ibid., p. 90.
9. ibid., p. 88.
10. Australian Industrial Relations Commission 2002, *Norske Skog Boyer Mill, Enterprise Bargaining Agreement 2001*, AG 813338, p. 4.
11. Norske Skog 2002, *Press Release*, 24 June.
12. Rimmer et al., op. cit., pp. 203–4.
13. T. Kochan & P. Osterman 1994, *The Mutual Gains Enterprise*, Harvard Business School Press, Boston.

GLOSSARY

360-degree feedback or appraisal: process of obtaining feedback from multiple sources, such as subordinates, peers, supervisors, customers and the employees themselves, p. 209

action research: research in which the subject often an organisation both influences and is influenced by the researcher and the research process, p. 306

adaptive strategic thinking: creative, intuitive approach to strategy-making; responding flexibly to opportunities as they emerge, p. 55

administrative expert: traditional human resource role, which is concerned with designing and delivering human resource processes efficiently while maintaining quality, p. 189

asymmetry of information: unequal knowledge of organisational 'insiders' and 'outsiders' concerning the performance of investment in 'intangibles', p. 347

authoritarianism: demanding strict obedience and adherence to person or persons in positions of authority and power, p. 234

balanced scorecard approach: those means of investigating both tangible and intangible organisational resources and giving them equal weight. It aims to force organisations away from their tendency to focus on short-term financial indicators of performance and instead view four perspectives of activities customer, internal, innovation and learning, and financial perspectives. p. 95

bases of power: factors that provide an individual with a foundation for exercising power, p. 268

benchmarking: the search among comparable organisations for best practices that lead to superior performance, p. 305

best practice: a holistic program for empowered teams to drive continuous improvement in all aspects of a business's operation, leading to world-class results in productivity and equity, pp. 108, 348

biological perspective: a metaphor for viewing organisational change as analogous to changes that occur in the natural world, particularly focusing upon Darwinian evolution and an organism's life-cycle, p. 9

breakpoints: radical, framebreaking change that triggers a fundamental review of organisational systems, processes, structure and design, p. 152

broadband intelligence: exhibited by people whose intelligence has been allowed to develop in a balanced way, stimulated by a wide variety of influences and activities. Leaders with broadband intelligence are able to draw on and make connections between the seven distinctive forms of intelligence: linguistic; logical mathematical; spatial; musical; bodily kinaesthetic; interpersonal; and intrapersonal. See also related endnote 21. p. 233

bullying: workplace behaviour that involves tyranny over the weak, sometimes leading to adverse social and health outcomes, p. 345

business process re-engineering: fundamental re-evaluation and redesign of a business's processes, retaining and improving only those that add value to the end user, p. 108

capital market 'short termism': the tendency for organisations to be influenced by capital market valuations to focus investments and activities on yielding short-term rather than long-term performance gains, p. 334

captains: leaders who exhibit a directive, authoritative leadership style. A style of leadership is successful when the followers are in favour of change and the group mindset accepts a directive approach. p. 253

cause-and-effect chart: also termed an Ishikawa or 'fishbone' diagram, a device used by quality circles or work teams to identify a hierarchy of causes affecting quality ranging from major causes to minor ones, p. 320

change agent: the role of helping the organisation build a capacity for change, p. 189

change checklist: key success factors that managers can monitor to gather systematic data to evaluate the change process, p. 322

change leadership: the assumption of responsibility by managers or other employees for planning, monitoring and reinforcing change, p. 350

change path or change trajectory: the experience of change unique to an organisation arising from its particular configuration of personal, organisational and environmental influences, p. 108

change planning tool or change model: a general recipe or formula for introducing change in all organisations, or a particular class of organisation, p. 108

change transitions: an approach to organisational change where the management of change transitions implies that the impact of organisational change is psychologically and emotionally traumatic for employees, p. 14

chaos theory: a systems-based view of change where the combination and accumulation of simple systems can lead to chaos and unpredictability, p. 17

charismatic leaders: those leaders who, through their personal attributes and strong interpersonal skills, are able to inspire and enthuse others to commit to their vision for the future, p. 253

coaches: those leaders who exhibit a hands-on, people-centred, consultative and informal leadership style. Coaches show a strong interest and belief in their followers, have excellent communication and listening skills, and have high expectations of themselves and others. p. 253

coercive change: top-down, mandated change that involves little or no consultation with subordinates, p. 254

coercive power: power based on the belief that the change driver can administer unwelcome penalties or sanctions, p. 268

commanders: those leaders who exhibit a top-down, directive leadership style. At its most extreme, this leadership style can be coercive, gaining compliance rather than commitment. p. 253

competencies: the behaviour patterns that an employee must have to perform their tasks and functions with competence. These are set as the criteria against which applicants can be measured and assessed. p. 186

complexity theory: a systems-oriented theory that considers some change as non-linear and emergent; a result of the complex interaction of organisational elements, p. 17

contingency model: a model by which managers select change strategy to fit organisational requirements and environment, p. 109

contingency perspective: the behavioural view of organisational change where managers should make decisions taking into account technology, structure and size, focusing on those that are the most directly relevant to circumstances, p. 13

continuous improvement: ongoing evaluation of work processes, systems and structures to see whether they can be improved, p. 44

control and measurement systems: reporting systems involving the collection, analysis and use of data to evaluate all aspects of performance, including the accomplishment of change to achieve best practice, p. 350

core capabilities: distinctive skills and technologies that provide a source of sustainable competitive advantage because they are valuable, rare/unique and not easily transferred to, or copied by, other firms, p. 92

core competencies: distinctive skills and technologies that provide a source of sustainable competitive advantage because they are valuable, rare/unique and not easily transferred to, or copied by, other firms, p. 94

core competencies: the capacity of a firm's human resources to perform its key tasks or activities, p. 184

core values: the enduring values of an organisation that guide strategies and practices, and influence employee values to align with the company's ideology and ambitions, p. 334

cost–benefit analysis: evaluation of the relative economic value of the inputs and outputs of organisational change, p. 333

critical success factors CSFs: variables, often related to cost, quality and delivery, that must be managed effectively for a business strategy to succeed, p. 308

cultural perspective: a view that the central issue in organisational change is the values, beliefs and norms shared by organisational members, which acts as a powerful mechanism of conformity, but is difficult to modify intentionally, p. 15

cultural renewal: identifying and challenging the core values, beliefs and assumptions that guide organisational thinking and action. This is about corporate cultural change. p. 56

decoupled: where a lack of coordination and control mechanisms results in the organisation's loss of focus and direction, p. 236

deliberate strategy: planned, premeditated, intended strategy that may or may not be realised, p. 73

deregulation: the removal of regulations governing the control of operations in, for example, the banking, telecommunications, automotive and agricultural industries. An example of deregulation is the reduction of tariff barriers on imported cars in the automotive industry. p. 40

discontinuous change: rapid, turbulent, unpredictable change, forcing a radical departure from the familiar, pp. 40, 250

double-loop learning: a form of organisational learning reinforced by two feedback loops. The first involves learning from the pursuit of existing goals. The second involves questioning and adjusting those goals to reflect new needs. p. 120

downsizing: the reduction of workforce numbers to improve the organisation's bottom line, p. 200

emergent strategy: strategy that has evolved as part of a 'pattern in a stream of actions', as opposed to a preconceived plan, p. 73

emotional intelligence: distinct from IQ and technical skills, a form of intelligence characterised by strong interpersonal skills, ability to work with others, and effectiveness in leading change, p. 72

employee benefits: elements of rewards given in addition to various forms of cash pay; for example, child-care facilities or a health club membership, p. 212

employee champion: the role of dealing with the day-to-day problems, concerns and needs of individual employees, and representing these concerns to management. It includes helping to increase the employee's commitment to the organisation and their ability to deliver results. p. 189

empowerment: making employees responsible and accountable for their actions by redistributing decision-making to involve employee or worker participation, pp. 56, 274, 350

endings: a stage in psychological adjustment to change that involves the identification and acceptance of loss, p. 338

expert power: power based on the belief that the change driver has superior knowledge relevant to the situation and the challenges presented to the organisation, p. 269

external fit: the alignment of change strategy to external environmental conditions, p. 112

first dimension of power: when power is exercised in open conflict or debate, p. 271

fourth dimension of power: when power is embedded in the very fabric of the system, constraining what is thought, what is seen and how it is seen, and providing the means of limiting the capacity for resistance, p. 273

framebending: change that focuses on individual organisational components/subsystems rather than the entire organisation, and that takes place within the existing organisational framework and culture, p. 252

framebreaking: systemic, organisation-wide change that challenges the status quo and involves fundamental changes to strategy, structure, systems and culture, and leads to new ways of perceiving the environment, the organisation and the relationship between the two, p. 252

global business environment: where competition is no longer constrained by national borders, creating a global village and economy, p. 40

goal-based single-loop learning: adult learning reinforced by feedback that performance meets targets, p. 120

haphazard learning: adult learning without clear objectives that is not reinforced by feedback, p. 120

high-performance work organisation (HPWO): a loosely defined group of practices relating to work organisation, human resources, industrial relations and quality management practices. Typically, these practices entail more cooperative production methods to increase productivity. p. 110

holistic: a systemic, organisation-wide approach to change that recognises the interconnectivity of an organisation's components, p. 45

holistic change: change to multiple parts of an organisational system where the benefits of change arise from synergies among changes in different parts of the system, p. 334

holistic model: a change model comprising interdependent elements, of which each is essential, p. 113

horizontal integration: moving into activities that are competitive with or complementary to a firm's existing activities, p. 153

human capital: the sum of the employees' knowledge, skills, and abilities and encompasses capabilities not directly related to task performance, including experiences and social skills, as well as values, beliefs, and attitudes, p. 190

human resource development: the broad set of activities concerned with the organisation's investment in learning and improving the performance of its human resources as a whole. It includes education, training and development, as well as career management and planning, and organisational learning. p. 185

human resources HR scorecard: an adaptation of the balanced scorecard to evaluate the contribution of human resources to strategic performance. It is a measurement system involving four dimensions: 1 human resource deliverables, 2 high-performance work systems, 3 alignment of the high-performance work system with strategy, and 4 efficiency in generating deliverables. p. 306

incremental adaptation: predictable, familiar change that is managed as a series of small, gradual steps made within the context, or frame, of the current set of organisational strategies and components. It focuses on individual organisational components/subsystems rather than the entire organisation; for example, improving work

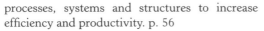

processes, systems and structures to increase efficiency and productivity. p. 56

incremental change: predictable, familiar change that is managed as a series of small, gradual steps within the context, or frame, of the current set of organisational strategies, structures and systems, p. 250

institutional perspective: a view of change that considers the shaping force to be the pressure within the industrial environment, including social, governmental, legal, cultural or other pressures, to encourage organisations to conform to common standards, p. 11

institutionalised resistance: when resistance behaviours are embedded in an organisation's legitimate structures, decision-making processes and resource allocation, and lead members to believe that there is no need for change, p. 284

internal fit: the alignment of change strategy to internal organisational characteristics, p. 113

job analysis: the process of recording and describing the purpose, characteristics and duties of a given job. The results are used for a variety of human resource activities. p. 195

job design: the structuring of the specific content, methods and relationships in a job to ensure it satisfies its role and function within the organisation, p. 195

just-in-time: a 'pull' system of inventory management guided by the target of zero inventory, p. 122

kaizen: team-based continuous improvement, p. 122

kanban: an order that activates production in a just-in-time system, p. 122

key performance indicators (KPIs): measures of critical success factors (CSFs) that may relate to the organisation as a whole or to its parts including work teams, p. 309

lean production: a continuous improvement and production system that minimises the use of inputs and inventory, p. 110

learning organisation: a cooperative system of work organisation in which semi-autonomous work teams, supported by appropriate technology and information systems, engage in double-loop learning, p. 110

legitimate power: power based on the belief that the change driver has the authority to give instructions as a direct consequence of their formal position or rank within the organisation, p. 268

life-cycle theory: an organisational change theory inspired by biological development that views change in organisations as inevitable through a series of linear stages from birth, development and maturity through to decline and death, p. 10

logical incrementalism: the deliberate development of strategy by 'learning through doing', p. 76

loosely coupled: where there is both integration and differentiation between an organisation's component parts — that is, where the business units or functional areas of an organisation assert both autonomy and interdependence, p. 236

manufacturing resource planning (MRP II): a computerised order and material tracking system used for inventory management, production planning, cost control and monitoring of shop-floor efficiency, p. 123

matrix structure: a combination of structures that can comprise either product and geographical divisions, or functional and divisional structures operating alongside each other in the one organisation, p. 152

motivational approach to empowerment: a way of understanding and practising empowerment that emphasises open communication and cooperative goal-setting designed to increase commitment and involvement, p. 276

multidivisional organisation: subdivision of an organisation into autonomous/semi-autonomous business units divisions on the basis of products, services, geographic areas or the processes of the firm, p. 152

mutual gains enterprise: a form of best practice in which employee commitment to change is based on sharing the benefits of productivity improvement, usually by the award of guaranteed job security and higher pay, p. 333

network multidivisional form: similar to the multidivisional organisation, but the network form of organising depends on cooperation for success. Therefore, the network multidivisional form emphasises horizontal communication; flexibility and boundary spanning; cross-divisional knowledge transfer and learning; and intra-organisational relationships and processes. p. 152

neutral zone: a confused intermediate stage in psychological adjustment to change that is characterised by discomfort, anxiety, problematic motivation and low productivity, p. 338

new beginnings: the final step in psychological adjustment to change that involves the internalisation or acceptance of new values, beliefs, actions and habits, p. 338

normative change: a change process that is inclusive and seeks the participation and involvement of all organisational members, p. 254

organisational capabilities: capabilities reflected in an organisation's shared values, assumptions and beliefs, which are manifested not only through its strategic focus, structures and systems, but also through the management style, skills and behaviour of its people. Similar to Mintzberg's definition of strategy as perspective, organisational capabilities represent the 'unconscious mind of the organisation, shaping how external change is interpreted, how strategic and tactical decisions are taken, and how internal change is managed'. p. 92

organisational culture: the pattern of beliefs and expectations that is common to members of a social unit and subsequently sets the behavioural standards or norms for all new employees, p. 284

organisational development: a change intervention tool involving team-building exercises informed by action research activities and supported by participative management. This approach to organisational change is premised upon the view that resistance to change can be understood and diminished if employees are considered as the pivotal organisational resources to be managed with care and sensitivity, pp. 14, 110

organisational learning: a process whereby the organisation and its employees continually learn and apply what they have learned to improve the way in which the organisation functions, p. 202

Pareto principle: also known as the 80:20 rule, the principal that a few of the causes usually account for most of the effect, p. 320

performance appraisal: the assessment of an individual's past performance, usually against set objectives, and the setting of future performance objectives. It may include the identification of development or training needs, and the determination of rewards or bonuses. p. 208

performance management systems: the process or set of processes designed to manage the performance of the individual, the group and the organisation against objectives. It includes the development of competencies that support the organisational strategy, and of recognition and rewards that are linked to critical behaviours and competencies for example, teamwork and information sharing as well as outputs. p. 182

performance-related pay: financial reward linked to individual, team, business unit or company performance. It also can be pay for particular skills and competencies, measured by the achievement of goals and objectives set through performance management systems, p. 212

phenomenological research: research based on the assumption that the researcher's values shape interaction with research subjects and, therefore, that valid findings must be situational or context bound, and reached through qualitative methods, p. 316

political perspective: a view that assumes organisational change is driven by the desire of individuals and groups to introduce new philosophies, approaches or ideas into an organisation, causing conflict and resolved by power, p. 15

politics: those activities within organisations to acquire, develop and use power and other resources to obtain one's preferred outcomes when there is dissension or uncertainty about choices, p. 265

population ecology: an organisational change theory that uses the concept of natural selection and biological evolution to model the effects of industrial change on organisations, p. 9

positivist research: research based on the assumption that the researcher is independent of the subject, is objective and can validate predictive generalisations about cause-and-effect relationships, p. 316

Post-Fordism: a production system requiring flatter and more flexible organisational structures and multiskilled/high-discretion work teams, catering for the customer requirements of a niche market, p. 109

postmodern perspective: the postmodern interpretation of change rejects attempts to explain organisations using universal, grand theories, instead taking the view that change is best understood through the ways organisational members construct their social reality, which can be manifestly different and can involve the simultaneous presence of competing or even contradictory trends and experiences, p. 18

power: the ability to get an individual or group to behave in a way they otherwise would not, or the ability of individuals to achieve desired outcomes, p. 264

psychological perspective: an approach to organisational change that concentrates on individuals' personal psychology and their reaction to change interventions, p. 14

punctuated equilibrium: a theory of change borrowed from an alternative view of biological evolution, where radical change interrupts

periods of relative stability or incremental change, p. 10

quality assurance (QA): formal management structures or systems to control quality. These systems allocate responsibility, designate tasks and prescribe measures. The elements of these systems are set down in Australian and international quality assurance standards. p. 125

quality circles (QC): teams of employees that engage in continuous improvement to achieve zero quality defects, p. 125

radical transformation: revolutionary, framebreaking organisation-wide change that addresses fundamental changes in the definition of the business, shifts of power and changes in organisational culture that is, changes in established behaviour patterns, routines and rituals, and so on, p. 56

rational perspective: a view concerned with the alignment between an organisation's structure and competencies and its environment, p. 10

rational strategic planning: a formal, systematic approach to strategy formulation, p. 55

referent power: power based on the belief that the change driver has desirable abilities and personality traits that should be copied, p. 268

relational approach to empowerment: a way of understanding and practising empowerment that includes significant structural change, particularly associated with the formal decentralisation of power, p. 276

resistance: any structural, systemic or human barriers that impede both deliberately introduced and externally pressured change, p. 264

resource perspective: resource dependence or resource-based theory takes the view that the acquisition and deployment of resources is the critical activity driving change in organisations, p. 12

return on equity: a financial ratio calculated by dividing the declared accounting profit of an organisation by accounting investment. It is a widely used financial measure of changes to performance. p. 305

reward management systems: systems designed to manage all forms of remuneration and non-financial benefits that employees receive as part of an employment relationship, p. 211

reward power: power based on the belief that the change driver has access to valued rewards that will be dispensed in return for compliance, p. 268

scenario planning: a tool for stimulating strategic thinking that goes beyond the traditional financial and forecast-based planning approaches, because it can be used to capture a range of options, to stimulate thinking about alternatives that otherwise may be ignored and to challenge the prevailing organisational mindset, p. 83

second dimension of power: when power is exercised to suppress conflict or debate, p. 271

self-leadership: taking charge of one's own destiny, one's own learning and development, p. 56

semi-autonomous work group: multiskilled work team that rotates tasks among members and exercises discretion over matters normally decided by supervisors or lower management, p. 119

shared vision: a vision that gives meaning and structure to the change efforts. It provides a focus and a sense of direction that, while offering a challenge, must be realistic and acceptable to the majority of the workforce. In addition, if the majority of stakeholders is to commit to this vision, then as many as possible must have had meaningful input into its substance. p. 241

smokestack: the industrial economy — a term that Stace and Dunphy attribute to Alvin Toffler, p. 152

socio-technical systems: a theory of work organisation that gives equal weighting to social and technical influences, p. 119

sources of power: the political instruments through which bases of power are obtained, p. 267

stakeholders: individuals or agencies with an interest or stake in the firm; for example, employees, customers, suppliers, government departments and agencies, p. 75

statistical quality control (SQC): a set of techniques to measure and control variation and ensure consistency in a process, p. 125

status quo: the existing state of affairs, or the 'way we do business around here', p. 83

strategic human resource management: the design and implementation of internally consistent policies and practices, which are aligned with the organisation's strategy, to ensure employees contribute to the achievement of business objectives, p. 182

strategic intent: relentless pursuit of a certain long-term strategic objective and concentration of strategic actions on achieving that objective, even if the organisation does not have the immediate capabilities and resources. It is about creating 'stretch', or a mis-fit between resources and aspirations. p. 80

strategic partner: the role of aligning the organisation's HR strategies and practices with business strategy and its execution, p. 189

strategic planning: traditional linear, rational, systematic approach to strategy formation and implementation, p. 72

strategic positioning: performing different activities from those of rivals or performing similar activities in different ways, p. 73

strategic thinking: creative, intuitive approach to the strategy-making process, in which strategy formation and implementation are interactive, interchangeable components, p. 72

strategy: the direction and scope of an organisation over the long-term — its managerial game plan for the future, which is influenced by environmental forces and resource availability, and the values and expectations of its power base the stakeholders, p. 72

stress: a psychological problem, sometimes manifested through physical health problems, arising from an excessive discrepancy between the demands placed on people and their skills and resources to deal with them, p. 342

sustainability: the maintenance of a change program to the point that it becomes accepted as prescribing a normal way of working and meets expectations of improved productivity performance, p. 333

systematic change: a long-term strategy requiring considerable human and financial commitment. It includes widespread organisational cultural change, right down to the levels of values and attitudes, p. 200

systemic change: holistic, organisation-wide change that recognises the interconnectivity of an organisation's component parts, p. 233

systems perspective: a change approach that views organisations as a constellation of interrelated and interdependent units or entities that work together, implying that change must be holistic, dealing with the range of organisational sub-systems with an awareness that change in one will affect the others, p. 16

tacit knowledge: the unique combination of skills and cooperative social arrangements that influences organisational performance, p. 314

Taylorism: A model of work organisation ascribed to F. W. Taylor involving the separation of mental and manual work, the design of simple and standardised manual tasks to eliminate scope for discretion, and the exercise of strict control over work effort, p. 110

third dimension of power: when power is a reflection of the institutional norms and procedures that constrain the domain and direction of conflict and its resolution, p. 271

total quality management (TQM): a holistic approach to quality improvement involving all parts of an organisation in the measurement, analysis and rectification of quality problems, pp. 108, 305

transitions: a process of personal, psychological adjustment to change, often distinguished from situational objective change, p. 332

triple bottom line (TBL): corporate reporting of social, environmental, and financial performance, p. 315

value-based strategic management: a technique to convert disaggregated performance data into a single, organisation-wide measure of shareholder value, p. 310

value-innovation focus: organisations pursuing value innovation adopt a strategic focus that is opportunistic and intent on creating fundamentally new and superior value, making their competitors irrelevant, p. 81

vertical integration: when a company owns or is involved in both upstream and downstream value chain activities. For example, a brewery producing its own input raw materials upstream and owning the distribution centres, namely retail outlets such as pubs and liquor stores downstream. p. 153

work redesign: a medium-term strategy aimed at reducing the work through changes to work design and processes, rather than cutting the number of employees, p. 200

workforce reduction: a short-term directional strategy aimed at cutting the number of employees through transfers, attrition, early retirement or voluntary severance packages, lay-offs and terminations, p. 200